Financial Accounting: A Case-Based Approach

Financial Accounting: A Case-Based Approach

Edited by
Thomas Abbington

WILLFORD PRESS
www.willfordpress.com

Published by Willford Press,
118-35 Queens Blvd., Suite 400,
Forest Hills, NY 11375, USA

ISBN: 978-1-68285-636-9

Cataloging-in-Publication Data

Financial accounting : a case-based approach / edited by Thomas Abbington.
    p. cm.
Includes bibliographical references and index.
ISBN 978-1-68285-636-9
1. Accounting. 2. Accounting--Case studies. 3. Financial statements.
I. Abbington, Thomas.
HF5636 .F56 2019
657--dc23

For information on all Willford Press publications
visit our website at www.willfordpress.com

Contents

Permissions

List of Contributors

Index

Preface

Financial accounting is a field of accounting that deals with the analysis and reporting of financial transactions related to a business. The preparation of financial statements is a crucial aspect of financial accounting. The primary components of financial statements are statement of cash flows, statement of profit and loss and statement of financial position. It facilitates a systematic record of transactions, understanding of the financial and solvency position of the business, rational decision-making, etc. The aim of this book is to present researches that have transformed the discipline of financial accounting and aided its advancement. From theories to research to practical applications, case studies related to all contemporary topics of relevance to this field have been included herein. Students, researchers, experts and all associated with financial accounting will benefit alike from this book.

This book has been the outcome of endless efforts put in by authors and researchers on various issues and topics within the field. The book is a comprehensive collection of significant researches that are addressed in a variety of chapters. It will surely enhance the knowledge of the field among readers across the globe.

It gives us an immense pleasure to thank our researchers and authors for their efforts to submit their piece of writing before the deadlines. Finally in the end, I would like to thank my family and colleagues who have been a great source of inspiration and support.

Editor

Accounting for Goodwill and Manipulation

Takefumi Ueno[1]*, Genki Sakakibara[2] and Sanshiro Uchino[3]

[1]Faculty of Management and Information Department, University of Shizuoka, Japan
[2]Shizuoka Bank, Shizuoka, Japan
[3]Graduate Schools of Management and Information of Innovation, University of Shizuoka, Japan

Abstract

We explored some links between earnings management and accounting fraud. Most previous studies ignored the connections between earnings management and accounting fraud. This study attempted to find the linkage between them by exploring some cases. In particular, we focused on M&A deals. Accounting for acquired goodwill has been subject to considerable debate for at least the past 50 years because the accounting tends to provide managers with discretion to manipulate accounting figures. The European Securities and Markets Authority (ESMA) reported that overall impairment losses on goodwill amounted to only €40 billion from the €790 billion of goodwill in spite of the EU sovereign debt crisis in 2011. This showed that managers tended to intentionally avoid impairments losses. Goodwill accounting gives managers opportunities to manipulate accounting figures. This study used two case studies to explore the accounting manipulation through M&A transactions. The first case is the scandal of Olympus Corporation (Olympus) which is one of the most famous accounting fraud. Olympus had hidden more than $1.5 billion of investment losses through M&A transactions until the scandal exposure in 2011. The second case is the unintentional mismanagement by HP. HP recorded $8.8 billion of the impairment loss of goodwill after the detection of Autonomy's fraud. The boundary between earnings management and accounting fraud is unclear. Managers have a broad discretion into the accounting for goodwill. This would lead to a high possibility that many companies poorly comply with the requirements of accounting.

Keywords: Goodwill; Accounting Fraud; Earnings Management; Amortization

Introduction

Many previous studies have already suggested that managers have an incentive to manipulate a financial result meeting their earnings targets. Managers tend to manipulate accounting figures through economic transactions [1]. If value for an economic transaction is bigger, manipulatable value is also larger. M&A is one of the biggest deals in management decision. There are many manipulation cases by handling M&A deals. Those cases were illegal and legal. The Olympus Corporation (hereafter Olympus) scandal in 2011 is a typical and the latest illegal case for M&A. Olympus had hidden more than $1.5 billion of investment losses through M&A transactions until the scandal exposure in 2011. One of the typical legal cases is Hewlett-Packard (hereafter HP) scandal. HP recognized goodwill value of $6.4 billion which is 5% in total assets by acquired Autonomy (Telecommunication Company in U.K.) after acquiring Autonomy (Telecommunication Company in U.K.) in 2011. HP recorded $8.8 billion of the impairment loss of Autonomy's goodwill in 2012. These types of scandals are usually revealed by bankruptcy, anonymous reporting, supervisor monitoring, and etc. Until the scandals are revealed, we cannot identify whether managers did the window dressing in their financial statements or not. Even if we identify manager's manipulation as legal bounds, some manipulation might be illegal. In addition, a manager could shift a legal manipulation to an illegal manipulation. The accounting area calls legal manipulation as "earnings management" and illegal manipulation as "accounting fraud" or "window dressing". Perols and Lougee [2] showed that fraud companies were more active in earnings managements than non-fraud companies in previous fiscal years. Our study explores links between earnings management and accounting fraud through case study. In particular, we focused on M&A deals. Accounting for acquired goodwill has been subject to considerable debate for at least the past 50 years [1]. As mentioned above, managers are likely to manipulate accounting figures through accounting procedures for M&A. Those manipulations can have a huge impact on their financial statements.

Methodologies-Case Studies

This study used two case studies to explore the accounting manipulation through M&A transactions. The first case is the scandal of Olympus Corporation (hereafter Olympus) which is one of the most famous accounting frauds. At first, we survey the summary of the Olympus scandal and the scheme. We mainly investigate the role of goodwill accounting under the scheme. This case will suggest the transition from its earnings management to the accounting fraud and the relationship between them. The second case is the unintentional error caused by HP. HP recorded $8.8 billion of the impairment loss of goodwill after the detection of Autonomy's fraud. HP treated goodwill in the appropriate way. However, this case raised a doubt about the management decision and the accounting process.

In next section, we explain what logic of accounting manipulation is and why managers tend to utilize M&A deals to control companies' performance.

Theory of Manipulation

Many previous studies have already suggested that managers have an incentive to manipulate a financial result meeting their earnings targets. Managers tend to manipulate company performance through accounting procedures of an economic transaction and events. Accounting manipulation occurs when managers manipulate economic transactions or events to record them in financial reporting. "Generally

---

*Corresponding author: Takefumi Ueno, Faculty of Management and Information Department, University of Shizuoka, Japan
E-mail: ueno@u-shizuoka-ken.ac.jp

Accepted Accounting Principles" (GAAP) allows managers to choose from various methods when they prepare financial statements. While earnings management is a discretional behavior within the framework of the GAAP, accounting fraud is a discretional behavior beyond the framework of the GAAP. Most previous studies have been clearly separated into the two behaviors. However, limited studies showed that earnings management may constitute accounting fraud. For example, Perols and Lougee [2] suggested that earnings management has a link to accounting fraud. They used a sample of 54 fraud and 54 non-fraud firms in the U.S to explore this connection. They found that the likelihood of fraud is significantly higher for firms that have previously managed earnings. They also found that firms that meet or beat analyst forecasts or inflate reported revenue are more likely to be committing fraud. This result might be a link between earnings management and accounting fraud. Collapses of Enron Co. and WorldCom Co. are one of the most famous and the biggest bankruptcy cases in the United States. Enron Co. had kept huge debts off the balance sheets until the company went into collapse. Enron Co. utilized loopholes within the GAAP [3]. The audit firms of Arthur Andersen cooperated with this this manipulation. WorldCom Co. underreported line costs by capitalizing them and inflated revenue in profits and losses. Their accounting fraud had been revealed just before their bankruptcy. Figure 1 showed a relation between accounting fraud and earnings management. There is a gray zone between accounting fraud and earnings management. Whether a procedure in the gray zone is accounting fraud or earnings management depends on a supervisor's judgment. The judgment may change with each case.

Manipulation and M&A

Accounting procedures for M&A

If the value of an economic transaction is larger, its manipulatable value is also larger. M&A is one of the biggest deals in management decision. There are many accounting manipulation cases by M&A deals. Procedures of M&A deals are related to accounting standards for business combinations, goodwill and intangible assets. Accounting standards have progressed to a convergence between International Financial Reporting Standards (hereafter IFRS) and Statement of Financial Accounting Standards in the U.S. (hereafter SFAS) since 2002[1]. Japanese Accounting Standards Setter (hereafter ASBJ) has accurately converged Japanese GAAP with IFRS since 2011[2]. SFAS 141

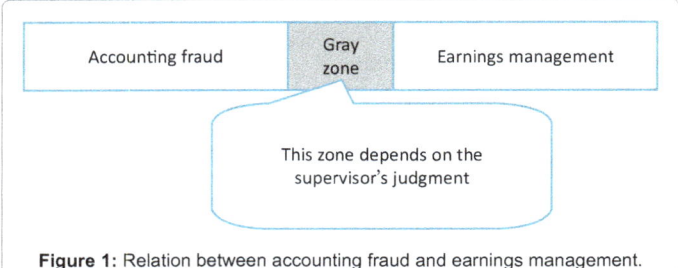

Figure 1: Relation between accounting fraud and earnings management.

[1]In October 2002, the International Accounting Standards Board (IASB) and the Financial Accounting Standards Board (FASB) announced the issuance of a memorandum of understanding ("the Norwalk Agreement"). Accordance to this agreement, the IASB and the FASB has cooperated to progress the convergence of IFRS and SFAS.
Please see the following URL: http://www.fasb.org/jsp/FASB/Page/SectionPage&cid=1176156245663
[2]In August 2007, the ASBJ and the IASB jointly announced an agreement ("the Tokyo Agreement") to accelerate convergence between Japanese GAAP and IFRS. In June 2011, the IASB and the ASBJ have announced their achievements under the agreement.
Please see the following URL: http://www.ifrs.org/news/press-releases/Pages/iasb-asbj-10-june-2011.aspx

and IFRS 3 define accounting procedures for business combinations. SFAS 141 and IFRS 3 have been adopted since 1st April, 2001 and 1st April 2004, respectively. These accounting standards prohibit the pooling-of-interests method. Managers must adopt the purchase method after adopting these standards [4,5]. Under the purchase method, managers must decide which companies is an acquirer or acquiree when a company merges or acquires with another company, while acquirer is a buyer in M&A deals, acquiree is a seller in the deals. The standards require an acquirer reevaluate all of an acquirer's all assets and debts based on the fair value measurements. The buyer obtains control of the seller at the acquisition date. The fair value is defined as the price that would be received to sell assets or be paid to transfer a liability in an orderly transaction between market participants at the measurement date. A fair value is made up one or more inputs. The most reliable indicator of fair value is quoted from an active market. When we can know a market price of the assets or liabilities (such as stock price), we use it as fair value. When this is not available, managers can use a valuation technique to measure fair value, maximizing the use of relevant observable inputs and minimizing the use of observable inputs. A large part of company assets and debts do not have a market price in an active market. As said above, the accounting standards for M&A require an acquirer to reevaluate the value of an acuiree's assets and liabilities at the acquisition date. It is difficult for outside stakeholders (e.g. investors) to verify these values because an acquire basically use a valuation technique to evaluate them. In accordance with accounting standards, an acquirer recognizes an identifiable intangible asset of the acquiree at the acquisition. An identifiable intangible asset includes computer software, patents, copyrights, customer lists and marketing rights. Accounting standards prohibit adding internal intangible assets up as assets in the balance sheet because their values lack objective measurement. An acquirer must recognize the intangible assets in the accounting process of M&A if they are separable from the entity and can be sold to another entity.

Accounting procedure for purchased goodwill

Purchased goodwill arises when a company is purchased by another company. Figure 2 shows a formula to calculate goodwill [6]. Goodwill is the excess of the purchase price over the fair value of net assets and identifiable intangible assets. The financial accounting treats as goodwill the future economic benefits arising from business combinations (M&A).

As the Figure 2 shows, the goodwill cannot be directly measured. The accounting standards in the IASB (IAS38) and the FASB (SFAS 142) require only impairment testing for goodwill at least once a fiscal year and prohibit its amortization while the Japanese GAAP needs the impairment test and periodic amortization within 20 years period. As said above, the ASBJ has already completed a convergence with the IFRS. However, there are some differences between them. The treatment for goodwill is one of the differences. Only impairment testing for goodwill

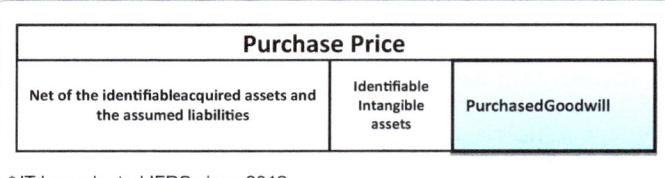

Purchase Price		
Net of the identifiableacquired assets and the assumed liabilities	Identifiable Intangible assets	PurchasedGoodwill

*JT has adopted IFRS since 2012.
(Unit price: million yen)
(Source: JT's annual reports)

Figure 2: Calculation for purchased goodwill.

means the value of goodwill continue to be on the balance sheet and is not expensed in the Profits and losses if goodwill is not impaired. This difference between IFRS, SFAS and the Japanese GAAP will change companies' net income. For example, Japan Tobacco Co. (hereafter JT) voluntary adopted IFRS in 2011. Net income of JT went up \82.8billion which is 22% higher than that of Japanese GAAP. Table 1 showed JT's trend of goodwill value and its amortization cost from 2009 to 2014. JT has voluntary adopted IFRS since 2011. Total assets to goodwill value have gradually increased in the period. Amortization costs heavily impacted JT's net income before 2010. JT didn't need to recognize amortization costs after the adoption of IFRS. JT's net income has been pushed up [7]. Needless to say, managers must recognize impairment losses in a lump sum at the impairment date for goodwill. JT has goodwill impairment risk.

Accounting procedure for M&A

Watts discussed that the procedures of goodwill impairment based on SFAS 142 rely on unverifiable fair value and managing can control impairment losses. As said above, acquirers must reevaluate all assets and liabilities of acquirees by using fair value. The fair values are basically estimated by specific techniques and unobservable inputs. Outside stakeholder cannot verify the values. The lack of verifiability provides managers with the opportunity to manipulate their performance in financial reporting.

Companies have three opportunities for discretion in the accounting for goodwill. The first opportunity is decision of purchase price. When they decide the purchase price, the purchase price fully depends on management decision. Purchase price is directly related to the value of goodwill. The second one is measurement of goodwill value. They can manipulate goodwill value by controlling the fair value measurement for net assets and identifiable intangible assets. The third is procedure of goodwill after the acquisition date. Managers might avoid goodwill impairment losses by manipulating a judgment for impairment (Figure 3).

	2009	2010	2011
Net income before tax (A)	262,143	276,054	280,497
Amortization cost	105,470	97,394	91,089
(B)/(A)	40%	35%	32%
GOODWILL (C)	1,453,961	1,387,397	1,147,816
Total assets (D)	3,879,803	3,872,595	3,571,927
(C)/(D)	37.5%	35.8%	32.1%
	2012	2013	2014
Net income before tax (A)	441,355	509,355	636,203
Amortization cost (B)	–	–	–
(B)/(A)	–	–	–
Goodwill (C)	1,110,046	1,316,476	1,584,432
Total assets (D)	3,667,007	3,852,567	4,611,444
(C)/(D)	30.3%	34.2%	34.4%

Table 1: JT's trend of goodwill value and amortization costs.

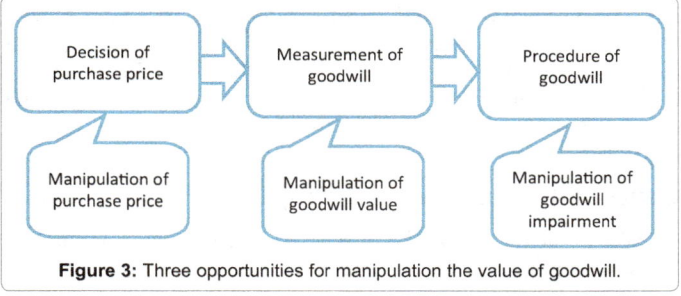

Figure 3: Three opportunities for manipulation the value of goodwill.

Determinants of the purchase price are hot issues in academic studies. There are many studies from various areas. In particular, they focus on why managers tend to overpay when buying a target company. The acquisition price must be lower than the merger synergies. The less managers pay to the target company, the more advantage they get. Rational and sophisticated managers try to buy a company at a low price. Managers do not intentionally overpay with acquisition if they want to hide something and deceive someone through M&A. However, some of them paid high acquisition premiums in many cases.

Kim et al. [8] explored why managers are likely to pay too much for acquisitions. They used a sample of firms in the American banking industry from 1994 to 2005. The number of sample was 878 acquisitions that were made by 401 firms. They estimated the models using a cross-sectional time series technique by pooling the longitudinal panel data. Kim et al. [8] found that firms with a low growth opportunity pay greater premiums than firms with a high growth opportunity. Hayward and Hannbrick [9] focused on a manager's emotion to explain overpayment for acquisition. They explored a relation between managers' hubris and overpayment. They used a sample of firms in the American publicly traded firms which paid over $100 million with acquisitions in 1989 and 1999. The number of sample is 53 in 1989 and 59 in 1992. 1989 was boom year for M&A while 1992 was a through. They consider different economic environments to test robustness for their experiment. They found that four indicators of managers' hubris: the acquiring company's recent performance, recent media praise for the CEO, and a measure of the CEO's self-importance and composite of these three factors. There was a positive correlation between managers' hubris and premiums.

Gu and Lev [10] explored the relation between acquires' overpricing shares and goodwill impairment losses. Their sample consists of all U.S. publicly traded firms that undertook mergers and acquisitions from 1990 to 2006. We include acquisitions of both U.S. and foreign enterprises, as well as acquisitions. The number of sample is 54,218. The number of bidder subsample which acquired companies in the period is 7,055 in the sample. They suggested that acquires' overpriced shares provide managers with strong incentives to exploit the overpricing by acquiring business. It often occurs overpayment for acquisition. In particular they showed acquires' overpriced shares positively correlated with the intensity of corporate acquisitions and the growth of goodwill value.

ESMA report

The European Securities and Markets Authority (ESMA) explored an overview of accounting practices related to impairment testing of goodwill. The sample is 235 European listed entities. The sample was selected through a two-step process to ensure representation of the largest European issuers with the most significant amount of goodwill, and a wide coverage of industries and balanced geographical representation across Europe[3].

The report showed managers are likely to avoid recognizing impairment losses of goodwill, particularly in the financial services and telecommunication industry. The €790 billion of goodwill recognized in the 2010 IFRS financial statements. Even though 43% of the sample showed a market value below equity (book value) on December 2011, total impairment losses on goodwill in 2011 amounted to €40 billion. These losses are only 5% into total goodwill value in 2010 [6]. This report questioned managers used the appropriate assumptions

[3]The ESMA report showed how the sample was selected. Please refer to ESMA (2012).

to do goodwill impairment tests. As mentioned before, goodwill is not amortized after initial recognition in accounting for goodwill. When the carrying amount of asset exceeds the recoverable amount, the managers should reduce the carrying amount and recognize an impairment loss. Goodwill acquired in a business combination has to be tested for impairment at least on an annual basis. Goodwill impairment loss cannot be recovered until the recoverable amount is recognized after recognizing impairment losses. The ESMA report suggested the accounting for goodwill (IAS36) gave managers discretions to manipulate accounting figures. ESMA also found that approximately 10% of companies are not accordance with disclosure requirements of IAS 36.

Case studies-Olympus Scandal

Increasing loss

As mentioned above, managers have a incentive to meet their performance expectations. Managers manipulate their perfomance to avoid a decline in the value of their stocks, a downgrade of the company's debt, debt covenant violations, and corporate bankruptcy. The Olympus scandal is one of the typycal case for accounting fraud. Managers had hiden companies' lossses until it was revealed.

Olympus was founded in 1919 and an one of the most famous and traditional camera brands. Its main products are precision machineries and istruments, degital cameras, madeical endscopes.

The root for the scandal was an aggressive financial assets management after 1985(the Japanese bubble period). This management caused the loss in the faincial assets after 1990 (the collapse of bubble economy). Olympus started investing risky financial products to recover the loss. Ironically, this investment increased the loss of financial assets and the unrealized loss piled up to about \95 billion around 1998 [11, 12]. At that time, the Japanese jurisdicton are working to adopt the fair value accounting in 2001. Few limited employees at Finance Grop with hired consaltants started seeking a way to aboid discloing the unrealized loss.

Loss separation scheme

They decided to use the measure ("Loss Separation Scheme"). Since1998, Olympus started selling the financial instruments incorporating the unrealized loss at the book value to the funds who were not a consoldate entity. This enabled Olympus to transfer the unrealozed loss to the funds. These funds are called "Receiver Fund". the Receiver Funds got loans secured with some assets of Olympus from LGT [11]. They also had Olympus set up business investment funds to provide funds to the Receiver Funds. This scheme was concealed by the top management and selected exucectives over 10 years.

Settlement of the loss

However, they recognized that it is impossible to eliminate the loss, beccause the receiver funds must repay the loans to the bank and the money invested into the funds had to be reimbursed. Under the situation, they worked out a plan taking advantage of the accounting for business combinations to change the separated loss to goodwill as an asset in the Olympus's balance sheet. The Figure 4 is a summary of the steps.

They had the Private Funds buy the three private small ventures. Olympus bought that shares for the price over 100 times as high as its actual value. The excess expenditure by overpricing was recognized as goodwill. This means that they succeed in moving the first unrecognized

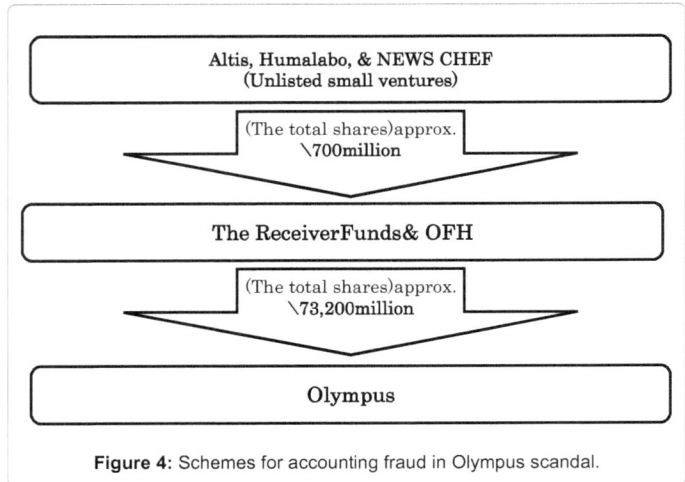

Figure 4: Schemes for accounting fraud in Olympus scandal.

loss to an asset as goodwill. Moreover, because of the overpricing, the Receiver Funds got enough money to repay the loans. Consequently, the bank deposit of Olympus got unnecessary. The invested money was also reimbursed.

The scandal

At first, Olympus planned to amortize the goodwill gradually over 10 to 20 years under the accounting for business combinations. However, in 2009, KPMG AZSA LLC noted the necessity of impairment for the shares and goodwill of Altis, Humalabo, and NEWS CHEF. In response to it, Olympus recognized \77 billion of impairment loss of goodwill. Eventually, in 2011, a Japanese financial magazine, FACTA, exposed the facts concerning the apparently high payments for acquisitions by Olympus in an article. Michael Woodford, COO of Olympus, found this article, investigated the facts and also engaged PwC to confirm the facts. Finally, he became a central figure in exposing the Olympus scandal. However, a problem is that the scandal had would not been exposed at the time if he has not blown the whistle.

Case studies Hewlett-Packard

HP is an American multinational information technology corporation which provides hardware, software and services to consumers, small- and medium-sized businesses and large enterprises. HP acquired Autonomy (Telecommunication Company in U.K.) in 2011 and recognized goodwill value of $6.4 billion which is 5% in total assets. The deal valued Autonomy at $11.7 billion with a premium of around 79% over market price at the acquisition date. Autonomy overstated own revenues by adding the future service revenues before HP bought Autonomy. HP could not understand the true state of Autonomy's financial representation. In November 2012, HP recognized an $8.8 billion impairment loss after the revelation of Autonomy's accounting fraud. HP has admitted overpricing for acquisition of Autonomy. HP Chief Executive Officer Meg Whitman told that HP's board relied on audited financials by Deloitte. On the other hand, she doesn't explain why HP paid $11 billion for Autonomy. HP unintentionally mismanaged the Autonomy merger. This case isn't illegal and is material omissions. Impairment testing alone approach might have an influence on HP's mismanagement.

Conclusion, Limitations and Implication

We verified through the case studies the current accounting standards provide managers with discretion to handle companies' performance. Managers can decide to the value of goodwill and control timing of goodwill impairment. Although the ESMA report shows the possibility that European issuers have not treated goodwill properly while the treatments were not illegal. The boundary between earnings management and accounting fraud is unclear. It is difficult for outside stakeholders to judge whether the accounting process for goodwill is proper or not. While HP's case was unintentional mismanagement, the management caused a loss to shareholders. Managers have a broad discretion into the accounting for goodwill. This would lead to a high possibility that many companies poorly comply with the requirements of accounting. The biases have an impact on earnings quality. The study use only case studies. We need further investigation about this topic.

References

1. Ramanna K, Watts RL (2007) Evidence on the use of unverifiable estimates in required goodwill impairment. Review of Accounting Studies 17: 749-780.

2. Perols JL, Lougee BA (2011) The relation between earnings management and financial statement fraud. Advances in Accounting 17: 39-53.

3. European Securities and Markets Authority (2013) European enforcers review of impairment of good will and other intangible assets in the IFRS financial statement.

4. Dechow PM, Sloan RD, Sweeney AP (1996) Causes and Consequences of Earnings Manipulation: An Analysis of Firms Subject to Enforcement Actions by the SEC. Contemporary Accounting Research 13: 1-36.

5. Healy PM (1985) The effect of bonus schemes on accounting decisions. Journal of Accounting and Economics 7: 85-107.

6. Hirschey M, Vernon JR (2003) Investor Underreaction to Goodwill Write-Offs. Financial Analyst Journal 59: 75-84.

7. Jennings R, LeClere M, Thompson RB (2001) Goodwill Amortization and the Usefulness of Earnings Financial Analysts Journal 57: 20-28.

8. Kim JJ, Haleblian, Finkelstein S (2011) When Firms are Desperate to Grow via Acquisition: The Effect of Growth Patterns and Acquisition Experience on Acquisition Premiumus. Administrative Science Quarterly 56: 26-60.

9. Hayward MLA, Hambrick DC (1997) Explaining the Premiums Paid for Large Acquisitions: Evidence of CEO Hubris. Administrative Science Quarterly 42: 103-127.

10. Gu F, Lev B (2011) Overpriced Shares, Ill-Advised Acquisitions, and Goodwill Impairment. The Accounting Review 86: 1995-2022.

11. Shalev R (2009) The Information Content of Business Combination Disclosure Level. The Accounting Review 84: 239-270.

12. Verrecchia RE (1983) Discretionary Disclosure. Journal of Accounting and Economics 5: 179-194.

2

Impact of Human Resource Management on Organizational Performance

Muhammad Hamid*, Sumra Maheen, Ayesha Cheem and Rizwana Yaseen
Department of Business Administration, University of Sargodha, Pakistan

Abstract

The objective of all organizations is to improve their performance so the aim of this study is to investigate the organizational performance of 200 employees of ufone and Mobilink franchises in Sargodha city. The population in this study has included all companies in telecommunication in Pakistan. We are conducting the exploratory factor analysis. In analyzing the data the descriptive statistics was used. Software used for data analysis was SPSS version 20. The results shows that the higher level of compensation management, organizational citizenship behavior and employee development practices that will lead to a higher level of organizational performance, also indicate that compensation management, organizational citizenship behavior and employee development is positively associated with organizational performance. Our result shows that there is positive or significant relationship between independent and dependent variables, so we reject the null hypothesis. There are some areas that need more development in future including the topics that relate to the study that can be conducted on manufacturing firms with more variables.

Keywords: Organizational performance; Organizational citizenship behavior; Compensation management; Employee development; Tele-communication sector

Introduction

The business of the telecom sector is not only capital intensive, where the important component of capital is to assess to ensure the growth of the strong network but also the core competencies, skills of management, qualification and abilities of management are the dense drivers to increase the achievement of organization profits and the sustainability of business.

No doubt that organization internationally isdetermined for achievement and high profit those in the same industry. For the purpose of this, organizations have to get and apply their human resource effectively and efficiently. Organizations have to be aware of human resource need to know about HRM more realistically and organizations have to keep their human resource up-to-date. Consequently, manager play significant role for the purpose of achieving company's goal and meet profits, basically the core functions of managers have to manage the human resource in a way that right number in right way. This paper therefore, examines the influence of human resource management that is compensation, employee's development and organizational citizenship behavior on the performance of the organization.

In any organization performance of organization is very important. The super objective of all organizations is to improve their performance. There may be three areas that create or to enhance the organizational performance: employee development of organization (EDO), compensation management of organization (CMO) and organizational citizenship behavior (OCB).

The main objective of this study is to measure the effect of compensation on organizational performance. Compensation is vital for organization's performance. As the employee compensation, training and rewards have risen the performance of human resource managementresultsgenerallyraisesthe satisfactionand performance. There are three independent variables citizenship behavior, employee's development, and compensation management and their combine effect on organizational performance.

According to Turnipseed and Russuli explained that when organization criticized in investment, which means organizational

citizenship behavior is "going beyond the call of duty" [1]. Poncheri [2] refers that organization citizenship behavior have significant impact on performance of organization. OCB not relevant to individual duties, it is related to the organization's functions and duties which is significant to improve the organizational effectiveness or performance Applebaumet et al. [3]. Morhd/Griffin explained that organizational citizenship behavior creativity and adaptation leads to the organizational effectiveness and work related management in HRM (1375, 132).

Torraco and Swanson [4] observed the positive relationship between employee development and organizational performance. Organizational performance can be achieved through the learning opportunities, through better employee performance on their jobs. The unit of analysis in the research is employee development which has an impact on performance but the less information is available. Learning opportunities are the part of employee development programs.

Research has established the significant impact on organizational performance. There is connection between HRM and organizational performance is considered a "black box" that is absence of clarity as to, what leads to what. Gerhart [5]. Therefore this study shows the significant positive relationship between independent variables and organizational performance either financial or non-financial.

In this study we fill the gap of previous studies and more observe the procedure through which HRM policies, procedures techniques and effect of organizational performance, it is important to conduct analysis in Pakistan context on the telecom sector. The main objective of this research is to examine how the HRM practices influence the performance of organization , to enhance the relationship instead of

*Corresponding author: Muhammad Hamid, Department of Business Administration, University of Sargodha, Pakistan
E-mail: Hamid_cheema@yahoo.com

two variables we take three variables that are employee development, compensation management and organizational citizenship. Next we present the hypothesis to be verified. The discussion is followed by methodology and evaluates the hypothesis. The following portion concentrates on important findings, their applied effects and argument. Lastly sum up the key of the research and focus the key purpose direction for additional study, contributions, limitations of the analysis and results.

General purpose of the study

In the light of above outline, the goal of this study is to test the effects of human resource management on performance of organizational within the telecom sector in Sargodha Pakistan.

Specific purpose

The sub goals included are as follow:

a) To examine the influence of compensation management on organizational performance.

b) The effect of employee development on performance of organization.

c) The impact of organizational citizenship behavior on organizational performance.

d) The purpose is to introduce the relationship of above these independent variables first time with dependent

e) Variable as organizational performance.

Literature Review

Employee development and organizational performance

Stiles and Kulvisaechana [6] observed the positive relationship between the human resource development and organizational performance according to the large and expand body of literature. Human Resource management in an independent and intangible variable, market value depends on intangible variable. Shih, Chiang, and Hsu [7] observed that the part of framework of human resource development is retaining and recruiting the perfect employees. The cooperative goals of the organizations can be shared and applied through knowledge, employee's capacity and competence hold by the organization through training and encouraging environment. Expansion in productivity and business performance expand the Future returns. Future returns depend on the employee's skills and abilities. Hardre [8] study the impact of resourcing and growth on the employee's attitude which include motivation, satisfaction and commitment. Personnel training and development and organizational development contribute to unleashing human expertise and to enhance performance [9]. Organizational performance and productivity is positively affiliated with comprehensive training activities [10]. The effectiveness and efficiency of public sector depends on the positive future oriented employee development [11]. The organizational performance depends on the training and development of human resource and the organization spends millions of money for this purpose. Organizational performance depends on the employee development because employee development enhances knowledge base of the organization [12].

There is a positive relationship between business performance and employee development. Performance management programs have impact on this relationship. Performance management programs include the incentives plans, feedback mechanism. This study suggests that low level of performance management programs and low employee development decrease the industrial performance [13]. The employee development depends on the two important measures, training and promotion. There is a significant relationship between investment in employee development and business performance. The factors effecting the employee development include the selection strategies, recruitment, evaluation of performance and planning procedure. There is an indirect relationship between employee development and organizational performance, relationship include the human resource practices [14].

The honest conversation regarding the employee development showed that there is the positive correlation with employee's attitudes; employee attitude includes the goal commitment and job satisfaction [15].

The four approaches are used for employee development which includes laissez-faire, autocracy, meritocracy and co-determination. Management behaviors directly or indirectly related to the employee development and situational outcomes [16]. Organizational performance and employee development are affected by the tuition assistance programs. Tuition assistance programs are a method that the organizations used to invest their resources in the human resource with the aim to develop more knowledgeable and educated workforce. Swanson [9] indicates that the independent variable is employeedevelopment which directly affects the organizational performance. Organizational performance positively affected by employee development because of effective use of employee empowerment practices.

Compensation management and organizational performance

Holt [17]employee receive compensation in the form of rewards, pay, benefit it is basically the output that management uses to increase the performance of organization.

Half of the cash flow is equal to the compensation of the organizationbut more than half in the service sector. Ivanceikh, Glueck [18]. For the purpose to increase performance of organization the key factor is tomotivate employees and attract the employees.

Compensation can be in the form of multiple pay plans and can be in the form of individually, merit pay to performance long incentives, bonus, and merit pay in the form of rewards. These are the different qualities and components of compensation that are in the form of individual performance and multiple pay plan performance, this research was conducted by Millvier and Newman. In order to increase the performance of organization pay plan is commonly used Chani. The most common appraisal of employee is pay plan by Heneman and warner.

The research conducted in ref. [19]. Pay have direct impact on the performance of employees the compensation and the pay structure directly impact the performance of the employees and the they provide the output according to the pay plan and pay structure according to the performance of employees. In 1999 the employees have fixed pay and the organization give rewards for their better performance that willgive the power job shorter orientedso there is relationship between compensation like pay and performance.

Simon, more and hunt, jahangar Suggested that rewards of managers supervisors significant positive relationship with performance of organization that is performance of employees, enhance productivity, satisfaction of employees organizational citizenship behavior and turnover. For the purpose of achievement of organizational performance either it is financial or non-financial compensation in the form of rewards or incentives are most important component to eradicate employees paying their energy to produce innovation in cress the performance of organization. The researches by employees' productivity can be increase by motivation which provide effective recognition as a result improve organizational performance.

The research on relationship between organizational performance and compensation in the form of pay suggested that pay is not directly related to the performance of organization but in many statements or claims merit increases the salary and hence increase the performance.

Their research concluded that significant positive relationship between HRM practices and organizational performance [20], HRM practices like selective hiring, compensation management, training and development, status differences,decentralization,information sharing, employment security, and use of groups on performance of organization as operational performance likeflexibility,cost reduction, quality, and commitment. HR administration structures in US study investigates that organizational performance has significant positive relationship to various HR practices compensation and benefits. Gerhart and Trevor [21], kochy McGrath [14], recruitment and selection.

HRM practices like compensation and rewards, training and development, recruitment and selection and performance management have positive effect on organization performance observed in 104 articles documented in 18 that four most important [22].

To measure the impact of HRM practices like training and development, compensation and rewards,performance appraisal, and employeesrecruitmentand selectiontheir relations on performance of organization that are (product quality, Product cost,, performance, market share compared with competitors and 19 organization performance relative to industry average) and in 20 companies of oil and gas establish significant positive relationship with HRM practices like compensation, training and development, employees development and performance of the organization.

Khan investigates Motivational factor for the employees are the compensation so proposes structure of compensation in which employees who perform better are paid more than average performing employees is important to increase the performance of organization Hewitt [23].

Organizational citizenship behavior and organizational performance

In 1770s OCB has been studied and its interest significantly increased. Denis Organ considered as the father of OCB. Organ explained "Individually behavior that is discretionary not directly or explicitly recognized by the formal reward system and that in aggregate promotes the effective functioning of the organization" (P.4). Duton et al. expressed that better standing of employees with organization that ultimately affect the organizational citizenship behavior [24].

Coole [25]indicates that the organizational citizenship performance speculate the overall performance and across all task performance levels. Morinson defines citizenship behavior as a function of employee's in-role and extra-role job behaviors [26]. Mc Ulster described organizational citizenship behavior is favorable for organization. To improve the organizational performance issues has been facing by senior management. The findings of [27] organizational citizenship behavior prove to be helpful to the organization. Podsakoff

and Mackenzie researched that OCB are significant to the performance of all organizations [28].

The type of OCB creates strong link between organizational performance and organizational workers [1]. Todd described that if we add the social work environment the overall performance of organization increases substantially [24]. According to Niehoff and Yen that the organization becomes more effective if there are more employees in organizational citizenship behavior. As a result we anticipated OCB to make the correlation between organizational performance and HR practices.

Hypothesis

H1: There is positive relationship between employee's development and organizational performance.

H2: There is positive relationship between compensation management and organizational performance.

H3: There is positive relationship between organizational citizenship behavior and organizational performance.

Conceptual framework

Our research consist of total four variables and three are independent such as employee development, compensation, and organizational citizenship behavior they have influence or effect on dependent variable organizational performance. According to refs. [29-35] the impact of human resource management practices on the performance of organization have some backing for positive relationship between human resource management like compensation, employee development and citizenship behavior and performance particularly profitability (Figure 1).

Methodology

The purpose of our research is to analysis the impact of human resource on organizational performance. There are the two major sources of research. The study was conducted on the bases of different publications on this field. The secondary source refers to the collection of qualitative data from faculty members of ufone and Mobilink franchises in Sargodha city. We use the structured questionnaires to get the sufficient information. The study conducted on Sargodha city [36-41].

Population and Sample size

The target sector of our study is Pakistan telecommunication. The target population of the study all companies in telecommunication. Franchises of ufone or Mobilink in Sargodha city are our sample size. By using convenience sampling technique, 200 employees of ufone

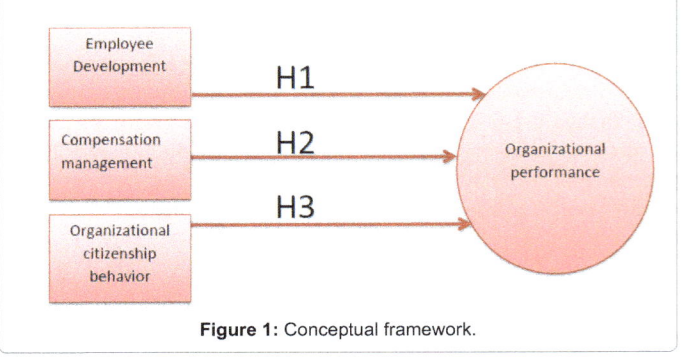

Figure 1: Conceptual framework.

and Mobilinkfranchises has been chosen. Sample subjects have been chosen on the basis of accessibility of the researchers.

Nature of data

Nature of data is qualitative which consist of feelings and behaviors of faculty members of ufone and Mobilink franchises in Sargodha city. We are conducting the exploratory Analysis.

Instrument: We use the Questionnaire technique on 5 likert scale which consist of the following scale

a) Strongly agree

b) Agree

c) Neutral

d) disagree

e) Strongly disagree

The questionnaire consists of 19 questions that are distributed in four different sections each section represents factors.

The questionnaire contained the two sections: the first section was designed to gather the information about the respondent's personal background. In the second section of the questionnaire, the respondents were asked to

Salient features ofufone and Mobilink Company. The questions asked in this section include those that measured the employee development, compensation management, organizational performance, and organizational citizenship.

The analyses were run to determine the response of responded about Ufone and Mobilink Company. Since this study is exploratory in nature.

The four to six items have been tested as a measure of the dependent variables and the three variables are taken as the independent variables.

Analysis technique: We use SPSS software for data analysis. In SPSS, we compute frequencies, descriptive analysis, reliability andvalidity of test, correlation and at the end we run regression; we analyze model summary,ANOVA and coefficient analysis.

Data Analysis

Demographic profile

There are 200 employees in Ufone and Mobilink franchises in Sargodha. According to the Table 1, there are 167 Male and 33 female. The age of respondents, 3 %was below 19 years old.19.5 % was between the ages of 20-29 years. 34 %was between the ages of 30-39 years. 28.5%were between the ages of 40-49 years.15% was above 50 years old.24% employees had less than 5 years worked experience.43 % employees in franchises had experience of 5- 10 years.12.5% employees had 11-15 years worked experience.17.5% employees had 16-20 years worked experience. 3% employees had working experience of more than 20 years (Table 1).

The23.5% employees were senior managers, 45% were middle managers, 19.5% were junior employees, 12% were other staff members.

Descriptive statistics

We describe this central position using a number of statistics, including the minimum, maximum, and mean. To describe this spread, a number of statistics are available to including the range, variance and

	Variables	Frequencies	Percentages
Gender	Male	167	83.5
	Female	33	16.5
Age	Below 19	6	3
Working	20-29	39	19.5
Experience	30-39	68	34
	40-49	57	28.5
	50 above	30	15
Respondent position			
	Less than 5 years	48	24
	5-10 years	86	43
	11-15 years	25	12.5
	16-20years	35	17.5
	More than 20 years	6	3
	Senior manager	47	23.5
	Middle	90	45
	Junior	39	19.5
	Staff	24	12

Table 1: Demographic profile.

Statistics

		Org. Performance	Org. Citizenbehaviour	Emp. Development	Comp. Management
N	Valid	200	200	200	200
	Missing	0	0	0	0
Mean		6.6750	8.4650	11.7450	7.0550
Median		6.0000	8.0000	12.0000	7.0000
Std. Deviation		2.76361	3.21097	4.16494	2.65655
Range		12.00	13.00	14.00	12.00
Minimum		4.00	5.00	6.00	4.00
Maximum		16.00	18.00	20.00	16.00
Sum		1335.00	1693.00	2349.00	1411.00

Table 2: Descriptive statistics.

Latent Variable	No. of Items	Cronbach's Alpha (>0.7)
Compensation Management	4	0.845
Employee development	6	0.872
Organizational citizenship behavior	5	0.909
Organizational performance	4	0.892

Table 3: Reliability analysis.

standard deviation. The mean value represent that the respondent's satisfaction regarding the human resource management practices in franchises (Table 2).

Reliability analysis

According to the cronbach's Alpha the reliability of the scale require the value of cronbach's alpha should be >0.6, the value more than 0.6 is called significant value.

To check the reliability of the scale and internal consistency of the measure, we use the cronbach's Alpha method. Internal consistency of the measure means that the suggested method gives the same results, when we apply the same test under the same condition again and again.

According to the Cuieford the Cronbach's alpha value should be more than 7 that identify the reliability of the measure (Table 3).

Reliability value

The scale that we used in our study is reliable for data analysis. The internal consistency of the measure is good and reliable because the cronbach's alpha value is >0.7. we get the results of inter item consistency and reliability coefficients of all independent variables (organizational citizenship behavior , compensation management, employee development) and dependent variable (Organizational performance). The calculated values of cronbach's Alpha are given in Table 3. The cronbach's alpha values that is near to α=1.0 is considered more significant and value that is less than α=0.6 is insignificant. We measured the organizational performance (telecommunication Pakistan) through 4 items and the value of cronbach's alpha is α=0.892. This value is near to α=1.0. We measured the compensation management through 5 items and the cronbach's alpha value is α=0.909, employee development was measured through the 6 items and the Cronbach's alpha value is 0.872 which is significant.

We also measured the organizational citizenship behaviors with 4 items and value of Cronbach's alpha is α=0.845 that is reliable.

Correlation (Table 4)

The first item organizational citizenship behavior is highly correlated with organizational performance with value of 0.586 it means that increase in citizenship behavior of employees increases the performance of organization. So it rejects the null hypothesis that is there is no relationship between organization citizenship and performance of organization.

The null hypothesis of employee development has no relation with organizational performance is also rejected because it also correlated with performance of organization with value of 350. There is medium correlation, not highly correlated but there is correlation.

Compensation management is also highly correlated with organizational performance with the value of 0.531 and it will reject the null hypothesis that it has no relationship with performance of organization. This means that it can be interpreted that there is positive relationship between compensation and performance of organization.

There is concluded that there is large Pearson correlation or

relationship with these above mentioned items with performance of organization with Pearson correlation of above 0.5 for each.

Regression

Model summary: The model summary of regression analysis consists of the values of R, R square, adjusted R square, standard error of the estimates. R called the Pearson R. Pearson R is equal to the R^2. R^2 is used to determine the model fitness. Coefficient of determination is also called R square. R^2 is equal to the regression divided by total sum of square which is given in ANOVA Table 5. R square is used to determine the variation in dependent variable that is explained by independent variables. According to Table 6, 37% variation in organizational performance id due to the predictors (Compensation management, organizational citizenship behavior and employee development). The rest of the 62.8% variation in organizational performance is explained by other factors that are not the part of our study (Table 5).

ANOVA (Table 6)

The results of ANOVA test reveal that the model is statistically significant that analyzed the factors affectingthe organizational performance. The above model demonstrates that the significance level is less than 0.05 that is a sign of approval that there exists a relationship between organizational performance and independent variables of the study.

Coefficients (Table 7)

The coefficient table includes unstandardized coefficient (beta and std. error) and also include standardized coefficient (beta) t value and significance. Beta value is value of Y it means value of dependent variable that is organizational performance when there is one unit change in independent variables (compensation, employee development, and organizational citizenship behavior) it would change in dependent variable. t Value is significant at 95 % confidence level

Correlations			ORGPER	ORGCITIZEN	EMPDEVELOP	COMPMANAGE
Pearson correlation		ORGPER	1.000			.
		ORGCITIZEN	0.586	1.000		
		EMPDEVELOP	0.350	0.456	1.000	
		COMPMANAGE	0.531	0.707	0.558	1.000
Sig. (1-tailed)		ORGPER	0	0.000	0.000	0.000
		ORGCITIZEN	0.000	.	0.000	0.000
		EMPDEVELOP	0.000	0.000	.	0.000
		COMPMANAGE	0.000	0.000	0.000	.
N		ORGPER	200	200	200	200
		ORGCITIZEN	200	200	200	200
		EMPDEVELOP	200	200	200	200
		COMPMANAGE	200	200	200	200

Correlation is significant at 0.01 (1-tail).
Correlation is significant at 0.05 (1-tail).

Table 4: Correlation.

Model	R	R Square	Adjusted R Square	Std. Error of the Estimate	Durbin-Watson
1	0.610[a]	0.372	0.362	2.20710	2.283

a. Predictors: (Constant), COMPMANAGE, EMPDEVELOP, ORGCITIZEN.

b. Dependent Variable: ORGPER.

Adjusted R square is based upon the sample size and the number of regressors (constant). The value of standard error of the estimates is calculated with the help of Mean square value of ANOVA Table. The standard error of the estimate is a measure of the accuracy of predictions. Model summary table also includes Durbin Watson value it should range from 1 to 4 here value is 2.283 it means there is auto correlation between the independent variables. (Vining, G. G. 2001). If its value is exactly 2 it means there is no auto correlation, but here there is some auto correlation.

Table 5: Model summary.

Model	Sum of Squares	Df	Mean Square	F	Sig.
Regression	565.104	3	188.368	38.669	0.000[b]
Residual	954.771	196	4.871		
Total	1519.875	199			
a. Dependent Variable: Orgper					
b. Predictors: (Constant), Compmanage, Empdevelop, Orgcitizen					

Table 6: ANOVA[a].

Model	Unstandardized Coefficients		Standardized Coefficients	t	Sig.
	B	Std. Error	Beta		
(Constant)	1.755	0.530		3.311	0.001
ORGCITIZEN	0.359	0.069	0.417	5.175	0.000
EMPDEVELOP	0.027	0.046	0.041	0.598	0.550
COMPMANAGE	0.222	0.090	0.213	2.467	0.014

Table 7: Coefficients.

that we are confident organizational performance is affected by these independent variables. Organizational citizenship, compensation is positively significant at 95% with t value 5.175 and 2.467, respectively. Employee development is positively insignificant with t value of 0.598.

Areas needing more contribution

Several areas in which HR is needed to play a role but were not yet working to fulfill the need and in which HR was already playing significant role but there was still gap in which HR should consider.

a) Scope of this study covers only employees in future this study can be conducted oncustomer.

b) The comparative research can be conducted between private and public sector.

c) The study conducted only on the Sargodha in future researcher conduct study on other cities of Pakistan as well.

d) In future the study can be conducted on manufacturing firms with more variables.

e) Due to time shortage there are few variables next research can be on human resource management and its impact on change management, financial performance of company.

Conclusion

The purpose of the present study is to empirically examine the impact of compensation management, employee development and organizational citizenship behavior on organizational performance of Ufone Company and Mobil inkCompany (telecommunication Pakistan). A questionnaire survey was conducted among ufone and Mobilink's faculty members. Its intention was to measure the impact of organizational citizenship behaviors, employee development and compensation with the perspective of employees on the performance of organization. The study's findings indicate that the establishment of higher levels of compensation management practices, employees development and organizational citizenship behavior that will lead to a higher level oforganizational performance. As a result, they indicate that compensation management is positively associated with organizational performance (ufone and Mobilink Company). Furthermore, the results also show that the effect of employees development and organizational citizenship behavior are also measures the organizational performance. There are some areas that need more development in future including the topics that relate to the study that can be conducted on manufacturing firms with more variables. There is need to conduct the research that include more variables i.e., human

resource management and its impact on change management, financial performance of company in other cities of Pakistan.

References

1. Turnipseed DL, Rassuli A (2005) Performance Perceptions of Organizational Citizenship Behaviours at Work: a Bi-Level Study among Managers and Employees. British Journal of Management 16: 231-244.

2. Poncheri RM (2006) The Impact of Work Context on The Prediction of Job Performance.

3. Appelbaum S, Bartolomucci N, Beaumier E, Boulanger J, Corrigan R, et al. (2004) Organizational Citizenship Behavior: A Case Study of Culture, Leadership And Trust. Management Decision 42:13-40.

4. Torraco RJ, Swanson RA (1995) The Strategic Roles of Human Resource Development. People and Strategy18: 10.

5. Gerhart B (2007) Horizontal and Vertical Fit In Human Resource Systems. Perspectives on Organizational fit.

6. Stiles P, Kulvisaechana S (2003) Human Capital and Performance: A Literature Review.

7. Shih HA, Chiang YH, Hsu CC (2006) Can High Performance Work Systems Really Lead To Better Performance? International Journal of Manpower 27: 741-763.

8. Hardré PL (2003) Beyond Two Decades of Motivation: A Review of the Research and Practice in Instructional Design and Human Performance Technology. Human Resource Development Review 2: 54-81.

9. Swanson RA (1995) Human Resource Development: Performance Is the Key. Human Resource Development Quarterly 6: 207-213.

10. Lee CH, Bruvold NT (2003) Creating Value for Employees: Investment in Employee Development. The International Journal of Human Resource Management 14: 981-1000.

11. Solkhe A, Chaudhary N (2011) HRD climate and job satisfaction: An empirical investigation. International Journal of Computing and Business Research 2: 1-20.

12. Nwuche CA, Awa HO (2011) Career Planning and Development: The Realities in Nigerian Organizations. International Business and Management 2: 117-127.

13. Mcdonald D, Smith A (1995) A Proven Connection Performance Management and Business Results. Compensation & Benefits Review 27 59-64.

14. Koch MJ, McGrath RG (1996) Improving labor productivity: Human resource management policies do matter. Strategic Management Journal 17: 335-354.

15. Tansky JA (1991) An Effective Employee Development Discussion: The Causes and Consequences.

16. Washington C (1996) A Proposed Model of Approaches to Front-Line Employee Development. In Proceedings of the Annual Conference of the Academy of Human Resource Development.

17. Holt DH (1993) Management: Concept and Practices.

18. Ivancevich, Glueck JMWF (1989) Foundations of Personnel/Human Management. 21397-409.

19. Lazear EP (1986) Salaries and Piece Rates. Journal of Business 59:405-431.

20. Ahmad S, Schroeder RG (2003) The Impact of Human Resource Management Practices on Operational Performance: Recognizing Country and Industry Differences. Journal of Operations Management 21: 19-43.

21. Gerhart B, Trevor CO (1996) Employment Variability under Different Managerial Compensation Systems. Academy of Management Journal 39: 1692-1712.

22. Boselie P, Dietz G, Boon C (2005) Commonalities and Contradictions in HRM and Performance Research. Human Resource Management Journal 15: 67-94.

23. Hewitt A (2009) Managing Performance with Incentive Pay. Journal of Personnel Management 7: 20-31.

24. Todd SY (2004) A Causal Model Depicting the Influence of Selected Task and Employee Variables on Organizational Citizenship Behavior.

25. Coole DR (2003) The Effects of Citizenship Performance, Task Performance, and Rating Format on Performance Judgments.

26. Morrison EW (1994) Role Definitions and Organizational Citizenship Behavior: The Importance of the Employee's Perspective. Academy of Management Journal 37: 1543-1567.

27. MacKenzie SB, Podsakoff PM, Fetter R (1993) The Impact of Organizational Citizenship Behavior on Evaluations of Salesperson Performance. The Journal of Marketing 57: 70-80.

28. Podsakoff PM, MacKenzie SB (1997) Impact of Organizational Citizenship Behavior on Organizational Performance: A Review and Suggestion for Future Research. Human Performance 10: 133-151.

29. Hyde J, Stup R, Holden L (2008) The Effect of Human Resource Management Practices on Farm Profitability: An Initial Assessment. Economics Bulletin 17: 1-10.

30. Anlesinya A, Bukari Z, Eshun P (2014) The Effect Of Employee Development On Performance Of Public Sector Organisations In Ghana: Evidence from Controller and Accountant General's Department, Accra.

31. Caudron S (1999) Free Agent Learner. Training & Development 53: 26-31.

32. Anlesinya A, Bukari Z, Eshun P(2014) The Effect Of Employee Development on Performance of Public Sector Organisations In Ghana: Evidence from Controller and Accountant General's Department, Accra.

33. Podsakoff PM, Ahearne M, MacKenzie SB (1997) Organizational Citizenship Behavior and the Quantity and Quality of Work Group Performance. Journal of Applied Psychology 82: 262.

34. Podsakoff PM, MacKenzie SB (1997) Impact of Organizational Citizenship Behavior on Organizational Performance: A Review and Suggestion for Future Research. Human Performance 10: 133-151.

35. Organ DW (1988) Organizational Citizenship Behavior: The Good Soldier Syndrome. Lexington Books/DC Heath and Com.

36. MacKenzie SB, Podsakoff PM, Fetter R (1993) The Impact of Organizational Citizenship Behavior on Evaluations of Salesperson Performance. The Journal of Marketing 57: 70-80.

37. Van Der Wiele T, Boselie P, Hesselink M (2002) Empirical Evidence for the Relationship between Customer Satisfaction and Business Performance. Managing Service Quality: An International Journal 12: 184-193.

38. Rawashdeh AM, karim Al-Adwan I (2012) The Impact of Human Resource Management Practices on Corporate Performance: Empirical Study in Jordanian Commercial Banks. African Journal of Business Management6: 10591.

39. Ijigu AW (2015) The Effect of Selected Human Resource Management Practices on Employees' Job Satisfaction in Ethiopian Public Banks. Emerging Markets Journal.

40. Boxall PF, John P, Wright PM (2007) The Oxford Handbook of Human Resource Management. Oxford University Press on Demand.

41. Montgomery DC, Jennings CL, Kulahci M (2015) Introduction to Time Series Analysis and Forecasting. John Wiley & Sons.

Change in Bank Equity Stakes before Merger Completion

Paitoon Chetthamrongchai[1]*, Lin Lin[2], Hsaio-Fen Hsiao[3] and Yu-LunHuang[2]

[1]*Department of Marketing, Kasetsart University, Bangkok, Thailand*
[2]*Department of Banking and Finance, National Chi Nan University, Taiwan*
[3]*Department of Finance, MingDao University, Taiwan*

Abstract

This study investigates the relationship between the changes in the shareholdings of the institutional financial/ investment professionals and the firm-specific characteristics of the acquiring companies prior to merger completion. The present study thus serves to identifying the factors dominating investment behaviors of acquiring firms. Both total and average changes in their ownership are considered to test the popular agency and signaling hypotheses. Evidence shows that commercial banks are more likely to increase their equity holdings of those businesses with increasing current liability and decreasing profitability. The former supports the signaling hypothesis but the latter suggests the agency cost hypothesis is correct. Investment banks, on the other hand, prefer those with increasing assets and a stable financial status. A competitive relation of these financial experts is also presented in terms of the pursuit of greater controlling power over the board against each other before the merger completion date.

Keywords: Bank holding; Financial expertise; Agency theory; Signaling theory; Corporate governance

Introduction

Financial institutions play an important role in the financial markets by not only serving as a key funding source for new enterprises but also, through the exchange process, monitoring a firm's operations and diagnosing a firm's financial condition. Within the realm of financial institutions, commercial banks and investment banks have a particularly strong effect on the firm's performance. Petersen and Rajan [1] pointed out that as firms and commercial banks build and maintain long-term relationships, both lenders and borrowers can reduce agency conflict and the information asymmetry problem [2-5]. Investment banks can provide professional advice to firms on investment projects including mergers and acquisitions (M&As) activities [6]. In particular, investment banks can gain access to the firm's inside information and thus more accurately estimate the true value in the underwriting process, reducing the possibility of credit risk [7,8]. In addition, an investment bank holding firm's stock can reduce underwriting fees because the firm can reduce the cost of equity financing [9].

It is a well-known fact that M&As come in waves. Jensen and Meckling [10] apply agency theory to the modern corporation and model the agency costs of outside equity. The corporate finance literature comes up with different answers to this question. Shleifer and Vishny [11] argue that ownership concentration enhances corporate control by improving the monitoring of management. With diffused ownership, shareholders have few incentives for monitoring. With concentrated ownership, the cost of shirking will be mostly borne by large shareholders who therefore have a strong incentive to monitor the firm's management.

Commercial bank holding firm's stock in order to reduce the agency problem between shareholders and creditors, when the smaller size of the firm, the higher the ratio of intangible assets, greater volatility, and lower profitability, so that firms have more serious information asymmetry and agency conflicts [2,3,12,13]. The bank holding to get control of the firms through effective supervision and control of the firm's plans for the choice, reduce the conversion of assets, over- or under-investment problems, bank holding can use earning of investment plan to make up for some of the diluted value of the bank loan to the firm. This can often lead to increased bank holdings of probability.

The past research only considered a single type of a bank holding firm's stock or treated the supervisor of the companies' directors as the research object. Under general conditions, a variety of financial institutions will hold the stock at the same time. The present research simultaneously considers the commercial bank and the investment bank holding firm's stock as the research object. In addition, the previous studies are mostly for a specific time to explore the external financial institutions to enter the directors of the Companies Board of Supervisors and the companies characteristics related to research [14-16]. However, each firm may have different, time-dependent shocks. In addition, at the point in time before the study, the financial institutions may have had early access to the firm's board of directors and the holding firm's shares. Because the use of a specific point in time may be difficult to illustrate, the of financial institutions into directors of the Companies Board of Supervisors or holding shares of the firm's motives. This study does not explore the motive of ownership of financial institutions at a particular point in time. The quarterly holding changes between the first six quarters for the merger completion date to determine whether to increase its holding and to research the change in the connection between shareholding of financial institutions and financial characteristics.

The organization of the remainder of this paper is as follows. Section 2 describes our model, while Section 3 discusses the date and reports the main estimation results. Finally, Section 4 offers some concluding thoughts and discusses some implications of our findings.

Model Implementation

This section briefly introduces the Logistic model used to investigate the bank's holdings increases and each bank's average holdings increase

---

*Corresponding author: Paitoon Chetthamrongchai, Department of Marketing, Kasetsart University, Bangkok, Thailand
E-mail: fbusptc@ku.ac.th

on the relationship between characteristics of the bidding firms. The commercial banks and investment banks were measured using the same method described as follows:

$$\Delta Y1a_i = \text{the commercial bank's holdings change by firm } i \qquad (1)$$

$$\Delta Y1b_i = \text{the each commercial bank's average holdings change by firm } i \qquad (2)$$

$$\Delta Y2a_i = \text{the investment bank's holdings change by firm } i \qquad (3)$$

$$\Delta Y2b_i = \text{the each investment bank's average holdings change by firm } i \qquad (4)$$

$$\text{each banks average holdings it} = \frac{\text{the bank holdings by firm } i \text{ in quarter } t}{\text{the bank number by firm } i \text{ in quarter } t}$$

where Y_i is equal to 1 if the bank's holdings increase for the period between the M&A announcement date to the completion date, and 0 otherwise.

The model

This paper analyses the relationship between the bank's holdings change and characteristics of the bidding firms. Following the methodology proposed by Kroszner and Strahan [14] and controlling for firm operating performance variables such as changes in financial position ($\Delta ZSCORE_i$); value of firms (Tobin's q_{it-6}); fame of firms ($FAME_i$) and change in investment quality ($\Delta EROIC_i$). First, based on agency theory and signaling effects, we examine the relationship between the commercial bank's holdings increase probability and changes in the bidding firm's characteristics. The basic regression model takes the following form:

$$\Delta Y_i = \alpha_0 + \sum_{j=1}^{3} \beta_j IND_j + \beta_4 CONTROL_{it} + \beta_5 TOBINQ_{it-6} + \beta_6 \Delta ZSCORE_i + \beta_{10} \Delta LnTA_i$$
$$+ \beta_7 \Delta VOL_i + \beta_8 \Delta VOL^2_i + \beta_9 PROFIT_i + \beta_{11} \Delta TANRATIO_i$$
$$+ \beta_{12} \Delta DEBTRATIO_i + \beta_{13} \Delta CDRATIO_i + \beta_{14} \Delta EROIC_i + FAME_i + \varepsilon_{it} \qquad (5)$$

Second, this paper examines the relationship between the investment bank's holdings change and characteristics of the bidding firms. The basic regression model takes the following form:

$$\Delta Y_i = \alpha_0 + \sum_{i=1}^{3} \beta_i IND_i + \beta_4 CONTROL_{it} + \beta_5 TOBINQ_{it} + \beta_6 \Delta ZSCORE_{it} + \beta_7 \Delta LnTA_i$$
$$+ \beta_8 \Delta INVRATIO_i + \beta_9 \Delta EQRATIO_i + \beta_{10} \Delta FAME_i + \varepsilon_{it} \qquad (6)$$

The coefficient α_0 is the intercept, β_j is the regression coefficient, and ε_{it} is an error term assumed to be normally distributed with a mean of zero, i is firm i, t is the six quarters before the M&A completion date, Δ is the change invariables in the six quarters before the M&A announcement date and the completion date. Because this study aims to examine changes in firm characteristics which affect a bank's holdings change, changes in the amount of use were also included as other independent variables (in addition to control variables, some of the powers, and Tobin's Q using the quarter in six quarters before M&A completion date).

Variables

Industry variables (IND_i): This paper uses codings in accordance with SIC CODE (Standard Industrial Classification Code) before the two-digit codes. Figure 1 shows the characteristics of the sample according to industry, which can be divided into four main categories (energy category, manufacturing sector, retail trade, and services

sector). These exclude the regulatory constraints of industry such as financial sector (SIC CODE=60~69) and public utilities (SIC CODE=49) (Figure 1).

IND_j is a dummy variable of industry in which j=1 is equal to 1 if the manufacturing sector (SIC CODE=20~48); j=2 is equal to 1 if the retail trade (SIC CODE=50 ~ 59); j=3 is equal to 1 if the services sector (SIC CODE=70~87).

Controlling power variables ($CONTROL_i$): This study suggests that holding a larger percentage of shares have greater controlling power before the M&A completion date. In other words, the commercial bank's holdings more than investment banks holdings in the bidding firms that commercial banks have greater controlling power, and vice versa. $CONTROL_i$ is a dummy variable of controlling power for bidding firms, which is equal to 1 if the commercial bank's holdings are more than the investment bank's holdings in the bidding firms and 0 otherwise.

In samples of commercial bank holdings changes, if the coefficient of controlling power was significantly positive, that commercial bank will continue to increase its holdings to maintain controlling power; if the coefficient is significantly negative, this indicates the investment bank of lower holding will increase its stake to gain controlling power. In samples of investment bank holdings changes, if the coefficient is significantly positive, this indicates the investment bank of lower holding will increase its stake to gain controlling power; if the coefficient is significantly negative, that commercial bank of higher holding has controlling power and will not continue to increase its holdings to maintain its controlling power.

Growth opportunities ($TOBINQ_{it-6}$): Firms with high levels of growth opportunities will have more demand for investment spending, and prior studies [17,18] empirically document such a relation. $TOBINQ_{it-6}$ is the proxy for growth opportunity. If Tobin's Q is higher, that Investors believe the companies governance and higher evaluation of asset quality, thus reducing the firm's proxy conflicts. According to the agency cost hypothesis, when Tobin's Q is greater that bank will reduce holdings. According to the signaling hypothesis, when Tobin's Q greater firms with high levels of growth opportunities [19,20]. Bank holdings may be earning higher profits for earning of the investment plan. Therefore it will increase holdings.

Changes in financial position ($\Delta ZSCORE_i$): Following Altman [21], we measured criteria by the Z-score model. In general, Z-scores are the proxies for the probability of financial distress. Firms that are not financially distressed show lower credit risks and are therefore easier to finance in the market. As a result, the conflicts between the shareholders and the creditor agency are usually small. According to the agency cost hypothesis, when bank holding for loan firms in order to reduce the agency conflicts, so bank holding will reduce for non-financial distress firms. According to the signaling hypothesis, firms that are not financially distressed have lower credit risks and their liquidity is higher. If bank holdings for loan firms in order to earn profits for earning of the investment plan, banks will increase holdings for firms of lower credit risk and more debt can be secure

---

1 $TOBINQ_{i,t-6} = (V_{i,t-6} + MVD_{i,t-6}) \div TA_{i,t-6}$, where $V_{i,t-6}$ is the market value of the shares of firm i, $MVD_{i,t}$ is the market value of debt; however, we use the book value of debt instead, and $TA_{i,t-6}$ is the book value of asset.

	two-digit SIC code	Industry name	Numbers	sub total	% of samples	sub total
Panel A	13	Petroleum and Natural Gas	9		3.46	
	15	Operative Builders	1		0.38	
	17	Construction	1		0.38	
				11		4.23
Panel B	20	Food Products	6		2.31	
	23	Apparel	1		0.38	
	26	Business Supplies	2		0.77	
	27	Printing and Publishing	6		2.31	
	28	Chemicals	23		8.85	
	29	Petroetroleum Refining	2		0.77	
	30	Rubber and Plastic Products	2		0.77	
	33	Steel Works Etc	1		0.38	
	34	Fabricated Products	3		1.15	
	35	Machinery	23		8.85	
	36	Electrical Equipment	38		14.62	
	37	Automobiles and Trucks	2		0.77	
	38	Measuring and Control Equipment	21		8.08	
	39	Recreation	2		0.77	
	44	Transportation	1		0.38	
	45	Airtransport	2		0.77	
	47	Arrange Trans-Freight and Cargo	1		0.38	
	48	Communication	7		2.69	
				143		55.00
Panel C	50	Computers and Software	2		0.77	
	51	Wholesale	5		1.92	
	53	Retail	2		0.77	
	54	Foodstores	1		0.38	
	56	Clothing Stores	5		1.92	
	57	Furniture	4		1.54	
	58	Restaraunts, Hotels, Motels	3		1.15	
	59	Other Retails	5		1.92	
				27		10.38
Panel D	70	Hotel	1		0.38	
	73	Business Services	60		23.08	
	79	Entertainment	2		0.77	
	80	Healthcare	6		2.31	
	82	Educational Services	3		1.15	
	87	Other Services	7		2.69	
				106		40.77
	Total		260		100	

Figure 1: Industry distribution of sample firms.

Note: In this study, the first two under the SIC-code code, the sample is divided into four parts, as follows: Panel A gold mine for the energy category (SIC CODE = 13 ~ 17) has 11 firms; Panel B for the manufacturing sector (SIC CODE = 20 ~ 48) has 143 firms; Panel C for the retail trade (SIC CODE = 50 ~ 59) has 27 firms; Panel D for the services sector (SIC CODE = 70 ~ 87) has 106 firms. However, all samples have 260 firms.

compensation. $\Delta ZSCORE_i^2$ is a dummy variable of financial position changes, which is equal to 1 if Z-score$_t$=1 and Z-score$_{t-6}$=0 or Z-score$_t$=1 and Z-score$_{t-6}$=1, and 0 otherwise.

Changes in asset size ($\Delta lnTA_i$) and changes in tangible assets ($\Delta TANRATIO_i$): When the firm has more assets or tangible assets to provide a higher guarantee for a loan, the creditor may conduct an auction of the collateral to back debt even if the firm is unable to repay the debt. Therefore, firms can increase the ratio of the assets or tangible assets to reduce agency conflicts between creditors and shareholders. According to the agency cost hypothesis, a bank maintaining a creditor

will not increase its holdings. According to the signaling hypothesis, the loan firms increase the ratio of assets or tangible assets to reduce the internal private information and increase transparency of information [22,23]. Therefore, banks holdings are negatively correlated to increase the proportion of assets or tangible assets. $\Delta lnTA_i^3$ is the change in asset size and $\Delta TANRATIO_i^4$ is the change in tangible assets.

Volatility of firm (ΔVOL_i): According to the agency cost hypothesis, the greater volatility of loan firms that have higher the risk of firm and agency conflict. It is more difficult to provide the firm with equity financing so the firm will rely more on bank lending. When the bank holding increases the stock of loan firm, indicating can reduce the

---

[2]Following Altman (1983) measured criteriaby Z-score model. $Z=1.2X_1+1.4X_2+3.3X_3+0.6X_4+0.999X_5$, where X_1 is *Operating capital/Total asset*, X_2 is *Retained earnings/Total asset*, X_3 is *Earnings before interest and tax/Total asset*, X_4 is *Equity market/Total debt*, X_5 is *Sales revenue/Total asset*. Z-score$_t$ is dummy variable of non-financial crisis firms which Z-score$_t$ is equal to 1 if Z-score$_t$ more than 2.675, and 0 otherwise.

[3]$\Delta lnTA_i = lnTA_t - lnTA_{t-6}$

[4]Following the definition of Guner et al. (2005) and Jagannathan (2004), $\Delta TANRATIO_i = (PPE_{i,t} - PPE_{i,t-6})/Average\ TA$, $PPE_{i,t}$ where net property plant and equipment, $Average\ TA = (TA_{i,t} - TA_{i,t-6})/2$.

agency problems from the identity of the creditor banks transferred to shareholders. As a result, a bank's holdings increase is positively correlated with firm volatility. On the other hand, according to the signaling hypothesis, if bank holdings by the loan firm in order to earn profits for earning of the investment plan, then bank's holding will reduce for higher volatility of firm. Kroszner and Strahan [14] show the lower volatility of firm that bank holdings will increase. ΔVOL_i is the volatility of the standard deviation of daily stock returns before the M&A completion date. ΔVOL_i^2 is the volatility of daily stock returns variance before the M&A completion date.

Profitability performance ($\Delta PROFIT_i$): According to the agency cost hypothesis, a firm's improved profitability can make the shareholders or creditors earn greater profits which works to reduce agency conflict. Therefore, the bank holdings are negatively correlated with the profitability performance of the firm. According to the signaling hypothesis, the bank holdings will increase for higher profitability firms in order to earn profits for earning of the investment plan. Then the bank holdings will be positively correlated with the profitability performance of firm. E $\Delta PROFIT_i$ is the profitability performance such as the return of asset (ROA).

Changes in debt ratio ($\Delta DBRATIO_i$): In general, the proportion of debt increase that the total assets of firm to use debt to buy assets in the proportion of improved while the financial risk of firm is increased, therefore, improve agency problem between shareholders and creditors. According to the agency cost hypothesis, the bank holding increases the stock of the loan firm, indicating can reduce the interest conflict problems between shareholders and the creditor. The bank's holdings increase is positively correlated with the debt ratio of firms. On the other hand, according to the signaling hypothesis, the bank holdings will increases for the loan firm in order to earn profits for earning of the investment plan. Bank holdings will then be reduced to increase the proportion of firm liabilities. Therefore, the bank holdings are negative correlated with the debt ratio of firms. $\Delta DBRATIO_i$ is a change in debt ratio.

Changes in short-term liabilities ratio ($\Delta CDRATIO_i$): According to Kroszner and Strahan [14] and Stearns and Mizruchi [24], short-term liabilities ratios are the proxies for the relationship between banks and are also the borrowing source of the loan firm. Fama [2] indicates that when firms have higher agency conflicts and asymmetric information, those firms cannot collect funds by equity financing. Rather, they must collect funds through financial institutions. According to the agency cost hypothesis, the bank holdings increase for the increased short-term liabilities of the firm in order to reduce the conflict of interest between stockholders and creditors. If the firm increases the proportion of short-term liabilities, then the information transparency will decrease. According to signaling hypothesis, the bank holdings will increase in order to control the internal information of firm. $\Delta CDRATIO_i$ is the change in short-term liabilities ratio.

Change in investment quality ($\Delta EROIC_i$): The firm increases the rate of investment to rapidly expand and thus create a higher return. When the firm has a high-quality investment project, it can work to reduce agency conflict between shareholders and creditors. According to the agency cost hypothesis, the bank holdings for the loan firm serve to reduce the conflict of interest between shareholders and creditors. As a result, the bank holdings decrease for firms that have high-quality investment projects. According to signaling hypothesis, the bank holdings for loan firms serve to earn profits for earning of the investment plan. Accordingly, bank holdings will reduce for i firms which have high-quality investment projects [25]. However, the firm

invest lower-quality project that cannot use signaling theory to explain the direction of bank holdings rate. In general, return on investment is used as the proxy variable of the investment quality. $\Delta EROIC_i^5$ is the change in investment quality.

Changes in investment ratio ($\Delta INVRATIO_i$): Capital expenditures are increased to show increased investment opportunities, so firm need investment banks to increase invest. Therefore, changes in the investment bank holding rate are positively correlated with the investment spending of firm. Capital expenditures are the proxies for investment opportunities. $\Delta INVRATIO_i^6$ is the change in investment ratio.

Changes in equity financing ratio ($\Delta EQRATIO_i$): When the firm issues equity financing, firms need investment banking to support securities underwriting. Investment banks may increase holdings to obtain the opportunity for securities underwriting. Therefore, expected changes in the equity financing ratio and changes in investment bank holdings are positively correlated. $\Delta EQRATIO_i^7$ is the change in equity financing ratio.

Data

This study examines the connection between the holding changes in the commercial banks (investment banks) and the financial characteristics of the bidding firms for the six quarters between the M&A announcement date and the completion date. First, we select the date for all firms of M&A announced between 2000 and 2005 using the SDC database (1,025 firms). The top fifty holdings in firms, the quarterly holding date of the professional financial institutions from the Thomson One Banker in the board database, the daily stock returns date from CRSP database, the quarterly accounting date from Compustat database, press News from LexisNexis database. Of the original 1,025 firms, 260 were retained in the final analysis: 444 firms were deleted because the transactions do not provide the firm's complete stock data, 91 were deleted because they did not provide the status of the outside directors of companies holding, 146 firms were deleted because they were firms which the financial industry (SIC CODE=60~69) and public utilities (SIC CODE=49), and finally 84 additional firms were deleted from the analysis because there were not six quarters between the M&A announcement date and the completion date (Figures 2 and 3).

As the study shows, while commercial banks and investment banks simultaneously holding the bidding firms shares. Figures 2 and 3 show nine cases from a change set of all banks shares hold proportion. Each bank's average shares hold proportion changes set in the six quarters between the M&A announcement date and the completion date. For example, there were nine cases in which the commercial bank holdings increased (decrease and no change) and the investment holdings increased (decrease and no change). Figure 2 shows the 86 commercial and investment bank firms for which holdings all increased (33.08% of the total sample). Figure 3 shows the 95 commercial and investment bank firms for which the average holdings all increased (36.54% of the total sample). However, commercial banks and investment banks simultaneously holding the bidding firms shares before the M&A completion date.

---

[5] $\Delta EROIC_i = EROIC_{i,t} - EROIC_{i,t-6}$, where $EROIC_{i,t}$=Net profit after tax/Capital investment spending

[6] $\Delta INVRATIO_i = (INVRATIO_{i,t} - INVRATIO_{i,t-6})$/Average TA

[7] $\Delta EQRATIO_i = (EQRATIO_{i,t} - EQRATIO_{i,t-6})$/Average TA, where $EQRATIO$=Total equity – Retained earnings.

	(a)	(b)			(c)		
		C+	C−	C.	I+	I−	I.
C+I−	61	61	-	-	-	61	-
C+I.	6	6	-	-	-	-	6
C+I+	86	86	-	-	86	-	-
C−I−	59	-	59	-	-	59	-
C−I.	2	-	2	-	-	-	2
C−I+	44	-	44	-	44	-	-
C. I+	0	-	-	-	-	-	-
C. I−	2	-	-	2	-	2	-
C. I.	0	-	-	-	-	-	-
Total	260	153	105	2	130	122	8

Figure 2: Sample of all bank holdings and the process of selection.

Note: Difference of all commercial banks and investment banks shareholdings in the six quarters before the M&A announcement date and the completion date. For example, nine cases from change set of commercial banks holding and investment bank holding. C is commercial banks; I is investment banks; + is holdings increase; − is holding decrease; · is holding no change (a) shows firm numbers which nine cases from change set of commercial banks holding and investment bank holding; (b) only firms numbers of commercial banks holding change; (c) only firms numbers of investment banks holding change.

	(a)	(b)			(c)		
		C+	C−	C.	I+	I−	I.
C+I−	60	60	-	-	-	60	-
C+I.	5	5	-	-	-	-	5
C+I+	95	95	-	-	95	-	-
C−I−	45	-	45	-	-	45	-
C−I.	1	-	1	-	-	-	1
C−I+	50	-	50	-	50	-	-
C. I+	0	-	-	-	-	-	-
C. I−	4	-	-	4	-	4	-
C. I.	0	-	-	-	-	-	-
Total	260	160	96	4	145	109	6

Figure 3: Sample of all bank average holdings and the process of selection.

Note: Difference of all commercial banks and investment banks average shareholdings in the six quarters before the M&A announcement date and the completion date. For example, nine cases from change set of commercial banks holding and investment bank each unit share hold. C is commercial banks; I is investment banks; + is holding increase; − is holding decrease; · is holding no change (a) show firms numbers which nine cases from change set of commercial banks holding and investment bank holding; (b) only firms numbers of commercial banks holding change; (c) only firms numbers of investment banks holding change.

Empirical Results

We first report the results of our main test regarding changes in financial institution holdings for the quarters prior to the merger completion date. In Panel A of Table 1, the commercial banks quarters holding proportion in 3.41%~4.71% and average commercial banks quarters holding proportion in 0.63%~0.86%. This indicates a significant increasing trend for bank holdings from the second to fourth quarter before the M&A completion date. The investment banks quarters holding proportion is 3.63%~4.96% and average investment banks quarters holding proportion is 1.16%~1.63% in Panel B. The results show a significant decreasing trend for the investment bank's holding proportion between the fifth and sixth quarters before the M&A completion date, but a significant increasing trend between the third and fourth quarters before the M&A completion date. The average investment bank's holding proportion indicated a significant increasing trend from the second to the third quarter after the M&A completion quarter. Panel C shows the insurance companies quarters holding proportion in 1.19%~1.28% and average insurance companies quarters holding proportion in 0.79%~0.92%. The results show that the insurance company holdings proportions did not significantly change in the quarter before or after the M&A completion quarter (Table 1).

Because of commercial banks, investment banks and insurance companies quarters holding proportion not significant difference. We therefore used a difference test for comparing holdings proportion changes between the M&A completion quarter and each quarter. In Panel A of Table 2, the results show a significantly increasing trend for the commercial bank's holdings proportion in the two periods six quarters before the M&A completion quarter and from the fourth to the sixth quarter after the M&A completion quarter. The average commercial bank's holding proportion also revealed a significantly increasing trend from the third to the sixth quarter before M&A completion quarter and from the third to the sixth quarter after the M&A completion quarter. In Panel B, the results show a significantly increasing trend for the investment bank's holding proportion from the third to the fifth quarter before the M&A completion quarter and from the second to the sixth quarter after the M&A completion quarter. The average investment bank's holding proportion significantly increased from the third to sixth quarter before the M&A completion quarter and from the third to the sixth quarter after the M&A completion quarter. In Panel C, the results show that the insurance companies holding proportion did not significantly change between the M&A completion quarter and the other quarters (Table 2).

Panel A-I: Commercial banks holding (%)

Quarter	-6	-5	-4	-3	-2	-1	0	1	2	3	4	5	6
Mean	3.41	3.46	3.54	3.77	3.99	4.12	4.23	4.34	4.38	4.47	4.63	4.69	4.71
Mid	2.69	2.79	2.98	3.33	3.39	3.56	3.89	3.58	3.90	4.02	4.32	4.44	4.36
Std. Dev	3.24	3.19	3.15	3.55	3.66	3.66	3.71	4.17	4.07	4.11	4.12	3.66	3.59
Min	0.00	0.00	0.00	0.00	0.00	0.00	0.00	0.00	0.00	0.00	0.00	0.00	0.00
Max	15.63	15.53	17.72	26.42	25.26	21.05	21.83	34.79	36.11	35.67	35.22	20.05	18.03
Tests of difference with next quarter													
	(0.64)	(1.07)	(1.90)*	(1.99)**	(1.51)	(0.96)	(0.71)	(0.39)	(1.00)	(1.46)	(0.42)	(0.13)	

Panel A-II: Average commercial banks holding (%)

Quarter	-6	-5	-4	-3	-2	-1	0	1	2	3	4	5	6
Mean	0.60	0.62	0.65	0.70	0.73	0.75	0.76	0.84	0.82	0.86	0.87	0.86	0.86
Mid	0.51	0.51	0.57	0.61	0.67	0.67	0.71	0.70	0.74	0.80	0.84	0.83	0.85
Std. Dev	0.55	0.56	0.57	0.67	0.62	0.63	0.59	0.93	0.79	0.85	0.77	0.69	0.63
Min	0.00	0.00	0.00	0.00	0.00	0.00	0.00	0.00	0.00	0.00	0.00	0.00	0.00
Max	3.28	3.41	3.46	5.92	3.57	3.34	3.39	11.60	9.03	8.92	7.04	5.54	3.18
Tests of difference with next quarter													
	(0.81)	(1.56)	(1.73)*	(1.12)	(0.94)	(0.61)	(1.67)*	(-0.67)	(1.61)	(1.16)	(-0.10)	(-0.15)	

Panel B-I: Investment banks holding (%)

Quarter	-6	-5	-4	-3	-2	-1	0	1	2	3	4	5	6
Mean	4.31	3.63	3.73	3.89	4.06	4.09	4.12	4.19	4.38	4.67	4.76	4.72	4.96
Mid	3.19	3.11	3.16	3.34	3.65	3.53	3.66	3.86	4.03	3.25	4.21	4.50	4.62
Std. Dev	4.82	3.20	3.25	3.14	3.30	3.44	3.43	3.13	3.33	3.61	3.70	3.45	3.53
Min	0.00	0.00	0.00	0.00	0.00	0.00	0.00	0.00	0.00	0.00	0.00	0.00	0.00
Max	35.26	19.49	20.13	17.20	16.58	21.09	22.64	19.58	18.81	20.36	20.80	21.47	19.13
Tests of difference with next quarter													
	(-2.70)***	(1.49)	(1.79)*	(1.65)	(0.39)	(0.25)	(0.61)	(2.12)**	(3.30)**	(1.17)	(-0.44)	(2.31)**	

Panel B-II: Average investment banks holding (%)

Quarter	-6	-5	-4	-3	-2	-1	0	1	2	3	4	5	6
Mean	1.17	1.16	1.17	1.20	1.25	1.27	1.30	1.34	1.34	1.50	1.57	1.59	1.65
Mid	0.97	0.97	0.98	1.10	1.22	1.12	1.21	1.21	1.25	1.32	1.39	1.35	1.48
Std. Dev	0.99	0.99	0.91	0.92	0.92	0.96	1.02	0.98	1.07	1.40	1.30	1.29	1.21
Min	0.00	0.00	0.00	0.00	0.00	0.00	0.00	0.00	0.00	0.00	0.00	0.00	0.00
Max	6.59	5.50	5.03	5.28	4.77	5.17	6.04	6.86	9.55	14.12	7.63	8.41	6.34
Tests of difference with next quarter													
	(-0.32)	(0.20)	(0.11)	(1.19)	(0.70)	(0.80)	(0.88)	(0.08)	(3.54)**	(1.50)	(0.37)	(1.44)	

Panel C-I: Insurance companies holding (%)

Quarter	-6	-5	-4	-3	-2	-1	0	1	2	3	4	5	6
Mean	1.19	1.25	1.26	1.21	1.25	1.24	1.29	1.27	1.28	1.20	1.21	1.18	1.12
Mid	0.23	0.28	0.28	0.35	0.36	0.31	0.35	0.28	0.33	0.29	0.39	0.33	0.34
Std. Dev	2.36	2.45	2.49	2.20	2.14	2.16	2.10	2.16	2.25	2.25	2.23	2.28	2.23
Min	0.00	0.00	0.00	0.00	0.00	0.00	0.00	0.00	0.00	0.00	0.00	0.00	0.00
Max	20.18	21.11	17.88	15.60	14.55	17.59	16.72	16.98	16.52	18.00	17.64	19.45	19.31
Tests of difference with next quarter													
	(0.95)	(0.03)	(-0.70)	(0.63)	(0.14)	(0.79)	(-0.37)	(0.29)	(-1.32)	(-0.13)	(0.56)	(1.13)	

Panel C-II: Average insurance companies holding (%)

Quarter	-6	-5	-4	-3	-2	-1	0	1	2	3	4	5	6
Mean	0.80	0.83	0.82	0.79	0.82	0.86	0.93	0.91	0.89	0.85	0.86	0.86	0.81
Mid	0.21	0.25	0.22	0.28	0.26	0.24	0.28	0.21	0.26	0.22	0.31	0.31	0.29
Std. dev	1.81	1.83	1.63	1.51	1.33	1.60	1.64	1.73	1.68	1.71	1.49	1.64	1.54
Min	0.00	0.00	0.00	0.00	0.00	0.00	0.00	0.00	0.00	0.00	0.00	0.00	0.00
Max	20.18	21.11	16.83	15.60	9.17	17.59	16.72	16.98	16.52	18.00	10.34	11.79	10.06
Tests of difference with next quarter													
	(0.61)	(-0.21)	(-0.68)	(0.39)	(0.72)	(1.40)	(-0.50)	(-0.38)	(-0.82)	(0.15)	(0.07)	(-1.25)	

Note: Panel A –I (B-I and C-I) display the quarterly holdings changes in commercial banks (investment banks and insurance companies) which five top ten holdings in the firm. T-tests were used to compare quarterly holdings. Panel A-II (B-II and C-II) is the quarterly average holdings of commercial banks (investment banks and insurance companies) which five top ten holdings in the firm. T-tests were used to compare quarterly holdings. Positive t-values indicate an increasing trend; negative values indicate a decreasing trend. *:10%, **:5%, ***:1% significance level.

Table 1: Summary statistics of all banks and the difference analysis for each quarter (sample is 260 firms).

Panel A-I: Commercial banks holding (%)													
Quarter	-6	-5	-4	-3	-2	-1	0	1	2	3	4	5	6
Mean	3.41***	3.46***	3.54***	3.77***	3.99*	4.12	4.23	4.34	4.38	4.47	4.63*	4.69**	4.71**
t-value	(4.67)	(4.42)	(4.15)	(2.81)	(1.69)	(0.96)		(0.71)	(0.83)	(1.22)	(1.85)	(2047)	(2.39)
Mid	2.69***	2.79***	2.98***	3.33***	3.39*	3.56	3.89	3.58	3.90	4.02	4.32*	4.44***	4.36***
z-value	(4.26)	(4.31)	(4.13)	(3.75)	(1.95)	(0.77)		(0.92)	(0.14)	(0.67)	(1.88)	(3.44)	(3.28)
Panel A-II: Average commercial banks holding (%)													
Mean	0.60***	0.62***	0.65***	0.70*	0.73	0.75	0.76	0.84*	0.82	0.86**	0.87**	0.86**	0.86***
t-value	(5.20)	(4.42)	(3.68)	(1.83)	(1.17)	(0.61)		(1.67)	(1.51)	(2.26)	(2.53)	(2.57)	(2.62)
mid	0.51***	0.51***	0.57***	0.61***	0.67	0.67	0.71	0.70	0.74	0.80*	0.84*	0.83***	0.85***
z-value	(5.00)	(4.55)	(3.99)	(3.20)	(1.37)	(0.14)		(1.36)	(1.02)	(1.85)	(1.89)	(3.07)	(3.29)
Panel B-I: Investment banks holding (%)													
Quarter	-6	-5	-4	-3	-2	-1	0	1	2	3	4	5	6
Mean	4.31	3.63**	3.73*	3.89*	4.06	4.09	4.12	4.19	4.38***	4.67***	4.76***	4.72***	4.96***
t-value	(-0.60)	(2.38)	(1.89)	(1.26)	(0.42)	(0.25)		(0.61)	(2.26)	(3.56)	(3.99)	(3.56)	(4.36)
Mid	3.12	3.11**	3.16	3.34	3.65	3.53	3.66	3.86	4.03***	4.25***	4.21***	4.50***	4.62***
z-value	(0.67)	(2030)	(1.56)	(0.73)	(0.43)	(1.08)		(1.43)	(2.48)	(3.79)	(4.31)	(4.82)	(4.80)
Panel B-II: Average investment banks holding (%)													
Mean	1.17*	1.16**	1.17**	1.20*	1.25	1.27	1.30	1.34	1.34	1.50***	1.57***	1.59***	1.65***
t-value	(1.84)	(2.16)	(2.30)	(1.86)	(1.20)	(0.80)		(0.88)	(0.77)	(3.06)	(4.32)	(4.37)	(5.49)
Mid	0.97**	9.97**	0.98**	1.10**	1.22	1.12	1.21	1.21*	1.25	1.32***	1.39***	1.35***	1.48***
z-value	(2.07)	(2.53)	(2.26)	(2.08)	(0.78)	(1.22)		(1.88)	(1.04)	(3.08)	(4.45)	(4.40)	(5.59)
Panel C-I: Insurance companies holding (%)													
Quarter	-6	-5	-4	-3	-2	-1	0	1	2	3	4	5	6
Mean	1.19	1.25	1.26	1.21	1.25	1.24	1.29	1.27	1.28	1.20	1.21	1.18	1.12
t-value	(0.81)	(0.27)	(0.25)	(0.73)	(0.44)	(0.79)		(0.37)	(0.03)	(0.90)	(0.71)	(0.86)	(1.27)
Mid	0.23	0.28	0.28	0.35	0.36	0.31	0.35	0.28	0.33	0.29	0.39	0.33	0.34
z-value	(1.39)	0.45)	(1.16)	(0.71)	(0.37)	(1.10)		(0.52)	(0.25)	(1.21)	(0.73)	(1.21)	(1.73)
Panel C-II: Average insurance companies holding (%)													
Mean	0.80	0.83	0.82	0.79	0.82	0.86	0.93	0.91	0.89	0.85	0.86	0.86	0.81
t-value	(1.44)	(1.10)	(1.36)	(1.81)	(1.45)	(1.40)		(0.50)	(0.69)	(1.14)	(0.81)	(0.65)	(1.15)
Mid	0.21	0.25	0.22	0.28	0.26	0.24	0.28	0.21	0.26	0.22	0.31	0.31	0.29
z-value	(1.86)	(1.06)	(1.46)	(1.46)	(1.70)	(1.25)		(0.91)	(0.85)	(1.10)	(0.45)	(1.36)	(1.46)

Note: The table shows quarterly holdings rate, number and average (median) holdings of commercial banks (investment banks and insurance companies) which five top ten holdings in the firm. We use T-tests (Wilcoxon rank-sum test) to test the mean (median) of M&A completion quarter holdings for a significant difference. *:10%, **:5%, ***:1% significance level.

Table 2: Difference analysis of all bank holdings for each quarter and the M&A completion quarter (sample is 260 firms).

In Panel A of Figure 4, the results show that 91.54% complete M&A since M&A announcement date to the completion date which need about three quarters. The results show 72.69% completed within the three months between the M&A announcement date and the completion date in Panel B. These results are similar to Wansley et al. [26]. Therefore, the M & A announcement date may be the second quarter before the M&A completion date and the financial institutional holdings show no significant change between the M&A announcement date and the completion date. This study was to explore the financial institutions holding behavior before M&A completion date (Figure 4).

According to the results obtained, the commercial (investment) banks have a higher holdings proportion and a significantly increasing trend before the M&A completion date. So the commercial banks and investment banks important than the insurance companies. The bidding firms acquire the M&A professional advice by investment banks holdings [27], and obtain debt expertise by commercial banks holding. Therefore, this study of commercial and investment bank holding changes before the M&A completion date is the main object of study, with the specific goal of testing the connection between the financial institutions holding proportion and the firm's financial characteristics.

In Panel A and B of Table 3 provides the descriptive statistics used to analyze the financial institutions of holding proportion increase that assets size increase level higher than financial institutions of holding proportion decrease from the sixth quarter before M&A completion date to the M&A completion date. The results show that firms increase the ratio of assets to reduce agency problems between shareholders and creditors. Furthermore, the financial institutions monitor profit more than costs, and the banks choose to increase holding proportion for the firms that increase higher ratio of asset size. Therefore, bank holdings were significantly positively correlated with increases in the proportion of assets. These results are inconsistent with both the agency cost hypothesis and signaling hypothesis. The results show that the profitability of firms improved to make the shareholders or creditors increase earned profits, thus reducing the agency conflict within the firms. Therefore, bank holdings were significantly negatively correlated with changes in the profitability performance of the firm. These results are consistent with the agency cost hypothesis in Panel A-I (-II).

In Panel A-II, the average commercial banks holdings by the loan firm in order to earn profits for earning of the investment plan, then banks holding will reduce for higher volatility of firm. The results show the average commercial bank's holdings are significantly negatively correlated with the volatility of the firm, consistent with the signaling hypothesis. Fama [2] found that when the firm had higher agency

Panel A : The quarters between M&A announced date and completed date									Total
Quarter	0	1	2	3	4	5-6	7-8	9-10	11-12	
Number of firms	99	107	32	10	6	2	2	1	1	260
% of samples	38.08	41.15	12.31	3.85	2.31	0.77	0.77	0.38	0.38	100

Panel B : The months between M&A announced date and completed date										Total
Months	0	1	2	3	4	5	6	7	8-13	15-37	
Number of firms	46	53	42	48	17	13	8	11	16	6	260
% of samples	17.69	20.38	16.15	18.46	6.54	5.00	3.08	4.23	6.15	2.31	100

Note: Panel A is the length difference by quarter; Panel B is the length difference by month (22 trading days).

Figure 4: Length of the average time from the M&A announcement date to the completion date.

Panel A-I: Commercial banks holding (%)

	Full Sample Number of firms = 258			Holding increase Number of firms = 158			Holding decrease Number of firms = 105			Test of difference
	Mean	Media	Std. Dev	Mean	Media	Std. Dev	Mean	Media	Std. Dev	t-value
$\Delta LNTA$	0.506	0.358	0.703	0.588	0.439	0.769	0.388	0.302	0.578	-2.382**
$\Delta TANRTIO$	0.064	0.025	0.141	0.068	0.028	0.128	0.058	0.018	0.158	-0.540
ΔVOL	1.064	0.954	0.513	1.025	0.937	0.436	1.116	1.037	0.598	1.261
$\Delta PROFIT$	0.011	0.008	0.056	0.004	0.005	0.045	0.022	0.011	0.067	2.258***
$\Delta CDRATIO$	0.030	0.000	0.192	0.033	0.000	0.196	0.025	0.000	0.185	0.357
$\Delta DEBTRATIO$	0.148	0.103	0.245	0.137	0.078	0.237	0.164	0.132	0.257	0.865
$\Delta EROIC$	0.004	-0.004	0.179	-0.005	-0.007	0.184	0.017	0.004	0.171	0.953
$TOBIN\ Q_{-6}$	3.810	1.817	8.450	4.280	1.814	10.359	3.134	1.820	4.417	-1.067
$FAME$	2.473	1.000	4.892	2.621	1.000	4.796	2.257	1.000	5.044	-0.586

Panel A-II: Average commercial banks holding (%)

	Mean	Media	Std. Dev	Mean	Media	Std. Dev	Mean	Media	Std. Dev	t-value
$\Delta LNTA$	0.508	0.358	0.705	0.561	0.431	0.745	0.419	0.314	0.626	-1.672*
$\Delta TANRTIO$	0.064	0.025	0.141	0.064	0.027	0.125	0.064	0.020	0.165	-0.017
ΔVOL	1.064	0.008	0.055	1.018	0.949	0.437	1.138	1.023	0.616	1.672*
$\Delta PROFIT$	0.011	0.008	0.055	0.004	0.006	0.043	0.023	0.013	0.069	2.278**
$\Delta CDRATIO$	0.030	0.000	0.192	0.046	0.000	0.219	0.003	0.000	0.134	-1.946*
$\Delta DEBTRATIO$	0.148	0.103	0.246	0.139	0.085	0.229	0.163	0.130	0.271	0.782
$\Delta EROIC$	0.004	-0.004	0.180	-0.005	-0.006	0.180	0.018	0.004	0.178	0.989
$TOBIN\ Q_{-6}$	3.831	1.831	8.480	4.148	1.773	10.131	3.310	2.022	4.632	-0.821
$FAME$	2.477	1.000	4.911	2.669	1.000	5.510	2.156	1.000	3.709	-0.821

Panel B-I: Investment banks holding (%)

	Full Sample Number of firms = 258			Holding increase Number of firms = 158			Holding decrease Number of firms = 105			Test of difference
	Mean	Media	Std. Dev	Mean	Media	Std. Dev	Mean	Media	Std. Dev	t-value
$\Delta LNTA$	0.519	0.391	0.707	0.660	0.467	0.758	0.370	0.296	0.618	-3.334***
ΔVOL	1.081	0.969	0.519	1.065	0.969	0.440	1.098	0.955	0.591	0.454
$\Delta PROFIT$	0.011	0.009	0.056	0.006	0.006	0.052	0.018	0.012	0.060	1.523
$\Delta CDRATIO$	0.031	0.000	0.194	0.033	0.000	0.161	0.029	0.000	0.225	-0.129
$\Delta DEBTRATIO$	0.155	0.104	0.250	0.158	0.096	0.251	0.152	0.121	0.250	-0.190
$\Delta INVRATIO$	0.011	0.007	0.049	0.016	0.009	0.049	0.005	0.003	0.048	-1.722*
$\Delta EQRATIO$	0.344	0.145	0.630	0.424	0.176	0.606	0.259	0.091	0.645	-2.058**
$TOBIN\ Q_{-6}$	3.872	1.842	8.541	4.687	2.042	11.270	3.017	1.718	3.921	-1.579
FAME	2.278	1.000	3.967	1.977	1.000	2.595	2.598	1.000	5.027	1.221

Panel B-II: Average investment banks holding (%)

	Mean	Media	Std. Dev	Mean	Media	Std. Dev	Mean	Media	Std. Dev	t-value
$\Delta LNTA$	0.515	0.386	0.706	0.644	0.456	0.730	0.344	0.241	0.638	-3.409***
ΔVOL	1.078	0.960	0.518	1.070	0.975	0.432	1.088	0.953	0.614	0.242
$\Delta PROFIT$	0.011	0.008	0.056	0.006	0.007	0.050	0.018	0.009	0.063	1.525
$\Delta CDRATIO$	0.030	0.000	0.193	0.039	0.000	0.200	0.019	0.000	0.185	-0.771
$\Delta DEBTRATIO$	0.153	0.104	0.250	0.152	0.104	0.229	0.156	0.098	0.275	0.139
$\Delta INVRATIO$	0.011	0.007	0.048	0.016	0.010	0.047	0.004	0.004	0.049	1.816*
$\Delta EQRATIO$	0.341	0.139	0.628	0.385	0.173	0.670	0.283	0.088	0.565	-1.258
$TOBIN\ Q_{-6}$	3.850	1.831	8.511	4.657	2.143	10.730	2.791	1.713	3.870	-1.922*
$FAME$	2.465	1.000	4.920	2.034	1.000	2.893	3.037	1.000	6.707	1.461

Note: *:10%, **:5%, ***:1% significance level.

Table 3: Descriptive statistics relating a financial institution's holdings proportion and the firm's financial characteristics.

conflicts and asymmetric information, the firm cannot collect funds by equity financing. Instead, such funds must be collected through financial institutions. The results show that the average commercial bank's holdings increase for the increased short-term liabilities of the firm in order to reduce the conflict of interest between stockholders and creditors. The results show that the average commercial bank's holdings were significantly positively correlated with changes in the short-term liabilities ratio, consistent with the agency cost hypothesis.

In Panel B-I of Table 3, capital expenditures increased to show that increase investment opportunities, so firm need investment banks to increase invest. Therefore, the results show that changes in an investment bank's holding rate are significant positively correlated with the investment spending of the firm, consistent with Panel B-II. When the firm issues equity financing, firms need investment banks to underwrite the securities. Investment banks may therefore increase holdings to obtain an opportunity for securities underwriting. Therefore, one may expect changes in the equity financing ratio and changes in the investment bank holdings to be significantly positively correlated. In Panel B-II, if Tobin's Q is greater that firms with high levels of growth opportunities [19,20]. The average investment bank's holdings may be earning higher profits for earning of the investment plan, and it will therefore increase holdings. The results show the average investment bank's holdings are significantly positively correlated with the firm's growth opportunities. These results are consistent with the signaling hypothesis (Table 3).

This paper used logistic regression analysis to examine the relationship between the changes in financial institutions holding proportion and the firm's characteristics. In order to avoid collinearity problems of the explanatory variables each other and to affect regression results between dependent variables and the stability of the explanatory variables. Therefore, this paper uses correlational analysis to examine the explanatory variables for the firm characteristics in Figure 5 (a Pearson correlation coefficient matrix). The results show the variables' correlation coefficients were lower than 0.3 or -0.3 which is a low degree of correlation except for debt ratio (or Tobin's q or equity financing ratio) and the size of the firm's assets that Pearson correlation is 0.472 (or 0.446 or 0.567) (Figure 5).

The commercial bank's holdings more than investment banks holdings in the bidding firms that commercial banks have greater controlling power in Table 4. In Panel A, the coefficient of controlling

power is significantly negative, indicating that investment banks with lower holdings will increase their stake to gain controlling power. In Panel B, the coefficient is significantly positive, indicating that investment banks with lower holding will increase their stake to gain controlling power. In Table 4, the results show that firms increase the ratio of assets to reduce agency problems between shareholders and creditors. Furthermore, the financial institutions monitor profits more than costs, and the banks choose to increase the holding proportion for those firms that have a higher ratio of asset size. Therefore, bank holdings are significantly positively correlated with the proportion of assets. These results are inconsistent with the agency cost hypothesis and the signaling hypothesis. In Panel A, the results show the profitability of the firm improved to make the shareholders or creditors increase earned profits to reduce agency conflict. Therefore, the bank holdings were significant negatively correlated with changes in profitability performance of the firm, consistent with the agency cost hypothesis.

In (c) and (d) of Panel A, the greater volatility of the loan firms have a higher risk of firm and agency conflict. It is more difficult for the firm to get equity financing so the firm will necessarily rely more on bank lending. The average commercial bank holdings by the loan firm in order to earn profits for earning of the investment plan, then banks holding will reduce for higher volatility of firm. The results here show that the lower volatility of firm that average commercial bank holdings will increase, consistent with the signaling hypothesis. The empirical results reveal a quadratic relation between the volatility of the firm and the average commercial bank's holdings proportion in (d) of Panel A.

Firms that are not financially distressed show a lower credit risk and have higher liquidity. They are therefore easier to finance in the market. In these cases, shareholder and creditor agency conflict is usually small. The investment bank's holdings for loan firms in order to earn profits for earning of the investment plan. The investment banks will increase holdings for firms with a lower credit risk and more debt can be secure compensation. These results are consistent with the signaling hypothesis (Table 4).

Conclusion

In this paper, we examined the effect that changes in a financial institution's holdings proportion for those quarters before the M&A completion date. The financial institution's holdings proportion for the bidding firms was the largest for investment banks, followed

	ΔLnTA	ΔVOL	ΔPROFIT	ΔTANRATIO	ΔCDRATIO	ΔDEBTRATIO	ΔINVRATIO	ΔEROIC	ΔEQRATIO	TOBINQ $_{-6}$	FAME
ΔLnTA	1.000										
ΔVOL	0.290 ***	1.000									
ΔPROFIT	0.245 ***	-0.042	1.000								
ΔTANRATIO	-0.104	0.119 *	-0.029	1.000							
ΔCDRATIO	0.102	0.121 *	-0.036	0.011	1.000						
ΔDEBTRATIO	0.472 ***	0.378 ***	0.186 ***	0.137 **	0.313 ***	1.000					
ΔINVRATIO	0.186 ***	0.269 ***	0.015	-0.024	-0.018	0.117 *	1.000				
ΔEROIC	0.231 ***	-0.007	0.007	0.209 ***	-0.083	-0.015	-0.023	1.000			
ΔEQRATIO	0.567 ***	0.015	0.105	-0.104	-0.110 *	-0.085	0.005	0.367 ***	1.000		
TOBIN Q $_{-6}$	0.446 ***	0.046	-0.060	0.058	-0.008	0.087	0.091	0.188 ***	0.320 ***	1.000	
FAME	-0.018	-0.042	0.028	-0.021	-0.019	-0.026	-0.041	0.000 ***	-0.015	-0.037	1.000

Note: *:10%, **:5%, ***:1% significance level.

Figure 5: Pearson Correlation coefficient matrix.

	Panel A: Commercial Bank				Panel B: Investment Bank	
	All Holding		Average Holding		All Holding	Average Holding
	(a)	(b)	(c)	(d)	(e)	(f)
Cons	0.594 (0.402)	-0.495 (0.180)	1.514 (2.324)	0.111 (0.008)	-2.189 (9.876)	-1.079 (3.470)
IND1	0.421 (0.260)	0.447 (0.287)	0.089 (0.011)	0.046 (0.003)	1.064* (2.716)	0.736 (1.656)
IND2	1.404 (2.309)	1.341 (2.067)	1.129 (1.396)	0.962 (0.997)	0.851 (1.305)	0.402 (0.347)
IND3	0.595 (0.508)	0.587 (0.483)	-0.204 (0.055)	-0.298 (0.114)	1.401** (4.293)	0.357 (0.349)
$CONTROL_{-6}$	-1.305*** (13.397)	-1.363*** (14.247)	-1.556*** (16.528)	-1.609*** (17.258)	1.433*** (21.121)	0.885** (6.198)
$TOBINQ_{-6}$	0.006 (0.035)	-0.006 (0.040)	0.020 (0.468)	-0.023 (0.610)	-0.006 (0.083)	0.026 (0.571)
FAME	0.010 (0.100)	0.005 (0.021)	0.053 (1.270)	0.046 (0.943)	-0.052 (1.393)	-0.047 (1.742)
$\Delta ZSORE$	0.030 (0.006)	0.041 (0.011)	0.369 (0.847)	0.419 (1.046)	0.574* (3.547)	0.737** (6.200)
$\Delta LNTA$	0.889* (3.236)	0.849* (2.866)	1.050* (3.356)	1.058* (3.173)	0.653** (5.015)	0.658** (4.819)
$\Delta TANRTIO$	0.149 (0.010)	0.175 (0.013)	0.842 (0.247)	-0.980 (0.318)	-	-
ΔVOL	-0.431 (1.722)	1.528 (1.385)	-0.828* (5.214)	1.848 (1.434)	-	-
ΔVOL^2	-	-0.664 (2.194)	-	-0.949* (2.824)	-	-
$\Delta PROFIT$	-8.130* (3.721)	-7.962* (3.545)	-11.365** (6.067)	-11.024** (5.681)	-	-
$\Delta DEBTRATIO$	-0.955 (0.761)	-1.100 (0.984)	-0.846 (0.480)	-1.069 (0.740)	-	-
$\Delta CDRATIO$	0.312 (0.118)	0.397 (0.194)	1.951 (2.605)	1.989 (2.732)	-	-
$\Delta EROIC$	0.490 (0.115)	0.295 (0.040)	0.772 (0.251)	0.379 (0.057)	-	-
$\Delta INVRATIO$	-	-	-	-	3.153 (1.015)	3.757 (1.523)
$\Delta EQRATIO_6$	-	-	-	-	0.172 (0.340)	-0.305 (0.904)
χ^2 for regression	33.761***	36.568***	48.696***	52.388***	41.445***	29.858***
-2 log likelihood	211.399	208.592	188.060	184.368	288.342	298.020
R^2	0.230	0.247	0.325	0.347	0.213	0.157
obs	180	180	178	178	238	240

Note: t-value in ( ).*:10%, **:5%, ***:1% significance level.

Table 4: Factors of financial institution's holdings proportion increase : Logistic model.

by commercial banks, and the smallest for insurance companies. Therefore, the investment and commercial banks significantly increase their holdings before the M&A completion date. The commercial banks and investment banks are therefore more important than insurance companies for the bidding firms.

This paper also uses descriptive statistics and logistic regression analysis to examine the relationship between the financial institutional quarters holdings proportion and the financial characteristics of the bidding firms. The results of the both analyses methods are consistent. The empirical results show that firms increase the ratio of assets to reduce agency problems between shareholders and creditors. Furthermore, the financial institutions monitor profit more than costs, and the banks choose to increase their holdings proportion for the firms which maintain a higher ratio of asset size. Therefore, banks holdings are significant positively correlated with proportion of assets.

These results are inconsistent with the agency cost hypothesis and signaling hypothesis.

The results show that the profitability of the firm improved to make the shareholders or creditors increase earned profits in order to reduce agency conflict. Therefore, the commercial bank holdings are significantly negatively correlated with changes in the profitability performance of the firm, consistent with the agency cost hypothesis. The average commercial bank's holdings by the loan firm in order to earn profits for earning of the investment plan, then banks holding will reduce for higher volatility of firm. The results show that the lower volatility of the firm that average commercial bank holdings will increase. These results are consistent with the signaling hypothesis.

Our findings using logistic regression analysis reveal that the commercial banks holdings are more than investment banks holdings in the bidding firms that commercial banks have greater controlling power. The results indicate that the investment banks with lower holdings will increase their stake to gain controlling power. Firms that are not financially distress have lower credit risk and their liquidity is higher. The investment banks holdings for loan firms in order to earn profits for earning of the investment plan. The investment banks will increase holdings for those firms with a lower credit risk and more debt can be secure compensation.

Overall, the investment and commercial bank holdings significantly increased before the M&A completion date. We also found that the financial institutional quarters holdings proportion and the financial characteristics of the bidding firms have a significant relationship.

References

1. Petersen MA, Rajan RG (1994) The benefits of lending relationships: Evidence from small business data. Journal of Finance 49: 3-37.

2. Fama EF (1985) What's different about banks? Journal of Monetary Economics15: 29-39.

3. Sharpe S (1990) Asymmetric information, banking lending, and implicit contracts: A stylized model of customer relationships. Journal of Finance 45: 1069-1087.

4. Diamond DW (1984) Financial intermediation and delegated monitoring. Review of Economic Studies 51: 393-414.

5. Shehzad CT, Haan J, Scholtens B (2010) The impact of bank ownership concentration on impaired loans and capital adequacy. Journal of Banking & Finance 34: 399-408.

6. Servaes H, Zenner M (1996) The role of investment banks in acquisitions. Review of Financial Studies 9: 787-815.

7. Boot AWA (2000) Relationship banking: What do we know? Journal of Financial Intermediation 9: 7-25.

8. James C (1992) Relationship-specific assets and the pricing of underwriter services. Journal of Finance 47: 1865-1885.

9. Burch T, Nanda V, Warther V (2004) The price of loyalty: an empirical analysis of underwriting relationships and fees, forthcoming.

10. Jensen M, Meckling W (1976) Theory of the firm: managerial behavior, agency costs and ownership structure. Journal of Financial Economics 3: 305-360.

11. Shleifer A, Vishny RW (1986) Large shareholders and corporate control. Journal of Political Economy 94: 461-488.

12. Smith CW, Warner J (1979) On financial contracting: An analysis of bond covenants. Journal of Financial Economics7: 117-161.

13. Diamond DW (1991) Monitoring and reputation: the choice between bank loans and directly placed debt. Journal of Political Economy 99: 689-751.

14. Kroszner RS, Strahan PE (2001) Bankers on boards: Monitoring, conflicts of interest, and lender liability. Journal of Financial Economics 62: 415-452.

15. Booth JR, Deli DN (1999) On executives of financial institutions as outside directors. Journal of Corporate Finance 5: 227-250.

16. Brockman P, Yan X (2009) Block ownership and firm-specific information. Journal of Banking and Finance 33: 308-316.

17. Shin HH, Park YS (1999) Financing constraints and internal capital markets: Evidence from Korean Chaebols. Journal of Corporate Finance 5: 169-191.

18. Chapman DR, Junor CW, Stegman TR (1996) Cash flow constraints and firms' investment behaviour. Applied Economics 28: 1037-1044.

19. Bushman R, Indjejikian R, Smith A (1996) CEO Compensation: The role of individual performance evaluation. Journal of Accounting and Economics 21: 161-193.

20. Ittner C, Larcker D, Rajan M (1997) The choice of performance measures in annual bonus contracts. The Accounting Review 72: 231-255.

21. Altman EJ (1983) Corporate financial distress: A complete guide to prediction of corporate bankruptcy. Journal of Finance 23: 589-609.

22. Harris M, Raviv A (1991) The theory of capital structure. Journal of Finance 46: 297-355.

23. Smith CW, Watts RL (1992) The investment opportunity set and corporate financing, dividend and compensation policies. Journal of Financial Economics 32: 263-292.

24. Stearns LB, Mizruchi MS (1993) Board composition and corporate finance: The impact of financial institution representation on borrowing. Academy of Management Journal 36: 603-617.

25. Leland H, Pyle D (1977) Information asymmetries, financial structure, and financial intermediation. Journal of Finance 32: 371-387.

26. Wansley JW, Lane WR, Yang HC (1983) Abnormal returns to acquired firms by type of acquisition and method of payment. Financial Management 12: 16-22.

27. Guner A, Malmendier U, Tate G (2005) The impact of boards with financial expertise on corporate policies. NBER Working Paper No. W11914.

4

Exploring the Disclosure of Intellectual Capital in Ghana: Evidence from Listed Companies

Nicholas Asare*, Joseph Mensah Onumah and Samuel Nana Yaw Simpson

Department of Accounting, Methodist University College, Ghana

Abstract

Intellectual Capital (IC) has become a prominent feature of business transactions and discourse. The rising interests in IC and Intellectual Capital Disclosure (ICD) issues in both developed and developing countries have necessitated insightful studies. This study explores ICD in Ghana and seeks to contribute to fill the dearth in the literature on ICD from the perspective of developing countries. The study examines the ICD of 25 companies listed on the Ghana Stock Exchange (GSE) over a five-year period (2006-2010) through content analysis of their corporate annual reports. The study revealed that the ICD level in annual reports in Ghana is quite high and descriptively reported and though disclosure of IC is improving but at a relatively marginal rate. Therefore looking at the trend of ICDs by the companies, the study recommends the need for accounting regulatory bodies and oversight agencies (local and global) to develop specific standards or guidelines on identifying, measuring and reporting IC. This paper is one of the few studies to have investigated the disclosure of IC in corporate annual reports in Ghana.

Keywords: Intellectual capital; Disclosure; Corporate annual reports; Stakeholders

Introduction

Intellectual Capital (IC) is a term now in common usage across different fields of academic and managerial activity [1]. Roslender and Fincham [2] note that, while the term 'IC' is relatively new, the substance of the debate goes back to at least the 1960s and 1970s when many of the same topics were debated under the headings of 'Human Asset Accounting' or 'Human Resource Accounting'. The term IC was first used in the 1960s, but became pronounced in the 1990s and as result became an accounting/ management practitioner-created concept [3-6]. Since then, organizations have attached increased importance to the recognition, measurement and reporting of IC especially in corporate annual reports [7]. The increased focus on IC seems to be more related to the emergence of intangible assets as a key driver of value within knowledge based corporations, which is in turn a reflection of major macroeconomic economic shifts in most economies [8]. Edvinsson and Malone [9] argue that the worth of a company lies not in bricks and mortar, but in intangible kind of asset, that is IC, which is hidden behind the company's book values. Currently, companies are reporting on their IC in a qualitative or semi-quantitative manner in addition to the traditional and formally required financial reporting [10]. This can partly be traced to the increased demand by stakeholders for relevant information, prompted by the many frauds and scandals of the last decade which has demonstrated the need for there to be better rules and practices for financial information disclosure to improve trust in accounting [11].

To a large extent firms have much incentive to provide additional disclosure as previous literature identifies several reasons that pinpoint that enhanced disclosure has favorable capital market implications [12-14]. Disclosure can mitigate the adverse selection problem [15,16] and improve market liquidity [13] by providing value relevant information to otherwise uninformed investors [17]. Extensively ICDs forms a relative chunk of these disclosures that places the firm in proper perspective for investors and other stakeholders. Thus, a major premise is that firms disclose IC to improve transparency, legitimize status and enhance reputation [11]. Such a premise accords with contention by [8] that knowledge-based firms have strong reasons to improve transparency by disclosing IC information to stakeholders. This could be done through the corporate annual reports which have become noted for disclosing important/essential information about the financial and non-financial performance of companies.

There is a rising discussion of issues of IC in the context of the current knowledge/ information economy more largely within the accounting literature. However, a substantial portion of this prior research especially it's disclosures in annual reports have been undertaken in developed countries [7,18,19]. Thus, Kamath [18] calls for studies based on developing countries as part of the global attempt to develop disclosure guidelines on IC. In fact, there are no far-reaching regulations and guidelines that require companies to adhere to in disclosing IC [20]. Moreover, the International Financial Reporting Standards (IFRS) do not specifically and expressly require companies to report on IC, despite evidence that IC has become a key resource of value creation in today's knowledge economy [21].

This study therefore contributes to the literature by exploring the ICDs of companies in Ghana. The choice of Ghana stems from evidence that the country is one of the fastest growing countries; economically and democratically post World Bank and IMF sponsored reform programmers. Ghana was the first country in Sub-Saharan Africa to gain political independence from European colonial powers. Moreover, the country is considered by many scholars, the veritable site for researching into issues on Africa and developing countries [22]. The country maintains a mixed nature economy, with a modestly strong State and vibrant private sector [23].

This paper is organized as follows: the next section provides a

*Corresponding author: Nicholas Asare, Department of Accounting, Methodist University College, Ghana, E-mail: sirnickasare@yahoo.com

review of literature in the area. This is followed by details of the research method. Empirical results are presented in fourth section and findings discussed in the penultimate section. The final section presents some concluding remarks.

Literature Review

The business landscape has changed tremendously in the twenty-first century as we are entering the knowledge society, in which the basic economic resources are no longer capital, natural resources, or labor, but are, and will be, knowledge [24]. The notion of the "knowledge economy" has motivated much recent research (by academics, professional accounting bodies and various European Union (EU) and national government and international agencies), into why information relating to investments in intangible assets (e.g. IC), might be important in terms of better assessing and managing the sources of value generation and the sustainability and risks associated with corporate strategies.

In spite of these numerous research on IC, there are various definitions of IC in the literature, but Stewart's [25] definition appears to have received appreciable attention in the IC literature [26,27]. Stewart [25] defined IC as intellectual material – knowledge, information, intellectual property and experience – that can be put to use to create wealth. Other definitions give impetus to the fact that IC can be used to boost the wealth creation and firm value for sustain a competitive edge. Edvinsson and Malone [9] delineate IC as the possession of the knowledge, applied experience, organizational technology, customer relationships, and professional skills that give a company competitive edge in the market. Moreover, human beings, organizational structures and capabilities, customer base, organizational rapport with other stakeholders are emphasized.

Accounting regulation (for example, in the form of IAS 38: Intangible Assets) is conservative and restrictive in the extent to which it allows recognition and measurement of intangibles [28]. The friction is between ICD and accounting regulation as applied these days thereby signaling a need for a "revolution in accounting regulations" in order to ensure the fair presentation of the economic state of the firm [17]. In this regard the question that comes up is what Nielsen et al. [29] asked and endeavored to answer, i.e. how can we build an accounting system that enables the classification and presentation of IC indicators? They then went ahead and stated that, an accounting system for ICD would need to take into consideration the indicators of IC; which in turn must be classified according to common categories spanning the IC categories.

Over the years, a variety of approaches have been advanced to measure and report IC [30]. A system for classifying IC developed by Edvinsson et al. [31,32] proposed three components of IC, which they defined as human capital (HC) - individual competence, structural capital (SC) - internal structure and relational capital (RC) - external structure respectively.

The idea of HC and its significance for economic development can be found in the work of Smith (1976) [33]. HC is generally concerned with the contribution of human resources to organizational success. It generates innovation – whether of new products and services, or improving business processes [34]. Sonnier [35] described HC as the knowledge, skill, expertise/ know-how, problem solving capacity, education, training, judgment, experience, abilities, and loyalty of the employees of the firm. A further indebt explanation of the concept was

by Abeysekera and Guthrie [36]. They referred to HC as "a combination of factors possessed by individuals and the collective workforce of a firm. It can encompass knowledge, skills and technical ability; personal traits such as intelligence, energy, attitude, reliability, commitment; ability to learn, including aptitude, imagination and creativity; desire to share information, participate in a team and focus on the goals of the organization". The HC is the brain behind the SC of every organization.

Moreover, SC encompasses the structure, processes, procedures, routines, systems and culture of the firm, including its databases, management tools, IT systems, strategies, structural design/mechanism, coordination mechanisms, policies, organizational learning capacity and networking systems [35]. Riahi-Belkaoui [34], also described it as "the knowledge that belongs to the organization as a whole in terms of technologies, inventions, data, publications, strategy and culture, structures and systems, organizational routines and procedures". It thus includes the complementary business assets that are often necessary to convert an innovative idea into a saleable product or service [6]. The HC and SC are both need if the organization is to have good RC assets to create value for various stakeholders.

On the other hand, RC is based on the idea that firms are considered not to be isolated systems but as systems that are, to a great extent, dependent on their relations with their environment [4]. Hormiga et al. [4] explained that RC refers to the value generated by relationships not only with customers or shareholders, but with all stakeholders, both internal and external. RC is thus the knowledge embedded in the relationships with any stakeholder that influences the organization's life [37]. This presupposes that in thriving as a firm, it is very important that the firm establishes and nurtures good and more progressive relationships with all its stakeholders.

These three IC categories can be perceived not to be disclosed proportionately in the corporate annual reports as there are no generally accepted stringent criteria for such disclosures especially in the context of Ghana. In that regard regulations/ standards in accounting regulate the reporting of information in corporate annual reports to the stakeholders. Accounting regulation is restrictive in the extent to which it allows recognition of intangibles. Nonetheless, prior evidence indicates that more disclosure can help solve problems of asymmetry in information between company insiders and investors [14,16,38]. Additional disclosure can lead to increased trading since it enhances firms' visibility and investors are more likely to invest in firms they are familiar with [12,39]. Moreover, investors are likely to price protect themselves against potential losses from trading with well-informed market participants [17]. As a result, a firm's cost of capital increases due to insufficient disclosure [14,38].

So firms have different motivations as to why they disclose IC. Generally, IC information disclosed in annual reports have the tendency to help various stakeholders especially investors to be familiar and satisfied with the affairs of firms so as to take informed decisions with regards to any dealings with the firms. The argument typically put forward by policy advisors appears to be that greater recognition, reporting and management of intangible assets e.g. IC could lead to significant improvements in corporate performance and that this information could provide both inside and outside stakeholders with valuable and relevant information concerning corporate risks and prospects [40]. Management of IC efficiently and effectively is the key to sustain competitive edge currently in specific industries.

Empirically, many of the ICD studies are based on evidence from the developed world and concentrated on organizations in the Nordic areas and English speaking countries, such as UK, USA, Canada and Australia [18,19]. Moreover, studies have relied on various media of disclosure, such as company websites, presentations to analysts and IPO prospectuses, but the annual report remains the most popular medium [41]. Furthermore, ICD in annual reports cuts across several sections of the reports. The sections include Chairman's Report (CR), Director(s) Report (DR), Auditor's Report, Corporate Governance Report (CG), Corporate Social Report (CSR), Financial Statements (FS) and Notes to the Financial Statements (N).

From the Australian context, Guthrie and Petty [42] report that IC is poorly understood, inadequately identified, inefficiently managed and not reported within a consistent framework when reported at all. European companies have pioneered the IC measurement and reporting field, and this trend is extending to Japan where guidelines for disclosure of IC have been issued. From the Scandinavia settings, many of the studies show sustained interest in accounting for the worth of employees, aptly identified via ICD [43]. They find that IC accounting developments in the UK is limited, thus has become the focus of interest within the sample of companies. Kansal and Singh [21] and Guthrie et al. [44] also find that levels of voluntary ICD by listed companies is low and in qualitative rather than quantitative form.

Focusing on intangible assets which IC is an example, report that firms with different background do not disclose intangible assets in the same way. These strengthen the view that ICD practices are not uniform across countries and firms. Abeysekera [45] argues that differences in ICD practices can be attributed to economic, social and political factors. More specifically Vergauwen and Alem [17] also pronounced that such difference can be explained by country-specific regulation and auditor conservatism. In spite of this, literature on the phenomenon in the context of developing countries and more specifically Sub-Saharan Africa may not be much to engineer evidence of ICD practices to international standard setters and stakeholders.

Recounting the few studies based evidence from Sub-Saharan Africa; Wagiciengo and Belal [7] reported that ICDs by South African companies have increased over the 5 years study period with certain firms and that out of the three components, HC is the most disclosed. Based on listed companies on the Nairobi Stock Exchange, Abeysekera [46] finds that those firms disclose more tactical SC and more strategic HC have larger boards. Tayib and Salman [47] also looked at Intellectual Capital Reporting (ICR) in Nigeria and found out that most of the IC indicators are not supported by accounting standards issued in Nigeria. More recently in Nigeria, Haji et al. [48], looked at ICD from a longitudinal perspective, the results show that the overall ICD of Nigerian banks increased moderately over the period and that human and internal capital disclosures dominated the banks' ICD.

Research Method

This study is primarily exploratory; there are little empirical studies on ICD in the context of developing countries and more specifically Ghana. The study draws on companies listed the Ghana Stock Exchange (GSE) as at the end of the year 2010. Out of the 36 listed firms as at that date, 25 were purposively sampled to include companies with at least five years annual reports. The reason for focusing the study on listed companies is that that they are more likely to disclose more information than unlisted companies and were assumed to appreciate issues of IC especially from the perspective that it could help them gain competitive advantage.

Annual report was the main source of data in light of evidence that it highly reliable and often used by managers of companies to signal what is important [49-51]. The annual report is an important document because it is the principal means for corporate communication of activities and intentions to stakeholders [52] it is produced regularly, the company has a substantial editorial input into it and it is widely distributed and read.

The 2006 – 2010 annual reports of the firms were gleaned and analyzed using content analysis method; widely used research methods in investigating the frequency and type of IC reporting. Content analysis involves codifying the text of writing (i.e. qualitative and quantitative information) into various pre-defined groups/classes or categories based on selected criteria in order to derive patterns in the presentation and reporting of information [51, 44].

There are several units of content analysis of ICD; word, sentence and paragraph counts. Gray et al. [53], argue that words have the advantage of lending themselves to more exclusive analysis even though sentences are preferred in written communication if the task is to infer meaning. Using sentences for both coding and measurement is likely to provide complete, reliable and meaningful data for further analysis [54]. The argument for paragraph method is that, it is more appropriate than word count in drawing inferences from narrative statements as we commonly establish meaning with paragraphs rather than through the reporting of a word or sentence [51]. The literature does not provide an overwhelming justification for any of the three units of analysis [55]. However, the use of words and/or sentences seems to be preferred by most researchers. Drawing on the advantages that sentence count has over other units [53,54] sentences are used as the recording unit just as previous studies. Wagiciengo and Belal [7] also add the need for an ICD framework.

On account of the exploratory nature of the current study and also based on a country specific study from Sub-Saharan Africa, Wagiciengo and Belal's [7] framework is adapted. Their framework was modified based on the Ghanaian regulatory environment, hence 30 indicators (i.e. 10 for each for the IC categories) assumed to be pertinent and applicable to all the firms were chosen (see table 1). The content analysis method was thus used to analyze the annual reports of the companies to determine the types of IC reported taken into consideration the various indicators/ attributes and categories of IC in the ICD framework. According to Guthrie et al. [51], the categories of classification must be clearly and operationally defined and objectively be clear that an item either belongs or does not belong to a particular category whilst a reliable coder is needed to be able to quantify the information.

An arithmetical coding format was used; an indicator reported (even repeated) was scored one (1) and a score of zero (0) if the indicator is not referred to [7]. The aggregate disclosure scores of IC indicators were aggregated to determine the ICD levels for a company and for each category of IC over the period. Also, in analyzing the ICD scores in the corporate annual reports, repeated ICD information was considered or recorded once.

Discussions of Findings

Drawing on the above framework, actual scores for a company and a category were out of a possible total disclosure score of 30 and 250 respectively. As can be seen from Table 2, the study shows that Ghana Commercial Bank Ltd and Standard Chartered Bank Ltd report

	Human Capital		Structural Capital		Relational Capital
1	Career planning/ development	1	Corporate culture	1	Partnerships and Alliances
2	Education	2	Information systems	2	Community Involvement
3	Employee demographics	3	Intellectual property	3	Competitors
4	Remuneration Incentives	4	Management philosophy	4	Customer& Supplier
5	Industrial relations	5	Management processes	5	Distribution channels
6	Innovation, Initiative, motivation	6	Organizational learningcapacity	6	Favourable contracts
7	Know-how and experience	7	Organizational structure	7	Financial relations
8	Occupational health and Safety	8	Policies and procedures	8	Investors
9	Teamwork capacity	9	Quality services/products	9	Licensing/franchising
10	Training &Work-related Competencies	10	R&D	10	Organisation name/ brands

Table 1: The ICD Framework.

Company	2006	2007	2008	2009	2010	Average
	Score	Score	Score	Score	Score	Score
Ghana Commercial Bank Ltd	21	21	23	23	24	22.4
Standard Chartered Bank Ltd	22	21	20	24	25	22.4
HFC Bank Ltd	21	20	21	23	24	21.8
Enterprise Insurance Company Ltd	21	20	20	22	24	21.4
SG-SSB Ltd	20	20	21	22	23	21.2
CAL Bank Ltd	21	20	20	22	22	21
Mechanical Lloyd Company Ltd	19	19	21	21	22	20.4
PZ Cussons Ltd	19	20	19	19	21	19.6
Pioneer Kitchenware Ltd	19	18	21	18	22	19.6
Total Petroleum Ltd	19	18	18	18	20	18.6
Aluworks Ltd	16	16	17	19	22	18
Accra Brewery Company Ltd	18	17	19	16	16	17.2
Guinness Ghana Breweries Ltd	13	15	15	21	22	17.2
Benso Oil Palm Plantation Ltd	16	16	16	17	19	16.8
Produce Buying Company Ltd	14	15	17	17	19	16.4
Unilever (Ghana) Ltd	14	15	17	18	17	16.2
Cocoa Processing Company Ltd	16	15	16	18	14	15.8
Fan Milk Ltd	11	16	16	18	18	15.8
Starwin Products Ltd	18	15	15	15	15	15.6
Golden Web Ltd	14	14	15	16	16	15
Camelot Ghana Ltd	12	14	12	13	15	13.2
Sam Wood Ltd	13	13	13	14	13	13.2
Clydestone Ltd	13	12	12	14	15	13.2
CFAO Ltd	8	10	14	11	13	11.2
African Champions Industries Ltd	10	11	10	12	12	11
Average	**16.32**	**16.44**	**17.12**	**18.04**	**18.92**	**17.37**

Table 2: Rankings by Companies' ICD Scores.

more on IC in their annual reports hence have the highest average ICD score of 22.40 over the period. On the other hand, African Champions Industries Ltd had the lowest ICD score with an average of 11.00 compared to the overall average of 17.35 of the total ICD indicators over the period. The overall average ICD score was 57.89% of the IC indicators. The average disclosure score for all the firms increased from 16.32 in 2006 to 18.92 in 2010 (i.e. 15.93% increase over the period); indicating that ICDs for the firms increased at marginal rates over the period. This illustrate the gradual way at which ICD in corporate annual reports is improving in such reports; and could indicates that the firms are not so enthused about increasing such disclosures at higher rates within the foreseeable future.

In the specific instance of Ghana Commercial Bank Ltd and Standard Chartered Bank Ltd, they are among the largest banks and/ or listed firms in the country in terms of their market share and market capitalization in the banking industry and GSE bourse respectively and as such do not seem to surprise the researchers that they disclose more

IC than any of the sampled companies. Moreover, firms in the banking, finance and insurance industry appear more conversant with IC issues as evidence from Table 2 indicates that all of them were ranked among the first ten. The first six firms are all from the banking, finance and insurance industry and they form the total number of companies from that sector included in this study. This could be attributed to their quest to achieve competitive advantage as a result of the competitive nature of that industry coupled with stringent regulatory regime of their industry.

Overall, the ICD level was relatively high as more than half of the IC indicators were disclosed by the listed firms on average over the period. This is somehow commendable and shows that Ghanaian listed firms have appreciable understanding of the practice of ICD.

With this observation the researchers went further to find out the IC category that was relatively disclosed than the others using the average ICD scores cautiously. It can be seen from Table 3 that SC (133 in 2006 to 157 in 2010) and HC (141 in 2006 to 153 in 2010) increased sporadically over the period, but RC (135 in 2006 to 158 in 2010) increased continuously, hence the relatively dominant component (mean of 149.6). This reveals that RC disclosures in corporate annual reports are relatively higher than HC and SC disclosures among listed firms in Ghana. It could be inferred by the researchers that in the quest of listed firms to provide adequate disclosures with respect to IC they disclose more RC indicators as probably they treasure relationships built with stakeholders. Though this findings differ from Wagiciengo and Belal [7] findings; the dominance of HC, it is consistent with findings that RC disclosures are relatively higher than HC and SC disclosures [21,56].

Also, from Table 4, RC indicators were relatively disclosed most, with an average 58.48% of companies disclosing on them over the period. Coincidentally RC is also quite the most disclosed in the annual reports and as such is not surprising that a greater number of companies are disclosing it in their annual reports than the others. This was followed closely by SC indicators i.e. with an average of 57.68% companies disclosing it over the period. The latter was not significantly different from the number of firms that disclosed the RC. A further perusal of the analysis using the 30 IC indicators used in this study indicated that, the most disclosed IC indicator was 'management processes'. This was on average disclosed by all the companies (i.e. 24.8 representing 99.2%) for the period. This was followed closely by 'Information systems/ technology'; an average of 24.4 representing 97.6% companies. The least disclosed indicator was 'Industrial Relations'.

These findings suppose that issues of management or technical processes (series of actions) implemented/ to be implemented to achieve specific results in the firms are always disclosed in the corporate annual reports coupled with information on systems or networking stuffs. Labor union relations and activities i.e. 'Industrial Relations' disclosures are hardly disclosed by majority of the listed firms.

In terms of the three categories; for the HC category, issues of remuneration and incentives are the one disclosed by most of the companies (i.e. 23.60 representing 94.40%); with SC, management processes was on average disclosed by all the companies (i.e. 24.8 representing 99.20%) and as such is the most disclosed by the companies over the period; RC's most disclosed attribute was "financial relations (i.e. references to recognized associations with financial institutions)", 23.60 firms representing 94.40% of the sampled firms.

The analysis of ICD by its locations in the sections of the annual reports as shown in Table 5 basically revealed that the chairman's report contains the most of ICDs (approximately 28% of the total ICDs over the period). 24% and 23% of all ICDs over the period were disclosed in notes to the financial statements and director(s) report sections correspondingly. The sections with the least amount of disclosures were the financial statements and corporate social report (i.e. 2% of total ICDs). The results for the directors' report as against the chairman's report and notes to the financial statements can be partly explained that considerable portion of what should be in the directors report and

financial statements is dictated by the companies code 1963 (i.e. in the context of Ghana) and accounting standards respectively. With regards to the accounting standards there are no clear cut standards enjoining firms to recognize IC in financial statements. Corporate governance issues have also hyped the chairman's report of the annual reports and could invariably be a factor as to what information is disclosed in that report.

Also, the disclosure of IC for all the sections of the annual reports increased irregularly over the period; pinpointing the gradual improvement with which ICDs in the various sections of corporate annual reports have been over the period. The low ICD in financial statements section certainly is clarified by the piece of evidence in this report that, most of the companies reported IC in qualitative form. According to Guthrie et al. [44], this ought to be expected, as there are no corporation laws or accounting standards that require the quantification of IC. The fact is that generally intangibles do not meet the stringent criteria of the monetary measurement concept as stipulated in the GAAP and are voluntarily disclosed in discursive form.

Consistent with Guthrie et al. [44], most of the ICDs were mostly in qualitative form (i.e. descriptive form); about 95% of total ICDs over the period (see Figure 1). This supports the general perception that ICDs in annual reports are mostly in words or descriptive form.

Conclusion

This study sought to examine the level of ICD of listed companies via content analysis of their corporate annual reports. A sample of 25 firms listed on the Ghana stock exchange was used in 0the study. The ICD level was relatively high and mostly in qualitative form. This obviously puts listed firms as being concerned with their ICD in the annual reports even though very little is being done to quantify those assets in monetary and numerical terms. The disclosures are fairly dominated by RC indicators and are mostly in the chairman's report section of the annual reports. Issues of management or technical processes (series of actions) implemented/ to be implemented to achieve specific results in the firms are always disclosed in the corporate annual reports coupled with information on systems or networking stuffs. Labour union relations and activities i.e. 'industrial relations' disclosures are hardly disclosed by majority of the listed firms. Besides, the banking & finance and insurance industry as a knowledge intensive sector have comparatively high ICDs as the all the 6 companies from that sector were ranked the top six in the ICD score rankings. On the whole, conclusion can be made that, the disclosure of IC in Ghana is improving but at a relatively low rate. Various ICD approaches could be adopted or adapted to raise disclosures to a more desirable or more excellent quality. The standards and guidelines will speed up the improvements in the ICD in the annual reports.

Companies should voluntarily increase the content, in terms of quantity and quality, of ICDs in corporate annual reports and other equally important reports. In that regard management should ensure that they are consistent in their ICD practices by instituting mechanisms

	2006	2007	2008	2009	2010	Average
HC	141	141	139	149	153	144.6
SC	133	131	137	148	157	141.2
RC	135	139	152	158	164	149.6
Average	136.33	137	142.67	151.67	158	145.13

Table 3: ICD Scores for IC Categories.

Human Capital	Average (2006-2010)	
	No. of Companies	%
Remuneration and Incentives	23.6	94.4
Innovation, Initiative, motivation	20.6	82.4
Know-how and experience	20.2	80.8
Education	16.8	67.2
Training &Work-related competencies	16.6	66.4
Teamwork capacity	12	48
Employee demographics	10.8	43.2
Career planning/development	10.2	40.8
Occupational health and Safety	9.8	39.2
Industrial relations	2.2	8.8
Average	**14.28**	**57.12**
Structural Capital		
Management processes	24.8	99.2
Information systems	24.4	97.6
Policies and procedures	24.2	96.8
Corporate culture	22.8	91.2
Management philosophy	15.2	60.8
Quality services/products	11.2	44.8
R&D	7.8	31.2
Intellectual property	5	20
Organizational learning capacity	3.2	12.8
Organisational structure	3.2	12.8
Average	**14.18**	**56.72**
Relational Capital		
Financial relations	21.6	86.4
Investors	20.2	80.8
Partnerships and Alliances	18.8	75.2
Customer &Supplier	17.8	71.2
Distribution channels	18.2	72.8
Organisation name/ brands	15.6	62.4
Community Involvement	14.6	58.4
Competitors	8.2	32.8
Licensing/franchising	7	28
Favourable contracts	4.6	18.4
Average	**14.66**	**58.64**

Table 4: Number of Companies by Reported Indicators.

Year	DR	CR	CG	AR	FS	N	CSR	Total
2010	184	231	98	80	16	190	16	815
2009	181	217	83	71	21	180	19	772
2008	175	202	81	70	16	182	12	738
2007	163	185	72	71	17	170	12	690
2006	169	197	88	71	14	173	12	724
Total	872	1032	422	363	84	895	71	3739
Percent (%)	23.32	27.6	11.29	9.71	2.25	23.94	1.9	100

Table 5: Location of ICDs in Corporate Annual Reports over the Period (2006-2010).

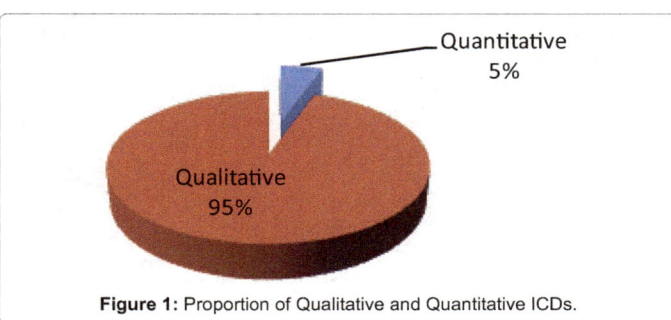

Figure 1: Proportion of Qualitative and Quantitative ICDs.

to ensure the provision of relevant and reliable IC information. Stakeholders are encouraged to incorporate IC information in their decisions since it will help them to make good decisions with regards to their dealings with companies.

As there is no distinctive model/approach for ICD, various approaches have been adapted to measure and report IC in the specific context of the companies and industries; thus showing how disparaging the practice of ICD in annual reports is across the country. There should be harmonization of the practices across the world by accounting standards. Efforts by accounting regulatory bodies should be intensified in coming out with specific standards. Therefore looking at the trend of ICDs by the companies i.e. is improving but at a relatively low rate, the study recommends the need for accounting regulatory bodies and oversight agencies (local and global) to develop specific standards or guidelines on identifying, measuring and reporting IC in corporate annual reports. Managers of listed companies on the other hand should continue to improve their disclosures by disclosing relevant and reliable information on IC for stakeholder use. In the light of these recommendations future research work could be undertaken to improve the ICD practices in Ghana.

A similar study could also be undertaken in unlisted companies and state owned enterprises. This current study looked at the extent and level of disclosure of IC in corporate annual reports. Future research may well be made to ascertain the quality of the disclosed IC and the willingness of management to make such disclosures in spite of its being primarily voluntary. The study focused on five years corporate annual reports. Imminent research could extend the time period covered in order to observe the development of ICD over a longer period.

This study was limited to selected listed companies on the GSE. Content analysis as a methodology, itself is subject to its own inherent limitations. The result of the study therefore may not necessarily represent the general situation in all companies in Ghana.

References

1. Gowthorpe C (2009) Wider still and wider? A critical discussion of intellectual capital recognition, measurement and control in a boundary theoretical context. Crc Perspect Account 20: 823–834.

2. Roslender R, Fincham R (2001) Thinking critically about intellectual capital accounting. Account, Auditing and Accountability J 14: 383–399.

3. Atalay M, Anafarta N (2011) Enhancing Innovation Through Intellectual Capital: A Theoretical Overview. J Mod Account and Auditing 7: 202-210.

4. Hormiga E, Batista-Canino RM, Sánchez-Medina A (2010) The Role of Intellectual Capital in the Success of New Ventures. IntEntrepManag J

5. Schneider A, Samkin G (2008) Intellectual Capital Reporting by the New Zealand Local Government Sector. J Intellectual Capital 9: 456-486.

6. Sullivan PH (1999) Profiting from Intellectual Capital. J Knowl Manage 3: 132-142.

7. Wagiciengo MM, Belal AR (2012) Intellectual Capital Disclosures by South African Companies: A Longitudinal Investigation. Advances in Accounting 28: 111-119.

8. McPhail K (2009) Where is the ethical knowledge in the knowledge economy? Power and potential in the emergence of ethical knowledge as a component of intellectual capital. Crc Perspect Account 20: 804–822.

9. Edvinsson L, Malone MS (1997) Intellectual capital: Realizing your company's true value by finding its hidden brainpower. Harper Business, New York.

10. Boekestein B (2009) Acquisitions Reveal the Hidden Intellectual Capital of Pharmaceutical Companies. J Intellectual Capital 10: 389-400.

11. Oliveira L, Rodrigues LL, Craig R (2006) Firm-Specific Determinants Of Intangibles Reporting: Evidence from the Portuguese Stock Market. J Hum Resource Costing & Account 10: 11-33.

12. Diamond DW, Verrecchia RE (1991) Disclosure, Liquidity, and the Cost of Capital. J Financ 46: 1325-1359.

13. Healy PM, Hutton AP, Palepu KG (1999) Stock Performance and Intermediation Changes Surrounding Sustained Increases in Disclosure. Contemp Account Res 16: 485- 520.

14. Leuz C, Verecchia RE (2000) The economic consequences of increased disclosure. J Account Res 38: 91-124.

15. Akerlof G (1970) The market for lemons: Quality uncertainty and the market mechanism. Q J Econ 84: 488-500.

16. Verrecchia RE (2001) Essay on disclosure. J Account Econ 32: 97-180.

17. Vergauwen PGMC, Alem FJC (2005) Annual Report IC Disclosures in the Netherlands, France and Germany. J Intellectual Capital 6: 89-104.

18. Kamath GB (2008) Intellectual Capital and Corporate Performance in Indian Pharmaceutical Industry. J Intellectual Capital 9: 684-704.

19. Seleim A, Ashour A, Bontis N (2004) Intellectual Capital in Egyptian Software Firms. Learning Organization 11: 332-346.

20. Bruggen A, Vergauwen P, Dao M (2009) Determinants of intellectual capital disclosure: evidence from Australia. Management Decision 47: 233-245.

21. Kansal M, Singh S (2011) Voluntary Disclosures of Intellectual Capital: An Empirical Analysis. J Intellectual Capital 12: 301-318.

22. Ayee JRA (2008) The Balance Sheet of Decentralization in Ghana. Found Local Gov: 233-258

23. Anaman KA (2006) What Factors Have Influenced Economic Growth in Ghana? Institute of Economic Analysis (IEA), Ghana Policy Analysis 2.

24. Ismail TH (2008) Intellectual Capital Reporting in Knowledge Economy: Evidence from Egypt. International Conference on Economic Directions III: Economic Policy in a Rapidly Changing World, College of Business Administration, Kuwait University, Kuwait.

25. Stewart TA (1997) Intellectual Capital: The New Wealth of Organizations. Doubleday Dell Publishing Group, Inc. New York, USA.

26. An Y, Davey H (2010) Intellectual capital disclosure in Chinese (mainland) companies. J Intellectual Capital 11: 326-347.

27. An Y, Davey H, Eggleton IRC (2011) Towards a comprehensive theoretical framework for voluntary IC Disclosure. J Intellectual Capital 12: 571-585.

28. Gowthorpe C (2009) Wider still and wider? A critical discussion of intellectual capital recognition, measurement and control in a boundary theoretical context. Crc Perspect Account 20: 823–834.

29. Nielsen C, Bukh P, Mouritsen J, Johansen MR, Gormsen P (2006) Intellectual capital statements on their way to the stock exchange: Analyzing new reporting systems. J Intellectual Capital 7: 221-240.

30. Vafaei A, Taylor D, Ahmed K (2011) The Value Relevance of Intellectual Capital Disclosures. J Intellectual Capital 12: 407-429.

31. Edvinsson L, Sullivan P (1996) Developing a model for managing intellectual capital. European Management Journal 14: 356-364.

32. Sveiby KE (1997) Intangible Assets Monitor. J Hum Resources Costing & Account 2: 73-97.

33. Smith A (1976) The theory of moral sentiments. Oxford: Oxford University Press.

34. Riahi-Belkaoui A (2003) Intellectual Capital and Firm Performance of US Multinational Firms: A Study of the Resource-Based and Stakeholder Views. J Intellectual Capital 4: 215-226.

35. Sonnier BM (2008) Intellectual Capital Disclosure: High-Tech Versus Traditional Sector Companies. J Intellectual Capital 9: 705-722.

36. Abeysekera I, Guthrie J (2004) Human capital reporting in a developing nation. Br Account Rev 36: 251-268.

37. Cabrita M, Vaz J (2006) Intellectual Capital and Value Creation: Evidence from the Portuguese Banking Industry. Electron J Knowl Manage 4: 11-20

38. Lambert RC, Leuz C, Verrecchia RE (2007) Accounting information, disclosure and the cost of capital. J Account Res 45: 385-420.

39. Chang M, D'Anna G , Watson I, Wee M (2008) Does Disclosure Quality via Investor Relations Affect Information asymmetry? Aust J Manage 33: 375-390.

40. Eustace C (2000) The intangible economy impact and policy issues. Report of the European High Level Expert Group on the Intangible Economy, European Commission. Enterprise Directorate-General, Brussels, Belgium.

41. Abhayawansa S, Abeysekera I (2008) An explanation of human capital disclosure from the resource-based perspective. J Hum Resource Costing & Account 12: 51-64.

42. Guthrie J, Petty R (2000) Intellectual Capital Literature Review Measurement, Reporting and Management. J Intellectual Capital 1: 155-176.

43. Roslender R, Fincham R (2004) Intellectual capital accounting in the UK. Account, Auditing and Accountability J 17: 178-209.

44. Guthrie J, Petty R, Ricceri F (2006) The Voluntary Reporting of Intellectual Capital Comparing Evidence from Hong Kong and Australia. J Intellectual Capital 7: 254-271.

45. Abeysekera I (2007) Intellectual capital reporting between a developing and developed nation. J Intellectual Capital 8: 329-345

46. Abeysekera I (2010) The influence of board size on intellectual capital disclosure by Kenyan listed firms. J Intellectual Capital 11: 504-518.

47. Tayib M, Salman RT (2011) Intellectual Capital Reporting in Nigeria: A way forward. 2ndAfrican International Business and Management Conference, in "Building Synergies for Better Performance", in Nairobi, Kenya August 25-26.

48. Haji AA, Gombak J, Mubaraq S (2012) The trends of intellectual capital disclosures: evidence from the Nigerian banking sector. J Hum Resource Costing & Account 16: 184-209.

49. Guthrie J, Petty R (2000) Intellectual Capital: Australian Annual Reporting Practices. J Intellectual Capital 1: 241-251.

50. April KA, Bosma P, Deglon DA (2003) IC measurement and reporting: establishing a practice in mining. J Intellectual Capital 4: 165-180.

51. Guthrie J, Petty R, Yongvanich K, Ricceri F (2004) Using Content Analysis as a Research Method to Inquire into Intellectual Capital Reporting. J Intellectual Capital 5: 282-293.

52. Holland L, Boon Foo Y (2003) Differences in environmental reporting practices in the UK and the US: the legal and regulatory context. Brit Account Rev 35: 1-18.

53. Gray RH, Kouchy R, Lavers S (1995) Constructing a Research Database of Social and Environmental Reporting by UK Companies: A Methodological Note. J Account, Auditing & Accountability 8: 78-101.

54. Milne M, Adler R (1999) Exploring the Reliability of Social and Environmental Disclosures Content Analysis. Account, Auditing & Accountability J 12: 237-256.

55. Williams SM (1999) Voluntary environmental and social accounting disclosure practices in the Asia-Pacific Region: an international empirical test of political economy theory. Int J Account 34: 209-238.

56. Oliveras E, Gowthorpe C, Kasperskaya Y, Perramon J (2008) Reporting Intellectual Capital in Spain.b Corporate Communications: An International Journal 13: 168-181.

5

How Advertising Intensity and Promotion Costs Effect Operating Profit in Four Type Indonesian Banking Industry

Krisnanto U*

Perbanas Institute, South Jakarta, Indonesia

Abstract

Kotler research found that there are four strategy in placing advertising i.e., uniform pulsing, maintenance pulsing, and impulse pulsing. There is relationship between sales and intensity advertising. This research is to find relationshipintensity bank advertising and bank promotion cost to bank operational profit. Intensity advertising obtained from a national daily newspaper, promotion cost and operating profit obtained from bank quarterly report publicly. Research object divided to four kind of bank i.e. state enterprise bank, private bank, regional bank, and Sharia bank. Research found that advertising behavior of the four banks same with Kotler theory, but promotion costs and operating profit not followed the theory. Quantititive analysis found that regional bank advertising did not effect the operational profit. Sharia banks did not determinate behavior advertising and promotion costs as an important thing to made operating profit. Recommendation as one shot research, it must be done in longitudinal research. It is better find another kind of promotion bank that could be analyzed.

Keywords: Banking; Profit; Advertising

Introduction

Launching banking products requires strategy. The marketing strategy of banking products requires an appropriate time. Banks that want to market their products need to schedule the right time to market its products and services both directly and indirectly.

The growth of digital advertising requires further research how the development of advertising in a particular industry. To market the banking products and services required costs. Costs related to promotion known from the banking performance report. While the sales of banking products and services result of a marketing plan or difference with the actual sales that is carried out at a certain time. Sales in the food industry have a stable relationship in the long run with the role of advertising, but not in the beverage industry as well as in the opposite direction with advertising issued by competitors Elliot [1]. This research supported by Andrasetal [2] that advertising and research effect earnings. Even advertising is closely related to the declining cost of capital [3]. Pulse advertising more recommended by Dube et al. [4] to optimize profit in certain period. Cost for advertisingwill be drained cash flow are considerably higher than the company that utilizes only for the sake of advertising necessary. Marketing of banking products can be done in various promotional mixes. Promotion mix will be effective if it can determine business type and targets to be achieved. For service businesses, word of mouth (personal selling) would be a very effective medium to reach consumers. Other promotional mix is also important to be used as a medium of communication from producer to consumer. Competitiontheory said the company that controls the advertising in two media ads will provide profit greater than companies that only monopolize the advertising media. Ads will be served by banks depends on the most appropriate schedule. Problem formulation divided into the following. When the apropriate time does the banking advertisements? How large is the promotional costs incurred? How large is the operating profit earned? What correlation incurred in advertising intensity and promotion cost to operational profit? The study only focused on the banking advertising during certain year in national newspaper daily and publish bank quarterly report. Based on the problem formulation and problem limitation stated above, the purpose of the study as follows. To study the behavior of the banking advertisements, to determine relevance number of banking ads and banking operating profit, to determine correlation promotion costs and banking profit operations, to determine the behavior banking ads effect andbanking promotional costs tobanking operating profit, to know the behavior of four kind of bank.

Material and Methods

Advertisingntensity

Advertising has a very important function for the company. According Saftiana [5] the higher the level of intensity of the ad, which can be measured with a high ratio of advertising costs to total sales will increase market share acquired. Instead the high intensity advertising of a product depends on the level of market concentration that can be measured concentration ratio. Advertising intensity is how much the strength of a company advertises its products so that ads can be seen by the public and the company will benefit.

Promotion costs

Carrying out promotional activities certainly require costs incurred by the company, therefore the cost of sale is the one used to finance sales promotion activities. Promotion cost is determined by aggregating all costs incurred by the company to carry out the promotion of goods. Some companies had different promotional tool, it relates to the company situation. Companies spend in promotion with a variety of promotional tools such as, advertising in mass media, electronic media, holding exhibitions, and others Rustami et al. [6]. Efforts to introduce the product to the consumer are the beginning of the promotional activities. Promotion is not just limited to introduce the product to consumers alone, but must be followed by influencing

*Corresponding author: Krisnanto U, Perbanas Institute, South Jakarta, Indonesia
E-mail: umbas@perbanas.id

it so that consumers can know the products offered by the company and then they are interested in and then buy the product or service offered. Promotion cost is the value that was sacrificed or incurred by a company for promotional purposes in connection with the marketing of products produced by the company. This promotion costs can directly affect the company profits. The higher promotional costs incurred by the company, the higher the profits to be obtained by the company. Bank's financial statements are published by Bank Indonesia or submitting their financial statements publicly.

Previous research

Saftiana [5] found that the ratio of the concentration ratio had linear positive effect on profitability, but ad intensity had not positive effect on profitability. Rustami et al. [6] found that production costs, promotional costs, and sales volumes simultaneously affect profit. Production, promotion, sales volume costs partially influence on earnings. Sales volume as a dominant influence on earnings. Andras et al. [2] found that advertising intensity effect on corporate earnings and R&D intensity effect on corporate profits. Widnyana et al. [7] found that promotion cost had positive effect on earnings and distribution costs positive effect on earnings.

Research framework

Todays' ccomptition very tight. Companiesusedmany ways to win competition. Every new strategy undertaken by a company always followed by others in order to win. Companies need coordination between marketing and finance departement for internal optimization to face of competition. Always balancing marketing target and equity issues [8]. From now on technology changed marketing approaches. Internetfacilities driving an increase in sales of motor vehicles Peng et al. [6]. The other way is to utilize markeing using natural disaster. Disaster made businesses contribute along with advertising. Research Zhang et al. [9] states that the more competitors, the more often companies make donations to natural disasters. On the other hand non promotional advertising is a new way to introduce a product to the consumer, for example through a proof of the originality of a product Vlachvei et al. [10]. Competition within an industry is also being studied by Willis and Rogers [11], the policy of the company to determine the frequency of ad placements, invite some comments from Mahajan [12], and Muller Mesak [13], and Park and Hahn [14]. Ad placement policies tend to be stable over time, at other times there are different frequencies. Ad placements different frequency bands adapted to the purpose of the ad placement as has been proposed by Kotler and Keller [15], for example at the time of going to launch a product required a fairly intensive advertising. Horsky [16], suggested that an ad placement hinge on the company's market share. All researchers agree that the placement of advertising depends on the sales strategy of the company. There are four types of advertising policies Kotler and Keller [15], namelyUniformAdvertisementpolicy of the company who advertise all the time. Pulsing MaintenanceAdvertisement, company's policy that advertisements based on different times tailored to the needs at that time. Pulsing Advertisement, company's policy that advertise with them within a certain time where no advertising because at that time waiting for a response if the consumer without ads. ImpulseAdvertisement, company's policy in advertisements only at one time and then not place ads on a longer time. The influence of sales to advertisement cycle Mesak [13]. It is assumed that the level of advertising and sales in a state of constant and linear. Has not found evidence that advertising affects sales at the same time (Simon [17], the framework is a synthesis of the relationship between variables is

compiled from a variety of theories that have been described. Based on the theories that have been described, analyzed critically and systematically, so aimlessly synthesis of the relationships between the variables studied (Sugiyono [18]. The framework below describes the influence of the intensity of advertising and promotion costs to operating profit bank (Figure 1).

Hypothesis formulation

The hypothesis is a temporary answer to the formula research problem, therefore the formulation of research problems are usually arranged in the form of a question sentence. Tesis to be temporary, because new answers given are based on relevant theory, not based on empirical facts obtained through data collection. So the hypothesis can also be expressed as a theoretical answer to the formula research problem, not the answer empirically Sugiyono [18].

Effect intensity Ad to bank operating profit: According Saftiana [5], the higher the level of intensity of the ad, which can be measured with a high ratio of advertising costs to total sales will drive the higher market share acquired. Instead the high intensity needed advertising of a product depends on the level of market concentration product that can be measured concentration ratio. Results of research conducted by Andras et al. [2] showed that the intensity of the ad significant positive effect on corporate profits. While Saftiana [5] shows the intensity of descriptive ads had no effect on operating profit. Based on the above, can be formulated hypotheses:

Ho_1: The intensity of the ad had no significant impact on bank operating profit.

Ha_1: Intensity ads had significant effect on bank operating profit.

Influence promotion cost to operating profit bank: Cost of sale is determined company by aggregating all costs incurred by the company to carry out the sale of goods or products. Some companies put a promotional tool that differs from one another, it relates to the promotion of what is suitable for the company. Companies spend in promotion with a variety of promotional tools such as, advertising in mass media, electronic media, holding exhibitions, and others (Rustami et al. [6] results of research conducted by Rustami et al. Saftiana [6] showed that the cost of the promotion had partial effect on operating profit and FirdausSaftiana [19] promotion cost had positive effect on sales volume. While Shoffiyana study Saftiana [6] showed that the cost of sale does not affect the volume of sales. Based on the above, can be formulated hypotheses:

Ho_2: Promoton Cost had no significant impact on bank operating profit.

Ha_2: Promotion Costhad significant effect on bank operating profit.

Research methods

In general, the research method is a scientific way to get data with

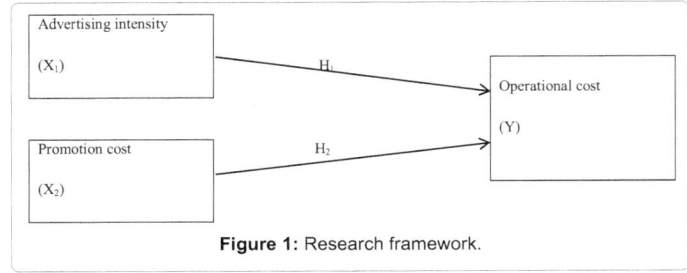

Figure 1: Research framework.

a specific purpose and usefulness (Sugiyono Saftiana [18]. This type of research used in this research is quantitative. Quantitative research is the analysis of quantitative data/statistics that aim to test the hypothesis that has been established with the population or a particular sample taken by random and data that can be used in the study of quantitative and qualitative data, quantitative data is the data that shaped figure, while the qualitative data is data that is not shaped figure (Sugiyono, Saftiana [18]. This research is a survey that takes secondary data derived from the newspaper for advertising and the bank's financial statements were published. Operational definitions of variables can be based on one or more source or reference to the reasons underlying the use of that definition. Once defined, the variables must be measured according to the rules or the size scale commonly accepted academically. To be examined and measured quantitatively, the variables in this study need to be operationally defined as follows: In this study, the dependent variable is the Operating profit on all banks in Indonesia which is obtained from the publication of financial statements of Central Bank. Operating profit in question in this research is the size of the profit earned by the company which has taken into account all the costs associated with the operations that cost of sales, cost of sales, general costs and administrative and depreciation expenses. In this study, using two independent variables, namely: Intensity ad in this research is how big and strength banks to advertise its products so that ads can be seen by the public and the company will benefit. The intensity is obtained from national newspaper ads. Promotioncosts in this study are all costs incurred by the bank for promotional activities, including advertising, sales promotion costs, direct sales costs, and the cost of publication. This promotion expenses derived from the Bank Financial Statements. Population is the generalization region consisting of: the object or subject that has certain qualities and characteristics yan set by researchers to learn and then drawn conclusions (Sugiyono, Saftiana [18]. The population in this study is all Banks. The sample is part of the number and characteristics possessed by this population (Sugiyono [18]. Sampling technique used in this study using purposive sampling, the sampling technique with consideration or criteria Sugiyono [18]. The sampling method by using purposive sampling method of making the goal that researchers get a sample corresponding to the desired researchers, making it easy to do research. Sampling based on banks ad at the national newspaper. Based on the above explanation of samples in this study are as follows: State enterprise Bank (All Population: 4 banks), Private Banks (13 from 65 banks), Regional Banks (15 from 26 banks), and Sharia Bank (7 from 11 banks). The data used in this research is secondary data. Secondary data is data that has been collected by the data collecting agency and published to the user community of data Kuncoro [20]. Secondary data for advertising intensity acquired from national newspaper ad in a year and the financial statements of the promotion costs and bank operating profit from bank's financial statements of each bank's website. There are some banks that did not follow the provisions of Central Bank which requires financial reports are published quarterly, making it difficult to sort out its quarterly report. For banks that do not advertise financial statements in accordance with the provisions, it had not taken the data. Advertising is done on an assumed quarter will increase consumption of banking products in the same quarter that may affect bank profits in the same quarter. Ads drawn from national newspapers, ads that are the object of the research is the ad placed by the bank concerned including advertising by bank coworkers (partner or sponsor). The data collection study was conducted from January 2 to December 31, except public holidays. There digit difference between profit, promotion, and advertising intensity, in order to be comparable is necessary to use ratio. The ratio is obtained from the average of each variable. To prove the influence and relationships used regression and correlation calculation. Meanwhile, to prove whether the intensity of advertising and promotion costs really beneficial profitable use ratio of each variable.

Data analysis method

This data is analyzed to see the behavior of advertising done by various banks daily and weekly. Behavioral promotion costs and profitability of each bank is also done. Then compared with the theory that has been put forward. These data were analyzed using statistical analysis using multiple linear regression analysis.

Testing Assumptions Regression Model

Normality test is done to see if the independent variables and the dependent variable has a normal distribution. To test it can be used a graphical method Normal P-P Plot of standardized residual cumulative probability, with identification when spreading are at about the normal, then the assumption of normality can be met. Additionally Test Kolmogorov-Smirnof also be used to see the normality of the identification if the p-value is greater than alpha, then the assumption of normality can be accepted. This test is performed to determine whether there is a correlation between confounding one another (non autocorrelation). To test there is no usable test autocorrelation Durbin Watson. To test whether there is a similarity variance of residuals from one observation to another observation. To test this used Scatterplot, where the X axis are the values of the prediction ZPRED=Predicted Value Regression Standardized with the Y-axis is the value that is ZRESID=Regression Standardized Predicted Value. When the graphs obtained showed a pattern generated by points are then said to have occurred Heteroscedasticity, but if they do not form a particular pattern then it is said does not happen heteroscedasticity. Multicollinearity that there is a linear relationship between changes definitely free. To determine whether there is a problem multicollinearity can use VIF (Variance Inflation Factory). If the value of VIF is still less than the 10 it was concluded not happen multicollinearity. The fulfillment of all the assumptions in the above linear regression, the model produced is considered good to use the influence of the independent variables on the dependent variable independent which further models can be used as a forecast tool. The next step is testing the reliability of the overall model (simultaneous test) and testing of the reliability of the variable portion (partial test). Analysis of the data used to determine the influence of each independent variable (advertising intensity and promotion costs) to bank operating profit is a multiple linear regression analysis aimed to determine the relationship between independent variables and the dependent variable whether each variable independently associated positive or negative and make predictions estimate the value of the dependent variable on the independent variable. This study used quantitative method with multiple regression analysis. In a multiple regression analysis to test the hypotheses that have been proposed, and to process and discuss the data obtained. Multiple regression analysis used by researchers intend to predict how the situation (up and down) the dependent variable, when two or more independent variables as predictors factors manipulated. Sample regression function permanence in assessing the actual value can be measured from the Goodness of Fit. Statistically, at least, this can be measured from the partial test, the value of coefficient of determination and the statistical F value. According Kuncoro [20] test statistic t basically shows how far the influence of the independent variable (the intensity of advertising and promotion costs) individually in explaining the variation of the dependent variable (operating profit). If a significant level of less than 0.05, then Ho is rejected and Ha accepted. Means the independent variables can explain the dependent variable. Conversely, if a significant level of more than 0.05 then Ho is accepted and Ha rejected. Means that the independent variable can not explain the dependent variable individually. The test measures can be explained as follows:1. Determine the hypothesis, 2. Determining the level of significance α (alpha) is used, α=5%, 3. Make a decision, 4. Make conclusions.

The statistical F test basically indicates whether all the independent variables included in the model have jointly influence the dependent variable (Kuncoro [20]. The null hypothesis (Ho) is tested all parameters in the model is equal to zero, or Ho: b1=b2=Bk=0. This means that if all the independent variables is not a significant explanatory on the dependent variable. The alternative hypothesis (Ha), not all parameters simultaneously equal to zero, or Ha: b1 ≠ b2 ≠ bk ≠ 0. This means that all independent variables simultaneously is a significant explanatory on the dependent variable. And to test this hypothesis with the F statistic used criteria decision making is when the F value is greater then Ho can be rejected at 5% confidence level. In other words we accept Ha (alternative hypothesis), that all independent variables simultaneously and significantly affect the dependent variable. Step-by-step test as follows:1. Determining Hypothesis, 2. Determining the level of significance (α) is used, α=5%, 3. Make a decision, 4. Make conclusions.

In the coefficient of determination (R^2) was used to measure how far the ability of the model to explain variations in the dependent variable (Kuncoro [20]. The value of coefficient of determination (R^2) reflects between zero and one. Small coefficient value determination means the ability of the independent variables in explaining the variation of the dependent variable are very limited. Likewise approximate value of the means of independent variables provide almost all the information needed to predict the variation of the dependent variable.

Results

Descriptive analysis

Based on the results of advertising intensity research quarterly on regional banks showed two peaks, first, in the second quarter and the last peak in the fourth quarter. Based on the results of the study advertising intensity every day for a week, there are two peaks, on Monday and the highest on Saturday, while the lowest on Tuesdays and Thursdays. In both areas reflects the bank's behavior as proposed by Kotler and Keller's theory Pulsing maintenance [15].

Based on the research results quarterly behavioral advertising on state-owned banks showed two peaks, the first and the highest, in the second quarter and the last in the fourth quarter. Based on the results

of the study behavioral advertising every day for a week at a state bank there is a peak t on Friday, while the lowest on Tuesday. In both behaviors reflect a state bank as proposed by Kotler and Keller's theory Pulsing maintenance [15].

Based on the results of behavioral advertising research quarterly on Islamic banks and private banks showed two peaks, the first, the second quarter and last, in the fourth quarter. Based on the results of the study behavioral advertising every day for a week on private and sharia banks there is a peak that on Friday, while the lowest on Tuesday. The two bank behaviors reflects Kotler and Keller Pulsing maintenancetheory [15].

Quantitative analysis

Statistical analysis summarized in Table 1:

Discussion

Based on the research results on behavioral advertising quarterly and behavioral advertising dailyin a week by regional, state enterprises, sharia, and private bank shows similarity theory as proposed by Kotler and Keller [15] i.e. Pulsing maintenance [16].

Based on the statistical analysis, the four banks had similarities concerning the promotional costs and profits. Research related to advertising and profits similar to. Regionalbanks advertising intensity had not positive influence on earnings as research conducted by Yulia [17-20].

Conclusion

1. The advertisement behavior of the four types of banks had not followed the theory. But the behavior of the promotion costs and operating profit did not follow behavioral advertising.

2. Correlation of regional bank advertising to operating income it very low, but the other three types of banks is high.

3. Correlation of regional bank promotion cost to operating income it very low, but the other three types of banks is high.

4. Correlation of sharia bank promotion cost to operational profit lower than the other three type of bank.

5. Advertisingintensity and promotion cost to operational profit had the same effect to the four type of bank but in the difference in number.

Analysis	Regional Bank	Private Bank	Sharia Bank	State enterprise Bank
Normality test	Normal distribution			
Autocorrelation test	Noautocorellation			
Homo scedastisity test	No heteroscedastisity			
Multi collinearity	No multicollinearity			
Multiple regression analysis	Y= 0,008 + 0,030X₁ + 0,460X₂	Y= -0,012 + 0,674X₁ + 0,941X₂	Y= 0,011 + 0,302X₁ + 0,386X₂	Y= -0,017 + 0,432X₁ + 0,884X₂
T test	• No significant effect on advertising intensity to operational profit (H₀ accepted and Hₐ not accepted) • No significant effect on promotion cost to operational profit (H₀ accepted and Hₐ not accepted)	Significat effect on advertising intensity to operational profit and promotion cost to operationanl profit (H₀ not accepted and Hₐ accepted)		
F test	Honot accepted and Ha accepted			
Determination analysis	0.594	0.855	0.303	0.530

Table 1: Statistical analysis. Source: statistical data.

Research Limitations

1. The study was only for one year.

2. Advertising intensity comes frome one national newspaper

Manajerial Implication

1. Yearly research study to know long-term behavior.

2. Data sources from all kind of promotion.

3. Need another research why regional and sharia bank have different behavior than the two other bank.

References

1. Caroline E (2001) A Cointegration analysis of advertising and sales data. Review of Industrial Organization 18: 417-426.

2. AndrasTL, Srinivasan SS (2003) Advertising intensity and R&D intensity: Differences across industires and their impact on form performance. International. Journal of Business and Economcs 2: 167-176.

3. Huang Y, Wei XS (2012) Advertising intensity, investor recognition, and cost of capital. Review Quantitatif Financial Accounting 38: 275-298.

4. Dube JP, Hitsch JG,Manchanda P (2005) An empirical model of advertising dynamics. Quantitative Marketing and Economics 3: 107-144.

5. Saftiana Y (2014) Analisis Hubungan Rasio Konsentrasi, IntensitasIklan, dan Profitabilitas Industri Kosmetik di Indonesia. Jurnal Manajemen Dan Bisnis Sriwijaya 12: 243-258.

6. Rustami P, Kirya IK, Cipta W (2014) Pengaruh Biaya Produksi, Biaya Promosi, dan Volume Penjualan Terhadap Laba Pada Perusahaan Kopi Bubuk Banyuatis. E-Jurnal Bisma Universitas Pendidikan Ganesha 2: 1-9.

7. Widnyana MJ, Nuridja IM, Dunia IK (2014) Pengaruh Biaya Promosidan Biaya Distribusi Terhadap Laba UD Surya Logam Desa Temukus Tahun 2010-2012. Journal Jurusan Pendidikan Ekonomi 4: 1-11.

8. Luo X, J de Jong P (2012) Does advertising spending really work? The intermediate role of analysts in the impact of advertising on firm value. Journal of the Academy of Marketing Science 40: 605-624.

9. Zhang, Ran, Jigao Z, Heng Y, Chunyan Z (2010) Corpcrate Philanthropic Giving, Advertising Intensity, and Industry Competition Level. Journal of Business Ethics 94: 39-52.

10. Vlachvei ANotta O, Ananiadis I (2009) Does advertising matter? An Application to the Greek Wine Industry. British Food Journal 111: 686-698.

11. Willis, Michael S, Richard TR (1998) Market Share Dispersion among Leading Firms as a Determinant of Advertising Intensity. Review of Industrial Organization 13: 495-508.

12. Mahajan V, Muller E (1986) Advertising pulsing policies for generating awareness for new products, Marketing Science 5: 89-106.

13. Mesak HI (1985) On modeling advertising pulsing decision Decision Science 16: 25-42.

14. Park S, Hahn M (1991) Pulsing in a dicrete model of advertising competition, Journal of Management Research 18.

15. Kotler P, Keller KL (2014) Marketing Management (14thedn) Pearson Education. 2000 Pearson Education, Inc., publishing as Prentice Hall, One Lake Street, Upper Saddle River, New Jersey 07458.

16. Horsky D (1977) An empirical analysis of the optimal advertising policy, Management Science 23: 1037-1049.

17. Simon H (1982) ADPULS: An advertising model with wearout and pulsation, Journal of Management Research 19: 221-234.

18. Sugiyono (2013) MetodePenelitianBisnis (17thedn) Bandung: Alfabeta.

19. FirdausY (2011) Peranan Biaya Promosi Dalam Meningkatkan Volume Penjualan. Jurnal Ekonomi Dan Informasi Akuntansi 1: 143-152.

20. Kuncoro M (2011) Metode Kuantitatif TeoridanAplikasi Untuk Bisnis and Ekonomi (4thedn) Yogyakarta: UPP STIM YKPN.

6

An Empirical Analysis on Asset Quality of Indian Banking Industry - Non-performing Assets to Advances

Chilukuri SS[1], Srinivas Rao K[2]* and Madhav VV[3]

[1]KLUBS, KL University, Guntur, Andhra Pradesh, India
[2]Vivek Vardhini College of PG Studies (AN), Hyderabad, Telangana, India
[3]Department of Management, KLUBS, KL University, Guntur, Andhra Pradesh, India

Abstract

The banking is the life blood of the economy acting as a catalyst in the regulation and monitoring of financial activities and contributes for economic growth. They play a crucial role as manufacturers and purveyors of money in effective allocation of idle savings to productive utilisation. As a fiduciary it provides leverage by bring money and money related assets to the access of needy borrowers or for any other developmental activities. In this process banks are prone to risk of loss due to the uncertainties of counterparty. The increase in default is leading to rise in Non-Performing Assets, impairing the profitability and quality assets in financial statements of banking industry. The present paper examines status of quality assets of Indian banking industry in relation to Non-Performing Assets to advances of all Scheduled Commercial Banks for 12 years from 2001-02 to 2012-13 based on secondary source of information retrieved from "Handbook of Statistics on the Indian Economy 2013-2014". The study observed that there is major penetration of advances from Public Sector Banks indicating higher share among all Scheduled Commercial Banks and there is tremendous increase in advances over the period of study, nevertheless the decline trend in NPAs shown improvement in the asset quality of Scheduled Commercial Banks of India.

Keywords: Non-performing asset; Advances; CAGR; Asset quality; Scheduled commercial banks

Introduction

The banking business is the life blood of economy, which has gained significance in regulating financial and economic aspects of the economy. The banking system forms the core of the financial sector of an economy meeting the financial needs of trade and industry and also to satisfy the institutions of the country. The role of banking and financial institutions is particularly important in underdeveloped countries. Banks are both manufacturers of money and purveyors of money. Through mobilization of resources and their better allocation, banking and financial institutions play an important role in the development process of underdeveloped countries. They play intermediation function in a fiduciary capacity and provide leverage to the accumulated funds through credit creation. Availing credit to borrowers is one means by which banks contribute to the growth of economies.

In the process of attainment of balanced regional developmental, banks promote social objectives by offering lending and investment activities in those regions or part of the country which are less developed. Even banks offer attractive saving schemes, ensuring safety of deposits and here by help in transforming idle savings/unproductive resources into effective and productive one. Banks also acts as a facilitator in generation of employment opportunities by lending money to priority sectors of the economy such as agriculture, MSMEs, retail traders, small borrowers, self-employed and etc.

Status of non-performing assets of BRICS nations-2015

The statistics were clearly explained at Table 1 [1]. *Parenthesis indicate previous year:* According to the statistics of World Bank among BRICS nations Russia stood at first position with 7.4% of NPA due followed by India 4.2%.

Research gap and implications

The 1991 Liberalisation policy opened doors to industrialists and entrepreneurs to setup new business and expand the operational efficiencies. To meet these requirements, the Indian Banking Sector was at the fate to finance the credit. In the global economic scenario, the vulnerability of Indian business houses has been expanded its operations. But due to various reasons Indian banking sector is evincing the increasing growth rate of Non-Performing Assets due to increase in non-payment of loan amount form individuals, entrepreneurs, industrialists and other borrowers. This is not only limited to the public sector banks but even by other scheduled commercial banks. Hence the present study is carried to study the trend level and to compare the NPA percent of various scheduled commercial banks.

Statement of problem

As lending is considered as the most important function banks exist to provide financial intermediation services while at the same time endeavour to maximize profit and shareholders' value. Even though loan is major source of banks income and constitutes their major

Country	NPA Ratio (%)
Brazil	3.1
Russia	7.4
India	4.2
China	1.2˙
South Africa	3.2

Table 1: Non-performing assets [1].

*Corresponding author: Rao KS, Assistant Professor of Commerce, Vivek Vardhini College of PG Studies (AN), Hyderabad, Telangana, India
E-mail: srikanrao2006@gmail.com

assets, it is riskier, due to uncertainty of counterparty the quality of loans are deteriorating and impairing the profits of the banks. This is leading to the increase of loss of loan assets or Non-Performing Assets.

Review of Literature

Comprehensive and exhaustive studies have been conducted on increase in the menace of Non-Performing Assets. A brief explanation of literature review is presented below.

Bhattacharaya [2], "Banking strategy, Credit Appraisal and Lending Decision", In the study researcher opined the fact that in an increasing rate regime, quality borrowers may tend to other avenues like capital markets, internal accruals to meet their credit requirements. In such context the banks may dilute the quality of borrowers there by increasing the probability of generation of NPAs.

Reddy [3] in his research paper on the topic, "A comparative study of Non Performing Assets in India in the Global context examined the similarities and dissimilarities, remedial measures", Financial sector reform in India has progressed rapidly on aspects like interest rate deregulation, reduction in reserve requirements, barriers to entry, prudential norms and risk-based supervision. The study reveals that the sheltering of weak institutions while liberalizing operational rules of the game is making implementation of operational changes difficult and ineffective. Changes required to tackle the NPA problem would have to span the entire gamut of judiciary, polity and the bureaucracy to be truly effective. This paper deals with the experiences of other Asian countries in handling of NPAs. It further looks into the effect of the reforms on the level of NPAs and suggests mechanisms to handle the problem by drawing on experiences from other countries.

Das [4], "Management of Non Performing Assets in Indian Public Sector Banks with special reference to Jharakhnad", in this study researcher rightly pointed the fact that expansion of credit is a must for a country like India. It was found that high credit growth may lead to high NPAs. He opined that the effective and regular follow-up of the credit sanctioned is necessary to ascertain any embezzlement or diversion of funds.

Malyadri [5], "A Comparative Study of Non Performing Assets in Indian Banking Industry", The study observed that during 2004-2010 the asset quality management of Indian Public sector and Private sector banks have improved in NPA management by the implementation of prudential regulations of accounting, income recognition, provisioning and exposure, introduction of CAMELS supervisory rating system and reduction of NPA's and up gradation of technology. But inorder to bring on par international level the government should formulate bank specific policies and should implement these policies through Reserve Bank of India enhancement of Public Sector Banks. The researcher noticed that NPA percentage has decline during their period of study i.e. From 2004 to 2010 as percentage of advances to weaker sections from 18.9% to 3% in case of public s to sector banks and from 12.15% to 0.5%

Srivastava [6], "A Study of trends of Non-Performing Assets in Private Banks in India", The share of public sector banks is almost 2/3rd shares of total advances in the economy in Indian banking industry. Substandard Assets showed increase from 1.1% in 2006-07 to 2.0% in 2008-09 but further decrease from 1.5% in 2009-10 to 0.6% in 2011-12. Doubtful Assets showed a reduction from 1.0% in 2006-07 to 0.9% in 2007-08 but further increase 1.5% in 2010-11 and also further decrease to 1.2 in 2011-12. Loss Assets showed increase from 0.2% in 2006-07 to 0.4% in 2010-11 and decrease to 0.3 in 2011-12. This indicates a up and down trend of financial soundness of private sector banks.

Balasubramaniam [7], "Non-Performing Assets and Profitability of commercial Banks In India: Assessment and Emerging Issues", The conceptual study revealed that in the competitive world bank are facing a challenges in their business operations with introduction of NBFC's and foreign banks and by following the Basel III norms to be introduce would make banks to bring financial stability in their performance.

Mohnani [8], "A Study of Non-Performing Assets on Selected Public and Private Sector Banks", The study suggested that banks should appoint a committee to review the credit appraisal of banks through well documented loan policy and review should be done weekly basis in order to curtail the increase of new accounts of NPA's. The researchers considered SBI, PNB, ICICI and HDFC and analysed the position of NPAs during 2003 to 2012. It was found that there has been marginal decrease in NPAs level over the period in all selected banks. SBI from 11.95% to 3.28%, PNB from 11.38% to 1.79%, HDFC from 3.18% 1.06% and ICICI position is about 5.08%.

Mahajan [9], 'Trends of NPAs in Indian Banking Sector', the researcher focused compare the status of Indian banking NPAs with BRICS nations. In his study it was identified the APEC countries consider a loan as non performing only after it has been in arrears for at least six months whereas in India it is considered as NPA if it is due for 90 days, but the recovery process in India is time taking process compared to developing countries. So finally the study concluded that magnitude of India banking NPAs are high compared to developing countries.

Sharma [10], "NPA:-A Comparative Study Of Public Sector And Private Sector Commercial Banks", The researcher studied trends in NPAs of public sector banks during 2001 to 2013 and analyzed the data using statistical tools. The research resulted showing there is constant rise in values of Gross NPA and Net NPA from 2000-2004 and decline trend from 2004-2008 and after that it is increasing at constant. Whereas the private sector banks it was observed that Gross NPA and Net NPA is in increased trend from 2000 to 2003 and decline trend up to 2006 and thereafter it showed increased trend.

Objectives of Study

An empirical attempt is made in the current paper to analyze Non Performing Assets based on following objectives.

1) To study the trend level of NPAs in Indian banking industry.

2) To compare Schedule Commercial Banks NPAs and Public Sector Banks NPAs.

3) To compare between Public Sector Banks NPAs, Private Sector Banks NPAs and Foreign Banks NPAs.

Methodology of Study

The source of information for the study is retrieved from Handbook of Statistics on the Indian Economy 2013-2014 [11].

Period of study

For the present study 12 years of period from 2001-02 to 2012-13 has been considered to compare and analyse the trends of NPAs in Scheduled Commercial Banks.

Tools for data analysis

The data is analyzed and tested with the statistical tool such as Geometric Progression Ratio CAGR (Compound Annual Growth

Rate) and percentages to examine the status of quality asset of Indian banking industry in relation to year-over-year growth in percentage of NPAs to advances.

$$\text{CAGR} (t_{o,} t_{n)} = [V (t_{n)}/V (t_{o)}]^{1/t_n - t_o} - 1$$

Where t_o = Beginning Value

t_n = Ending Value

$t_n - t_o$ = Number of Years

Data Analysis and Interpretation

The Table 2 and Figure 1 depicts that there is a steady increase in Advances of both Scheduled Commercial Banks and Public Sector Banks from 2001-02 to 2012-13 [11]. The study observed that the movement of absolute NPAs has a mixture of increasing and decreasing trends. The NPAs CAGR of the Scheduled Commercial Banks and Public Sector stood at 8.87 and 10.23 respectively, which indicates that the major part of NPAs in Scheduled Commercial Banks is from Public Sector Banks. In contrast to that the percent of NPAs CAGR of Scheduled Commercial Banks is -9.32 and Public Sector Banks is -8.49 [12].

The Table 3 and Figure 2, studies the quality of assets in relation of NPAs to advances of Public Sector Banks, Private Sector Banks and Foreign Sector Banks [11]. The empirical comparison of advances of Public Sector Banks, Private Sector Banks and Foreign Banks have increased. This acknowledges that all the banks at their capacity improved in penetration of advances. The percent CAGR is near to each other betweeb Public Sector Banks and Private sector Banks as 20.43 and 20.96 respectively. The foreign Sector Banks stood at 15.11 which is less compared to the other sector banks. The study examines that the absolute values of NPAs in Public Sector Banks has mixed trend upto 2007-08 and later it increased. The absolute values of NPAs in Private Sector Banks possess mixed trend all over the period of study. The study also observed that the percent NPAs of Foreign Sector Banks cautiously slided up to maximum of 1.9 and minimum of 0.6 and stood as 1 by the end of 2012-13. The percent NPAs CAGR is performing good as -5.21 compared to -8.49 and -18.06 of Public Sector Banks and Private Sector Banks. The reason can be attributed as existence of Foreign Sector Bank opertaions are fewer when compared to others [13].

From the Table 4, Figures 3a and 3b on thorough observation of statistical information portrayed that over the period of study

Years	Scheduled Commercial Banks			Public Sector Banks		
	Advances	NPAs	% NPAs	Advances	NPAs	% NPAs
2001-02	6458.59	355.54	5.5	4806.81	279.58	5.8
2002-03	7404.73	296.92	4	5493.51	248.77	4.5
2003-04	8626.43	243.96	2.8	6313.83	193.35	3.1
2004-05	11156.63	217.54	2	8489.12	169.04	2.1
2005-06	15168.11	185.43	1.2	11062.88	145.66	1.3
2006-07	19812.37	201.01	1	14401.46	151.45	1.1
2007-08	24769.36	247.3	1	17974.01	178.36	1
2008-09	29999.24	315.64	1.1	22592.12	211.55	0.9
2009-10	34970.92	387.23	1.1	27013	293.75	1.1
2010-11	42987.04	417	1.1	33056.32	360	1.2
2011-12	50735.59	652	1.3	38773.07	593	1.5
2012-13	58797.03	986	1.7	44727.74	900	2
CAGR%	20.21	8.87	-9.32	20.43	10.23	-8.49

Source: RBI, Handbook of Statistics on the Indian Economy 2013-2014 [11].

Table 2: Comparison between scheduled commercial banks and public sector banks - (amount in INR billions).

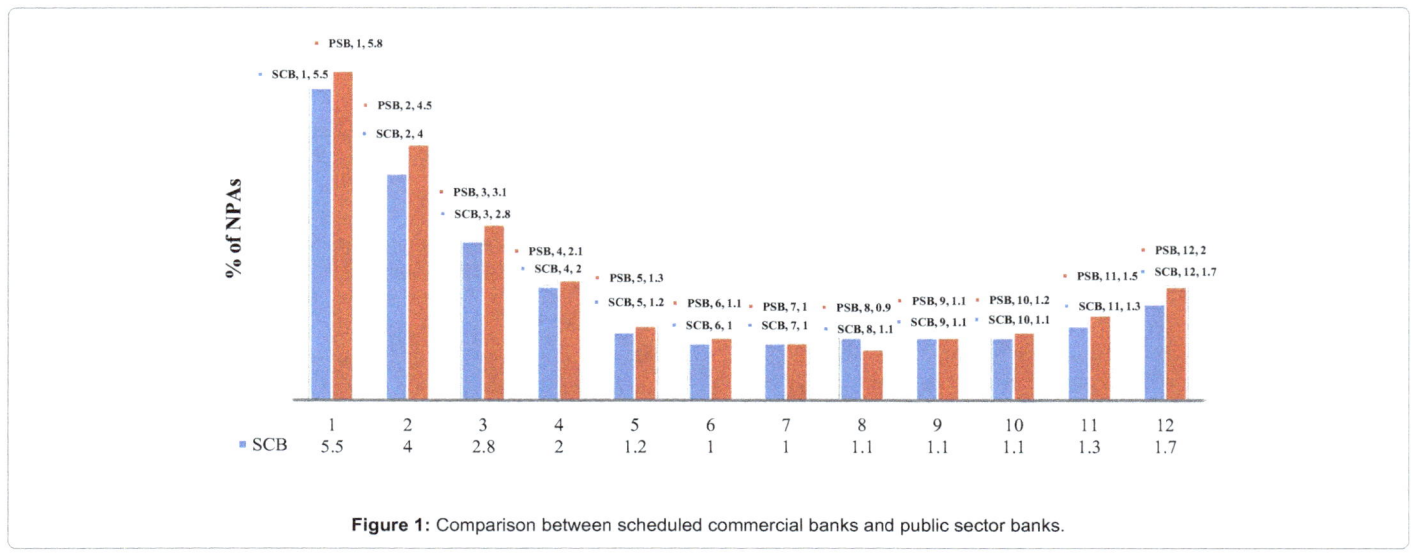

Figure 1: Comparison between scheduled commercial banks and public sector banks.

Years	Public Sector Banks			Private Sector Banks			Foreign Sector Banks		
	Advances	NPAs	% NPAs	Advances	NPAs	% NPAs	Advances	NPAs	% NPAs
2001-02	4806.81	279.58	5.8	1164.73	66.76	12	487.05	9.2	1.9
2002-03	5493.51	248.77	4.5	1389.51	39.63	6.7	521.71	9.03	1.7
2003-04	6313.83	193.35	3.1	1707.54	41.28	5.5	605.06	9.33	1.5
2004-05	8489.12	169.04	2.1	1913.97	42.12	4.6	753.54	6.39	0.8
2005-06	11062.9	145.66	1.3	3129.62	31.71	2.5	975.62	8.08	0.8
2006-07	14401.5	151.45	1.1	4147.52	40.28	2	1263.4	9.27	0.7
2007-08	17974	178.36	1	5184.03	56.47	1.9	1611.3	12.47	0.8
2008-09	22592.1	211.55	0.9	5753.28	74.11	2.3	1653.9	29.96	1.8
2009-10	27013	293.75	1.1	6324.94	65.05	1.9	1632.6	29.77	1.8
2010-11	33056.3	360	1.2	7975.33	43	1.1	1955.4	12	0.6
2011-12	38773.1	593	1.5	9664.02	43	1	2298.5	14	0.6
2012-13	44727.7	900	2	11432.48	59	1.1	2636.8	26	1
CAGR%	20.43	10.23	-8.49	20.96	-1.02	-18.06	15.11	9.04	-5.21

Source: RBI, Handbook of Statistics on The Indian Economy 2013-2014 [11].

Table 3: Comparison between public sector banks, private sector banks and foreign sector banks NPAS (amount in INR billions).

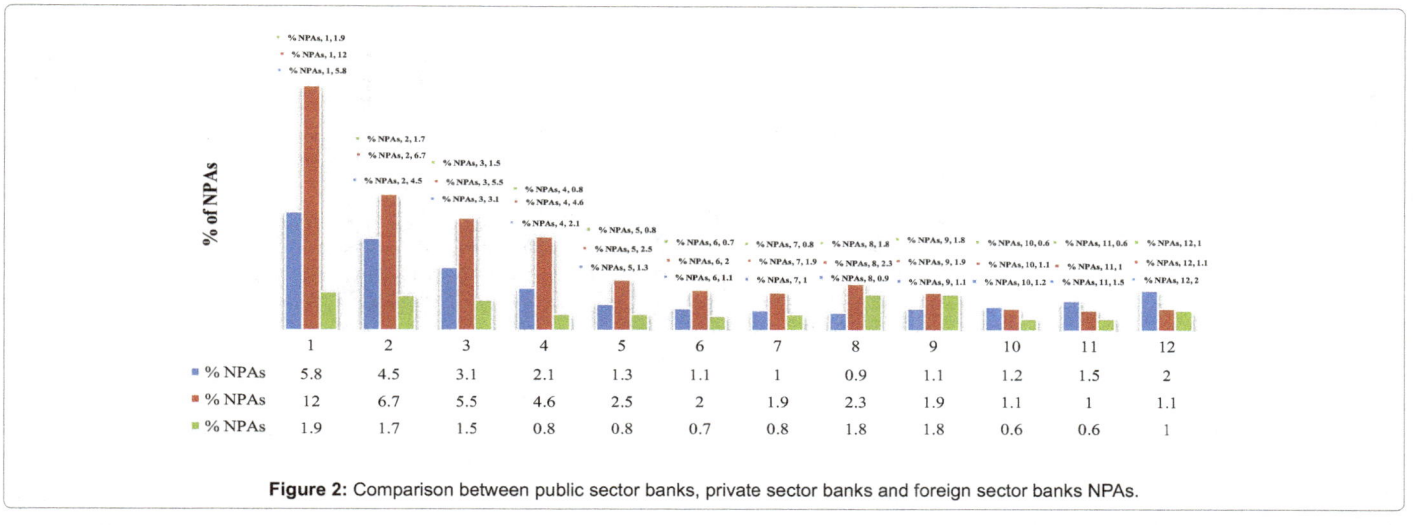

Figure 2: Comparison between public sector banks, private sector banks and foreign sector banks NPAs.

Years	Public Sector Banks		Private Sector Banks		Foreign Banks		Scheduled Commercial Banks	
	Advances	NPAs	Advances	NPAs	Advances	NPAs	Advances	NPAs
2001-02	4806.81 (74.4)	279.58 (78.6)	1164.73 (18)	66.76 (18.8)	487.05 (7.5)	9.2 (2.9)	6458.59 (100)	355.54 (100)
2002-03	5493.51 (74.2)	248.77 (83.8)	1389.51 (18.8)	39.63 (13.3)	521.71 (7.04)	9.03 (3.04)	7404.73 (100)	296.92 (100)
2003-04	6313.83 (73.2)	193.35 (79.6)	1707.54 (19.8)	41.28 (16.9)	605.06 (7.01)	9.33 (3.9)	8626.43 (100)	243.96 (100)
2004-05	8489.12 (76.1)	169.04 (77.7)	1913.97 (17.6)	42.12 (19.7)	753.54 (6.8)	6.39 (2.9)	11156.6 (100)	217.54 (100)
2005-06	11062.88 (72.9)	145.66 (78.6)	3129.62 (20.6)	31.71 (17.1)	975.62 (6.4)	8.08 (4.4)	15168.1 (100)	185.43 (100)
2006-07	14401.46 (72.7)	151.45 (75.3)	4147.52 (20.9)	40.28 (20)	1263.39 (6.4)	9.27 (4.6)	19812.4 (100)	201.01 (100)
2007-08	17974.01 (72.6)	178.36 (72.1)	5184.03 (20.9)	56.47 (22.8)	1611.33 (6.5)	12.47 (5.04)	24769.4 (100)	247.3 (100)
2008-09	22592.12 (75.3)	211.55 (67)	5753.28 (19.1)	74.11 (23.8)	1653.85 (5.5)	29.96 (9.5)	29999.2 (100)	315.64 (100)
2009-10	27013 (77.2)	293.75 (75.9)	6324.94 (18.1)	65.05 (16.8)	1632.6 (4.7)	29.77 (7.7)	34970.9 (100)	387.23 (100)
2010-11	33056.32 (76.8)	360 (86.3)	7975.33 (18.6)	43 (10.3)	1955.39 (4.54)	12 (2.9)	42987 (100)	417 (100)
2011-12	38773.07 (76.4)	593 (90.9)	9664.02 (19)	43 (6.6)	2298.49 (4.53)	14 (2.1)	50735.6 (100)	652 (100)
2012-13	44727.74 (76.1)	900 (91.3)	11432.5 (19.4)	59 (6)	2636.8 (4.48)	26 (2.6)	58797 (100)	986 (100)

Source: RBI, Handbook of Statistics on the Indian Economy 2013-2014 [11].

Table 4: Share of public sector banks, private sector banks and foreign sector banks in total scheduled commercial banks advances and NPAs (amount n INR billions).

the Public Sector Banks have higher share in NPAs and advances of Scheduled Commercial Banks on comparison with Private Sector Banks and Foreign Sector Banks.

Findings

The empirical observations primarily revealed that the performances of NPA in terms of absolute value are high from Public Sector Banks in

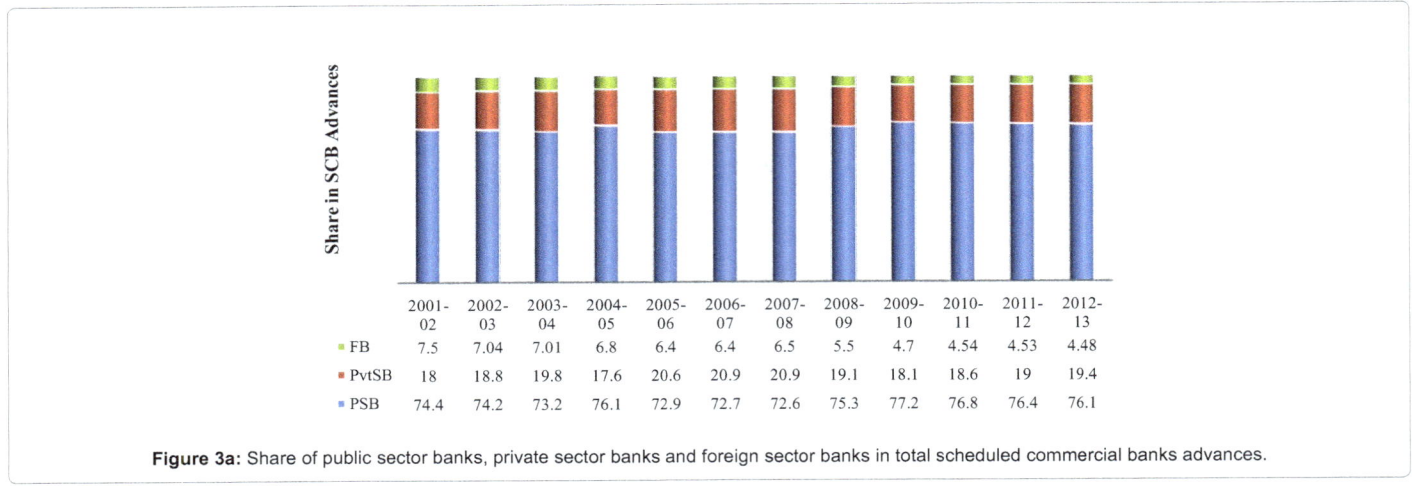

Figure 3a: Share of public sector banks, private sector banks and foreign sector banks in total scheduled commercial banks advances.

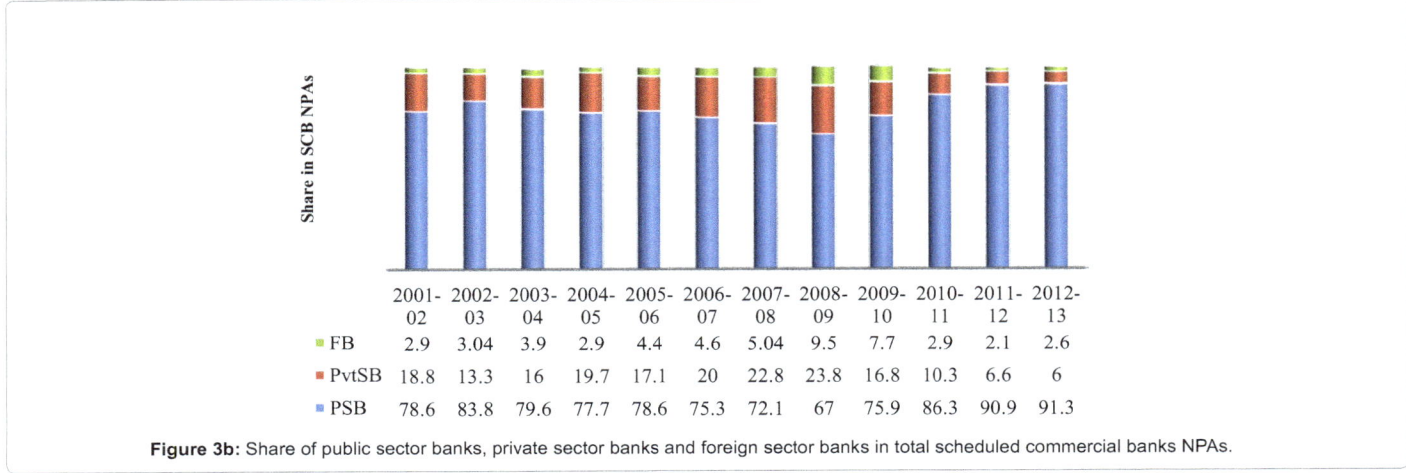

Figure 3b: Share of public sector banks, private sector banks and foreign sector banks in total scheduled commercial banks NPAs.

total of Scheduled Commercial Banks. The examination of the data over the 12 years period of study from 2001-02 to 2012-13 has found that the asset quality of all sectors banks made a consistent improvement in asset quality. This can be acknowledged through trend in the percentages of NPAs of absolute value of NPAs i.e., trend ratio of NPAs to advances of Public Sector Banks from 5.8% to 2%, Private Sector Banks from 12% to 1.1% and Foreign Sector Banks from 1.9% to 1%. By end period of study as the percent of NPAs to advances are in decline trend says that all Scheduled Commercial Banks are consistently trying to reduce the cost of creation of NPAs and to improve the asset quality. The study even revealed that there is major penetration of advances from Public Sector Banks indicating higher share among all Scheduled Commercial Banks [14].

Conclusion

The study observed that there is tremendous increase of advances over the 12 years period of study, nevertheless the decline trend in NPAs shown improvement in the asset quality of Scheduled Commercial Banks of India. The success in enhancement of asset quality and improving the financial health of Scheduled Banks can be accredited to the respective banks management in compliance with the prudential norms, income recognition norms and provisioning norms.

However in order to reduce the menace and intensity of NPA banks should develop efficient management information system and should

employ the specialized and trained staff who can use their expertise and deal the situations cautiously. Frequent review of statements of outstanding advances, defaulters, identifying the reasons for rise in NPAs, timely action can trim down the rise in NPAs and can improve the asset quality of banking industry.

Further Scope for Research

1)   An in-depth analysis of asset quality can be done by analyzing individual banks performance.

2)   Analysis of NPAs based on sectorial performance can be dealt to give accurate results of asset quality of Scheduled Commercial Banks.

References

1. http://data.worldbank.org

2. Bhattacharaya H (2001) "Banking strategy, Credit Appraisal & Lending Decision: A Risk-return Framework. Oxford Scholarship Online, New Delhi, India.

3. Reddy PK (2002) A comparative study of Non-Performing Assets in India in the Global context examined the similarities and dissimilarities, remedial measures.

4. Das S (2007) Management of Non-Performing Assets in Indian Public Sector Banks with specual reference to Jharakhnad.

5. Malyadri P, Sirisha S (2011) A Comparative Study of Non-Performing Assets in Indian Banking Industry. International Journal of Economic Practices and Theories.

6. Srivastava V, Bansal D (2012) A Study of trends of Non-Performing Assets in Private Banks in India. International Journal in Multidisciplinary and Academic Research 2.

7. Balasubramaniam CS (2012) Non-Performing Assets and Profitability Of commercial Banks in India: Assessment and Emerging Issues. Journal of Research in Commerce & Management.

8. Mohnani P, Deshmukh M (2013) A Study of Non-Performing Assets on Selected Public and Private Sector Banks.

9. Mahajan S (2014) Trends of NPAs in Indian Banking Sector. International Journal of Innovative Research and Studies 3: 498-512.

10. Sharma SJ, Arora J (2014) Npa:-A Comparative Study Of Public Sector And Private Sector Commercial Banks.

11. (2014) Handbook of Statistics on the Indian Economy.

12. Kumar M, Singh G (2012) Mounting Npas In Indian Commercial Banks.

13. Muniappan GP (2002) The NPA Overhang - Magnitude, Solutions, Legal Reforms.

14. Poongavanam.S (2011) Non-Performing Assets: Issues, Causes and Remedial Solution.

7

International Financial Reporting Standard (IFRS): Prospects and Challenges

Katta Ashok Kumar[*]

Research Scholar and Assistant Professor, Saveetha University, Chennai, India

[*]**Corresponding author:** Katta Ashok Kumar, Research Scholar and Assistant Professor, Saveetha University, 162, Poonamalle HighRoad, 600077, Chennai, India, E-mail: yoursashok1984@gmail.com

Abstract

Consistent, comparable and understandable financial information is the lifeblood of commerce and making investment. The idea of global harmonization of accounting standards stems from lack of comparability of financial statements across the country. Increasing cross border investing and proliferation of financial products have posed a challenge to companies as they faced multiple standards. Harmonization and convergence with IFRS can greatly contribute to the efforts to build global financial reporting infrastructure. This resulted in international initiative of convergence of Accounting Standards to a common standard viz. the International Accounting Standards/ International Financial Reporting Standards (IFRS).

In India, the ICAI formulates the accounting standards on various issues. But since last few years, the aim has been following the IFRS to the extent possible. Henceforth, while issuing accounting standards, IFRS need to be adopted suitably. However, deviations from IFRS have been noted due to some unavoidable reasons like legal and regulatory requirements, economic environment, level of preparedness, conceptual differences etc. Thus, it can be argued that even if there has been a lot of deliberation on convergence of Indian accounting standards with IFRS, it is difficult to adopt IFRS considering the indigenous problems. In order to resolve this problem, the ICAI has given a roadmap through which, IFRS can be adopted in India in a phased manner.

This analytical Paper deals with concept, objective and benefits of convergence with IFRS and explores the way how we converge the Indian GAAP with IFRS. Problems and challenges faced in the process of convergence in Indian perspective have been thoroughly discussed. This paper also focuses on IFRS prospects in Indian scenario. This paper puts forward a view point that convergence will bring forth galore benefits to investors, industry, professionals and the economy as a whole.

Keywords: Accounting standards; IFRS; IAS; Convergence

Introduction

Consistent, comparable and understandable financial information is the lifeblood of commerce and making investment. The idea of global harmonization of accounting standards stems from the lack of comparability of financial statements across the country. In particular, a company having presence in different countries has to prepare financial reports as per Generally Accepted Accounting Principles (GAAP) of the country of operation and then it is required to reconcile all such reports for the purpose of consolidation as per GAAP of the country to which the parent belongs. This increases the cost of preparing the financial reports and also performance measurement across the geographical region becomes difficult because of noncomparable accounting rules.

In India, the Central Government prescribes accounting standards in consultation with the National Advisory Committee on Accounting Standards (NACAS) established under the Companies Act, 1956. NACAS, has been engaged in the exercise of examining Accounting Standards prepared by ICAI. It has adapted the international norms established by the International Financial Reporting Standards [1] issued by the International Accounting Standards Board. The Central Government notified 28 Accounting Standards (AS 1 to 7 and AS 9 to 29) in December 2006 in the form of Companies (Accounting Standard) [2] Rules, 2006, after receiving recommendations of NACAS. The Government has adopted a policy of enabling disclosure of company accounts in a transparent manner at par with widely accepted international practices, through a process of convergence with the International Financial Reporting Standards (IFRS). The initiative for harmonization of the Indian accounting standards with IFRS, taken up by NACAS in 2001 and implemented through notification of accounting standards by the Central Government in 2006.

Such increasing complexity of business operations and globalization of capital markets makes [3] mandatory a single set of high quality reporting standards. This space can aptly be filled in with the emergence of International Financial Reporting Standards (IFRS), as formulated by the International Accounting Standards Board. IFRS has emerged as a new force in aligning the global firms on a single line.

International Financial Reporting Standards are set by the International Accounting Standards Board (IASB). The mission of IASB is to develop, in the public interest, a single set of high quality, understandable and International Financial Reporting Standards (IFRS) for general purpose financial statements. IASB is an independent standard-setting board, appointed and overseen by a geographically and professionally diverse group of Trustees of the IASC Foundation who are accountable to the public interest. It is supported by an external advisory council (SAC) and an interpretations committee (IFRIC) to offer guidance wherever divergence in practice occurs. The IASB cooperates with national accounting standard setters to achieve convergence in accounting standards around the world.

In India the Institute of Chartered Accountants of India (ICAI) has decided to fully converge with IFRS issued by the International Accounting Standards Board for accounting periods commencing on or after April 1, 2011. The Ministry of Corporate Affairs (MCA) issued various press releases on the IFRS roadmap and convergence plan for India specifying the convergence date to be 1 April, 2011, through 2014 for select Indian companies.

Since the timeline in the roadmap is no longer valid for Phase I companies, the new implementation date for Ind AS is awaited from the MCA. It is unclear if the MCA will release a fresh roadmap or just amend the implementation date. Convergence will bring forth galore benefits to investors, industry, professionals and the economy as a whole. This is a significant move towards the emergence of IFRS as a global accounting language.

What is IAS Regulation and IFRS

IAS is International Accounting Standards (IAS) which was issued between 1973 and 2001 by the International Accounting Standard Committee (IASC). On 1 April, 2001, IASC was replaced by International Accounting Standards Board (IASB). Since then International Accounting Standards Board (IASB), based at London - UK is now responsible to issue International Financial Reporting Stan IASB is an independent body and consists of members from nine different countries around the globe having variety of functional backgrounds. During its first meeting the Board adopted existing IAS and SICs. The IASB has continued to develop standards calling the new standards IFRS.

International Financial Reporting Standards (IFRS)

Standards, Interpretations and the Framework for the Preparation and Presentation of Financial Statements set and adopted by the International Accounting Standards Board. IFRS has replaced the older term international accounting standard. Many of the standards forming part of IFRS are known by the older name of International Accounting Standards (IAS). IFRS are considered 'principles based' set of standards in that they establish broad rules as well as dictating specific treatments.

Objectives of IFRS

Harmonization is the necessity of modern globalized era because various factors like cross border investments, interdependence on trade, increase of business complexities, global financial crisis, global slowdown and mobility of capital and people across the globe, are significantly influencing the world economy. Therefore, the main objective of IFRS development is harmonization in financial statements reporting. Some additional objectives are:

- To create the global financial reporting infrastructure.
- To generate sound business sense among the beneficiaries.
- To generate the dimensions of fair presentation of financial statement.
- To maintain higher transparency of financial statement and mobility of capital.

Benefits of Convergence with IFRS

It is sensible to make a careful preliminary assessment and a cost/benefit analysis of whether or not under the particular circumstances, an adoption of IFRS would be desirable and also examine different scenarios concerning timing of adopting IFRS. The number of companies which elect to adopt IFRS is growing and this is because IFRS reporting [4] offers a wide scope of benefits. Examples of these benefits include the following:

- IFRS significantly improves the comparability of entities and provide more consistent financial information.
- IFRS are accepted as a financial reporting framework for companies seeking admission to almost all of the world's stock exchanges (including US).
- The enhanced comparability of the companies' financial information and the improved quality of communication to their stockholders, decrease investor uncertainty, reduce risk, increases market efficiency and eventually minimizes the cost of capital.
- IFRS eliminates barriers to cross border trading in securities, by ensuring that financial statements are more transparent.
- Management reporting for internal purposes under IFRS, can improve the quality and consistency of information that management needs in order to make effective, efficient and timely decisions for the business.
- IFRS adoption may be used as a chance to make some strategic improvements to the finance systems and processes as well as to reduce costs in the longer term.
- IFRS financial statements that are universally understood and comparable can both improve and initiate new relationships with customers and suppliers across national borders.
- Because of the positive effect IFRS financial information has on credit ratings, a company's position strengthens in negotiations with credit institutions and cost of borrowings are reduced.
- IFRS can also result in more accurate risk evaluations by lenders and to a lower risk premium. It also helps companies to take advantage of alternative forms of finance.
- In the case of groups it removes the need for individual companies to prepare two set of financial statements, if all individual companies in the group apply IFRS. It also allows multinational groups to have a common accounting language, thereby improving management reporting and decision making.

As IFRS hit the market, analysts and investors will become more sophisticated very quickly and will be less forgiving towards companies which provide the market with the poor disclosures [5, 6].

Convergence with IFRS: Indian Prospects

As per European Commission the requirement of compliance of IFRS by all listed companies in their CFS from 2005 (IAS Regulation) onwards will help eliminate barriers to cross boarder trading in securities by ensuring that company accounts throughout the European Union (EU) are more reliable and transparent. If the Indian companies prepare their accounts in accordance with IFRS, they can be more easily compared with their accounts with EU companies and other IFRS user countries. This will, in turn, increase market efficiency and reduce the cost of raising capital for companies, ultimately improving competitiveness and helping boost economy.

In India, manipulations of accounts become a key factor in presentation of financial statements. The Financial Accounting Standards Board (FASB), USA, is having a convergence project with the IASB and is broadly adopting the principle-based approach instead of rule based approach. IFRS are principle-based standards which have distinct advantage that the transactions cannot be manipulated easily to achieve a particular accounting. Examples are:

- IAS 17, Leases, distinguishes finance lease from operating lease based on principle of 'substance over form', whereas corresponding US GAAP lay down rules for making such distinction.
- IAS 27, Consolidated and Separate Financial Statements, lays down criteria of power to govern financial and operating policies for identification of subsidiaries. The corresponding US GAAP lay down requirement for majority ownership of shares only. In India, the Companies Act definition is based on either majority ownership or board control.

The advantages to investors are clear. IFRS make it easier to compare the accounts of companies in different countries. Today, India is one of the fastest growing economies in the world with a compounded average growth rate of 5.7 per cent over the past two decades. Comparability and transparency of financial statements would increase inflows of FDI and foreign capital which is urgently required by the Government of India to implement its plans to transform India into a developed nation by 2020.

Substance over form

IFRS lay down treatments based on the economic substance of various events and transactions rather than their legal form. The application of this approach may result into events and transactions being presented in a manner different from their legal form. To illustrate, as per IAS 32, preference shares that provide for mandatory redemption by the issuer are presented as a liability. The dividend payable on cumulative redeemable preference shares is treated as expense and not as distribution of profits.

Non-financial Disclosures

As per the IASB:

Framework for the Preparation and Presentation of Financial Statements: The objective of financial statements is to provide information that is useful to a wide range of users in making economic decisions. The Framework recognizes financial statements do not provide all the information required for decisions. To achieve, the objective the financial reports may include additional information in the form of non-financial disclosures. In India, non-financial information played a significant role in making economic decisions. Non-financial disclosure may include information about:-

- Nature of business, Objectives and Strategies, Key resources, Risks, Results Prospects, etc. Such disclosures are usually contained in Management Report. To deal with the aspect, the IASB is developing a separate IFRS on Management Commentary. Recently, a discussion paper on the subject has been issued.

Issuing accounting standards interpretations on matters related to accounting standards: With a view to resolve various intricate interpretational issues arising in the implementation of new accounting standards that have already been issued, the ICAI has issued thirty accounting standards interpretations.

Issuance of background materials on accounting standards: To facilitate discussion at seminars, workshops, etc., ICAI has issued background material on newly issued accounting standards. The background material deals, inter alia, with the key requirements of the accounting standards with examples and Frequently Asked Questions (FAQs), which accountants and auditors may encounter in the application of accounting standards.

Issuance of Guidance Notes on accounting matters: ICAI has issued various Guidance Notes in order to provide immediate guidance on accounting issues arising due to issuance of new accounting standards and to provide immediate guidance on new accounting issues arising due to changes in legal or economic environment and/or other developments. These guidance notes form an important part of the generally accepted accounting principles in India and need to be referred to on a regular basis by people involved in the preparation and presentation of financial statements, as well as by people involved in auditing these statements.

IFRS Auditing Standards: Indian Perspective

A single set of accounting standards would enable international auditing firms to standardize training and ensure better quality of their work on a global scale. It would also permit international capital to flow more freely, enabling auditing firms and their clients to develop consistence global practices on accounting problems [7]. It would be beneficial to regulators too, as the complexity associated with needing to understand various reporting regimes would be reduced. Auditing Standards are codification of existing best practices in the area of auditing. International Standards on Auditing (ISA) are issued by the IAASB of IFAC. In India, the ICAI formulates Auditing and Assurance Standards (AAS). Basic considerations behind AAS formulation are:

- Harmonization with ISA, to the extent possible – a Membership obligation for ICAI
- Applicable laws in India.
- Customs, usages & business environment in India.

These standards apply whenever independent audit carried out and irrespective of size, legal form or commercial motives of the client. It may appropriately apply to other functions of auditors.

Convergence with IFRS: Major Challenges

The problem of differences in accounting standards will continue to exist for some time. From a regulatory perspective, convergence to IFRS would require amendments to the Companies Act and the Income Tax Act, to mention the major ones. Currently industries such as banking and insurance are also regulated by specific acts that prescribe accounting norms. Today, IFRS does not provide industry specific standards so there would be additional transition challenges as and when progress is made. IFRS requires valuations and future forecasts, which will involve use of estimates, assumptions and management's judgments. The ICAI and the Ministry of Corporate Affairs have already made noteworthy progress in moving towards IFRS [8].

Legal and regulatory considerations

In some cases, the legal and regulatory accounting requirements in India differ from the IFRS. In India, Companies Act of 1956, Banking Regulation Act of 1949, IRDA regulations and SEBI guidelines prescribe detailed formats for financial statements to be followed by respective enterprises in their financial reporting. In such cases, strict adherence to IFRS in India would result in various legal problems [9, 10].

Economic Environment

Some IFRS require fair value approach to be followed, for example:

- IAS 39, Financial Instruments: Recognition and Measurement
- IAS 41, Agriculture

The markets of many economies such as India normally do not have adequate depth and breadth for reliable determination of fair values. With a view to provide further guidance on the use of fair value approach, the IASB is developing a document. Till date, no viable solution of objective fair value measures is available.

SME Concerns

In emerging economies like India, a significant part of the economic activities is carried on by small- and medium-sized entities (SMEs). Such entities face problems in implementing the accounting standards because of:

- Scarcity of resources and expertise with the SMEs to achieve compliance.
- Cost of compliance not commensurate with the expected benefits.

In India, exemptions/ relaxations have been provided to SMEs. These exemptions/ relaxations are primarily related to disclosure requirements, though some exemptions/ relaxations from measurement principles have also been provided, e.g., AS 28 - Impairment of Assets and AS 15 - Employee Benefits. Keeping in view the difficulties faced by the SMEs, the IASB is developing an IFRS for SMEs.

Training to Preparers

Some IFRS are complex. There is lack of adequate skills amongst the preparers and users of Financial Statements to apply IFRS. Proper implementation of such IFRS requires extensive education of preparers.

Interpretation

A large number of application issues arise while applying IFRS. There is a need to have a forum which may address the application issues in specific cases. In India, the Institute of Chartered Accountants of India has constituted the Expert Advisory Committee to provide guidance on enterprise specific issues.

Conclusion

Irrespective of various challenges, adoption of IFRS in India has significantly changed the contents of corporate financial statements as a result of:

- More refined measurements of performance and state of affairs, and
- Enhanced disclosures leading to greater transparency.

With the rapid liberalization process experienced in India over the past decade, there is now a huge presence of multinational enterprises in the country. Furthermore, Indian companies are also investing in foreign markets. This has generated an interest in Indian GAAP by all concerned. In this context, the roles of Indian accounting standards, which are becoming closer to IFRS, have assumed a great significance from the point of view of global financial reporting. More than 12,000 companies and about 109 countries presently require or permit use of IFRS in preparation of financial statements in their country. By 2011, this number is expected to reach 150. The Indian GAAP has conceptual differences with IFRS and our legal and regulatory frameworks need to be amended to adopt IFRS. The bridge to successful IFRS reporting can be crossed only with strenuous efforts of experienced professionals.

India's blue-chip companies have begun to align their accounting standards to the International Financial Reporting Standards (IFRS), two years ahead of the mandatory time for the switchover. The list of companies includes IT firms like Wipro, Infosys Technologies and NIIT, automakers like Mahindra & Mahindra and Tata Motors, textile companies like Bombay Dyeing and pharma firm Dr Reddy's Laboratories. KPMG India launches IFRS Institute which will help companies and individuals to transition from Indian GAAP to IFRS. It has also launched online IFRS institute to provide information updates and view on IFRS.

References

1. Ball R (2005) International Financial Reporting Standards (IFRS): Pros and Cons for Investors. Accounting and Business Research, Forthcoming.

2. Manoharan T N (2007) President, ICAI. International Standards and Practices for Accounting, Audit and Non-financial Disclosures.

3. Armstrong CS, Barth Mary E, Jagolinzer Alan D, Riedl Edward J (2009) Market Reaction to the Adoption of IFRS in Europe. Accounting Review Forthcoming.

4. Daske Holger, Hail Luzi Leuz, Christian, Verdi Rodrigo S (2008) Mandatory IFRS Reporting Around the World: Early Evidence on the Economic Consequences. ECGI - Finance Working Paper No. 198/2008; Chicago GSB Research Paper No. 12.

5. De Jong, Abe, Rosellón Cifuentes, Miguel Angel and Verwijmeren, Patrick (2006) The Economic Consequences of IFRS: The Impact of IAS 32 on Preference Shares in the Netherlands. ERIM Report Series Reference No. ERS-2006-021-F&A.

6. Lantto, Anna-Maija and Sahlström Petri (2009) Impact of International Financial Reporting Standard adoption on key financial ratios. Accounting and Finance, 49, 341–361.

7. Agrawal Nitin, Baingani Vikash (2005) Indian Accounting Standards and IFRSs: A Comparative Study - The Chartered Accountant- Journal of the ICAI- Feb 2005.

8. Martin M (2008) Dy. President ICAEW – International conference 'Global Convergence of Accounting – Road Ahead' on accounting profession – Shining Bridge Between Global Economies – ICAI at Jaipur from Nov.20-22, 2008.

9. Mihular Reyaz (2008) past president ICA Srilanka - International Conference 'IFRS Preparing Industry for Compliance' on Accounting Profession – Shining Bridge Between Global Economies – ICAI at Jaipur from Nov.20-22, 2008.

10. ShardaNP past President ICAI - International Conference on Accounting Profession – Shining Bridge Between Global Economies– ICAI at Jaipur.

8

Financial Stability of Islamic Banks in the MENA Countries during Financial Crisis and Political Uncertainty: An Emperical Investigation

Ameni Ghenimi[1]*, Khaled Oweis[2] and Mohamed AO[3]

[1]Economic Sciences and Management of Tunisia, Tunisia
[2]Accounting Department Rafha Community College, Northem Border University, Kingdom of Saudi Arabia
[3]Accounting Department College of Business Administration, Northem Border University, Kingdom of Saudi Arabia

Abstract

The recent financial crisis has triggered a series of failures of many conventional banks and led to the rise of the interest in the Islamic banks. In this study, we seek to address the following question: What was the effect of the financial crisis and the political uncertainty on the financial stability of both Islamic and conventional banks? The conditional variance (volatility) of returns was used to measure financial stability. The various GARCH models were used to estimate volatility due to their ability to take into account the leverage effect; however they depend on the log likelihood results. The study covers a sample of 11 Islamic banks (IBs) and 17 conventional banks (CBs) for three major regions (the GCC, the Mediterranean and the MENA) for the period from (09/11/ 2005 to 09/12/2013). Our major findings are as follows. First, we document a significant increase in the volatility of conventional banks (CBs) during the period of the financial crisis whereas this crisis has had no significant effect on the volatility in Islamic banks (IBs). Second, the volatility of IBs has increased during the recent political turmoil and that of their conventional counterparts remain low in the Golf countries and the MENA region but more than in the Mediterranean region, this increase remained very moderate. In general, the findings are important for the understanding of the role of financial crisis and the Arab spring on the financial stability of IBs and CBs, suggesting that they are of great significance to investors.

Keywords: Islamic banks; Conventional banks; Financial crisis; Arab spring; Political uncertainty; Financial stability

Introduction

The subprime mortgage crisis erupted in the USA in 2007 and the failure of Lehman brothers in September 2008 caused an economic panic throughout the world. This crisis has triggered a series of failures of many conventional banks. The economy was also affected by the global credit crisis followed by the political crisis of 2010. However, a major political event like this can also have an explosive effect on the stock market volatility because of its economic and social implications. According to the OCDE [1], the financial crisis has shown that banks' funding structure is important to their resilience. Although a financial or a political crisis severely affects stock returns of IBS and CBS, we assume that these two crises have different impacts on financial stability of IBS and CBS, or else the impact of a financial crisis on volatility of the stock returns of banks may be as high as that of a political crisis. Political uncertainty caused by unrest could manifest itself in stock market cycles and volatility reactions shaking international investors' confidence in the region. Furthermore, these crises also draw the attention to Islamic finance. Khan [2] argues that the theoretical model of Islamic banks can successfully fill the failure of conventional banks in maintaining stability. IBs are different from CBs because they operate upon the principles of the Islamic law which prohibits the payment or receipt of interest and encourage risk sharing [3]. More precisely, since Islamic financial products are based on the idea of sharing profit and loss, they are very attractive to the people who require financial services consistent with their religious beliefs. In light of the high specific nature of the financing tools used by Islamic banks, the risks they incur, the management methods, and the governance they use reflect very different realities to which conventional banks are subject. The financial crisis is an opportunity to test and compare financial stability

between Islamic banks and their conventional counterparts. According to Shamshad Akhtar[1], IBs have illustrated a degree of stability to the recent crisis but have been impacted because of their higher exposure to real estate and limited reliance on risk sharing. To our knowledge, the only articles that analyzed the financial stability of IBs and CBs are Cihak and Hesse [4], and Boumediene and Caby [5]. These authors conclude that IBs contributed to financial and economic stability of CBs during the financial crisis.

This paper attempts to analyze and compare the effects of financial crisis and political uncertainty on the three regions in terms of financial stability of both groups of banks (share price volatility). Given the growing importance of all the MENA region in the world economy, in general, and the Islamic financial assets in particular, there is a pressing need for a rigorous research to examine the effects of the global financial crisis and the Arab Spring uprising in order to better understand the relationship between the financial crisis, political uncertainty and financial stability. Furthermore, this paper adds to the growing literature studying the determinants of financial stability. Several studies have examined financial stability during the financial crisis and no research has studied this theme during the financial crisis and the political crisis for each region separately at the same time. It remains relatively unclear whether and to what extent the financial crisis and the recent political turmoil have affected volatility of stock returns of

---

[1]The Ex-Vice-President of the World Bank for MENA in her speech during the 'Sympisium on Islamic Finance in Roma: Developments in MENA region', Bank Italia, Rome, Italy, November, 11th, 2009.

*Corresponding author: Ameni Ghenimi, Economic Sciences and Management of Tunisia, Campus Universities, El Manar BP 248, El Manar II, 2092, Tunis, Tunisia, E-mail: ameni.fsegs@gmail.com

IBs and CBs. In this paper, we attempt to fill this gap by examining the volatility of the stock returns of IBs and CBs in three regions during the financial crisis and the Arab Spring movements. Firstly, we consider a matched sample of IBs and CBs for each region separately. Secondly, we use not only the various GARCH models as done by Boumediene and Caby [5], Al Ali and Yousfi [6], but also a multiplicative dummy variable in the best volatility model that assesses the impact of these crises on two groups of banks. Our matched data comprise the daily returns of 11 IBs and 17 CBs from three regions covered during the period 09/11/2005 to 09/12/2013 which enables us to assess the effect of both crises on the financial stability of IBs and CBs. The volatility of the stock returns of IBs and CBs was estimated using the GJR-GARCH model during the financial crisis and the political crisis in the Arab countries.

Our major findings are as follows. We find that IBs were more stable than their counterparts during the global financial crisis. It seems that CBs were operating with greater risk exposure than their Islamic peers during the crisis, however, during the political uncertainty; they saw their initially-low volatility increase during that period. Although this increase remained very moderate, CBs saw their volatility initially decline during the crisis. Therefore, it seems that both crises are different regarding the risk.

The structure of this paper is as follows, section 2 provides a short overview of the specifics of Islamic banking. Section 3 presents the literature review of the financial stability in IBs and CBs. The variables, the data and the econometric methodology are presented in section 4. Section 5 presents and discusses the empirical results. Finally, our concluding remarks are summed up in the last section.

Specific Characteristics of Islamic Banks

Many economists, such as Cihak and Hesse [4], Khan [2], Syed Ali [7] found two principles of transactions, the Mudharabah and Musharakah, as the only instruments of profit and loss sharing. Traditional banking intermediation is based on debt and allows the transfer of risk, whereas Islamic banking is based on the assets and risk sharing. The mechanisms allow Islamic banks to keep their net worth and avoid the imbalance of their balance sheets during the crises. On the liabilities side of the balance sheet, the Mudharabah transaction between the bank and customers is unlimited so that the management of the bank is free to invest money in what seems to comply with sharia.

On the asset side of the balance sheet, the funds are invested through a limited Mudharabah contract. The bank also accepts deposits in current accounts. Bank deposits can be divided into demand and time deposits. The total amount of these demand deposits is guaranteed, and current account depositors are aware that their deposits are used for risky projects. Two basic methods are offered by Islamic banks, the first depends on the profit and loss sharing and includes Musharakah and Mudharabah, and the second involves the sale and purchase of goods and services on credit. Islamic banks follow the sharia principles in their operations. The other types of Islamic financial modes, which are based on mark-up including (Murabaha, Ijaras, and Istisnaa), require that a real asset underlies the financial transaction. Consequently, financial assets and derivatives based on other debt financial assets cannot be traded. The linkage prevents the exposure of Islamic banks to speculative behavior that leads to instability. These funding models and the balance sheet structure inevitably have implications on Islamic banks' exposure to risk (default risk, solvency risk; liquidity risk).

On the income distribution side, Islamic banks distribute profits to investment depositors even when they return loss and pay the benefits of equity. Zainol and Kassim [8], Cevik and Charap [9] found that current practice does not make a clear distribution between the rights of shareholders and investment account holders.

Hence, in terms of capital, investment firms sell their capital to the public in the form of shares, and the shareholders have the right to control the direction of the company and exercise the right to vote. In Islamic banks, customers have no right to interfere with the management of the bank. Because of their engagements and the principle of sharing profits and losses, Islamic banks have better immunity to external shocks than conventional banks. Finally, IBs may not fully respect Shari'ah principles in their activities. For example, Chong and Liu [10] claim that Malaysian banks are not very different than conventional banks in terms of the adoption of the PLS principles.

Literature Review Related to Financial Stability

The stability of the banking system is important and therefore more attention should be given to the Islamic and Conventional banks after the period of the global financial crisis. Therefore, the literature that treated these issues is presented as follows:

Measurement indicators of financial stability can be divided into two groups: Measurement indicators by Z-score or GARCH (Table 1).

Data and Methodology

Data

Our dataset consists of daily prices for both conventional and Islamic banks from three regions, namely the GCC, the Mediterranean and the MENA over the period from 09/11/2005 to 9/12/2013. The dataset was gathered via DataStream [5]. The stock returns used to investigate banks' stability are calculated using the following formula:

$$R_t = \ln\left(\frac{p_t}{p_{t-1}}\right) \tag{1}$$

Where, P_t and P_{t-1} are the daily closing prices of the stocks index at time t and t-1. This choice is justified by the importance of shocks for the banking during this period.

Methodology

We adopt the generalized autoregressive conditional heteroscedasticity (GARCH) framework to examine whether, and to what extent, the financial crisis and political turmoil have affected the financial stability of both banks in the three regions. We perform inter-temporal and inter-bank comparison using the wilcoxon signed-rank test.

Measuring bank stability

The measurement of stability has a distinctive role in the operational framework of the financial system stability. It helps ensure the accountability of the authorities in charge and support the implementation of the chosen strategy to achieve the goal in real-time. The stability of banks is measured by the volatility of their returns on shares quoted on the stock exchange market. However, the level of bank stability is measured using the GARCH indicator (Generalized Autoregressive Conditional Heteroscedasticity). In the literature of Islamic banking, this indicator is used by Boumediene and Caby [5] Al-Ali and Yousfi [6].

Illing and Liu [11] observed that the GARCH method provided the best measure of stress on capital markets. This research uses a symmetric GARCH model and examines the asymmetric reactions of

Authors	Methodology	Objective	Results
Čihák and Hesse [4]	Model: Z-score Period: 1993 to 2004 Frequency: 77 Islamic banks and 397 commercials banks in Bahrain, Bangladesh, Brunei, Egypt, Gambia, Indonesia, Iran, Jordan, Kuwait, Lebanon, Malaysia, Mauritania, Pakistan, Qatar, Saudi Arabia, Sudan, Tunisia, United Arab Emirates, West bank and Gaza, and Yemen.	Studied the impact of Islamic banks on financial stability	The researchers found that (i) large commercial banks were financially more solid than large Islamic banks; (ii) small Islamic banks were financially more solid than conventional banks of the same size; and (iii) small Islamic banks tend to be financially stronger than large Islamic banks, which may reflect challenges of credit risk management in large Islamic banks.
Boumediene and Caby [5]	Model: GARCH, E-GARCH and GJR-GARCH Period: 2007-2009 Frequency: 14 Islamic banks and 14 commercials banks in UAE, Saudi Arabia, Bangladesh, Bahrain, Egypt, UK Bretagne, Kuwait, Pakistan, and Qatar	Examine the financial stability of Islamic banks during the subprime crisis.	The researchers showed that conventional banks were highly volatile than Islamic banks, and that Islamic banks were at least partially immune to the subprime crisis. These banks are not subject to the same risks as conventional banks.
Al ali and Yousfi [6]	Model: GARCH, E-GARCH and GJR-GARCH Period: 2005 to 2010 Frequency: ten conventional banks and one Islamic bank in Jordan	Investigated, measured and compare the financial stability of Jordanian Islamic and conventional banks in pre and post financial crisis.	The researchers showed that Islamic bank were more stable than conventional banks, which may due to their links with the real economy. They recommended that Islamic banks in Jordan need to improve the branch network throughout the country, and conventional banks must open Islamic branches, to benefit from this worthy system and to diversify their risks.
Rahim, Hassan and Zakaria [16]	Model: Z-score. Period: 2005-2010 Frequency: 17 Islamic banks and 21 commercial banks in Malaysia	Studied the difference in the level of financial stability of Islamic banks as compared to commercial banks of Malaysia	They showed that Islamic banks are more stable than commercial banks.
Gamagita and Rokhin [23]	Model: Z-score. Period: 2004-2009 Frequency: 12 Islamic banks and 71 conventional banks in Indonesia	studied the stability comparison between Islamic and conventional banks in Indonesia	They show that the level of stability comparison between Islamic and conventional banks is significantly different. The results show that the Islamic banks have a lower degree of stability compared to the conventional counterparts. The researchers show that the small Islamic banks relatively have the same degree of stability with small conventional banks. Islamic and conventional banks tented to have the same relative degree of stability during the crisis period of 2008-2009.
Shahid and Abbas [24]	Model: Z-score. Period: 2005-2010 Frequency: 55 banks which 5 Islamic banks in Pakistan	Analyze the financial stability of Islamic banks and its comparison with conventional banks in Pakistan.	They found in Pakistan that the (i) small Islamic banks tend to be financially stronger than small conventional banks, (ii) large conventional banks tend to be financially stronger than large Islamic banks, (iii) small Islamic banks were financially more solid than large Islamic banks, which may reflect challenges of credit risk management in large Islamic banks; and (iv) the market share of Islamic banks had a significant impact on the financial strength of other banks.
Abdulkadhim Altaee, AnisTalo and Mohammad Adam [25]	Model: Z-score. Period: 2003-2010 Frequency:42 IBs and 55 CBs in Bahrain, Kuwait, Oman, Qatar, Saudi Arabia, and United Arab Emirates	studied the stability of Islamic and conventional banks in the gulf countries and They compared changes in certain aspect pre-and post-crisis	These researchers found that there was no significant difference between the financial stability of conventional and Islamic banking for the periods 2003-2010, 2003-2007, and 2008-2010. Conventional banks tend to be financially stronger than Islamic banks to pre-financial crisis.
Hasan and Dridi [26]	Model: Z-score. Period: 2005 to 2009 Frequency:85 Conventional banks and 37 Islamic banks in five GCC countries (Bahrain, Kuwait, Qatar, Bahrain, Saudi Arabia, and the UAE), three non-GCC countries, (Jordan, Turkey, and Malaysia)	compared the crisis effect on the Conventional and Islamic banks in eight countries	The researchers show that in the aspect of profitability, Islamic banks experienced a significant decline in profitability during the crisis period, although on average still relatively similar to conventionalbank profitability. In terms of assets and loans, Islamic banks showed much higher growth compared to the conventional banks in times of crisis and the assessment of external rating agencies indicates relatively stable ratings for Islamic banks.

Table 1: The studies that studied the financial stability of Islamic and conventional banks.

the conditional mean and volatility by using the GARCH, E-GARCH, and GJR-GARCH.

GARH (1,1): In 1986, the lag of the ARCH models became too large. Bollerslev [12] proposed adopting the generalized ARCH, known as the GARCH model (General Autoregressive Conditional Heteroskedasticity), which is an extension of the ARCH model developed by Engel [13]. The GARCH model is a representation of the autoregressive conditional variance process. The general form of this model by Bollerslev [2], which is called the GARCH (p,q) model, is given by:

$$h_t = \sigma_t^2 = \omega + \sum_{i=1}^{p} \alpha_i \xi_{t-i}^2 + \sum_{i=1}^{q} \beta_i h_{t-i} \qquad (2)$$

(2)Where the GARCH parameters are restricted to $\omega > 0$, $\alpha_i > 0$ and

$\beta_i > 0$, q is the order of the autoregressive GARCH terms and p is the order of the moving average ARCH terms. Therefore, the GARCH (1, 1) model for one period can be summarized as follows:

$$h_t = \omega + \alpha\xi_{t-1}^2 + \beta h_{t-1} \qquad (3)$$

Where, $\omega > 0; \alpha, \beta > 0$ and $\alpha + \beta < 0$

EGARCH (1,1): The exponential general autoregressive conditional heteroskedastic (E-GARCH) model proposed by Nelson is another form of the GARCH model. The E-GARCH model with the exponential nature of the conditional variance captures the effect of external unexpected shocks on the predicted volatility. This model allows for testing the asymmetries. When the residual is negative, volatility is impacted by two terms in the equation that includes the residual. The E-GARCH model also gives good results in the case of violent shocks. This model is formulated as:

$$Log(h_t) = \omega + \alpha\frac{\xi_{t-1}}{\sqrt{h_{t-1}}} + \gamma\frac{\xi_{t-1}}{\sqrt{h_{t-1}}} + \beta log(h_{t-1}) \qquad (4)$$

Where ω, α, θ and β are constant parameters

GJR-GARCH (1,1): Engel [13] tested the various asymmetric volatility forecasting models. They demonstrated that the one that most effectively models is the GJR-GARCH. The GJR-GARCH model was introduced independently by Glosten, Jagannathan, and Runkle [14]. The model has a positive and a negative shock on the conditional asymmetric variance. The formula for GJR-GARCH (1, 1) is as follows:

$$h_t = \omega + \beta h_{t-1} + \alpha\xi_{t-1}^2 + \gamma S_{t-1}^-\xi_{t-1}^2 \qquad (5)$$

Where S-t-1= 1 if ξt-1<0, S-t-1= 0 if ξt-1≥0. ω, α, γ and β are constant parameters.

Model specifications

We use a specification test model to see which form of the equation of conditional volatility best fits the series. The three models used to capture the common characteristics of the financial asset return variance are; the standard symmetric GARCH model, the asymmetric GARCH (GJR-GARCH) model of Glosten et al. [14] and the exponential GARCH (EGARCH) of Nelson [15]:

$$h_t = \omega + \alpha\xi_{t-1}^2 + \beta h_{t-1} \text{ [GARCH]}$$

$$log(h_t) = \omega + \alpha\frac{\xi_{t-1}}{\sqrt{h_{t-1}}} + \gamma\frac{\xi_{t-1}}{\sqrt{h_{t-1}}} + \beta log(h_{t-1}) \text{ [EGARCH]}$$

$$h_t = \omega + \alpha\xi_{t-1}^2 + \gamma I[\xi_{t-1} < 0]\xi_{t-1}^2 + \beta h_{t-1} \text{ [GJR-GARCH]}$$

Where ξ_{t-1} is the innovation at time t-1, I is a dummy variable and I=1 if ξ_{t-1}<0, I=0 otherwise.

(γ) determines the effect of negative return shocks on the conditional variance and indicates that a negative shock has a greater impact on future volatility than a positive shock; therefore it has a greater influence on the conditional variance. To select the best model for each individual series, we use the log-likelihood function (log L) criterion.

Volatility effect of the financial crisis and the political uncertainty on the financial stability of IBs and CBs

To determine whether the financial and political crises have led to an increase or decrease in the volatility of stock prices in the three regions, we include a multiplicative dummy variable in the best equation of the conditional variance according to the procedure described above. In this paper, the best model is the GJR-GARCH conditional volatility equation:

$$h_t = (1 + \lambda_d Dt)\omega + \alpha\xi_{t-1}^2 + \gamma I[\xi_{t-1} < 0]\xi_{t-1}^2 + \beta h_{t-1} \qquad (6)$$

Where D_t is an event dummy variable which takes a value of the unity after the financial crisis, and zero otherwise, and that of the unity after the Arab Spring, and zero otherwise. A significant estimate for parameter λ_d would indicate an increase in stock returns bank in the three regions during these crises[2].

Results and Discussions

Preliminary analysis

First, we applied the unit root test (augmented dickey fuller test). This test indicates that all the return series for both types of banks are not stationary during the three periods of the study.

We notice the volatility between conventional and Islamic banks suggesting a comparable stability. In addition, the stock returns of conventional and Islamic banks appeared to be volatile during the recent crises, reflecting the effect of the financial global crisis, the political uncertainty and further ARCH effects for most returns in the data over the last two crises. We also computed the descriptive statistics of the daily stock returns for Islamic and conventional banks for three regions (the Golf, the Mediterranean and the all MENA) before and, during the recent financial crisis and, Political uncertainty. These statistics are calculated and reported in Table 2. The Jarque-Bera normality test for conventional and Islamic banks during the three periods of the study strongly rejects the null hypothesis of normality distribution at 1% significance level. We also noted that conventional and Islamic banks in two regions, (the GCC and in all the MENA countries) during the Arab spring, have a positive Skewness, which indicates that the right tail of the distribution is longer. However, the other series have a negative Skewness, which means that the return distribution is highly skewed to the left. The kurtosis is higher than 3 for both types of banks during the financial crisis and political uncertainty, however, this is not for the Islamic banks in three regions before the crisis. This is said to be a leptokurtic distribution. All the Ljung-Box (LB) statistics for the returns of both types of banks for three regions during three periods are statistically significant, indicating that our return series are longer serially correlated.

Effects of the financial crisis and the Arab spring on the financial stability of IBs and CBs

In this paper, we attempt to examine the impact of the financial crisis and the recent political crisis in the Arab countries (i.e. Arab Spring) on the financial stability of the IBs and CBs in three regions.

We demonstrated the performance of a model using the specification test reported in Table 3 which indicates that (according to log L), the best model for IBs and CBs during the three periods of the study is the GJR-GARCH (1, 1), whereas the GARCH (1,1) was preferred for CBs for the MENA region before the financial crisis. To investigate the impact of the financial crisis and the Arab Spring on the financial volatility of IBs and CBs, as in equation 3, we first showed the results of returns for the conventional banks during the financial crisis. In all cases, the moving average parameters α are close to 0 and autoregressive parameters β tend to be close to 1. It can be seen that the coefficients describing the conditional variance are positive and significant at 1% and 5% in only the Mediterranean and MENA regions,

---

[2]This analytical framework is similar to that adopted by Chaua, Deescmsaka and Wang (2014) in the context of the political uncertainty and stock market volatility in MENA.

Region Returns banks	GCC		Mediterranean		MENA	
	Islamic	conventional	Islamic	conventional	Islamic	conventional
Panel A: Before financial crisis						
Mean	-0.0001	-0.0005	0.0007	-0.0001	-0.0001	0.0006
Std dev	0.0119	0.0102	0.0136	0.0122	0.0128	0.0083
Skew	-0.2446	-0.2744	-0.0799	-0.6412	-0.1192	-0.4068
Kurt	2.0909	5.8968	0.3692	3.5816	1.0658	4.9511
ADF	-10.6930	-12.0593	-11.6177	-11.6876	-16.7528	-8.5781
LB(12)	12.185**	9.143**	10.235**	11.257*	11.123**	13.257**
	(0.04)	(0.0 3)	(0.05)	(0.07)	(0.01)	(0.03)
ARCH(12)	28.6839***	5.8106	23.7631**	21.4520***	43.0583***	1.09
	(0.0043)	(0.9253)	(0.0219)	(0.0003)	(0.0000)	(0.2147)
JB	84.5328***	643.0123***	2.967	265.3317***	43.7381***	236.019***
	(0.0000)	(0.0000)	(0.2268)	(0.0000)	(0.0000)	(0.0000)
Nb obs	440	440	440	440	440	440
Panel B: during financial crisis						
Mean	-0.0002	-0.0005	0.0004	-0.0009	-0.0003	-0.0007
Std dev	0.0111	0.0101	0.0122	0.0115	0.0117	0.0108
Skew	-0.9929	-0.5635	-1.1120	-0.4289	-1.0664	-0.4928
Kurt	5.5631	4.4133	9.8987	3.1972	8.2384	3.7469
ADF	-20.1952	-14.5267	-19.6042	-14.6621	-20.1952	-14.5267
LB(12)	11.257**	11.235**	10.144*	9.125*	11.231*	14.236**
	(0.05)	(0.02) 183.6041***	(0.06)	(0.06)	(0.06)	(0.02)
ARCH(12)	44.1102***	(0.0000)	13.634	161.3929***	163.7716***	219.7809***
	(0.0003)	771.1105***	(0.3247)	(0.0000)	(0.0000)	(0.0000)
JB	1296.7791***	(0.0000)	3825.6146***	407.28***	5383.2207***	1115.7708***
	(0.0000)	892	(0.0000)	(0.0000)	(0.0000)	(0.0000)
Nb obs	892		892	892	892	892
Panel C: during Arab Spring						
Mean	0.0011	0.0004	0.0006	-0.0003	0.0011	0.0003
Std dev	0.0146	0.0084	0.01	0.0213	0.0146	0.0203
Skew	0.2731	0.1599	-2.6864	-5.4108	0.2731	0.1584
Kurt	6.1116	4.5016	34.6778	80.9352	6.1116	4.8316
ADF	-14.6765	-21.2361	-19.8971	-21.2693	-28.2796	-28.34
LB(12)	13.254**	10.231**	12.101**	14.234**	10.231**	11.234**
	(0.03)	(0.02)	(0.03)	(0.03)	(0.03)	(0.016)
ARCH(12)	247.2954 ***	28.8279 ***	39.9004***	10.1544	5.883	104.2932 ***
	(0.0000)	(0.0041)	(0.0000)	(0.999)	(0.9219)	(0.0000)
JB	1217.3651***	659.345***	39867.2009***	585915.9172***	1217.3651***	1518.0232***
	(0.0000)	(0.0000)	(0.0)	(0.0000)	(0.0000)	(0.0000)
Nb obs	777	777	777	777	777	777

Notes: Std. Dev: indicates standard deviation, skewness measures the asymmetry series' distribution around the mean, kurtosis measures the flatness of series' distribution. For a normal distribution, the value of the skewness coefficient is zero and that of kurtosis is 3. LB (12) is the Ljung-Box test of serial correlation for the return, ARCH (12) is the Lagrange multiplier test for ARCH effect.
***Significant at 1%, **Significant at 5%, and *Significant at 10%.

Table 2: Summary statistics of stock returns of IBs and CBs.

Region Returns banks	GCC		Mediterranean		MENA	
	Islamic	conventional	Islamic	conventional	Islamic	conventional
Panel A: Before financial crisis Performance criteria: Log L						900.7739
GARCH	1342.207	1437.6204	1275.8940	1317.0312	2613.2188	890.0567
E-GARCH	1336.5615	1411.5742	1267.5582	1316.104	2598.1578	898.1571
GJR-GARCH	1342.6558	2704.9334	1277.5662	2592.8879	2615.1203	
Panel B: during financial crisis Performance criteria: Log L						5769.9447
GARCH	2863.8490	2963.2390	2807.3208	2811.2059	5664.2296	5667.757
E-GARCH	2858.4626	2910.7239	2727.7238 2	767.3739	5556.1455	5667.757
GJR-GARCH	2871.2644	2966.513	2807.5635	2817.8938	5667.2758	5778.4380
Panel C: during Arab Spring Performance criteria: Log L						
GARCH	898.8988	2629.8963	2499.9101	5227.8321	4652.6801	4001.3279
E-GARCH	889.4031	2613.5346	2499.8324	5226.0718	4652.8189	3980.121
GJR-GARCH	900.7155	2630.6737	2505.6370	5607.0607	4655.1189	4002.9741

Note: This table summarizes the results from an extensive GARCH model specification test. The standard GARCH model is compared with the asymmetric GJR-GARCH and the EGARCH:

Table 3: Results of specification tests for various GARCH models.

with the exception of γ in the Golf countries. Moreover γ is positive and significant, which indicates that the bank returns volatility is highly persistent and asymmetric. Concerning the coefficient estimates obtained for the dummy variable λ_d, the evidence suggests that the conditional variance for the Golf countries and the MENA region had

significant changes in their volatility during the period of the financial crisis. This change, which was not present in the Mediterranean region, was induced by the subprime crisis. Similarly, the results of returns for Islamic banks with the exception of γ in the Mediterranean region indicate that the relevant coefficients in the variance equation are significant. The parameter γ is positive and significant at 1%, 5% and 10% in only the GCC and MENA regions, which indicates that the bank returns volatility is highly persistent and asymmetric. The λ_d coefficient was found in the Islamic bank returns, which indicates that there was no change in that period. These results explain the confidence of investors in financial stability and economic growth in the Islamic banks of the region. These results are equivalent with prior evidence which suggests that financial crisis adversely affects conventional banks than Islamic banks Al Ali and Yousfi [6]; Boumediene and Caby [5]; Rahim et al. [16]. Secondly, concerning the effect of political uncertainty on the volatility of conventional bank returns; in all cases, with the exception of γ of the Golf countries, the coefficients in the variance equation are significant at 1%, 5% and 10%. Moreover, γ is negative and significant, which indicates that bad news has no impact on the volatility of conventional bank returns, which may be explained by the confidence of investors. The estimated coefficient obtained for the dummy variable λ_d is significant at 5% and 10%, except for the Mediterranean region. λ_d indicates that volatility for the Mediterranean region has not changed during that period. The evidence suggests that the conditional variance for the Golf countries and the MENA region had a significant change in their volatility during the period of the Arab spring. This change was induced in the recent revolution. Similarly, the results of Islamic bank returns except for γ of the MENA region indicate that the relevant coefficients in the variance equation are significant at 1% and 5%. Parameter γ is positive and significant, which indicates that the bank return volatility is highly persistent and asymmetric. In that period, the λd indicates that the volatility of Islamic bank returns in the Mediterranean region did not change but had a significant change in the Golf countries and the MENA region around that period. This change is explained by the recent revolution and political instability. These results are equivalent with prior evidence which suggests that political uncertainty adversely affects banks stability [17,18] and not conform to prior evidence which suggests that no difference effect of the political uncertainty and stability of Islamic banks [19].

Our findings for Islamic bank returns are more relevant than for conventional banks during the crisis period. This can be explained by the specificities of Islamic finance which prohibits speculation. In addition, during political uncertainty, Islamic banks saw their volatility-initially low- increase during the crisis whereas that of their conventional counterpart remained low during the crisis because of the panic. Therefore, the major MENA stock markets were affected, at the same time, by the Arab spring uprising and the instability in the stock markets in the MENA region [20]. These crises are not subject to the same risks and to the same regulations. Finally, these results confirm both the hypotheses that Islamic banks were at least partially immune to the financial crisis than conventional banks and Islamic banks were not subject to the same risks as conventional banks. However, due to their links with the real economy, they really suffered the consequences of the financial crisis and the political turmoil, which suggests that in general, the Islamic market provides further investment opportunities.

$$h_t = \omega + \alpha\xi_{t-1}^2 + \beta h_{t-1} \text{ [GARCH]}$$

$$\log(h_t) = \omega + \alpha\frac{\xi_{t-1}}{\sqrt{h_{t-1}}} + \gamma\frac{\xi_{t-1}}{\sqrt{h_{t-1}}} + \beta\log(h_{t-1}) \text{ [EGARCH]}$$

$$h_t = \omega + \alpha\xi_{t-1}^2 + \gamma I[\xi_{t-1} < 0]\xi_{t-1}^2 + \beta h_{t-1} \text{ [GJR-GARCH]}$$

The best-performing model is chosen on the basis of several information criteria, including the log-likelihood function (log L). The best model according to each criterion is highlighted in bold while the selected specifications used in our analysis are reported in the final column (Table 4).

Estimates of conditional variances

Before the crisis, volatility and risk in Islamic banks in the three regions were higher than conventional banks. This indicates the confidence of investors in the markets in general. During the financial crisis, the volatility of conventional banks increased whereas that of the Islamic banks decreased. This means mainly that conventional banks show a higher volatility than Islamic banks mainly in the Golf countries and the MENA region, but not for the Mediterranean region. The fact that the crisis has no impact on the volatility of Islamic banks indicates that investors have confidence in Islamic banks.

Similarly, during the Arab Spring, the volatility of conventional banks increased in both regions (the Mediterranean and the MENA), but did not increase in the GCC region whereas that of Islamic banks decreased for the GCC region and the Mediterranean region and increased for the entire MENA region. This explains that the investors' confidence in Islamic banks was not affected by this crisis. Therefore, this crisis had more impact on the conventional banks than on Islamic banks. The volatility of Islamic and conventional banks in the MENA region increased during the political crisis. This can be explained by the widespread of political protests, which seriously threatened the old order in the MENA region, and caused political uncertainty. Islamic and conventional banks' results show a positive skewness for both groups of banks for three regions during three periods. This indicates that the right tail of the distribution is longer. The kurtosis is higher than 3 for both types of banks in the three regions during three periods. However, this indicates that the distribution and fat tails are sharper than a normal distribution. They are leptokurtic. We conclude that Islamic banks were more stable than conventional banks during the financial crisis and the Arab Spring. However, investors had more confidence in this type of banks during periods of crises than before the financial crisis (Table 5).

Volatility of Islamic and conventional banksbefore, during the financial crisis and during the Arab spring

Okpara [21] indicated that the Wilcoxon signed-rank test is a non-parametric alternative to the two-sample t-test when the population cannot be assumed to be normally distributed. Wilcoxon rank-sum test is utilized to examine whether the difference in volatility between both groups of banks in three periods is statistically significant. The mean volatility of conventional banks in the three regions is significantly higher than that of Islamic banks at 1% level for the three periods [22]. These results corroborate the hypothesis that Islamic banks were at least partially immune to the financial crisis and the Arab spring. This indicates that bad news (the financial crisis and the Arab spring) has no impact on the financial stability of Islamic banks. Besides, the underlying hypothesis states that Islamic banks are not subjects to the same risks as conventional banks, due to their links with the real economy and their main principles as risk sharing (Table 6).

Conclusion

The recent financial crisis has induced a series of failures of many conventional banks followed by a political uncertainty, and led many economists to advocate the development of Islamic banks in the MENA region regarding stability during two crises. In light of the study objectives, we have examined the financial volatility of Islamic banks and that of their conventional peers in three major regions (the GCC, the Mediterranean, and the MENA) during periods of calmness, of

Region	GCC		Mediterranean		MENA	
Returns	Islamic	conventional	Islamic	conventional	Islamic	conventional
Panel A: during financial crisis						
Selected model	GJR-GARCH	GJR-GARCH	GJR-GARCH	GJR-GARCH	GJR-GARCH	GJR-GARCH
ω	0.0002***	0.0003***	0.0022*	0.0004***	0.0051***	0.0005***
	(4.8612)	(3.2266)	(1.8912)	(3.3689)	(3.3529)	(3.1991)
α	0.0997**	0.1397***	0.1275***	0.0998***	0.0921***	0.1022***
	(2.1339)	(6.1358)	(4.3739)	(5.2952)	(3.9887)	(4.5472)
β	0.5361***	0.8276***	0.8583***	0.8526***	0.8418***	0.8187***
	(7.6359)	(32.035)	(29.6877)	(39.6144)	(24.7179)	(24.4964)
γ	0.3022***	0.0411	0.0185	0.0561**	0.056**	0.0874***
	(3.6812)	(1.579)	(0.6611)	(2.3573)	(2.2391)	(2.6981)
λd	0.0413	0.0535**	0.0146	0.0440	0.0202	0.0722**
	(1.0417)	(1.9956)	(0.3902)	(1.5339)	(0.73003)	(2.5314)
Panel B: during Arab spring						
Selected model	GJR-GARCH	GJR-GARCH	GJR-GARCH	GJR-GARCH	GJR-GARCH	GJR-GARCH
	0.000005***	0.00001*	0.00005***	0.000002***	0.0000007***	0.00001***
ω	(3.4051)	(1.8089)	(8.3018)	(7.2343)	(3.5820)	(7.5998)
	0.0434***	0.1396***	0.1859***	0.1318***	0.0285***	0.2659***
α	(2.6326)	(2.8965)	(3.6238)	(10.5552)	(4.6594)	(9.2046)
	0.8568***	0.6954***	0.2434***	0.938***	0.9628***	0.7679***
β	(31.6477)	(5.196)	(3.2953)	(177.0566)	(251.9716)	(48.5829)
	0.1133***	-0.0490	0.264***	-0.1356***	0.0097	-0.0706**
γ	(3.7983)	(-0.9592)	(3.4163)	(-10.7582)	(1.0816)	(-2.0791)
	0.0579**	-0.0797*	0.0486	0.0101	0.056**	-0.0598**
λd	(2.1382)	(-1.8294)	(1.58774)	(0.57692)	(2.0253)	(-2.1381)

Note: This table reports the parameter estimates for each of the selected best-performing GARCH model with a multiplicative dummy; where Dt is a dummy variable takes on a value of unity after the start of Arab Spring and zero otherwise. A significant and positive estimate for λd would indicate an increase in MENA stock market volatility during the period of political uncertainty. The hetero scedasticity-consistent t-statistics are shown in parentheses.
*Statistical significance at the 10% level.
**Statistical significance at the 5% level.
***Statistical significance at the 1% level.

Table 4: Effects of the Financial Crisis and the Arab Spring on returns volatility for IBs and CBs in three regions.

Region	GCC		Mediterranean		MENA	
Returns banks	Islamic	conventional	Islamic	conventional	Islamic	conventional
Panel A: Before financial crisis						
Mean	0.000140	0.000097	0.000193	0.000150	0.000168	0.000059
Std dev	0.000048	0.000032	0.000060	0.000031	0.000058	0.000065
Skew	2.948579	4.557180	1.969955	5.325066	2.469855	7.458784
Kurt	11.839327	29.815458	6.179983	53.343534	8.969604	63.624394
Panel B: during financial crisis						
Mean	0.000115	0.000127	0.000116	0.000123	0.000137	0.000102
Std dev	0.000107	0.000145	0.000107	0.000035	0.000170	0.000032
Skew	5.932591	5.365517	5.941769	7.344585	5.369954	3.595792
Kurt	50.957795	45.113088	51.0664	119.102341	3.306710	19.3636448
Panel C: during Arab Spring						
Mean	0.000050	0.000083	0.000115	0.000470	0.000206	0.000340
Std dev	0.000025	0.000083	0.000107	0.000656	0.002194	0.000325
Skew	5.828766	10.864930	5.932591	23.962737	39.392011	3.801900
Kurt	51.393504	166.479973	50.95779	725.047224	1552.481731	26.879051

Notes: Std.Dev: Indicates standard deviation, skewness measures the asymmetry series' distribution around the mean, kurtosis measures the flatness of series' distribution. For a normal distribution, the value of the skewness coefficient is zero and that of kurtosis is 3.

Table 5: Statistical Estimates of Conditional Variances.

financial crisis and of political uncertainty. To this end, we considered a matched sample comprising returns of 11 IBs and 17 CBs using the GJR- GARCH model. Our analysis produced some interesting results which indicate that the global financial crisis has contributed to the volatility of conventional bank returns. Moreover, the volatility of Islamic banks increased during the recent political turmoil in these regions. Consequently, the results showed that there is a significant difference between IBs and CBs in terms of the effect of the financial crisis on the banking stability but little or no significant difference in terms of the effect of the Arab spring on the banking stability. Therefore, this does not mean that both crises are different from each other in terms of types of risks and that the impact of a political crisis on stock prices largely arises due to the psychological reactions. However, Islamic banks are more stable than conventional banks in general. This stability seems to be partially due to the different types of risks, the management methods and the governance of both types of banks. Overall; the results are consistent with our hypotheses. This in turn suggests that bank returns volatility is driven by financial and

	Before the crisis	financial crisis	Arab Spring
IB GCC	0.0002	0.0004	0.0003
CB GCC	0.001	0.0053	0.0067
Statistic*	14.354	21.231	11.231
P-value	0.000	0.000	0.000
IB Mediterranean	0.0006	0.0005	0.0003
CB Mediterranean	0.0037	0.0008	0.0074
Statistic*	5.470	7.253	13.254
P-value	0.001	0.000	0.000
IB MENA	0.0004	0.0004	0.0003
CB MENA	0.001	0.0023	0.0064
Statistic*	14.354	11.352	14.251
P-value	0.000	0.000	0.000

Notes: *Wilcoxon Two-Sample Test statistic. The null hypothesis is that the mean value of volatility is equal for both types of banks; the p-value is the probability that the null hypothesis is rejected at 1% significance level in favor of the alternative hypothesis that the stability is higher for Islamic banks.

Table 6: Mean Volatility of Islamic and Conventional Banks Before the crisis, During the Financial Crisis and During the Arab Spring.

economic factors, and to a lesser extent, by political events.

Overall, these findings complement the literature on the relationship between financial crisis and, political crises, and volatility of bank returns. Our results are very important in understanding the role of the financial crisis and that of the Arab spring on the financial stability of both types of banks. Therefore, they are of a great significance to international investors.

References

1. OCDE (2010) Competition, concentration and stability in the banking sector.

2. Khan M (1987) Islamic interest-free banking: A theoretical analysis. Theoretical studies in islamic banking and finance. The institute of Islamic Studies 15-36.

3. Siddiqi MN (2006) Islamic banking and finance in theory and practice: A survey of state of the art. Islamic Economic Studies 13: 2-48.

4. Cihák M, Hesse H (2010) Islamic banks and financial stability: An Empirical. Journal of Financial Services Research 38: 95-113.

5. Boumediene A, Caby J (2009) The financial stability of Islamic banks during the subprime crisis.

6. Al-ali A, Yousfi I (2012) Investigation of Jordanian Islamic and conventional Banks' Stability: Evidence from the recent financial crisis. European Journal of Economics, Finance and Administrative Sciences 44: 1450-2275.

7. Syed AS (2007) Financial distress and bank failure: Lessons from closure from Ihlas Finans in Turkey. Islamic Economic Studies 14: 1-52.

8. Zainol Z, Kassim SH (2010) An analysis of Islamic bank's exposure to rate of return risk. Journal of Economic Cooperation and Development 31: 59-83.

9. Cevik S, Charap J (2011) The behavior of conventional and islamic bank deposit returns in Malaysia and Turkey.

10. Chong SC, Liu MH (2009) Islamic banking: Interest free or interest-based?. Pacific-Basin Finance Journal 17: 125-144.

11. Illing M, Liu Y (2003) An index of financial stress for canada. Bank of canada working paper, n°2003-14.

12. Bollerslev T (1986) Generalized Autoregressive Conditional Heteroskedasticity. Journal of Econometrica 31: 307-327.

13. Engel RF (1993) Measuring and testing the impact of news on volatility. Journal of Finance 48: 1749-1778.

14. Glosten LR, Jagannathan R, Runkle DE (1993) On the relation between the expected value and the volatility of the nominal excess returns on stocks. Journal of finance 48: 779-801.

15. Nelson DB (1991) Conditional heteroskedasticity in asset returns: A New Approach. Journal of econometrica 59: 347-70.

16. Siti RM, Norsilawati MH, Roza HZ (2012) Islamic Vs. conventional bank stability: A case study of Malaysia. Prosiding perkem 2.

17. Micco A, Panizza U, Yanez M (2007) Bank ownership and performance: Does politics matter? Journal of Banking and Finance 31: 219-241.

18. Baum C, Caglayan M, Talavera O (2010) Parliamentary election cycles and the Turkish banking sector. Journal of Banking and Finance 34: 2709-2719.

19. Ghosh S (2015) Political transaction and bank performance: How important was the Arab Spring? Journal of Comparative Economics.

20. World Bank (2011) MENA facing challenges and opportunities, World Bank Middle East and North Africa Region, Regional Economic Update.

21. Okpara G (2010) Microfinance banks and poverty alleviation in Nigeria. Research gate.

22. Allen WA, Wood G (2006) Defining and achieving financial stability. Journal of Financial Stability 2: 152-172.

23. Gamaginta RR (2011) The Stability comparison between Islamic banks and conventional banks: Evidence in Indonesia. 8th International Conference on Islamic Economics and Finance.

24. Shahid MA, Abbas Z (2012) Financial stability of Islamic banking in Pakistan: An empirical study. African Journal of Business Management 6: 3706-3714.

25. Altaee HA, Talo IM, Adam MH (2013) Testing the Financial Stability of Banks in GCC Countries: Pre and Post Financial Crisis. International Journal of Business and Social Research (IJBSR).

26. Hasan M, Dridi J (2010) The effects of the global crisis on Islamic and conventional banks: A comparative study. International Monetary Fund (IMF).

International Financial Reporting Standards

Srinivasa Rao K[1] and Malyadri P[2]*

[1]*Assistant Professor of Commerce, Vivek Vardhini College of P.G. Studies, (Affiliated To Osmania University), Jambagh, Koti, Hyderabad-500095, India*
[2]*Principal, Government Degree College, Affiliated to Osmania University Patancheru, Hyderabad, Telangana State, India*

Abstract

Globalisation is causing a convergence of economic, trading, political and social process. Recent years have seen major changes in financial reporting worldwide under which the most obvious is the continuing adoption of IFRS worldwide. An upcoming economy on world economic map, India, too, decided to converge to International Financial Reporting Standards (IFRS). While regulators, standard setters and law makers sit together to rollout the road map for implementation of IFRS in India, a wide section of the industry is already debating about the impact that they are going to have on transitioning to IFRS. This paper explores the impact of adoption of IFRS, challenges that will come up and its adoption procedure in India. It also discusses the problems faced by the stakeholders (Regulators, Accountants, and Firms etc) in the process of adoption of IFRS in India. This paper discuss the IFRS adoption procedure in India and the utility for India in adopting IFRS, the problems and challenges faced by the stakeholders and its impact on India.

Keywords: IFR; Adoption of IFRS; Changes in financial reporting

Introduction

International Financial Reporting Standards (IFRS) are designed as a common global language for business affairs so that company accounts are understandable and comparable across international boundaries [1]. They are a consequence of growing international shareholding and trade and are particularly important for companies that have dealings in several countries. They are progressively replacing the many different national accounting standards. The rules to be followed by accountants to maintain books of accounts which is comparable, understandable, reliable and relevant as per the users internal or external. IFRS, with the exception of IAS 29. Financial Reporting in Hyperinflationary Economies and IFRIC 7 Applying the Restatement Approach under IAS 29, are authorized in terms of the historical cost paradigm. IAS 29 and IFRIC 7 are authorized in terms of the constant purchasing power paradigm. IFRS began as an attempt to harmonize accounting across the European Union but the value of harmonization quickly made the concept attractive around the world [2]. However, it has been debated whether or not the harmonization has been successful. IFRS are sometimes still called by the original name of International Accounting Standards (IAS). IAS was issued between 1973 and 2001 by the Board of the International Accounting Standards Committee (IASC). On 1st April, 2001, the new International Accounting Standards Board (IASB) took over from the IASC the responsibility for setting International Accounting Standards. During its first meeting the new Board adopted existing IAS and Standing Interpretations Committee standards (SICs) [3]. The IASB has continued to develop standards calling the new standards "International Financial Reporting Standards".

IFRS

A single set of high quality, understandable and enforceable global accounting standards that require high quality, transparent and comparable information in financial statements and other financial reporting to help participants in the world's capital markets and other users make economic decisions effectively [4].

Financial Statement and Information

Financial statements are a structured representation of the financial positions and financial performance of an entity. The objective of financial statements is to provide information about the financial position, financial performance and cash flows of an entity that is useful to a wide range of users in making economic decisions. Financial statements also show the results of the management's stewardship of the resources entrusted to it [5].

To meet this objective, financial statements provide information about an entity's:

- Assets
- liabilities
- equity;
- income and expenses, including gains and losses;
- Contributions by and distributions to owners in their capacity as owners; and
- Cash flows.

This information, along with other information in the notes, assists users of financial statements in predicting the entity's future cash flows and, in particular, their timing and certainty [6].

IFRS - general features

Fair presentation and compliance with IFRS: Fair presentation requires the faithful representation of the effects of the transactions, other events and conditions in accordance with the definitions and recognition criteria for assets, liabilities, income and expenses set out in the Framework of IFRS.

Going concern: Financial statements are present on a going concern basis unless management either intends to liquidate the entity or to cease trading, or has no realistic alternative but to do so [7].

---

*Corresponding author: Malyadri P, Principal, Government Degree College, Affiliated to Osmania University Patancheru, Hyderabad, Telangana State, India
E-mail: drpm16@gmail.com

Accrual basis of accounting: An entity [8] shall recognise items as assets, liabilities, equity, income and expenses when they satisfy the definition and recognition criteria for those elements in the Framework of IFRS.

Materiality and aggregation: Every material class of similar items has to be presented separately. Items that are of a dissimilar nature or function shall be presented separately unless they are immaterial.

Offsetting: Offsetting is generally forbidden in IFRS. However certain standards require offsetting when specific conditions are satisfied such as in case of the accounting for defined benefit liabilities in IAS 19 and the net presentation of deferred tax liabilities and deferred tax assets in IAS 12.

Frequency of reporting: IFRS requires that at least annually a complete set of financial statements is presented. However listed companies generally also publish interim financial statements (for which the accounting is fully IFRS compliant) for which the presentation is in accordance with IAS 34 Interim Financing Reporting [9].

Comparative information: IFRS requires entities to present comparative information in respect of the preceding period for all amounts reported in the current period's financial statements [10]. In addition comparative information shall also be provided for narrative and descriptive information if it is relevant to understanding the current period's financial statements [11]. The standard IAS 1 also requires an additional statement of financial position (also called a third balance sheet) when an entity applies an accounting policy retrospectively or makes a retrospective restatement of items in its financial statements, or when it reclassifies items in its financial statements. This for example occurred with the adoption of the revised standard IAS 19 (as of 1 January 2013) or when the new consolidation standards IFRS 10-11-12 were adopted (as of 1 January 2013 or 2014 for companies in the European Union).

Consistency of presentation: IFRS requires that the presentation and classification of items in the financial statements is retained from one period to the next unless: (a) it is apparent, following a significant change in the nature of the entity's operations or a review of its financial statements, that another presentation or classification would be more appropriate having regard to the criteria for the selection and application of accounting policies in IAS 8; or (b) an IFRS standard requires a change in presentation [12].

Applicability of IFRS

IFRS in India, issued by ICAI in October 2007, the IFRS should be applicable to Public Interest Entities (PIE). PIE has been defined to include:

- All listed companies;
- All banking companies;
- All financial institutions;
- All scheduled commercial banks;
- All insurance companies; and
- All NBFC

Benefit sections: The convergence with IFRS entails benefit to the following:

The Investors: The investor will be benefited in as the way accounting information made available to them will be more reliable, relevant, timely and most importantly the information will be comparable across different legal framework. It will develop better understanding and confidence among the investors [13].

The Professional: The professional, both in practice and in employment will get benefits as they will be able to provide their services in various part of the world, as few years after everybody will follow the same reporting standards.

The Corporate world: The Indian corporate reputation and relationship with international finance community will elevate because of achievement of higher level of consistency between reporting structure and requirements; better access to international markets; improving confidence among the international investors [14]. The international comparability will also get improve strengthening the industrial and capital markets in the country.

Challenges to IFRS Adoption in India

The practical challenges that may be faced in INDIA as a result of implementing the IFRS needs. The challenges are discussed as follows:

Level of Awareness: The transition plan to IFRS and its implications for preparers and users of financial statements, regulators, educators and other stakeholders have to be effectively coordinated and communicated. This should include raising awareness on the potential impact of the conversion, identifying regulatory synergies to be derived and communicating the temporary impact of the transition on business performance and financial position [15]. The implementation of IFRS requires considerable preparation both at the country and entity levels to ensure coherence and provide clarity on the authority that IFRS will have in relation to other existing national laws.

Accounting education and training: Practical implementation of IFRS requires adequate technical capacity among preparers and users of financial statements, auditors and regulatory authorities. Countries that implemented IFRS faced a variety of capacity-related issues, depending on the approach they took. One of the principal challenges may encounter in the practical implementation process, shall be the shortage of accountants and auditors who are technically competent in implementing IFRS. Usually, the time lag between decision date and the actual implementation date is not sufficiently long to train a good number of professionals who could competently apply international standards [16].

Training resources: Professional accountants are looked upon to ensure successful implementation of IFRS. Along with these accountants, government officials, financial analysts, auditors, tax practitioners, regulators, accounting lecturers, stock-brokers, preparers of financial statements and information officers are all responsible for smooth adoption process. Training materials on IFRS are not readily available at affordable costs in India to train such a large group which poses a great challenge to IFRS adoption.

Tax reporting: The tax considerations associated with the conversion to IFRS, like other aspects of a conversion, are complex. IFRS conversion calls for a detailed review of tax laws and tax administration. Specific taxation rules would have to be redefined to accommodate these adjustments .For instance, tax laws which limit relief of tax losses to four years should be reviewed [17]. This is because transition adjustments may result in huge losses that may not be recoverable in four years. Accounting issues that may present significant tax burden on adoption of IFRS, include determination of Impairment, Loan loss provisioning and Investment in Securities/Financial Instruments (Figure 1).

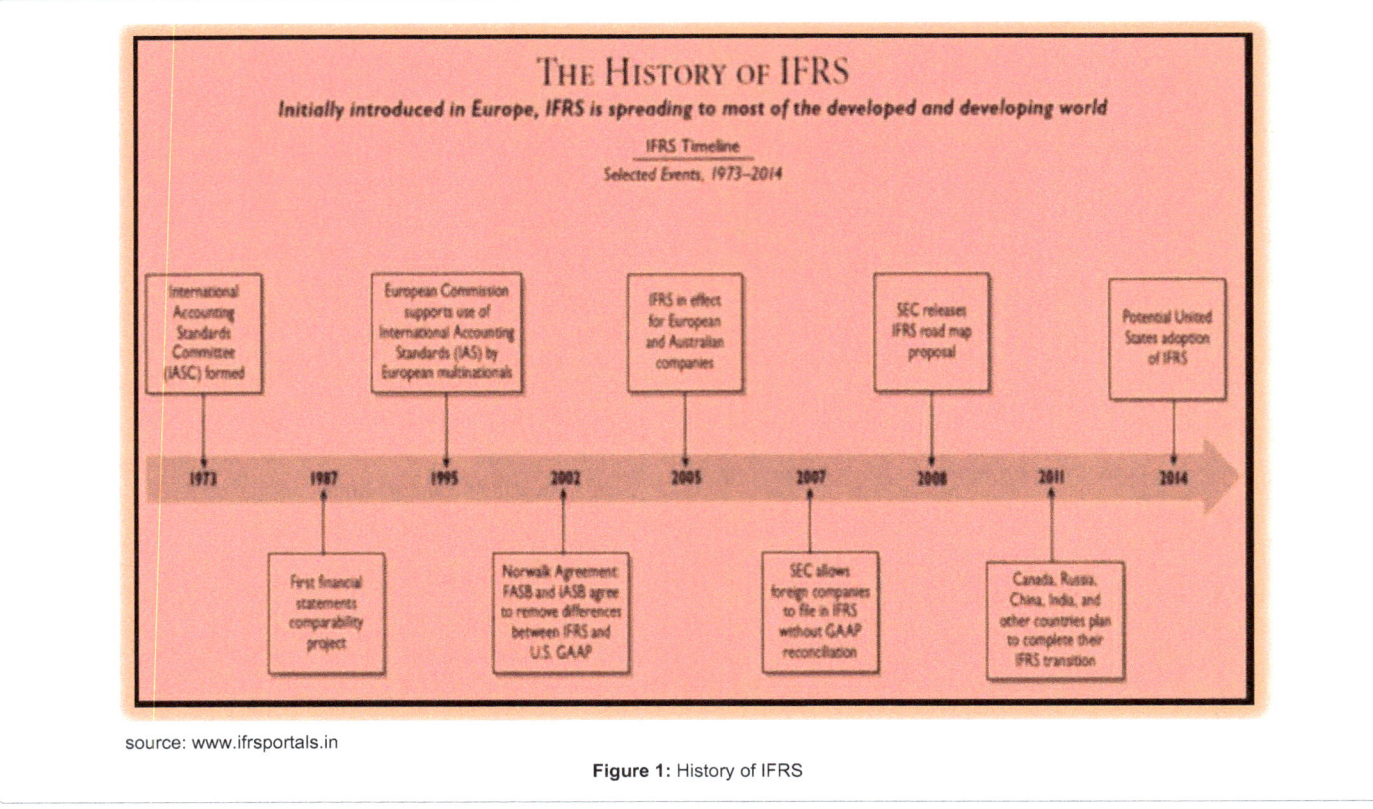

Figure 1: History of IFRS

Amendment to existing laws: In India, accounting practices are governed and issued by the Indian Accounting Standards Board (IASB) and other existing laws such as Indian Stock Exchange Act, these provide some guidelines on preparation of financial statements in India. IFRS does not recognize the presence of these laws and the accountants have to follow the IFRS fully with no overriding provisions from these laws. Indian law makers have to make necessary amendments to ensure a smooth transition to IFRS [18].

IFRS roadmap overview

The MCA roadmap has provided specific dates for adoption of IFRS in India on the basis of a company's net worth as indicated by the exchange on which they are traded. The IFRS conversion roadmap for Banks and Insurance companies will follow separately.

- Phase 1 companies are required to start reporting IFRS results from the first quarter of year beginning 1 April, 2011. Also, depending on how a company elects to present comparative information in the first year, the actual date of transition could be as early as 1 April 2010 [19].

- The core group and its sub-group 1, constituted by the MCA for IFRS convergence, shall determine IFRS conversion roadmap for banking and insurance companies separately by 28 February 2010.

- Non-listed companies with net worth of less than INR 500 crore and other small and medium-sized companies (SMCs) have been given an option to continue to either follow non converged standards (hereinafter referred to as "Indian GAAP") or to adopt IFRS.

- The draft of the Companies (Amendments) Bill, proposing for changes to the Companies Act, 1956, will be prepared by February, 2010.

- The Institute of Chartered Accountants of India (ICAI) has submitted to the MCA revised Schedule VI to the Companies Act, 1956 [20]. The NACAS shall review the draft and submit a revised Schedule VI to the MCA by 31 January 2010. Amendments to Schedule XIV will also be carried out in a time bound manner.

- Convergence of all the accounting standards with IFRS will be completed by the ICAI by 31 March 2010 and the NACAS will submit its final recommendations to MCA by 30 April 2010.

Conclusion

Effective implementation of IFRS is a pre-requisite in today's business world. It is necessary to have unique procedures of financial reporting systems and procedures. These procedures must be minimised and more meaningfulness. An interpretation does not require understanding in such a away the procedures has to be formulated and to be implemented time to time to ensure the correctness and credibility in the minds of investors. IFRS adoption improves the functioning of global capital markets by providing comparable and high-quality information to investors. In this connection corporates have to disclose the realities of their business activities and professionals in turn to interpret and report as per the standards without any violations.

References

1. Ashbaugh H, Pincus M (2001) Domestic accounting standards, International Accounting Standards, and the predictability of earnings. Journal of Accounting Research 39: 417-434.

2. Barth ME (2008) Global financial reporting: Implications for US academics. The Accounting Review, 83: 1159-1179.

3. Callao S, Jarne JI, Lainez JA (2007) Adoption of IFRS in Spain: Effect on the comparability and relevance of financial reporting, Journal of International Accounting, Auditing and Taxation 16: 148-178.

4. Christensen HB, Lee E, Walker M (2007) Cross-sectional variation in the economic consequences of international accounting harmonization: The case of mandatory IFRS adoption in the UK. The International Journal of Accounting 42: 341-379.

5. Daske H (2006) Economic benefits of adopting IFRS or US-GAAP: Have the expected costs of equity capital really decreased? Journal of Business Finance and Accounting 33: 329-373.

6. El-Gazzar SM, Finn PM, Jacob R (1999) An empirical investigation of multinational firms' compliance with international accounting standards. The International Journal of Accounting 34: 239-248.

7. Goodwin J, Ahmedand K, Heaney R (2008) The Effects of International Financial Reporting Standards on the Accounts and Accounting Quality of Australian Firms: A Retrospective Study. Journal of Contemporary Accounting & Economics 4: 89-119.

8. Haller A, Ernstberger J, Froschhammer M (2009) Implications of the mandatory transition from national GAAP to IFRS-Empirical evidence from Germany. Advances in Accounting 25: 226-236.

9. Iatridis G (2010) International Financial Reporting Standards and the quality of financial statement information, International Review of Financial Analysis 19: 193-204.

10. Jermakowicz EK, Gornik-Tomaszewski S (2006) Implementing IFRS from the perspective of EU publicly traded companies. Journal of International Accounting, Auditing and Taxation 16: 170-196.

11. Lang MJ, Raedy J, Yetman M (2003) How representative are firms that are cross listed in the United States? An analysis of accounting quality. Journal of Accounting Research 41: 363-386.

12. Marchal S, Boukari M, Cayssials JL (2007) L'impact des normes IFRS sur les données comptables des groupes français cotés, Bulletin de la Banque de France 163: 27-42.

13. Mahender K, Sharma (2013) IFRS & India – its problems and challenges. International Multidisciplinary Research Journal 1: 1-5.

14. Nobes CW (1981) An empirical investigation of international accounting principles: A comment. Journal of Accounting Research 19: 268-280.

15. Poria, Saxena, Vandana (2009) IFRS Implementation and Challenges. MEDC Monthly Economic Digest.

16. Perramon J, Amat O (2007) IFRS Introduction And Its Effect On Listed Companies In Spain, Social Science Electronic Publishing, Inc.

17. Sunita Ajaykumar Rai (2012) IFRS- Problems and Challenges in First Time Adoption. International Indexed & Referred Research Journal 1: 2250-2556.

18. Ann Tarca (2012) The Case for Global Accounting Standards: Arguments and Evidence. Social Science Electronic Publishing, Inc.

19. The Institute of Chartered Accountants of India (2007) 58th Annual Report, New Delhi.

20. Van Tendeloo B, Vanstraelen A (2005) Earnings management under German GAAP versus IFRS. European Accounting Review 14: 155-180.

10

Corporate Governance and Financial Performance of Listed Deposit Money Banks in Nigeria

Abdulazeez DA*, NdibeL and Mercy AM
Federal University of Technology, Minna, Niger, Nigeria

Abstract

Effective management of organizational resources requires good corporate governance practice particularly in banking industry where there is management/shareholders separation. Since the introduction of corporate governance code after the CBN consolidation exercise in 2005, corporate governance has attracted an unprecedented attention of researchers. However, the sample sizes as well as the number of years covered by previous researches were considered inadequate to generalize findings. It is against this backdrop that the study examined the impact of corporate governance on the financial performance of all listed deposit money banks in Nigeria for a period of seven (7) years (after consolidation). Data for the study were quantitatively retrieved from the annual reports and accounts of the studied banks. Multico linearity test was conducted via Pearson correlation and further confirmed through VIF test. Regression was used to analyze the data and it was found that larger board size contributes positively and significantly to the financial performance of deposit money banks in Nigeria. The study however, recommended among others that banks should increase their board size but within the maximum limit set by the code of corporate governance.

Keywords: Corporate governance; Audit committee; CEO duality; Board size; Board composition; Firm size; Return on asset

Introduction

Corporate governance has become a topical issue which has attracted the attention of academic scholars and practitioners. Revelations of corporate fraud all over the world in the past years have clearly shaken investors' confidence and historical antecedents in financial practices have indicated that financial crisis is the direct consequence of poor corporate governance [1]. For instance, the Enron saga and the crash of sub-prime mortgage institutions which led to the last global financial crisis. These problems transferred to other parts of the world through globalization which makes countries of the world to be interconnected as a result of trade liberalization and advancement in technology (telecommunication and transportation).

Africa particularly Nigeria had its own share of the contagious financial crises. In the recent past, financial institutions in Nigeria witnessed untold financial distress in which banks that were considered healthy by investors happened to be the most distressed. This made the Securities and Exchange Commission (SEC) in 2003 to posit that, the financial sector attracted poor corporate governance as a result of the fact that about 40% of companies including banks quoted in the exchange had recognized code of corporate governance. Subsequently, in 2003, the Nigerian Securities and Exchange Commission rolled out a code of best practices on corporate governance for all public quoted companies.

The banking sector crisis remained a subject of concern because of its role in facilitating and stimulating economic development. This however made the apex bank (CBN) to take a bold step in revitalizing the banking sector through the stipulation of N25 billion naira capital bases for all banks in Nigeria. This led to the emergence of 25 commercial banks in Nigeria as 31st December, 2005. In 2006, the Central bank of Nigeria issued a code of corporate governance to complement the existing one and the provisions of the new code were said to be indispensable in achieving viable and successful banking practice.

Since the issuance of the code of corporate governance by the CBN,

efforts have been made to evaluate its impact on the performance of banks. From empirical perspective, efforts aimed at studying the impact of corporate governance among scholars have yielded varying outcome where a consensus is yet to be reached. This led to continuous study in the area of corporate governance and the performance of banks in the post consolidation era. Most of the resent post consolidation studies on corporate governance and bank performance covered five years period with some of them using primary data. Majority of those that used secondary data have either used statistical package for social sciences (SPSS) as analytical software or covered less than the listed banks, example of studies in this category are [2-5]. There is therefore the need to increase the number of years of study, the sample size and to use different statistical software so as increase the reliability of findings. It is based on this vacuum created by previous studies that this study intends to fill.

The thrust of this study therefore is to examine the impact of corporate governance on the performance of Nigerian banks after consolidation.

Literature Review

Corporate governance

According to the Central Bank of Nigeria (CBN) code of corporate governance for banks and other financial institutions in Nigeria, corporate governance is the process by which the business activities of an institution are directed and managed. Adeusi et al. [6], explained

*Corresponding author: Abdulazeez DA, Federal University of Technology, Minna, Niger, Nigeria, E-mail: daniyad3rd@yahoo.com

that corporate governance is a set of rules and incentives through which the management of an organization is being directed and controlled. However, Lemo [7] emphasized that corporate governance consists of body of rules of the game by which companies are managed. This view was extended by Demaki [8] that, corporate governance is an institutional arrangement that checks the excesses of controlling managers. The whole essence of corporate governance according to Kajola [9] is to ensure that the business is run well and investors receive a fair return. A firm is said to have observed corporate governance rule if the firm is managed with diligence, transparency, responsibility and accountability aimed at maximizing shareholders' wealth [10]. Akinsulire [11] explained that, corporate governance is a term which covers the general mechanisms by which management is led to act in the best interest of the company owners. Corporate performance according to Adegbemi et al. [3] is an important concept which relates to the ways and manners in which the resources (human, machine, finance) of an institution are effectively used to achieve the overall corporate objective of an organization. What keeps an organization in business is simply its ability of judiciously use its available resources and make sure that the providers of economic resources and its managers mutually benefit from the use of the resources.

Though there exist different views about how scholars integrate the concept of governance but, however, at the end, they tend to point toward the same direction which is to ensure the well-being of the owners of organizations. A wider or broader rather than a narrow view of corporate governance should be adopted in the banking sector because of the peculiar contractual nature of banking which requires the extension of corporate governance benefit to depositors [4]. This broader view makes a lot of sense because apart from using owners' found in business transactions, money deposited by depositors are also used for business investment purposes, hence the need for broader view.

Review of related empirical studies

Generally studies which examine the relationship between corporate governance and firm performance can be grouped into two. The first group relates to examination of the relationship between corporate governance variables and some performance indicators across firms in various industries. This area is largely dominated by the studies of [6,8,12,13]. The second group consists of cross-sectional analysis which analyses specific governance variables or proxies against selected performance measures in a given industry such as banking over a period of time. Quite a large number of studies in this second category have been carried out some of which are found relevant to this research.

Board size and financial performance

Ajola et al. [4] studied the effect of corporate governance on the performance of Nigerian banking sector using the Pearson Correlation and Regression to analyze the relationship between corporate governance variables and banks' performance and found that a negative but significant relationship exist between board size and the financial performance of the selected banks covering a period of five years. Bawa and Lubabah [2] examined corporate governance and financial performance of banks on twelve banks in Nigeria covering a period of five years (2006-2010) and found negative relationship between board size and profitability of banks.

However, the study carried out by Akpan and Rima [5] on eleven (11) selected banks in Nigeria using linear regression analysis arrived at a conclusion which also tallies with the finding of Asuagwu [14], that smaller board size positively and significantly enhance performance and Yoshikawa and Phan [15] added that larger board size increases agency cost.

Mansi and Reeb [16] argued that larger board is better than smaller board size in that larger board size have the ability to push the managers to track lower cost of debt because creditors believe that such firms are more effective monitors of accounting process. This position is in consonance with the findings of Adeusi et al. [6] who also examined the effect of board size on the performance of ten selected banks for a period of six years (2005-2010) using econometric model of linear regression and found that increasing number of board size increases the performance of banks. The findings of Prakash and Martin (ND) on a study of corporate governance and efficiency in Nepalese commercial banks revealed that bigger board size lead to efficiency in commercial banks.

Board composition and financial performance

Weisbach, Hermalin and Weisbach [12], posited that the proposition of board composition is to help reduce agency problem. From this position, a positive relationship is expected between firm performance and the proportion of outside directors sitting on the board. Conflicting empirical evidence has evolved with respect to board composition in the recent past.

There exist mixed results from empirical studies on the effects of board composition and performance. Kajola [9] examined corporate governance and firm performance on some Nigerian listed banks between 2000 and 2006 and found no significant relationship between board composition and firm performance. This outcome has also, the support of [2,6,12,17] who further added that the performance of banks tends to be worse when there are more external board members.

However, the findings of Prakash and Martin (n.d.) on twenty-nine (29) Nepalese banks for a period of six (6) via the use of regression analysis, shows that outside directors have positive and significant effect on the bank performance. This is also the position taken by Bawa and Lubabah [2] and Ezzamel and Watson [18]. The code of corporate governance emphasizes board composition that has qualitative, qualified, experienced members and people of proven integrity [2]. Benerd et al. [19] argued that the board of directors' ability to monitor and advise a firm depends on their influence, competence and experience. This will reduce fraud and increase performance.

Audit committee size and financial performance

Shareholders' interests are protected through the activities of audit committee because management may not always act in the interest of corporation's owners. Studies in favour of larger audit committee posited that when more people are involved in checking the activities of managers, wrongdoings will be reduced and performance will be enhanced. A number of studies which revealed positive relationship between audit committee size and firm performance include [20,21]. However, other researchers like [9,22] reported that there is no positive relationship between audit committee size and the performance of firms. From the foregoing, there exist a mixed reaction with respect to the relationship between audit committee size and firm performance. The position of Prakash and Martins make logical sense as the interest of shareholders can be protected by a number of individuals who will be difficult to manipulate especially when they are large in number.

Chief Executive Officer (CEO) duality and financial performance

When an organization is structured in a way that the Chief Executive Officer (CEO) also serves as the Chairman of the board of directors of the same firm, then there is duality in the function of the CEO [23]. Orwall and Gentile cited in Mansur and Bawa [2] posited that CEO duality does not encourage effective communication between the CEO and the board. In order to enhance performance therefore, CEO duality should be discouraged in its totality.

Though there is evidence that having independent Chairman still does not prevent misconduct and malpractices [24]. Studies which examined the relationship between CEO duality and performance include Daily and Dalton, cited in Mansur and Bawa [2] and Calligham [23] and they found significant relationship between CEO duality and firm performance while Rhoades, Rechner and Murthy [25] found no significant relationship in firms having executive duality and performance. Also, in the work of Yermeela, cited in Kajola [9], evidence from 452 sampled USA public firms revealed that agency problems are higher when the same person occupies the position of CEO as well as that of the Chairman of the board.

From the reviewed empirical studies on the effect of corporate governance on the performance of banks in Nigeria, scholars appear to have varying conclusions. The position of scholars that posited that larger board size influences performance makes logical sense. This is because when more individuals are brought into the board, it increases the managerial ability of the bank as divergent views that will lead to proper positioning of bank are brought to bear thereby contributing meaningfully to the organization. This study also takes side with scholars' position on increased non-executive members on the board but the level of competence and experience of these non-executives is also of utmost important.

The significant positive relationship between audit committee and performance is also logical as that will protect the interest of the owner since manipulations will be difficult without collusion. Also CEO duality appears the best way for managing the activities of an organization because decision taken by one person can be challenged by another person thereby propelling the organization towards better performance.

Theoretical framework

Smith was the earliest known economist that addressed the theoretical issues of the role of board of directors in the governance of firms [14]. Smith further observed that as a result of the fact that managers control resources other than theirs, it should not be expected that they will watch over the business with anxious vigilance as possibility of negligence abound. Negligence is the direct consequence of the separation of ownership from control which is very common in Modern Corporation [12]. The need to explain the theoretical framework within which the owners' and managers' relationship exist becomes indispensable.

Theories which are used to explain corporate governance and firm performance include and not limited to the following:

The stewardship theory: Donaldson and Davis, cited in Akingunola et al. [1], explained that managers are good stewards who diligently work to attain high level of profit and shareholders' returns. This theory is based on the assumption that managers are motivated by achievement. Non-executive directors on the board serve this purpose better.

The stakeholder's theory: This theory states that the firm is a system of stakeholders operating within a larger system of the society which provides the required legal and market infrastructure for the firm to thrive. The purpose of the firm in this case is to serve the general public who may have direct or indirect relationship with the firm. The management and the provision of information should be directed at satisfying the interest of the general public rather than shareholders.

Agency theory: This theory sees shareholders as the principals and management as their agents. Sanda et al. [12] explained further that the presence of information asymmetry can make agents to pursue interest that may be detrimental to the interest of the principal. The process of aligning these two interests can ignite conflict between the interest groups. In agency theory unlike stakeholder theory managers only optimize principal's objective rather optimizing multiple objectives.

From the foregoing, agency theory practically explains corporate governance and firm performance especially in the banking sector where the basic tenet of corporate governance is to protect the interests of absentee owners (shareholders) who are also the principal of the management (agents). On the basis, this study adopts agency theory alongside [1,12,14] as the theoretical basis for explaining corporate governance and bank performance.

Methodology

Research design

This study employs ex-post facto research design using panel data for the periods under study (2006-2012) as it allows for the collection of past and multi-dimensional data which provide basis for the full establishment of the relationship between corporate governance and the financial performance of banks in Nigeria.

Population and sample size

The study uses all the banks that scale through the Central Bank of Nigeria (CBN) consolidation exercise which ended on the 31st December, 2005. These banks were so used because they were considered viable and were seen to have the required financial wherewithal to carry on banking business in Nigeria. Also, the CBN code of corporate governance which regulates the operating activities of the consolidated banks was issued shortly after consolidation in 2006. As at December, 2005 (year of consolidation), only twenty five (25) banks emerged as most healthy banks in Nigeria. Table 1 therefore, shows the list of those banks.

From the above listed banks, a working population was drawn base on certain criterion. The criterion used in selecting the working population was based on the listing status of the banks on the Nigeria stock exchange. This is because only listed banks can be termed public banks (Plc.) which are also expected to comply fully with the requirements of CBN code of corporate governance. Also, being listed enabled the researcher to have access to the banks' annual reports.

Table 2 therefore shows the list of banks listed on the Nigeria stock exchange with their respective years of listing.

The working population of this study consists of fifteen listed banks. However, these banks are also taken as the sample size of the study. This is done to; apart from the fact that the required data for all the aforestated banks are available, provide wider range of generalizing the findings as previous studies in this area covered fewer banks. Functionally, wp = n, where wp equals working population

S. No	Name of Banks
1	Access Bank
2	Afri Bank
3	Eco Bank
4	Equitorial Trust Bank
5	Diamond Bank
6	Guarranty Trust Bank
7	Fidelity Bank
8	First City Monument Bank
9	First Bank
10	First Inland Bank
11	IBTC Chartered Bank
12	Intercontinental Bank PLC
13	Nig. Intercontinental/City Bank
14	Oceanic Bank
15	Platinum Bank
16	Skye Bank
17	Spring Bank
18	Stanbic Bank
19	Standard Chartered Bank
20	Sterling Bank
21	United Bank For Africa
22	Union Bank
23	Unity Bank
24	Wema Bank
25	Zenith Bank

Source: CBN press conference release, 16th January, 2006
Table 1: Study population.

S/N	Banks	YEAR OF LISTING
1	Eco Bank PLC	2006
2	Guarranty Trust Bank (GTB) PLC	1996
3	Fidelity Bank PLC	2005
4	Stanbic IBTC PLC	2005
5	Sterling Bank PLC	1993
6	Wema Bank PLC	1991
7	First Bank PLC	1971
8	United Bank For Africa (UBA) PLC	1970
9	Diamond Bank PLC	2005
10	First City Monument Bank (FCMB) PLC	2004
11	Skye Bank PLC	2005
12	Union Bank PLC	1970
13	Unity Bank PLC	2005
14	Zenith PLC	2004
15	Access Bank PLC	1998

Source: Generated from NSE fact book 2012
Table 2: Listed (public) banks in Nigeria.

and 'n' equals sample size. Bawa and Lubabah [2], also used working population as sample size in their study.

Variables specification and measurements

There are two basic variables used in this study. They are corporate governance (independent) and financial performance (dependent) variables respectively.

Dependent variable and its measurement

The dependent variable used in this study is the performance of banks which the researcher proxied by; Return on asset (ROA) measured by dividing the netprofit after tax by the total assets to examine how productive the banks' assets have been used to generate wealth. This method of measurement is in line with the work of Akpan [5].

Independent variable and its measurement

Corporate governance is the independent variable with the following proxies and measurements.

Board size (BS): This is the total number of directors sitting on the board of a particular bank which in line with the code of corporate governance should not be more than 20. This study examines the extent to which bank performance will be affected by the size of the board.

Board composition (BC): This is the number of non-executive directors on the board and it is measured by the percentage of outside directors (non-executive directors) on the total board members.

CEO duality (CD): CEO duality exists when a single person holds both the position of chairman and MD/CEO of the company. For banks with CEO as the chairman, a one (1) value is assigned and zero (o) otherwise [12].

Audit committee (AC): This is taken as the total number of members in the audit committee. It is expected that the higher the number though within the limit set by code of corporate governance, the better the performance [26].

Control variable

Firm size (FS) is used as the control variable which is measured by the total value of each bank's assets. Because the values for total assets were too large for the regression analysis, then log of the assets was used to reduce the values. This control variable was introduced because of the notion that performance may also be affected by other factors not captured in the independent variables in which firm size is one [6].

Method of data collection and data analysis

The data used in this research were generated from the audited annual financial statements of the 15 banks under study covering a period of 7 years (2006-2012). This method of data collection was adopted because of the availability of data, convenience as well as the nature of the research design which required past and documented facts as basis for performance evaluation. This study used regression analysis in measuring the collected data via statistical software 'stata version 11' to examine the relationship between the identified variables andto confirm the viability of previous findings.

Model specification

This study adopts and modifies the econometric model used by Adeusi et al. [6] which is given as follows:

$$Y_{it} = a_0 + \beta_1 CG_{it} + \beta_2 C_{it} + e_{it}$$

Where: Y_{it} represents bank performance variable; Return on Assets (ROA) for bank in time t, a_0 is the constant term, CG_{it} is a vector of corporate governance variables; Board Size (BS), Board Composition (BC), CEO duality (CD), Audit committee (AC), C_{it} is a vector of control variable 'Size of the firm' (FS) and e_{it}, is the error term. The model is modified thus;

$$ROA_{it} = a_0 + \beta_1 BS_{it} + \beta_2 BC_{it} + \beta_3 CD_{it} + \beta_4 AC_{it} + \beta_5 FS_{it} + e_{it}$$

Data Analysis and Discussion

The data sets are summarized in Table 1 below, which provides the summary statistics. The correlation matrix between the variables is also provided in Tables 2 and 3.

Of the 15 banks studied, the mean board size is about fourteen (14) which suggests that banks in Nigeria have relatively moderate board sizes as the mean value 14 is greater than the average of the maximum number of board size of 20. Also, with a maximum board size of twenty (20) and standard deviation of 2.47319, it implies that banks in Nigeria have relatively similar board sizes. The mean description for board composition is high compare to the maximum board composition suggesting that the ratio of outside directors to the total number of directors in Nigerian banks is very high. Generally, the summary for the standard deviation reveals that factors that influence performance are evenly distributed across all the banks. However CEO duality will be omitted from subsequent analyses because of lack of collinearity (Table 4).

There is no high correlation among the determinant variables used in measuring return on asset which shows that the predictive ability of each of the combined independent variables are different (Table 5).

Multi-collinearity exists when the predictor variables are themselves highly correlated. If the variables have VIF of above 10 and TV less than 0.10, then there is a strong indication of the existence of excess correlation, Gujarati. With the above values of VIF, all of which are less than 10 and the values of TV which are also more than 0.10, there is therefore absence of multi-collinearity (Table 6).

The regression results presented in Table 3 above show that both board composition and firm size are negatively and insignificantly related to the performance of banks. However, audit committee has positive but insignificant relationship with performance.

Board size is positive and significant at 5 per cent on bank performance. The result indicates that increase in board size would increase the performance of the banks. The R^2 of 0.0608 suggests that the independent variables used can only account for about 6% of the banks' performance while other factors and variables not included in this study account for the remaining percentage.

From The above regression result, it shows that increase in board size would increase the performance of the banks. This result therefore takes side with studies that support the view that larger board size is better for corporate performance than smaller board size because in larger board, members have a wide range of expertise to help make better decisions and are also difficult for a powerful CEO to dominate.

The finding of this study is consistent with the findings of Adeusi [6] who all found bigger board size better than smaller board size in terms of contribution to performance of banks. This study therefore, does not support the views of [4,5,14,27] who all concluded that smaller board size contributes more to performance than larger board size [28-30].

Conclusion and Recommendation

The relationship between corporate governance and the financial performance of listed deposit money banks in Nigeria from 2006 to 2012 has been explored using data collected from the financial statements of all the fifteen listed (15) deposit money banks in the Nigerian stock exchange and it was discovered that bigger board size contributes more to performance than smaller board size. Also, when a board size is large, it will be difficult for a person (may be CEO) to dominate the board and decisions reached by the board are seen to have emanated from sound and constructive arguments. The result of the summary statistics revealed that the proportion of non-

Variable	Obs	Mean	Std.Dev.	Min	Max
roa	105	0.2955683	2.569893	-0.22713	26.3155
bs	105	14.13333	2.47319	7	20
bc	105	0.6143722	0.0899756	0.285714	0.857143
cd	105	0	0	0	0
ac	105	5.990476	0.325081	4	8
fs	105	20.00392	1.152296	14.23428	21.73438

Source: generated from the financial statements of the studied banks using stata (version 11)

Table 3: Descriptive Statistics of the Variables.

	roa	bs	bc	ac	fs
roa	1	1			
bs	0.2338	0.0068			
bc	-0.0706	-0.0223	1		
ac	0.0029	-0.0223	0.0088	1	
fs	-0.0218	0.0269	-0.0231	-0.0149	1

Source: generated from the financial statements of the studied banks using stata (version 11)

Table 4: Correlation matrix for the variables.

Variable	VIF	1/VIF
bc	1.01	0.987146
fs	1.01	0.987308
ac	1	0.998302
bs	1	0.998796
Mean VIF	1.01	

Source: generated from the financial statements of the studied banks using stata (version 11)

Table 5: Test of Multi-collinearity

roa	coef.	Std.Err.	t	P > [t]	[95%Conf.Interval]	
bs	0.244452	0.100764	2.43	0.017	0.044538	0.444365
bc	-2.082735	2.76892	-0.75	0.454	-7.576192	3.410732
ac	0.0663171	0.7664216	0.09	0.931	-1.454242	1.586876
fs	-0.662644	0.2162941	-0.31	0.76	-0.4953858	0.362857
-Cons	-0.9514985	6.743251	-0.14	0.888	-14.32992	12.42692

R^2 = 0.0608

Source: Generated from the financial statements of the studied banks using stata (version 11)

Table 6: Regression Result.

executive director serving in the boards of banks are high and this is in compliance with the specification of corporate governance code which specifies that the number of non-executive directors should be higher than the executive directors. Of to continue to enjoy the advantage of larger board size, efforts should be directed at bringing on board those with relevant credentials, competence and wide range of experience.

Sequel to the findings of this study, it is recommended that the size of the board (membership) should be increased but not exceeding the maximum number specified by the code of corporate governance for banks.

References

1. Akingunola RO, Olusegun B, Adedipe (2013) Corporate governance and banks performance in Nigeria (post bank consolidation). European Journal of Business and Social Sciences 2: 89-111.

2. Lubabah M, Bawa A (2013) Board composition, executive duality and performance of banks in the post consolidated era in Nigeria. International Journal of Academic Research in Economics and Management Sciences 2: 109-122.

3. Adegbemi O, Donald IE, Ismail O (2012) Corporate Governance and Bank Performance: A Pooled Study of Selected Banks in Nigeria. European Scientific Journal 8: 155-164.

4. Ajola O, Amuda T, Arulogum L (2012) Evaluating the Effects of Corporate Governance on the Performance of Nigerian Banking Sector. Review of Contemporary Business Research 1: 32-42.

5. Akpan E, Roman HB (2012) Does corporate governance affect bank profitability Evidence from Nigeria. American International Journal of Contemporary Research 2: 135-145.

6. Adeusi S, Akeke N, Aribaba F, Adebisi O (2013) Corporate Governance and Firm Financial Performance: Do Ownership and Board Size Matter. Academic Journal of Interdisciplinary Studies 2: 251-258.

7. Lemo T (2010) Keynote address of the 34th conference of ICSAN. Lagos.

8. Demaki GO (2011) Proliferation of codes of corporate governance in Nigeria and economy development. Business Management Review 1: 1-7.

9. Kajola S (2008) Corporate governance and firm performance: The case of Nigerian listed firms. European Journal of Economic, Finance and Administrative Sciences 16-28.

10. Pandey IM (2005) Financial management. 9th edtn, Vikas Publishing House RT Ltd, India

11. Akinsulire O (2006) Financial management. 4th edtn, Lagos: Gemosl Nigeria Ltd, Nigeria

12. Sanda A, Mikailu S, Garba T (2005) Corporate governance mechanisms and firm financial performance in Nigeria. African Economic Research Consortium, Nairobi, Kenya.

13. Brown LD, Caylor MI (2004) Corporate governance and firm performance. Georgia State University, Georgia, USA.

14. Asuagwu G (2013) Implication of Corporate Governance on the Performance of Deposit Money Banks in Nigeria. Arabian Journal of Business and Management review (OMAN Chapter) 2: 107-119.

15. Yashinkawa T, Phan P (2003) The performance implication of ownership-driven governance reform. European Management Journal 21: 698-706.

16. Anderson R, Mansi S, Reeb D (2004) Board Characteristics, Accounting Report, Integrity and the Cost Of Debt. Journal of Accounting and Economics 37: 315-342.

17. Bhagat S, Black B (2002) The non correlation between board independence and long term firm performance. Journal of Corporation Law 27.

18. Essamel M, Watson R (1993) Organizational form, ownership structure and corporate performance: A contextual empirical analysis of UK companies. British Journal of Management 4: 161-176.

19. Benard J, Chrourou, Courteau L (2004) The effect of audit committee expertise, independence and activity on aggressive earnings management. Auditing Journal of Practice and Theory 23: 13-35.

20. Blao X, Wallace N, Peter J (2003) Earnings management and corporate governance: The roles of the board and the audit committee. Journal of Corporate Finance 9: 295-316.

21. Kyereboah CA (2007) Corporate governance and firm performance in Africa: A dynamic panel data analysis. A paper prepared for the international conference on corporate governance in emerging markets, Global Corporate Governance Forum and Asian Institute of Corporate Governance, Istanbul, Turkey.

22. Hardwick P, Adams M, Zou H (2003) Corporate governance and cost efficiency in the United Kingdom life insurance Industry. European Business Management School, London, UK.

23. Callaghan MA (2005) The relationship between chief executives officer's duality and subsequent corporate financial performance. Being a dissertation submitted to the University of Capall in partial fulfillment for the award of Doctor of Philosophy.

24. Damato K (2004) SEC to seek independent chairmen on fund boards. The wall Street Journal.

25. Rhoades D, Rechners P, Sundaramurthy C (2001) A mental analysis of board leadership structure and financial performance: Are two heads better than one' corporate governance.

26. Klein A (2002) Audit committee, board of directors' characters and earnings management. Journal of Accounting and Economics 33: 375-400.

27. Bawa A, Lubabah M (2012) Corporate Governance and Financial Performance of Banks in the Post Consolidated Era in Nigeria. International Journal of Science and Humanity Studies 4: 1309-8063.

28. (2006) CBN Code of Corporate Governance.

29. Choe H, Lee B (2003) Korean bank governance reform after Asian financial crisis. Pacific-Basin Finance Journal 11: 483-508.

30. Gujarati DN (2004) Basic Econometrics. 4th edtn, McGraw-Hill, USA.

11

Adoption and use of IFRS: Evidence from Brazil

Marta Cristina Pelucio-Grecco[1]*, Cecília Moraes Santostaso Geron[2] and Gerson Begas Grecco[3]

[1]*PhD in Business Administration by Mackenzie Presbyterian University, Professor at Financial and Actuarial Accounting Research Institute Foundation - FIPECAFI Faculty,Brazil*
[2]*Department of Accounting, University of São Paulo, Professor at Mackenzie Presbyterian University, Rua São Bento, 545 – 5SL, São Paulo, 01011-904, Brazil*
[3]*Department of Accounting, Mackenzie Presbyterian University, Rua Dr. Gabriel dos Santos, 794 – apto 111, São Paulo, 01231-010, Brazil*

Abstract

We did a survey based on DOI - Diffusion of Innovation Theory, made with preparers and users concerning IFRS in Brazil. Both recognize the improvement in the quality of the accounting information after the Brazilian convergence to IFRS. The Full IFRS adoption contributes to improving the company image, representing relative advantage of accounting and of the preparers, when they are most valued in the market. The analysts trust more in the audited and published statements, though great part of the preparers in general only do it when obligatory. The preparers that work in SME recognize more the IFRS benefits than the ones that work in larger companies. The IFRS financial statements are also utilized for making internal decisions, especially by micro enterprises and by small sized companies. The analysts highlight that they still have difficulties in understanding the financial statements in the light of IFRS.

Keywords: IFRS; SME; DOI

Introduction

IFRS (International Financial Reporting Standards) is present in 138 jurisdictions around the world, including all the countries belonging to G20. In most of these jurisdictions IFRS is also required or allowed to privately held companies and in 50% of such jurisdictions IFRS for SME is allowed or required [1].

Small and medium sized corporations are extremely important for the financial health and stability of global economy. They represent most of the Gross Domestic Product (GDP) of the planet, besides generating most of the jobs and having the key for the recovery of the world economy [2]. According to IFRS [3], it is estimated that 96% of the companies around the world are SME.

IFRS Foundation has already signed bilateral agreements – Memoranda of Understanding (MoUs) with other international boards (Accounting Standards Advisory Forum – ASAF; European Securities and Markets Authority – ESMA; International Actuarial Association – IAA; International Federation of Accountants – IFAC; International Integrated Reporting Council – IIRC; International Organization of Securities Commissions – IOSCO; International Valuation Standards Council – IVSC) and with three jurisdictions (Brazil, Japan and the United States) [4].

Many studies have been directed to analyze the impact of IFRS adoption around the world and specially to analyze the quality of the accounting information in the period post implementation. The perception of academics and professionals related to the area is that the convergence to IFRS is beneficial to the market as a whole [5]. Additionally Macías and Muiño [6] noticed that in the European countries where there is a local accounting norm for individual accounting statements concomitant with IFRS for consolidated account statements, the quality of the accounting information is inferior compared to the countries that do not have such duality. Some countries, especially the ones under development process, have faced difficulties in the IFRS implementation process [7] and mainly to suit IFRS for SME in the local reality [8].

In Brazil, all listed companies and financial institutions are required to issue IFRS since 2010. For the local standardization, CPC - Accounting Pronounce Board, was created, its norms are issued in compliance with IFRS, with no modifications. Being so, by means of local standardization, full IFRS is required from all large sized companies (Full CPC, equivalent to Full IFRS).

For all other Brazilian companies, the ones that are not considered large sized companies, IFRS for SME is required, by means of an equivalent local norm named CPC PME; those companies are allowed to apply Full IFRS.

In addition, Brazilian companies considered micro enterprises can still make use of a local norm, instead of IFRS for SME, named Simplified Bookkeeping, which is not equivalent to IFRS.

Another important issue to be taken into account is the local cultural influence in the accounting, as observed by Masca [9] in his study regarding IFRS for SME in Europe. In Brazil, there has always been a history of influence of tax legislation in the accounting practices adopted in the country, although the process of Brazilian convergence to IFRS has fetched a detachment of accounting for corporate purposes from tax purposes, this influence was always noticed in Brazil.

Studies in Brazil and around the world analyze the effective use of new accounting practices in small and medium sized companies. In Brazil, studies show that the new practices have not been widely adopted [10,11], the reasons are: (a) There is not a penalty for not adopting IFRS for SME in Brazil and use of accounting practices before 2008, before the IFRS adoption in Brazil [12]; (b) the accounting information of small and medium sized companies are not used by external users of those companies; (c) there is the influence of fiscal rules in accounting

*Corresponding author: Marta Cristina PELUCIO-GRECCO, PhD in Business Administration by Mackenzie Presbyterian University, Professor at Financial and Actuarial Accounting Research Institute Foundation - FIPECAFI Faculty,Brazil
E-mail: marta.pelucio@praesum.com.br

of our country [12]; (d) low level of efforts for its adoption concerning accounting professionals as well as the companies [13]. It is interesting to notice that Gonzáles and Nagai [13] and Masera and Orth [14] state that IFRS for SME has legal efficacy once its adoption is legally required.

In other parts of the world, the discussion is similar to Brazil: (a) the compliance to these practices is not monitored as it happens in the listed companies [15] and the country tax system can be an obstacle to the adoption [16,17]. Besides that, Quagli [18] observed a vast research in continental Europe, where the responsible ones for the preparation of the accounting statements showed a stronger opposition to the accounting practices implementation for small and medium sized companies and the users of such information are favorable to the new practices.

Based on the described scenario, it has been highlighted the following research problem: What is the acceptance of the Brazilian accounting practices set by its preparers and by external users?

The general objective of this paper was to verify which set of accounting practices is adopted by the financial statements preparers of companies which adoption is alternative and the acceptance of this set of norms by external users in order to verify effectively which ones are used in the practice of their analyses.

To meet the overall objective of this paper, some specific objectives were observed:

• Identify which are the variable demographic determiners in the adoption process, according to the Theory Reasoned Action Fishbein and Ajzen [19];

• Identify which are the perception differences in relation to the applicable norms set, among preparers and external users according to Theory Reasoned Action Fishbein and Ajzen [19];

• Identify which are the factors realized by the preparers and the external users in their decisions for the innovation accounting adoption in Brazil, according to Diffusion of Innovations, Rogers [20].

Theoretic and Practical Justification

From 2014, the Provisional Measure 627/13, converted into law 12.973/14, defines the fiscal treatment of the new accounting practices adopted in Brazil. This way, as it occurred in the decree law issue 1.598 in 1977, fiscal law adopts the accounting practices and there is the possibility of a greater adhesion by small and medium sized companies due to fiscal demanding. Therefore, researches play an important role in order to check if the fiscal law becomes a motivating factor instead of a demotivating factor of the new accounting practices for small and medium sized companies.

Besides that, it is important to verify the perception of external users regarding the accounting practices, once according to IFRS for SME, this is the objective of the norm, to provide information for these users. Concerning this issue, there is not any Brazilian research about the theme.

It is expected that the results of this Project contribute with relevant information to (a) preparers of accounting information for identifying the expectations of the users regarding financial information; (b) class entities, for identifying the determiners for the adoption of accounting practices for small and medium sized companies, for determining training future policies for the accounting information preparers; (c) IFRS foundation and International Accounting Standards Board (IASB), for understanding the necessities of financial information that the market has, for collaborating in the alteration studies of such pronounces.

Theoretic References

Brazilian accounting practices

Due to the convergence process to IFRS, there are three sets of applicable accounting norms in Brazil since 2010, according to the company size: Full IFRS for listed companies and large sized companies; IFRS for SME and Simplified book keeping (local norm that is not equivalent to IFRS) for micro enterprises.

In Brazil, the concept of a large sized company is determined by the Law11.638/07: they are companies under common control, that in the previous year presented assets superior to R$ 240 million or annual gross revenue superior to R$ 300 million. These companies must apply Full IFRS.

Small and medium sized companies are the ones that do not correspond to the explanation above and must apply IFRS for SME. Nevertheless, these companies can opt for using the Full IFRS.

IFRS for SME was adopted by CFC (Federal Accounting Council), that rules the accounting profession and is in charge of issuing Brazilian Accounting Norms, named by this board as NBC TG 1000 (Brazilian accounting norm general technic 1000), through the resolution CFC no 1.255, December 10, 2009.

Micro enterprises and small sized companies in Brazil (companies with revenue up to R$ 3,6 million annually) has its bookkeeping very simplified, which must be performed in compliance with ITG 1000, approved by resolution CFC 1.330/11, named Simplified Bookkeeping. Nevertheless, they still can opt for IFRS for SME or Full IFRS.

In Table 1 the types of companies are described and its respective set of applicable accounting norms.

According to the research released by IBPT- Brazilian Institute of Planning and Tax, there were 16.002.903 companies in Brazil in 30/09/13. In Table 2, the percentage of these companies per size.

According to the size division of IBPT, represented in Table 2, there is not distinction of large sized companies, according to the concept of the law 11.638/07, there to say, revenue over R$ 300 million. Among large sized companies, according to IBPT, a set of companies with revenue varying from R$ 48 and R$ 300 millionshould be included, but according to the law 11.638/07, they would be considered SME.

Type of company	Size of company	Norm to be applied	Permitted alternative
Corporation and large sized companies	Total Assets >R$ 240 million or Revenue >R$ 300 million	Full IFRS	It does not exist
Small and medium sized companies	Total Assets <R$ 240 million or Revenue from R$ 3,6 million to $ 300 million	IFRS for SME	Full IFRS
Small sized company and micro enterprises	Revenue <R$ 3,6 million	Simplified Bookkeeping (ITG 1000)	IFRS for SME or Full IFRS

Table 1: Set of applicable accounting norms per type and size of the company.

It is noticed in Table 2, that great part of Brazilian companies is placed in the range where there is the possibility of opting for the set of applicable accounting norms. Small sized companies and micro enterprises, that can opt for the Simplified Bookkeeping, IFRS for SME or Full IFRS, correspond to 52,66% of the companies (approximated 8,4 million companies). Medium sized companies, that can opt for IFRS for SME or Full IFRS correspond to 14,79% of the companies (approximated 2,4 million companies). Besides those that would be classified as large sized companies according IBPT, cited above.

The fiscal treatment for the changes in the Brazilian accounting practices is defined by the Law 12.973/14 (Provisory Measure 627/13) that changes the Decree Law1.598/77. This way, from 2014, for the companies that adopt in advance and from 2015 for all Brazilian companies, the fiscal effect of the alteration in the accounting practices that started in 2008, will have legal basis. The difference between accounting and fiscal treatments must be tracked by fiscal authorities, considered accounting subaccounts.

Fiscal laws define the taxes calculation basis over the profit from the accounting income, defining additions and exclusions that will adjust this accounting basis for meeting tax basis. Many times, small and medium sized companies record the events using fiscal rules instead of accounting rules, for simplifying necessary internal control to segregate differences between the accounting and fiscal basis.

If high quality accounting practices (IFRS and IFRS SME) were adopted in Brazil, the companies that do not have securities in stock market or that do not depend on banks resources and do not undergo audits, would have less incentive to effectively adopt such practices due to the complexity of controlling the differences between accounting and fiscal bases in subaccounts and proper systems for attending the fiscal law.

According to Schutte and Buys [21], SME are particularly vulnerable and affected by cultural differences [22]. Stopping attending the fiscal rules to attend norms based on principles, even legally valid as in Brazil, is a great step for SME. Nevertheless, the use of a global accounting standard for SME represent a very important step on the way to the convergence to the world accounting practices, once those companies represent the majority companies of the planet [23].

Theory of diffusion of innovation

According to Rogers [20], innovation refers to ideas, practices or objects considered new by the adopter. It is noticed that the concept is very wide and it does not necessarily refer to something new, but to something considered new by the user. Being so, the analysis for the acceptance of new accounting practices will be performed according to the theory of diffusion of innovation.

Diffusion of innovation (DOI) developed by the author in his work

in 1983, defines the following noticed characteristics that influence the adoption of a technological innovation:

(a) Relative Advantage, the more the innovation is perceived as better than its precursor, the greater the chance to be adopted;

(b) Compatibility, the innovation is perceived as consistent with values, necessities and experiences of potential users;

(c) Complexity refers to the difficulty degree of the use of innovation. This aspect makes it difficult the adoption of innovation;

(d) Trialability, how the innovation can be tested or experienced before the adoption.

(e) Observability of its benefits, how the results of innovation are observed;

Rogers [20] still suggests other variables connected to internal factors to the organization, that also contribute to the adoption of the innovation, such as the type of decision for the innovation, there to say, the mental process that varies from the initial knowledge of the innovation, the formation of the attitude regarding the innovation, the decision for adopting or rejecting it, the implementation and the conformity of the decision. Other important factors are the nature of the communication means by which the innovation is introduced in the company, the nature of the involved social system and the role of the changing agent in this process.

Moore and Benbasat [24] add other perceived characteristics that influence in the adoption of a technologic innovation:

(a) Image, how the use of the innovation is perceived to improve the image of an entity that can be considered as an aspect of the Relative Advantage of Rogers.

(b) Voluntary use, the perception of the user of being free to decide for the implementation of the innovation. However, the common sense and experience indicate that there are levels of volunteering concerning the behavior of the company. Therefore, the authors cite the perception of voluntary use and not a real voluntary use of the innovation.

Theory of reasoned action

The Theory of Reasoned Action- TRA, that has its origin in the Social Psychology developed by Fishbein and Ajzen [19], considers that people evaluate what they have to lose and to win at the moment of decision.

The external variables that should be analyzed for determining the behavior, take into account the demographic variables, attitudes related to the object and personality traces.

For the development of this work, questions will be applied to verify if the following demographic variables can influence in the decision of applicable norms: gender, age, place of working and academic degree.

Concerning the relative attitudes to the object, questions will be applied to verify which of the following beliefs and motivators influence in the decisions of the motivators: difficulty in the implementation, perceived fiscal risk, perceived cost and benefits.

Methodological Procedures

This research has exploratory and descriptive nature, for according to Deslauriers and Kérisit [25] such studies explore determined questions and describe certain social situations. We used the quantitative method for treating data, because according to Bryman

Size	%	Annual Revenue
Large	2,07%	Over R$ 48 Milllion
Medium	14,79%	Over R$ 3,6 Millionto R$ 48 Million
Small	10,78%	Over R$ 360 Thousand to R$ 3,6 Million
Micro enterprises	41,88%	Up to R$ 360 Thousand
Individual enterpreneur	21,47%	Up toR$ 60 Thousand
Non-profit and Government Entities	9,01%	Regardeless of the revenue
Total	100%	

Source: IBPT (2013)

Table 2: Percentage of companies per size.

[26], it permits the highlight of differences among the people in terms of characteristics and provides consistent tools for doing so. We applied the Mann-Whitney and Kruskal Wallis non-parametric tests for comparison of variables means.

Population of this study is composed of preparers and external users of financial statements in Brazil. The sample, by convenience, was composed of ANEFAC associates- National Association of Finance Executives, Administration and Accounting; it has approximate 1500 members in different states around Brazilian territory. This association was selected for the sample due to its representativeness in different states as well as for having members with different profiles that are mentioned in this study: preparers and external users.

Data collection was performed through questionnaires sent by digital means, without identification of the respondents who accepted to take part in the research as volunteers agreeing with an informed consent form. The studies variables were highlighted using as basis DOI and TRA according to Table 3.

Results Analyses

Respondents' profile

We obtained 147 responses, being 125 preparers (P) and 22 external users (U). Most of the respondents are men (81%) and work in São Paulo city (81%), 45% of them are over 45 years old. Most of them have attended some IFRS course of short, medium or long duration (78%), only 7,5% has not attended any training course regarding IFRS and 14,3% had contact with IFRS only during graduation period. Most of them have Accounting degree (86,4%) besides having a post-graduation degree (93,2%), only 6,8% does not have post-graduation degree. In Table 4, the distribution of the respondents' profile is described into two studied categories.

Regarding the professional area, the respondents work in either small and medium sized companies or large sized companies (listed companies or not). The preparers mainly work in accounting area (51,2%), 40,6% of them render Consulting services, 26,6% work in outsourcing companies and 23,4% of them is auditors. External users

are mainly investments analysts 36, 4% or de credit analysts 27, 3% (Table 5).

Use of financial statements and influence in the accounting choices

For the understanding of the percentage presented in Table 6, it is important to notice that the accounting information preparers can use more than one set of norms in their work, once they can prepare statements for more than one company. Among the preparers, it is included service renderers that can use different sets of accounting norms for each client.

Regarding the set of adopted norms by the preparers of the financial statements, 66% say that make use of Full IFRS as basis for this preparation, being 23% of the cases, this adoption is by choice and not by obligation according to some specific legislation. Thus, it is possible to infer that companies that could use IFRS for SME or Simplified book keeping, use indeed Full IFRS. The perception that the adoption is voluntary boosts the decision for technological innovation [24], besides the compatibility of this innovation with the values of the information preparer [20]. Approximately one third (35%) of the respondents state that use IFRS for SME, what can be considered very important. According to Rogers [20], strong adhesion of an innovation occurs from a perception of relative advantage, in other words, the preparers realize IFRS as a set of accounting standards of higher quality than the previous one.

The percentage of the respondents that use fiscal standards for preparing the companies accounting where they work or their clients', in case of services renderers, is 12% which shows the influence of the fiscal laws in the Brazilian accounting practices.

Table 7 shows the external users' demands concerning financial statements. Similar to Table 6, the percentage shows that the users of financial statements can demand more than a type of information for their analyses, for example, they can demand audited financial statements and the accounting information presented in the Corporate Income Tax Return (DIPJ) of the analyzed company.

Questionnaires	Studies variables	Theoretic foundation
Identification	Age, Gender, city and stateof work, activity andsize of the company, specific training, Graduation and Post-Graduation.	TRA – demographic variables
Questionnaires for Preparers	Statement Publication	DOI – Image
	Statement auditing	TRA – demographic variables
	Set of adopted norms	DOI – volunteer use
	External public demanding (banks, clients, suppliers)	DOI – Compatibility
	Knowledge of the mangers and accountants. Joint analysis of managers and accountants. Knowledge of tax laws.	DOI – Trialability
	Perception of managers regardingtheBenefits and personal perception. Use for management.	DOI – Observability
	Difficulties in the implementation, IT problems, lack of clarityandnorms understanding	DOI – Complexity
	Position of tax authorities. Tax contingency, tax adjustments and tax effects on accounting practice.Motivating factors in the selection of norms sets	TRA – Relative attitudes to the object
Questionnaires for external users	Knowledge level	DOI – Trialability
	Importance of the use. Facility.Improvement in the quality. Quality regarding the type of norm. Comparison to other countries.	DOI – Trialability
	Relative demanding, auditing	DOI – Compatibility
	Statements Publication	DOI – Image
	Specific preference, useof tax information	DOI – Voluntary use
	Understanding difficult	DOI - Complexity
Accounting information quality	Quality regarding the type of norm. Higher quality. Higher transparency	DOI - Relative advantage

Table 3: Studies variables and theoretic foundation.

	Frequence			Percentage		
	P	U	Total	P	U	Total
Total	**125**	**22**	**147**	**85,0%**	**15,0%**	**100,0%**
Gender						
Male	101	18	119	80,8%	81,8%	81,0%
Female	24	4	28	19,2%	18,2%	19,0%
Age						
Up to 25 years old	7	3	10	5,6%	13,6%	6,8%
From 26 to 35 years old	34	7	41	27,2%	31,8%	27,9%
From 36 to 45 years old	33	3	36	26,4%	13,6%	24,5%
Over 45 years old	51	9	60	40,8%	40,9%	40,8%
Origin						
SP capital	99	20	119	79,2%	90,9%	81,0%
SP country side	8	1	9	6,4%	4,5%	6,1%
RJ	8	0	8	6,4%	0,0%	5,4%
MG	2	0	2	1,6%	0,0%	1,4%
BA	3	0	3	2,4%	0,0%	2,0%
DF	1	0	1	0,8%	0,0%	0,7%
PR	1	0	1	0,8%	0,0%	0,7%
RS	1	0	1	0,8%	0,0%	0,7%
Abroad	2	1	3	1,6%	4,5%	2,0%
Training course *						
None	7	4	11	5,6%	18,2%	7,5%
Short–Executive graduation	55	13	68	44,0%	59,1%	46,3%
Medium– Especialization	16	2	18	12,8%	9,1%	12,2%
Long – Post-Graduation	42	1	43	33,6%	4,5%	29,3%
Graduation	18	3	21	14,4%	13,6%	14,3%
Graduation *						
Accounting	111	16	127	88,8%	72,7%	86,4%
Administration	20	4	24	16,0%	18,2%	16,3%
Economy	2	4	6	1,6%	18,2%	4,1%
Others	11	3	14	8,8%	13,6%	9,5%
Post-Graduation*						
Especialization or Post-Graduation	65	6	71	52,0%	27,3%	48,3%
Another especialization course or post-graduation	32	8	40	25,6%	36,4%	27,2%
Academic mastering in accounting or related areas	12	6	18	9,6%	27,3%	12,2%
Another academic mastering	5	1	6	4,0%	4,5%	4,1%
Professional masteringin accounting or related areas	16	0	16	12,8%	0,0%	10,9%
AnotherProfessional mastering	0	2	2	0,0%	9,1%	1,4%
Doctoratein accounting or related areas	6	0	6	4,8%	0,0%	4,1%
Another doctorate	5	0	5	4,0%	0,0%	3,4%
I have not attended any post-graduation course	8	2	10	6,4%	9,1%	6,8%

* Multiple responses were allowed than total of percentages exceeds 100%

Table 4: Repondents' profile.

Most of the external users that answered to the research demand audited financial statements (58%). In Brazil, only companies defined as large sized companies by corporate law are obliged to have their financial statements audited. Companies are considered large when they had earnings superior to R\$ 300 million or had total assets superior to R\$ 240 million in the previous period.

From the total of the respondents, 42% use non audited financial statements, once the company is not considered large sized company and there is not a demand for audit from the headquarters, they are not obliged to be audited.

Given to the great influence of fiscal law in the accounting practices in Brazil, 30% of the external users use accounting information for tax purposes, present in the annual Corporate Income Tax Return (DIPJ).

According to Table 6, 12% of the preparers use only the set of fiscal standards in the financial statements. Besides this, 17% of the users do not use formatted accounting information, or demand financial statements, but use questionnaires about main figures and operations of the analyzed company for decision making.

Table 8 presents the reasons for the choice of accounting norms set adopted by the information preparer and the preferences of external users about the financial statements.

Concerning the decision of which set of norms to use, 53% of the respondents state that there was not participation of the company management in this choice; only the preparer of the financial statements. Accounting measures and shows the operations of a company. It is

	Frequence			Percentage		
	P	U	Total	P	U	Total
Size of the company *						
ME	16	1	17	12,8%	4,5%	11,6%
Small Sized company	17	2	19	13,6%	9,1%	12,9%
Small and medium Sized company	69	7	76	55,2%	31,8%	51,7%
SGP	30	7	37	24,0%	31,8%	25,2%
Privetely held company	35	3	38	28,0%	13,6%	25,9%
Listed company	28	9	37	22,4%	40,9%	25,2%
Preparers company activity						
Industry	20			16,0%		
Trade	13			10,4%		
Service	26			20,8%		
Accounting service	64			51,2%		
Third party	0			0,0%		
Other	2			1,6%		
Accounting service type **						
Audit	15			23,4%		
Accounting outsourcing	17			26,6%		
Advisory	6			9,4%		
Consulting	26			40,6%		
External users activity						
Credit analyst		6			27,3%	
Investment analyst		8			36,4%	
Investor		7			31,8%	
Other		1			4,5%	

* Multiple responses were allowed than total of percentages exceeds 100%.

** Percentage regarding accounting services.

Table 5: Respondents' professional area.

	Frequence	Percentage
Simplified bookkeeping	19	15%
IFRS for SME	44	35%
Full CPC (by choice)	29	23%
Full CPC, (by obligation)	54	43%
Only bookkeeping for tax purposes	15	12%
Other	3	2%

Table 6: Set of adopted norms by preparers.

	Frequence	Percentage
Audited financial statements	72	58%
Financial statements without audit need	53	42%
Accounting information for tax purposes (DIPJ)	38	30%
Unformatted accounting information (questionnaires)	16	13%
No demand for financial statements	5	4%

Table 7: External demands.

understood that the involvement of other managers of the company in how the company will be represented is important.

As already presented in other questions, the influence of fiscal legislation is very important in the choice of accounting practices in Brazil: the mean of agreement to this question was 6,80. Only in 2014, the fiscal law was amended to encompass and provide fiscal treatment to the accounting changes occurred in the IFRS implementation in the country. From this year, Brazilian fiscal authorities understand that the companies adopted new accounting practices. Perhaps this fact reinforces a greater adhesion to IFRS in Brazil.

According to the preparers of financial statements, the search

for improvement in this information is very important (mean of agreement 7,7 and mode 10). The pursuit for quality is related to the belief that IFRS represent an advance over previous practices and therefore, represent relative advantage (Rogers, 2003). In addition, the presentation of higher quality information gives the company and the preparer of the accounting information a better image [24].

According to Rogers [20], the complexity or difficulty of using an innovation hinders its adoption. Despite the mode 10 concerning the agreement to the statement that the complexity influences the choice of accounting practices set, the respondents agreed with mean of 5,98 with this statement, or, lower, probably due to the obligation of the use

	Score (percentage)											Min	Max	Mean	Mode
	0	1	2	3	4	5	6	7	8	9	10				
Questionnaire for preparers															
Joint analysis between manager and accountant	4	6	10	9	15	9	6	19	10	3	10	0	10	5,34	7
Fiscal influence in the choice of the norms	3	2	3	6	4	14	6	10	17	13	21	0	10	6,80	10
Search for quality is fundamental in the choice of the norms	1	2	2	3	3	9	5	8	21	10	35	0	10	7,70	10
Complexity is fundamental in the choice of the norms	9	5	5	6	4	14	6	8	18	7	18	0	10	5,98	10
External demands are fundamental in the choice of the norms	2	2	6	3	4	9	5	13	18	15	23	0	10	7,17	10
Internal demands are fundamental in the choice of the norms	4	2	8	6	5	12	7	16	16	7	18	0	10	6,38	10
Banks demand financial statements	2	2	5	7	6	17	9	8	13	13	20	0	10	6,66	10
Clients demand financial statements	10	9	8	14	4	18	7	7	10	5	8	0	10	4,67	5
Suppliers demand financial statements	10	8	11	15	5	19	9	5	9	2	6	0	10	4,34	5
Questionnaire for external users															
Use of financial statements by users	-	-	-	5	14	5	9	14	5	23	27	3	10	7,54	10
Demand for financial statements in compliance with the type of the company	5	14	-	-	14	5	9	5	14	23	14	0	10	6,27	9
Preference for Full IFRS	9	5	-	-	9	14	5	5	14	18	23	0	10	6,68	10
Use of tax information for analyses	14	5	-	-	5	-	23	18	14	14	9	0	10	6,09	6
Joint use of financial and tax statements	14	5	-	-	5	14	5	23	14	14	9	0	10	6	7
Importance of financial statements in relation to tax information	5	-	-	-	5	5	14	9	14	32	18	0	10	7,64	9

Table 8: Accounting choices and use of financial statements.

	Frequence	Percentage
Publish by obligation	55	44%
Publish by choice	27	22%
Not	61	49%

Table 9: Financial statements publication.

	Frequence	Percentage
Yes, because of legal obligation	52	42%
Yes, only because of internal obligation (headquarters or investors)	33	26%
Yes, by choice	27	22%
Not	34	27%

Table 10: Financial statements audit.

of a determined set of norms, despite the complexity of the adoption and maintenance (mode 10 and mean 7,17). Therefore, the obligation of the use of the norm is very important, but also it is not definitive: the quality also influences.

Additionally, it is noticed that external demands are slightly more important than internal demands. The fact of a law, a regulator board, the company headquarters or yet, the creditor (bank) determines which set of accounting norms to be adopted is slightly more important than an internal manager decision of the company to be reported. On the other hand, the preparers of the accounting information understand that the demand of external users, such as clients and suppliers is inferior to the other users (mode 5).

In order to know the preferences and requirements of external users, the first question was if they effectively use financial statements in their analyses. 5% did not agree in some degree with the use of financial statements and 14% were indifferent. Thus, over 80% use the accounting information, and the mode to agree with this statement was 10. External users are worried about demanding the appropriate set of

norms according to the company to be analyzed (mean 6,27 and mode 9), but prefer Full IFRS (mean 6,68 and mode 10).

Therefore, it is possible to infer that the use of Full IFRS can contribute to improving the image of the company [24] in relation to external users. Besides this, this fact can be considered a relative advantage [20] of the companies that use IFRS and of the preparers of the accounting information that will be most valued in the market.

Regarding the perception of these users about the information prepared for fiscal purposes, in some cases these information are used (mode 6 and mean 6,09) or used in conjunction with accounting information prepared according to IFRS (mode 7 and mean 6). The preference of external users is using the financial statements prepared according to IFRS (mode 9 and mean 7,64).

Disclosure and audit

In Table 9, the total of percentage is over 100% because the preparers of financial statements can render services for more than one company, in other words, they can prepare information for companies that will publish their statements and for companies that will not.

Among preparers and third parties, 49% of the respondents state they do not publish their financial statements, 44% publishes by obligation and only 44% by choice. On the other hand, when asked to the users if they trusted more in the published financial statements in a range of 0 to 10, the obtained mean was 8 and the mode 9. It is noticed that, though, the analysts prefer using published financial statements, the preparers and third parties do not publish them. The image of the company [24] and the relative advantage [20] can be affected by the option for publishing or not the financial statements (Table 9).

Similar to the previous table, the percentage is over 100% because the preparers can render this service for more than one company. According to Brazilian law, large sized companies must be audited (42%). Nevertheless, 26 % of the preparers of financial information state that the reported company is audited by obligation from the headquarters and 22% by choice. These numbers show the preoccupation about either the image of the company or the relative advantage for having the statements audited once the external users prefer analyzing audited financial statements according Table 7. Additionally, the option for publishing and auditing the financial statements is related to the observability or visibility of the benefits that an innovation can bring to the company to be reported (Table 10).

The results shown in Table 11 indicate that external users prefer analyzing published and audited information. These results corroborate for the improvement in the company image.

Perception regarding accounting information quality and IFRS implementation

In the respondents' opinion, Brazilian convergence to IFRS was responsible for higher quality and transparency in accounting information and they also believe that the detachment of accounting for tax purposes causes improvement in the quality.

Not only the preparers but also the analysts admit the quality in the financial statements performed by Full IFRS and by IFRS for SME. Nevertheless, the perception is different concerning the simplified bookkeeping, because only 59% of the respondents attributed a score over 5 in this question. On Table 12, the respondents' perception is described regarding the quality of the accounting information.

The answers of the preparers according to Table 13 and by the users according to Table 14 are similar. The means of both groups for each question are not meaningfully different according to the applied Mann-Whitney test. Despite this, the preparers are slightly more optimistic in relation to higher quality and transparency in the accounting information after IFRS implementation in Brazil. In addition, although the preparers use the simplified bookkeeping in service rendering, they do not believe that they present high quality [27-29].

External users according to Table 14 do not believe that the Simplified Bookkeeping can result in high quality financial statements. Besides this, 19% understands that the detachment of corporate accounting from tax accounting does not result in higher quality in the accounting information.

All in all, the respondents believe that the accounting information has higher quality after IFRS implementation, except for Simplified Bookkeeping. Additionally, IFRS for SME presents information with as good quality as Full IFRS, in the preparers' perception as well as the users of such financial statements. Therefore, the preparers' perception and the users' are in agreement with IFRS adoption shown in Table 6, there to say, caused not only by legal demand but based on the market beliefs. In this case, compatibility is observed; the innovation is noticed as consistent with values, necessities and potential users' experiences [20].

Based on the data presented in Table 15, the benefits and difficulties of the preparers of accounting information in IFRS adoption will be analyzed. Besides, the perception of the accounting information users about financial statements in IFRS will be presented.

	Score (percentage)														
	0	1	2	3	4	5	6	7	8	9	10	Min	Max	Mean	Mode
Greater confidence in published financial statements	-	-	-	-	5	9	9	5	23	27	23	4	10	8,04	9
Greater confidence in audited financial statements	-	-	-	-	5	9	5	9	9	23	41	4	10	8,41	10

Table 11: Users' confidence.

	Score (percentage)														
	0	1	2	3	4	5	6	7	8	9	10	Min	Max	Mean	Mode
Full IFRS	-	1	1	1	3	4	4	10	24	26	27	1	10	8,22	10
IFRS for SME	2	-	3	1	5	12	6	10	29	10	22	0	10	7,38	8
Simplified bookkeeping	5	4	4	5	5	17	10	16	16	7	11	0	10	6,02	5
Higher quality after IFRS	-	-	1	1	5	4	4	14	24	16	32	2	10	8,16	10
Greater transparency after IFRS	-	-	1	3	3	3	8	15	22	15	30	2	10	8,01	10
Higher quality after tax detachment	1	1	1	4	4	7	7	11	17	15	32	0	10	7,76	10

Table 12: Respondents' perception regarding the quality of the accounting information.

	Score (percentage)														
	0	1	2	3	4	5	6	7	8	9	10	Min	Max	Mean	Mode
Full IFRS	-	1	1	2	2	5	3	10	22	28	27	1	10	8,24	9
IFRS for SME	2	-	3	2	4	11	5	10	28	11	24	0	10	7,44	8
Simplified bookkeeping	6	5	5	5	5	17	8	16	15	7	12	0	10	5,984	5
Higher quality after IFRS	-	-	1	2	4	5	3	15	23	14	34	1	10	8,16	10
Greater transparency after IFRS	-	-	2	3	2	4	6	16	22	14	31	1	10	8,04	10
Higher quality after tax detachment	1	1	1	5	3	8	6	10	16	14	36	1	10	7.856	10

Table 13: Preparers' perception regarding the quality of the accounting information.

	Score (percentage)														
	0	1	2	3	4	5	6	7	8	9	10	Min	Max	Mean	Mode
Full IFRS	-	-	-	-	5	-	9	14	36	14	23	4	10	8,09	8
IFRS for SME	-	-	-	-	9	14	14	14	36	5	9	4	10	7,05	8
Simplified bookkeeping	-	-	-	9	9	18	18	18	18	5	5	3	10	6,23	5
Higher quality after IFRS	-	-	-	-	9	-	9	5	27	27	23	4	10	8,14	9
Greater transparency after IFRS	-	-	-	-	9	-	18	9	23	18	23	4	10	7,82	8
Higher quality after tax detachment	5	-	-	-	9	5	9	18	23	23	9	0	10	7,18	9

Table 14: Users' perception regarding the quality of the accounting information.

The accounting information preparers state that, in a range of 0 to 10, in parts it is agreed (mean 5,46 and mode 5) that they admit the benefits of IFRS adoption. This position is opposite to the information users that prefer analyzing the financial statements according to IFRS, besides it is said that IFRS adoption facilitated the analyses and improved the quality of the information presented to them (mode 8). The benefits (Rogers, 2003) noticed by external users are better than the ones noticed by the preparers of the information. Despite this, the preparers believe that the benefits with the adoption overcome the costs (mean 6,14 and mode 8).

Although the information is for external users, the preparers of the information noticed that the financial statement according to IFRS is also used by the company's internal users. The mean of agreement for this affirmation is 6,06 and the mode 7. The difficulties found in the implementation refer to problems faced in the parameters settings of the ERP and also in the understanding of applicable rules (mode 8) (Table 15).

The fiscal law was only defined with the issue of the Law12.973 in 2014 after being defined the treatment to be given to the new accounting practices. Once the changes of such practices occurred in two steps in Brazil, 2008 and finished in 2010, in practice, the market had expectation regarding the fiscal treatment for seven years. Therefore, the lack of clarity about tax over accounting income is a very important item for the accounting information preparers (mean 6,74 and mode 8). On the other hand, the worry about the appearance of some fiscal contingence is inferior (mean 6, 17 and mode 5), once the law allowed the changes in the accounting practices in Brazil before a scenario of "fiscal neutrality".

The comprehension of external users that answered our research, despite discussing on a higher quality in the accounting information analyzed after IFRS implementation, states that there were some difficulties in understanding financial statements prepared from this set of norms in the period of accounting practices transition (mean 6,23 and mode 7) and that there still is little difficulty (mean 5,55 and mode 7).

Most of the statements analyzed by external users are prepared based on Full IFRS (mean 7,27 and mode 9) they are not based on IFRS for SME (mean 4,23 and mode5). One of the reasons declared by CVM – Securities Commission in Brazil for the adoption of IFRs in the country refers to the facilitation to compare statements prepared in Brazil; this would facilitate and leverage the investments in our country. Nevertheless, according to the answers in our research, the internal users do not agree with this affirmation (mean5,14 and mode 8).

Knowledge of applicable standardization

According to the opinion of the financial statements preparers who answered our research, the managers of the companies that report know little about the accounting practices adopted by those companies

(mean 5,18 and mode 5). On the other hand, the knowledge of whom effectively prepares the information is higher (mean 7,44 and mode 8). It is interesting to notice that despite declared knowledge of the issue, the effective adoption and the affirmation of external users about the preference to use financial statements prepared according to IFRS, the preparers of the accounting information do not recognize as many benefits as the users.

Concerning the knowledge of applicable norms (IFRS), the external users of the information declare that they reasonably know about the issue (mean 6,05 and mode 7). Despite declaring lower knowledge than the preparers, the users prefer these information to the previous ones utilized in the country and yet, in relation to the simplified bookkeeping or fiscal information (Table 16).

Profile analyses versus respondents' perception

In order to verify the perception differences regarding the respondents' profile, according to the theory reasoned action Fishbein and Ajzen [19], the Kruskal Wallis test was applied about all the questions, in relation to: age, gender; working place, company size, graduation degree (training courses, graduation and post-graduation).

In Table 17, questions about perception differences according to the respondents' profile, according to the Kruskal Wallis test with significance level of 5%,

It is noticed that the most experienced ones believe that the detachment of corporate and fiscal accounting causes better quality in the accounting information than the others. The most experienced recognize more the quality of IFRS for SME than the others. Respondents younger than 25 years old and over 45 years old have more confidence in audited financial statements than the others.

Female respondents whose age range from 26 to 35 years old are the ones that demand less the financial statements in compliance with the type of the company to be analyzed.

It is noticed that analysts (external users) who work in São Paulo have better knowledge about different types of norms than the others and also use more tax information (alone or in conjunction with financial statements). The analysts who do not work in São Paulo analyze primarily IFRS for SME.

This result suggests that the analysts with more contact with IFRS for SME and less contact with Full IFRS use less tax information than the others.

Professionals who work exclusively with micro enterprises and small sized companies demonstrate more that the complexity and external demands are fundamental for choosing the norms to be used, in other words, if there is not an external agent that demands accounting information according to IFRS, they will not be prepared like this. Respondents who work in large sized companies and small sized companies use more IFRS information for taking internal

	Score (percentage)											Min	Max	Mean	Mode
	0	1	2	3	4	5	6	7	8	9	10				
Questionnaire for preparers															
Managers recognizethe benefits brought by IFRS	5	6	5	11	9	15	8	12	15	5	9	0	10	5,46	5
Use of IFRS for taking internal decisions	3	2	7	8	4	14	11	17	14	7	11	0	10	6,06	7
IFRS brought benefits superior to the involved costs	2	1	9	5	9	15	10	13	17	9	10	0	10	6,14	8
Difficulties in the IFRS implementation due to IT problems	2	2	5	6	5	12	7	12	22	12	14	0	10	6,61	8
Difficulties in the IFRS implementation due to lack of clarity of understanding	3	4	2	6	10	12	8	14	22	11	7	0	10	6,25	8
Difficulty in the IFRS implementation due to lack of understanding of Fiscal authorities positioning	2	1	7	3	6	10	7	14	19	14	14	0	10	6,74	8
Risk of fiscal contingence	5	2	9	4	2	18	10	11	14	12	13	0	10	6,17	5
Questionnaire for external users															
IFRS facilitates analyses	-	-	-	9	9	18	9	9	27	9	9	3	10	6,64	8
Higher quality in the accounting information with IFRS	-	-	-	5	9	14	5	9	32	5	23	3	10	7,32	8
Difficulty in understanding the financial statements during the transition period to IFRS	5	-	-	5	18	9	14	18	18	-	14	0	10	6,23	7
Still have difficulties to understand the financial statements according to IFRS	9	-	5	5	9	14	18	23	9	5	5	0	10	5,55	7
Most of the analyzed financial statements are according to Full IFRS	5	-	-	5	5	-	14	18	18	23	14	0	10	7,27	9
Most of the analyzed financial statements are according to IFRS for SME	18	-	5	18	-	27	9	14	9	-	-	0	8	4,23	5
Facility to have International comparison after IFRS	32	-	-	5	-	-	5	5	50	5	-	0	9	5,14	8

Table 15: Benefits and difficulties with IFRS.

	0	1	2	3	4	5	6	7	8	9	10	Min	Max	Mean	Mode
Questionnaire for preparers															
Managers knowledge about applicable accounting norms	2	5	10	11	10	17	13	9	15	6	2	0	10	5,18	5
Accountants knowledge about applicable accounting norms	-	1	3	2	5	7	9	14	24	21	14	1	10	7,44	8
Questionnaire external users															
Analysts knowledge about different accounting norms	-	-	-	23	-	5	23	27	18	5	-	3	9	6,05	7

Table 16: Knowledge about fiscal norms.

Age	Up to 25	From 26 to 35	From 36 to 45	Over 45		
Demand for financial statements according to the type of company	6,00	3,43	6,67	8,44		
Greater confidence in audited financial statements	9,67	7,71	6,00	9,33		
IFRS for SME	5,90	6,80	7,36	8,03		
Better quality after fiscal detachment	6,50	7,05	8,00	8,30		
Gender	**F**	**M**				
Demand for financial statements according to the type of company	2,00	7,22				
Local	**SP**	**Others**				
Analysts knowledge regarding different types of norms	6,35	3,00				
Use of tax information the analyses	6,65	0,50				
Joint use of financial and tax statements	6,55	0,50				
Most of the analyzed financial statementsare in compliance with IFRS for SME	3,90	7,50				
Size	**ME or EPP**	**SME**	**SGP/SA**	**Div**		
Complexity is fundamental in the choice of the norms	8,00	5,77	6,46	4,64		
External demand is fundamental in the choice of the norms	8,50	6,89	7,59	6,36		
Use of IFRS for taking internal decisions	6,90	5,77	6,74	4,96		
Banks demand financial statements	8,40	6,00	7,33	5,88		
IFRS brought benefits to the involved costs	7,20	5,32	6,74	6,04		
Training	**N**	**CP**	**MP**	**LP**	**G**	**Div**
Complexity is fundamental in the choice of the norms	5,86	6,84	3,57	5,74	6 53	4,0
Use of IFRS for taking internal decisions	3,43	6,27	7,43	5,58	6,29	7,3
Greater transparency after IFRS	6,36	7,81	9,25	8,33	7,85	8,8

Table 17: Perception differences according to the respondents'profile.

decisions than the others. Banks demand more financial statements from micro enterprises and large sized companies than small and medium sized companies.

Respondents who work in micro enterprises and small sized companies recognize more that IFRS brought benefits that overcome the involved costs. It is observed that when the respondents work in different sized companies, the complexity and external demands are less important in the accounting choice, they are also less demanded by the banks and are the ones to use less IFRS for taking decisions.

The persons who have not attended any kind of training course about IFRS do not believe that there was greater transparency after the Brazilian convergence and they do not use IFRS for taking decisions either, supposedly due to lack of knowledge.

Final Considerations

It is general opinion that accounting information has higher quality and transparency after IFRS implementation and the detachment of fiscal accounting. The preparers see these benefits in a more positive way. The perception is different regarding Simplified Bookkeeping. It is interesting to observe that the preparers use a set of norms that according to them do not provide high quality information. It is possible to infer that the limitation of financial, technological and personnel resources are the reasons for using simplified rules that do not satisfy even their preparers.

In contrast to the preparation, the adoption benefits of IFRS are also noticed by preparers and also by the analysts, but the analysts are the ones who see them in a more positive way. The most related difficulties by the preparers are referred to the implementation, though they consider the fiscal contingency risk lower and that the benefits overcome costs. Regarding the understanding of the norms, the respondents in general still have insecurity.

Another important finding was that the users do not consider that IFRS adoption facilitated the comparison of statements, in antithesis to the reasons stated by CVM at the time of Brazilian convergence.

We observed that the respondents who have not attended any type of IFRS training course cannot see a higher transparency with IFRS like the others and they also do not use IFRS for taking decisions. Thus, it is noted that the most specific knowledge of IFRS increases the credibility of the individual in the transparency of accounting information in the light of IFRS.

Legal requirement, by regulator board, by the headquarters or yet by the banks are more important than the internal manager's demand. It is emphasized additionally, that there is a greater demand for financial statements from the banks to micro enterprises and small sized companies that the others.

External users require the set of norms appropriate for the analyzed company, but they prefer Full IFRS. It may suggest that Full IFRS adoption contributes to improving the company image, representing relative advantage of accounting and the preparers', when they are most valued in the market.

Although analysts prefer using and also have more confidence in published financial statements, less than a quarter of the companies do it voluntarily. The same occurs to audit. It is possible to suppose that companies that do it voluntarily show preoccupation with the company image and search for relative advantage with initiative.

We emphasized that although users show less knowledge than the preparers, they prefer this information to the ones previously used in the country and yet, concerning the simplified bookkeeping or fiscal information.

References

1. IFRS (2014b) Analysis of the IFRS jurisdiction profiles.

2. IFAC (2012) Helping Small- and Medium-Sized Practices Meet the Challenges and Seize the Opportunities of Tomorrow Interview with Giancarlo Attolini, Chair, IFAC Small and Medium Practices (SMP) Committee. New York.

3. IFRS (2014a) About the IFRS for SMEs.

4. IFRS (2014c) Jurisdictional and International MoUs.

5. Rezaee Z, Smith LM, Szendi, JZ (2010) Convergence in accounting standards: Insights from academicians and practitioners. Advances in accounting 26: 142-154.

6. Macías M, Muiño F (2011) Examining dual accounting systems in Europe. The International Journal of Accounting 46: 51-78.

7. Alp A, Ustundag S (2009) Financial reporting transformation: The experience of Turkey. Critical Perspectives on Accounting 20: 680-699.

8. Aboagye-Otchere F, Agbeibor J (2012) The International Financial Reporting Standard for Small and Medium-sized Entities (IFRS for SMES): Suitability for small businesses in Ghana. Journal of Financial Reporting and Accounting 10: 190-214.

9. Masca E (2012) Influence of Cultural Factors in Adoption of the IFRS for SMEs. Procedia Economics and Finance 3: 567-575.

10. Favarin MC (2012) Um estudo sobre os Estágios de Adoção do CPC PME sob a ótica da Teoria Institucional. Dissertation of the Master. Mackenzie Presbyterian University. São Paulo.

11. Botinha RA, Lemes S (2014) IFRS para Pequenas e Médias Empresas: Percepção Sobre a Adoção das Normas Internacionais no Brasil. Revista de Administração e Contabilidade da FAT 5: 117-135.

12. Santos GM (2012) Critérios Utilizados pelos Escritórios Contábeis na Adoção Inicial do Pronunciamento CPC PME. Dissertation of the Master. Mackenzie Presbyterian University. São Paulo.

13. Gonzáles A, Nagai C (2013) A eficácia social do pronunciamento técnico para pequenas e médias empresas sob a ótica da Teoria dos Jogos. Enfoque: Reflexão Contábil 32: 3-13.

14. Masera PD, de Oliveira Orth C (2012) Normas Internacionais de contabilidade: Um estudo acerca da legalidade e obrigatoriedade de adoção da IFRS nas pequenas e médias empresas do Brasil. Revista Eletrônica do Curso de Ciências Contábeis.

15. Buys PW, Schutte D (2011) A Consideration of IFRS Education and Acceptance From Culturally Diverse Backgrounds: A South African Perspective. International Business & Economics Research Journal (IBER) 10: 49-58.

16. Bohušová H, Blašková V (2012) In What Ways are Countries, which have Already Adopted IFRS for SMEs Different. Acta Universitatis Agriculturae et Silviculturae Mendelianae Brunensis.

17. Turegun N, Kaya CT (2014) Repeated Cross Sectional Analysis of Acuity of Turkish CPAs on the Adoption of IFRS for SMEs for Turkish SMEs. Research Journal of Finance and Accounting 5: 49-55.

18. Quagli A (2010) How is the IFRS for SME accepted in the European context? An analysis of the homogeneity among European Countries, users and preparers in the European Commission Questionnaire. Advances in Accounting Incorporating Advances in International Accounting.

19. Fishbein M, Ajzen I (1975) Belief, attitude, intention and behavior: An introduction to theory and research.

20. Rogers EM (2003) Diffusion of innovation. (5thedn) New York: The Free Press.

21. Schutte D, Buys P (2011) Cultural considerations and the implementation of IFRS: A focus on small and medium entities. Journal of Social Sciences 26: 19-27.

22. Guerreiro MS, Rodrigues LL, Craig R (2014) Institutional Change of Accounting Systems: The Adoption of a Regime of Adapted International Financial Reporting Standards. European Accounting Review 1-41.

23. Neag R, Masca E, Pascan I (2009) Actual aspects regarding the IFRS for SME– Opinions, debates and future developments. Annales Universitatis Apulensis Series Oeconomica 11: 32-42.

24. Moore GC, Benbasat I (1991) Development of an instrument to measure the perceptions of adopting an information technology innovation. Information systems research 2: 192-222.

25. Deslauriers JP, Kérisit M (2008) O delineamento de pesquisa qualitativa.

26. Bryman A (2004) Social research methods. (2ndedn), Oxford: University Press.

27. Brasil. Resolução CFC no. 1.255, de 10 de dezembro de 2009. Aprova a NBC T 19.41 – Contabilidade para Pequenas e Médias Empresas. Diário Oficial da União, Brasília, DF, 17 dez. 2009.

28. Medida Provisória no. 627, de 11 de novembro de 2013. Diário Oficial da União, Brasília.

29. (IBPT) Instituto Brasileiro de Planejamento e Tributação (2013) Perfil Empresarial Brasileiro.

International Financial Reporting Standards (IFRS) Adoption on Financial Decisions

Katta Ashok Kumar*

Business Management Department, Saveetha University, Chennai, India

Abstract

Expansion of business environment in 1990s changed the financial set up of India from the conventional bank based borrowings to market based one. This necessitated companies to address global stakeholders. The regulatory requirement of different countries also necessitated companies to do multiple reporting i.e., one as per home country standard and the other as per the host country standard. To avoid multiple reporting and to address global stakeholders, a uniform system of reporting was felt necessary to facilitate comparisons, which resulted in the establishment of International Accounting Standard Board (IASB) which issued International Financial Reporting Standards (IFRS). Financial reporting is to present financial information about the status of a company which is used by the stakeholders before any decisions are made with regard to investment, finance, dividend etc. Users of financial reports are; investors, creditors, employees, customers, competitors, government, public etc. and purpose of usage of these reports differ from person to person.

Certain Indian companies having listed in foreign stock exchanges are reporting IFRS voluntarily in their financial statements. The present study tries to understand the impact of this voluntary adoption of International Financial Reporting Standards on the financial decision makers, through a case analysis of Wipro Ltd. The analysis compared the major financial parameters under IFRS and Indian GAAP as reported by Wipro Ltd. for a period of four years from 2009-10 to 2012 - 13. The results postulate an increase in liquidity ratio; equity ratio; interest coverage ratio; marginal increase in debt equity ratio; and no significant increase in profitability ratios except net profit ratio which rose marginally in the year 2013.

Overall the results indicate that the adoption of fair value accounting and strict requirement in adhering to accounting standards have strengthened the financial indicators and provided the decision makers a transparent, true and fair accounting highlighters.

Keywords: Financial markets; Globalization; Financial reporting; Financial standards; Accounting standards

Introduction

Developments in Socio-economic fabric in India have changed financial environment of businesses in India from traditional bank based system to market oriented, which paved way for globalization and consequently expansion of financial markets worldwide necessitating companies to raise funds abroad and address investors outside the home country. As a result, companies were required to comply with regulatory requirement of filing financial reports as per home country and global standards, which led to multiple reporting. To avoid multiple reporting and to have a transparent system of reporting which facilitates; comparisons, reduces cost of raising capital, and also fulfills regulatory requirements of different countries, a uniform system of accounting was felt necessary. The establishment of International Financial Reporting Standards (IFRS), a common accounting system and framework, which is perceived as transparent, and fair to local and global investors, and which lead to increased compatibility and comparability among different financial statements across the globe [1]. This perception is supported by the findings of Hope [2] that countries adopt IFRS to improve investor protection, to make capital market more accessible to foreign investors, and to improve comparativeness and comprehensiveness of their financial information.

In the past, companies submitted their annual financials to regulators and banks as a mandatory disclosure, as users of these financial statements were few, with creditors being major stakeholder. Others are investors, employees, customers and management. Employees were happy as long as they were rewarded with good return; employees with their salaries and benefits; customers with quality product at competitive prices. The necessity to read financial statements was never felt by these stakeholders. Even, focus of financial statement was on providing financial information to stockholders and creditors to measure management's performance, and for taxation purpose. However, globalization has given new twist to financial market with a change in focus from traditional stewardship to a broader stakeholder focused fair valuation. The framework of IFRS also emphasizes that financial information provided should help stakeholders to make economic and other decisions.

Today, doing business is not only attractive but complex with higher level of expectations by various stakeholders with different phases of economy and stages of product/services. Business solutions, although look simple have taken a manifold deliverables with shared governances with various aspects, parties, compliances, standards etc. in a multi-country focus of businesses. Investors are always on the lookout for newer investment opportunities in any part of the world, which would add value to them. Expansion of markets internationally

*Corresponding author: Katta Ashok Kumar, Research Scholar and Assistant Professor of Business Management, Saveetha University, Chennai, India
E-mail: yoursashok1984@gmail.com

has deprived local companies of the home market advantage. Even small and medium industries are exposed to competition, in and around the world. Employees and Customers take pride in identifying themselves with brands. The reputation associated with good financial reporting is more when brands become associated with a company's name [3]. As financial statements are the means through which businesses communicate to these various stakeholders, requirement of a uniform system of financial reporting became necessity. Supporters of International Financial Reporting Standards (IFRS) consider that financial statements prepared are to meet needs of various stakeholders [4].

Purpose of any financial reporting is essentially to reduce information asymmetry between corporate managers and parties contracting with their firm [5]. It is for corporate managers to reduce this information asymmetry by providing transparent financial reports. The IFRS framework IASB [6] provides four principal quality features: relevance, reliability, understandability and comparability. Information is said to have relevance only when it helps users in decision making process by evaluating various options. Jendrichovska [7] postulated that accounting information needs to be appropriate as this report provides the stakeholder what they want in taking investment decisions. As users of financial statements do not have access to books and records based on which financial statements are prepared, they depend on companies audited financial statements, which are presumed to be both reliable and relevant. To ensure the reliability and relevance of financial statements, companies in US frequently employ Certified Public Accountant (CPA) firms to validate that the companies' financial information adhered to Generally Accepted Accounting Principles (GAAP) [8]. Any information provided must also have reliability. Information is said to have reliability when it is free from any error and prejudice. Without reliable financial information, decision makers cannot rely on financial statements for making sound economic decisions [9]. Ashbaugh and Pincus [10] indicated IFRS implementation increases quality of reporting and reduces absolute analyst forecast errors. Financial statements must be presented in such a way that there should not be any ambiguity in reporting and give scope for interpreting it in multiple ways. Comparability of financial statement is another important aspect of IFRS, main purpose for which uniform accounting standard was initiated. Stakeholders should be able to read financial statement of two different companies and analyze financial performance and position of the company. The International Accounting Standards Board (IASB) seeks a workable solution to alleviate the existing complexity, conflict and confusion created by inconsistency and the lack of streamlined accounting standards in financial reporting [11].

Users of these financial reports are many, such as investors, creditors, employees, customers, competitors, government, public and so on. Purpose of usage of these reports also differs from person to person. Alexander [12] divide users of financial reports into Equity investors, Loan Creditors, Employees, Analysts, Suppliers, Customer, Competitors, Government and Public. Shareholders use it to determine the company's financial position to decide whether to invest in the company or not; Creditors to view liquidity position of the company so that they get their payments on time; Employees to know health of the company; Government to monitor the compliances followed and taxation. Companies will be able to initiate new relationships with investors, customers, suppliers and other stakeholders internationally as IFRS provides a globally accepted reporting platform which will ultimately raise reputation and relationship of the corporate and give them a competitive advantage in building their brand [1].

The introduction of IFRS has fuelled the expectations of users of financial statements on potential benefits of adoption. Studies have confirmed the benefits of IFRS adoption such as comparability of financial statements among companies functioning under different regulatory authorities, low cost of capital, and access to international capital markets and greater international investment [3,13]. Many studies done in Europe and Canada who were early adopters of IFRS have confirmed that the adoption has resulted in changes in key accounting parameters and financial ratios of the companies. Though literature finds difference in accounting standards affecting accounting parameters and financial ratios, no study has focused on to find the impact, these differences have on financial decisions. This pertinent case analysis is an attempt to highlight the impact IFRS may have on financial decisions of Wipro Ltd.

Literature Review

IFRS is comprehensive principles based accounting with emphasis on real economic transactions [14]. Advocates of IFRS argue that if all companies follow one accounting standards, financial reports of companies would be uniform which facilitates easy comparison. Ding [15] IFRS enhances the quality of financial reporting, improves the credit worthiness of financial statements, and provides creditors with more information about the company's ability to repay the debt in time and thus leading to better borrowing terms [16]. A further argument in support of IFRS is that the detailed information provided by way of notes to accounts will improve the ability of users to guage management performance, as the introduction of fair value allows for better assessment of manager ability. Eventually, due to smoother communication between managers, shareholders and other interested parties, agency costs would become lower, which will lead to lower cost of debt financing [16]. Barth [4] present roof that IFRS communicate new information to the market which helps investors in taking investment decisions, analyzing company's future financial performance. The improved financial communication helps users in taking decisions as this extended information helps them to understand the dynamics of financial reporting better [3].

Dunne [3] in his study on implementation of IFRS in UK, Italy and Ireland on whether IFRS enables stakeholders make better informed decisions, reports Italians were very supportive, UK respondents agreed but the Irish were more negative. This was attributed to the negative views of UK and Irish auditors and preparers. Since profitability is one of the key indicator, showcasing the health of a company, proponents of IFRS claim that adoption of IFRS results in increase in these ratios. Studies by Lantto and Sahlstom [17] examined the impact of IFRS adoption on key financial ratios of Finnish companies. The results showed that, IFRS changes the magnitude of accounting ratios due to the adoption of fair value accounting and stricter requirement on certain accounting issues. The results indicated increase in profitability and gearing ratios and decrease in PE, equity and quick ratios. The study by Punda [18], on UK companies found that, though UK GAAP and IFRS are very much similar in many aspects, still there was sizeable difference in financial ratios after conversion to IFRS, with respect to profitability and liquidity ratios.

Hung and Subramanyam [19] investigated the effects of IFRS on Financial statements of German Companies during the period 1998-2002. The study found increase in total assets and book value of equity under IFRS and also variability of book value and income. Henry [20] examined the reconciliation between US GAAP and IFRS of EU cross-listed firms from 2004 to 2006. Their findings indicate differences in net income and shareholders' equity between industries. Firms reported higher net income and lower shareholder equity under IFRS than US GAAP. Dunne [3] states that the main reason for European countries to adopt IFRS is due to its potential benefits: improvements of investor protection, capital market accessibility to foreign investors, comparability and quality of financial statements.

Rahmonova [21] found substantial difference between financial ratios for companies reporting under IFRS versus US GAAP. These differences increased the need of investors and other financial statement users to understand the changes that results from the new set of standards to make well informed and sound financial decisions. According to Price water house Coopers [22]. "Executives can expect that IFRS conversion could affect business fundamentals, such as, communications with key stakeholders, operations and infrastructure, tax and human capital strategies". Even it is expected that, some rules and guidelines concerning assets and liabilities, revenues and expenses, equities are going to change according to IFRS.

Methodology

Research questions

As few of the Indian companies listed in European Union and New York stock exchanges have adopted IFRS voluntarily as early as 2007 (without waiting for Government announcement). The present case study analysis is an attempt to explore the impact of this voluntary adoption of International Financial Reporting Standards on financial decisions. The study compares major financial parameters under IFRS and Indian GAAP as reported by Wipro for a period of four years from 2009-10 to 2012-13, and its possible impact in terms of benefits/drawbacks to all the external/internal stakeholders.

The study analyses financial statements of Wipro, both balance sheet and income statement from 2009-10 to 2012-13 (four years). Financial ratios, both under IFRS and Indian GAAP are the focal areas of analysis. Further, the study draws the differences in financial ratios under both standards and builds on the inherent information to financial decision makers.

Financial ratios provide a benchmark for comparability of firms to review their growth in relation to previous years or with competing companies or against industry standard. Thus, nine financial ratios have been identified and are grouped into four categories i.e., Liquidity, Debt, Equity and Profitability.

Liquidity ratio measures the company's ability to meet its short term obligations. The stability of the business, its financial health and all reflected through these ratios. These are ratios which are generally looked into my creditors, analysts and potential investors before taking any decisions regarding lending or investing. Liquidity ratios considered for the study are current and quick ratios.

Under Debt category, debt equity ratio and interest coverage ratio are considered for study. Debt equity ratio shows the relation between the funds provided by the shareholders and the funds lent by the creditors. A ratio of interest to both the shareholders and creditors, as the debt position of the company reflects the managerial efficiency with which the capital is utilized and also the financial health. Interest coverage ratio indicates the ability of the company to pay interest on its debt. Higher coverage indicates the margin of safety the company has in repaying interest from its earnings.

The equity ratio indicates the amount of fund investors have contributed towards the assets of the company in relation to the total equity. This ratio highlights the long term solvency and sustainability of the business and hence was found important.

Profitability ratios are used to assess a company's earning capacity in relation to its equity, expenses, capital and assets. These are ratios which are considered by the stakeholders before any taking any financial decisions. Return on equity show how much a company earns in relation to the shareholders equity. This ratio helps investors in deciding on investing in a particular company by comparing it with its peers.

Fixed assets turnover ratio reflects the sales generated by the company out of investments made in fixed assets. This ratio helps in understanding how efficiently and effectively a company uses its fixed assets to earn revenue. Return on capital employed measures the returns a company generates out of capital employed. This ratio indicates the efficiency and profitability of company's investments. The Net profit ratio indicates the percentage of in net income. The ratio also indicates how a company manages its expenses in relation to its net sales. Higher ratio indicates better management of resources and return to stakeholders.

Matrixe

Liquidity ratios

- Current Ratio: Current Assets/Current Liabilities.

- Quick Ratio: Current Assets- (Inventory + Prepaid Expenses)/Current Liabilities.

Debt ratios

- Debt Equity Ratio: Total Liabilities / Stockholders Equity.

- Interest Coverage Ratio: *EBIT / Interest Expense.

Equity ratio

- Proprietary Ratio: Stockholders Equity/(Total Assets-Intangibles).

Profitability ratio

- Net Profit Ratio: Net Profit after tax/Net Sales.

- Return on Equity: Net Income/Stockholders Equity.

- Fixed Assets Turnover Ratio: Net Sales/Average Total Assets.

- Return on capital employed: *EBIT/(Total Assets - Current Liabilities).

* Earnings before Interest and Tax.

The % difference between the ratios under IFRS and Indian GAAP is calculated by:

$$\%\text{Difference} = \frac{(\text{Ratio under IFRS} - \text{Ratio under Indian GAAP})}{\text{Ratio under Indian GAAP}} \times 100$$

Data

Wipro Ltd (Wipro) is one of the largest IT services companies of India. Established in 1945 as an edible oil company, it later forayed into IT business. Wipro is also into other businesses such as Consumer Care, Lighting and Infrastructure Engineering. The company is predominantly equity financed, with its total loans and borrowings amounting only to 18% of capital mix as on March 31, 2013. The market capitalization of the company as on March 31, 2013 is `1075 bn. Over the last six years the growth of revenue and profit are noticed at a CAGR of 20% and 14% respectively. The company's operations are found in 54 countries with an intellectual strength of 142,000+ across services/countries. Primarily, the companies stocks are listed at National Stock Exchange and Bombay Stock Exchange. The company's American Depositary Receipts (ADR) representing equity shares are listed in New York Stock Exchange. Wipro started reporting under IFRS from 2009-2010, with transition date of 01.04.2008. The company reports its financials both under Indian GAAP and IFRS. Data has been extracted from both Indian GAAP and IFRS as reported by Wipro to calculate, compare, and for analysis.

First time adopters of International Financial Reporting Standards are required to explain the reasons for difference in figures from Indian GAAP to IFRS with a reconciliation of Equity and Profit and Loss Account as on the date of transition. This explanation along with the notes to the consolidated financial statements has been used to interpret the reasons for the difference in ratios calculated.

Analysis and Interpretation

Liquidity ratios

Liquidity ratios are a measure of company's ability to meet short term financial obligations and it reflects on the margin of safety management maintains to overcome any adverse situations. Table 1 postulate that, both the current and quick ratios have increased significantly from a negative 15% difference in 2010 to a positive 17% in 2013. This gives a positive signal to lenders / bankers as they look into the solvency of a company before financing. A good liquidity position helps managers not only to address fixed obligations of company but also helps them in taking decisions with regard to declaration of dividend, expansion, diversification etc. From shareholder perspective if liabilities are less, it is good news to them as the company is adding value to them in form of financial assets.

A reduced current liabilities and strengthened current asset is the reason for this significant improvement in liquidity ratios. Where Indian GAAP provides for dividend before it is approved by shareholders, IFRS requires approval before payment of dividend. This reduces provision for liability to a considerable extent. IFRS recognizes lease advance and rentals as current assets and available

for sale financial assets are measured at fair value at reporting date. Indian GAAP treats lease advance and rentals in PPE and available for sale financial assets are measured at cost or market value whichever is lower. This reporting difference has boosted current asset in IFRS and resulted in a better liquidity position.

Debt equity ratio

Debt Equity ratio is a long term solvency ratio which indicate relation between portion of assets provided by stockholders and portion of assets financed by creditors. A high debt equity ratio means company is at risk, as it has to earn not only to reward the stockholders but also to fulfill the commitment to lenders.

Table 2 shows that difference in ratio has decreased marginally from a negative 13.34% in 2010, 14.74% in 2013. Low debt symbolizes low risk and gives confidence to the lenders that their debt would be repaid in time. Low debt also means that earnings of the company are not spent on repaying interest but to reward shareholders for the risk undertaken. An average debt equity ratio for four years hovering around 0.57 under IFRS as against 0.66 under Indian GAAP reflects financial health and managerial efficiency of the company to external stakeholders.

Decreased liability is on account of reporting difference under IFRS in accounting of provision for dividend and application of fair value principle.

Interest coverage

Interest Coverage is a financial ratio which indicates the company's ability to pay interest charges on its debt. The coverage aspect of ratio indicates the number of times interest could be paid from available earnings, thereby providing a sense of safety margin a company has, for paying its interest for any period. Table 2 shows difference in interest coverage ratio between Indian GAAP and IFRS as very volatile ranging from a negative 6.28% in 2010 to a positive 7.08% in 2013.

Low interest coverage in IFRS and a greater difference in ratio reflected in the years 2010(-6.28) and 2011(-58.68) are due to

Ratios	IGAAP				IFRS				Difference In %			
	2010	2011	2012	2013	2010	2011	2012	2013	2010	2011	2012	2013
Current Ratio	2.26	2.27	1.99	1.82	1.90	2.31	2.32	2.12	-15.61	1.86	16.52	16.96
Quick Ratio	2.16	2.16	1.92	1.80	1.83	2.21	2.23	2.10	-15.24	2.49	16.60	16.98

Table 1: Liquidity Ratios: Wipro Ltd.

Ratios	IGAAP				IFRS				Difference In %			
	2010	2011	2012	2013	2010	2011	2012	2013	2010	2011	2012	2013
Debt Equity Ratio	0.78	0.63	0.60	0.64	0.68	0.55	0.52	0.54	-13.34	-13.76	-12.16	-14.74
Interest coverage Ratio	45.72	81.35	21.30	28.19	42.85	33.61	20.98	30.19	-6.28	-58.68	-1.51	-6.28

Table 2: Debt Ratios: Wipro Ltd.

Ratios	IGAAP				IFRS				Difference In %			
	2010	2011	2012	2013	2010	2011	2012	2013	2010	2011	2012	2013
Proprietary Ratio	0.67	0.72	0.74	0.70	0.72	0.77	0.79	0.74	7.21	6.58	5.63	6.97

Table 3: Equity Ratios: Wipro Ltd.

Ratios	IGAAP				IFRS				Difference In %			
	2010	2011	2012	2013	2010	2011	2012	2013	2010	2011	2012	2013
Net Profit Ratio	0.17	0.17	0.15	0.16	0.17	0.17	0.15	0.18	-0.36	0.70	-0.13	8.46
Return on Equity	0.25	0.23	0.21	0.23	0.23	0.22	0.20	0.22	-6.80	-5.26	-5.56	-6.69

Table 4: Profitability Ratios: Wipro Ltd.

exchange fluctuation of foreign currency borrowings which is shown as deduction to other income in the profit and loss account in Indian GAAP, whereas in IFRS it is shown as an interest expense. Because of this, interest coverage under IFRS in the years 2010 and 2011 were very low (especially in 2011) compared to Indian GAAP. But following the companies bill of 2011 which was initiated to align Indian GAAP with IFRS, the exchange fluctuation on foreign currency borrowings was also shown as an interest expense in Indian GAAP from 2012 onwards, instead of adjusting with other income. As a result of which the difference between ratios has narrowed from 2012 onwards and has strengthened under IFRS in 2013.

By including the risk on foreign currency borrowings along with fixed obligations, IFRS strengthens the internal control systems of the company which also reflect on the Management's perspective. As the ability to pay interest on borrowings is a tool for testing the solvency of the company, a higher ratio portrays a positive signal to the lenders and margin of safety to the shareholders.

Proprietary ratio

Proprietary ratio indicates relationship between owners' funds and total assets. It reflects extent to which owners funds are invested in different types of assets and financial strength of the company. Higher ratio indicates long term solvency position of the company and lower ratio indicates greater risk to the creditors.

As per Table 3, the % difference has been around 6% in almost all the years. A high proprietary ratio under IFRS indicates the soundness of the capital structure, healthier long term solvency of the company, a good return to the shareholders and a greater security for creditors.

Net profit ratio

Net profit ratio measures the efficiency of a company. It reflects on companies pricing policy, cost structure and production efficiency. A low profit indicates low margin of safety for stakeholders as decline in sales in subsequent years would erode profits.

Table 4, Net profit remains more or less the same under both Indian GAAP and IFRS except in the year 2013 where the % difference between Indian GAAP and IFRS is 8.46%. This is due to demerger and discontinuation of operations by of certain subsidiary companies, by which assets and liabilities of these companies are adjusted against reserves of Wipro as on March 31, 2012. However, IFRS continues to show the profits of the discontinued (demerged) operations separately in its income statement in 2013, which has resulted in the difference of 8.46% in the ratios. With profits of continued and discontinued (demerged) operations separately in the income statement, a transparent communication is sent to all the stakeholders reading the report to take appropriate decisions.

High and consistent profitability of the company is looked into by investors to assess the risk of investing, creditors for determining repaying capacity of debts and Governments to compute taxes.

Return on equity

Return on Equity is the measure of financial efficiency of a company. Higher values indicate efficiency of the company in generating income from investment to its stockholders. Table 4 shows minor difference in ratios under IFRS and Indian GAAP which is on account of minority interest of company recognized within equity in IFRS and is presented separately from equity in Indian GAAP. This presentation difference between IFRS and Indian GAAP has resulted in increase in equity

under IFRS, resulting in low return to stockholders. But by reporting minority interest within equity, IFRS facilitates stakeholders, investors and lenders to identify their share on returns of the company, after taking into account stake of minority interest.

Fixed asset turnover

Fixed asset turnover ratio measures sales generated by the company out of investment made in fixed assets. Higher ratio is a good indicator as it signifies greater level of usage of fixed assets.

Negative and low difference found (Table 4) is on account of leases of land which are classified as operating leases in IFRS and lease advance and rentals are recognized as income in profit and loss account, whereas in Indian GAAP, these are treated as finance lease and are taken to Property, Plant and Equipment (PPE). The treatment of lease accounting not only affects fixed asset turnover ratio but also ratios such as return on equity and EBITDA etc. and also changes the user's decision making about their investment.

Return on capital

Return on capital employed measures the efficiency with which investments made by stakeholders and creditors are used. By comparing net income to sum of a company's debt and equity capital, investors get a picture of how leverage impacts company's profitability. Analysts consider ROCE as a measurement of comprehensive profitability indicator because it gauges management's ability to generate earnings from a company's total pool of capital.

The difference in ROCE shows a gradual decline under IFRS from a positive 10.19 in 2010 to - 8.40 in 2013. The fair value measurement, balance sheet approach for tax calculation under IFRS has resulted in a decreased ROCE.

To Sum-up

This study supports the literature on the impact of adoption of IFRS on accounting figures and key financial ratios of Wipro Ltd used by investors, creditors, analysts etc. Results indicate considerable increase in liquidity ratios, equity ratio and interest coverage ratio, marginal increase in debt equity ratio and no significant increase in any of the profitability ratios. The major reasons for difference in ratios could be attributed to principle based IFRS standard which requires fair value accounting, difference in accounting for leases, balance sheet approach to deferred taxes, and timing of providing provision for proposed dividend.

As users of financial statements are not experts in reading and taking decisions based on reports, explanation provided by way of notes to accounts under IFRS makes it easier for even a novice to understand the reports. As IFRS adoption requires providing more extensive information; transparency, quality and control systems of companies get strengthened. Thus IFRS not only impact the accounting figures but also brings in changes within the organization by strengthening their internal systems and processes. Overall the results indicate that adoption of fair value accounting and strict requirement in adhering to accounting standards have strengthened the financial figures and provided decision makers a transparent, true and fair accounting picture. Though the initial cost involved in transition is high, companies need to adopt IFRS to participate in a globalized financial market, to enable investors and other users of financial statements.

References

1. Yadav (2012) Convergence to IFRS: What needs to be done by Indian Corporate to meet the emerging challenges? IJCEM International Journal of Computational Engineering & Management 15: 2230-7893.

2. Hope OK, Jin J, Kang T (2005) Empirical evidence on jurisdictions that adopt IFRS. Journal of International Accounting Research 5: 1-20.

3. Dunne T, Finningham G, Hannah G, Power D, Fox A, et al. (2008) The implementation of IFRS in the UK, Italy and Ireland. The Institute of Chartered Accountants of Scotland.

4. Barth ME, Landsman WR, Lang MH (2007) International Accounting Standards and Accounting Quality. Journal of Accounting Research 46: 467-498.

5. Ball R (2001) Infrastructure requirement for an economically efficient system of public reporting disclosure. Brooking-Wharton papers on Financial Services 127-169.

6. International Accounting Standards Committee (1989) IASC.

7. Jendrichovska J (2008) International Differences in Accounting: The Birth of Accounting Harmonization Process. Anglo-American University in Prague 1-7.

8. McFarland K (2005) How to play safe on document retention. International Financial Law Review 24: 1-7.

9. Molyneaux D (2004) After Andersen: An experience of integrating ethics into undergraduate accountancy education. Journal of Business Ethics 54: 385-398.

10. Ashbaugh SH, Pincus M (2001) Domestic Accounting Standards, International Accounting Standards, and the Predictability of Earnings. Journal of Accounting Research 39: 417-434.

11. Pologeorgis N (2013) The Impact of combining the US GAAP and IFRS.

12. David A, Anne B, Ann J (2005) International Financial Reporting and Analysis. (2ndedn), Thomson Learning, London.

13. Aharony J, Barniv R, Falk H (2010) The Impact of Mandatory IFRS Adoption on Equity Valuation of Accounting Numbers for Security Investors in the EU. European Accounting Review 19: 535-578.

14. Galbraith, Clyde, Kevin E, Flynn (2009) Convergence Pennsylvania Institute of Certified Public Accountants.

15. Ding Y, Hope OK, Jean T, Stolowy C (2007) Differences between domestic accounting standards and IAS: Measurement, determinants and implications. Journal of Accounting and Public Policy 26: 1-38.

16. Iatridis G (2010) IFRS Adoption and Financial Statement Effect: The UK case. International Research Journal of Finance and Economics 38: 165-172.

17. Lantto AMb, Sahlstrom P (2009) Impact of International Financial Reporting Standard adoption on key financial ratios. Accounting and Finance 49: 341-361.

18. Punda P (2011) Impact of International Financial Reporting Standards (IFRS adoption on key financial ratios) - Evidence from the UK. Master's Thesis, Aarhus School of Business.

19. Mingyi H, Subramanyam KR (2004) Financial Statement Effects of Adopting International Accounting Standards: the Case of Germany. Review of Accounting Studies, Forthcoming.

20. Henry E, Lin S, Yang Y (2009) The European-U.S. GAAP Gap: IFRS to US GAAP Form 20-F Reconciliation. Accounting Horizons 23: 121-150.

21. Rahmonova (2009) IFRS versus US. GAAP: How Numbers in Financial Statements Change, Accounting and Finance Department Summer Student Research Program at the University of Nebraska at Kearney.

22. PricewaterhouseCoopers (2008) IFRS and US GAAP similarities and differences.

13

Dynamics of the Exchange Rate in India

Rabia Najaf[1]* and Khakan Najaf[2]

[1]Department of Accounting and Finance, University of Lahore, Islamabad Campus, Pakistan
[2]Riphah International University, Islamabad, Pakistan

Abstract

Exchange rate is act as the main role in the integral part of the economic development. India is also facing this issue like other Asian countries impact of increase exchange rate on the growth of the economy. It is source of the external funds and act as the channel between risk and investment. In this research, we have taken the data from 1998 to 2008 and applied the ADF test, normality test and Jarqu e-Bera statistics test for taking the proper results about the impact of exchange rate on the development of India. Normality test explains the nature of the data. Our results are showing that increase exchange rate has negative impact on the stock exchange of India. Our suggested that Government should focus about the exchange rate policy.

Keywords: Economic development; Asian countries; ADF test; Nor-mality data; Exchange rate policy

Introduction

In simple words, exchange rate volatility is also known as the name of risk and uncertainty. Most of the studies have shown that volatility in prices has two types 1) upwards 2) downward both are showing that exchange rate can be appreciate and can be depreciate. Exchange rate depends upon the supply and demand. Stock market return is considered the most important metric for the shareholders of the organization. Why the share prices are flocking it is most interesting topic for every researchers. Fr enhancing the economic condition stock market is come on most of sensitive assets which makes the causal association between macroeconomic variables and stock prices. This topic did not take the attention of policy makers also take the attention of economists. Shaock prices are best way for policy makers to predict about the upcoming policies.

In the modern area, globalization has created the different links for the development of financial market.

Impact of exchange rate volatility on the growth of the stock exchange

Robust of the studies have been observed that there is causal association between stock market and exchange rate. Exchange rate is crucial element for analysis the performance of the stock exchange. Stock prices have the main tool through which investors can take proper decision about the future investments. For the better investment public must be aware about the stock market prices. It is also act as the risk seeker. There are no of variables, which have influenced on the stock market performance. Exchange rate is such the shock that can block the stock market. Therefore most of the researchers take it for analysis the performance of the stock market. Exchange rate is also affected on the industries production. This thing has proved that there is negative association between increase exchange rate and stock market.

Overview of Bombay stock exchange

Bombay stock exchange is the oldest stock exchange of India. It is most faster stock exchange regarding to trade. It was organized in 1876. It has the 11th no in the world. Near about 5700 companies listed in it. Large capitalization is the reason that huge no of investors want to invest their money in it. According to rules and regulation of securities act, Bombay stock exchange was known as the recognized stock exchange. It is also famous with the name of derivate market. In the

Bombay stock exchange the operation system is electronic. In this way; investors can invest their money throughout the world and at any time.

Objectives

1) The prime objective of this paper is to find out the impact of exchange rate of Indian stock exchange

2) Impact of stock exchange from the last few years.

3) In this paper, we have also shown the capitalization of Bombay stock exchange.

4) How can increase the foreign investors in Indian stock exchange.

Problem statement

Impact of exchange rate on the Bombay stock exchange is shown in Figure 1.

Literature Review

Rabia najaf, khakan najaf, explored the impact of exchange rate on the stock market of Malaysia. For this purpose, they had taken the data from year 1998 to 2008 and applies the VAR model. Their results are showing that there is negative association between exchange rate volatility and stock market. This study suggested that policy makers should work in the case of decrease the exchange rate [1].

Aggarwal analyzed the impact of exchange rate on the stock market Austria. For this purpose, they had taken the data from year 1999 to 2009 and applies the ECM model. Their results are showing that there is negative association between exchange rate volatility and stock market. This study suggested that policy makers should work in the case of decrease the exchange rate [2].

Babu and Prabheesh examined the impact of exchange rate on

*Corresponding author: Rabia Najaf, Department of Accounting and Finance, University of Lahore, Islamabad Campus, Pakistan
E-mail: rabianajaf@hotmail.com

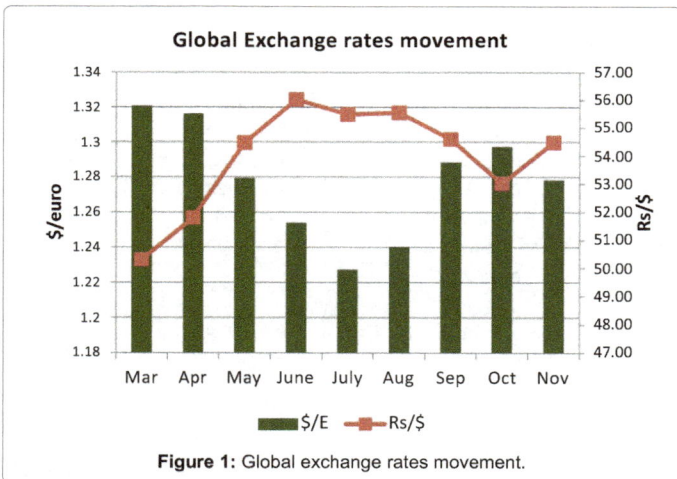

Figure 1: Global exchange rates movement.

the stock market of Bahrain. For this purpose, they had taken the data from year 1996 to 2006 and applies the unit root model. Their results are showing that there is negative association between exchange rate volatility and stock market. This study suggested that policy makers should work in the case of decrease the exchange rate [3].

Ajayi and Mougoue observed the impact of exchange rate on the stock market of Indonesian. For this purpose, they had taken the data from year 1993 to 2004 and applies the regression analysis model. Their results are showing that there is negative association between exchange rate volatility and stock market. This study suggested that policy makers should work in the case of decrease the exchange rate [4].

Doong et al. studied the impact of exchange rate on the stock market of Bahamas. For this purpose, they had taken the data from year 1999 to 2012 and applies the VAR analysis model. Their results are showing that there is negative association between exchange rate volatility and stock market. This study suggested that policy makers should work in the case of decrease the exchange rate [5].

Joseph, N, Analyzed the impact of exchange rate on the stock market of India. For this purpose, they had taken the data from year 1998 to 2008 and applies the OLS model. Their results are showing that there is negative association between exchange rate volatility and stock market. This study suggested that policy makers should work in the case of decrease the exchange rate [6].

Yau and Nieh, observed the impact of exchange rate on the stock market of Bangladesh. For this purpose, they had taken the data from year 1995 to 2015 and applies the Autogressive model. Their results are showing that there is negative association between exchange rate volatility and stock market. This study suggested that policy makers should work in the case of decrease the exchange rate [7].

Wu explored the impact of exchange rate on the stock market of USA. For this purpose, they had taken the data from year 1998 to 2008 and applies the multi regression model. Their results are showing that there is negative association between exchange rate volatility and stock market. This study suggested that policy makers should work in the case of decrease the exchange rate [8].

Takeshi viewed the impact of exchange rate on the stock market of UK. For this purpose, they had taken the data from year 1995 to 2005 and applies the OLS model. Their results are showing that there is negative association between exchange rate volatility and stock market.

This study suggested that policy makers should work in the case of decrease the exchange rate [9].

Parkinson examined the impact of exchange rate on the stock market of Malaysia. For this purpose, they had taken the data from year 1997 to 2007 and applies the ECM model. Their results are showing that there is negative association between exchange rate volatility and stock market. This study suggested that policy makers should work in the case of decrease the exchange rate [10,11].

Gaps in literature

1) In the prior studies nobody had discussed about the impact of exchange rate on the other variables.

2) From the last few decades, nobody has viewed both increase and decrease impact on the Bombay stock exchange.

3) Impact of stock exchange on the monetary policy of India.

4) Which factors are affected on the growth of economy?

Theoretical framework

Theoretical framework is shown in Figure 2.

Methodology

In the paper, we are viewing the linkage between Indian stock rate movements and volatility. For these proper results, we have used the daily data (Tables 1 and 2).

$$r = \ln P(t) / P(t-1)$$

Empirical analysis

In methodology, there are four main steps1) normality test 2) jarqu e-bera statistics 3) ADF. The purpose of normality test to determine the nature of the data and Jarqu e-bera statistics for the disturbing purpose.

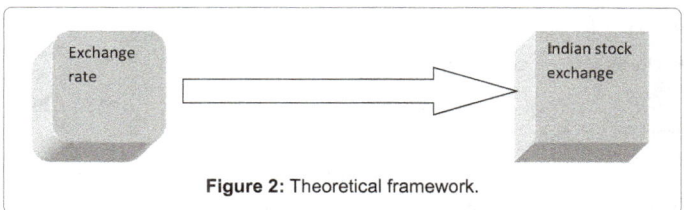

Figure 2: Theoretical framework.

	Stock Returns	Exchange Rates
Observations	355	355
Mean	-0.001165	0.000126
Median	-0.001715	0.000217
Maximum	0.061572	0.031269
Minimum	-0.110131	-0.011267
Std. Deviation	0.016261	0.003247
Skewness	-0.195281	0.197228
Kurtosis	4.112681	9.026138
Jarque-Bera	47.11652	540.1171
Probability	0	0
Sum	-0.719532	0.282188
Sum Sq Dev.	0.218016	0.018118
Result	Not Normal	Not Normal

ADF Test Statistic -9.522262: 1% Critical Value* -3.9892; 5% Critical Value -3.42272; 10% Critical Value -3.1375.

*MacKinnon critical values for rejection of hypothesis of a unit root.

Table 1: Results of augmented dickey fuller test.

	Coefficient	Std. Error	t-Statistic	Prob.
RETURN(-1)	-1.15124	0.120893	-9.52636	0
D(RETURN(-1))	0.203939	0.104893	1.944731	0.0591
D(RETURN(-2))	0.187599	0.090453	2.073497	0.0327
D(RETURN(-3))	0.158121	0.074293	2.128202	0.032
D(RETURN(-4))	0.040239	0.054393	0.739231	0.469
C	0.000119	0.002893	0.039136	0.9612
1	-1.45E-05	1.44E-02	-1.0061	0.3122
R-squared	0.479675	Mean dependent var	5.87E-09	
Adjusted	R-0.4703256 S.D. dependent var	0.035239		
S.E. of regression	0.0261577 Akaike info criterion	4.442913		
Sum squared resid	0.228498	Schwarz criterion	4.350219	
Log likelihood	762.1738	F-statistic	51.31296	
5Durbin-Watson	2.009114	Prob(F-statistic)	0	
	Stock exchange Returns	Exchange Rates		
Nifty Returns	7	-0.08678		
Exchange Rates	-0.0978	9		

Table 2: ADF on return series.

We also checked that data is stationary or not. The values of Skeweness and Kurtosis are showing that these are normally disturbed. Skeweness value are 0.28538 and 0.247329 respectively. Mean and variance are constant here, ADF results are -9.522393 and -8.078962 respectively, at level form data are stationary.

Conclusion

The prime objective of our study to find out the association exchange rate and stock maker; According to William there is long run association between stock exchange and stock market. For this purpose, they have applied the latest models to find out the better results. According to pettron there is inverse relationship between stock market and exchange rate.

Policy recommendation

1) There is need of proper polices for the investment in stock exchange in the condition of decreasing exchange rate.

2) Government should give attention towards the issue of high stock exchange.

3) There should make polices about the controlling exchange rate, it is best way to increase the investors.

References

1. Najaf R, Najaf K (2016) Dynamics of the Exchange Rate in Malaysia. International Journal of Academic Research in Management and Business 1: 104.

2. Aggarwal R (2003) Exchange rates and stock prices: A study of the US capital market sunder floating exchange rates. Akron Business and Economic Review 12: 7-12.

3. Babu MS, Prabheesh K (2007) Causal Relationships between Foreign Institutional Investments and stock returns in India. International Journal of Trade and Global Markets 1: 259-265.

4. Ajayi RA, Mougoue M (1996) On the dynamic relation between stock prices and Exchange Rates. Journal of Financial Research 19: 193-207.

5. Doong SC, Yang SY, Wang AT (2005) The Emerging Relationship and Pricing of Stocks and Exchange Rates: Empirical Evidence from Asian Emerging Markets. Journal of American Academy of Business, Cambridge 7: 118-123.

6. Joseph N (2002) Modeling the impacts of interest rate and exchange rate changes on UK Stock Returns. Derivatives Use, Trading & Regulation 7: 306-323.

7. Yau HY, Nieh CC (2006) Interrelationships among stock prices of Taiwan and Japan and NTD/Yen exchange rate. Journal of Asian Economics 17: 535–552.

8. Wu Y (2000) Stock prices and exchange rates in a VEC model-the case of Singapore in the 1990s. Journal of Economics and Finance 24: 260-274.

9. Takeshi I (2008) The causal relationships in mean and variance between stock returns and Foreign institutional investment in India. IDE Paper Discussion 3: 19-337.

10. Parkinson JM (1987) The EMH and the CAPM on the Nairobi Stock Exchange. East African Economic Review 13: 105-110.

11. Naeem M, Abdul R (2002) Stock Prices and Exchange Rates: Are they related? Evidence from South Asian Countries. The Pakistan Development Review 41: 535-550.

14

Are All Bank Acquisitions Equal? The Impact of Bank Mergers and Acquisitions around the 2007-2009 Financial Crisis: Evidence from TARP

Timothy King[1]* and Ruhua Kong[2]

[1]Research Officer, Accounting and Finance, Leeds University Business School, UK
[2]Imperial College Business School, London

Abstract

The large wave of bank mergers, which had affected the US bank sector in the years leading 2007-2009 crisis, experienced a sudden decline in both volume and value in the post-financial crisis period. This study examines whether TARP banks, i.e. banks that received government financial support during the recent 2007-2009 crisis, differed in terms of M&A financial performance outcomes in the pre and post financial crisis periods compared to non-TARP recipients. We find significant and differences in the post-merger financial performance of TARP recipients compared to non-TARP recipients in the post financial crisis period but no significant differences in their pre-merger performance. Our results infer differences in merger motivations for TARP and non-TARP banks.

Keywords: Banks; Bank bailouts; Government capital injections; TARP mergers and acquisitions

Introduction

The number of commercial banks in the U.S. has decreased rapidly in the last decade. Number of U.S. commercial bank charters fell by 13.7 percent (from 8,579 to 7,391) between 2000 and 2006, and by an additional 17.5 percent (from 7,391 to 6,101) between 2007 and 2012 [1]. These trends were shaped by on-going unassisted mergers throughout the 2000s; along with an increase in number of failed banks and the decrease in number of new charters issued around the financial crisis.

Previous research identifies conflicting results as to the casual impact of bank consolidation activities on bank performance. As the trend of deregulation in the financial industry, academic studies start to examine acquisitions across geographic locations and production lines, and several of them identify improvements in post-merger performance for mergers with certain deal characteristics [2,3]. Other research examines the pre-merger characteristics of target and acquiring banks, and identifies changes in operating efficiency, as well as the trend of mean reversion in the post-merger period [4-6]. However, the majority of studies to date, focus on M&As completed in the period prior to the financial crisis of 2007-09. Although, many studies examine merger related outcomes in relation to changes in government regulatory factors, almost all overlook the impact of government assistance, i.e. FDIC assisted mergers in the US, on the changes in bank performance around mergers [7-9].

Building on extant M&A research, this paper contributes to literature by providing a first examination as to whether large US bank recipients of Troubled Asset Support Program (TARP) funds in 2008 exhibited significant differences in merger performance compared to non-TARP banks over the period of 2007-2012 by examining differences in pre and post-merger financial outcomes between TARP and Non-TARP banks. We are motivated to do so based on existing work that suggests differences between TARP and Non-TARP banks.

By way of preview, our results highlight significant and important differences in the financial performance outcomes of bank acquisitions between TARP and Non-TARP banks in the post financial crisis period. In particular, we find that TARP banks experience significantly larger deteriorations in post-merger performance compare to non-TARP recipients in terms of changes in operating cash flows and declines in profit efficiency, operating efficiency and asset quality indicators.

The decrease in asset quality is more likely to be caused by the large scale of loan defaults in the background of sub-mortgage crisis and recession. The decrease in operating efficiency may be explained as the banks focus more on expanding bank asset size, thus lead to acquisition of less efficient banks. The decrease in profit efficiency is due to use interest-earning assets less efficiently, and this can be caused by the deterioration in loan quality and increasing valuation uncertainty in the financial market around the financial crisis.

Our results have implications for bank supervisors and regulators in the wake of post crisis financial sector reforms and underscore the continuing importance of M&As as an important avenue that can serve to affect bank performance in terms of changes including capital structure, market power, efficiency of operations, and financial performance. Furthermore, our results provide further support to the notion that banks will continue to seek growth through M&A activities in order to benefit from too-big and/or too-systemically-important-to-fail guarantees [10].

The rest of the paperis organised as follows. Section 2provides an overview of M&As in the U.S. banking industry in the post-2000 period including a review of paper methodologies and results from the bank M&As literature. In addition, we also outline two hypotheses which are tested in the present study. Section 3discusses sample selection and provides descriptive statistics of the sample and bank performance characteristics.

Theoretical Background and Literature Review

The U.S. banking industry in the post-2000 period

Mergers and acquisitions (M&As) in the U.S. banking industry in

---

*Corresponding author: Timothy King, Research Officer, Accounting and Financ, Leeds University Business School, UK
E-mail: t.p.king@leeds.ac.uk

the 2000s were driven by changes in the competitive landscape including financial deregulation, technology innovation and financial innovation. The Interstate Banking and Branching Efficiency Act (IBBEA) of 1994, and the Gramm-Leach-Bliley Act (GLBA) of 1999, encouraged interstate banking; allowing commercial banks to undertake the role of investment banks and insurance companies. Importantly, these financial deregulations enabled commercial banks to expand into geographic markets and product markets through consolidating activities [11]. In addition, rapid developments in computer science and communication technology have contributed to technological innovations in the back-office processing, front-office delivering system and payment systems, help improved the operating efficiency, enabled the branching strategy that aimed to take advantage of geographical diversification and the economies of scale [12]. Separately, financial innovations such as financial engineering, new risk management tools and the more sophisticated derivatives markets drastically changed the operational and competitive strategies to be considered by bank holding companies, and enabled banks to take advantage of product diversification and the economies of scope [13].

Banks that were larger and better diversified, particularly geographically, were more likely to survive in the merger wave period; prior to the financial crisis of 2007-09. In contrast, smaller and/or less financially sound banks tended to become takeover targets to larger and better diversified competitors [11]. A motivating factor was the rapid development in evolvement of financial system which increased the market competition and market concentration. Wheelock (2011) points out that deposit concentration continued - the 10 largest banks hold 49 percent of total U.S. deposits by the end of 2010, while this figure was 28 percent by 1999. Importantly, in the context of the present study, we highlight that bank consolidation activities in the period 2007-12 show different features compare to merger in period 2000-06.

As discussed, the recent financial crisis shaped the consolidation activities in the U.S. market with a decline in number of deals, along with a shift from M&As involve both financial soundness institutions to mainly acquisitions of failed or distressed institutions by comparably soundness institutions [14]. To illustrate, the total number of banks eliminated by both FDIC-assisted and unassisted mergers decreased by 26 percent, from 2,272 banks between 2000 and 2006, to 1,695 banks between 2007 and 2012, while the percentage of total unassisted mergers decreased to 72.6 percent of total number of eliminated banks during 2007-2012, compare to the figure of 94.9 percent during 2000-2006 (Appendix 1). Changes in trends of assisted and unassisted mergers around the financial crisis are partly influenced by the subprime mortgage crisis, which posed pressure on banks' ability to stay financial soundness and maintain assets quality with increasing uncertainty in the valuation of mortgages and mortgage-backed securities [15]. Meanwhile, short-term financing sources dried up to financial institutions, in which a large proportion of debt instruments were used. The interbank market became inactive due to the perceived default and the significantly increase in the liquidity risk [16]. A shortage of liquidity in the short-time financing market, along with the uncertainty in asset valuation, led to the decrease in number of unassisted mergers. In addition to the attempts of mergers to achieve 'too-big-to-fail' status in the pre-crisis period, comparably soundness banks started to take advantage of the market conditions and acquire less soundness banks with asset size which allows the merged bank to achieve a size large enough to become systematically important.

The U.S. Department of the Treasury introduced the Troubled Asset Relief Program (TARP) in order to prevent the economy from falling into great recession on September 19, 2008. The U.S. Congress passed the modified version of TARP, and the department of Treasury revised the TARP and announced the Capital Purchase Program (CPP) as a sub-program of TARP on October 14, 2008. This revision allocated 250 billion USD to purchase senior preferred stocks and warrants from certain depository financial institutions, thus help them restore from the liquidity drain-up being caused by the inactive inter-bank market and declining value of toxic and illiquid assets. Treasury provided capital injection to 707 financial institutions under CPP. Recent research suggests that pre-crisis characteristics of banks are related to the probability of receiving TARP funds [17-19]. An important empirical question yet to be suitably examined, which we address in the current paper, pertains to whether the M&As undertook by TARP recipients have different impact on post-acquisition performance compare to non-recipients around the financial crisis of 2007-09.

The impacts of M&As on U.S. banking industry: a review of methodologies and results of literatures

Previous research evaluates post-acquisition performance in relation to different factors, and identifies inconsistent results for M&As in the U.S. banking industry prior to the financial crisis of 2007-09. Evaluations of the consequences of consolidation activities are conducted using two main approaches, the operating performance approach and the shareholder value approach [20]. The operating performance approach measures post-acquisition economic performance through analysing changes in bank's cost function and profit function, while the shareholder value approach measures post-acquisition performance through analysing market abnormal returns around the merger announcement or in a longer timeframe.

The operating performance approach is used to measure the economic changes in post-acquisition directly using accounting variables method or efficiency method. The accounting variables are largely used as a measure of operating performance in studies about M&As happened prior to the financial crisis. Some research in the 1990s compares financial ratio indicators for pre- and post-merger periods to examine impacts of mergers on operating costs and profits. Cornett and Tehranian [21] examine the post-merger performance of large US bank mergers during 1989-1987 using a return metric being generated through dividing operating cash flows by the market value of asset, and find that on average merged banks outperform the banking industry. They use additional bank performance indicators to identify the sources of improvements in operating cash flow, and find significant improvements in the ability to attract loans and deposits, in employee productivity, and in portfolio asset growth. Kwan and Wilcox [7] compare changes in operating costs between merged banks and the control group of similar sized banks and find significant declines in labour cost and occupancy expense in US bank mergers during the 1990s. They remove the pure accounting effects through adjusting the differences in expense data treatments between the purchasing and pooling methods, find significant reduction in operating costs and evidence of accounting methods being able to hide a significant portion of cost cuts.

Research in the 2000s built on earlier literature, by examining additional firm performance metrics. More specifically, more sophisticated methodologies are employed in order to examine additional factors/chanels of performance improvements; as well as to investigate correlations between these factors. For example, Knapp et al. [22] adopt lagged regression analysis on four industry-adjusted profitability ratios, and identify significant negative coefficients for each individual year, which provide evidence for the strong mean reversion trend in merged bank profitability. This indicates that profit performance of merged bank tends to move back towards the industry mean overtime, regardless it outperform or underperform the industry in one year after the merger. In addition, they find that merged banks significantly outperform the industry in the first five years after the merger once adjust the profitability measure for mean revision.

Other studies seek to identify the sources and channels governing changes in post-acquisition performance [3]. Cornett et al. [8] find that large, activity-focusing or geographic-focusing mergers during 1990-2000 produce greater performance gains compare to small or diversifying mergers, and the performance improvements are traced back to both revenue enhancements and cost reduction activities. Hagendorff and Keasy [3] find no evidence of improvements in the overall post-merger performance for mergers announced during 1996-2004, and this is consistent with their findings of revenue enhancements due to improvements in both interest and non-interest income, and efficiency deterioration due to increase costs and lower productivity. Al-Khasawnen and Essaddam [20] identify two main weaknesses of the operating performance approach based on accounting ratios. First of all, the accuracy and reliability of financial ratios as the measure of bank performance is questionable. There are also limitations using accounting data as the only measure of company performance. In addition, although corporate financial reporting is regulated by the US General Accepted Accounting Principles being adopted by the US Securities and Exchange Commission, the regulation cannot absolutely eliminate data manipulation and window-dressing. Secondly, performance ratios are not suitable measures of cost and profit efficiency since ratios cannot measure and represent differences in input prices and output mix.

Efficiency measures such as scale efficiency and X-efficiency are used as alternative methods to evaluate post-acquisition economic performance. This type of methodology is concerned with inputs and outputs thus provide solution to the second limitation of accounting measures, and are used to investigate merger's efficiency gains on the perspective of both cost and revenue. Rhoades [23] finds that although acquiring banks generally have strength in operating efficiency compare to target banks in mergers happened during 1981-1986, and the horizontal mergers are supposed to bring considerable deposit overlap thus lead to the economies of scale, those mergers do not yield efficiency gains. Peristiani [24] develops the Distribution-Free Approach (DFA) into measuring the managerial efficiency (X-efficiency) of merged banks, and find a small but significant decline in pro forma X-efficiency and concludes that mergers during the 1980s are not beneficial to banks managerial efficiency. Asaftei [5] analyses the impact of GLBA of 1999 on bank consolidation activities applying the return on assets (ROA) change decomposition methodology, and find that contribution of product mix was significant and offset losses from technical change and declining operating efficiency. He also identifies that large banks benefit more than community banks through accessing the recent financial innovation and deregulation at lower costs and switching to an optimal output portfolio mix.

The efficiency concept is better understood through the lens of Stochastic Frontier Analysis (SFA) and Data Envelopment Analysis (DEA) to analyse the relation between post-acquisition performance and banks' position at the efficiency frontier, and to compare the efficiency gains related to certain bank criteria, for example bank size and size of the merger [5,6,25]. Al-Sharkas et al. [6] find significant improvement in profit efficiency for both large and small bank mergers through using non-standard profit efficiency model. They also use DEA to investigate the sources of efficiency gains associated

with bank mergers, and find that small bank mergers generate greater cost efficiency improvements compare to large bank mergers, while this efficiency gain is due to improvements in technical efficiency as a result of using the most efficient technology available, and allocation efficiency as a result of launching cost minimizing input mix. This type of more sophisticated frontier methods can be used to investigate and quantify the impacts of factors such as technological progress, product and geographic diversification, risk diversification and economics of scale through a more econometric-based approach.

The shareholder value approach is used to investigate market reaction to merger announcement through measuring the market abnormal returns using variables like cumulated abnormal returns (CARs) and cumulated average abnormal returns (CAARs) applying different event window, and determine whether merger announcement generates shareholder wealth effect. Cornett and De [26] examines the value creation of interstate bank mergers through using a standard event study methodology to calculate an abnormal return of each security for event day t, and testing for significance. They find significant positive stock price reaction to merger announcement for both target and acquiring banks. Madura and Wiant [27] examine the long-term valuation effects of mergers through generating average abnormal returns and CAARs using monthly data, and then test for significance. They find that banks experienced significant negative abnormal returns on average for the period three years following the merger. Penas and Unal [28] find evidence of bondholder gains of acquiring banks, as a result of diversification, the achievement of too-big-too-fail status and synergy gains. They also identify significant positive correlation between announcement-month bond and equity returns, which proves that bank merger wealth creating rather than shifting wealth from shareholders to bondholders. Knapp et al. [22] find negative returns to shareholders of acquirers in large bank mergers happened between 1987 and 1998. DeLong [29] finds that market reacts differently to different types of mergers. Market reacts positively to geographic-focus and product-focus mergers, while the cumulate abnormal returns are positively connected to the relative target to bidder size and negatively connected to the pre-merger performance of target banks. Hagendroff et al. [30] identify stronger positive value effects to acquiring bank when the target bank is located in markets with lower level investor protection. They find that bidders targeting banks which operate in high investor protection regimes (the US and the UK) generally generate negative market reaction, since it is more difficult to realize gains following the acquisition. The assumptions behind the stock market event study approach are, first of all, the market is efficient and can react to large corporate event announcement, and secondly, the market will adjust the corporation market cap to reflect the economic implications, for example any potential changes in profit and cost efficiency as a result of the merger.

Some research uses a combination of operating performance approach and the shareholder value approach. Cornett and Tehranian [21] find a significant correlation between announcement period abnormal returns and operational performance measured by various accounting ratios, which indicates that the market participants are able to identify in advance the improvements in merged bank performance. Chronopoulos et al. [25] examine the relation between changes in cost and profit efficiency and the announcement-period abnormal returns. They find a positive relation between change in profit efficiency and acquirer's CARs, which indicates that market participants are able to identify merger-related profit efficiency gains upon merger announcement, while the relation between change in cost efficiency and the acquirer's CARs is not statistically significant.

Hypotheses development

We hypothesise, based on existing literature, that M&As undertook by TARP banks around the financial crisis 2007-09 have different features and motivations compared to merger activity in periods when systematic risk is relatively low. Our first hypothesis is that bank consolidation activities around the financial crisis 2007-09 lead to changes in bank profitability, operating efficiency and liquidity in three years after the acquisition. The null hypothesis is that the difference between pre- and post-merger performance are not significantly different from zero. The alternative hypothesis is that mergers improve bank performance.

Recent research investigates the impact of M&As on bank performance using post 2000 data. Dunn et al. [9] examine the non-government-assisted mergers of commercial banks closed during 2004-2010. They investigate the nature of bank mergers happened prior to and during the financial crisis period through testing the valuation discrepancy, the efficient discrepancy and the capital discrepancy, and the value creation effects through observing changes in shareholder value around the merger announcement. Brune et al. [31] examine acquisitions of capital-constrained and unconstrained banks between 1990 and 2008 to determine differences in post-merger performance of these two groups of banks and to identify deal characteristics that prompt better post-merger performance. Chuang [32] investigates the relation between the deal advisor and the extent of shareholder wealth effect around merger announcement with an observing period during 1995-2010. Hagendroff and Keasey [3] examine the relation between post-acquisition strategy and merged bank performance using deals announced during 1996-2004. To the best of our knowledge there is limited empirical research into operating performance changes of mergers around the financial crisis. This hypothesis will contribute to previous research through identifying any difference in post-acquisition in attribution to financial crisis, a period with high systematic risk and financial instability.

The second hypothesis is that changes in post-acquisition performance are different between TARP banks and Non-TARP banks, and the difference is due to differences in various bank characteristics. The null hypothesis is: the difference between pre- and post-merger performance of Non-TARP banks is not significantly different from the difference between pre- and post-merger performance of TARP banks. The alternative hypothesis is: TARP banks have a performance significantly worse than Non-TARP banks.

Several recent studiesassess the influence and effectiveness of TARP. Farruggio et al. [33] suggest that the liquid capital available from TARP-CPP can be used to take on new assets and diversify bank's asset portfolio, as long as the correlation decreases after rebalancing the overall asset portfolio. Berger and Bouwman [12] support the argument that capital holding is positively connected to the survival and market shares for small, medium and large banks during banking crisis. However, although TARP recapitalized troubled banks, there is a decline in operating efficiency for all banks during the crisis, while TARP banks experience a more significant decline in operating efficiency, possibly due to the moral hazard related to the reducing incentives of bank managers to improve asset quality [34].

Most existing literatures focus on TARP and TARP's impacts on the performance of individual bank and the banking industry, investor and market confidence and financial stability. To the best of our knowledge there is no research on how being a part of the TARP and receive government capital injection will affect post-acquisition

performance. In addition, most research excludes the government-assisted mergers since the accounting of failed bank takeover can bring bias into the post-acquisition performance thus affect the output. Although this research does not cover FDIC assisted merges, it is supposed to contribute to the study of mergers and acquisitions in the banking industry through investigating government policy's impact on the operating performance of acquired banks. This hypothesis will fill the gap that little previous research connects, i.e. are bank's pre-merger soundness and systematically important explanatory factors influencing post-acquisition performance. Recent research examines TARP's effectiveness on recipient bank performance, credit creation ability and the financial industry stability, and to build onto previous research, this hypothesis will examine the effectiveness of TARP on banks' consolidation activities.

Sample Construction and Performance Measures

Sample selection and data cleaning

The sample of merger deals used in this study were obtained from the M&As database within the Thomson One platform maintained by Thomson-Reuters. The following restrictions were imposed based on prior studies:

1. Sample M&A deals are announced during 2007-2012.

2. The sample deals are completed, and transfer the majority ownerships to the acquirers with the percent of shares owned after transaction more than 50 percent.

3. The acquirers and targets are limited to commercial banks located in the U.S. only. Thrifts are excluded because thrift charter has greater flexibility in affiliation and faces different statutory lending limits.

4. FDIC-assisted purchase of failing banks is excluded.

5. For acquirers engaged in M&A activities for more than once, the sample keeps the first merger announced throughout the observation period.

The quarterly financials for three years prior to and after the year of merger completion were then extracted from the Compustat North America database which is available through the Wharton Research Data Services (WRDS) platform. The final sample contains 114 acquiring banks with merger announcements during 2007-2012. The full list of TARP recipients was then sourced from SNL Financial, and matched with our dataset of acquiring banks. A dummy variable "*TARP*" was introduced, with 0 indicates non-recipients and 1 indicates TARP recipients.

Table 1 summarises the deal numbers of the sample obtained using methods described above. The largest portion of mergers happened in 2007 (39 mergers, which constitutes 34 percent of total mergers), with 22 acquirers engaged in mergers again following the first merger. 61 percent of total mergers were undertaken by TARP banks, while only 39 percent were undertook by Non-TARP banks. For TARP bank mergers, 64 percent were announced during 2007-09, while more than half of these acquiring banks engaged in more than one merger. For banks undertaking multiple mergers, 73 percent are TARP recipients. The descriptive table shows that financial crisis 2007-09 has large impact on bank consolidation activities with number of deal announced dropped rapidly since the crisis began. TARP banks undertake mergers more frequent and intensive before the launch of CPP on the fourth quarter of 2008 than Non-TARP banks, while large portion of TARP banks engaged in multiple mergers. This may indicate that TARP banks use M&As as a strategy to expand and achieve systematically important, thus increase their possibility of receiving government capital injection (Tables 1-3).

Table 2 summarizes the value of transactions for deal with disclosed value. The mean deal value is 192.21 million U.S. dollar in 2007, which drops rapidly to 48.39 million U.S. dollar in 2008 and remains at a relatively low level thereafter. For deals announced during 2007-09, TARP banks have a much larger deal value compare to Non-TARP banks. For deals announced after 2008, TARP banks have a much smaller deal value than Non-TARP banks. Since the TARP programme was first introduced on September 19, 2008, it suggests again that commercial banks may use mergers to expand bank size to become systematically important. In addition, the mean value of TARP bank involved mergers dropped significantly in 2009, which may be interpreted as TARP banks achieved their size expansion strategy and got included in the capital injection list, thus ceased from bidding. However, this decline in mean deal value may due to TARP banks' deterioration in financial performance thus not being able to afford consolidation activities.

Cornett and Terhanian [21], and Hagendroff and Keasey [3] both exclude deals with a total value less than 100 million to ensure the merger is an important corporate event to the acquiring bank and will therefore likely generate identifiable changes in operating performance. However, this study does not put a lower-bound on the size of the deal value. This is partly due to the relatively smaller size of mergers in the post-financial crisis period. The second reason is, this research considers consolidation activities as a strategy to maintain and improve bank operating performance in the changing economic background and regulatory environment. Therefore merger affects bank performance as a strategy derives from the bank management and organisational culture, rather than an isolated corporate event.

Operating performance measures

Similar to previous research, the operating cash flow returns on assets (OPCFROA) is used to examine the profitability of banks [3,8,21]. The operating cash flow is calculated using the following equation:

$OPCFROA=$(*Income before extraordinary items* [*ibcomq*]+*Total income taxes* [*txtq*]+*Interest on other borrowed money* [*xinsq*])/*Total assets* [*atq*]   (1)

The pre-tax operating cash flow is estimated use income figure from cash flow statement, and is then divided by the book value of assets.

Table 3 summarises the OPCFROA of the combined sample for three years before and after the merger. Acquiring banks experienced a rapid deterioration in OPCFROA from 0.2105 percent the year before to 0.0424the year after merger completion. Although it shows a steadily recovery for the three years after merger, the performance by the end of the third year is still worse than the year before merger. The decrease in medium and minimum OPCFROA in the post-merger period indicates that the deterioration is driven by the number and extents of underperformed banks. The descriptive table shows that merger leads to deterioration in bank operating performance. However, this may be a result of deteriorations in the performance of general banking industry, since individual bank performance can be highly correlated with other banks performance. An industry performance benchmark can be introduced to analyse the change in individual bank performance in relation to the industry performance [3,7,8,21]. This research does not introduce an industry benchmark because it aims to analyse the

difference in post-merger performance for TARP recipients and non-recipients, which is specified to the period of Financial Crisis 2007-09 and changes in regulatory environment.

Similar to extant research, a list of common bank indicators is used to identify the sources of changes in OPCFROA. The definition and calculations of each measure is presented in Appendix2.

Empirical Methods, Results and Discussion

Operating cash flow analysis

In order to examine the first null hypothesis of which the differences between pre- and post- merger performance are not significantly different from zero, we use student t-test to examine mean equality and Mann-Whitney-Wilcoxon test to examine median equality [35,36].

Table 4 presents the pre- and post- operating cash flow performance for different groups of acquirers. The mean OPCROA for the combined sample banks experienced a decrease from 0.3103 percent three years before merger to 0.1161 percent three years after merger, and the decline is statistically different from 0 at 1 percent level. This indicates that acquiring bank performance generally deteriorate after merger completion. Since this research does not introduce an

Year	Combined		Non-TARP banks		TARP banks	
	No.	% Total	No.	% Total	No.	% Total
2007	39 (22)	34% (19%)	6 (3)	14% (7%)	33 (19)	48% (28%)
2008	19 (9)	17% (8%)	8 (5)	18% (11%)	11 (4)	16% (6%)
2009	14 (7)	12% (6%)	7 (2)	16% (5%)	6 (5)	9% (7%)
2010	18 (6)	16% (5%)	12 (4)	27% (9%)	6 (2)	9% (3%)
2011	10 (2)	9% (2%)	6 (1)	14% (2%)	4 (1)	6% (1%)
2012	14 (1)	12% (1%)	5 (0)	11% (0%)	9 (1)	13% (1%)
Total	114 (47)	100% (41%)	44 (15)	100% (34%)	69 (32)	100% (46%)

Notes: The number and percent inside the brackets summarize the number of deals undertake by banks engaged in multiple mergers at their first time being observed.

Table 1: Summary statistics on the deal numbers in the sample of commercial bank mergers.

Year	Combined		Non-TARP		TARP	
	Observations	Mean	Observations	Mean	Observations	Mean
2007	37	192.21	6	96.59	31	210.71
2008	15	48.39	6	16.61	9	69.57
2009	5	21.84	4	25.23	'	8.31
2010	12	35.34	9	40.33	3	20.40
2011	7	23.65	5	31.57	2	3.84
2012	14	48.15	5	78.52	9	31.28
Total	90	102.34	35	48.387	55	136.67

Notes: 24 mergers in the observation sample do not have a disclosed value of transaction.

Table 2: Summary statistics on the value of transactions in the sample of commercial bank mergers.

	Mean	Median	St. Dev	Minimum	Maximum
t=-3	0.3354	0.3698	0.2641	-1.7191	1.0060
t=-2	0.3107	0.3458	0.3491	-4.0199	1.7440
t=-1	0.2861	0.3223	0.3590	-3.9355	2.5631
t=1	0.0727	0.2280	0.6412	-5.7238	2.0487
t=2	0.1170	0.2426	0.5104	-4.1797	1.9607
t=3	0.1705	0.2754	0.5055	-6.0021	0.9389

Table 3: Summary statistics on the operating cash flow measure of all banks engaged in mergers.

industry benchmark to control the industry-wide factors, for example, the aftermath of the financial crisis, it is difficult to draw a conclusion that M&As is the only factor destroys commercial bank's operating performance. Both TARP and Non-TARP acquirers experience significant decreases in post-merger performance at 1 percent level, while TARP banks experienced a larger decline in mean OPCFROA compare to Non-TARP banks.

The result from Table 5 highlight that bank operating performance deteriorate significantly after merger completion, while TARP banks experienced more rapid deterioration compare to Non-TARP banks. The sources of changes are then investigated using the list of common bank indicators.

Common bank indicators: analysis

Table 5 presents the changes in operating performance indicators of commercial banks around the merger. The changes in pre- and post-merger value are examined to identify statistically significant changes in bank performance.

Profit efficiency indicators: For all banks engaged in mergers, the operating performance deteriorates in the post-merger period. The return on average assets and return on average equity both decrease and significant at 1 percent level, while return on average equity decreased to -0.0393, which indicates losses for some sample banks. Although the difference in return on average equity are statistically significant

for both TARP and Non-TARP banks, TARP banks experience a more rapid decline to a mean of -0.6436. This may be caused by the significant decrease in TARP banks' net interest margin, which indicates a less effective use of bank's interest earning assets in relation to the interest cost of funding them.

Net interest income indicators: The result shows that both TARP and Non-TARP banks experience significant decreases in net loans to assets, while TARP banks have significant higher net loans to asset rate compare to Non-TARP banks. This indicates decreases in loan commitment level in the post-merger period for all banks, while TARP banks still have a higher level of loan commitment activities. This also confirms that TARP banks' deterioration in profitability may be caused by decreases in net interest margin, rather than the loan commitments level.

Operating efficiency indicators: The non-interest expenses to assets ratio experience significant increase in the post-merger period, while Non-TARP banks experience a more rapid increase compare to TARP banks, to a level not significantly different from the post-merger level of TARP banks. This indicates that Non-TARP banks experienced a larger increase in operating expenses and a more rapid decrease in operating efficiency. Employment costs as a percentage of operating expenses also increases significantly for the post-merger period for all banks, which may suggest that combined operation of banks increases the employment expenses.

	Pre-merger			Post-merger			Differences	
	No. obs.	Mean	Median	No. obs.	Mean	Median	Mean	Median
All banks	1316	0.3103	0.3456	1228	0.1161	0.2437	0.1942***	0.1020†
Non-TARP banks	494	0.3149	0.3456	468	0.2131	0.2865	0.1018***	0.0592†
TARP banks	822	0.3075	0.3454	760	0.0564	0.2058	0.2512***	0.1396†

Notes: The differences are calculated through deducting post-merger performance from pre-merger performance. ***, ** and * denote significance at 1, 5 and 10 percent levels, respectively, according to t-statistics on two sample with equal variance. † denotes Wilcoxon rank-sum test is significant at 5%.

Table 4: Pre- and post-merger operating cash flow performance for different groups of acquirers.

	Combined	Non-TARP	TARP
Profit efficiency indicators			
Return on average assets	0.1309***,†	0.0680***,†	0.1695***,†
Return on average equity	2.0359***,†	1.1006***,†	2.6110***,†
Net interest margin	0.0486*	-0.0141	0.0857***
Net-interest income indicators			
Net interest income to assets	0.0190***	0.0074	0.0262***
Net interest income to operating income	0.0011	0.0133	-0.0064
Net loans to assets	2.3507***,†	2.9397***,†	1.9769***,†
Operating efficiency indicators			
Cost-to-income ratio	46.7249†	120.0624	1.8609†
Non-interest expenses to assets	-0.0418***,†	-0.0365***,†	-0.0452***,†
Employment cost to operating expenses	-0.0364***,†	-0.0596***,†	-0.0220***,†
Asset quality indicators			
Loan loss provisions to net interest income	-14.0789***,†	-6.1974***,†	-18.9345***,†
Non-performing loans to gross loans	-2.0693***,†	-1.5415***,†	-2.3875***,†
ORED to assets	-0.3385***,†	-0.2846***,†	-0.3700***,†
Deposits to assets	-0.0249***,†	-0.0354***,†	-0.0186***,†
Capital adequacy indicators			
Tier 1 capital ratio	-0.3320**,†	0.6014**,†	-0.9105***,†
Capital surplus	-682.35***,†	-213.99***,†	-965.16***,†
Equity to assets	0.0066***	0.0139***	0.0024*

Notes: The differences are calculated through deducting post-merger performance from pre-merger performance. ***, ** and * denote significance at 1, 5 and 10 percent levels, respectively, according to t-statistics. † denotes Wilcoxon rank-sum test is significant at 5%.

Table 5: Common bank performance indicators for different group of acquirers.

Asset quality indicator: The result shows significant deteriorations in asset quality in the post-merger period for all banks. The loan loss provisions to net interest income increases from 11.2732 to 25.3521 for all banks, which indicates that for every one hundred dollar net interest income, banks need to hold 25.3531 dollars as the loan loss provisions in the post-merger period. Banks also experience significantly increases in non-performing loans and other real-estate acquired as loan obligations. The deterioration in post-merger bank's asset quality may be caused by low asset quality of target firms. However, this deterioration is more likely a result of the ongoing financial crisis, since the majority of merger happened in 2007, the post-merger observation period is also the period under the subprime mortgage crisis's impacts.

Capital adequacy indicators: Table 6 shows significant increases in Tier 1 capital ratio and total capital ratio for all banks, while the results are imbalanced for TARP and Non-TARP banks. This imbalance is due to TARP banks' lower capital ratios in the pre-merger period compare to Non-TARP banks, and the merger helps TARP banks to improve their capital structure. While for the Non-TARP banks, they improve the efficiency of the use of spare capital through involving in consolidation activities.

Differences-in-differences regression: performance changes of TARP recipient and non-recipient banks

A differences-in-differences estimation is introduced to examine the second null hypothesis, which is the difference between the changes in pre- and post-merger performance for TARP recipient and non-recipient banks is not different from zero. The TARP banks are viewed as the treatment group and the Non-TARP banks are viewed as the control group. This research assumes that the outcome in treatment and control group would follow the same time trend in the absence of the treatment, which means changes in post-merger performance will be in the identical trend and scale in comparison with the pre-merger trend and scale for both TARP and Non-TARP banks.

The change in OPCFROA of TARP banks is compared with change in OPCFROA of Non-TARP banks for the period before and after the merger completion. The regression model is:

$$OPCFROA_{ist} = \alpha + \gamma Tarp_s + \lambda Event_t + \delta(Tarp_s * Event_t) + \varepsilon_{ist} [2]$$

Where:

$OPCFROA_{ist}$ is the operating cash flow measure for commercial banks.

$Tarp_s$ is a dummy which is equal to 0 if the observation is a Non-TARP bank, is equal to 1 if the observation is a TARP bank.

$Event_t$ is a dummy which is equal to 0 if the observation is from pre-merger period, is equal to 1 if the observation is from post-merger period.

$Tarp_s * Event_t$ is the interaction between the two dummies mentioned above.

ε_{ist} is the residual.

The regression result is reported in Table 6. Non-TARP banks' pre-merger OPCFROA is slightly better than TARP-banks, by a 0.007 percent, which is statistically different from zero. Non-TARP banks' post-merger OPCFROA is better than TARP banks by 0.157 percent, which is significantly different from zero at 1 percent level. Non-TARP banks experience a decrease of 0.102 percent from the pre-merger period to the post-merger period, while Non-TARP banks experience a decrease of 0.251 percent. Both decreases are significant at 1 percent level. The overall result indicates that TARP and Non-TARP banks do not have significant differences in pre-merger performance, while TARP banks perform significantly worse compare to Non-TARP banks in the post-merger period. This may indicates that TARP recipient banks do have strategic differences concerning the consolidation activities compare to Non-TARP banks, which lead to underperform of TARP banks in the post-merger period (Table 6).

Ordinary-least-square estimation: factors contributed to the differences in TARP recipients and non-recipient banks

A linear regression is introduced to investigate factors that may have impact on bank operating performance.

Variable	Non-TARP banks	TARP banks	Difference, TARP – Non-TARP
Pre-merger OPCFROA	0.315	0.308	-0.007
	(32.77)	(27.29)	(-0.52)
Post-merger OPCFROA	0.213	0.056	-0.157***
	(8.05)	(3.34)	(-5.12)
Change in pre- and post-OPCFROA	-0.102***	-0.251***	-0.149***
	(-4.17)	(-8.96)	(0.035)

Notes: z-value is reported inside the brackets. Significance inference: ***p<0.001; **p<0.05; *p<0.01.

Table 6: Regression results for the differences-in-differences estimation without covariates.

	Independent variables	Interactions with TARP
TARP		0.3275**
Event dummy	-0.0436**	-0.0759***
Multiple M&A Dummy	0.0724***	-0.0609**
Size	0.0640***	0.0000
Deal value	0.0124**	-0.0119*
Loan loss provision	-0.0094***	0.0020***
Non-interest expenses	-0.6248***	-0.1343***
Net interest margin	0.1858***	-0.0513**
_cons	-0.37798***	

Notes: This table reports the coefficients for independent variables and interactions between TARP and each independent variable. ***, ** and * denotes significance at 1 percent, 5 percent and 10 percent level.

Table 7: Regression results for the ordinary-least-square estimators with interactions.

$$OPCFROA_{ist} = \alpha + \beta_1 Event_t + \beta_2 MultiM\&A_i + \beta_3 Size_i + \beta_4 DealValue_i + \beta_5 LoanLoss_i + \beta_6 Noninterest_i + \beta_7 Netinterest_i + \varepsilon_{ist} \qquad (3)$$

The dependent variable is the mean of OPCFROA. $Event_t$ is the event dummy. ε_{ist} is the residuals. The following list of independent variables is introduced to analyse other bank specific factors' impact on the operating performance:

$MultiM\&A_i$: The multiple merger dummy is 0 if the acquiring bank engaged in only one merger, and is 1 if the acquiring bank engaged in more than one merger throughout the observation period. It is expected that banks engaged in multiple merger has more extra capital and more efficient in the aspect of operating efficiency.

$Size_i$: Size is measured as the natural logarithm of acquiring bank's book value of total assets. Banks with larger asset size is supposed to be more efficient and have a better post-merger performance.

$Deal Value_i$: Deal value is measured as the ratio of value of transaction to the book value of acquiring bank's assets. Post-merger performance is expected to deteriorate as the relative size of transaction increases, because larger deal size may indicates increased complexity to combine the operation of two separate entities.

$Loan Loss_i$: Loan loss provision is expressed as a percentage of net interest income. Loan assets takeover from target banks may lead to deterioration in acquiring banks' asset quality.

$Noninterest_i$: Non-interest expense is measured as a percentage of total assets. This is used to measure bank's operating efficiency exclude the impact of net-interest expense and net-interest margin.

$Netinterest_i$: Net interest margin measures how effectively the bank is utilizing its interest earning assets in relation to the interest cost of funding them.

The Chow test (presented in Appendix 3) rejects the null hypothesis of coefficientsequality between TARP and Non-TARP banks, thus afitted interacted model is used instead of the pooled model in equation [3]:

$$OPCFROA_{ist} = \alpha + \beta_1 Event_t + \beta_2 MultiM\&A_i + \beta_3 Size_i + \beta_4 DealValue_i + \beta_5 LoanLoss_i + \beta_6 Noninterest_i + \beta_7 Netinterest_i + \gamma_1 * Tarp + \gamma_2 Tarp * Event_t + \gamma_3 Tarp * MultiM\&A_i + \gamma_4 Tarp * Size_i + \gamma_5 Tarp * DealValue_i + \gamma_6 Tarp * LoanLoss_i + \gamma_7 Tarp * Noninterest_i + \gamma_8 Tarp * Netinterest_i + \varepsilon_{ist} \qquad (4)$$

Where:

$Tarp$ is equal to 1 for the group of TARPrecipient banks, and is equal to 0 for group of non-recipient banks. γ_n indicate interactions between $Tarp$ and independent variables from equation [3].

Table 7 presents regression result of equation [4]. TARP banks have better overall operating cash flow return performance compare to Non-TARP banks with a coefficient of 0.3275 of the TARP dummy. For the Non-TARP banks, operating cash flow performance deteriorates in the post-merger period, while TARP banks have a larger decrease in OPCFROA compare to Non-TARP banks at 1 percent significant level. The sources of change are analysed using loan loss provision, non-interest expenses and net interest margin. The regression results indicates that 1 percent increase in loan loss provision to net interest income will lead to 0.0094 percent decrease in OPCFROA for Non-TARP banks, while it will lead to a smaller decrease for TARP banks. This suggest that TARP banks has a relatively stronger tolerance towards loan loss provision, thus an decrease in Non-TARP banks' asset quality will reduce the differences in operating cash flow returns between TARP and Non-TARP banks. Net interest margin is positively related

to operating cash flow return, with 1 percent increase in net interest margin leads to 0.1858 percent increase in OPCFROA. TARP banks' reaction to increase in net interest margin is smaller than Non-TARP banks by 0.0513, and the difference is significant at 5 percent level. The results suggest that differences in asset quality, operating efficiency, and profit efficiency lead to differences in operating performance of TARP and Non-TARP banks.

The regression also analyses the deal characteristics that may impact on bank performance around the merger completion. Banks' practice of undertaking multiple mergers is positively correlated with operating cash flow return, while TARP bank's engagement in multiple mergers reduces the difference in operating performance between TARP and Non-TARP banks. This may suggest multiple M&As undertake by Non-TARP banks are aimed to improve operating performance, and is driven by the bank's demand to use spare capital. While Non-TARP banks engage in multiple mergers simply to expand, with less consideration on mergers' impact on operating performance. The size of acquiring bank is also related to increases in OPCFROA for Non-TARP banks, while it does not have significant impact on the differences in performance between TARP and Non-TARP banks.

Concluding Remarks

U.S. banking industry experiences dynamic and structural changes during last decades. Government plays a more important role in protect public benefits and maintain financial stability through increasing intervention and regulation. The introduction of CPP aimed to help banks and other financial institutions to stay solvency and to maintain the loan commitment level, thus contribute to the recovery of the U.S. economy after the crisis. However, banks continually engaged in M&As in the period of high systematic risks, and it worth investigating the motives behind and impact of consolidation activities during this period.

This paper examines post-merger performance changes for U.S. commercial banks following M&A activity during 2007-2012 in terms of changes in operating cash flows. The main empirical results lead to the conclusion that bank operating performance deteriorates significantly in the period of three years after merger completion. The deterioration is mainly caused by significantly decreases in profit efficiency, operating efficiency and asset quality. Although the result is specified to the period around financial crisis 2007-09, the study suggests that M&As may not be the most effective strategy to maintain bank operating performance in a market with high systematic risks.

Our results also infer differences in merger motives for TARP recipient banks to engage in more aggressive M&A based consolidation activities. A possible explanation for this observable difference in business strategy for TARP banks may stem from a desired motive to expand to a status of systematically importance, thus increase the possibility of receiving government capital injection in the period prior to the launch of CPP. This leads to the assumption that changes in post-merger performance will be different between TARP and Non-TARP banks, since mergers aim to achieve quickly expansion may lead to deterioration in operating performance.

Although the Capital Purchase Program (CPP) was not introduced until October 14, 2008, we introduce a dummy variable TARP for banks receiving government funds, despite the facts that several mergers undertook by TARP banks have effective date prior to the announcement of revised-TARP. This enables us to examine merger activities based on banks' soundness and systematically importance, especially in the background of high systematic risk in the market. The empirical results suggest that acquirers receive TARP capital injection tends to have a worse post-merger performance compare to non-recipients. This may due to TARP banks' actively engaged in consolidation activities to expand asset sizes, while put less attention on how the merger will affect bank operating performance.

The diff-in-diff regression identifies significant differences between the changes in post-merger performance for TARP versus Non-TARP banks. This suggests the interesting interpretation that TARP banks react differently in the post-merger period compare to TARP banks. In addition, TARP banks experience significantly larger deteriorations in post-merger performance compare to Non-TARP banks, which may provide evidence that as TARP banks concentrating on expand bank asset size, they pay less attention on the potential impacts on bank fundamentals. OLS repressions with interactions confirm the deterioration in post-merger performance, as well as the gain in operating cash flow return through engaging in multiple mergers. It also suggests that the differences in the changes in post-merger performance of TARP and Non-TARP banks are also caused by differences in asset quality, operating efficiency and profit efficiency. The differences in the coefficients of deal characteristics of TARP and Non-TARP banks also provide evidence that TARP banks focus more on the size expansion and increasing possibility of receiving TARP funds, rather than improve post-merger operating efficiency.

References

1. Federal Deposit Insurance Corporation (2015) Historical Statistics on Banking.

2. Campa JM, Hernando I (2006) M&As performance in the European financial industry. Journal of Banking & Finance 30: 3367-3392.

3. Hagendorff J, Keasey K (2009) Post-merger strategy and performance: evidence from the US and European banking industries. Accounting & Finance 49: 725-751.

4. Knapp M, Gart A, Chaudhry M (2006) The impact of mean reversion of bank profitability on post-merger performance in the banking industry. Journal of Banking & Finance 30: 3503-3517.

5. Gabriel A (2008) The contribution of product mix versus efficiency and technical change in US banking. Journal of Banking & Finance 32: 2336-2345.

6. Al-Sharkas AA, Hassan MK, Lawrence S (2008) The impact of mergers and acquisitions on the efficiency of the US banking industry: further evidence. Journal of Business Finance & Accounting 35: 50-70.

7. Kwan SH, Wilcox JA (1999) Hidden cost reductions in bank mergers: accounting for more productive banks.

8. Cornett MM, McNutt JJ, Tehranian H (2006) Performance changes around bank mergers: revenue enhancements versus cost reductions. Journal of Money, Credit and Banking 38: 1013-1050.

9. Dunn JK, Intintoli VJ, McNutt JJ (2015) An examination of non-government-assisted US commercial bank mergers during financial crisis. Journal of economics and business 77: 16-41.

10. Brewer III E, Jagtiani J (2013) How much did banks pay to become too-big-to-fail and to become systemically important. Journal of Financial Services Research 43: 1-35.

11. DeYoung R, Evanoff DD and Molyneux P (2009) Mergers and acquisitions of Financial Institutions: A review of the post-2000 literature. Journal of Financial Services Research 36: 87-110.

12. Berger AN, Bouwman CHS (2013) How does capital affect bank performance during financial crises. Journal of Financial Economics 109: 146-176.

13. DeYoung R (2007) Safety, Soundness, and the Evolution of the U.S. Banking Industry. Economic Review 92: 41-66.

14. Adams RM (2012) Consolidation and Merger Activity in the United States Banking Industry from 2000 through 2010. Washington DC: The Federal Reserve Board.

15. Allen F, Carletti E (2010) An overview of the crisis: causes, consequences, and solutions. International Review of Finance 10: 1-26.

16. Brunnermeier MK (2009) Deciphering the liquidity and credit crunch 2007-2008. Journal of Economic Perspectives 23: 77-100.

17. Fahlenbrach R, Prilmeir R, Stulz RM (2012) This time is the same: using bank performance in 1998 to explain bank performance during the recent financial crisis. Journal of Finance 67: 2139-2185.

18. Cornett MM, Li L, Tehranian H (2013) The performance of banks around the receipt and repayment of TARP funds: Over-achievers versus under-achievers. Journal of Banking & Finance 37: 730-746.

19. King T, Srivastav A, Williams J (2016) What's in an education? Implications of CEO education for bank performance. Journal of Corporate Finance 37: 287-308.

20. Al-Khasawneh J A, Essaddam N (2012) Market reaction to the merger announcements of US banks: A non-parametric X-efficiency framework. Global Finance Journal 23: 167-183.

21. Cornett MM, Tehranian H (1992) Changes in corporate performance associated with bank acquisitions. Journal of Financial Economics 31: 211-234.

22. Knapp M, Gart A, Becher D (2005) Post-Merger Performance of Bank Holding Companies, 1987–1998. The Financial Review 40: 549-574.

23. Rhoades SA (1993) Efficiency effects of horizontal (in-market) bank mergers. Journal of Banking and Finance 17: 411-422.

24. Peristiani S (1997) Do Mergers Improve the X-Efficiency and Scale Efficiency of U.S. Banks. Evidence from the 1980s. Journal of Money, Credit, and Banking 29: 326-337.

25. Chronopoulos DK, Giardone C, Nankervis JC (2013) How Do Stock Markets in the US and Europe Price Efficiency Gains from Bank M&As. Journal of Financial Services Research 43: 243-263.

26. Cornett MM, De S (1991) Common stock returns in corporate takeover bids: evidence from interstate bank mergers. Journal of Banking & Finance 15: 273-296.

27. Madura J, Wiant KJ (1994) Long-term valuation effects of bank acquisitions. Journal of Banking & Finance 18: 1135-1154.

28. Penas MF, Unal H (2004) Gains in bank mergers: Evidence from the bond markets. Journal of Financial Economics 74: 149-179.

29. DeLong GL (2001) Stockholder gains from focusing versus diversifying bank mergers. Journal of Financial Economics 59: 221-252.

30. Hagendorff J, Collins M, Keasey K (2008) Investor protection and the value effects of bank merger announcements in Europe and the US. Journal of Banking and Finance 32: 1333-1348.

31. Brune C, Lee K, Miller S (2015) The effects of bank capital constraints on post-acquisition performance. Journal of Economics and Finance 39: 75-99.

32. Chuang KS (2014) Financial advisors, financial crisis, and shareholder wealth in bank mergers. Global Finance Journal 25: 229-245.

33. Farruggio C, Michalak TC, Uhde A (2013) The light and dark side of TARP. Journal of Banking and Finance 37: 2586-2604.

34. Harris O, Huerta D, Ngo T (2013) The impact of TARP on bank efficiency. Journal of International Financial Markets, Institutions and Money 24: 85-104.

35. Berger AN, Humphrey DB (1992) Megamergers in banking and the use of cost efficiency as an antitrust defense. The Antitrust Bulletin 37: 541-600.

36. Wheelock DC (2011) Banking Industry Consolidation and Market Structure: Impact of the Financial Crisis and Recession. Federal Reserve Bank of St. Louis Review 93: 419-438.

15

How the Libyan Context can Shape Corporate Social Responsibility Disclosure in Libya

Nagib Salem Mohammed Bayoud*

Department ofAccounting & Management, University ofTripoli, Libya

Abstract

This research has showed the relationship between the Libyan context regarding to sociocultural context, political context and economic context with corporate social responsibility disclosure (CSRD). The research has been used the literature review related this topic by books, papers, and master degree and PhD research. This research has covered the stage between 1970 until 2010. The results of this research revealed that the sociocultural context, political context and economic context can influence corporate social responsibility disclosure (CSRD) in Libya.

Keywords: Corporate social responsibility disclosure; Sociocultural context; Political context; Economic context

Introduction

Corporate social responsibility (CSR) and disclosure has become an important issue in the business world, because of some major corporate ethical disasters regarding the environment, human resources, and the community. In addition, there has been a growing demand for public firms to voluntarily disclose their CSR activities in the annual reports sent to stakeholders such as customers, suppliers, employees, investors, and activist organisations. The World Business Council for Sustainable Development defined CSR as the continuing commitment by business to behave ethically and contribute to economic development while improving that quality of life of the workforce and their families as well as of the local community and society at large.

In addition, corporate social responsibility disclosure (CSRD) is an extension of the financial disclosure system, which reflects the wider anticipation of society concerning the role of the business community in the economy. Furthermore, CSRD has an impact on companies in terms of financial performance, employee commitment, and corporate reputation. As a result, many studies in Australia, the United States, and the United Kingdom have focused on defining the relationship between CSRD and organisational performance. Although they have found the relationship between CSRD and organisational performance to be positive, other studies have found negative results, or a mixed relationship. In developing countries, despite growing concern for CSRD in various industries, only a few studies have focused on the impacts of CSR on organisational performance [1]. For example, Rettab et al (2009) found the relationship between CSR and organisational performance to be positive.

The research was undertaken in Libya, because Libya has an important standing in the world economy and uniqueness "a different political and economic system". Moreover, it is a particularly interesting country, as socialist and Islamic factors have impacted on the nature of CSRD. As a result, the level of CSRD has increased in Libya since 2000 due to pressures from stakeholders for information which may influence organisational performance for Libyan companies.

This research is organised into two sections. The first section includes the Libyan context which contains sociocultural context, political context and economic context. The final section shows the research conclusion.

The Libyan Context

A number of environmental factors influence the level and quality of business disclosures and of CSRDs in particular. The factors include social, cultural, political, economic, and legal factors, the last of which plays an important role in identifying levels of corporate disclosure.

Sociocultural context

Culture encompasses social, political, and other factors such as religion that can affect individuals' behaviours [2]. Aghila [3] explains that language and religion are considered vital cultural factors in Arabic countries, in particular Libya, which means these factors have a significant impact on the attitudes and behaviour of people.

Language: The official language in Libya is Arabic, although English is in common use, particularly among educated classes, in tourist areas, and in international business centres. Italian is the third most commonly used language due to the Italian colonization. Libya's private education system has ensured the ongoing use of English. In addition, some Libyan company (public and private) websites use English and Arabic. However, all Libyan companies prepare their annual reports in Arabic, as required by law. Nevertheless, a few Libyan companies (public and private) issue their annual reports in Arabic and English.

Religion: Religion is one of the most important aspects of Libyan society as most Libyans are religious. Religion has thus shaped the country's cultural background. Although all native Libyans are Muslim, more than one million foreigners live in Libya and most of them belong to various Christian denominations or Indo-Chinese religions [4]. There are churches and other places of worship for most of these religious groups.

The Libyan Constitution of September 11, 1969, declares in article 1 that Islam is the official state religion. Islamic values are practiced and

*****Corresponding author:** Nagib Salem Mohammed Bayoud, Department of Accounting & Management, University of Tripoli, Libya, E-mail: bayoudns@gmail.com

confirmed in numerous state ceremonies. In November 1973, a new code of law was established that emphasises Islam Sharia in all aspects of Libyan law.

Islam is one of the most significant drivers behind the increase in CSR activities in Libya. Islam is the main factor that leads and regulates the attitudes and behaviour of Arabic societies. Islamic societies are varied in terms of their CSR practices and understandings of CSRD. As such Libya is a particularly interesting country, as societal and Islamic factors have influenced the nature of disclosure. According to Pratten and Mashat (2009), "the Islamic influence adds further demands on legislation, behaviour, and industrial change." According to Ali [5], Islam organises the social life within the family and in other social organisations and supports their endurance and influence.

Geography, Population, Demographics: Located in North Africa, Libya is considered one of the most important Arabic countries. Libya not only links eastern and western Africa and Southern Europe and Africa. Libya is bounded by Egypt to the east, the Mediterranean Sea to the north, Tunisia and Algeria to the west, Sudan to the southeast, and Niger and Chad to the south; It is the fourth largest state in Africa. It also has a Mediterranean coastline of almost 2,000 km (1,250 miles). Although the land of Libya is 94.73% desert, 3.94% agricultural, and 0.29% forests%, the total area of Libya is approximately 1,775,500 km². Otman and Karlberg (2007) indicate that Libya consists of three regions: Tripoli in the northwest, Cyrenaica in the east, and Fezzan in the southwest.

In 2006, Libya had a population of nearly 575 million, made up of approximately 51% male and 49% female (Table 1). According to available data, approximately 4 million people live in coastal cities of Benghazi, Misurata, Zawia, and Derna, but especially in the capital city of Tripoli, where about 2.5 million people live.. At 3.5 percent, Libya has one of the highest population growth rates in the world. Furthermore, Libya has one of the highest urbanization rates in the world, with almost 86 percent of its population living in urban areas. About 50 percent of Libya's population is under 20 years old [6].

The family is considered an essential unit in Libyan society, a family and its members are assigned to a hierarchical order based on age and generation. El Fathaly (cited in Ahmad & Gao [7]) states that the father, grandfather, and oldest son represent leadership and authority in the Libyan family. Islam and Arabic custom support the role of the family in Libyan society and its status, which is based on the afore-mentioned hierarchy [8]. Bjerke and Al-Meer [8] note that, in Libya, while leaders hold authority at the community level, fathers hold authority at the family level.

The organisation of Libyan society is similar to that of other Arabic countries and is divided into extended families, villages, clans, and tribes. Agnaia [9] states that these social units play a major role in people's relationships and community life. More specifically, because one's loyalty to the law and one's profession is occasionally weaker than one's loyalty to one's village, tribe, clan, and family, it is more common for career promotions and business connections to be obtained through family contacts and personal relationships than through one's academic qualifications or practical experience [9].

International accounting literature has focused on the impact of society and culture on accounting practice in general and in particular on corporate disclosure [2]. Numerous studies investigate the effects of society and culture on the structure of business and accounting, and in particular on corporate disclosures [10-14]. These studies arrive at the following conclusion: society and culture are considered among the most important factors affecting business performance and accounting.

Clearly, public organisations should contribute and disclose their activities that lead to the well-being of society. Thus, this argument might support the stakeholder theory, which claims that in a society concerned with social issues, user groups (i.e., stakeholders) may use more power, possess greater legitimacy, and have their claims viewed with greater urgency. In this vein, just as societal values can affect managerial values, so might decision makers (such as managers) in societies with a strong interest in or concern with social issues, be more aware of stakeholder claims and therefore place more importance on them.

Political context

The political system in Libya's began September 1, 1969, when a group of army officers called the Revolutionary Command Council (RCC) took power. The principles of the RCC were Freedom, Socialism, and Unity. The RCC renamed Libya the Libyan Arab Republic. As the leader of the RCC, Muammar Gaddafi became the Prime Minister and the Defence Minister Gaddafi. In the 1970s, Gaddafi presented his Green Book, which presented in three parts (political, economic, and social programs), his Third Universal Theory. Moreover, the Third Universal Theory was presented as representing the Libyan policies until Feb 2011.

Gaddafi presented Libya's new political system in 1977, which

Population	Ages	Number in population			Percentage of total population			
		Male	Female	Total	Male	Female	Total	
1995	Total	2231079	2158660	4389739	50.82	49.18	100	
2006	Total	2695145	2628846	5323991	50.62	49.38	100	

Source: Libyan Higher Committee for Statistics and Census 2006 (Otman & Karlberg 2007).

Table 1: Distribution of Libyan Population, 2005 and 2006.

	1967	1975	1980	1985	1990	1997
GDP (LD million):	748	3,674	10,554	7,852	7,750	12,976
Oil sector	403	1,961	6,526	3,500	2,741	2,978
Non-oil sector	345	1,713	4,028	4,352	5,009	9,998
Per Capita (LD million)	430	1,369	3,252	2,140	1,600	2,426
Per Capita ($)	1,250	4,624	10,985	7,228	4,320	6,064

LD = Libyan currency (Libyan Dinar)
Source: The Libyan Secretary of Planning (1998), Economical and Social Development Achievements in 28 years; The Secretary of Planning (1997), Economic and Social Indicators (1962-1996).

Table 2: GDP and Per Capita Income in Libya in the period 1967-1997.

introduced five major reforms leading to basic changes in the country's structure. This system was then accepted in an extraordinary session of the General People's Congress G.P.C. under Muammar Gaddafi's chairmanship. The five reforms were (1) the official name of Libya became the Socialist People's Libyan Arab Jamahiriya (SPLAJ), (2) the Holy Book of Islam became the official social code, (3) the authority is for the all Libyan people and no one else as this system represented the basis of the political system in the SPLAJ, (4) the People's Congresses, People's Committees, Syndicates, Unions, Professional Associations, and the G.P.C became functions that define and maintain law and order and through which the Libyan people exercised their power (Figure 1).

Figure 1 show that Libyan people debate and made decisions through the Basic People's Congress. The Basic People's Congress collected and reformatted the people's decisions, then passed them on to the General People's Congress for consideration and implementation as national policy. There were at least 1,500 Basic People's Congresses in Libya. Each congress has its own budget and legislative and executive powers. They also elected a secretariat to represent them in the General People's Congress. Twice a year the General People Congress met to pass resolutions, adopted laws and decrees, and nominate ministers to the General People's Committees (or the cabinet). Finally, the responsibility of every Libyan citizen was homeland defence and all citizens received arms and general military training. Law defines the methods of training military institutions and the general military. This system finished in the SPLAJ.

Libya's political system affects the behavior of organizations and the people in certain ways. It has been argued that Libya's political and governmental stability affect accounting in numerous ways. Alhashim and Arpan 1992 (Saleh 2001) indicate that in societies where the government sets accounting rules, then when major changes happen in the people governing, these changes may lead to changes in the accounting procedures of the country. The degree of political rights and civil liberties evident in a country's political and civil structure is based on the degree of political and civil freedom in that country. As a result of violations of political rights and civil liberties associated with certain forms of political structures, the restriction of political and civil

freedoms are likely to pose obstacles to full and fair disclosure. In light of this, a number of studies have examined the relationship between political systems and accounting practices. For example, Goodrich (1986) found a significant relationship between accounting practices and political systems, "Political factors, like political system types and international organizational membership, are significantly linked to the accounting groups." Williams (1999) also found a positive correlation between the degree of social and environmental information in companies' annual reports and civil repression and the level of political freedom for Asia-Pacific companies.

Economic and business context

Libya is a rich developing country that is just beginning to change to a market-based economy. It is also attempting to rapidly move towards economic growth (UNDP 2007). Briefly stated, the history of economic development in Libya has occurred as follows: Agriculture was considered as the primary sector of the Libyan economy before the discovery of oil in 1959. Benjamin Higgins, who worked as an economic adviser to Libya in the twentieth century, described the Libyan economy between 1950 and 1963 as a deficit economy.

Higgins (1959) indicated in his book that Libya's great merit as a case study is as a prototype of a poor country. We need not construct abstract models of an economy where the bulk of the people live on a subsistence level, where per capita income is well below US$ 50 per year, where there are no sources of power and no mineral resources, where agriculture expansion is severely limited by climatic conditions, where capital formation is zero or less, where there is no skilled labour supply and no indigenous entrepreneurship ... Libya is at the bottom of the range in income and resources and provides a reference point for comparison with all other countries.

The International Bank for Reconstruction and Development (IBRD) (1960) also mentioned that as a result of the deficit of the Italian economy in their period of colonization of Libya, this situation led to the neglect of Libyan education and technical skill and excluded the Libyan employees from any significant careers, in particular in the administration of Libya, which did not allow them to improve

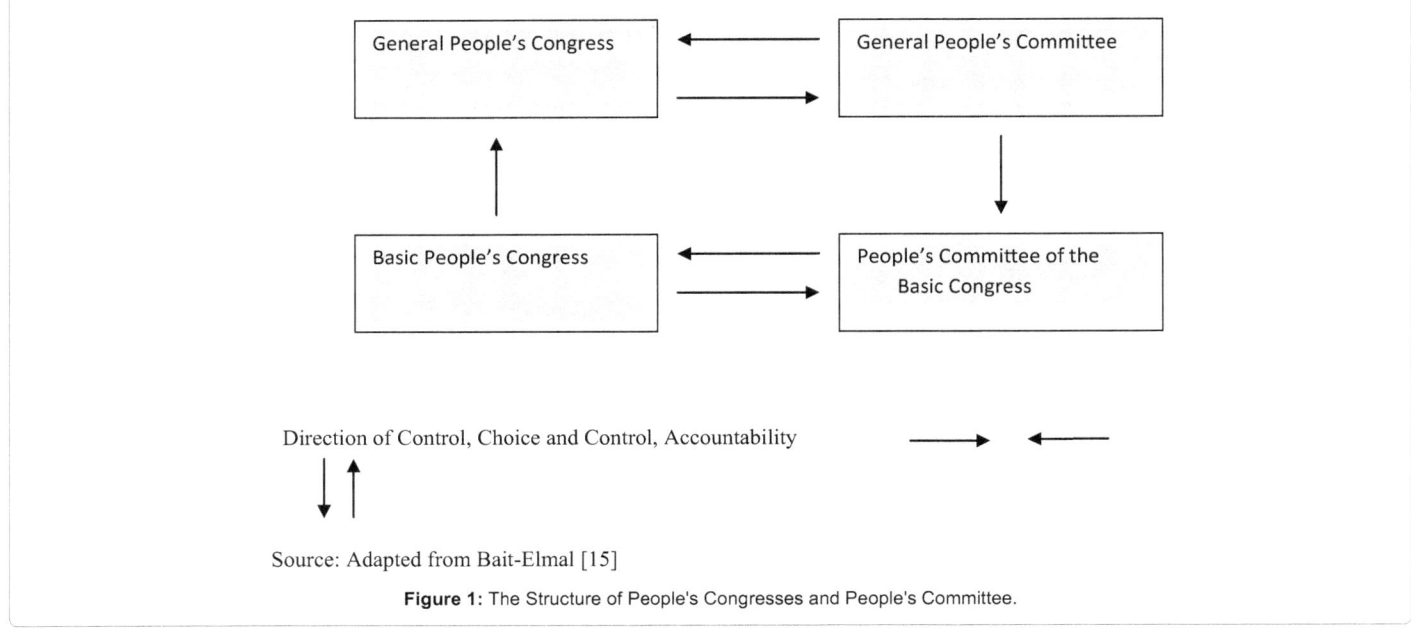

Source: Adapted from Bait-Elmal [15]

Figure 1: The Structure of People's Congresses and People's Committee.

their skills and experience. IBRD (1960) emphasized that as a result of these causes, Libya has focused on the training of Libyans to fill foreign administrative and technical positions, and this process is still the trickiest of all the problems related to the Libyan economic development. At this stage, the Libyan economy was characterized by low levels of literacy and health, chronic trade deficits, low levels of consumption and domestic production, and underexploited natural resources. Therefore, the Economic and Social Council (ESC) of the United Nations issued a decree at the beginning of 1950 to treat these problems by supplying foreign aid to promote the Libyan economy.

The discovery of oil in 1955 led to the end of foreign aid and major modifications in all aspects of Libyan life. In just five years, Libya changed from a poor country to one of the richest country in the world. Bait El-mal [15] indicates that the discovery of oil attracted many foreign oil companies to Libya; in particular USA and UK oil companies. Western advisers in Libya thus designed Libyan petroleum laws in 1955 to encourage foreign companies to explore, carry out oil development operations, and release oil from the Libyan Desert. In addition, by 1969 some 2,000 international companies from non-oil sectors registered manufacturing concerns in Libya. Some Libyans worked in these companies, but foreigners built and controlled the administrations of these companies.

A number of changes occurred in the Libyan economy after September 1, 1969. The leaders of the 1969 revolution took steps to restructure the economy. They were observed that the benefits accruing from oil heavily favoured foreign and international companies rather than Libya, and hence there was a need to nationalize the control of Libyan oil. Kilani (1988) stated that this stage witnessed the rapid disappearance of the private sector due to the revolutionaries' opposition to capitalism; however, this stage was also characterized by the rapid development of the and non-oil revenues (Table 2) to develop the economy. Libyan economy, the formation of an extensive range of public organisations, and the establishment of publicly owned organisations. In this respect, the Libyan government prepared to employ its three plans by using oil revenues.

The short-term plans specified finance infrastructure projects, such as roads, water, and hospitals. The medium-term plans involved the development of economic sectors, such as agriculture, services, and industry. The long-term plans aimed to expand and convert the Libyan economy from that of a developing to a developed economy. El- Jehaimi (1987) notes that prior plans also aimed to focus on agriculture and industry more than other sectors, to reduce agricultural and industrial imports from foreign countries, and to achieve self-sufficiency in the agricultural and industrial sectors, to redirect revenues from the oil sector to finance the requirements of the other sectors, and to limit foreign participation and focus on the role of national workers in the development effort.

The new economic system was based on the "Third Universal Theory" from the Green Book, written by Muammar Gaddafi. The Green Book is titled The Third Universal Theory. Gaddafi claimed this theory resolved Libya's economic problems by giving workers the right to benefit from the products being produced, whether as a public or private establishment; whereas, all prior theories attempted to resolve the economic problems from either the perspective of ownership of the means of production or from that of the wages for production. These prior attempts failed due to being based on "a wage system."

In 1970, Gaddafi's reforms gave Libyan workers the right to manage their own organisations. People's Committees (PC) were chosen by workers in most Libyan companies. The economic reforms stemming from the Green Book meant workers were not wage workers but partners in managing Libyan companies. The Green Book also stated that

If we analyse the economic factors of production from ancient times till now we always find that they are composed of these essentials: raw materials, an instrument of production and a producer. The natural rule of equality is that each of the factors has a share in this production, for if any of them is withdrawn, there will be no production. Each factor has an essential role in the process of production and without it production comes to a halt. As long as each factor is essential and fundamental, they are all equal in their essential character within the process of production. Therefore they all should be equal in their right to what is produced. The encroachment of one factor on another is opposed to the natural rule of equality, and is an attack on the right of others. Each factor, then, has a share regardless of the number of factors. If we find a process of production, which can be performed by only two factors, each factor shall have half of the production. If it is carried out by three factors, each shall have a third of the production.

The People Committee's are responsible for managing organisations in Libya. Each employee in a Libyan company can be a member of the People's Committee, which includes the head of the company. Thus, the top of the hierarchical structure can be managed by employees, who contribute to decision making. This process may lead to poor decisions, however, because most employees have inadequate experience or educational qualifications. This means that society's values stem from the economic activities and decisions rendered by all Libyan organisations. All Libyan organisations, thus should again study the issues related to employee rights and protections as well as their impacts on Libyan organisations. In addition, employees in Libya are dealt with as partners, not as wage-earners. However, public organisations are more focused on providing basic services and goods to citizens, rather than focusing on maximizing profits.

Economic development plays an important role in the development of accounting practices, particularly in reporting and disclosure. Economic development can directly and indirectly influence corporate disclosure in a country. Williams(1999) asserts that one of the most important factors that received wide attention recently is the level of economic development and its impact on accounting. Economic development in a country encompasses economic growth and structures and social changes. To evaluate the performance of every organisation in terms of productivity and efficiency, the three previous factors (economic growth and structures as well as social changes) need to use financial and reporting tools.

The role of accounting in any country affects economic development, "accounting information has the potential to play a very important part in many of the debates on the issues of affecting economic development". All companies and government authorities need to receive financial information within relevant certain time frame for a number of reasons, including to efficiently allocate and use economic resources, to control and safeguard assets, to price services and goods, to value assets, and to measure and evaluate performance. Novin and Baker (1990) asserted that it is difficult and complicated for all companies and government authorities to dispense reliable and sufficient accounting information within the relevant time, to allow effective control and management.

Additionally, a number of studies have examined the relationship between accounting and economic development. This relationship is observed due to the major role accounting plays in providing information on macro- and micro-economic activities to make effective decisions at various levels. The accounting function plays a stewardship and reporting role and a budgeting and forecasting role at the micro level, and also encompasses the creation of adequate information for planning and administering purposes, and for controlling the economy and demanding accountability at the macro level. Clearly, there is a significant and strong interplay between the macro and micro levels of accounting, on the one hand, and the macro and micro levels of the economy, on the other. In this regard, micro data are used for macro accounting, while macro and micro data use macro accounting for assessing and decision making. More specifically, the macro accounting framework combines the accounting and the economic frameworks. Although micro accounting forms a significant and effective part of the macro accounting database, it is concerned with measuring and reporting results of economic activities of micro units in an economy. Both micro and macro accounting and economic frameworks, therefore, should be used to improve information quality.

The Research Conclusion

This research has showed the Libyan context and its effect on corporate social responsibility disclosure (CSRD). It can be seen that Libya has a unique economic, political, and social system. It is based on the "Third Universal Theory" of the Green Book and Islamic instructions. The Libyan economy is neither classical political economy nor a bourgeois political economy.

Additionally, this research has described the social and environmental concerns in Libya. It has revealed that changes in the Libyan social environment have influenced corporate social responsibility (CSR) and corporate social responsibility disclosure (CSRD). It has also showed the importance of CSRD and stakeholders' pressure in particular after the establishment of a stock market in Libya.

The future research can cover the following points in the Libyan context: the relationship between regulatory system and corporate social responsibility disclosure. How education system can shape corporate social responsibility disclosure.

References

1. Kang KH, Lee S, Huh C (2010) Impacts of positive and negative corporate social responsibility activities on company performance in the hospitality industry. International Journal of Hospitality Management 29: 72-82.

2. Hamid S, Craig R, Clarke F (1993) Religion: a confounding cultural element in the international harmonization of accounting? Abacus 29: 131-48.

3. Aghila EA (2000) Job satisfaction and work commitment in the context of Libya. The Manchester Metropolitan University, Manchester, UK.

4. Attir Moa, Al-Azzabi K (2004) The Libyan Jamahiriya: Country, People, Social and Political Development. Doing business with Libya, Kogan Page Ltd, London, UK.

5. Ali A (1996) Organisational development in the Arab World. Journal of Management Development 15: 4-21.

6. Arab Banking Corporation: ABC (2001) The Arab Economic: Structure and Outlook, Manama, Bahrain Kingdom.

7. Ahmad Na, Gao S (2004) Changes, Problems and Challenges of Accounting Education in Libya. Accounting Education: International Journal 13: 365-90.

8. Bjerke B, Al-Meer A (1993) Culture's consequences: management in Saudi Arabia. Leadership & Organization Development Journal 14: 30-5.

9. Agnaia AA (1997) Management Training and Development within its Environment: the Case of Libyan Industrial Companies. Journal of European Industrial Training 21: 117-23.

10. Archambault JJ, Archambault ME (2003) A multinational test of determinants of corporate disclosure. The International Journal of Accounting 38: 173-94.

11. Cravens KS, Oliver EG (2000) The Influence of Culture on Pension Plans. The International Journal of Accounting 35: 521-37.

12. Doupnik TS, Salter SB (1995) External Environment, Culture, and Accounting Practice: A Preliminary Test of a General Model of International Accounting Development. International Journal of Accounting 30: 189-207.

13. Gray SJ (1988) Towards a Theory of Cultural Influence on The Development of Accounting Systems Internationally. Abacus 24: 1-15.

14. Hofstede GHa, Bond MH (1988) The Confucius Connection: From Cultural Roots to Economic Growth. Organisational Dynamics 16: 5-21.

15. Bait-Elmal A (2000) The Role of Management Control Systems in Libyan Organizations: A Libyan Development Policy Case Study with Special Reference to the Industrial Sector. Manchester Metropolitan University, Manchester, UK.

16

Audit Committee Effectiveness: Relationship with Audit Committee Characteristics and Interaction with the Internal Audit Department: Case of Egypt

Elsayed Nasser DAA*

Banking and Finance Department, Hekma School of Business, Dar Alhekma University, Jeddah, Kingdom of Saudi Arabia

Abstract

This study examines whether specific audit committee (AC) characteristics, including indpendence, knowledge, experience and training, and interaction between audit committee members and the internal audit function are associated with AC effectiveess. We find that AC effectiveness is higher when members are more independent affected mainly by their ability to express an opinion regarding doubt of continuity and having compensation within the acceptable limits, knowledge and experience affected mainly be the existence of at least one member who as strong accounting, financial and auditing expertise, and effective interaction with internal audit function measured mainly by AC reviews of the programs and procedures related to risk management process and AC determination of the internal audit annual budget. These findings are consistent with an increased demand for higher quality auditing by audit committees, and by firms that make greater use of internal audit.

Keywords: Audit committee; Internal audit; Auditing expertise; Risk management process

Introduction

Developing nations in general and Egypt in particular suffer from serious economic and financial problems, including: weak and illiquid stock markets, economic uncertainties, weak investor protection, frequent government intervention; high levels of ownership concentration; state ownership of companies, weak legal and judiciary systems, weak institutions, and limited human resources capabilities [1-7].

To overcome these serious problems, Egypt is actively working to develop the tools and institutions necessary to implement sound governance principles on a national scale. It is interesting to note, however, that one of the key obstacles to the successful implementation of governance standards is the private sector's lack of awareness about the subject and the benefits it provides.

Corporate governance is one of the tools that will help Egypt to realize high and sustainable rates of growth, increase confidence in the national economy, deepen capital market and increase its ability to mobilize savings. In addition, it results in raising investment rates, protecting the rights of the minority shareholders or small investors. Also, it encourages growth of private sector by supporting its competitive capabilities, helping to secure financing for projects, generating profits, and creating job opportunities [8].

Although the audit committee is only one dimension of broad-based CG, a lack of appropriate audit committee oversight can ultimately contribute to corporate failure and diminish public confidence in the mechanism [9]. The audit committee forms an important requirement of Egypt corporate governance code. Egypt started to develop a CG code only in 2005. The Egyptian Code of Corporate Governance (ECCG) was formally established in October 2005 and was largely derived from the recommendations of the Cadbury Report (1992), the Hampel Report (1998) and the Combined Code in the UK.

There are two CG codes that are now available in Arabic and English: The first is the "Guide to Corporate Governance Principles in Egypt" by Dr. Zeyad Bahaa El Din and Mr. Maged Shawqi, 2005, published by the Center for International Private Enterprise (CIPE) and the second is the "Corporate governance executive regulations project for Egyptian Listed Companies", by the Capital Market Authority, Nov. 2006. Giving the fact that the two codes are not more than 14 pages for each and the AC section in both is not more than a page, specifying the composition of the AC, their functions and frequency of meetings without giving any details regarding the determinants of AC effectiveness to be able to perform such functions, the interaction with the internal audit department or the external auditor.

AC was formally required for all listed companies in Egypt beginning 2008 by Capital Market Authority (CMA) now the Egyptian Financial Supervisory Authority (EFSA) (CMA Board of Directors Decision No. (94) of 2008 issued on 22/9/2008; Audit Committee was mentioned in article 7). At the beginning of 2009 all listed companies on the Egyptian Exchange (EGX) have to submit the audit committee report starting from the first quarter of 2009 (ending March 31) and the companies that did not submit the audit committee report by the two months deadline were required to pay a fine of LE 15,000. Given this fact combined with the fact that the Egyptian Code is very briefed in terms of AC effectiveness, the paper tries to answer this question: what are the determinants of audit effectiveness in Egypt given the briefness of the Egyptian Code of corporate governance?

Although many researchers have examined audit committee effectiveness and its determinants in developed nations, much less academic study has been made of developing and emerging nations, given the pressures related to globalization, international trade, and international investment practices [10]. Moreover, developing and emerging countries have tended to mimic the practices of developed

***Corresponding author:** Elsayed Nasser DAA, Banking and Finance Department, Hekma School of Business, Dar Alhekma University, Jeddah, Kingdom of Saudi Arabia, E-mail: daliaadel2000@yahoo.com

nations, despite evidence, for example from Rabelo and Vasconcelos, show that the factors that give rise to the need for corporate governance in developing nations and those in developed nations differ. Moreover the Egyptian setting involves firms that are smaller in size than those in the USA, where most of the studies related to AC characteristics and interaction between AC members and the internal audit function have been performed. Kapardis and Psaros reported that CG is not a new phenomenon and it has been addressed by various authoritative committees such as Cadbury Report, Greenbury, Hampel Report, Turnbull Report and Higgs. Indeed, Mertzanis noted that the effort to reform CG began in the USA as early as the 1970s [11-17]. Consequently, while CG is anything but a new area of enquiry, it has taken on greater international significance since the mid-1990s, in particular, for developing economies (including that of Egypt).

This paper examines whether, in an Egyptian setting, specific characteristics of an audit committee and the interaction between the audit committee and the internal audit department enhances AC effectiveness. Higher audit committee effectiveness implies higher audit quality (Francis). A higher quality audit should improve the quality of financial reporting and reduce the risk of the auditor providing an incorrect audit opinion.

Giving the fact that the Audit Committee report became mandatory starting from 2009 for all listed companies in the EGX, We contribute to the growing body of published literature in this area in a number of ways.

Finally, we extend the models used in previous studies by providing additional measures of audit committee independence and including: independence, knowledge and experience, and interaction with the internal audit function.

We also find that the use of internal audit is associated with higher audit committee effectiveness. This result suggests that firms that engage in greater internal monitoring through the use of internal audit also demand higher quality external auditing. This implies that directors of these firms recognize the importance of both types of audit as mechanisms to strengthen corporate governance.

The paper investigates the determinants of audit committee effectiveness in Egypt. It contributes to audit committee effectiveness and governance literature by studying audit committee effectiveness determinants in a developing country like Egypt, which is distinguished from most developed nations by three important characteristics [18]. Firstly, most companies are closely held, secondly there is considerable state ownership of privatized companies, thirdly that board independence is weak. While Bremer and Ellias note that Egyptian businesses are starting to appreciate the need for corporate governance mechanisms, they argue that together with Fawzy's three characteristics, weakness in the economic structure, and lack of awareness of corporate governance concepts and benefits, hinder the development of corporate governance in Egypt [19]. Thus the results of this research may be useful for regulators in developing and emerging nations with similar characteristics as they continue to deliberate appropriate corporate governance requirements in their own nations.

Also, this paper introduces a more comprehensive set of determinants of audit committee effectiveness including: *Independence* determined by the followings: AC members are external directors, have/manage stock ownership in the Co. or in another affiliated Co., can protect the external auditor in case of expressing an opinion regarding doubt of continuity, provide consulting services to the Co., AC members Knowledge, experience and training determined by: having at least one member who has strong accounting, auditing, and

financial expertise, having at least one member who has supervisory financial expertise that requires broad financial responsibilities, and at least one member who has professional certification that—to the best of the authors' knowledge—have been not tested before in an Egyptian context in relation to AC effectiveness as an important element of corporate Governance. Our findings relating to the determinants of audit committee effectiveness for 2013 are relatively lower than those reported by KPMG, although many regulation changes have taken place in Egypt such as the formation of the Egyptian Financial Supervisory Authority (EFSA), and the update of the CG code. All these changes aim to enhance CG including audit committee effectiveness [20].

Despite the importance of CG, there is surprisingly little professional guidance on which factors to consider in assessing the effectiveness of AC. In recognition of the need to enhance the level of confidence of foreign portfolio investors in the Egyptian capital market, the ministry of investment through the Egyptian Institute of Directors (EIoD) introduced a corporate governance code in 2005 for companies listed in the stock market, especially those being actively trading. The Egyptian Corporate Governance Code (ECGC) is initially prepared in accordance with the Guidelines on Corporate Governance of State-Owned Enterprises in the Organization for Economic Cooperation and Development (OECD). Subsequently, a team of Egyptian experts drafted the initial code, which was then subjected to in-depth examination and extended discussions. At the end, the code was reviewed by experts fromthe OECD, the International Finance Corporation (IFC) and also theWorld Bank.

However, the Report on the Observance of Standards and Codes (ROSC): A Corporate Governance Country Assessment for The Arab Republic of Egypt argued that Egypt can take a major step forward in closing these gaps by: 1. requiring companies to implement the Egyptian Corporate Governance Code (ECGC) on a 'comply-or-explain' basis, 2. amending the ECGC to better meet good practice, 3. strengthening enforcement capacity, and 4. supporting the EIoD to roll-out its director training program, focusing on family-owned businesses outside the EGX 30 [21].

Numerous publications issued by accounting firms have advocated approaches and guidelines for more effective ACs [22]. A number of these recommendations have been made legally mandatory (e.g., Egypt through Egypt Corporate Governance Code). Accounting academics also have participated in the quest for AC effectiveness. For example, archival studies have sought to identify and assess factors (e.g., degree of independence and expertise of AC members) that are correlated with proxies of effectiveness.

The remainder of the paper is structured as follows. The next section discusses the background to the study and develops our hypotheses. The third section describes the research design. The results of our study are reported in the fourth section while in the final section conclusions are drawn and the implications of the study are discussed.

Background and Hypotheses

Existence of an audit committee

The expectation that audit committees exercise an active monitoring of the company financial reporting process is well established and this role has been confirmed by many CG codes and professional pronouncements over the last 10-15 years.

Davidson reported that prior published literature indicates that the effectiveness of an audit committee is dependent, in part, on the extent to which the committee is independent, its frequency of meetings and its size. It is contended that audit committees are unable to function effectively when members are also executives of the firm. Both the published literature and governance reports suggest that audit committees should consist exclusively of non-executive or independent directors. This is supported by research that demonstrates a relationship between audit committee independence and a higher degree of active oversight and a lower incidence of financial statement fraud.

The academic literature and recent CG pronouncements recognized the pivotal role of audit committees in financial reporting. The Cadbury Report, in the UK, highlighted the audit committee as a central mechanism for ensuring good financial reporting and internal control. In the USA, the BRC (1999) made specific recommendations on how to improve the effectiveness of audit committees.

The recommendation of the Egyptian's CG code to establish audit committees in listed companies includes some recommendations concerning audit committee features and potential tasks. The most important of these is the notion that committee formation and composition in general should be exclusively content-driven. These tasks are considered in No. 6 of the Code. The ECCG prescribes a series of characteristics an effective audit committee should possess. The ECCG extends the notion of director independence that has been widely applied to boards to emphasize that audit committees should also be independent. The rationale is that independent directors serving on audit committees are more likely to be free from management's influence in ensuring that objective financial information is conveyed to shareholders. Second, to monitor effectively the quality of financial information that is disclosed by the firm, committee members should have essential skills in understanding and interpreting that information correctly. The ECCG suggests that audit committees should be composed of at least three non-executive board members. At least one of its members should have financial and accounting expertise. If the number of non-executives on the BOD is less than three, one or more members may be appointed from outside the corporation. Also, the board should constitute at minimum an audit committee consisting of a number of non-executive board members. The audit committee shall be responsible for the oversight of the internal audit department and the corporation's procedures.

Audit committee characteristics and audit effectiveness

AC team should not be less than 3 members and no more than 6, one of them at least should possess financial expertise and the others should be financially literate. All the members should have integrity, objectivity, confidence and informed judgment.

KPMG s Global Audit Committee Survey captures the views of some 1800 audit committee members around the world on a number of issues, including factors affecting audit committee effectiveness. Many Survey respondents point to the need for "additional expertise" (e.g., IT, M&A, and risk) as a key to improving the committees effectiveness.

Additional expertise and greater diversity of thinking and backgrounds would most improve the AC composition and effectiveness. In light of the increasing complexity of the global risk environment and the pace of technology change, it is perhaps not surprising that most survey respondents said the audit committees effectiveness would be most improved by additional expertise (e.g., IT, risk, M&A, industry knowledge) at the highest rank 64%, and "greater diversity of thinking, background, perspectives, and experiences among members in the second rank, 50%.

Overall, respondents gave the lowest ratings to the audit committees ability to stay up to speed on changes impacting the company (e.g., accounting, risk, IT).

Canadian analysis suggests that AC effectiveness is to some extent related to the background that members possess in terms of expertise and independence, which is consistent with the present regulatory approach that regulators have favored for some time, which consists (more or less coercively) of specifying prime features needed by AC members (especially in terms of expertise and independence), and to make these features visible through disclosures.

It is reasonable to argue that regulators to a large extent grope along in their quest to make ACs more effective. It is also difficult to make sense of conflicting findings or claims in literature. For example, while archival studies generally suggest that the quality of financial reporting is positively related to members degree of independence from corporate management and experience in financial reporting matters, a number of stakeholders are keen to point out that some of the largest corporate governance failures involved ACs that were described in corporate proxies as being made up of independent, financially literate members [23].

Independence: Independence of the committee members is necessary to safeguard the credibility of the organization. As a prerequisite to the effective performance of the AC, the BD should formulate a clear definition of the AC"s authority. It should define the purpose of the charter: to help the BD fulfill its oversight responsibilities with a detailed description of the authority of AC [24]. Moreover, independence of AC members influences the construction of AC effectiveness. Independence means unrelated directors.

Here, independence is conceived of as one's ability to be detached from managers' reports, which allegedly allows members to review financial documents in a way that unquestioningly benefits shareholders. Outside directorship is believed to be sufficient to provide members with an inner ability to examine documents and reports from an angle different than that of management, thereby pointing to a potentially significant difference between attendees_ conception of member independence and that of regulators. (Independence and leadership are found to be important if the self assessment process is to be meaningful leading to improvement, as it will highlight whether there is a need for a "fresh set of eyes", or a greater diversity of views?. The results of prior research provide support for a positive association between audit committee characteristics and AC effectiveness. Therefore, we test the following hypothesis:

Skills, experience, and training: The Egyptian AC Code was very brief about the expert, "One member should be a financial and accounting expert". Auday finds that the AC financial expert should possess professional experience that will be relevant to the operations of the AC, such as: (1) thorough understanding of AC's oversight function; (2) expertise in financial matters as well as having a through grasp of financial statements;(3) the capacity to ask the right questions to decide whether the corporation's financial statements are accurate and complete; (4) the size of the organization with which the individual has experience; (5)the scope of that corporation's operations; and (6) the complexity of its accounting and financial statements. Previous experience in accounting jobs by itself does not validate the BD to hire a given applicant as an AC Financial Expert; the BD must guarantee that it names an AC Financial Expert who embodies the highest values of professional and personal integrity. Companies must include the Financial Expert disclosure in their AC section of the annual report.

When the company reaches the maximum number of AC members; then it could hire Financial Experts as advisors to the AC, where they should be financially qualified and have experience of working in the concerned country.

Gendron and Be´dard argued that formal competencies, extensive financial and accounting background may generate feelings of self-confidence in AC members minds, thereby possibly affecting their performance during meetings (e.g., being more confident may translate into members asking more challenging questions or, alternatively, it may prevent members from asking "naive" but fundamental questions).

Similarly, managers and auditors appeared to take into account members_ expertise background when constructing effectiveness. For example, boards of directors put their "stronger heads" on the AC—because ACs deal with matters for which boards tend to be sued. In the following quote, B_s external auditor links the effectiveness of the company's AC to the credential profile of its members.

Formal competencies are a manageable input. The more professional accountants on the AC, the more "effective" is the AC in terms of adhering to best practices. The longer the members have been on the AC, the better enabled they are to deal with specifics.

With regard to experience and training, The Egyptian AC Code stated; "Gather all the international developments in accounting and auditing and notify the BD, including what AC believes is important for the company" [25]. In order to formulate a more detailed CG Code to develop the AC practice in Egypt, the researcher proposes the following provision: Training should be offered to all members of the AC on a timely and ongoing basis and should include an understanding of related company bylaws and recent developments in financial reporting. The training may take many forms including seminars and internal company talks, formal conferences and courses, and briefings by external advisers. There should be more focus on training new AC members. Every member of the AC must be financially literate; specifically, AC members must have expertise, or access to expertise, that goes beyond mere familiarity with financial statement. Potential gaps in AC members' business and technical knowledge should be identified and offers training made as needed. Corporations, with a stated market capitalization, must have AC members financially literate or who will become financially literate within a reasonable time after their appointment. The AC should identify, and agree with the BD on the skills required; the required set of skills should be periodically reviewed.

The results of prior research provide support for a positive association between audit committee characteristics and AC effectiveness. Therefore, we test the following hypothesis: Regulators emphasize the need for audit committees to be comprised of members who are independent and at least some of whom have financial expertise. These views are supported by the results of research studies that show that audit committee characteristics impact the committee's effectiveness [26].

Abbott argue that independent audit committee members might both demand a higher level of assurance and also support the auditor's demand for more testing leading to higher audit quality [27]. This support is likely to be greater when committee members have the financial and auditing expertise that enables them to better understand the risks associated with a lower quality audit. Furthermore, audit committees that meet frequently are likely to be better informed and more diligent in performing their duties.

From the previous discussion, we can propose the following hypotheses:

H1: Higher AC effectiveness is associated with more independent AC members.

H2: Higher AC effectiveness is higher when AC members have financial, accounting, and auditing experience.

Internal Audit Function

A strong internal audit function begins with a strong AC. With regard to the Internal Audit Process, The supervisory authority's regulations state that, "The company should maintain a tight internal control system established by the BD members and directors". The same function was also required in the Sarbanes-Oxley act. The responsibility of AC to hire the CAE was mentioned in the Egyptian Code but in the part dealing with the IAF as follows: "The audit department's head is appointed, reappointed, financial terms arranged and dismissed by the CEO; subject [to] the approval of the AC" [28].

In the time of economic crises and cost cutting, the IAF should not be part of this, in fact it should be asked to do extra work especially in these times. AC should create an agenda or approve the CAE's agenda for next year [29]. Two researchers emphasized the AC's responsibility to review the IAF budget and plan to match them against the CPA firm's objectives. Another study asserted that IAF team performance should be parallel to the performance of the rest of employees in the company to develop their experience. The Egyptian AC Code included only some details in this part stating that the AC should, "Review the reports submitted by the internal auditor and any corrective measures taken". Therefore, Auday proposed the following provisions that the Egyptian Code missed to enhance implementation of CG practice: The internal audit function should have a direct reporting relationship with the AC and the AC should provide oversight of its activity. The AC and the internal audit team should maintain a strong positive relationship. The CAE should have a solid line reporting relationship to the AC. The AC should create an agenda for the coming year or approve and review the CAE's agenda. The BD and senior management may desire objective assurance and advice on control and risk. An adequately resourced internal audit function may provide such assurance and advice. The AC should review the internal audit function, including the internal audit budget and proposed audit plans for the coming year and how such plans reflect the CPA firm's objectives. The AC should guarantee that the function has resources and access to information to fulfill its mandate, and is equipped to perform in line with appropriate professional standards for internal auditors. In times of cutting costs, the internal audit function should not be the victim of a company downsizing; in fact, it should be doing extra monitoring at precisely this time.

In relation to the evaluating of the IAF, Auday 2010 noted the need for the quality assurance program for the IAF to be done by an independent reviewing team from outside the organization. Another researcher asserted that the HR also has some role in the evaluation of the IAF in parallel with the overall organizational strategy. The Egyptian AC Code did mention the evaluation of the IAF briefly, stating: the AC should "Review and discuss the internal audit department plan and its efficiency". Due to proposing the following: The AC should ensure that the internal auditor team has direct access to the BD's chairman and to the AC and is accountable to the AC. Companies should establish an Improvement and Quality Assurance Program that includes both periodic and ongoing internal QAs and undergoes an external QA a minimum of once every 5 years, by a qualified independent reviewer or review team from out-side the organization. Internal audit's behavior should be parallel with the organization's overall HR strategies to enhance the employees' experiences. AC should meet annually with executive managers and the CPA firm to discuss the performance of CAE.

AC members mentioned paying careful attention to the extent to which managers adopt appropriate measures to solve deficiencies highlighted in internal audit reports.

Ideally, the internal auditor should report directly to an audit committee comprised of non-employee members of the board of directors. Reporting at this level should allow the auditor the greatest access to all levels of the institution, and assure prompt and independently objective consideration of audit results. It also enables the auditor to assist the AC members in fulfilling their responsibilities. The AC should regularly receive a report of all internal audit activity. This report should include the status of all audits on the internal audit schedule, and summaries of all audits completed during the period including audit conclusions. In addition, this report should provide the resolution status of previous internal audit findings and recommendations. If the internal auditor does not report to the board or its audit committee, the reporting line should be to an individual with no financial or operational responsibilities.

Data Statistics Analysis

Sample and method of data collection

A survey was presented to professionals involved in the auditing profession including AC members, auditors and accounting professors. Most of the auditors surveyed were from leading accounting firms in Egypt while the professors were from the Accounting Department at the different universities in Egypt. Collecting the opinions of different categories of respondents was necessary to get a non-biased opinion, rather than narrowing participants to only the AC members. Using Likert scales, respondents were asked, if they agree or disagree with each statement; expressing each answer using a scale, from one to five, to reflect the degree of acceptance or rejection. Auday 2010 assessed the opinion of the participants concerning the determinants of AC effectiveness. Respondents are Surveyed using the traditional method (Paper and pencil questionnaires) and through the internet (surveymonkey).

After decoding and transforming the data into the computer for data processing, the 17th version of the statistical tool SPSS was used to perform data statistical analysis of the field study as follow:

First : Reliability and Validity coefficients

Second:Testing the hypothesies

The researcher will discuss each of the previous elements in details as follow :

First : Reliability and Validity coefficients: With Cronbach's alpha tool the the reliability is tested and the validity for the proposed determinants. The reliability coefficient (Cronbach's Alpha) measures the internal consistency of an assessment by comparing the answers to related questions. This measurement indicates the extent to which reliability is without bias (free of error) and offers consistent measurements of variables and so, the extent to which the results of the field study could be generalized, while the validity test measures the strength of our proposition, inferences or conclusions. This measurement will provide the expected score of variables in the same domain even if the domain is diverse. These tools were used to identify possible explanations for the responses.

Reliability and validity coefficients of the study variables were calculated. In Table 1 it is clear that values of reliability and validity coefficient are reasonable for all variables. The reliability coefficient ranged from 0.641 for " Competence " to 0.981 for "Characteristics of the Audit Committee" , while the validity coefficient ranged from 0.801 to 0.990 respectively (the value of validity coefficient is the square root of the reliability coefficient). It could be said that it is a coefficient with good significance for research aims, and could be usefuel in results generalizatin.

Second: Testing the hypothesis: The first hypothesis: 'There is no significant relationship between characteristics of the audit Committee and AC effectiveness'

To test this hypothesis was tested Sub hypotheses:

H1: 'There is no significant relationship between the independence of committee members and AC effectiveness '

To test this hypothesis we can use Correlation and Regression model as follows:

Correlation coefficients

Table 2 provides the correlation coefficients of the variables used in the multivariate analysis. As it can be seen, the correlation coefficients reported indicated that there is a strong positive correlation between (Audit committee members compensation is within the acceptable limit) and dependent variable (AC effectiveness) where the value of the correlation coefficient is (0.748), it is a significant at the significan level of 1%. Generally, there is a positive relationship between the dependent variable and the independent variables (The independence of committee members), and it is significant at significance level 1%.

Regression model

Table 3 represents the stepwise regression model of independent variables (The independence of committee members) on the dependent variable (Audit Committee effectiveness).

It is clear the significance of the regression model as the F value (61.399) and it is significant at a significan level of 1% as the value of (Sig= 0.000) is less than the significant level 1%, a significant regression coefficients and constant show through T test and the value of p-value as it is significant at the significant level 1%, The most important independent variables that affect the dependent variable (AC effectiveness) are: AC compensation is within the acceptable limit (0.748) and then for AC members to be external directors ().744).The determination coefficientis (0.627), which means that the independent variables explain 62.7% of the changes that occur in the dependent variable (Audit fees).

From the above H1: is incorrect and we accept the alternative hypothesis:

'There is significant relationship between the independence of committee members and AC effectiveness.

H2: There is no significant relationship between committee members' knowledge and experience and AC effectiveness.

To test this hypothesis we can use Correlation and regression model as follows:

Correlation coefficients

Table 4 provides the correlation coefficients of the variables used in

Variables	Cronbach's Alpha	Validity
Characteristics of the Audit Committee	0.981	0.990
Independence	0.911	0.954
Financially Literate	0.803	0.896
The extent of interaction between the audit committee and the internal audit function	0.928	0.963

Table 1: Reliability and Vliadtiy coefficient of the measurements used in the questionnaire.

Independence	AC Effectiveness
Audit committee members are external directors.	.744**
Audit committee members have stock ownership in the Company.	.619**
Audit committee can protect the external auditor in case of expressing an opinion regarding doubt of continuity.	.753**
Audit committee members provide consulting services e.g, financial consultation to the Co.	.554**
Audit committee members compensation is within the acceptable limit	.748**
Audit committee members manage/have stock ownership in another affiliated business.	.741**
Audit committee members have personal relations with current or prior officers, legal consultants, bank officers, main suppliers or customers officers.	.601**
Audit committee members have cooling off periods in case of historical work relations.	.612**
The more the independence the audit committee the stronger the audit committee and the more willingness to incur higher audit fees to secure a higher level of assurance.	.662**

** Correlation is significant at the 0.01 level (2-tailed).

Table 2: Correlation coefficients between the independence of committee members and AC effectiveness.

P-value	t	β		R²	F (P-value)
.009	-2.669	-.640	Constant		
.000	6.089	.683	x2.1.5	0.627	61.399 (0.000)
.001	3.635	.374	x2.1.9		

Table 3: The stepwise regression.

the multivariate analysis. As it can be seen, the correlation coefficients reported show that there is a strong positive correlation between the financial, accounting, and auditing literacy of the audit committee members (indpendent variable) and the effectiveness of the AC (dependent variable) where the value of the correlation coefficient is (0.843). It is significant at the significan level of 1%.

Regression model

Table 5 represents the stepwise regression model of independent variable (The experience and training of committee members) and the dependent variable (AC effectiveness).

It is clear the significance of the regression model as the F value is (92.954) and it is significant at a significan level of 1% as the value of (Sig= 0.000) is less than the significant level 1%, a significant regression coefficients and constant shown through T test and the value of p-value as it is significant at the significant level 1%, The most important independent variables (derminants) that affect the dependent variable are the existence of at least one member who has strong accounting, financial, and auditing expertise (0.834) and the existence of at least one independent accounting consultant to train AC members on important accounting issues.

From the above H2 is incorrect and we accept the alternative hypothesis:

'There is significant relationship between committee members' knowledge, experience, and training and AC effectiveness.

H2: There is no significant relationship between the extent of interaction between the audit committee and the internal audit function and AC effectiveness.

To test this hypothesis we can use Correlation and regression model as follows:

Correlation coefficients

Table 6 provides the correlation coefficients of the variables used in the multivariate analysis. As shown, the correlation coefficients show a strong positive correlation between Audit committee review of the programs and procedures related to coordination of activities with external auditors.) and dependent variable (AC effectveness) where the value of the correlation coefficient is (0.786), it is a significant at the significant level of 1%. Generally, there is a positive relationship between the dependent variable (AC effectiveness) and the independent variable (The extent of interaction between the audit committee and the internal

Committee members' knowledge, experience, and training	AC Effectiveness
There is at least one independent accounting consultant to train AC members on important accounting issues.	0.759**
There is at least one member who has strong accounting, financial, and auditing expertise.	0.834**
There is at least one member who has supervisory financial expertise that requires broad financial responsibilities.	0.654**
There is at least one member who has professional certification such as CPA	0.643**

** Correlation is significant at the 0.01 level (2-tailed).

Table 4: Correlation coefficients between Committee members' knowledge and experience and AC effectiveness.

P-value	t	β		R²	F (P-value)
.000	-4.712	-.884	Constant		
.001	3.433	.442	x2.2.4		
.001	3.453	.298	x2.2.1	0.795	92.954 (0.000)
.002	3.263	.331	x2.2.3		

Table 5: The stepwise regression.

The extent of interaction between the audit committee and the internal audit function	AC Effectiveness
The chief internal auditor CIA meets regularly with the audit committee	.754**
Internal audit reports to the Audit Committee	.656**
The audit committee is involved in the dismissal of the CIA.	.432**
The Audit Committee determines Internal Audit's annual budget	.759**
Audit committee reviews the programs and procedures related to the internal audit budget regularly	.739**
Audit committee reviews the programs and procedures related to the internal control reports	.682**
Audit committee reviews the programs and procedures related to coordination of activities with external auditors.	.786**
Audit committee reviews the programs and procedures related to risk management processe	.764**

** Correlation is significant at the 0.01 level (2-tailed).

Table 6: Correlation coefficients between the extent of interaction between the audit committee and the internal audit function and AC effectiveness.

Audit Committee Effectiveness: Relationship with Audit Committee Characteristics and Interaction with the Internal Audit...

105

audit function), and it is significant at a significant level 1%.

Regression model

Table 7 represents the stepwise regression model of independent variables (The independence of committee members) on the dependent variable (AC effectiveness).

It is clear significant regression model as the F value (65.994) and it is significant at a significan level of 1% as the value of (Sig= 0.000) is less than the significant level 1%, a significant regression coefficients and constant show through T test and the value of p-value as it is significant at the significant level 1%, The most important independent variables that affect the dependent variable are:

- Audit committee reviews the programs and procedures related to coordination of activities with external auditors.

- Audit committee reviews the programs and procedures related to the internal audit budget regularly.

- Internal audit reports to the Audit Committee

- The Audit Committee determines Internal Audit's annual budget

The determination coefficientis (0.825), which means that the independent variables explain 82.5% of the changes that occur in the dependent variable (Audit fees).

From the above H3: is incorrect and we accept the alternative hypothesis:

Conclusion

There is significant relationship between the extent of interaction between the audit committee and the internal audit function and AC effectiveness. From the above the second hypothesis is incorrect and we accept the alternative hypothesis: There is significant relationship between interation between AC members and internal auditors and AC effectiveness.

References

P-value	t	β		R²	F (P-value)
.000	-6.488	-1.311	Constant		
.033	2.176	.262	x2.3.13		
.000	5.371	.662	x2.3.11	0.825	65.994 (0.000)
.000	4.530	.486	x2.3.3		
.000	5.127	.939	x2.3.2		
.000	4.550	.745	x2.3.8		

Table 7: The stepwise regression.

1. Ahunwan B (2002) Corporate governance in Nigeria. Journal of Business Ethics 37: 269–287.

2. Gugler K, Mueller D, Burcin Y (2003) The Impact of Corporate Governance on Investment Returns in Developed and Developing Nations. Economic Journal 113: 511-539.

3. Rabelo F, Vasconcelos F (2002) Corporate governance in Brazil. Journal of Business Ethics 37: 321–335.

4. Reed D (2002) Corporate Governance in Developing Countries. Journal of Business Ethics 37: 223-247.

5. Tsameny M, Enninful-Adu E, Onumah J (2007) Disclosure and corporate governance in developing countries: Evidence from Ghana. Managerial Auditing Journal 22: 319-334.

6. Mensah S (2002) Corporate governance in Ghana: Issues and challenges.

7. Young M, Peng M, Ahlstrom D, Bruton G, Jiang Y (2008) Corporate governance in emerging economies: A review of the principal–principal perspective. Journal of Management Studies 45: 196-220.

8. Dahawy K (2008) Developing Nations and Corporate Governance: The Story of Egypt. The Global Corporate Governance Forum. The International Financial Corporation (IFC).

9. Cohen J, Hanno D (2000) Auditors' consideration of corporate governance and management control philosophy in preplanning and planning judgments.

10. DeZoort F, Hermanson D, Archambeault D, Reed S (2002) Audit committee effectiveness: A synthesis of the empirical audit committee literature. Journal of Accounting Literature 21: 38-75.

11. Kapardis MK, Psaros J (2006) The implementation of corporate governance principles in an emerging economy: a critique of the situation in Cyprus. Corporate Governance 14: 126-39.

12. Cadbury A (2000) The corporate governance Agenda. Corporate Governance 8: 7-15.

13. Greenbury (1995) Greenbury Recommendations.

14. Hampel Report (1998) Committee on Corporate Governance, final report.

15. Turnbull Report (1999) Control-Guidance for Directors on the Combined Code, Institute of Chartered Accountants in England and Wales, London.

16. Higgs D (2003) Review of the Role and Effectiveness of Non-Executive Directors

17. Mertzanis HV (2001) Principles of corporate governance in Greece. Corporate Governance: An International Review 9: 89-100.

18. Fawzy S (2004) How Does Corporate Governance in Egypt Compare with Selected MENA and Emerging Markets? The Egyptian Center for Educational Studies, Cairo University, Egypt.

19. Bremer J, Ellias N (2007) Corporate Governance in Developing Economies –The Case of Egypt. International Journal of Business Governance and Ethics 3: 430-445.

20. KPMG, 2013

21. World Bank (2009) Report on the observance of standards and codes (ROSC): A corporate governance country assessment for The Arab Republic of Egypt. Egypt: Cairo June.

22. KPMG (1999) Fraud survey results. New York.

23. Gendron Y, Be´dard J (2006) On the constitution of AC effectiveness. Accounting, Organizations and Society 31: 211-239

24. Harrington C (2004) Internal Audit's New Role. Journal of Accountancy 198: 57-63.

25. Capital Market Authority (2006) Executive Regulations Project for Listed Companies, Cairo, Egypt: Capital Market Authority.

26. Abbott L, Park Y, Parker S(2000) The effects of audit committee activity and independence on corporate fraud. Managerial Finance 26: 55-67

27. Abbott L, Parker S (2000) Auditor selection and audit committee characteristics. Journal of Practice and Theory 19: 47-66.

28. Egyptian Institute of Directors (2005) Guide to Corporate Governance Principles in Egypt. Ministry of Investment, Egyptian Institute of Directors. Cairo: Center for International Private Enterprise.

29. AICPA (2008) The AICPA AC Toolkit Public Companies. New York, USA: American Institute of Certified public Accountants.

African Capital Markets Conference December.

17

Internet Banking, Customer Perceived Value and Loyalty: The Role of Switching Costs

Samar Rahi* and Mazuri Abd Ghani
University of Sultan Zainal Abdin, Malaysia

Abstract

Purpose: This study aims to examine the relationship between internet banking, customer perceived value, switching cost and customer loyalty. Furthermore, this study also examines if switching cost moderates the relationship between internet banking, Customer perceived value and customer loyalty.

Design/methodology/approach: Data collected in a survey that yielded 437 respondents. Questionnaire was adapted from research work of Eriksson, Kerem, and Nilsson; Gefe; Levesque and McDougall; Zeithaml, Berry, and Parasuraman. Quantitative Approach was used for the analysis. Pearson correlation, multiple and moderating regression were used to examine the hypothesized relationship.

Findings: The findings confirm that internet banking and customer Perceived value brought significant change on customer loyalty. Moreover, results prevailed that there was significant qasi moderation between variables. Switching costs moderate the relationship between internet banking, customer perceived value, and customer loyalty.

Research limitations/implication: Further research is indicated, to identify effects of these variables on other services provider companies. Banking sector in Pakistan should pay more attention on Internet banking services, Customer Perceived Value and switching cost in order to enhance the customer loyalty.

Originality/value: This study is the first study that tests the western model on south Asian countries like Pakistan. Hence, there is no research work found that reflects on internet banking and customer perceived value with moderating effect of switching cost. This study contributes to the field of e-commerce marketing and will help managers to adopt appropriate strategies that will lead banking sector towards prosperity.

Keywords: Internet banking; Customer perceived value; Switching costs; Customer loyalty; Moderating Regression

Introduction

Banks are dealing in various transactions like receiving, transferring, paying, lending, and investing in order to achieve consumer's insights Wolf et al. [1]. As per [2-4]; Liao and Cheung [5] one of the major force behind this change is technology. Burgetz [6] research investigates that internet has great impact on progress of Small medium enterprises. According to [7-9] by using technology you can get better information about their customer needs and wants.

Furst, Lang, and Nolle [10], Kardaras & Papathanassiou [11] argues that banking sector is the most important sector to analyze and get the advantage by using E-commerce services. As per [12,13] electronic banking is low cost alternative [14,15]. Explain internet banking process will helpful for customer satisfaction [16-18]. Research focus is on the importance of internet banking [19-23]. Argues that online transaction is the future of our companies.

Loyalty for any products or services have been seen the core element of marketing activities and its promotion [24,25]. Shamma and Hassan [26] highlight the importance of customer perceived value in their research with relation to customer loyalty. Woodruff [27] defines the meaning of customer perceived value where the ratio of benefits would be equal the cost that customer is paying in return of that product. Richard L Oliver [28] also nail down the definition of customer perceived value, where customer outcome/input ratio is equal to the befts of the customer outcome/input ratio and where customer get satisfaction with what he is getting in return of what he is paying.

Literature Review

Theoretical background

Customer preferred to use internet banking because it is convenientGupta, Rao, and Upadhyaya [29]. Shariq [9] says internet banking plays a role of delivery channel. Deng, Lu, Wei, and Zhang [30] define switching cost, where the customer endeavor from one service provider to another service provider and it includes the monetary cost or it may be in sense of facing of new firms as psychological perspectives or in the shape of time or effort that involved to use the new product or services. Oliver [31] narrate perceived value where the ratio of outcome and input is equal to the ratio of customer satisfaction and its perceiving outcome what he input during the purchase.

Internet banking

Now the trend has been changed the ratio of internet users is growing day by day globally the trend of using internet is growing. Liao and Cheung [5] described technology has changed the way of the business now customers want convenience with latest features and companies are focusing to improve their technological features. Weick

*Corresponding author: Samar Rahi, University of Sultan Zainal Abdin, Malaysia, E-mail: sr_adroit@yahoo.com

and Quinn [32] argues that information technology is important in any business. Nabi [33] defines internet it is a network that combine the computers all over the world [11,21,22]. Describe the importance of e-commerce it is an application that provide facilities to customer for the purpose of business and exchanges between two or more customers moreover it bring effectiveness in business process.

Orr [12]; Shariq [9] explain that the use of internet and technology is the most important element to improve efficiency in business. Jayawardhena [34]; Reichheld and Schefter [35] explain that website should be user friendly [36]. Also explain in their research that if you are using internet properly it would be powerful for your business and it will enhance the image and loyalty. Domegan [2]; Tari and Sabater [37] narrate that use of internet is the best way to attract your customer anywhere at any time. Lichtenstein and Williamson [38] narrate that internet banking is better than traditional banking, thus the following hypothesis generate.

Hypothesis a

H1: Customer Loyalty will be positively influenced by internet banking

Customer perceived value

Customer value has various types of element Sweeney and Soutar [39] explain that value matter where you have your potential customer and it must be equal to what customer is paying and in return what he is getting. Sheth, Newman, and Gross [40] argued that there are number of dimension for customer perceived value like functional value where the operation comes, conditional value depend on conditions of the business nature moreover emotional value also matter like your customer intention towards your product hence social value also count and lastly epistemic values. Woodruff [27] explains the dimension of perceived value, functional value where the intention of purchase while emotional value where you create curiosity towards particular product and perceive it emotionally however, in this study we will focus on overall perceived value that will focus on complete process from purchase to use and its outcome.

Oliver [31] describe the equity theory it include the ratio of outcome/input in both perspective from customer as well as seller point of view. R N Bolton [41] also explains customer perceived value it is a process of evaluation that what customer is paying and what he is getting in return moreover perceived value also include monetary and non monetary concepts like how much time your customer consume, endeavor to find a product and in return what he gets it include all efforts physically to mentally. R.L. Oliver [31] explicitly described and emphasize the concept of outcome to input must be appropriate to enhance the customer perceived value. Moreover, research also describe the importance of perceived value as a marketing tool on behalf of this literature we can generate following hypothesis

Hypothesis-b

H1: Customer Loyalty will be positively influenced by customer perceived value

Switching cost

Lee, Lee, and Feick [42] describe that switching cost when users switch from one service to another service, it also include the cost of monitoring and endeavors that customer perform during switching. Kim, Kliger, and Vale [43] describe psychological cost more precisely the cost that involves curiosity and uncertainty and user face it when

switch from one product to another, this research also highlight that switching cost can be used as a barrier for customer because it will take time to learn new things. Dick [24] explains that switching cost is used as a barriers thus it can be a best tool to enhance the customer loyalty and marketer use this tool always to bound their customer with their product for long time. According to Bauer et al. [14], there are three dimensions of switching cost and each dimension has its own importance foremost, procedural cost that usually includes set up cost and the process of evaluation that how customer evaluate the product before switching one product to another product, secondly financial cost as it appears with its name finance and its related cost that what customer is getting and what he is paying in the meanwhile finally, the relational cost that is also important in banking sector to maintain good relation it include relation with the management relation with product and its organizational environment.

Anderson, Fornell, and Lehmann [44] explain that switching cost has direct impact on customer loyalty the big advantage is the binding of the customer due to switching cost sometime customer hesitate to switch due to extra effort. Klemperer [45] narrates that frequently customer reluctant to switch because they know the risk he may face during switching it includes all types of switching dimension it may be procedural or it may be financial cost. Deng et al. [30] explain that switching cost is the key tool for customer loyalty due switching cost you can avail one more chance to entertain your customer hence, in banking sector it is difficult to switch, you have to familiar with other banking website operations like how to create online account what will be the charges against transactions, users look towards switching cost with different perspective and ultimately they become loyal to learn and use the same product.

Customer loyalty

Customer Loyalty aim is retaining and making the customers loyal towards a brand or a product [14,46]. Brown [47] narrates that customer loyalty have always been key factor for enhancing customer experiences, almost every entrepreneur has realized the importance of customer loyalty and know that it is tough to attain a new customer rather than to retain your old customers via customer loyalty. Chaudhuri [48] customer loyalty directly impact on companies sales and for companies it is essential that they must prioritize their customer needs and wants to make them loyal towards product.

Customer loyalty is regarded as necessary for successful competition in all types of business. Dick [24] narrates that if your customer is loyal with your product it must have favorable attitude during purchase of your product. Johnson [49] explain that you can see customer loyalty in different perspective moreover different business have different types of requirement to make their customer loyal.

As per Andreassen [50] managers must focus on the development of customer loyalty because customer loyalty means that future purchase will be higher if your customer is loyal with your products they will buy your products again and again. Edvardsson, Johnson, Gustafsson, and Strandvik [51] explain that confidence about the product motivate your customer towards customer loyalty moreover the value you are giving to your customer is also enrich the customer loyalty. Hallowell [52] explain that customer perceived value also impact on customer loyalty.

Hallowell [52] narrates that customer loyalty is the key factor for your business and if you are doing business online it is more important to gain customer trust for customer loyalty. Flavián, Guinalíu, and

Gurrea [53], explain that loyalty is close to psychological process and commitment that your customers have with your product. Hallowell [52] described the attitudinal and behavioral loyalty. Flavián, Guinalíu, and Gurrea [53] enlighten on behavioral component of customer loyalty it based on the customer visit to a shop to make a purchase with a special frequency. Nilsson and Olsen [54] explained behavioral and attitudinal loyalty however for internet banking we will chose attitudinal loyalty it is a state where your customer stay committed with your product otherness behavioral dimension is just a state of effectiveness Eshghi, Haughton, and Topi [55] also elaborate that attitudinal loyalty is best fit on internet banking. After reviewing the whole literature following hypothesis generate.

Hypothesis-c: H1c: The higher the level of switching costs, the greater is the likelihood that internet banking will lead to greater customer loyalty.

Hypothesis-d: H1d: The higher the level of switching costs, the greater is the likelihood that customer perceived value will lead to greater customer loyalty.

Research Framework

After reviewing the literature a research framework builds that shows how internet banking and customer perceived value can influence on customer loyalty with moderation of switching cost. Following is the research model (Figure 1).

Research Methodology

For this research author has used positive paradigm. Ontology and epistemology approach have been used Creswell and Clark [56]. According to Collis et al. [57] deductive approach where theory already existed. This method is generally used for assumptions examination Collis et al. [57]. Precisely quantitative method has been used in this research Grinnell Jr and Unrau [58]. Focus of this method is on fresh data collection Collis et al. [57]. Arkin narrated that the quantitative strategy works on objectives and measures through actions and opinions.

Target population

Sector: Professionals of Government and private sector, Account

Manager of SME, Common people who are familiar with internet Banking Services. The first section of questioner was designed to capture the characteristics information of respondents for instance gender, age, education and region. Table 1 depicts the demographic information of respondents.

Sample and data collection

Sample size is selected from 500 customers through structured questionnaire. Only 437 usable response were received. Stratified-Random sampling technique has been used for data collection.

Measure Validation

Internet banking

Internet Banking has been measured with 8-item, Likert type scale. A sample of item is "Internet banking has made communication with banks easier" adapted from research work of Eriksson et al. [59].

Switching cost

Switching cost has been measured with 3-item Likert type scale. A sample item is "Switching to other internet banking service will be expensive" adapted from research work of Gefen [60].

Customer perceived value

Customer Perceived Value has been measured with 4-item Likert type scale. A sample item is "Compared to branch banking services internet banking provides more free services" adapted from study of Levesque and McDougall [61].

Customer loyalty

Participant will be measured with a 5-item Likert type scale. A sample item is "I will use that company's Product in the future" adapted from Zeithaml et al. [62].

Data Analysis

For the purpose of data analysis, a help was taken from SPSS (Statistical Package for Social Sciences) 20. Data was entered in software SPSS-20 and various tests were applied to check the validity

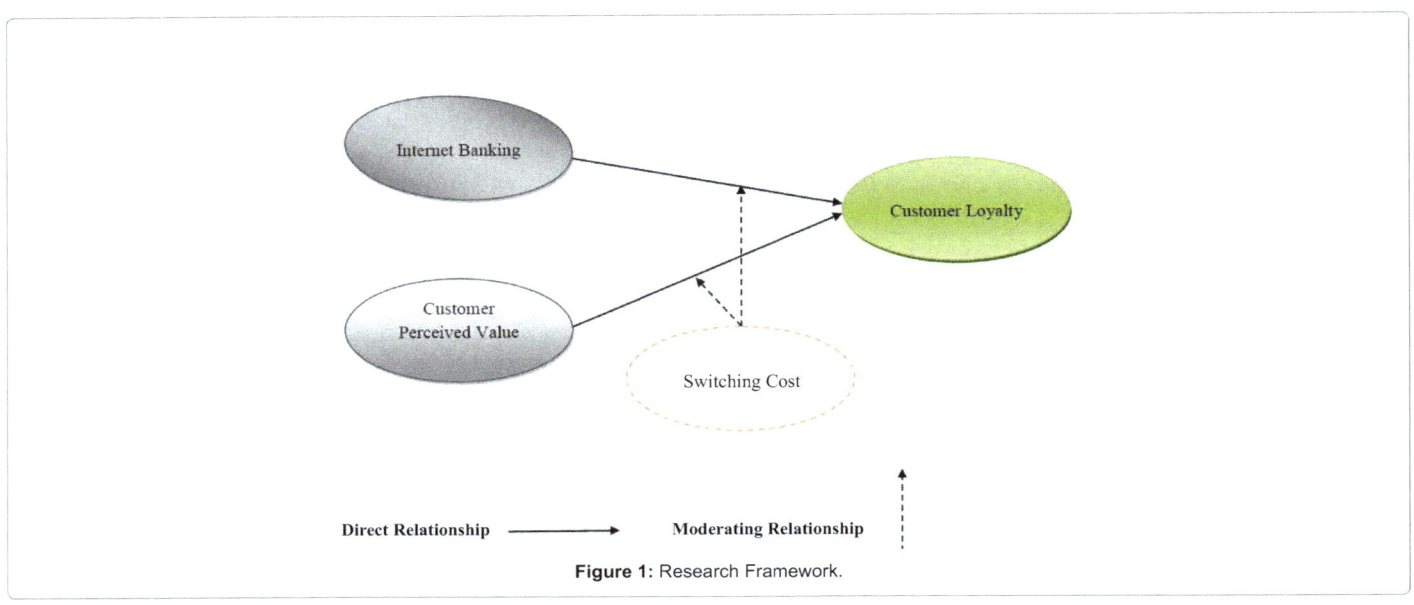

Figure 1: Research Framework.

Demographic Characteristics	Percentage (%)
Gender	
Male	52.6
Female	47.4
Age	
Less than 25 years	32.5
26-35 years	35.5
36-45 years	20.6
46 years and above	11.4
Education	
Below high School	1.6
Attended High School	5.5
Attended College	8.7
Graduate	52.6
Post Graduate	31.6
Region	
Urban	49.4
Country Side	50.6

Table 1: Demographic Profile of Respondents.

Constructs	Valid-N	Number of Items	Cronbach's Alpha
Customer loyalty	437	5	.752
Customer Perceived value	437	4	.905
Switching Cost	437	3	.810
Internet Banking	437	8	.776

Table 2: Reliability Analysis.

and reliability of the instrument as well with the help of response received in return of this survey. Relationship between the dependent and independent variables was also checked and other statistical tests were also applied to strengthen the study, which were further presented into the data analysis section.

Validity and reliability

To reconfirm the reliability of the instruments, Chronbach's Alpha test was employed with the help of SPSS software which are presented in the next section with detailed explanation and interpretation.

Coding

Data collection instrument was developed in which 20 statements were asked from the respondent on 5-point Likert scale (Strongly Agree 5), (Agree 4), (Neutral 3), (Disagree 2), (Strongly disagree 1).

Findings and Analysis

Interpretation of reliability analysis

As quantitative research depends on the accuracy and reliability of the data so for this purpose Cronbach's Alpha test has been employed. For a reliable instrument of data collection the value of Chronbach's Alpha must be equal to or greater than 0.70. Table 2 depicts that all values are greater than 0.70, Customer Loyalty 0.75, Customer Perceived Value 0.90, Switching Cost 0.81 meanwhile internet banking 0.77 that shows significant validity of the questionnaire.

Interpretation of Pearson correlation

Pearson correlation has been employed for the checking of the relationship among variables. Researcher examined the results Customer Loyalty with other variables Customer Perceived Value, switching Cost and Internet Banking is 0.88, 0.87, and 0.94. Customer Perceived Value has significant relationship with other variables

Customer Loyalty, switching Cost and Internet Banking 0.88, 0.99 and 0.89. Meanwhile switching cost relationship with other variables, Customer Loyalty, Customer Perceived Value and Internet Banking is found 0.87, 0.99, 0.89. Hence, Internet Banking relationship with other variables Customer Loyalty, Customer Perceived Value and switching cost is found 94, 89, 89. So proposed research frame work accepted because values shows there is a significant relationship between Internet banking, customer perceived value, switching cost and customer loyalty (Table 3).

Interpretation of regression analysis

Regression analysis has been employed to check the level of dependency of customer loyalty with internet banking and customer perceived value. Result shows that there is a significant relationship between variables. Table 4 depicts the value of constant -4.358 and value of B for internet banking 0.178 and Customer Perceived value 0.123. Further more significance value is less than 0.05. Thus we will accept the H1-a, and H1-b that evoke there is significant relationship between of Internet banking, Customer Perceived Value, and Customer Loyalty.

Necessary statistics

Table 4.1 depicts the overall model fitness in which significance of F-test is less than 0.01 and on behalf of these values it can be concluded that model is good fitted. Furthermore value of adjusted R square is 0.945 which show the combined effect of all independent variables on customer loyalty and in other words it can be explained that both independent variables Internet banking and Customer perceived Value, have a combined effect of 94% on Customer loyalty.

Moderation

To check the moderation between variables moderated regression analysis was employed. A moderator variable can be defined as a variable that systematically modifies either the form and/or strength of the relationship between a dependent variable and independent variable De Ruyter, Wetzels, and Bloemer [63]. Sharma, Durand, and Gur-Arie [64] differentiate two methods to identify moderator variables.

(1) Moderated regression analysis

(2) Subgroup analysis.

MRA involves the comparison of three regression models De Ruyter, Wetzels, and Bloemer [63]. The full model contains three terms: the dependent variable, the hypothesized moderator variable and the interaction term of these two. The restricted model omits either the interaction term or the hypothesized moderator. Tests are carried out by comparing the restricted model to the full model. In subgroup analysis the hypothesized moderator variable is used to split the sample. After subdividing the sample, regression analysis is carried out between the dependent and independent variables. A number of authors have recommended the use of MRA, since subgroup analysis is characterized by several shortcomings De Ruyter, Wetzels, and Bloemer [63]. In applying MRA we will need three regression models. In this particular case the following three regression models are relevant to examine the effect of Brand Image as moderator. If models (1), (2) and (3) are significantly different from each other (b2 b3 0), then switching costs is a quasi moderator Sharma et al. [64].

Moderating Regression Equation

1. $LOYi = a + b1 * IB$

Correlation Matrix		Customer Loyalty	Customer Perceived Value	Switching Cost	Internet Banking
Customer Loyalty	Pearson Correlation	1	.886**	.870**	.947**
	Sig. (2-tailed)		.000	.000	.000
Customer Perceived Value	Pearson Correlation	.886**	1	.996**	.897**
	Sig. (2-tailed)	.000		.000	.000
Switching Cost	Pearson Correlation	.870**	.996**	1	.890**
	Sig. (2-tailed)	.000	.000		.000
Internet Banking	Pearson Correlation	.947**	.897**	.890**	1
	Sig. (2-tailed)	.000	.000	.000	
**Correlation is significant at the 0.01 level (2-tailed)					

Table 3: Pearson Correlation Matrix.

Regression	Unstandardized Coefficients		Standardized Coefficients	T	Sig.
	B	Std. Error	Beta		
Constant	-4.358	.343		-12.707	.000
Internet Banking	.178	.038	.194	4.724	.000
Customer Perceived Value	.123	.028	.113	4.393	.000

Table 4: Regression Analysis

R^2	Adj. R^2	F-Statistic	Prob. (F-Statistic)
.945	.945	2.486E3	.000a

Table 4.1: Necessary Statistics.

Hypothesis (H1c)	Regression Equation	Adj R2	F
Model 1	LOY=-1.160+.869 -3.102***61.354***	.896	3.764E3***
Model 2	LOY=-1.092+.762+.203 -2.963***24.980***3.937***	.900	1.953E3***
Model 3	LOY=8.305+.376+-.556+.031 4.579***4.764***-3.656***5.284***	.905	1.392E3***

***Significance level between variables

Table 5: Moderation Of Switching Cost With Internet Banking And Customer Loyalty.

Hypothesis (H1d)	Regression Equation	Adj R2	F
Model 1	LOY=4.491+.964 10.346***39.898***	.785	1.592E3***
Model 2	LOY=7.229+2.789+-2.614 12.794***10.763***-7.071***	.807	910.565***
Model 3	LOY=7.234+2.789+-2.614+2.526 2.985***8.526***-6.679***.002	.808	605.645***

***Significance level between variables

Table 6: Moderation of Switching Cost with Customer Perceived Value on Customer Loyalty.

2. $LOY_i = a + b1 * IB + b2*DSc$

3. $LOY_i = a + b1 * IB + b2*DSc + b3 * (IB * DSc)$

Moderation of switching cost with internet banking on customer loyalty

Table 5 depicts that Switching Cost is a moderator variable for the relationship between Internet Banking and customer loyalty, as the partial regression coefficient of the interaction term (IB*DSc) is significantly different from 0. More particularly, Switching Cost is a quasi moderator for the relationship between Internet Banking and Customer Loyalty, because the three models are significantly different from each other. On behalf of these differences we accept hypothesis H1c- that suggest the higher the level of switching costs, the greater is the likelihood that internet banking will lead to greater customer loyalty.

Moderation of switching cost with customer perceived value on customer loyalty

Moderating Regression Equation

1. $LOY_i = a + b1 * CPV$

2. $LOY_i = a + b1 * CPV + b2*DSc$

3. $LOY_i = a + b1 * CPV + b2*DSc + b3 * (CPV * DSc)$

As can be seen in Table 6 Switching Cost is a moderator variable for the relationship between Customer Perceived Value and customer loyalty, as the partial regression coefficient of the interaction term (IB*DSc) is significantly different from 0. More particularly, Switching Cost is a quasi moderator for the relationship between Customer Perceived Value and Customer Loyalty, because the three models are significantly different from one another. Thus we accept H1d: the higher the level of switching costs, the greater is the likelihood that customer perceived value will lead to greater customer loyalty.

Discussion

The findings suggest that customer loyalty can be generated through Internet banking, Customer perceived value and switching cost in banking sector. Hypothesis mentioned above is accepted and shows significant impact on customer loyalty. Researcher took the descriptive statistic analysis first in which gender of respondent their age, region and education measured. Moreover to check the data normality statics mean employed. Hence to check the reliability of the instrument researcher have employed the Chronbach's Alpha test and found significant values, all values are more than 0.07 that show instruments are valid and useable for further statistical testing.

To check the relationship between hypotheses, researcher have applied correlation test. The very first step is to check which test should be applied either Pearson of spearman correlation. Through scatter plot Researcher found that person correlation will be applied. In Pearson correlation it has been proved that all variables have significant relationship.

Simple regression test has been employed to check the direct impact of internet banking, and Customer Perceived Value on Customer Loyalty. The result shows that all independent variable have significant impact on Customer loyalty. Meanwhile moderation relationship of switching cost on customer loyalty has also been checked. All the hypothesis depict moderation with Switching cost furthermore the level of moderation was qasi, on behalf of this detailed analysis researcher concluded that in banking sector internet banking, Customer Perceived value with moderating variable of switching cost have significant impact on Customer loyalty.

Conclusions and Recommendations

Findings

Major finding was to calculate the moderation of switching cost. Research proved that switching cost has qasi moderation between internet banking and customer perceived value on customer loyalty.

Conclusion

The results evoked from structured questionnaires indicate that banks striving for customer loyalty should focus on internet banking services and customer perceived value. In addition the moderating effect of switching cost on customer loyalty through internet banking and customer perceived value are contingent upon the level of internet banking and customer perceived value.

Recommendation

After conducting this detailed research it is very clear that for all private and Governemnts. Banks should introduce internet banking in Pakistan. Internet banking is the key service for customer loyalty. Moreover if managers want that their customers must be loyal with bank they should focus on customer perceived value.

Limitations

This research only explores the banking consumer of city Lahore and Islamabad because data collected from Lahore and Islamabad. Further research may be conduct on other cities of Pakistani so that

marketer will be able to find the needs and desires of banking consumer from different regions.

Future research

Further research may be conducted with other variables like Customer Satisfaction and Public relation within banking context.

References

1. Wolf S, Awschalom D, Buhrman R, Daughton J, Von Molnar S, et al. (2001) Spintronics: a spin-based electronics vision for the future. Science 294: 1488-1495.

2. Domegan CT (1996) The adoption of information technology in customer service. European Journal of Marketing 30: 52-69.

3. Earl MJ (1994) The new and the old of business process redesign. The Journal of Strategic Information Systems 3: 5-22.

4. Goetsch DL, Davis S (2004) Effective Customer Service: Ten Steps for Technical Professions. Pearson Prentice Hall.

5. Liao Z, Cheung MT (2002) Internet-based e-banking and consumer attitudes: an empirical study. Information & Management 39: 283-295.

6. Burgetz B (1992) Project design: The critical step to successful systems. CMA Magazine 66: 10.

7. Bharadwaj AS, Bharadwaj SG, Konsynski BR (1999) Information technology effects on firm performance as measured by Tobin's q. Management science 45: 1008-1024.

8. Chaffey D (2007) E-business and E-commerce Management: Strategy, Implementation and Practice: Pearson Education.

9. Shariq S (2006) Internet banking in Pakistan. Master thesis, Business Administration. Department of Business Administration and Social Sciences, Division of Industrial marketing and e-commerce.

10. Furst K, Lang WW, Nolle DE (2002) Internet banking. Journal of Financial Services Research 22: 95-117.

11. Kardaras D, Papathanassiou E (2001) Electronic commerce opportunities for improving corporate customer support in banking in Greece. International Journal of Bank Marketing 19: 292-298.

12. Orr HA (2000) Adaptation and the cost of complexity. Evolution 54: 13-20.

13. Tan M, Teo TS (2000) Factors influencing the adoption of Internet banking. Journal of the AIS.

14. Bauer HH, Hammerschmidt M, Falk T (2005) Measuring the quality of e-banking portals. International Journal of Bank Marketing 23: 153-175.

15. Singh B, Malhotra P (2004) Adoption of Internet banking: An empirical investigation of Indian banking Sector. Journal of Internet Banking and Commerce 9: 9909-9905.

16. Gerrard P, Cunningham JB (2003) The diffusion of internet banking among Singapore consumers. International Journal of Bank Marketing 21: 16-28.

17. Mattila M, Karjaluoto H, Pento T (2003) Internet banking adoption among mature customers: early majority or laggards. Journal of services marketing 17: 514-528.

18. Polatoglu VN, Ekin S (2001) An empirical investigation of the Turkish consumers' acceptance of Internet banking services. International Journal of Bank Marketing 19: 156-165.

19. Barnes-Vieyra P, Claycomb C (2001) Business-to-business e-commerce: models and managerial decisions. Business horizons 44: 13-20.

20. Daniel E (1999) Provision of electronic banking in the UK and the Republic of Ireland. International Journal of Bank Marketing 17: 72-83.

21. Jayawardhena C, Foley P (2000) Changes in the banking sector–the case of Internet banking in the UK. Internet Research 10: 19-31.

22. Mols NP (2000) The Internet and services marketing–the case of Danish retail banking. Internet Research 10: 7-18.

23. Zhuang Y, Lederer AL (2004) The impact of top management commitment, business process redesign, and IT planning on the business-to-consumer e-commerce site. Electronic Commerce Research 4: 315-333.

24. Dick BK (1994) Customer loyalty: Toward an integrated conceptual framework. Journal of the Academy of Marketing Science 22: 99-113.

25. Sirohi N, McLaughlin EW, Wittink DR (1998) A model of consumer perceptions and store loyalty intentions for a supermarket retailer. Journal of retailing 74: 223-245.

26. Shamma HM, Hassan SS (2009) Customer and non-customer perspectives for examining corporate reputation. Journal of Product & Brand Management 18: 326-337.

27. Woodruff RB (1997) Customer value: the next source for competitive advantage. Journal of the Academy of Marketing Science 25: 139-153.

28. Oliver RL (1993) Cognitive, affective and attributes of the satisfaction response. Journal of consumer research 20: 418-430.

29. Gupta M, Rao R, Upadhyaya S (2008) Electronic Banking and Information Assurance Issues. Advances in Banking Technology and Management: Impacts of ICT and CRM.

30. Deng Z, Lu Y, Wei KK, Zhang J (2010) Understanding customer satisfaction and loyalty: An empirical study of mobile instant messages in China. International Journal of Information Management 30: 289-300.

31. Oliver RL (1999) Whence consumer loyalty. Journal of Marketing 63: 20-38.

32. Weick KE, Quinn RE (1999) Organizational change and development. Annual review of psychology 50: 361-386.

33. Nabi F (2005) Secure business application logic for e-commerce systems. Computers & Security 24: 208-217.

34. Jayawardhena C (2004) Personal values' influence on e-shopping attitude and behaviour. Internet Research 14: 127-138.

35. Reichheld FF, Schefter P (2000) E-loyalty. Harvard business review 78: 105-113.

36. Norsworthy JK, Griffith GM, Scott RC, Smith KL, Oliver LR (2008) Confirmation and control of glyphosate-resistant Palmer amaranth (Amaranthus palmeri) in Arkansas. Weed Technology 22: 108-113.

37. Tari JJ, Sabater V (2004) Quality tools and techniques: are they necessary for quality management? International Journal of Production Economics 92: 267-280.

38. Lichtenstein S, Williamson K (2006) Understanding consumer adoption of internet banking: an interpretive study in the Australian banking context. Journal of Electronic Commerce Research 7: 50-66.

39. Sweeney JC, Soutar GN (2001) Consumer perceived value: the development of a multiple item scale. Journal of retailing 77: 203-220.

40. Sheth JN, Newman BI, Gross BL (1991) Why we buy what we buy: a theory of consumption values. Journal of business research 22: 159-170.

41. Bolton RN, KNL (1999) A Dynamic Model of Customers' Usage of Services: Usage as an Antecedent and Consequence of Satisfaction. Journal of Marketing Research.

42. Lee J, Lee J, Feick L (2001) The impact of switching costs on the customer satisfaction-loyalty link: mobile phone service in France. Journal of services marketing 15: 35-48.

43. Kim M, Kliger D, Vale B (2003) Estimating switching costs: the case of banking. Journal of Financial Intermediation 12: 25-56.

44. Anderson EW, Fornell C, Lehmann DR (1994) Customer satisfaction, market share, and profitability: findings from Sweden. The Journal of Marketing 53-66.

45. Klemperer P (1987) The competitiveness of markets with switching costs. The RAND Journal of Economics 138-150.

46. Chirico P, Anna LP (2008) A customer loyalty model for services based on a continuing relationship with the provider. Journal of Marketing 3: 168-171.

47. Brown T, Dacin P (1997) The company and the product: Corporate associations and consumer product responses. Journal of Marketing 61: 68-84.

48. Chaudhuri A, Morris BH (2001) The chain of effects from brand trust and brand affect to brand performance: the role of brand loyalty. Journal of Marketing 65: 81-93.

49. Johnson MK (2006) Dissociating medial frontal and posterior cingulate activity during self-reflection. Social Cognitive and Affective Neuroscience 1: 56-64.

50. Andreassen TW (1999) What drives customer loyalty with complaint resolution? Journal of Service Research 1: 324-332.

51. Edvardsson B, Johnson MD, Gustafsson A, Strandvik T (2000) The effects of satisfaction and loyalty on profits and growth: products versus services. Total Quality Management 11: 917-927.

52. Hallowell R (1996) The relationships of customer satisfaction, customer loyalty, and profitability: an empirical study. International journal of service industry management 7: 27-42.

53. Flavián C, Guinalíu M, Gurrea R (2006) The role played by perceived usability, satisfaction and consumer trust on website loyalty. Information & Management 43: 1-14.

54. Nilsson OS, Olsen JK (1995) Measuring consumer retail store loyalty.

55. Eshghi A, Haughton D, Topi H (2007) Determinants of customer loyalty in the wireless telecommunications industry. Telecommunications policy 31: 93-106.

56. Creswell JW, Clark VLP (2007) Designing and conducting mixed methods research: Wiley Online Library.

57. Collis J, Hussey R, Crowther D, Lancaster G, Saunders M, et al. (2003) Business research methods: Palgrave Macmillan, New York.

58. Grinnell RM, Unrau YA (2010) Social work research and evaluation: Foundations of evidence-based practice: Oxford University Press.

59. Eriksson K, Kerem K, Nilsson D (2005) Customer acceptance of internet banking in Estonia. International Journal of Bank Marketing 23: 200-216.

60. Gefen D (2002) Customer loyalty in e-commerce. Journal of the association for information systems 3: 27-51.

61. Levesque T, McDougall GH (1996) Determinants of customer satisfaction in retail banking. International Journal of Bank Marketing 14: 12-20.

62. Zeithaml VA, Berry LL, Parasuraman A (1996) The behavioral consequences of service quality. The Journal of Marketing 31-46.

63. De Ruyter K, Wetzels M, Bloemer J (1998) On the relationship between perceived service quality, service loyalty and switching costs. International journal of service industry management 9: 436-453.

64. Sharma S, Durand RM, Gur-Arie O (1981) Identification and analysis of moderator variables. Journal of Marketing Research 291-300.

18

The Effect of Fundamental Determinants on Voluntary Disclosure of Financial and Nonfinancial Information: The Case of Tehran Stock Exchange

Abdolreza Ghasempour*and Mohd Atef bin MdYusof
Department of Accounting, Universiti Utara Malaysia, Sintok, Kedah, Malaysia

Abstract

Recent tendency of businesses towards voluntary disclosure has improved the quality of financial reporting. High-quality financial reporting helps users of financial information trust the business, and thus, creates value for the business. The present study divided voluntary disclosure in two groups of financial and non-financial information and investigated the effects of fundamentals on voluntary disclosure by businesses. The population was composed of 65 companies listed on the Tehran Stock Exchange from 2005 to 2012. The hypothesis testing results showed that firm size, business complexity, earnings volatility, and firm value had a significant and positive impact on voluntary disclosure whereas financial leverage had a significant and negative impact on voluntary disclosure, while no relationship was observed between voluntary disclosure and financial performance.

Keywords: Voluntary disclosure; Fundamental variables; Financial reporting; Financial performance

Introduction

With the development of privatization and economic growth, shareholding grows to become a public trend. The increasing number of shareholders and active institutions in the financial sector, including but not limited to investment companies, rating agencies, mutual funds, brokerage firms, and investment advisory firms, necessitates broad studies on finance and accounting. Due to the sudden changes in the stock market structure, policy makers need to enact laws and regulations for companies to minimize the possibility of misrepresentation and encourage disclosure of information. These policies prepare companies for global stock exchange markets.

Among the most important areas are studies investigating information disclosure by companies as well as investor behavior, attempting to identify the fundamentals underlying different investor decision making under equal circumstances. Scholars, analyzers, and empiricists including Verrecchia [1], Darrough and Stoughton [2], and Hughes [3] have concerned themselves with the incentives of companies for voluntary disclosure. Recent decades have observed numerous researchers trying to identify variables defining the behavior of shareholders and other stakeholders. The present study is an attempt to further the mentioned studies.

Global investors and creditors base their decisions on the information reported in different economic, financial, and nonfinancial reports provided by stock exchange enlisted companies. Prior to decision-making concerning investment on a specific share, investors and creditors also take into account profitability, financial particulars, and nonfinancial particulars including staff information, Board Members" salary and benefits, and internal stock transfers. Therefore, voluntary disclosure, undertaken by many companies enlisted on world's most credible stock exchange markets, is a logical development of basic information disclosure in annual financial reports, necessarily reflecting the information pertaining to the economic realities of a company in a meaningful, transparent, and comparable manner. In Iran, with the enactment of Internal Auditing By-Law as well as the By-Law of Corporate Governance the first steps have been taken towards voluntary disclosure on the part of companies. However, traditional and not so comprehensive and detailed disclosure of general information in

the reports of Board of Directors or exclusive websites of companies, and verylittle in notes accompanying financial reports are still the only sources for optional and voluntary disclosure of information by Iranian companies.

Studies on voluntary disclosure have been conducted in many developed countries. In order for protecting the interests of public investors and the other parties in the market, a legal and efficient system of disclosure needs to be devised. With the development of securities market in many developed countries including the US (10-K Act) or East Asian countries such as China, a large amount of legal information concerning public disclosure of information has been published by the enlisted companies on Stock Exchange Markets for public consideration. Yet, scholars, analysts, and empiricists have regrettably not considered specific laws focusing on the incentives of firms for voluntary disclosure. Analytical studies indicate the fact that how competition influences disclosure levels [1,2], and how disclosure is employed as a signal for firm's value [3]. The present study is specifically concerned with the voluntary disclosure of information on the intellectual capital and knowledge assets in Tehran Stock Exchange. This approach fills out some of the mentioned research gaps and further develops the related literature in a global level.

Theoretical framework and review of the related literature

Disclosure, in its simple and general sense, is defined as transferring and presenting economic information associated with the financial status and performance of firms, whether financial or nonfinancial, quantitative or in other forms. If it is made compulsory through sources

---

*Corresponding author: Abdolreza Ghasempour, Department of Accounting, Universiti Utara Malaysia, Sintok, Kedah, Malaysia
E-mail: reza52_gh@yahoo.com

of law, this disclosure is referred to as "Mandatory Disclosure", and if it is not mandated by any specific regulation, it is considered "Voluntary Disclosure". Furthermore, disclosure implies presenting a minimum amount of information in firm reports, based on which a reasonable evaluation of the firm's relative risks and value can be drawn and which can assist information users in this regard [4].

Both traditional (mainly monetary) and voluntary disclosure (mainly non-monetary) are efficient sources of information for stakeholders. Empirical studies on voluntary disclosure maintain a rather long history, commenced by Cerf and followed by a plethora of complementarystudies concerned with investigating the influence of other company features on disclosure, including size, type of stock exchange admission, leverage, and administrative structure.

Expenses for development and collection of detailed information can be rather higher for small companies compared to large corporations. As, in large corporations, the mentioned information has already been developed for internal reporting to the administration, therefore, its disclosure shall not incur extra expenses Owusu-Ansah [4] also maintain that production and dissemination of information is a costly activity and larger corporations probably have the required resources and expert staff for the dissemination of financial reports with high disclosure levels and consequently higher compliance with the disclosure regulations. It can thus be concluded that disclosure costs per unit are reduced and as a result large corporations disclose higher amounts of information. As quoted by Owusu-Ansah [4], Stigler [5] considering the available economic facilities for information production and storage, large corporations are inclined to spend more resources for information production, and disclosure of information is higher in large corporations rather than small companies. Stigler [5] found out that the response to larger negative earnings is mostly obtained through voluntary disclosure by companies. Many studies today indicate the effects of disclosure on the cost of capital [6] and the cost of debt [7]. There are also numerous studies on corporate governance and disclosure [8-13]. In Iran, it seems, there are significant research gaps in this area. Little research has been conducted on the subject under discussion in Iran, with each one addressing only small portions of voluntary disclosure literature [14-17]. Taking into account different stakeholder groups, the present study has attempted to further develop the literature in many aspects nationally and in a few aspects worldwide.

O'Dwyer [18] investigated first-hand the incentives of directors for social information disclosure in annual reports. The results showed that directors maintain that social pressures necessitate the accountability of companies and disclosure of information in annual reports is deemed as a gesture of redeeming their legitimacy.

Another study which investigated the influence of governance, corporate governance mechanisms, and firm-specific characteristics on the voluntary disclosure of Shanghai Stock Exchange listed companies. The results indicated that sole proprietorship, existence of an audit committee, firm size, and leverage are significantly related to voluntary disclosure. Their findings moreover indicated an understanding of disclosure behavior in state-owned entities during the privatization process in China. This study intends to investigate different governance variables and firm-specific characteristics within the framework of Stakeholder Theory.

In Australia, Deegan et al. [19] utilized Legitimacy Theory to explain the changes in disclosure of environmental reports by enterprises for periods in which authorities, including the government and Environmental Protection Organization, emphasized compliance with environmental protection regulations. The results portrayed that during the years companies were pressured to comply with environmental protection regulations, their disclosure tended to be more desirable and comprehensive in this regard, as compared to the other years. They also found out that regulatory requirements concerning environmental protection coerces enterprises to turn to environmental disclosure. It seems that business entities struggle to retain their legitimacy via voluntary disclosure when they have violated a social contract.

Deegan et al. [19] conducted a study on the methods of social and environmental disclosure employed by Australian companies. The results supported the legitimacy-seeking incentives of directors of socio-environmental information-disclosing companies.

In another study, Kashanipoor et al. [17] investigated the relationship between voluntary disclosure of a company and the number of its non-executive directors. Their sample was composed of 239 companies. Their disclosure checklist listed 71 items. Their results showed that there was not a significant relationship between voluntary disclosure and the percentage of non-executive directors on the Board.

Sajadi et al. [15] studied the relationship between five nonfinancial characteristics of Tehran Stock Exchange listed companies and the quality of their financial reporting. To measure the financial reporting quality, an index was employed containing 155 items, following Iran Accounting Standards and other disclosure pertaining regulations, to investigate possiblerelationships between the firm size, type of auditing institute, type of industry, ownership structure, and company age, and financial reporting quality, using models of multiple regression. The results showed that firm size, company age, and type of industry maintained significant positive relationships while ownership structure had a negative relationship with the financial reporting quality, whereas the relationship between type of auditing institute and financial reporting quality was not significant.

In their applied descriptive-survey study, Yazdi et al. [14] investigated the feasibility of social reporting by Tehran Stock Exchange listed companies, collecting the data using questionnaires. They concluded that social reporting is not well-received for a couple of reasons, namely: absence of a proper accounting information system, reluctance of directors to disclose company's social costs, absence of legal standards, and high costs of developing social reports. They also provided evidences indicating that directors are more inclined to disseminate measures they have taken concerning employee welfare and health, charity, and environmental protection.

In addition to the above-gone examples, many scholars have struggled in the recent decades to identify the defining variables in explaining shareholder behavior and other stakeholders. The present study is an attempt to further develop these studies.

Methodology

This is a descriptive-library study in terms of data collection, an applied study in terms of the objective, and concerning hypothesis testing, this study is classified as correlational, adopting a deductive-inductive approach, and of causal-comparative type. In terms of sampling method it is a semi empirical study. Initially the population was studied, including Tehran Stock Exchange listed companies who have been active from March 2005 through to 2012. Of course, for mean calculation for some of the variables, the period was extended to include March 2002. Then the companies lacking the required characteristics were excluded, and the sample was ultimately selected from among the remaining companies. The designated variables were later on extracted from different information sources, databases, and financial reports of the sample companies, and consequently the hypotheses were tested.

Sample and sampling procedure

The population of the present study was Tehran Stock Exchange listed companies who have been active from March 2005 through to 2012. Approximately 330 companies have been active on Tehran Stock Exchange since March 2002. However, for mean calculation of some variables, the period has been extended to include March 2002, adding up to a number of 320 active companies. Tehran Stock Exchange Organization was the research location. Research period is from March 2002 to March 2012. As for hypothesis testing, the companies were selected as sample only if:

1. The company is not in the financial intermediation industry, as the capital structure of these institutes are different

2. The company has been enlisted on Tehran Stock Exchange since March 2002

3. The company's ticker symbol does not suffer a significant halt (i.e. does not suffer a halt of more than 3 months on the stock market board)

4. The company's data are available

Having considered the above-gone conditions, the population shrank to 182 companies, out of which 65 companies were randomly selected and analyzed as the sample. The pertinent data was investigated for a 7 year period, i.e. a total of 455 observations (year-company) were tested for hypothesis testing.

$$n \geq \frac{NZ_{a/2}^2 \times P(1-P)}{(N-1)\in^2 + Z_{\frac{a}{2}}^2 \times P(1-P)} = 65$$

Research hypotheses

To achieve the objectives, the research hypotheses are addressed in two separate divisions.

Primary hypotheses

A. There is a significant relationship between company fundamentals and voluntary disclosure of financial information

B. There is a significant relationship between company fundamentals and voluntary disclosure of nonfinancial information

Secondary hypotheses group 1:

A1: There is a significant relationship between the company's market value and levels of voluntary disclosure of financial information;

A2: There is a significant relationship between the firm size and levels of voluntary disclosure of financial information;

A3: There is a significant relationship between access to growth opportunities and levels of voluntary disclosure of financial information;

A4: There is a significant relationship between complexity of business and levels of voluntary disclosure of financial information;

A5: There is a significant relationship between financial performance and levels of voluntary disclosure of financial information;

A6: There is a significant relationship between earnings volatility and levels of voluntary disclosure of financial information;

Secondary hypotheses group 2:

B1: There is a significant relationship between the company's market value and levels of voluntary disclosure of nonfinancial information;

B2: There is a significant relationship between the firm size and levels of voluntary disclosure of nonfinancial information;

B3: There is a significant relationship between access to growth opportunities and levels of voluntary disclosure of nonfinancial information;

B4: There is a significant relationship between complexity of business and levels of voluntary disclosure of nonfinancial information;

B5: There is a significant relationship between financial performance and levels of voluntary disclosure of nonfinancial information;

B6: There is a significant relationship between earnings volatility and levels of voluntary disclosure of nonfinancial information;

Research variables and how they are calculated

Research variables are listed below as employed in the first section:

Voluntary disclosure index (VolDiscT): Voluntary disclosure is defined as disclosure of information by companies besides what mandated by Iranian Accounting Standards, including the entire financial and nonfinancial items, not enlisted on the Adequacy of Disclosure Checklist [20].

Different studies in the pertinent literature, have adopted various criteria and scores for measuring voluntary disclosure: management forecasts, managerial speeches, self-constructed scores, and standard scores constructed by credible rating agencies (Association for Investment Management and Research (AIMR)) Scores and Standard & Poor's (S&P) Transparency and Disclosure Scores, for instance), to mention a few. The self-constructed score was selected for measuring voluntary disclosure for two reasons: they have stated that self-constructed scores are more trustworthy, and properly measure what they stand for (validity). Self-constructed rating scores are more successful than standard disclosure indices especially in cases where many questions are raised concerning the efficiency of externally designed measuring indices (e.g. whether this rating procedure is capable of properly measuring the changes in disclosure approaches taken by the company?). To extract voluntary disclosure index, this study employed a weighted disclosure index for measuring the disclosure score of each and every company; a disclosure index was developed to meet this end, composed of approximately 112 financial and 131 nonfinancial items [21].

Every individual item was assigned with a unique score, depending on the perceived importance, and weight and extent of disclosure by the company. These scores were mostly retrieved from the company's website and Board reports. Voluntary disclosure index can therefore be defined as:

$$VolDisc_j = \frac{1}{n_j} \sum_{i=1}^{n_j} w_i d_i$$

In which:

$VolDisc_j$ is the disclosure weight index for the company j, and W_i represents the assigned weight to the informational item i, as disclosed by the company

1. j represents the assigned weight

2. Access to Growth Opportunities (M/B) = market/book ratio or price/earnings ratio (P/E).

3. Leverage = Total Average Debt/Total Average Assets

4. Size = natural logarithm of the company's total average stock market value;

5. Complexity: total receivables and inventory/total assets.

6. Firm Value: to calculate Tobin's Q, the model proposed by Perfect and Wiles (1994) was employed. Their proposed index follows:

$$Q = \frac{MV(Eqity) + BV(Debt)}{BV(Asset)}$$

The ultimate proposed models for investigating the effects of company fundamentals on

Voluntarydisclosure was extracted as follows:

$$VolDiscT = \alpha_0 + \alpha_1 Fvalue + \alpha_2 Size + \alpha_3 M/B + \alpha_4 Leverage + \alpha_5 Complexity + \alpha_6 ROE + \alpha_7 EarnVol + \psi$$

$$VolDisc1 = \alpha_0 + \alpha_1 Fvalue + \alpha_2 Size + \alpha_3 M/B + \alpha_4 Leverage + \alpha_5 Complexity + \alpha_6 ROE + \alpha_7 EarnVol + \psi$$

$$VolDisc2 = \alpha_0 + \alpha_1 Fvalue + \alpha_2 Size + \alpha_3 M/B + \alpha_4 Leverage + \alpha_5 Complexity + \alpha_6 ROE + \alpha_7 EarnVol + \psi$$

Descriptive Statistics of Research Variables					
	Mean	Median	Max	Min	Standard
Variable					Deviation
Business Complexity	0.474	0.4597	3.757	0.029	0.327
Leverage	0.661	0.672	1.093	0.186	0.168
Growth Opportunity (M/B)	3.84	2.092	47.566	0.104	4.96
Size	12.884	12.725	16.945	9.5	1.546
Return on Equity	0.61	0.407	5.672	-1.177	0.733
Secondary Disclosure Index (VOLDISC1)	94.598	84.5	312	0	57.446
Secondary Disclosure Index (VOLDISC2)	14.687	12	110	0	13.883
Secondary Disclosure Index (VOLDISC3)	29.57	16	260	0	38.128
Secondary Disclosure Index (VOLDISC4)	6.744	3	57	0	9.624
Secondary Disclosure Index (VOLDISC5)	5.798	3	43	0	6.262
Secondary Disclosure Index (VOLDISCT)	151.361	126	646	13	105.255

Table 1: Descriptive Statistics of Research Variables.

Model	ModelIT	Model1	Model2
F-Stastics	1.728	1.861	1.169
Prob>F	0.0013	0.0003	0.2069
$\chi^2 - Statistic$	116.919	124.691	0.0319
$Prob > \chi^2$	0.0001	0	86.523
Number of Observations	573	573	573
Model Type	Panel	Panel	Mixed

Table 2: Panel or Mixed Model Identification(F-LimerTest).

Research Findings

Descriptive analyses

Table 1 shows the descriptive statistics of research variables. The values were obtained and analyzed using SPSS, Eviews, Stata, and Excel. Results from analyzing descriptive statistics revealed that the obtained scores for the total voluntary disclosure index fluctuated between 13 and 646. This high dispersion of scores indicates the absence of a unified approach among companies for information disclosure. Mean disclosure index score (VOLDISCT) was 126, with a standard deviation of 105.255. High standard deviation of the obtained scores is probably due to the major difference in firm sizes of companies enlisted on Tehran Stock Exchange. Furthermore, average obtained scores for secondary voluntary disclosure indices, namely, shareholder value creation (VOLDISC1), customers and products (VOLDISC2), intellectual capital and human resources (VOLDISC3), social and environmental reporting (VOLDISC4), and lastly corporate governance (VOLDISC5), were obtained at 94.598, 14.687, 29,570, 6.744, and 5.798, respectively, indicative of the fact that companies are more inclined to disclose the information pertaining to their financial performance and much less their nonfinancial information, especially that pertaining to their corporate governance and socio-environmental reporting.

Normality test

Since the analyses in this section are conducted using Dynamic PanelEstimator (GMM), data normality is not prioritized. Nevertheless, Jarque-Bera and Shapiro-Wilk tests were followed through for data normality, and cases of non-normality, were normalized using features of STATA software.

Step one: panel or mixed model identification (F-Limer test): Prior to model estimation, it needs to be identified that whether the model is with single or multiple y-intercepts, i.e. whether there is a panel or mixed distribution. F-Limer test was utilized to meet this end. Results of the mentioned tests for models pertaining to the first theory are presented in Table 2.

Here, the H_0 implies non-panel distribution. As shown by the results, except for sub model 2 (Model2), the models maintain panel distribution. As stated above, panel data has singly y-intercept, while mixed data has multiple y-intercepts.

Step two: random effects test and hausman test: Having determined the type of y-intercept, the next issue to deal with is whether the discussed y-intercepts are fixed or random. From a theoretical point of view, if all the y-intercepts of the population are present, the model will be fixed effect model. It, however, should be kept in mind that in case the conditions justify random effect estimation theory, a Hausman Test needs to be conducted primarily, and if that rejects, fixed effect model is the correct procedure. The H_0 of Hausman test proved that the model is a random effects model. The important point to be considered here is that the basis of Hausman test is that the test is required to be estimated randomly first, only then can the Hausman test be conducted. Results from the above tests for the first model are presented in Table 3.

As shown by the results, the main model as well as submodel 1 is required to be estimated as the random effects of y-intercepts.

Step three: heteroscedasticity test: One of the problems of regression model is the Heteroscedasticity of modeling errors, imposed by the violation of the hypothesis $Var(U_i) = \sigma^2 I$. Such an issue in the regression will cause the OLS result to be no longer efficient. The H_0 is Homoscedasticity.

Model	ModelT	Model1	Model2
Wald chi2 (7)	9.167	8.532	-
Prob> chi2	0.241	0.288	-
Final Result	Random Effects	Random Effects	

Table 3: Random Effects and Hausman Tests for the Research Models.

Model	ModelT	Model1	Model2
y-intercept	3.222	3.024	0.813
	(9.351)***	(9.912)***	-1.624
Access to Growth Opportunities	-0.189	-0.130	-0.449
	(-2.505)***	(-1.921)**	(-3.167)***
Size	0.135	0.097	0.291
	(2.958)***	(2.402)***	(4.471)***
Financial Leverage	0.169	0.069	0.183
	(1.483)	(0.671)	(1.114)
Complexity of Business	0.134	0.141	0.175
	(2.746)***	(3.246)***	(2.665)*
Financial Performance	0.012	0.009	0.037
	(0.330)	(0.287)	(0.725)
Earnigs Volatility	0.009	0.029	-0.123
	(0.267)	(0.914)	(-2.432)**
Firm value in the Past Year	0.014	0.111	0.230
	(0.206)	(1.823)	(2.474)
AR(1)	-	-	0.202
			(3.416)
Adj_R2	0.065	0.076	0.098
F	4.660	5.238	4.778
Prob>chi2	0.000	0.000	0.000
D.W.	1.700	1.87	1.84
Number of Observations	366	356	278

***, **, and * indicate significant at 1%, 5%, and 10% respectively

Table 4: Final Estimate of Regressive Models.

Generalized least squares were adopted for cases of approved Heteroscedasticity.

Step four: autocorrelation test: Another recurrent problem in a regression model is autocorrelation between the residuals. Autocorrelation is violation of one of the standard assumptions of the regression model (the assumption: COV $(u_i, u_j) = 0$. The OLS estimation technique, thus, loses the Best Linear UnbiasedEstimator (BLE) feature, and as a result, the statistical inference would render unreliable. The autocorrelation problem can exist as first order Autoregressive Process (AR(1)), higher orders, or Moving Average Process (MA(q)). The H_0 here is the absence of autocorrelation. In cases observed with first order autocorrelation, coefficient estimates such as AR(1) were used to obviate autocorrelation.

Step five: final estimate of regressive models: The final model is consequently estimated in the final step subsequent to diagnostics. Results of model estimates are given in Table 4. As observable from the results depicted in Table 4, the t-statistics pertaining to the variables of firm size and complexity of business have significant and positive relationship with the voluntary disclosure levels of financial and nonfinancial information at the significance level of 0.05 in all the three models. The mentioned statistics for the same variables is 2.958 and 2.746 in the main model respectively. In other words, the results show that larger corporations and companies with higher business complexity are more inclined to disclose their information, probably due to the fact that they are interested to ensure their shareholders that the company's resources are properly managed and administered by the company.

Imposed pressures on behalf of the government, other organizations, and media can also be regarded as contributing factors. The negative coefficient of access to growth opportunities, on the other hand, implies that the company may have access to a range of opportunities for possible sales promotion, and is reluctant to further disclose pertinent information to maintain its competitive edge. The t-statistics of this variable is -2.505 in the main model. In contrast, according to Table 4, there is no significant relationship between variables of financial leverage, financial performance (profitability), and earnings volatility and voluntary disclosure, i.e. desirable financial conditions does not necessarily trigger higher information disclosure, and possibly other leverages are the contributing factors in this case.

Discussion and Conclusion

This study investigated voluntary reporting of companies concerning two divisions of financial and nonfinancial information and analyzed the effects of company fundamentals on such reporting. Results from hypothesis testing maintained that the variables of firm size and complexity of business have significant and positive relationship with the voluntary disclosurelevels of financial and nonfinancial information, as evidences to the point that larger corporations and also companies with higher business complexity are more inclined to disclose their information, probably due to the fact that they are interested to ensure their shareholders of the proper management of the company's resources. Pressures from the government, other organizations, and the media can also be regarded as additional contributing factors. The negative coefficient of access to growth opportunities, on the other hand, implies that the company may have access to a range of opportunities for possible sales promotion, and is reluctant to further disclose pertinent information to maintain competitive edge. Furthermore, there is no significant relationship between variables of financial leverage, financial performance (profitability), and earnings volatility and voluntary disclosure, i.e. desirable financial conditions does not necessarily trigger higher information disclosure, and possibly other leverages are the contributing factors.

Accordingly, most of the research hypotheses, except for the two variables of financial performance and earnings volatility, are proven at the significance level of 0.05. Findings of the present study in terms of the majority of the variables are consistent with similar studies conducted in other countries [6-12].

The results of the present study suggest that in their investment decisions, analyzers should take into account voluntary disclosure. It is also suggested that Tehran Stock Market devises incentives for smaller companies to further encourage voluntary disclosure.

References

1. Verrecchia R (1983) Discretionary disclosure. Journal of Accounting & Economics 5: 179-1948uality and the Cost of Debt, The Accounting Review 73: 459-474.

2. Chtourou SM, Bedard J, Courteau L (2001) Corporate governance and earnings management. Working Paper, Universite Laval, Canada.

3. KleinA (2002) Audit committee, board of director characteristics, and earnings management. Journal of Accounting and Economics. 33: 375-400.

4. Peasnell KV, Pope PF, Young SE (2001) The characteristics of firms subject to adverse rulings by the financial reporting review panel. Accounting and Business Research. 31: 291-311.

5. Xie B, Davidson WN, DaDalt PJ (2001) Earnings management and corporate governance: the roles of the board and the audit committee, Journal of Corporate Finance 9: 295-316.

6. Beekes W, Pope P, Young S (2004) The link between earnings conservatism and board composition: Evidence from the U.K. An International Review, 12: 47-59.

7. Eng LL, Mak YT (2003) Corporate governance and voluntary disclosure,Journal of Accounting and Public Policy, 22: 325-345..

8. Yazdi HK, Hemmati K, BayatA (2012) The Assessment of Social Reporting on behalf of Accepted Corporations Listed in Tehran Stock Exchange, Business Intelligence Journal (BIJ),5: 214-223.

9. SajadiH, Mansour Z, Alireza J (2009) Nonfinancial characteristics effective on financial disclosure quality in Tehran Exchange market listed companies, Accounting and Auditing Assessments Journal 16: 51-68.

10. ForoughiD, Morteza M, ShahshaniS, Poorhossein (2008) Directors attitude towards disclosure of social information: Stock Market listed companies (2007), Accounting and Auditing Assessments Journal 15: 55-70

11. Kashanipoor, Mohammad, Ali Rahmani, and Parchini (2009) The relationship between voluntary disclosure and non-executive directors, Accounting and Auditing Assessments Journal 16: 85-100.

12. O'DwyerB (2002) Managerial Perceptions of Corporate Social Disclosure: An Irish Story, Accounting Auditing and Accountability Journal 15: 406-436.

13. DeeganC, RankinM, Tobin J (2002) An Examination of the Corporate Social and Environmental Disclosures of BHP from 1983-1997: A Test of Legitimacy Theory". Accounting, Auditing & Accountability Journal15: 312-343.

14. Franncis F, Nanda D, Olsson A (2008) Voluntary Disclosure, Earnings Quality, and Cost of Capital", Journal of Accounting Research 46: 53-99.

15. BayatAli (2012)The relationship between the levels of voluntary disclosure, the cognitive styles of decision-making, and information asymmetry: according to Stakeholder Theory,Ph.D. Dissertation in Accounting, Islamic Azad University, Science and Research Branch, Faculty of Management and Economics.

19

Role of Technology Business Incubators to Nurture Entrepreneurship: A Study on Pakistani Universities

Sammer Mumtaz[1], Farheen Shafi[1*] and Fareeha Zafar[2]

[1]National College of Business Administration and Economics, DHA, Lahore, Pakistan
[2]Government College University, Lahore, Pakistan

Abstract

The purpose of this study is to explore how technology business incubation centers established in different universities of Pakistan playing their role to cultivate the entrepreneurial culture and providing support to startups. These incubation centers are also facilitating those who have some new innovative ideas to get them converted in successful business by providing professional support, business advices and exposure to entrepreneurial networks. One of the objectives of these incubators is to promote the entrepreneurial culture among students from the start of their study programs to change their mindset from job seeker to job provider. Based on observation this study identifies that technology business incubation centres provide the wide scope of resources and facilities to assist the startups ranging from prototype development to learning how to commercialize technological ideas, bridging the gap between academia and industry to providing the platform to industry as well in resolving their issues by providing the effective solutions. Tenants firms provided with opportunity to learn from multipurpose experiences of big industry icons by arranging informative workshops and seminars..

Keywords: Business incubators; University-industry linkage; Technology transfer; Entrepreneurship

Introduction

Entrepreneurship is a dynamic capability to innovatively act in order to create incremental gain. The company must master the ability to market its new product to obtain high commercial gains and achieve success. The purpose of Business Incubation Center (BIC) is to provide a conducive environment to nurture small businesses. Pakistani Universities are emphasizing on establishment of Technical Business Incubation Centres thus supporting researchers/young entrepreneur / startups, to develop promising early-stage business ventures.

A business incubator's prime goal is to create and grow small businesses, duly supporting them with required technical and financial assistance. Young graduates are enabled to commercialize new technologies, thereby strengthening local and national economies. The well-knit coordination among the entrepreneurs, universities and industry greatly influence the economy by facilitating networking with stakeholders.

The history of business Incubation Centres in Pakistan dates back to 2005 at National University of Science and Technology, Islamabad. Over the years we have Plan9 – PITB's Tech Incubator, SMEDA, IBA, NUST TIC, Lahore University of Management Sciences (Lums), COMSATS and many more Business Incubation Centres working successfully in Pakistan. "Young, fresh and inventive entrepreneurs fall back in developing the right connections, industrial know-how and gaining attention. At Plan9, we provide an environment conducive to the success of a startup that resolves all afore-mentioned predicaments." (Punjab Information Technology board-PLAN9 TECH INCUBATORS). In 2016, there has been a noteworthy rise in the trend of entrepreneurship. Many micro-companies were started from scratch by student entrepreneurs and also there were grown professionals who started their IT ventures. Many supporters provided mentorships and keen investors who supported the startups financially.

According to Zeenia Faraz, who runs the British Council's social enterprise programme in Pakistan, "**Social enterprise presents an ideal mechanism to enlist young people in Pakistan in developing their innovative ideas into businesses that deliver social and economic impact, address key development issues and contribute positively to society.**"

The British Council, along with **SEED (Social Education Environmental Development) Pakistan,** will work towards **building the capacity of the university incubation centres** to develop start-up ideas evolving from the social enterprise trainings. The British Council has planned to launch the programme in **50 universities of Pakistan by 2018.**

"In partnership with the universities, we expect to provide support and training to over 250 social enterprises start-ups through the incubation centres, and expect that 50 of these will become sustainable and successful businesses," said the British Council's Zeenia Faraz.

Literature Review

In order to build human capital for the forthcoming society, Entrepreneurship education is inevitable. Entrepreneurship flourishes in ecosystems in which various stakeholders, such as Governments at International, National, Regional, and Local level, Individuals and intermediaries such as NGOs and entrepreneurs, Entrepreneurial academic institutes and businesses, play key roles. Academic Institutions play a vital role in shaping attitudes, skills and behavior of the youth. On the other hand, critical role is played by stakeholders working outside the academia, thus influencing formal and informal educational programmes and simultaneously reaching out to underserved target groups. Here collaboration and multi-stakeholder partnerships become indispensable [1].

*****Corresponding author:** Farheen Shafi, National College of Business Administration and Economics, DHA, Lahore, Pakistan
E-mail: farheenshfi@gmail.com

Business Incubation is a process which supports the progress and development of enterprises in their early phase. The Business Incubators offers entrepreneurs a conducive environment for development of their new enterprise, providing assistance in launching the enterprise at minimal costs and boost the confidence and enhance the capacity of the entrepreneur. It also provides the entrepreneur with the necessary networking with the resources essential in starting and scaling a viable initiative. The business incubators accept entrepreneurs for a certain specified time period till the target profit or sales revenue is obtained [2]. It is difficult to identify an enterprise in its early phase that will grow meaningfully, if nurturing environment is provided.

The Business Incubation functions as a venture capitalist by investing in management, instead of just ideas. The Business Incubator calculates the ability of the entrepreneur as well as the market potential of the venture to determine the business potential. Various tools and methods are used to assess the entrepreneur and business potential. This requires the involvement of financiers, industry and business development experts. Highly successful entrepreneurs have high internal locus of control and a profound need for achievement. They are less risk averse and have high level of education [2]. Pakistan to become a part of the emerging economies requires channelizing its entrepreneurial efforts towards having export-focused start-ups; in order to contribute significantly in economic growth [3]. There is a U-shaped relationship between the entrepreneurial activity and economic development. The entrepreneurship is higher in countries which are at extreme ends of the GDP per capita. For example the GDP per capita of Philippines and Indonesia is less than $5000 whereas the rates of early stage entrepreneurship are amongst the highest in the world. On the other hand, Australia, having a GDP per capita of $32000 with entrepreneurial activity only 11.9% [3] (Figure1).

University-industry collaboration is a critical constituent of efficient nationwide innovation systems. Experience of developed countries can be studied in order to learn and benefit from various types of university industry collaborations [4-10]. The high intensity university industry collaboration in found in research partnerships, and shared infrastructure for development and commercial exploitation of technologies pursued by academic inventors through a company they partly own. In Pakistan, "TechHub Connect is a project of Punjab Information Technology Board. We are Pakistan's first co-working space for freelancers. We also act as the bridge between industry, academia and the government by assisting the formation of fruitful partnerships and collaborations among and within these organisations. "(Punjab Information Technology board-PLAN9 TECH INCUBATORS) Connect is an online portal which shapes a community where well-known IT companies can brand themselves as employers. Students can realize the latest industry trends to refine their talent for present-day and future industry requirements. Through connect; Professors can build their profiles to cater to the research need of the industry. Virtual recommendations can be received by the students thus facilitating them to apply for jobs (Figure 2).

Case study of university incubators in Taiwan

Taiwan is also working a lot for the incubation centers. We have analyzed the three national university incubation centers in Taiwan to check their policy. National Cheng Kung University (NCKU), National Taiwan University (NTU) and National Chiao Tung University (NCTU). "According to The Times (British) World University Ranking 2012-2013, National Cheng Kung University ranking is 321, National Taiwan University ranking is 134 and National Chiao Tung University

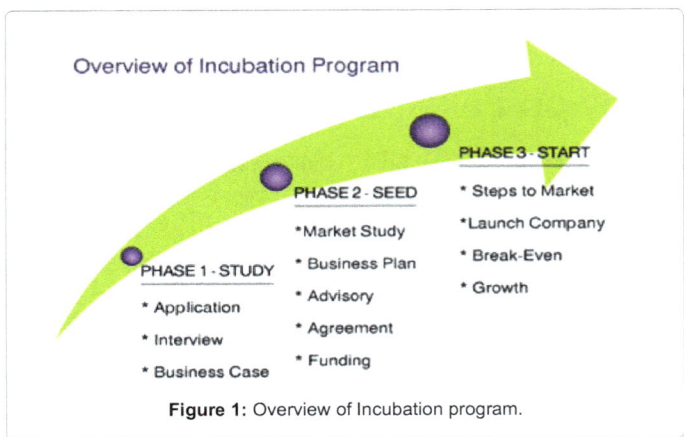

Figure 1: Overview of Incubation program.

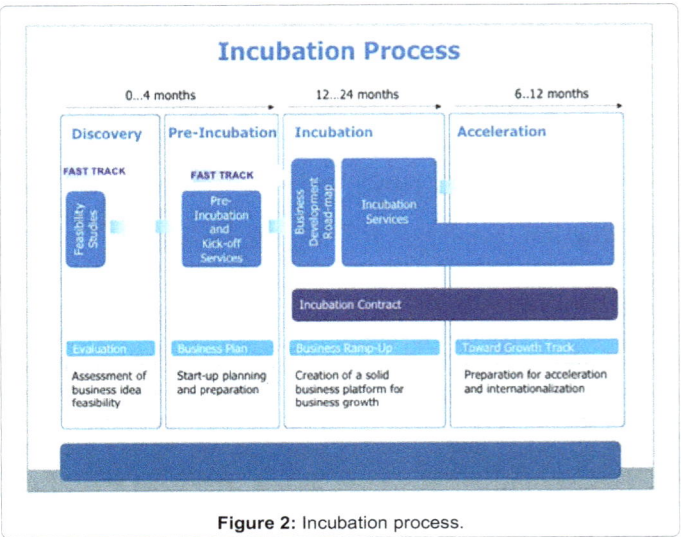

Figure 2: Incubation process.

ranking is 252 they are all well-known for science & technology in Taiwan and working efficiently and showing very good results in order to make incubation policy in Taiwan [11-16].

Methodology

We have used the survey method to carries out our study. We selected the five best universities who are running the business incubation centers in their universities. LUMS Center of Entrepreneurship, COMSATS Incubation Center, University of Engineering and technology- Peshawar, TIC-NUST University and Punjab University Incubation Center. The tools which have been used to conduct the survey are self-administered questioner. The questionnaire has been designed and that measured the importance and effectiveness of five incubation centers services incorporated in this study.

The sample for Survey Questions for business Incubation Centers are:

1. How long has your company been located at the Business Incubation Centre?

2. Are you participating in an Enterprise Platform Program?

3. What level of support are you receiving from the staff of the Incubation Centre?

4. Do you collaborate with the academic staff of the host Institute?

5. Do you have links with other companies located in other Business Incubation Centre's across Ireland?

We also measure the number of incubated companies in each incubation center of different universities mentioned above. Following is the performance of each incubation center (Figure 3).

LUMS Center of entrepreneurship has high percentage among all studied universities they have 72 incubated companies that has been successfully converted in the small enterprises [17-24].

Conclusions and Recommendations

Conclusion

In Pakistan ten public and private universities are successfully running the business incubation centers in their premises, assisting the startup companies to excellently establish their businesses, creating jobs, helping to earn revenues, transforming students innovative business ideas in to full fledge businesses, bridging the gap between academia and industry by arranging informative lectures, workshops for the learning of students, entrepreneurs. These incubation centers are playing their vital role to nurture and inculcating the entrepreneurial culture among students and promoting them to be a job provider and instead of job seeker. The 1st business incubation center was established in National University of Science and Technology, Islamabad in 2005 and slowly and steadily this culture starts prevailing in other universities as well. LUMS center of Entrepreneurship has reported 72 incubated companies that have been converted in successful business now. They have raised the investment of 180 Million and revenue generated by these incubates are Rs. 300 Million. Thousand plus job has also been created by these centers. It is also reported that in last two years 65% of investment was made by startups companies there were supported by different entrepreneurship program running in academic institutions as well as local entrepreneurial centers in Pakistan. Like in other developing countries, the entrepreneurs in Pakistan have lack of many resources that prove big hurdle in their way to success. They have lack of managerial skills, financial resources, technology, and marketing channels. But now these incubation centers are facilitating the startups and entrepreneurs by helping to overcome the different barriers they are facing to run their business smoothly and making them competitive enterprises form incubated companies.

Recommendations

In order to promote entrepreneurial culture the Higher education commission should start these incubation centers in other universities as well where this facility is not being provided yet to university students. It will help to inculcate the concept of entrepreneurship in the mind of students rather they put their efforts to find the jobs after completing their study. We should also put in the efforts to build strong academia industry linkages and networking through these incubation centers so that when they bring their problems to these centers for the solutions, students do research on it and give their innovative ideas to resolve the industry issues. These incubators help them in research and development as well. The government should also play its role by making some policy to fund these incubation centers in order to help the small & medium enterprises in Pakistan, to relief the entrepreneurs from taxes for the 1st five years and should also announce the interest free loans for the startups and new entrepreneurs.

References

1. Volkmann C, Wuppertal BU, Wilson KE, Partners GV (2009) Educating the next wave of entrepreneurs. World Economic Forum, Switzerland.

2. Khalil M, Olafsen E (2010) Enabling Innovative Entrepreneurship through Business Incubation. The Innovation for Development Report.

3. Terjesen S, Hessels J (2009) Varieties of export-oriented entrepreneurship in Asia.

4. Wang W, Hung Y, Wang C (2013) University-Industry business incubators in Taiwan. Open Journal Of Business And Management.

5. Lee S, Osteryoung J (2004) A comparison of critical success factors for effective operations of University business incubators in the United States and Korea. Journal of Small Business Management 42: 418-426.

6. Almeida P, Dokko G, Rosenkopf L (2002) Start-up Size and the Mechanisms of External Learning: Increasing Opportunity and Decreasing Ability. Working paper, Washington, DC, USA: Georgetown University.

7. Oh DS (2002) Technology-Based Regional Development Policy: Case Study of Taedok Science Town, Pajeon Metropolitan City, Korea. Habitat International 26: 213-228.

8. Colombo MG, Delmastro M (2002) How Effective are Technology Incubators? Evidence from Italy. Research Policy 31: 1103-1122.

9. Finer B, Holberton P (2002) Incubators: There and Back. Journal of Business Strategy 23: 21-24.

10. Hickman C, Raia C (2002) Incubating Innovation. Journal of Business Strategy May/June 23: 14.

11. Wiggens J, Gibson DV (2003) Overview of US incubators and the case of the Austin technology Incubator. International Journal of Entrepreneurship and Innovation Management 3: 56.

12. Yunos MGM (2002) Building an innovation-based economy: The Malaysian technology business incubator experience. Journal of Change Management 3: 177-188.

13. Lalkaka (2010) Technology business incubators to help build an innovation-based economy. Journal of Change Management 3: 2.

14. Begley TM, Tan WL, Schoch H (2005) Politico-economic factors associated with interests in starting a business: a multi-country study. Entrepreneurship Theory and Practice 29: 35-55.

15. Bhabra-Remedios RK, Cornelius B (2003) Cracks in the egg: improving performance measures in business incubator research. In: Small Enterprise Association of Australia and New Zealand 16th Annual Conference, Ballarat.

16. Bollingtoft A, Ulhoi JP (2005) The networked business incubator — leveraging entrepreneurial agency? Journal of Business Venturing 20: 265-290.

17. Chan KF, Lau T (2005) Assessing technology incubator programs in the science park: the good, the bad and the ugly. Technovation 25: 1215-1228.

18. Clarysse B, Wright M, Lockett A, Velde EVD, Vohora A (2005) Spinning out new ventures: a typology of incubation strategies from European research institutions. Journal of Business Venturing 20: 183-216.

19. Collinson S, Gregson G (2003) Knowledge networks for new technology-based firms: an international comparison of local entrepreneurship promotion. R&D Management 33: 189-208.

20. CSES (2002) Benchmarking of business incubators. Enterprise Directorate General. European Commission, Brussels.

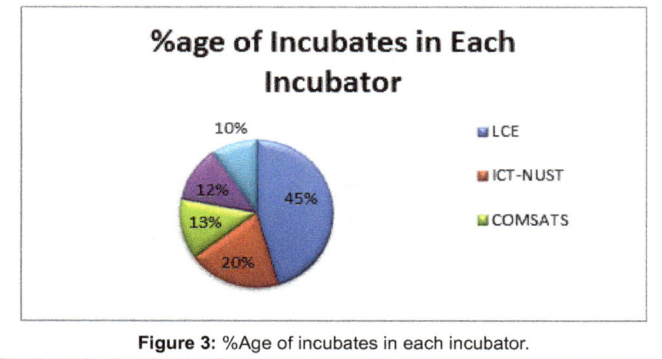

Figure 3: %Age of incubates in each incubator.

21. Grimaldi R, Grandi A (2005) Business incubators and new venture creation: an assessment of incubating models. Technovation 25: 111-121.

22. Hackett SM, Dilts DM (2004a) A real options-driven theory of business incubation. Journal of Technology Transfer 29: 41-54.

23. Hackett SM, Dilts DM (2004b) A systematic review of business incubation research. Journal of Technology Transfer 29: 55-82.

24. Hannon PD (2003) A conceptual development framework for management and leadership learning in the UK incubator sector. Journal of Education and Training 45: 449-460.

20

The Impact of Terrorism on Foreign Direct Investment in Jordan

Rabia Najaf*

Department of Accounting and Finance, University of Lahore, Islamabad Campus, Pakistan

Abstract

The main objective of this paper is to find out the long run relationship between terrorism and foreign direct investment of Jordan. For this purpose, we have taken the monthly data from 1996 to 2014. We have found that data are stationary at first difference. For the analysis of finding the long run association, we have applied the Johnson co integration approach. The results are showing that terrorism have negative relationship with the foreign direct investment. This study suggested that there is need of proper planning for the improvement of the foreign direct investment.

Keywords: Foreign direct investment; Cointegration; Jordan; Long run association

Introduction

From last few decades, it is very interesting topic to discuses that impact of terrorism on the foreign direct investment of all developing and under developing countries. The discussion about the decisiveness of foreign direct investment is the very burning topic for all researchers. For foreign direct investment has crucial role for the development of the poverty. Foreign direct investment is the best way to enhance the managerial skills and latest technology. All the emerging countries are formulating the latest polices for the better performance. According to William foreign direct investment is the basic element for the development of the economy. There is need of rigorous view to understand the importance of the foreign direct investment. Unfortunately, only few countries are getting benefit from the foreign direct investment [1-5]. Most of the scholars had worked out on this issues that why rate of foreign direct investment is moving towards decline position. According to different surveys, it is proved that Pakistan has the come at the low that due to terrorism activities the foreign direct investment is at very critical position. The terrorism activates are increasing day by day due to lack of security system. Since 2006, the ratio of terrorism actives are at the peak. Due to terrorism actives the economics of Pakistan is facing the problems like declines the productivity. According to poon the current position of the Jordan economy is going towards decline position. According to Akhtar after 1947 the inflows level of foreign direct investment is low in Jordan due to political instability. Our study is trying to show that terrorism has very worst impact on the economy of Jordan. The main reason of increasing the terrorism activists mismanagement of security. Foreign direct investment is known as the single way for the strength of the national markets [6-10]. Therefore, most of the emerging countries are keen about the increasing inflows level of foreign direct investment. In Jordan, there is not proper source to fulfill the gap between saving and investment. It is seen that foreign direct investment is the single tool through which any country can enhance the managerial skills. In 1980s, the inflows of foreign direct investment of Jordan were 17$ billion. During the period of 2005, the growth rate was 2.5$. Consequently, the foreign direct investment rate is going to decline due to poor policies [10-30].

Objective

1) The impact of terrorism on the foreign direct investment of Jordan.

2) The impact of terrorism on the foreign investors.

3) The impact of foreign direct investment on the welfare of the society.

Problem statement

The Impact of terrorism on the stock exchange of Jordan (Figure 1).

Literature Review

Abadie and Gardeazabel analyzed the impact of terrorism on performance of the stock market of Pakistan. For this purpose, they were collected the data from 1998 to 2008 and applied the VAR model. Their results are showing that terrorism had negative influences on the stock market of Pakistan. They suggested that Government should have focused on such sort of terrorism activities [1].

Accam observed the impact of terrorism on performance of the stock market of India. For this purpose, they were collected the data from 1999 to 2010 and applied the ECM model. Their results are showing that terrorism had negative influences on the stock market of India. They suggested that Government should have focused on such sort of terrorism activities [2].

Agrawal and Ramaswami applied the impact of terrorism on performance of the stock market of Malaysia. For this purpose, they were collected the data from 1995 to 2005 and applied the OLS model. Their results are showing that terrorism had negative influences on the stock market of Malaysia. They suggested that Government should have focused on such sort of terrorism activities [3].

Agrawal analyzed the impact of terrorism on performance of the stock market of UK. For this purpose, they were collected the data from 1993 to 2001 and applied the ARDL model. Their results are showing that terrorism had negative influences on the stock market of UK. They suggested that Government should have focused on such sort of terrorism activities [4].

*Corresponding author: Najaf R, Department of Accounting and Finance, University of Lahore, Islamabad Campus, Pakistan
E-mail: rabianajaf@hotmail.com

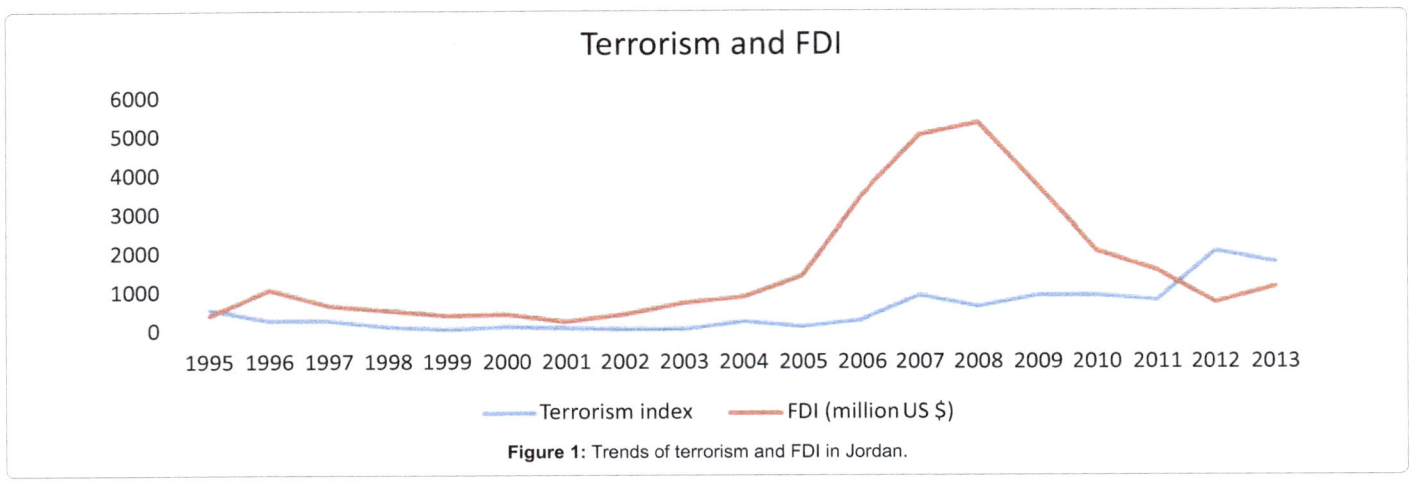

Figure 1: Trends of terrorism and FDI in Jordan.

Ali and Sharafat employed the impact of terrorism on performance of the stock market of USA. For this purpose, they were collected the data from 1986 to 2004 and applied the multiregression equation. Their results are showing that terrorism had negative influences on the stock market of USA. They suggested that Government should have focused on such sort of terrorism activities [5].

Asiedu and Freeman analyzed the impact of terrorism on performance of the stock market of France. For this purpose, they were collected the data from 1989 to 2009 and applied the ECM model. Their results are showing that terrorism had negative influences on the stock market of France. They suggested that Government should have focused on such sort of terrorism activities [6].

Bandera and White observed the impact of terrorism on performance of the stock market of France. For this purpose, they were collected the data from 1989 to 2009 and applied the ECM model. Their results are showing that terrorism had negative influences on the stock market of France. They suggested that Government should have focused on such sort of terrorism activities [7].

Belington viewed the impact of terrorism on performance of the stock market of Libya. For this purpose, they were collected the data from 1983 to 2001 and applied the unit root model. Their results are showing that terrorism had negative influences on the stock market of Libya. They suggested that Government should have focused on such sort of terrorism activities [8].

Bloomberg and Ashoka applied the impact of terrorism on performance of the stock market of Nigeria. For this purpose, they were collected the data from 1989 to 2009 and applied the ADRL model. Their results are showing that terrorism had negative influences on the stock market of Nigeria. They suggested that Government should have focused on such sort of terrorism activities [9].

Bloomberg et al. examined the impact of terrorism on performance of the stock market of China. For this purpose, they were collected the data from 1981 to 2005 and applied the VAR model. Their results are showing that terrorism had negative influences on the stock market of China. They suggested that Government should have focused on such sort of terrorism activities [10].

Theoretical framework

Research methodology was explained in Figure 2.

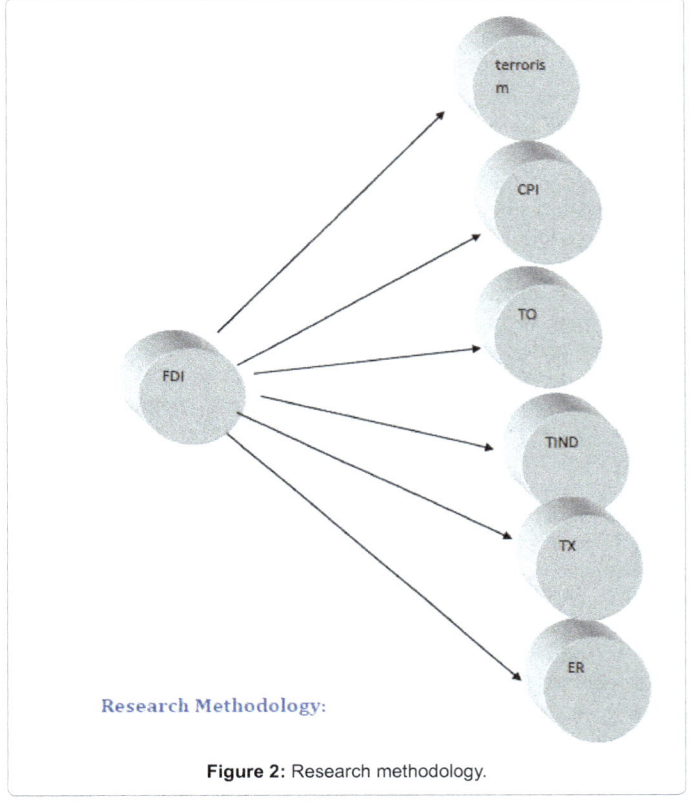

Research Methodology:

Figure 2: Research methodology.

Research Methodology

Data

In this paper, analyzed that there is long run relationship between terrorism and foreign direct investment, for this purpose taken the data from 1996 to 2014 and applied the different tests. Foreign direct investment is the considered dependent variable and CPI, trade openness, exchange rate and terrorism (Tables 1-6).

Mathematically the relationship between the variables can be presented as follows

$$LnFDI=\beta_0+\beta_1 Ln\,GDP+\beta_2 LnER+\beta_3 LnTX+\beta_4 LnCPI+\beta_5 LnTO+\beta_6 LnTIND+\varepsilon$$

	LNFDI	LNGDP	LNCPI	LNER	LNTO	LNTX	TIND
LNFDI	1						
LNGDP	0.1152	1					
LNCPI	-0.1083	-0.1272	1				
LNER	-0.2123	-0.1212	0.94018	1			
LNTO	-0.3739	0.24169	-0.6568	-0.4712	1		
LNTX	-0.0778	-0.3254	0.85238	0.7589	-0.7046	1	
TIND	0.04086	-0.1393	0.68658	0.46717	-0.7669	0.70274	1
Mean	-0.0008	0.02	0.0045	-0.0058	0.0014	-0.0024	5.6487
Maximum	0.3392	0.7968	0.0309	0.0234	0.1162	0.1762	7.6293
Minimum	-0.1896	-0.582	-0.0433	-0.0354	-0.0898	-0.2216	4.1097
Std. Dev.	0.0487	0.1023	0.008	0.0062	0.0195	0.0265	1.0187
Skewness	1.7055	2.4538	1.478	0.3715	0.8945	-2.5358	0.2188
Kurtosis	18.0377	33.2953	9.0028	8.5808	15.8577	45.9997	2.0284
Jorque-Bera	1614.83	6396.95	304.002	215.266	1144.52	12732.4	7.7142

Table 1: Mathematically the relationship between the variables.

Variables	ADF test at level	PP test at first difference	At level	At first difference
LnFDI	-5.075038	-12.03272		
LnGDP	-2.3354	-5.57621	-2.519	-11.48708
LnCPI	-5.88733	-4.324997		
LnTX	-1.2266	-15.05503	-1.2262	-15.05505
LnTO	-5.48509	-12.03412		
LnER	-0.4587	-3.641328	-1.0127	-8.68566
LnTINDX	-5.354386	-12.00103		
At Critical Level				
1% level	-6.92204	-6.918331		
5% level	-2.8748	-2.874933	-2.8742	-2.87444
10% level	-5.148487	-5.147063		

Table 2: Mathematically the relationship between the variables.

	Eigenvalue	Trace statistic	0.05 Critical value	Prob.
None	0.1504	136.6	125.6155	0.0092
At most 1	0.13619	99.8538	95.75367	0.0254
At most 2	0.09214	66.918	69.81888	0.0834
At most 3	0.08046	45.1702	47.85612	0.0372
At most 4	0.06402	26.2992	29.79702	0.11
At most 5	0.04378	11.3973	15.49472	0.1383
At most 6	0.00587	1.3216	3.841467	0.2504

Table 3: Mathematically the relationship between the variables.

Variables	Coefficient	Standard error	t-Statistics
LnGDP	1.725829	0.40739	3.08872
LnCPI	-8.73469	3.12065	2.55353
LnTO	3.615505	1.43799	-2.51428
LnTX	-2.283366	2.73637	-0.83447
LnER	-9.131476	3.23279	-2.82566
LnTIND	1.775638	0.41443	-4.28462

Table 4: Mathematically the relationship between the variables.

Empirical Results and Conclusion

Table 1 is showing that there is positive association between GDP and FDI. There is found negative association between exchange rate and foreign direct investment. There is moderate correlation between trade openness and foreign direct investment. Our results are showing the tax and terrorism index are negatively correlated with foreign direct investment. In this paper, the relationship is analyzed with the help of the co-integration. Our results are showing that data are stationary at level 1 at first difference. Then used Phillips-Perron test and found that there is weak dependency in all variables. The value of Schwarz criterion is showing that it is at lag2. There are found spurious results, so, OLS is not the best here, therefore we applied the co-integration. Different

	Obs.	F-Statistic	Prob.
RGDP does not Granger Cause RFDI	227	4.94924*	0.0078
RFDI does not Granger Cause RGDP	0.7898	0.4553	
RCPI does not Granger Cause RFDI	227	3.62107**	0.0285
RFDI does not Granger Cause RCPI		6.34972*	0.0022
RTO does not Granger Cause RFDI	227	1.62632	0.198
RFDI does not Granger Cause RTO	3.18838**	0.0432	
RTX does not Granger Cause RFDI	227	2.60786***	0.077
RFDI does not Granger Cause RTX		0.44477	0.6416
RER does not Granger Cause RFDI	227	0.34312	0.7098
RFDI does not Granger Cause RER	0.3114	0.7329	
RTIND does not Granger Cause RFDI	227	0.43669	0.6477
RFDI does not Granger Cause RIND Source: author's calculations		1.05449	0.3502

Table 5: Mathematically the relationship between the variables.

	S.E.	LNFDI	LNGDP	LNCPI	LNTX	LNTO	LNER	LTIND
1	0.05849	100	0	0	0	0	0	0
2	0.09492	99.8654	0.00024	0.00267	0.04076	0.05743	0.0078	0.02598
3	0.13293	99.4409	0.00427	0.0317	0.11504	0.27219	0.01785	0.11827
4	0.16825	98.8788	0.00754	0.10208	0.17628	0.55467	0.02976	0.25102
5	0.20196	98.1387	0.01106	0.24035	0.23063	0.91547	0.03969	0.42424
6	0.23393	97.2639	0.0138	0.45777	0.27783	1.31885	0.04642	0.62166
7	0.26454	96.2518	0.01588	0.76768	0.31938	1.76044	0.04918	0.8357
8	0.29399	95.1169	0.0178	1.17452	0.35593	2.22992	0.04826	1.05696
9	0.3226	93.8636	0.01949	1.68024	0.38804	2.72456	0.04453	1.27967
10	0.35028	92.5008	0.02148	2.28198	0.41608	3.24162	0.03927	1.49869

Table 6: Mathematically the relationship between the variables.

researchers studied that there is positive impact of long run market size and foreign direct investment. Here, there has also found long run relationship between inflation and foreign direct investment. There is significant negative association between trade openness and foreign direct investment. It is proved that there is negative association between terrorism and foreign direct investment. This thing is showing that due to terrorism activates investors are feel fear to invest in Jordan. Table 5 is showing that there has found both unidirectional and bidirectional relationship. There is unidirectional relationship between FDI and GDP and bidirectional relationship between CPI and FDI. There is not found lead lag relationship between FDI, terrorism and exchange rate. Table 6 is showing that there is 99% volatility in FDI. The main variables are trade openness and terrorism, which has main role in the volatility of FDI.

References

1. Abadie A, Gardeazabel J (2008) Terrorism and world economy. European Economic Review 52: 1-27.

2. Accam B (1997) Survey of measurement of exchange rate instability. Mimeo.

3. Agarwal S, Ramaswami S (1992) Choice of foreign entry mode: Impact of ownership, location and internalization factors. Journal of International Business Studies 23: 1-27.

4. Agrawal S (2011) The impact of terrorism on foreign direct investment: which sectors are more vulnerable?

5. Ali, Sharafat (2014) Inflation, income inequality and economic growth in Pakistan: A cointegration analysis. International Journal of Economic Practices and Theories.

6. Asiedu E, Freeman J (2009) The Effect of corruption on investment growth: Evidence.

7. Bandera VN, White JT (1968) US. Direct investments and domestic market in Europe. Economia International 21: 117-133.

8. Belington N (1999) The location of foreign direct investment: An empirical analysis. Applied Economics 31: 65-76.

9. Bloomberg B, Ashoka M (2005) How severely does violence deter international investment? Typescript. Department of Economics, Claremont McKenna College, Claremont, CA.

10. Bloomberg B, Hess G, Orphanides A (2004) The macroeconomic consequences of terrorism. Journal of Monetary Economics 51: 1007-1032.

11. Chandprapalert A (2000) The determinants of U.S. Direct investment in Thailand: A survey on managerial Perspectives. Multinational Business Review 8: 82.

12. Coleman AK, Tetty KF (2008) Effect of exchange rate volatility on foreign direct investment in Sub Saharan Africa: A Case of Ghana. Journal of Risk Finance 9: 52-70.

13. Dunning JH (1980) Toward an eclectic theory of international production: some empirical tests. Journal of International Business Studies 11: 9-31.

14. Enders W, Sandler T, Parise F (1992) An econometric analysis of the impact of terrorism on tourism 45: 531-554.

15. Erdal F, Tatoglu E (2002) Locational determinants of foreign direct investment in an emerging market economy: Evidence from Turkey. Multinational Business Review 10: 21.

16. Gaibulloev K Sandler T (2008) Growth consequences of terrorism in Western Europe. Kyklos 61: 411-424.

17. Hartman D (1984) Tax policy and foreign direct investment in the United States. National Tax Journal 37: 475-487.

18. IMF (2010) Transactions with Fund. International Monetary Fund Website.

19. Jackson S, Murkowski S (1995) The attractiveness of countries to foreign direct investment. Journal of World Trade 29: 159-180.

20. Kemsley D (1998) The effect of taxes on production location. Journal of Accounting Research 36: 321-341.

21. Kok R, Ersoy B (2009) Analyses of FDI determinants in developing countries. International Journal of Social Economics.

22. Lv N, Lightfoot WS (2008) Determinants of foreign direct investment at the regional level in China. Journal of Technology Management in China 1: 232-278.

23. Mirza D, Verdier T (2007) Impact of terrorism on financial markets of Pakistan. European Journal of Social Sciences.

24. Osinubi TS, Amaghionyeodiwe LA (2010) Foreign private investment and economic growth in Nigeria. REBS Review of Economic and Business Studies 3: 105-127.

25. Osorio GM (2008) Foreign direct investment and economic growth in Mexico: An empirical analysis. Applied Economic 34: 45-89.

26. Rasheed H, Tahir M (2012) FDI and terrorism: Co-integration and granger causality. International Affairs and Global Strategy.

27. Root F, Ahmed A (1978) Empirical determinants of manufacturing direct foreign investment in developing countries. Economic Development & Cultural Change 27: 751.

28. Ahmed SZ, Qazi M (2003) The determinants of FDI in Pak: an empirical investigation. The Pakistan development, Review 42: 697.

29. Swenson DL (1994) The impact of us tax reform on foreign d rect investment in the United States. Journal of Public Economics 54: 243-266.

30. Udoh E, Egwaikhide FO (2008) Exchange rate volatility, inflation uncertainty and foreign direct investment in Nigeria. Botswana Journal of Economics.

21

The Causal Relationship between Inflation and Economic Growth in Nigeria

Rabia Najaf*

Riphah International University, Islamabad, Pakistan

Abstract

In this paper, analysed that Nigeria is the poor country and facing the problem of inflation from last few years. The prime objective of this paper is to analysis the impact on all the developing and under developing countries. We have applied the regression analysis and taken the tile series data. Our results are showing that there negative relationship between Nigeria stock exchange and rate of inflation from last few years. We are also trying to expose that importance of stock exchange in all over the country and due to high inflation rate there is very worst impact on the progress of the economy. Our study suggested that government should make inflation control policies for the better performance.

Keywords: Nigeria; Regression analysis; Time series data; Stock exchange

Introduction

Nigeria is known as the lower middle income country with the inhabitants about 5.6 million. The phenomenon in inflation in enhancing is due to three factors. 1) Lack of policies of monetary policies. 2) Lack of policies fiscal policies. 3) Weak structure for the Nigeria economy. The objective of this paper is to analysis the impact of inflation on the economy of Nigeria. Nigeria is facing the problem of inflation from last few years and it has become international issues from last few years. We have taken some companies, which are listed in the stock market.

Stock exchange has the crucial role the development of the economy. Stock exchange is the way through which progress of the economy can be increased. According to William stock exchange is bridge between development and underdevelopment. It acts as the backbone of the economy. Stock exchange is the best way to enhance the capital and skills of the any country. Inflation is considered as the barrier for the economic development. Commonly, the inflation is the reason of increase and decrease the unemployment level l, wages level, and level of productivity. Inflation has very worst impact on the facial and monetary policy. It is widely believed that inflation has worst impact on the stock market development. Stock exchange is the way to start new financing progress. According to survey, 2008-09 the rate inflation in Nigeria was 14.3%. According to ESP 2012-13 it is seen that inflation rate was 10.9%. Most of the studies have proved that increase in money supply might be increase the level of inflation. Investment is also way to increase and decrease the inflation level (Figure 1).

Objectives of the study

1) Inflation process in Nigeria.

2) Relationship between inflation and stock prices.

Problem statement

Impact of inflation on the stock exchange of Nigera (Table 1).

Literature Review

Analyzed the impact of inflation rate on the stock exchange of USA. For this purpose they had taken the data from 1998-2008 and applied the ADF unit root test. Their results are showing that there is negative association between inflation and stock market. They suggested that government should focus on the polices of about inflation [1].

Examined the impact of inflation rate on the stock exchange of UK. For this purpose they had taken the data from 1991-2001 and applied the multi regression model. Their results are showing that there is significant negative association between inflation and stock market. They suggested that government should focus on the polices of about inflation [2].

Observed the impact of inflation rate on the stock exchange of India. For this purpose they had taken the data from 1994-2005 and applied the OLS model. Their results are showing that there is negative association between inflation and stock market. They suggested that government should focus on the polices of about inflation [3].

Viewed the impact of inflation rate on the stock exchange of china. For this purpose they had taken the data from 1998-2008 and applied the ECM model. Their results are showing that there is negative association between inflation and stock market. They suggested that government should focus on the polices of about inflation [4].

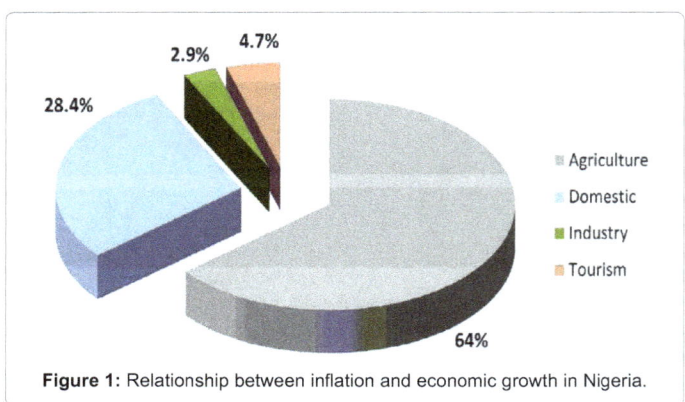

Figure 1: Relationship between inflation and economic growth in Nigeria.

***Corresponding author:** Rabia Najaf, Riphah International University, Islamabad, Pakistan, E-mail: rabianajaf@hotmail.com

2016	8	17.86	13.5	16.63	13.24	17.7
2016	9	17.62	12.75	16.44	12.70	17.21
2016	8	17.14	12.05	15.81	12.16	16.93
2016	7	16.49	11.38	15.31	11.67	16.22
2016	6	15.59	10.76	14.87	11.22	15.05
2016	5	13.73	10.19	13.18	10.79	13.35
2016	4	12.78	9.76	12.75	10.47	12.17
2016	3	11.39	9.38	11.36	10.18	11.04
2016	2	9.63	9.14	10.65	10.02	8.84
2015	11	9.56	9.02	10.58	9.9	8.73
2015	12	9.38	8.89	10.33	9.78	8.73
2015	11	9.4	8.77	10.14	9.68	8.74
2015	8	9.5	8.8	10.3	9.6	8.9
2015	9	9.4	8.7	10.2	9.6	9
2015	8	9.3	8.6	11	9.6	8.8
2015	7	9.3	8.5	11	9.5	8.4
2015	6	8	8.4	9.9	9.5	8.3
2015	5	8.8	8.3	9.6	9.5	7.7
2015	4	8.6	8.3	9.5	9.5	7.5
2015	3	8.5	8.2	9.5	9.5	7
2015	2	8.3	8.2	9.3	9.5	6.8
2014	13	9	9	9.3	9.5	6.2
2014	12	7.8	9	9.2	9.5	6.3
2014	11	8.2	9	9.4	9.5	6.3
2014	6	8.4	9	9.8	9.5	6.3
2014	9	8.6	9	11	9.5	6.3
2014	8	8.4	9	9.8	9.5	7.1
2014	7	8.3	9	9.9	9.5	8.1
2014	6	9	9	9.8	9.4	7.7
2014	5	7.8	8.2	9.5	9.4	7.5
2014	4	7.9	8.3	9.4	9.5	6.8
2014	3	7.8	8.4	9.3	9.5	7.2
2014	2	9	8.5	9.4	9.6	6.6
2013	11	9	8.6	9.4	9.7	7.9
2013	12	7.8	8.9	9.4	9.8	7.8
2013	11	7.9	9.3	9.4	10	7.6
2013	8	9	9.6	9.5	10.1	7.4
2013	9	8.3	9.9	9.8	10.2	7.2
2013	8	8.8	11	11	10.2	6.6
2013	9	8.5	10.5	9.7	10.4	5.5
2013	6	8	10.9	9.4	10.5	6.2
2013	5	9.2	11.2	11	10.8	6.9
2013	4	8.7	11.5	9.6	11	7.2
2013	3	9.6	11.8	12	11.2	11.2
2013	2	8	11.8	10.2	11.1	11.3
2012	13	13	12.3	10.4	11.3	13.7
2012	12	12.5	12.2	11.7	11.4	13.1
2012	11	11.8	11.8	11.2	11.2	12.4

Table 1: Rate of inflation in Nigeria from last few years.

Analyzed the impact of inflation rate on the stock exchange of France. For this purpose they had taken the data from 1995-2005 and applied the VAR model. Their results are showing that there is negative association between inflation and stock market. They suggested that government should focus on the polices of about inflation [5].

Examined the impact of inflation rate on the stock exchange of Japan. For this purpose they had taken the data from 1995-2005 and applied the VAR model. Their results are showing that there is negative association between inflation and stock market. They suggested that government should focus on the polices of about inflation [6].

Analyzed the impact of inflation rate on the stock exchange of srilanka. For this purpose they had taken the data from 1990-2010 and applied the ECM. Their results are showing that there is negative association between inflation and stock market. They suggested that government should focus on the polices of about inflation [7].

Examined the impact of inflation rate on the stock exchange of Singapore. For this purpose they had taken the data from 1999-2009 and applied the V ECM. Their results are showing that there is negative association between inflation and stock market. They suggested that government should focus on the polices of about inflation [8].

Years	ARBK	CABK	JOIN	JOEP	NPSC	ZAR	JOPH	ACDT	ELZA	DADI	CPI
1999	0.28	-0.2	-0.045	0.125	-0.257	-0.17	0.192	-0.25	0.033	-0.52	0.024
2000	0.096	-0.089	-0.13	-0.046	-0.367	-0.13	0.039	-0.312	-0.16	-0.366	0.066
2001	0.306	-0.292	0.015	0.18	-0.16	-0.08	0.118	0.012	-0.22	0.148	0.04
2002	-0.336	-0.218	0.035	-0.234	-0.3	-0.15	-0.593	-0.177	-0.13	-0.12	0.032
2003	-0.09	0.067	0.158	0.149	0.126	0.466	0.736	0.122	-0.077	-0.48	0.006
2004	-0.3	-0.162	0.06	-0.088	0.023	-0.06	-0.57	0.08	-0.234	-0.189	-0.03
2005	0.296	-0.123	-0.302	0.247	0.087	0.115	0.289	0.09	-0.044	0.713	0.018
2006	-0.085	-0.273	0.089	-0.063	-0.24	0.97	-0.288	0.236	-0.012	0.457	0.019
2007	0.654	1.376	0.563	0.548	2.102	0.52	0.688	0.093	0.624	-0.019	0.017
2008	-0.228	0.823	0.88	0.34	0.76	-0.18	0.267	0.08	-0.285	0.158	0.034

Table 2: Change in CPI and stock prices for the selected companies in the Nigeria stock exchange for the period from (1998-2007).

Observed the impact of inflation rate on the stock exchange of Canada. For this purpose they had taken the data from 1990-2010 and applied the OLS. Their results are showing that there is negative association between inflation and stock market. They suggested that government should focus on the polices of about inflation [9].

Viewed the impact of inflation rate on the stock exchange of Taiwan stock exchange. For this purpose they had taken the data from 1996-2010 and applied the VAR model. Their results are showing that there is negative association between inflation and stock market. They suggested that government should focus on the polices of about inflation [9].

Gaps in literature

1) In the prior studies, nobody had discussed about the impact of inflation on the future development

2) In the last studies, nobody had analyzed the inflation impact on the investors

3) Last few decades nobody has discussed about inflation on the purchasing power.

Theoretical Frame Work

Theoretical frame work is shown in Figure 2.

Methodology

We have used the time series data to collect the impact of inflation on the stock prices of Nigera. For this purpose, we have collected the data from 1999 to 2008 and used the regression analysis to analysis that there is positive impact or negative impact on the stock prices of Nigeria. The changes in the prices can be measured.

$$PC = (P_2 - P_1) / P_1$$

Where P_1, and P_2 represents the stock price or CPI index in time one and two respectively (Table 2).

Conclusion

Stocks are known as the claim to real assets, in the case of increase the prices of things will affect on the economy of all the emerging and developed countries. Our study is showing that inflation has impact all the companies in the varies sharp. Stocks are negatively related with the inflation. In some conditions, the impact of inflation on the stock prices may be positive may be night.

Recommendation

1) Government should focus regarding polices to how to control the inflation rate.

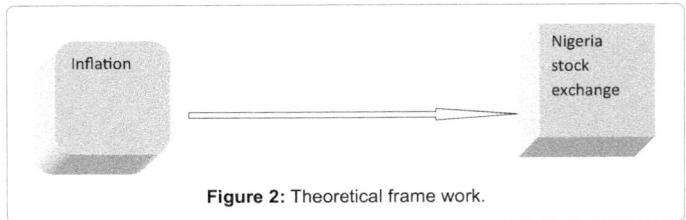

Figure 2: Theoretical frame work.

2) State bank should focus on the policies regarding currency.

3) Decrease the prices of subsidies inflation rate can be controlled.

References

1. Rose S, Marquis H (2006) Money and Capital Market. (9thedn) Mcgrawhill.

2. Madura J (2006) International Corporate Finance. (8thedn) Thomson.

3. Bodie ZKA, Marcus A (2005) Invesetments. (6thedn) Mcgrawhill.

4. Boucher (2004) Stock prices, Inflation and stock returns predicatively.

5. Giammarino R (1997) Central Bank Policy, Inflation, and Stock Prices.

6. Chao W (2006) Inflation and Stock Prices: No Illusion. Journal of Money, Credit and Banking 42:325-345.

7. Al-Rjoub SAM (2006) The Adjustments of Stock Prices to Information about Inflation: Evidence Form MENA Countries. Palgrave Macmillan UK.

8. Al-Khazali O (2010) Empirical Tests of the Proxy Hypothesis: Evidence from Jordan.

9. Ioannides K, Lake (1979) The relationship between stock market returns and inflation.

22

Performance Evaluation of Iranian Banking Industry through CAMELS Framework

Mohammad Khodaei Weleh Zagherd[1] and Mehrdad Barghi[2*]

[1]Assistant Professor, University of Tehran, Iran
[2]Faculty of Management, University of Tehran, Iran

Abstract

This research performs an empirical study on the performance evaluation of Iranian banking industry through CAMELS framework. The research method is applied in terms of objective, and correlational according to the type of method. Time domain of research is from 2007 to 2015. The research data are annually collected and extracted from financial statements of operating banks in the Iranian banking industry. Pooled and Panel hybrid regression model with fixed effects are used to analyze the research data and test the hypotheses. Based on the results of research model, the impact of capital adequacy, asset quality, management quality, liquidity quality, and sensitivity to market risk indicators is direct and significant on the return on assets of banks in the Iranian banking industry, but the effect of earnings quality is rejected on the return on assets of banks in the Iranian banking industry.

Keywords: Return on assets (ROA); CAMELS indicators; Capital adequacy; Asset quality; Management quality; Earnings quality; Liquidity quality; Sensitivity to market risk; Iranian banking industry

Introduction

This research performs an empirical study on performance evaluation of Iranian banking industry through CAMELS framework. There are numerous studies on banking performance evaluation. CAMELS framework, which is one of the most analyses for performance evaluation of banking sector compared the important parameters that reflects the results of banking sector performance [1]. On the other hand, CAMELS compounds as the bank performance indicators refer to the managerial performance from various financial and management aspects [2]. It is expected that there will be a relationship between CAMELS framework and bank performance [3]. Given that the identification of relationship between CAMELS framework and bank performance can provide very useful information about identification of risk-taking behavior in banks [4], this study aims at investigating the relationship between CAMELS framework and bank performance through evaluating the performance of Iranian banking industry [5]. CAMELS model has been widely applied in some countries especially the United States of America in order to evaluate the return on assets of financial institutions particularly the banks. This method is put in the group of modern performance evaluation methods. The financial ratios, which are derived from financial statements, are used to evaluate CAMELS framework [6].

The main objective of financial reporting is to express the economic effects of financial events and operations on the status and performance of business unit in order to help the active and potential users to make financial decisions for business unit [7]. The performance evaluation of banks is a major topic of accounting, management and economy discussion.

Theoretical principles of research

Research literature: The total return on assets of a bank is as a result of company performance and activities in relation to their use. Calculation of return on assets is one of the criteria for performance measurement, and measures to the ability of banks to make profits according to the amount of investment in bank and is calculated by dividing the net operating profit of bank by the resources [8]. The credit of return on assets depends on the appropriate measurement of applied earnings and assets of bank. Return on assets can be calculated by DuPont system. This rate is measured according to the asset turnover ratio and net profit margin ratio. The asset turnover is obtained from dividing the sales by the sum of assets. Furthermore, the net profit margin is measured by dividing the net profit belonging to common stockholders on the sales [9].

Return on assets of an indicator of bank earnings is dependent on the total assets of that bank. Return on assets gives us an idea about efficient management in applying the assets in order to generate profit (productive assets), and it is calculated through dividing the annual profit by the total bank assets [10].

The adequate and appropriate capital is one of the requirements for protecting the health of banking system; and each of the banks and credit institutes should always establish an appropriate ratio between capital and risk of their assets in order to ensure the stability and sustainability of their activities [11]. The main function of this ratio includes the bank protection from unexpected losses, and also the depositors and creditors' support [12].

The aim of calculating the CAMELS ratios is the accurate and consistent assessment of financial conditions and performance of bank in the field of capital adequacy [13], asset quality [1], management quality [14], earnings quality [15], liquidity quality [14], and sensitivity to market risk. CAMELS ratios in banks are not only applied as the reporting tools, but also as the intra-organizational tool for measurement of risk and its management as well as the optimal resource allocation. This system contains all processes of factor identification and their measurement and quantification. Researchers can assess the financial risk of banks by this system [6].

*Corresponding author: Mehrdad Barghi, Faculty of Management, University Tehran, Iran, E-mail: barghimehrdad68@gmail.com

The final result of all programs, activities, financial and production decisions is reflected in earnings activity of bank. Most of the required data for executive operation of bank is directly obtained from the profit and loss statement which is the summary of operations and financial and production activities in the bank. However, the executive operation should be related to the assets which create the operation results. Furthermore, the results of operation should indicate the outsiders' understanding of operation and income of institute.

The compared profit and loss statement in several consecutive periods of a bank indicates the useful information about the performance of management and the financial situation of bank. However, most of the people, who benefit from the banking affairs in terms of investment, giving the credit, or efficiency of its activity, often pay attention to the rate of profit and the profitability of that bank [12].

Profitability refers to the ability of company to achieve revenues and earnings. Net income or earning is the only criterion for measuring the profitability. The investors and creditors have a great interest to assess the current and future profitability of a company. To provide the required capital, the companies are forced to earn enough profit to obtain the appropriate returns for investors and creditors. In the case that the companies do not obtain enough profit, they will not be able to provide the capital needed to run a variety of projects through shareholders or creditors. In the long term, the survival of a company depends on its ability to earn money to carry out all obligations and provide necessary returns for main shareholders.

CAMELS' framework: In recent years one of the most used models for the estimation of a bank performances and soundness is represented by the CAMELS framework [7]. Actually, the analytical framework is based on the CAMELS rating system, a device created by federal banking regulators to assess the overall performance of banks [16]. In order to evaluate banks' overall financial condition, CAMELS supervisory rating system is built and introduced first in USA for onside monitoring. Now, it is used both onsite and off-site monitoring purposes [17]. The central banks that are responsible for supervising the banks in each country use rating system to assess the soundness of the banks [18]. Due to lack of sufficient historical data about bank defaults, bank rating system are usually based on empirical assessment techniques [19]. Creadit agencies, auditors and bank regulators have traditionally relied on the CAMELS model [5]. Actually the most effective way to enforce financial rules and regulations in the financial supervisory system is to conduct financial examinations [20]. The most popular approach is based on the CAMELS framework, which involves the consideration of six major factors [18]. The CAMEL acronym stands for Capital adequacy, Asset quality, Management, Earning and Liquidity. Regulators created an additional measure, Sensitivity, to evaluate market risk associated with changing interest rates and other factors [21], especially in the financial crisis [3].

Literature review

According to Sarker [22], CAMELS method is a type of financial analysis which is applied to assess the financial management of banks in order to determine the health and safety. The results of empirical research indicate that the profits are related to the performance of companies.

Based on the conducted studies by Hu and Zhou [23] and Ghosh [24], the use of company leverage has an impact on the company performance.

In an article entitled "Financial strategic management from theory and practice", Rose and Hudgins [16] studied these strategies and their application in improving the company performance. According to this article, the strategy of company is a tool which is established based on how a company achieves its goals. All of the strategy management models have been implemented as a pilot. The financial strategy plays a very important role among these strategies. This study investigates the financial strategy in small, large and medium companies. According to the results, there is a significant positive relationship between financial strategies and performance of companies in these companies. In other words, the performance of companies can be improved by utilizing the financial strategies.

Okpara [25] evaluated the performance of the Nigerian banking industry with a focus on the factors affecting the risk management of banks. They investigated the impact of macro-economic factors and intra-banking characteristics on the risk management of banks through application of panel data for a period of 2003-2009. According to the results, the economic growth and inflation respectively have positive and negative effects on the ratio of capital in Nigerian banks. Among the intra-banking indicators, the liquidity ratio, bank size, and market risk have positive impact, but the credit risk has a negative impact on the capital ratios of Nigerian banks. In fact, the research results indicate the important point that the banking risk management not only depends on the intra-banking factors, but it is also influenced by the macroeconomic factors.

Kumar et al. [26] assessed the financial abilities of governmental banks in India through CAMELS model. The capital adequacy, asset quality, management quality, earnings quality, and liquidity quality have studied in all governmental banks in India, and each of these indicators have been ranked in each bank.

Daud [27] studied the impact of banking diversity on the return on assets of banks through CAMELS rating approach and examined the impact of income diversification, diversification of income-generating assets, and diversity of under balance sheet line items on the return on assets. According to the results of their research, the diversity of income and income-generating assets during the financial crisis has an inverse impact on the return on assets of banks.

Golam [28] assessed the return on assets in two large banks in Bangladesh. This evaluation is done through CAMELS indicators as the latest model of financial analysis. This paper ranks the customer' feedback and their satisfaction with banks by indicators of this model namely the capital adequacy, management quality, asset quality, liquidity quality, and earnings quality.

Mandic [29] used fuzzy multi-criteria decision-making method in order to facilitate the performance evaluation of banks. The results of this study, which is conducted in Serbia, the stock criteria, portfolio, resources, floating assets, liquidity, etc., are considered as the performance evaluation criteria of banks.

Research Model

Research methodology

The statistical population and spatial domain of research consist of the Iranian banking industry. The research data is annually collected, extracted and investigated during the time domain of 2007 to 2014. A total of 17 banks operating in the Iranian banking industry are selected in a period of 9 years. Due to the use of panel data, a total of 153 hybrid bank-year observations are examined for testing the research hypotheses.

Hypotheses

Main hypothesis: CAMELS indicators explain the bank performance

H_1: **Capital adequacy has a significant effect on banking performance:** Capital adequacy indicates the measurement of a bank's financial strength. In this study, capital adequacy ratio was measured related to overall use of financial leverage in the bank given that banks with higher financial leverage are expected to face more volatility in earnings behavior than banks with lower financial leverage. As it indicates up to what level the institutions cover inherent risk in their operations, capital adequacy was defined as the overall use of financial leverage in the bank [13]. Nimalathasan [30] viewed capital adequacy as the capital position of the banks, which at the same time protect depositors from the potential losses incurred by banks. Therefore, capital adequacy was used as a variable under the CAMEL model. In this case, capital adequacy was viewed as the enhancer of bank financial performance.

H2: Asset quality has a significant effect on the banks performance in the Iranian banking industry: Asset quality takes into account the performance of assets, especially loans made by the bank. Based on a study by Teck [14], the main factors that affect asset quality are the degree of asset diversification, the size and duration of loans, the growth of loan portfolios, quality of collateral backing for each loan, the presence of directed or policy lending, and related party lending. In addition, it shows the risk level of assets and rate of financial strength within the bank [1].

H3: Management quality has a significant effect on the banks performance in the Iranian banking industry: Management competency plays an important role in determining bank performance. It is a pre-condition for the growth and success of any banking institution. Good management practice can result in stable profit. So, based on work by Teck [14], management practice should display a high standard of integrity, professional competence, and quality of service.

H4: Earnings quality has a significant effect on the banks performance in the Iranian banking industry: Earnings quality of an institution depends on the institutional effectiveness and efficiency of assets and liabilities management. The rise of earnings performance should inspire confidence among depositors, investors, creditors, and the public. The ability to support present and future bank operations depends on the profile of the earnings and profitability [15].

H5: Liquidity quality has a significant effect on the banks performance in the Iranian banking industry: Liquidity refers to a bank's ability to meet depositors' withdrawals, maturing liabilities and loan requests without delay [14]. Liquidity is important because banks need to meet short term financial obligations and satisfy customer loan demand. While the banks might be desperate to borrow short term funds and emergency loans at an excessive interest rate to cover the need for immediate cash, doing so leads to reduction in earnings. The soundness of liquidity management will lead to good bank performance.

H6: Sensitivity to market risk has a significant effect on the banks performance in the Iranian banking industry: Market risk is the risk of losses in liquid portfolio arising from the movements in market prices and consisting of interest rate, currency, equity and commodity risks. Interest rate and currency risk are the main parts of the market risk in the Iranian banking sector [31]. This article intended to calculate the Bank Performance from the return on assets (ROA) (Table 1).

Model 1

$$ROA_{i,t} = \beta 0 + \beta 1 CA\ i,t + \beta 2 AQi,t + \beta 3 MQi,t + \beta 4 EQi,t + \beta 5 LQi,t + \beta 6 SM\ i,t + \varepsilon i,t$$

Hypothesis test

Descriptive statistics: The conceptual model of research consists of a dependent variable (Table 2).

Return on assets (ROA) is a dependent variable. This variable has a hundred and fifty-three annual observations. With a mean of about 0.013032, this variable indicates the return on assets (ROA) of banks during sampling years. The residual value domain magnitude of fitted model indicates the return on assets (ROA) in studied banks. Distribution of this variable has positive skewness and kurtosis. According to these indicators, the remote observation is located on the right domain of distribution and has a serious difference with normal distribution. The observation density on the axis of central indicators is more severe, and has a serious difference with normal distribution.

Normality distribution test and unit root of research variables: The distribution normality of studied variables is one of the fundamental justifiable assumptions in parametric tests. However, the normal distribution is not a necessary condition, and the parametric tests can be used if the sample size is large or sample distribution does not have severe skewness and even if it does not have normal distribution. The static or stationary regression analysis is another test assumption. In other words, the possibility under which it is in a certain distance in current time is like any other time in the past and future. If the time series variables are unstable, there is not any theoretical relationship between dependant and independent, but the high coefficient of determination will be estimated for model. Jarque-bera test is used to test the distribution of studied variables of research; and the calculated significance level is compared with basis of 0.05. The possibility of higher error than 0.05 indicates the normal distribution, but its smaller value indicates the lack of normal distribution. Based on the results of Jarque-bera test, there is not any normal distribution of research variables, which have ratio data, but the use of regression analysis can be justified due to the large sample size, the single-exponential nature, and the lack of very high skewness. "Levin, Lin and Chu" and "Fisher-Phillips-Perron (pp)" tests are used in order to test the reliability of

Calculation Method	Variable role	Variable	Variable name
Net profit divided by total assets	Dependent	Return on assets	ROA
Equity divided by assets	Independent	Capital adequacy	CA
Total assets divided by equity	Independent	Asset quality	AQ
Joint income divided by operating costs	Independent	Management quality	MQ
Income facilities granted divided by total income	Independent	Earnings quality	EQ
Facilities granted divided by total bank deposits	Independent	Liquidity quality	LQ
Subtracting current liabilities from current assets divided by total capital	Independent	Sensitivity to market risk	SM

Table 1: Calculation method of variables.

research variables. The significance level of "Levin, Lin and Chu" test is less than 0.05 for all variables except for the asset quality at the confidence level of 90%, and thus it supports the reliability of variables at this level. The significance level of "Fisher- Phillips-Perron (pp)" test is less than 0.05 for all variables, so it supports their reliability at this level. The results of two different tests are presented in Table 3.

Study of collinearity relationship: The collinearity relationship indicates that an independent variable is a linear function of other independent variables. The existence of a strong relationship between independent variables leads to the creation of collinearity, thereby the incorrect inferences. There are several methods to identify the

collinearity relationship; and study on the correlation between independent variables is one of them. Pearson correlation coefficient test is applied in order to investigate the collinearity in this study. Based on the extracted results, there is not any severe relationship between the explanatory variables which have ratio scales, and thus the concurrent inclusion of explanatory variables into the model will not result in collinearity problem. The results of Pearson correlation coefficient test between explanatory variables of research are presented in Table 4.

Results of regression analysis of conceptual model: The lack of autocorrelation and normal distribution of residuals is one of the assumptions of applied regression analysis. The residuals of model

	Independent variables						Independent variable
	Sensitivity to market risk	Liquidity quality	Earnings quality	Management quality	Asset quality	Capital adequacy	Performance financial
Mean	1.702794	1.092426	0.569265	3.448603	13.87757	0.137132	0.013032
Median	0.740000	0.820000	0.650000	2.095000	13.26500	0.080000	0.010134
Max	18.46000	5.460000	0.990000	11.11000	60.06000	0.560000	0.077121
min	0.010000	0.460000	-0.620000	0.410000	1.790000	0.020000	-0.019464
S.D	2.616283	0.893597	0.311958	2.790168	9.497553	0.136381	0.013417
Skewness	4.273690	3.201833	-1.244280	0.974521	1.311041	1.772979	1.176257
Kurtosis	26.05825	13.03381	4.851519	2.596780	6.439908	5.033107	5.801366
Number observations	153	153	153	153	153	153	153

Table 2: Descriptive statistics of variables of model.

variables		Distribution Research variables		Reliability test of variables			
Research variables		Jarque-Bera Test results		Pesaran and Shin W- stat Test		Levin, Lin & Chu	
		Prob	Statistic	Prob	Statistic	Prob	Statistic
Return on assets	ROA	0.000000	85.31010	0.0000	83.6651	0.0000	-4.13986
Capital adequacy	CA	0.000000	94.67494	0.0005	65.0364	0.0168	-2.12371
Asset quality	AQ	0.000000	106.0136	0.0001	70.1298	0.9641	1.80028
Management quality	EQ	0.000000	54.51932	0.0786	46.2357	0.0000	-6.46783
Earnings quality	LQ	0.000000	802.8780	0.0015	63.7303	0.0816	-1.39457
Liquidity quality	MQ	0.000013	22.44767	0.0009	65.7437	0.0549	-1.59940
Sensitivity to market risk	SM	0.000000	3426.862	0.0000	81.9935	0.0057	-2.53215

Table 3: Reliability test of variables.

SM	MQ	LQ	EQ	CA	AQ	Test index	Explanatory variables
					1.000000	Correlation coefficient	Asset quality
					-----	T-statistic	
					-----	Probability of Error	
				1.000000	-0.698916	Correlation coefficient	Capital adequacy
				-----	-11.31220	T-statistic	
				-----	0.0000	Probability of Error	
			1.000000	-0.529090	0.310299	Correlation coefficient	Earnings quality
			-----	-7.217656	3.778480	T-statistic	
			-----	0.0000	0.0002	Probability of Error	
		1.000000	-0.093321	0.184577	-0.151666	Correlation coefficient	Liquidity quality
		-----	-1.084999	2.173991	-1.776209	T-statistic	
		-----	0.2799	0.0315	0.0780	Probability of Error	
	1.000000	-0.276146	0.578073	-0.304649	-0.029867	Correlation coefficient	Management quality
	-----	-3.325945	8.200742	-3.702567	-0.345889	T-statistic	
	-----	0.0011	0.0000	0.0003	0.7300	Probability of Error	
1.000000	-0.281836	-0.137344	-0.023828	-0.329156	0.681584	Correlation coefficient	Sensitivity to market risk
-----	-3.400326	-1.605078	-0.275905	-4.035107	10.78241	T-statistic	
-----	0.0009	0.1108	0.7830	0.0001	0.0000	Probability of Error	

Table 4: Correlation analysis results.

should be independent of each other, and there should not be any correlation between them. In other words, the error between the actual and predicted values should have the independence. The results of performed tests are explained in Tables 5 and 6.

H1: Capital adequacy has a significant effect on banking performance: Since the capital adequacy coefficient is equal to 0.49, one percent increase in the capital adequacy will lead to the increase of 0.49% in return on assets with probability of 0.07 (sig <0.05). The adjusted coefficient of determination is equal to 0.31, which should be from 0 to 1; and Durbin-Watson Statistic is 1.81, which should be from 1.5 to 2.5, and thus the capital adequacy has a significant effect on the return on assets in the Iranian banking industry.

H2: Asset quality has a significant effect on the banks performance in the Iranian banking industry: Since the capital asset quality is equal to 0.008, one percent increase in the asset quality will lead to the increase of 0.008% in return on assets with probability of 0.05 (sig <0.05). The adjusted coefficient of determination is equal to 0.31, which should be from 0 to 1; and Durbin-Watson Statistic is 1.81, which should be from 1.5 to 2.5, and thus the asset quality has a significant effect on the return on assets in the Iranian banking industry.

H3: Management quality has a significant effect on the banks performance in the Iranian banking industry: Since the management quality coefficient is equal to 0.008, one percent increase in the management quality will lead to the increase of 0.008% in return on assets with probability of 0.05 (sig <0.05). The adjusted coefficient of determination is equal to 0.31, which should be from 0 to 1; and Durbin-Watson Statistic is 1.81, which should be from 1.5 to 2.5, and thus the management quality has a significant effect on the return on assets in the Iranian banking industry.

H4: Earnings quality has a significant effect on the banks performance in the Iranian banking industry: Since the earnings quality coefficient is equal to 0.008, one percent increase in the earnings quality will lead to the increase of 0.008% in return on assets with probability of 0.05 (sig <0.05). The adjusted coefficient of determination is equal to 0.31, which should be from 0 to 1; and Durbin-Watson Statistic is 1.81, which should be from 1.5 to 2.5, and thus the earnings quality has a significant effect on the return on assets in the Iranian banking industry.

H5: Liquidity quality has a significant effect on the banks performance in the Iranian banking industry: Since the liquidity quality coefficient is equal to 0.008, one percent increase in the liquidity quality will lead to the increase of 0.008% in return on assets with probability of 0.05 (sig <0.05). The adjusted coefficient of determination is equal to 0.31, which should be from 0 to 1; and Durbin-Watson Statistic is 1.81, which should be from 1.5 to 2.5, and thus the liquidity quality has a significant effect on the return on assets in the Iranian banking industry.

H6: Sensitivity to market risk has a significant effect on the banks performance in the Iranian banking industry: Since the sensitivity to market risk coefficient is equal to 0.008, one percent increase in the sensitivity to market risk will lead to the increase of 0.008% in return on assets with probability of 0.05 (sig <0.05). The adjusted coefficient of determination is equal to 0.31, which should be from 0 to 1; and Durbin-Watson Statistic is 1.81, which should be from 1.5 to 2.5, and thus the sensitivity to market risk has a significant effect on the return on assets in the Iranian banking industry.

Conclusion and Interpretation of Research Results

This study suggests six hypotheses in order to investigate the impact of CAMELS indicators on the return on assets of banks in the Iranian banking industry and examines the impact of capital adequacy, asset quality, management quality, earnings quality, liquidity quality, and sensitivity to market risk on the return on assets. The hypothesis, extracted results, interpretation and comparison of previous research results are presented as follows.

According to the test indicators, the capital adequacy has a significant impact on the return on assets of Iranian banking industry. This index indicates that the increase or decrease of capital adequacy will lead to the significant changes in the return on assets of the Iranian banking industry. Therefore, the capital adequacy is a strong explanatory variable for return on assets of the Iranian banking industry. The result of this hypothesis is consistent with findings of research by Siti Nurain Muhmad & Hafiza Hashim [20]. Siti Nurain Muhmad and Hafiza Hashim investigated the impact of CAMELS indicators on the return on assets of Malaysian banking industry.

According to the test indicators, the asset quality has a significant

Type model	remaining distribution Test		Durbin-Watson Test		linear relationship Test	
	Prob.	Jarque-Bera Test	Expected	Statistic	Prob.	F statistic
Regression model	0.088149	4.855744	2.5-1.5	1.817248	0.000819	2.5211

Table 5: Results of model remnants.

Dependent variable: financial performance, number of course: 9, number of sections: 17, number of healthy observed: 153					
Prob.	t-Statistic	Std. Error	Coefficient	Variable	
0.0036	2.990809	0.105348	0.315075	C	Constant coefficient
0.0710	1.822185	0.270011	0.492009	CA	Capital adequacy
0.0592	1.911295	0.004483	0.008569	AQ	Asset quality
0.0000	4.304041	0.038388	0.165222	MQ	Management quality
0.1205	1.567829	0.146054	0.228987	EQ	Earnings quality
0.0011	3.372592	0.204222	0.688758	LQ	Liquidity qua ity
0.0802	1.769943	0.003921	0.006939	SM	Sensitivity to market risk
1.817248	Durbin-Watson stat		0.329236	R-squared	
			0.318645	Adjusted R-squared	
			0.014128	S.D. dependent var	
			2.521120	F-statistic	

Table 6: The results of CAMELS indicators on financial performance.

impact on the return on assets of the Iranian banking industry. This index indicates that the increase or decrease in the asset quality will lead to the significant changes in the return on assets of the Iranian banking industry. Therefore, the asset quality is a strong predictor for return on assets of the Iranian banking industry. The result of this hypothesis is consistent with findings of research by Siti Nurain Muhmad and Hafiza Hashim [20]. Siti Nurain Muhmad and Hafiza Hashim investigated the impact of CAMELS indicators on the return on assets of Malaysian banking industry.

According to the test indicators, the management quality has a significant impact on the return on assets of the Iranian banking industry. This index indicates that the increase or decrease in the management quality will lead to the significant changes in the return on assets of the Iranian banking industry. Therefore, the management quality is a strong predictor for return on assets of the Iranian banking industry. The result of this hypothesis is inconsistent with findings of research by Siti Nurain Muhmad and Hafiza Hashim [20]. Siti Nurain Muhmad and Hafiza Hashim investigated the impact of CAMELS indicators on the return on assets of Malaysian banking industry.

According to the test indicators, the earnings quality does not have any significant impact on the return on assets of the Iranian banking industry. This index indicates that the increase or decrease in the earnings quality will not lead to the significant changes in the return on assets of the Iranian banking industry. Therefore, the earnings quality is not a strong predictor for return on assets of the Iranian banking industry. The result of this hypothesis is inconsistent with findings of research by Siti Nurain Muhmad & Hafiza Hashim [20]. Siti Nurain Muhmad & Hafiza Hashim investigated the impact of CAMELS indicators on the return on assets of Malaysian banking industry.

According to the test indicators, the liquidity quality has a significant impact on the return on assets of the Iranian banking industry. This index indicates that the increase or decrease in the liquidity quality will lead to the significant changes in the return on assets of the Iranian banking industry. Therefore, the liquidity quality is a strong predictor for return on assets of the Iranian banking industry. The result of this hypothesis is consistent with findings of research by Siti Nurain Muhmad & Hafiza Hashim [20]. Siti Nurain Muhmad & Hafiza Hashim investigated the impact of CAMELS indicators on the return on assets of Malaysian banking industry.

According to the test indicators, the sensitivity to market risk has a significant impact on the return on assets of the Iranian banking industry. This index indicates that the increase or decrease in the sensitivity to market risk will lead to the significant changes in the return on assets of the Iranian banking industry. Therefore, the sensitivity to market risk is a strong predictor for return on assets of the Iranian banking industry. The result of this hypothesis is consistent with findings of research by Siti Nurain Muhmad & Hafiza Hashim [20]. Siti Nurain Muhmad & Hafiza Hashim investigated the impact of CAMELS indicators on the return on assets of Malaysian banking industry.

References

1. Dincer H, Gencer G, Orhan N, Sahinbas K (2011) A Performance Evaluation of the Turkish Banking after the Global Crisis Via CAMELS Ratios. Procedia Social and Behavioral Sciences 24: 1530-1545.

2. Salhuteru F, Wattimena F (2015) Bank Performance with CAMELS Ratios towards earnings management practices In State Banks and Private Banks. Advances in Social Sciences Research Journal 2: 23-36.

3. Kandrac J (2014) Modelling the causes and manifestation of bank stress: an example from the financial crisis. Applied Economics 46: 4290-4301.

4. Venkatesh D, Suresh C (2014) Comparative Performance Evaluation of Selected Commercial Banks in Kingdom of Bahrain Using CAMELS Method, Chithra, Comparative Performance Evaluation of Selected Commercial Banks in Kingdom of Bahrain Using CAMELS Method 1: 12-36.

5. Pasiouras F, Gaganis C, Zopounidis C (2006) The impact of bank regulations, supervision, market structure, and bank characteristics on individual bank ratings: A crosscountry analysis. Review of Quantitative Finance and Accounting 27: 403-438.

6. Valahzaghard M, Jabbari S (2013) A study on relationship between CAMELS Index's and Risk taking: A case study of Iranian banking industry. Management Science Letters 3: 1175-1180.

7. Roman A, Şargu AC (2013) Analysing the financial soundness of the commercial banks in Romania: an approach based on the camels framework. Procedia economics and finance 6: 703-712.

8. Chantapong S (2003) Comparative Study of Domestic and Foreign Bank Performance in Thailand: The Regression Analysis. Economic Change and Restructuring 38: 63- 83.

9. Chen JH, Chen CS (2010) The Effects of International off-site surveillance on Bank Rating Changes. Journal of Springer science.

10. Idris F (2010) Predicting Bank Financial Conditions Using a Log it Regression Approach: Empirical Evidence from Malaysia. Interdisciplinary Journal of Contemporary Research in Business 1: 179-97.

11. Douglas E, Lont D, Scott T (2014) Finance Company Failure in New Zealand During 2006–2009: Predictable Failures. Journal of Contemporary Accounting and Economics 10: 277-95.

12. Tarawneh M (2006) A Comparison of Financial Performance in the Banking Sector: Some Evidence from Omani Commercial Banks. International Research Journal of Finance and Economics 2: 101-12.

13. Freahat KIAA (2009) Evaluating Performance of Commercial Banks: An Empirical Study in Jordan (2004-2008). Universiti Utara Malaysia.

14. Teck YK (2000) A Comparative Study of the Performance of Commercial Banks, Finance Companies and Merchant Banks in Malaysia, 1990-1998. Iowa State University.

15. Shar AH, Shah M, Jamali H (2010) Performance Evaluation of Banking Sector in Pakistan: An Application of Bankometer. International Journal of Business and Management 5: 81-86.

16. Rose P, Hudgins S (2010) Bank Management and Financial Services. McGrawHill/Irwin.

17. Kaya YT (2001) Türk Bankacılık Sektöründe CAMELS Analizi,. Bankacılık Düzenleme ve Denetleme Kurumu, MSPD Çalıģma Raporları.

18. Doumpos M, Zopounidis C (2010) A multicriteria decision support system for bank rating. Decision Support Systems 50: 55-63.

19. Sahajwala R (2000) Supervisory risk assessment and early warning systems. Basle Committee on Banking Supervision.

20. Kao C, Liu ST (2004) Predicting bank performance with financial forecasts: A case of Taiwan commercial banks. Journal of Banking & Finance 28: 2353-2368.

21. Hays FH, De Lurgio SA, Gilbert AH (2009) Efficiency Ratios and Community Bank Performance. Journal of Finance and Accountancy 1: 1-15.

22. Sarker A (2005) CAMELS rating system in the context of Islamic banking: A proposed 'S'for Shariah framework. Journal of Islamic Economics and Finance 1: 78-84.

23. Hu Y, Zhou X (2008) The performance effect of managerial ownership: Evidence from China. Journal of Banking and Finance 32: 2099-2110.

24. Ghosh S (2007) Leverage, managerial monitoring and firm valuation: A simultaneous equation approach. Research in Business 61: 84-98.

25. Okpara G (2011) Bank reforms and the performance of the Nigerian Banking Sector: An empirical analysis. International Journal of Current Research.

26. Kumar M , Kumar S, Parvesh A (2013) A Camel Model Analysis of State Bank Group. World Journal of Social Sciences 3: 36- 55.

27. Daud NA (2013) Prestasi Perbankan Di Malaysia: Analisis Camel. Prosiding Perkem VIII: 1331-1339.

28. Golam M (2014) Use of CAMEL Model: A Study on Financial Performance of Selected Commercial Banks in Bangladesh. Universal Journal of Accounting and Finance 2: 151-160.

29. Mandic K (2014) Analysis of the financial parameters of Serbian banks through the application of the fuzzy AHP and TOPSIS methods. Economic Modelling.

30. Nimalathasan B (2008) A Comparative Study of Financial Performance of Banking Sector in Bangladesh – an Application of Camels Rating System. Economic and Administrative Series 2: 141-52.

31. Aykut E (2016) The Effect of Credit and Market Risk on Bank Performance: Evidence from Turkey. International Journal of Economics and Financial, 427-436.

23

The Impact of the Audit Quality on that of the Earnings Management: Case Study in Tunisia

Affes H* and Smii T

Department of Economics and Management Sciences, University of Sfax, Tunisia

Abstract

The purpose of this article is to examine the impact of the audit quality on that of the accounting earnings. We chose the accrual quality, the accounting conservatism and the profit relevance as a measure of the quality of the accounting earnings. The empirical study, which was carried out in this article on a sample of 20 Tunisian firms listed on the TSE (Tunisian Stock Exchange) for the period (2005-2009), confirms the significant impact of the audit quality on that of the accounting earnings. The study results also show that the variables: size of the audit firm, sector-based specialization of the audit firm, the co-auditing and the size of the audit committee, improve the quality of the accounting earnings.

Keywords: Profit relevance; Accounting conservatism; Earning management; Audit quality

Introduction

The financial crises that have been observed for a decade along with the recent financial scandals (Enron) have created a revolution in the design and evaluation of the audit quality. In fact, they reinforced the need for its improvement. In this context, several studies focus on the quality of the financial statements and specifically that of the accounting earnings considered as "priority information [1-3].

In this conceptual framework, most of these studies use accounting accruals as a measure of the quality of the accounting earnings. (Francis Hall and Wang; Piot; Becker et al.) [4-6]. others use the accounting relevance as a measure of accounting earnings [3,7,8]. Besides, further researches use accounting conservatism as a measure of the quality of the accounting earnings in a way that it systematically affects the profits (Basu, Watts, Givoly and Hany, Penman and Zang) [9-12].

Regarding this perception, the aim of our study is to check if the quality of the external audit is a constraint for the quality of the disclosed accounting earnings. Our objective is to investigate to what extent the quality of the accounting earnings depends on that of the external audit. As a consequence, we propose the earnings relevance, the accounting conservatism and the accruals quality as a measure of the quality of the accounting earnings.

Theoretical framework

In accordance with the agency theory, the leader is supposed to follow an opportunistic behavior to maximize his utility function. To cope with such opportunistic behavior, the shareholders use a third party (external auditor) to monitor the managers and check the quality of the disclosed information. Within the framework of theoretical reflection, the role of the external audit, as means of controlling and reducing the agency costs, is twofold: it helps, on the one hand, reduce the information asymmetry and, on the other hand, strengthen the mechanisms of corporate governance.

The concept of asymmetric information and the unequal information distribution between the shareholders and the managers is the basis of the signal theory. To deal with these problems, the external auditor has always played a fundamental role in the process of solving the problems of the information asymmetry since his intervention can discipline the opportunistic behavior of the managers, particularly in terms of accounting information manipulation [6,13]. The role of the external audit is therefore twofold; the external auditors are not only a means of controlling the decisions of the business leaders concerning the choice of their accounting policies, but also a means of ensuring the reliability of the disclosed financial information.

Perception of the audit quality

Most of the studies agree that the assessment of the audit quality is based on two basic concepts: the auditor's competence and independence [14,15], Lemon and Taffler [15]. However, recent financial scandals and the collapse of one of the audit giants, "Arthur Anderson's firm" showed the incapacity of these concepts to understand the audit quality on their own. It should, therefore, be necessary to rethink the current valuation rules and propose new measures that take into account the complexity of the audit work [3,16]. In this perspective, other criteria appeared to be reliable indicators of the audit quality. Accounting literature highlighted several measures of the audit quality, such as:

The sector-based specialization: By auditing several firms in the same auditing sector, the auditors require a good experience and then become experts in the processes and procedures related to this sector. In this sense, several studies predict that the audit firms specialized in a particular sector has considerable experience and significant investment in the technology adopted in this activity sector. They are the most competent in this sector and are likely to offer a relatively high quality of services [17-19]

The size of the audit firm: It is generally accepted that the Big 4 produce better audits since they have greater financial resources than others and better human skills. In this sense, De Angelo [14] considers that the size of the audit firm is an implicit guarantee of the quality of the performed tasks [6,20,21].

*Corresponding author: Affes H, Associate Professor, Department of economics and management Sciences, University of Sfax, Tunisia
E-mail: Habib.affes@yahoo.fr

The reputation of the audit firm: the reputation of the audit firm is usually the most commonly used indicator empirically to assess the audit quality. However, several studies show that the long-term audit relationship may impair the auditors' independence or inversely improve the auditors' conditions of the work exercise and therefore the quality of the performed audit [22-24].

The audit committee: the implementation of the audit committee in a company is one of the controlling mechanisms that ensure the relevance and consistency of the accounting policies adopted for the preparation of the financial statements. In this context, the presence of an audit committee within the firm is likely to improve the transparency of the information disclosure and limit the degree of the managers' involvement in the process of the earning management [25,26].

The audit fees: the fees received by the auditor were considered by literature as a means to measure the quality of service provided by the auditor. Frankel et al. [27] show that high fees help reduce the audit management result. Indeed, high audit fees may also reflect an increased audit effect and therefore a better audit quality.

The Conceptual Framework

Sector-based specialization and the quality of accounting earnings

Several studies show that the auditors who specialize in a well definite industry benefit from specific knowledge. They have the ability to make a good quality service, achieve cost savings on their audit and provide a better audit quality [17,20,21].

Thus, Balsam, Krishnan and Yang [18] anticipate a positive and significant relationship between the sector-based specialization of the audit firms and the quality of the accounting earnings. Gul et al. [28] found that sector-based specialization of the audit firms reduces the discretionary accruals and improves the quality of the accounting figures of the firms. In this regard, Carcello and Nagy [23] expect a negative relationship between the auditors' specialization and the reporting of fraudulent financial statements.

Hypothesis 1: The quality of the accounting earnings is positively associated with the sector-based specialization of the audit firms.

The size of the audit committee and the quality of the accounting earnings

Piot and Janin [21] find that the French firms having an audit committee have lower discretionary accruals than others. The establishment of an audit committee within a company can limit the power of the leaders and subsequently reduce the results management.

Several other researches admit that the presence of an audit committee within the firm limits the results management. The researches of Defond and Jiambalvo [25] and Dechow et al. [26] seem to confirm this hypothesis. Moreover, other studies consider that the audit committee can contribute to the improvement of the quality of the financial statements preparation process [14,23,29].

Hypothesis 2: The quality of the accounting earnings is positively associated with the size of the audit committee.

The size of the audit firm and the quality of accounting earnings

The size of the audit firm is the most important criterion used in the empirical literature to assess the quality of the external audit.

It is generally accepted that the Big 4 produce better quality audits. Chalmers and Godfray [30] show that the Big 4 help, on the one hand, reduce the problem of the information asymmetry between the managers and the shareholders, and on the other hand, improve the quality of the accounting income of their customers.

Several studies find a positive and significant relationship between the big auditors and the quality of the accounting earnings. These studies suggest that the large audit firms may conduct a checking of a higher quality. This hypothesis is also backed by: Francis and Yu [8]; De Angelo [14], Chalmers and Godfrey [30] Palmarosa [31] and Defond Jiambalvo [25] Krishnan [32].

Hypothesis 3: The quality of the accounting earnings is positively associated with the auditors' belonging to an international network (BIG 4).

The reputation of the audit firm and the quality of the accounting earnings

Several studies consider that a long audit relationship improves the conditions of the auditors' work performance and subsequently the quality of the carried out audit. Furthermore, some authors show that a long audit relationship improves the conditions of the audit work performance. In this case, the duration of the audit relationship can have a positive impact on the quality of the accounting earnings of the audited firms. [20,23,33-35].

However, other studies consider a long relationship audit could corrupt the auditors' independence, and thus the existence of a negative relationship between the duration of the audit relationship and audit quality [36]. The most recent work Hamilton et al. [37], Reynolds and Francis [8] confirm the negative association between the duration of the audit relationship and the abnormal component of the result.

Hypothesis 4: The quality of the accounting earnings is positively associated with the duration of the audit relationship.

The expertise of the audit committee's member and the quality of the accounting earnings

To handle the financial statement preparation process, and in order to carry out their missions, the committee members must hold a degree in finance and (or) in accounting or other qualifications in related fields [38,39]. Therefore, several studies find that firms having audit committee members with financial expertise have relevant accounting earnings [40,41].

Empirically, the results broadly support that the presence of an expert in accounting or finance within the audit committee can improve the performance of the company [39]. Similarly, Bryan et al. [41] and Rich argue that an audit committee with financial expertise can increase the relevance of the benefits.

Hypothesis 5: The quality of the accounting earnings is positively associated with the expertise of the audit committee's member.

The existence of majority shareholders and the quality of the accounting earnings

Several studies show that the agency costs in firms, where the capital is concentrated in the hands of a small number of shareholders, result in conflicts of interest between the majority and minority shareholders [42].

Indeed, the majority shareholders typically have a degree of influence and control over the company. They can later force the managers to work for their benefit by opposing their decisions which contradict the objective of maximizing the shareholders' wealth.

This can be reflected in an increase of the audit request. Similarly, Jeanjean [43] and Rajgopal, and Venhatachalam Jiambalvo [44] have argued that the existence of such shareholders provides a control mechanism that can prevent the results management. However, Bryan et al. [41], show that the existence of such shareholders negatively affects the relevance of financial information. These studies make us decide on the following hypothesis:

Hypothesis 6: The quality of the accounting earnings is positively associated with the presence of majority shareholders.

Concentration of the audit firms and the quality of the accounting earnings

To strengthen the independence of statutory auditors and improve the services provided by the auditors, some companies require the existence of two audit firms. On the institutional level, however, this differs from the Anglo-Saxon environments by the obligation to have the consolidated financial statements certified by at least two separate auditors.

The existence of two audit firms enables the audited entity to promote the audit quality both in terms of independence and of competence. Like the researches carried out on the control of the audit profession, Piot [5] deducted the positive effect of co-statutory auditor on the audit independence, on the safeguard of the interests of financial investors, and subsequently on the quality of the achieved results.

Hypothesis 7: The quality of the accounting earnings is positively associated with the concentration of the audit firms.

The Empirical Analysis Sample

The study sample which consists of 20 companies listed on the Tunis Stock Exchange (TSE) belongs to the non-financial sector. This study covers the period from 2005 to 2009.

The model

To test our research hypotheses, we use the following model:

$$EQ_{ki} = \beta_0 + \beta_1 BIG_{ij} + \beta_2 SPEC_{ij} + \beta_3 REPU_{ij} + \beta_4 COMM_{ij} + \beta_5 EXPER_{ij} + \beta_6 ACTI_{ij} + \beta_7 CONC_{ij} + \beta_8 ANAL_{ij} + \beta_9 TAILL_{ij} + \beta_{10} END_{ij} + \varepsilon_i$$

With:

EQ_{1i}: The relevance of the accounting earnings,

EQ_{2i}: That one of the accounting conservatism,

EQ_{3i}: The discretionary accruals to measure earning management.

The variables

The variables to be explained: the quality measurement of the accounting earnings

It will be measured by

The accounting conservatism: Among the researchers who presented a variety of definitions of the accounting conservatism, we find Bazu [9] who defined conservatism as "the tendency of the accountants to require a higher degree of verification so as to take into account the good news as gains rather than to recognize the bad news. The principle of the accounting conservatism affects the company's financial statements in a direct manner and the accounting profit in a specific way. In this regard, Givoly and Hayn [11] define conservatism

as a selection criterion among several accounting principles that lead to the minimization of reported benefits due to the delay in the consideration of the income, the rapid recognition of expenses and the lowest evaluation of assets and the highest one of the liabilities. These studies predict that the published results reflect the good news rather than the bad news.

To measure accounting conservatism, we will use the same approach as that of Basu [9]: a reverse profit regression compared with the performance of companies of which we present the following sequence:

$$P_{j,t-1} = a'_{0j} + a'_{1j}D_{jt} + â_{0j}\text{stocks Returns}_{jt} + â_{1j}D_{jt}*\text{stocks Return}_{jt} + â_{jt}$$

With:

Profits (j t): Profits of company j for year t, divided by the market value or the share price at the beginning of year t-1 (P_{jt-t}).

D_{jt}: Mute variable (1 if the returns of year t are negative, 0 if they are positive).

Stocks Return: equity returns for company j for year t.

The answers factors for the good and bad news are represented by β_{0j} and $(\beta_{0j} \beta_{1j})$.

The β_{1j} coefficient is a response coefficient which helps detect the effect of the bad news. Basu and Walker (1999) as well as Givoly and Hayn (2000) measure conservatism on the basis of the $\frac{(\beta_{0j}+\beta_{1j})}{\beta_{0j}}$, ratio, which gives the following formula:

$\text{Conservatism} = \frac{(\beta_{0j}+\beta_{1j})}{\beta_{0j}}$ A large value of the variable "conservatism" shows that there is an accounting conservatism and therefore quality benefits.

The relevance of the accounting earnings: According to Core, Guay, and Buskirk [45], Kothari and Shanken [2], the relevance of accounting information can be defined as the ability of the accounting figures to summarize the underlying information at the share cost.

Empirically, Borth, Beaver and Landsman [7] consider that an accounting figure is a relevant value if it is association with the market value of the company that published it. In this regard, the previous studies dealt with the relevance through the association between the accounting earnings and the stock returns.

The response coefficient of the generated profit of this regression is the measurement of the earnings relevance [45].

To estimate the earnings relevance, Francis and Schipper [13] and Bushman, Chen, Engel and Smith [46] use the following model:

Returns (j, t) = δ (0, j) + δ (1, j) Profit (j, t) + δ(2,J) Δ Profit (j, t)

With:

Returns (j, t): equity returns for company j for year t.

Profits (j, t): Profits for company j for financial year t, divided by the market value or the share price at the beginning of financial year t.

Francis and Shipper [13], LaFond, Olsson and Schipper [47] measure the benefits relevance on the basis of the adjusted R^2 arising from the regression model per company already mentioned. Therefore, Relevance=Adjusted R2

The earning management: Schipper [48] defines the results management as "a deliberate intervention in the presentation of the financial information in order to obtain personal gain." Therefore, the quality of disclosed information depends on whether there is a phenomenon of results management or not.

Thus, many studies referred to the practices of earnings management in order to assess the quality of the accounting earnings [27,49].

The literature review identifies two perspectives included in the approach of the earnings management to measure the quality of the accounting earnings: the prospective of the total accruals and that of the discretionary ones

Regarding our research, we suggest estimating the quality of the accounting earnings on the basis of the discretionary ones as proposed in the modified model of Jones [26]. Consequently, the model is as follows:

$$\frac{TA_t}{A_{t-1}} = \alpha_1(\frac{1}{A_{t-1}}) + \alpha_2(\frac{\Delta REV_{t-\Delta REC_t}}{A_{t-1}}) + \alpha_3(\frac{IMMO_t}{A_{t-1}}) + \varepsilon_t$$

Several models aim at assessing the discretionary component of the accruals and start with the basic accounting equation by taking total accruals (TA) the sum of discretionary accruals (DA) and the non-discretionary ones (AND)=AD AND ACT. Therefore, to do so, we must first calculate, for each firm i and year t, the total accruals according to the direct approach which is as follows:

ACT=RN-FTE

With:

ACCT: the total accruals.

RN: the net book profit.

FTE: The net operating cash flow

The discretionary accruals, which are obtained by the difference between the total accruals for each firm and the normal accruals, will then be estimated using the modified Jones model, therefore we obtain:

$$ACD_t = e_{it} = \frac{ACT_t}{A_{t-1}} - [\alpha_1\left(\frac{1}{A_{t-1}}\right) + \alpha_2\left(\frac{\Delta REVit - \Delta CCit}{A_{t-1}}\right) + \alpha_3\left(\frac{IMMO_t}{A_{t-1}}\right)]$$

With

ACD: discretionary accruals

ACT: total accruals.

A: total assets

ΔREV: Income variation

ΔCCL: Accounts receivable

IMMOB: Gross assets excluding financial assets

The explanatory variables: measurement of the audit quality: At this case and regarding our model, we have:

- **Size of the audit firm "Big4":** the dummy variable that takes value 1 if the firm is audited by the "Big4" and 0 otherwise [4,14,30,49].

- **Auditor's reputation "REPU":** the dummy variable that takes value 1 if the period is three years and 0 if it is shorter [23,24,34].

- **Size of the Audit Committee "COMM":** The dichotomous variable that takes value 1 if the members of the audit committee are at least three and 0 otherwise [29,50].

- **The expertise of the Audit Committee's member "EXPER":** It is a binary variable that takes value 1 if at least one member of the audit

committee is an expert in financial management or accounting, and 0 otherwise [41,50,51].

- **The existence of majority shareholders "ACTI":** this variable will be measured by the number of the shareholders who own more than 5% the company's stake [31,43,52].

- **The concentration of the audit firms "CONC":** this variable will be measured by a dummy variable that takes value 1 if the firm is audited by two firm's auditors and 0 otherwise [5].

   The control variables: We distinguish the following control variables: 2005

- **The tracking analyst "ANAL":** It is a binary variable that takes value 1 if the audited firm has a financial analyst and 0 otherwise.

- **The size of the audited firm "TAILL":** the firm's size is assessed in accordance with the logarithm of total assets [5,53].

- **The Indebtedness "END"**=Total Debt/Total Assets [6,18]

Result Analysis

The univariate test

The previous Table 1 presents the results obtained from the univariate tests related to the explanatory variables of the Tunisian non-financial firms. The results in this table show that the variables BIG, COMM, and EXPER affect significantly and positively the quality of the accounting benefits, as measured by the approach of the earning relevance and its management. The variables ANLY, ITAC and END significantly and negatively affect the quality of the accounting earnings, as measured by both the relevance and conservatism approaches [54].

It appears from this table that the existence of shareholders owning more than 5% of the capital and the sector-based specialization of the audit firms positively and significantly affects the quality of the accounting benefits as measured by the conservatism approach [55].

In fact, this table has a R^2 coefficient of about 39.33%, 55.35% and 19.56% respectively for the three measures of the accounting earnings quality, namely the relevance, conservatism and results management. We can say that the explanatory power of this model is significant. Therefore, we can conclude that the independent variables used in this model do well explain the studied phenomenon, namely the quality of the accounting earnings [56].

To better examine the impact of the audit quality on that of the accounting earnings, it is important to conduct a multivariate analysis taking into account the simultaneous effect of all the studied variables [57].

Tests on the panel data

The panel data have two dimensions: one for individuals (in our model they are the firms) and another for time. They are generally identified by indices i and t respectively. It is often useful to identify the effect associated with each individual, an effect which does not vary in time, but varies from one individual to another. This effect can be fixed or random. This is summarized in the test for the presence of individual effects, the Hausman and the correlation tests [58].

Test for the presence of individual effects

This test is to verify the presence of individual effects in our data. Our analysis will focus on the modeling of U_i individual effects for the panel data as follows: $Y_{it} = Y + X_{it}\beta + e_{it}$. In fact, we seek to test the $H_0: U_i = 0$ null hypothesis in the previous regression. This hypothesis is about the absence of individual effects (Table 2).

	Model 1			Model 2			Model 3		
	Std-Error	T-Statistics	PER	Std-Error	T-Statistics	CONS	Std-Error	T-Statistics	ACD
BIG	4.65888	1.95371	9.102 (0.053)	5.7127	-3.1763	-18.145 (0.002)	2332.89	3.41393	7964.366 (0.001)
SPEC	5.70603	-0.86078	-4.911 (0.391)	6.99677	3.308518	23.148 (0.001)	2857.24	1.61994	4628.583 (0.108)
REPU	10.0713	3.59482	36.204 (0.000)	12.3496	-1.34127	-16.564 (0.183)	5043.16	0.04862	245.230 (0.961)
COMM	5.62522	1.19989	6.749 (0.233)	6.89768	-0.65996	-4.552 (0.511)	2816.78	1.67023	4704.679 (0.098)
EXPER	5.85301	3.96198	23.189 (0.000)	7.17700	-1.48204	-10.636 (0.141)	2930.84	1.22343	3585.716 (0.224)
ACTI	1.33415	-5.15723	-6.880 (0.000)	1.63594	5.85411	9.577 (0.000)	668.064	-3.37468	-2254.508 (0.001)
CONC	4.87881	-0.47035	-2.294 (0.639)	5.98243	-1.51785	-9.080 (0.132)	2443.02	-2.19131	-5353.443 (0.031)
ANALY	7.36410	-2.82759	-20.822 (0.005)	9.02992	1.38593	12.514 (0.169)	3687.51	-1.20052	-4426.939 (0.233)
TAILL	0.00016	3.37320	0,005 (0.001)	0.00020	3.86582	0,00079 (0,000)	0.08369	0.08247	0.006 (0.934)
END	0.00024	-3.06103	-0,0005 (0.002)	0.00029	0.27878	8.33 (0.781)	0.12208	-0.27235	-0.033 (0.786)
		R²	0.39339			0.553567			0.195652
		R² adjusted	0.33264			0.508923			0.115218

Table 1: Univariate test on the subsample of the Tunisian non-financial firms.

	PER	CONS	ACD
Chi 2 Test	12,922	0,435	2,789
	(0,000)	(0,509)	(0,094)

Table 2: Test for the presence of individual effects.

	PER	CONS	ACD
Chi 2Test	5,039	15,323	1,121
	(0,080)	(0,000)	(0,570)

Table 3: Hausman test.

The results of this test for the subsample of non-financial firms can make us accept H_0 and check the absence of individual effects for the conservatism model. However, for the other two models of the results relevance and management, we can say that this test can reject H_0 and accept the alternative hypothesis, that it is to say, the hypothesis about the presence of individual effects . In this case, we should use the Hausman test to define whether the effects are fixed or random [59].

Hausman Test: The Hausman test is a specification one which helps determine if the coefficients of both estimates (fixed and random) are statistically different. The idea of this test is that, under the null hypothesis of independence between the errors and the explanatory variables, both estimators are unbiased and hence, the estimated coefficients should differ slightly. The Hausman test compares the variance-covariance matrix of both estimators [60].

$$W = (\hat{a}F - \hat{a}a)' var(\hat{a}F - \hat{a}a)^{-1}(\hat{a}F - \hat{a}a)$$

The null hypothesis of this test (H0) refers to the random effect, if p-value is greater than 10%, we use the random effects which are more effective (Table 3).

In our case, the Hausman test shows probabilities lower than 10% for both the relevance and conservatism models; that is (8% and 0%). However, concerning the results management model, the probability is greater than 10%; that is (57%) [61].

The results of this test therefore show that the individual effects are random and non-stationary for the results management model, whereas the individual effects are fixed and non-random for the other two measures of the accounting earnings quality, namely the relevance and conservatism.

The correlation test between the explanatory variables

The last test to be checked in the panel data framework is the absence of a of multi Collinearity problem between the variables included in our model. We will then examine Sperman's correlation matrix of the independent variables including the control ones [62].

In Table 4, we find that the correlation coefficients are significantly smaller than 0.8, which corresponds to the line drawn by Kennedt from which we generally begin to have serious problems of multicollinearity. As a result, we can say that there is no multicollinearity problem between the variables.

As argued by O'Keefe et al. [19], Piot [5], Carcello and Nagy [23], the auditors who specialize in certain industries will benefit from specific sector-based knowledge, and therefore will be able to produce a quality service which subsequently helps improve the quality of the results.

Similarly, Balsam et al. [18] found, on a sample of U.S. firms, that the sector-based specialization of the audit firms reduces the discretionary accruals and improves the relevance of the accounting income.

It appears that the results obtained in our study are consistent with the previous studies and support the hypothesis previously issued: The quality of the accounting earnings is positively associated with the sector-based specialization of the audit firms for the variables regressions of interests, conservative, and earning management.

Like the results released by Franci and Yu [49], Chalmers st Godfrey [30], our results obtained about the effect of the audit firm's size on the interest variables confirm the hypothesis previously issued and reflect a positive and significant relationship between the 'Big 4' auditors

	BIG	SPEC	REPU	COMM	EXPER	ACTI	CONC	ANALY	TAILL	END
BIG	1									
SPEC	-0.0821	1								
REPU	0.2536*	0.1873	1.0000							
COMM	0.0503	-0.3572**	-0.1147	1.0000						
EXPER	-0.0657	-0.3120**	-0.3505**	0.0545	1					
ACTI	0.3387**	0.1888	0.2880*	-0.033	0.0433	1				
CONC	0.5334**	0.1667	0.1873	0.1531	0.1336	0.3237**	1			
ANALY	0.0985	0.2287*	0.0964	0.2100*	0.3363**	0.0278	0.2287*	1		
TAILL	-0.0319	0.1539	0.163	-0.0815	-0.1356	0.1692	0.0265	-0.4294**	1.0000	
END	0.2370*	-0.1499	0.1408	0.0517	0.0326	0.0432	0.2723*	-0.0617	0.0317	1.0000

*Correlation is significant at 1%; **Correlation is significant at 5%.

Table 4 : Pearson's correlation.

and the quality of the accounting earnings as measured by the results management, the profit relevance and the accounting conservatism. This means that the large audit firms produce higher quality services because they have better techniques and well informed human skills [63-66].

As for the expertise variable of the audit committee's member, the obtained results confirm that the quality of the accounting earnings is positively associated with the member expertise of the audit committee. Anderson, Deli and Gillan [40] and Bryan et al. [41] showed that firms whose audit committees have members with financial expertise get relevant earnings. Similarly, Bryan and al. [41] argue that an audit committee with a financial expertise increases the earnings relevance [67].

Regarding the variable "auditor's reputation", the obtained results show a positive and significant effect on the model of the relevance of the accounting earnings, and a negative and significant effect on that of the results and accounting conservatism management. Theoretically, this contradictory effect of the "auditor's repuation" variable is justified by the findings of Libby and Frederick [33]; Myers et al. [34], Carcello and Nagy [23] who argued that the relationship length between the auditor and audited improves the conditions of carrying out the audit task. Hamilton et al. [37], Meyers et al. [36], JR Francis [8], find a negative association between the relationship length in years between the auditor and audited and the abnormal component of the result.

The effect caused by the existence of one or more shareholders confirms the hypothesis previously advanced [68]. This hypothesis says that the quality of the accounting earnings is positively associated with the presence of shareholders, and therefore corroborates the theoretical statements of Shleifer and Vishny [42], who reported that the concentration of the capital increases the control efficiency of the staff by the shareholders [69-71].

Jeanjean [43] and Rajgopal, Venhatachalam and Jiambalvo [44] argued that the existence of such shareholders provides a control mechanism that can hinder the earnings management. Unlike the expected results, the variable size of the audit committee positively affects only the model of the results management. Such a contradiction can be explained by the divergence of the results obtained in the studies of DeAngelo [14], Carcello and Nagy [23] and DeFond Jiambalvo [25].

Like in the researches carried out by Piot [5] on the control of the audit profession where the effect of co-statutory auditor on the audit independence was concluded, the obtained results show a significant effect of the variable "concentration of the audit firms" only for the model of the results management. This implies that the co-statutory auditor limits the managers' authority and therefore generates quality benefits.

Regarding the control variables, the obtained results suggest a positive relationship between the quality of the firms' accounting earnings and respectively the company's size and the presence of tracking financial analysts. These results imply that these elements are reasons that contribute to the improvement of the quality of the accounting earnings on which indebtedness has no significant impact [72].

Conclusion

As a governance mechanism, the external audit's main objective is to ensure the reliability of the accounting data published by the firms. Therefore, the agency and the signal theories are a theoretical basis for the positive impact of the external audit on the quality of the accounting earnings measured by different approaches such as the relevance, conservatism and results management.

In our study, we tried to check whether the quality of the external audit can improve the quality of the accounting earnings using three different approaches of measurement such as, the relevance, the level of conservatism and the results management. The empirical analysis in the Tunisian context helped us to show that a better external audit quality improves that of the accounting earnings.

More specifically, the developed study shows that the auditors' belonging to an international network (Big 4), the reputation of the audit firm, the existence of an accounting expert in the audit committee, the existence of an audit committee and the size of the audited company have a positive impact on the relevance of the accounting earnings for both sectors (financial and non-financial).

The results show that other variables of the external audit, such as the existence of majority shareholders holding more than 5% of the capital, the co-statuary auditor and the presence of a financial analyst within the company being audited, improve the quality of the accounting earnings.

References

1. Dechow PM (1994) Accounting earnings and cash flows as measures of firm performance: the role of accounting accruals. The Journal of accounting and economics 18: 3-42.

2. Dechow PM, Kothari SP, Watts RL (1998) The relation between earnings and cash-flows. The Journal of Accounting and Economics 25: 133-168.

3. Ball R, Brown P (1968) An empirical evaluation of accounting income numbers. Journal of Accounting Research 6: 159-178.

4. Francis, Wang D (2006) The joint effect of investor protection and Big 4 audits on earnings quality around the World. Contemporary Accounting Research 25: 157-191.

5. Piot C (2004) Effort d'audit et taille de l'entreprise: barème réglementaire et économie d'échelle dans le commissariat aux comptes des PME-PMI. Finance-Contrôle-Stratégie 7: 151-169.

6. Becker CL, Defond ML, Jiambalvo J, Subramanyam KR (1998) The effect of audit quality on earning management. Contemporary Accounting Research 15: 1-24.

7. Barth ME, Beaver WH, Landsman WR (2001) The relevance of the value relevance literature for financial accounting standard setting: Another view. Social science Research Network.

8. Francis J, Schipper K, Vincent L (2002) Earnings announcements and competing information. Journal of Accounting and Economics 33: 313-342.

9. Basu S (1997) The conservatism principle and the asymmetric timeliness of earnings. The Journal of Accounting and Economics 24: 3-37.

10. LaFond R, Watts RL (2008) The information role of conservative financial statement. The Accounting Review 83: 447-478.

11. Givoly D, Hayn C (2000) The changing time-series properties of earnings, cash flows and accruals: Has financial reporting become more conservative. The Journal of Accounting and Economics 29: 287-320.

12. Penman SH, Zhang X (2001) Accounting conservatism, the quality of earnings, and stock returns. The Accounting Review 77: 237-246.

13. Francis J, Schipper K (1999) Have financial statements lost their relevance. Journal of Accounting Research 37: 319-352.

14. De Angelo LE (1981a) Auditor size and audit quality. Journal of Accounting and Economic 3: 183-199.

15. Citron DB, Taffler RJ (1992) The audit report under going concern uncertainties: an empirical analysis. Accounting and Business Research 22: 337-345.

16. Carcello JV, Hermanson RH, McGrath NT (1992) Audit quality attributes: the perceptions of audit partners, preparers, and financial statement users. Auditing: A Journal of Practice and Theory 11: 1-15.

17. DeFond MI, Wong TJ (2000) Auditor industry specialization and market segmentation: evidence from Hong Kong. Auditing a journal of practice and theory 19: 51-66.

18. Balsam S, Krishnan, Yang JS (2003) Auditor Industry Specialization and Earnings Quality. Auditing: A Journal of Practise and Theory 22: 71-97.

19. O'Keefe TR, King RD, Gaver (1994) Audit Fees, industry specialization, and compliance with GASS reporting standard. Journal of practice and theory 13: 41-55.

20. Hammersley JS (2006) Pattern identification and industry-specialist auditors. The Accounting Review, mars.

21. Piot C, Janin R (2004) Audit quality, corporate governance and earning management in France. Annual Congress of European Accounting Association, Gothenburg.

22. Myers L, Skinner D (1999) Earnings momentum and earnings management.

23. Carcello JV, Nagy AL (2004) Client size, auditor specialization and fraudulent financial reporting. Managerial Auditing Journal 19: 5.

24. Mansi SA, Maxwell WF, Miller DP (2004) Does auditor quality and tenure matter to investors? Evidence from the bond market. Journal of Accounting Research 42: 755-793.

25. DeFond ML, Jiambalvo J (1994) Debt covenant violation and manipulation of accruals. Journal of Accounting and Economics 17: 145-176.

26. Dechow P, Sloan R, Sweeney A (1995) Detecting earnings management. The Accounting Review 70: 193-226.

27. Frankel R, Johnson M, Nelson K (2002) The Relation between auditors' fees for non-audit services and earning management. The Accounting Review 77: 71-105.

28. Gul AF, Fung KYS, Jaggi S (2009) Earning quality: Some evidence on the role of auditor tenure and auditors' industry expertise. Journal of Accounting and Economics 47: 265-287

29. Spira L (1999) Independence in Corporate Governance: The Audit Committee Role. A European Review 4: 262-273.

30. Chalmers K, Godfrey JM (2004) Reputation costs; the impetus for voluntary derivate financial reporting. Accounting Organization and Society 29: 95-125.

31. Palmrose Z-V (1988) An analysis of auditor litigation and audit service quality. The Accounting Review 63: 55-73.

32. Krishnan JY, Steven B (2003) Auditor industry specialization and the earning response coefficient.

33. Libby R, Frederick DM (1990) Experience and the ability to explain audit finding. Journal of Accounting Research 22: 348-367.

34. Meyrs JN, Meyrs LA, Omer T (2003) Exploring the term of the auditor-client relationship. The Accounting Review 78: 779-799.

35. Chen KY, Zhou J (2006) Auditor brand name, industry specialization, and earnings management: evidence from Taiwanese companies. International Journal of Accounting, Auditing and Performance Evaluation 3: 194-219.

36. Meyrs MJ, Regsby JT, Boone J (2007) The impact of auditor-client relationship on the reversal of first time audit qualification. Managerial Auditing Journal 22: 53.

37. Hamilton J, Ruddock CMS, Stokes DJ, Taylor SL (2005) Audit Partner Rotation, Earnings Quality and Earnings Conservatism, SSRN.

38. Lee T, Stone M (1995) Competence and independence: the congenial twins of auditing. Journal of business finance and accounting.

39. Abbott LJ, Parker S, Peters G (2002) Audit Committee Characteristics and Financial Misstatement: A Study of the Efficacy of Certain Blue Ribbon Committee Recommendations. SSRN.

40. Anderson L, Deli N, Gillan L (2003) Boards of Directors, Audit Committees and Information Content of Earnings. SSRN.

41. Bryan D, Liu C, Tiras SL (2004) The Influence of Independent and Effective Audit Committees on Earnings Quality. SSRN.

42. Shleifer A, Vishny R (1997) A survey of corporate governance. Journal of Finance 52: 737-783.

43. Jeanjean T (2001) Incentives and constraints on earnings management.7: 62-76.

44. Jiambalvo J, Rajgopal S, Venkatachalam M (2002) Institutional ownership and the extent to which stock prices reflect future earnings. Contemporary Accounting Research 19: 117-145.

45. Core JE, Guay WR, Buskirk AV (2003) Market valuations in the new economy: An investigation of what has changed. Journal of Accounting and Economics 34: 43□67.

46. Bushman RM, Chen Q, Engel, Smith EA (2000) Financial accounting information, organizational complexity and corporate governance systems. Journal of Accounting and Economics 37: 167-201.

47. Ashbaugh H, Collins DW, Lafond R (2004) Corporate governance, risk and the cost of equity capital. Accounting and Business Research 24: 195-2007.

48. Schipper K (1989) Commentary on earnings management. Accounting horizons 3: 91-102.

49. Francis JR, Yu MD (2009) Big 4 Office Size and Audit Quality. The Accounting Review. 84: 1521-1552.

50. Rich K (2009) Audit Committee Accounting Expertise and Changes in Financial Reporting Quality.

51. Knapp MC (1991) Factors that audit committee members use as surrogates for audit quality. Auditing: A Journal of Practice and Theory 10: 615-637.

52. Jensen MC, Meckling WH (1976) Theory of the firm, managerial behavior, agency costs and ownership structure. Journal of Financial Economics 3: 305-360.

53. Mayangsari S (2007) The Auditor Tenure and the Quality of Earnings: Is Mandatory Auditor rotation Useful. Unhas Makssar 26-28: 1-25.

54. Basu S (1999) Discussion of the international differences in the timeliness, conservatism, and classification of earnings. Journal of Accounting Research 37: 89-99.

55. Antle R (1982) The auditor as an economic agent. Journal of Accounting Research 20: 503-527.

56. Antle R, Nalebuff B (1991) Conservatism and auditor- client negotiations. Journal of Accounting Research 29: 31-59.

57. Bushman RM, Smith AJ (2001) Financial accounting information and Corporate Governance. Journal of Accounting and Economics 32: 237-333.

58. Datar S, Feltham G, Hughes J (1991) The role of audits and audit quality in valuing new issues. Journal of Accounting and Economics 14: 3-49.

59. Dunn KA, Mayhew BW (2004) Audit Firm Industry Specialization and Client Disclosure Quality. Review of Accounting Studies 9: 35-58.

60. Maydew FJE, Sparks H (1996) Earning management opportunities, auditor quality, and external monitoring.

61. Healy PM (1985) The effect of bonus schemes on accounting decisions. Journal of Accounting and Economics 7: 85-107.

62. Healy PM, Wahlen M (1999) A Review of earnings management literature and its implications for standard settings. Accounting Horizons 13: 365-395.

63. Hermanns S (2005) Financial Information and Earnings Quality: a Literature Review. SSRN.

64. Janin R, Piot C (2007) External Auditors, Audit Committees and Earnings Management in France. European Accounting Review 16: 429-454.

65. Jenkins DS, Kane GD, Velury U (2006) Earnings quality decline and the effect of industry specialist auditors: An analysis of the late 1990s. Journal of Accounting and Public Policy 25: 71-90.

66. Labelle R, Piot C (2003) Governance, audit and accounting manipulations. Financial Review 139: 84-90.

67. Piot C (2001) Agency costs and audit quality: Evidence from France. The European Accounting Review 10: 461-499.

68. Schipper K, Vincent L (2003) Earnings Quality. Accounting Horizons.

69. Van Tendeloo B, Vanstraelen A (2005) Earnings management under German GAAP versus IFRS. European Accounting Review 14: 155-130.

70. Watts RL (2003b) Conservatism in accounting, Part II: evidence and research opportunities. Accounting Horizons 17: 287-301.

71. Watts R, Zimmerman J (1990) Positive accounting theory: a ten year perspective. The Accounting Review 65: 131-156.

72. Watts RL (2003a) Conservatism in accounting, Part I: explanations and implications. Accounting Horizons 17: 207-221.

24

The Paradox of Variables' Effects on Channel Type

Mostafa Bakr¹* and Henri Masson²

¹*Scientist and Independent Scholar*
²*Professor Emeritus, University of Antwerp, Belgium*

Abstract

Purpose: This study aims to offer management with a structured decision-making approach to manage the conflicting impacts of different variables on the distribution channel type.

Problem statement: Different variables may possibly have opposite impacts on channel's type. When significant variables trigger the employment of direct channels, other significant variables may trigger indirect channels for the same product, leading to high complexity in channel decision making.

Design methodology approach: By means of a comprehensive survey covering 1400 retailers in Egypt and targeting three packaged milk categories, Structural Equation Modeling was used to group different variables, Logistic Regression was appliedto calculate the standardized beta coefficient of group variables.

Findings: Not all significant variables are equally important. Shelf life was found to be the most important variable with the highest standardized beta coefficient across 13 significant variables affecting distribution channel type.

Keywords: Channels of distribution; Food products; Egypt

Introduction

The complexity of distribution channel decision making becomes evident when different variables work in opposite directions. When a given variable triggers a direct channel of distribution, while another variable triggers an indirect channel type, decision makers have to manage the paradox of conflicting impacts of different variables. Previous empirical studies offered decision makers with variables found to be statistically significant. Previous studies offered as well broad and high-level grouping of variables, in addition to the rich conceptual interpretation of variables' significance and their logical relations with distribution channel type. Empirical works stopped at this level and did not make explicit propositions on how to take channel decisions when two groups of variables work simultaneously, but in opposite directions for a given product. This paper studies channel structures for different producers of different milk products in Egypt. The milk category clearly reflects the paradox of conflicting group variables with opposite stimulus to different channel types. Short shelf life and the temperature controlled environment for some milk products like chilled dairy trigger high levels of control by manufacturers and justifies direct channels of distribution. In the same time, purchase in small quantities and high purchase frequency of the same milk products require high logistical services and triggers the hiring of distributors and intermediaries. If it is believed that decision makers are taking channel decisions in a purely qualitative manner (Bucklin et al., 1996), therefore studying the paradox of group variables' conflicting impact on channel structure will be more appropriate to be done in an emerging market like Egypt, where resources are limited and the cost of correction of wrong channel decisions, if any, will not be easily absorbed by milk manufacturers. High conversion rates from unpackaged milk products to packaged milk products in Egypt [2] is one final reason which justifies making the study in Egypt. Making statistical inferences from the sample drawn from the study may provide chances for generalizing results applicability on other food manufacturers in other emerging markets. This paper is grouping variables into four main groups. The paper tests the propositions that different groups have opposite impacts on the channel type. The objective is to manage the complexity of conflicting impacts across groups through understanding which of the four group variables tends to have the highest impact on the channel type?

Literature Review

After studying 220 products coming from 167 manufacturers, Diamond [3] identified six typical product flows that would reflect all possible paths adapted by suppliers studied in his sample to reach their customers [3,4]. The six product flows are displayed in Appendix A.

The most obvious and clear proposition on how to manage variables with opposite impacts on channel's structure was raised by Bucklin et al. [1]. Bucklin's sample included 1019 strategic business units (SBUs). The study included 12 variables grouped under two broad services outputs: "Logistical and informational" in addition to one additional control group capturing the scale and shared market variables underneath. Bucklin et al. [1] stated that "the integrated model shows that higher end-user information needs produce an effect upon channel structure that is diametrically opposite from that of high logistical services needs."

Bucklin made an explicit comment regarding the mentioned conflict between opposite impacts when he stated that "These results suggest that if the end user needs for information and logistics increases in the future, channels with bifurcated (separate) structures for each output may become more prevalent." These comments remain propositions and final notes concluding the study without being empirically tested.

Other than Bucklin's et al. [1] study it was not evident that previous studies made any propositions on how to take channel decisions when different variables work simultaneously in different directions. Either the nature of the products in scope did not allow enough variability to reflect the claimed conflict across variables' impact like Anderson

---

*Corresponding author: Mostafa Bakr, Scientist and Independent Scholar
E-mail: mebakr@yahoo.com

and Coughlin's [5] study. Or the research objective was limited to the understanding of the significant variables only like Lilien's [4] study. Or the research objective was specific focusing deeply on one particular aspect of channel's structure like Wadinambiaratchi [6], El-Ansary and Stern [7], Etgar [8], Høst et al. [9], Towson [10], Aithal [11] and finally Xaba and Masuku [12].

Anderson and Coughlan [5] were mainly concerned about the distribution channel type appropriate for a given manufacturer interested in introducing his products to a foreign market. The results show that exporters tend to leverage existing channels of distribution for the introduction of new products. Differentiated products, as well as products characterized by high asset specificity, tend to be distributed through direct channels. "The fact that the analysis was restricted only to industrial products and one industry (semiconductor) undoubtedly reduces the amount of variation in data" [5]. Direct channels looked to be the dominant suitable approach for industrial products, demanding a high level of training due to differentiation and asset specificity. Accordingly, the conflicting impacts of different group variables were not probably observed in Anderson and Coughlan's study due to the mentioned lack of variability in data.

Lilien [4] study was comprehensive enough to include diverse variables which belonged to different groups, Lilien studied 131 industrial products. Variables found statistically significant were product complexity, the size of the firm, the stage in the product's life cycle, the size of an average order and the purchase frequency. Variables found statistically significant could be possibly grouped into different groups like Information group, logistical group, and size group, yet no clear or direct reference was made on how to manage potential opposite impacts of different group variables, possibly because the research objective was to understand the significant variables affecting channel type.

Other empirical studies could be characterized by an in-depth focus on one aspect of the channel structure. Wadinambiaratchi's [6] comparative study was mainly focusing on economic development and its relation to channel structure. El-Ansary and Stern [7] zoomed on power across channel members. Etgar's [8] concentrated on the level of control the channel leader exercises on other channel members in the distribution chain. Høst et al. [9] were primarily interested in the variables impacting the adoption of internet based marketing channels. Towson [10] identified the key factors impacting the supplier's decision to start an online direct sales channel. Aithal [11] studied factors impacting the length of channels in rural India. In the scope of food products, Xaba and Masuku [12] studied small farmers' decisions to market their food products. It was not evident as per our scanning to empirical works and the conceptual framework of channel structure that the paradox of conflicting variables' impacts was explicitly raised and discussed by previous scholars.

Methodology

Research design

This paper is studying the channels of distribution for packaged milk producers in Egypt. Channel decision making for milk products is quite a controversy and may not seem to be as straightforward as other products. Other products may reflect a clear dominance for one service group over the other. Like the frozen food products for example, where products are differentiated due to the temperature controlled environment, storage conditions are complex and require a high level of after sales service and direct sales support. Or backed food

products as another extreme, which are more frequently sold in more retail shops compared to frozen food, without any or much information service support. Unlike these two products, milk products stay midway between two extremes, with the highend-user need for both logistics and information services in the same time.

Product categories in scope: Within the packaged milk category, three subcategories are studied to ensure data variability to allow for the the testing of some variables that would not have been possible to test in case of having only one product category in scope. These subcategories are chilled dairy, ultra heat treated (UHT) products, and powdered milk. This variability allows for different shelf lives (14 days for chilled, 180 for UHT, and 540 for powdered milk). The variability also allows for testing different storage conditions (temperature controlled for chilled, ambient conditions for powdered milk and both conditions for UHT). For each product category of the three mentioned subcategories, two brands were studied, mainly the two market leaders regarding market share.

Variables grouping: To assess the impact of different variables having opposite effects on the distribution channel type, high-level grouping was required to consolidate the 13 variables studied in the scope of this paper into four main groups. These groups are "Information," "Size," "Control" and "Logistics." "Information" group includes asset specificity, auxiliary services, and customer concentration. "Size" group included firm's size and Purchasing power. "Control" includes perishable product, the stage in the product life and safety. Finally, the group "Logistics" includes broad assortment, purchase frequency, purchase in small quantity, and distance. It is believed that safety and purchasing power are empirically tested for the first time in the context of channels of distribution.

The directness of distribution is measured through a binary dependent variable with two values, 0 for indirect channels of distribution and 1 for direct channels. Figure 1 lists all variables and all group variables. Appendix B lists, the survey questions, showing how each variable was operationalized, and from which source the relevant data was collected?

Research proposition

Hypothesis 1: Ho: there is no difference in the effect of each group variable on the directness of distribution. The four group variables (information, size, control and logistics) have similar and equal effects on the directness of distribution.

Total effect of group information=Total effect of group size=Total effect of group control=Total effect of group logistics

Data collection

Data was collected from both primary and secondary sources. The primary source of the data collection was the retailer selling the products in scope. A questionnaire was designed to collect data from retailers on some variables, while secondary sources were used for data collection for other variables. For the retailer's survey, data was collected through a professional sales team which belongs to one of the brands studied in the scope of this paper. The sales team managed to fill in the survey during their routine sales visits to retailers. It should be noted that retailers do not uncover data to unknown independent researchers for confidentiality purposes. Retailers expressed concerns that unknown researchers may belong to tax authorities or other governmental authorities. Moreover, the business relationship between

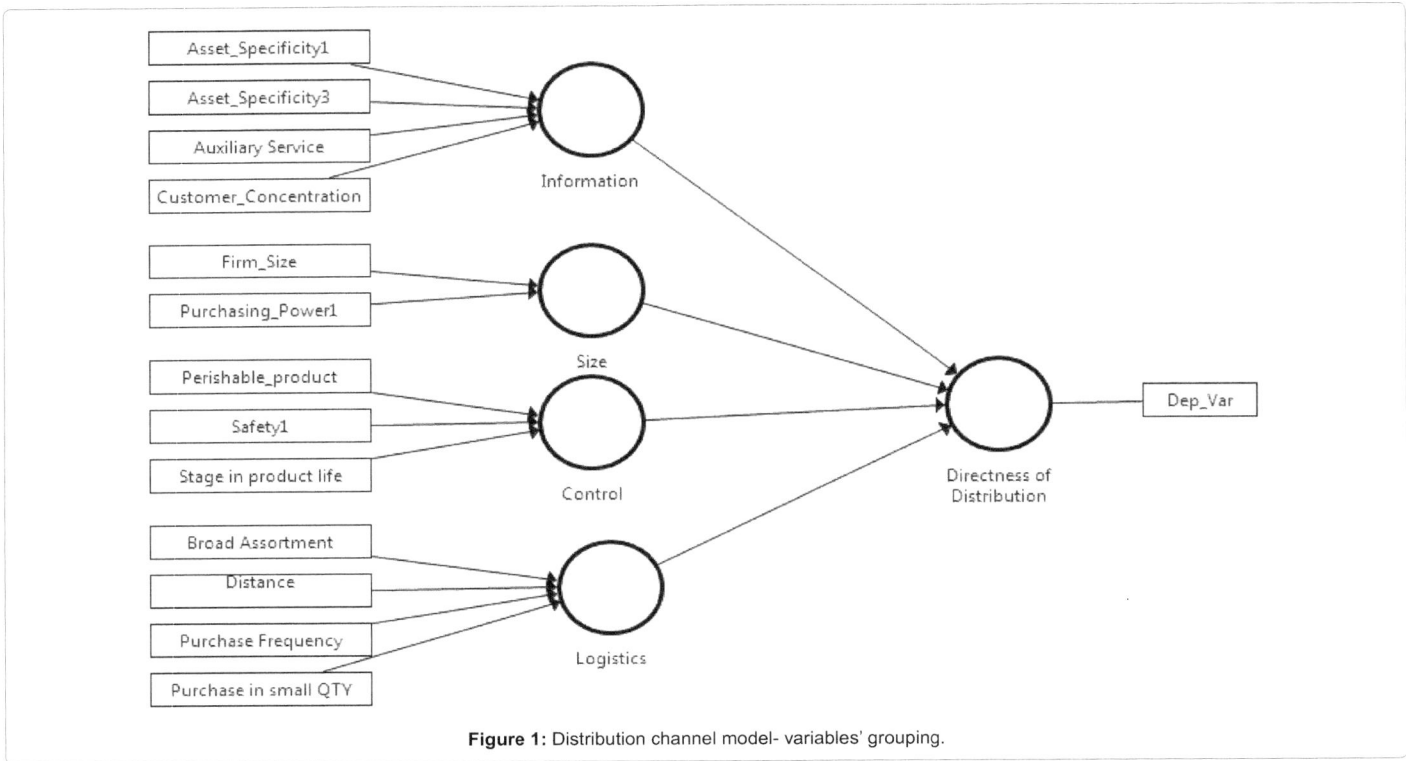

Figure 1: Distribution channel model- variables' grouping.

a given retailer and the concerned salesman secured the required time for explaining and filling in the survey.

Use of methods

Partial Least Squares Structural Equation Modeling (PLS–SEM) was used to group variables and to measure the significance and the relative importance of each variable/indicator forming the four group variables (logistics, information, size, and control). Smart PLS–SEM was also used to measure the significance of each of the four groups. Due to the binary nature of the dependent variable, Logistic Regression (LR) was used after that to measure the impact of each group on the directness of distribution. The standardized Beta coefficient is calculated to measure the relative importance of each group variable using the MS Excel function developed by King [13].

Results

Variables grouping and significance using SMART PLS-SEM

The relative importance of each indicator is measured by outer weight [14]. Our results indicate that the top three indicators are perishable products or shelf life followed by auxiliary service and firm size. Shelf life is clearly the highest significant contributor to the control group and the model in general. 11 out of 13 indicators were found statistically significant at the 1% probability of error level. The remaining two indicators were significant at the 5% level. The results reflect challenges facing channel decisions making due to the impact of numerous and significant variables.

Grouping did not allow any filtering or elimination as all groups were found significant at different levels and with opposite directional effects on the dependent variable. The "Control" group had the highest impact on the directness of distribution followed by "Information," "Size" and finally "Logistics." Out of the four group variables, the

total effect of each of the three groups (control, information, and size) was found statistically significant at the 1% probability of error level. Logistics' group total effect on the directness of distribution was barely found significant at the 5% probability of error level. The top two groups regarding their effect and significance had opposite impacts on the directness of distribution. While the group "Control" had a negative correlation with the dependent variable, the group "Information" had a positive correlation. Table 1 lists the total effects for the four groups; the outer weights for the 13 indicators, their related T Statistics' and finally their respective P values

Group variables significance testing using Logistic Regression (LR)

The binary dependent variable calls for the application of LR to understand the impact of each group on the directness of distribution. The group variable logistics violated the linearity of logit assumption. The interaction between the variable and its Ln (natural log transformation) was found statistically significant at p=0.000. Accordingly, the group logistics was excluded from the final LR model.

The omnibus test model coefficient chi-square was found statistically sig at p=0.000 which gives confidence in the predictive capacity of the model. The Nagelkerke R Square value implied that 52% of the variability in the dependent variable could be explained by the independent variables. Finally, the Wald test scores indicated that three group variables: control, information, and size were found statistically significant at 1% probability of error level.

The negative sign of the control group beta coefficient indicates that packaged milk manufacturers' tendency to rely on direct channels of distribution decreases, as the shelf life in days increases, the product moves from launch to maturity stage, and finally the number of traffic accidents increases in a given region. On the contrary, the positive beta

Group Variables	Total Effect	T Statistics	P Value
Control	-0.514	20.231	0.000
Information	0.183	5.970	0.000
Logistics	0.048	1.939	0.053
Size	-0.085	3.547	0.000
Indicators			
Indicators (group variable)	Outer Weight	T Statistics	P Value
Asset_Specificity1 – Information	.161	2.311	.021
Asset Specificity 3 – Information	.286	3.929	.000
Auxiliary Service – Information	0.853	34.694	.000
Broad Assortment – Logistics	0.427	4.249	.000
Customer Concentration – Information	0.355	7.496	000
Distance – Logistics	-0.291	3.229	.001
Firm Size – Size	0.767	9.829	.000
Perishable Product – Control	0.973	73.958	.000
Purchase frequency – Logistics	0.689	7.277	.000
Purchase in Small Quantity – Logistics	0.256	2.529	.011
Purchasing Power – Size	0.657	7.164	.000
Safety- Control	-0.347	8.440	.000
Stage in Product Life – Control	-0.118	2.609	.009

Table 1: PLS - Groups' Total Effects and Indicators' Outer Weights.

	B	Wald	Sig	Exp (B)	95% C.I for EXP (B)	
					Lower	Upper
Control	-2.016	198.310	.000	0.133	0.101	0.176
Information	0.419	29.159	.000	1.520	1.306	1.771
Size	**-0.202**	8.434	.004	0.816	0.712	0.936

Table 2: LR Outcome for the 3 Group Variables.

coefficient of the information group indicates that the manufacturer's tendency to rely on direct channels increases as the end user's need for information service increases. As a recall, information services operationalized in this paper is a composite of asset specificity, auxiliary service, and customer concentration. Control and information groups ranked the highest regarding their total effect on the directness of distribution based on their p values have different signs, indicating a conflicting impact on the channel decision to the same manufacturer.

Surprisingly group size had a negative beta coefficient, indicating a negative correlative between firm's size and purchasing power from one side and the directness of distribution from the other side. This outcome is not matching with Lilien's [4] results that size is positively correlated with the directness of distribution. Group "Size" as operationalized in this paper consisted of two indicators: firm's size (measured by the number of annual sales in tons for the brand/product in scope) and purchasing power in a given geographic region. Since the latter was reported on regional geographical level, it was found more or less similar across the six brands representing the six firms studied. For the firm's size, it was evident that the size of one manufacturer only outweighed the cumulative size of the other five manufacturers all together according to Ads (personal communication, June 17, 2015). This manufacturer was found relying more on indirect channels of distribution compared to direct channels. The positive relation between firm's size and the directness of distribution could be clearly observed for the rest of the five manufacturers, yet LR reported negative correlation might have been possibly impacted with the concentration towards indirectness of distribution for one giant manufacturer regarding size.

Table 2 lists beta coefficients, Wald test scores, significance levels and Exponential (B) for the three groups: "Control," "Information" and "Size."

Based upon LR Wald test scores, their levels of significance, and based upon PLS Group variables' total effect and their P values we tend to reject the null hypothesis that the four group variables (information, size, control and logistics) have similar and equal effects on the directness of distribution.

The paradox of channel decision making observed by PLS-SEM results is confirmed by LR outcome. The three group variables were found statistically significant with different beta signs indicating different stimulus to channel types. Standardized beta coefficients will be calculated to rank different group variables based on their strength of prediction. "The predictors are placed on a common scale so that each has the same mean and standard deviation. Variables having larger standardized beta weights (in absolute value) are considered to be stronger predictors in the equation" [13].

Standardized beta coefficient calculation using MS Excel and LR: King [13] used the mean of the predicted probability of the dataset, the un-standardized beta weight for a given variable, and the standard deviation to calculate the standardized beta for the same variable. Control group variables standardized beta weight came on top of all variables scoring (-0.453), followed by information group scoring (0.101), and finally size group scoring (-0.049). Appendix C lists the equations for computing standardized beta weights for all groups.

The reported results imply that a one standard deviation increase in Control decreases the predicted probability of employing direct channels by 45%, while a one standard deviation increase in Information increases the mean predicted probability of employing direct channels by only 10%. Finally, a one standard deviation increase in size decreases the mean predicted probability by only 5%. As per the standardized beta weight coefficient, it can be concluded that the effect of Control group is as much as 4.5 times the effect of the Information group and as much as nine times the effect of the size group. This piece of information if made available shall put an end to any hesitation in the decision-making process due to the existence of three group variables found all to be statistically significant and with opposite impacts on the channel type. It is now clear that the "control" group singled out as the main and most important contributor among a set of significant contributors [14-17].

Managerial implications

The finding that the control group had the highest impact on the channel distribution type for milk products in Egypt could be primarily explained by the perishable nature of milk products which had its implications on the consumer, the retailer and accordingly the manufacturer. Consumer's concerns about freshness in addition to the retailer's concerns about potential write-offs in case of bad goods, might have possibly influenced the manufacturer to seek a higher level of control through direct and short channels to distribute products with short shelf life. The mean of predicted probability of using direct channels of distribution increases from a weak 3% for long shelf life products like packaged powdered milk (545 days), to a moderate 44% for medium shelf life products like packaged UHT (180 days), to a significant 70% for short shelf life products like chilled dairy (only 14 days).

The logical interpretation is that losses accrued due to the employment of long distribution paths, to distribute short shelf life products, are not recoverable. Financial losses would equal to the total product value if such products happened to expire in the distributor's warehouse or the retailer's stores. Losses will also touch the consumers and will affect the brand's images if the products expired on the shelf due to inappropriate channel type or long paths. Manufacturers tend to exercise higher levels of control through short, and direct paths for short shelf life products due to significant financial losses and unrecoverable brand damage. Losses related to safety are also believed to be non-recoverable either in their effect on the corporate reputation or their effect on the staff morale in the case of irreversible injuries. Safety, as measured by the number of traffic accidents per region, is also believed to correlate with the directness of distribution negatively. Last but not least, newly launched product if not introduced through the right and proper channels,the product launch may fail. Therefore, suppliers tend to exercise higher levels of control in the launch stage. To summarize, the three variables forming the control group (and most importantly shelf life) have impacts which could not be compensated for in case of using the inappropriate channel type or in the case of using long channel paths for the distribution of short life products. This may explain why the Control group variable had the highest effect on channel type compared to Information, Size and Logistics groups.

Conclusion

While the information group is positively correlated with the directness of distribution, the control group is negatively correlated with the same. This conflict of group variables' impact on the distribution channel type must leave the channel decision maker with a substantial level of complexity to manage while taking channel decisions. Is the right decision to use direct channels in response to end user's needs to high information services, which is the case of UHT products, which require temperature-controlled environment for the display of products inside chillers? Chillers require routine maintenance and after sales service usually referred to as Auxiliary Services. Or the right decision is to use indirect channels for the same UHT products with relatively long shelf life nearly six months? While

both group variables are statistically significant with P values=0.000, the calculation of standardized beta coefficient shows clearly that the control group is much more important than the information group. The total effect of "Control" is as much as four times greater than the effect of "Information" group. Group variables found to be statistically significant are not equally important.

The group "Control" consisting of shelf life, the number of accidents per region and stage in product life is obviously the most important group. Shelf life is clearly the most impactful variable for milk products. One reason is the perishable nature of food products. Another possible reason is the non-recoverable losses in case of taking wrong channel decisions especially for products with short shelf lives. If the results derived from the milk products study could be generalized in other food products, then this will improve the channel decision making for food products, highly characterized by too many significant variables with opposite impacts on channel's structure.

To conclude, when all or numerous variables are found statistically significant, when a grouping of variables lead to different and opposite impacts, and finally when channel decision makers seek one criterion for food products to determine their channel type on, then it is shelf life. Short shelf lives trigger short and direct channel paths, and long shelf lives trigger long and indirect channel lives.

Limitations and recommendations

One limitation of this study is the limited number of products tested, which is believed to have impacted the directional relationship between size group and the dependent variable leading to the unexpected negative correlation, due to the substantial size of one of the six producers which happened to depend more on direct channels. A greater sample size including more producers is recommended for future studies to confirm the directional relationship between size and the directness of distribution. A greater sample sizeis also recommended to include more diverse brands other than milk products to confirm that milk findings are applicable for other and rest of food categories as well.

References

1. Bucklin LP, Ramaswamy V, Majumdar SK (1996) Analyzing channel structures of business markets via the structure-output paradigm. International Journal of Research in Marketing 13: 73-87.

2. El-Beheiry Z (2012) Juhayna food industries. Cairo, Egypt: NAEEM.

3. Diamond WT (1963) Distribution Channels for Industrial Goods. Ohio State University Press, Columbus, Ohio.

4. Lilien GL (1979) Exceptional paper-ADVISOR 2: Modeling the marketing mix decision for industrial products. Management Science 25: 191-204.

5. Anderson E, Coughlan AT (1987) International market entry and expansion via independent or integrated channels of distribution. Journal of Marketing 51: 71-82.

6. Wadinambiaratchi G (1965) Channels of distribution in developing economies. Business Quarterly 30: 72-82.

7. El-Ansary AI, Stern LW (1972) Power measurement in the distribution channel. Journal of Marketing Research 9: 47-52.

8. Etgar M (1977) Channel environment and channel leadership. Journal of Marketing Research 14: 69-76.

9. Høst V, Mols NP, Nielsen JF (2001) The adoption of Internet-based marketing channels. Homo Oeconomicus 17: 463-488.

10. Towson XL (2010) Coping with manufacturers' dilemma in the e-commerce era: Arelational model and a strategic framework. International Journal of E-Business Research 6: 52-69.

11. Aithal RK (2012) Marketing channel length in rural India: Influence of the external environment and rural retailer buyer behavior. International Journal of Retail and Distribution Management 40: 200-217.

12. Xaba BG, Masuku MB (2012) Factors affecting the choice of amarketing channel by vegetable farmers in Swaziland. Sustainable Agriculture Research 2: 112.

13. King JE (2007) Standardized coefficients in logistic regression. In: Annual meeting of the Southwest Educational Research Association. San Antonio, TX.

14. Hair JF, Hult GTM, Ringle CM, Sarstedt M (2016) A Primer on partial least squares structural equation modeling (PLS-SEM). Los Angeles, CA: SAGE Publications.

15. Distance Calculator (2015) Distance between 6th of October city, Giza Governorate. Egypt and Helwan, Cairo Governorate, Egypt.

16. Egyptian Central Authority for Public Mobilization and Statistics (2014) Key indicators for the income and consumption for 2012/2013.

17. National Center for Social and Criminological Research (2014) The annual report: Road accidents in Egypt.

Appendix A

Distribution Channel Paths

After studying 220 products coming from 167 manufacturers, Diamond (1963) identified six typical product flows that would reflect all possible paths adapted by suppliers studied in his sample to reach their customers (Diamond, 1963 as cited by Lilien, 1979).The six product flows are displayed in figure 1 hereunder.

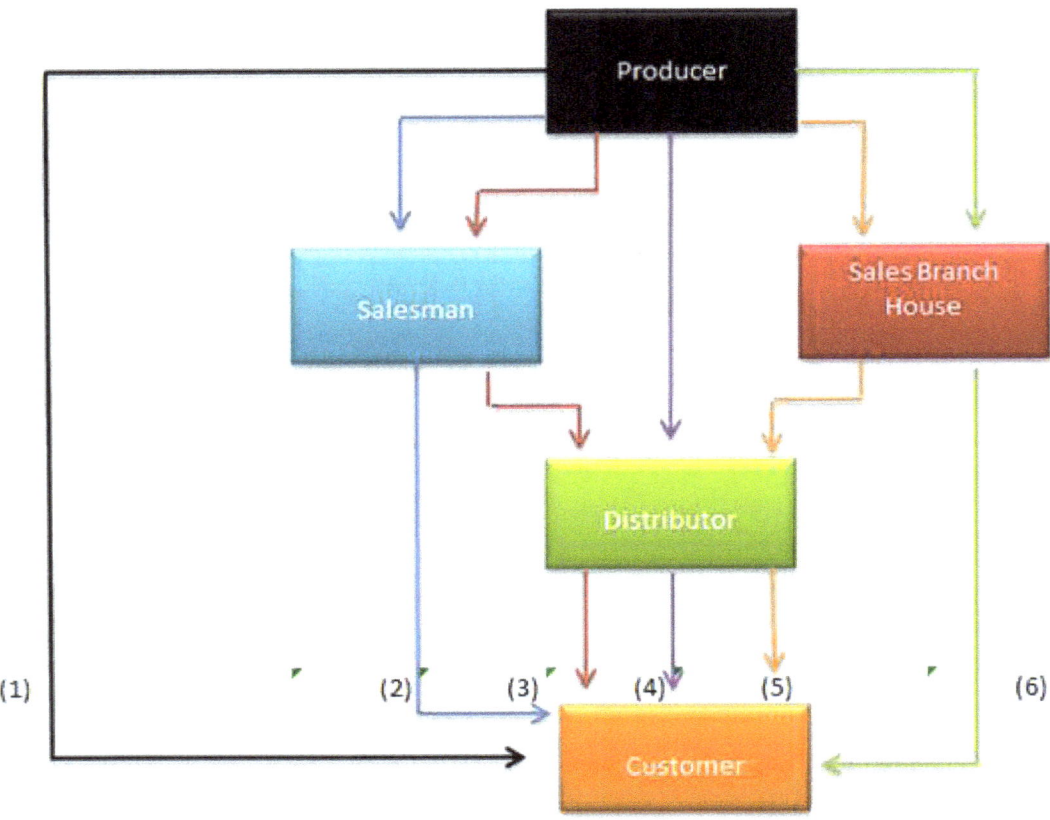

Figure 1: The Most six common industrial channels.

Source: Diamond (1963) as cited by Lilien (1979)

Out of the six possible paths, three are considered to be direct and three are indirect. Generally speaking, any path that passes through an intermediary, whether a distributor or a wholesaler is considered to be an indirect path. Any path from the supplier to the customer that bypasses an intermediary is considered a direct path. Diamond's 6 possible paths did not include the e-commerce channel path , which could be still direct if the manufacturer decided to respond to electronic orders received on own web portal and ship to consumers directly, or it could be an indirect path if the manufacturer decided to use an intermediary.

Appendix B

Research Variables

Group Variable	Variable	Source	Question
Logistics Services	Purchase in Small Quantity	Retailer's Survey	Upon purchase from the seller, what is the quantity purchased? Convert all quantities into pieces. If one case includes 12 pieces, therefore insert 12 pieces in case of purchasing 1 case.
Logistics Services	Distance	Secondary Sources – Distance Calculator	What is the distance in KM between the manufacturer and the retailer?
Logistics Services	Purchase Frequency	Retailer's Survey	What is the frequency of purchasing this product from the seller in your retail outlet? If you tend to purchase daily, then insert 30, if you tend to purchase every other day, then insert 15, if you tend to purchase twice a week, then insert 8. If others, please specify
Logistics Services	Broad Assortment	Retailer's Survey	Does the manufacturer offer a broad range of assortment compared to other manufacturers? 0) the manufacturer does not offer a broad range of assortment. 1) Yes the manufacturer offers a broad range
Information Services	Customer Concentration	Retailer's Survey	What is the type of the retail outlet? 0) Traditional Trade. 1) Super Market. 2) Wholesaler. 3) Key account
Information Services	Auxiliary Services	Retailer's Survey	Is the product stacked and displayed on ashelf or in chillers in your retail outlet? With thepoint of sale material or without apoint of sale material (POSM)? 0) On shelf without POSM. 1) On theshelf with few POSM. 2) On theshelf with a lot of POSM. 3) In chillers without maintenance. 4) In chillers once a year maintenance. 5) In chillers twice a year maintenance. 6) In chillers quarterly maintenance. 7) On shelf without POSM and in chillers with once a year maintenance.

Information services	Asset Specificity 1	Retailer's Survey	Did the salesman provide you any training in your retail outlet on how to **store** the product? 0) Very Little. 1) Little. 2) No Training. 3) High training. 5) Very high training.
Information services	Asset Specificity 3	Retailer's Survey	Did the salesman provide you any training in your retail outlet on how to **sell** the product? 1) Very Little. 1) Little. 2) No Training. 3) High training. 5) Very high training.
Control	Stage in the Product Life	Retailer's Survey	Since how many months this product has been launched? 0) Less than one month. 1) 1:6 months. 2) 6:12 months. 3) 12:24 months. 4) More than 36 months.
Control	Safety 1	Secondary Sources – National Center for Social and Criminological Research (2014)	What is the number of traffic accidents per governorate in Egypt?
Control	Perishable Product	Retailer's Survey	What is the shelf life of the product in days? If two weeks then insert 14. If six months then insert 180. If one year, then insert 365
Size	Firm's size	Secondary Sources – Personal Communication	What is the annual sales in tons for each of the six companies selling the six products in the scope of this study?
Size	Purchasing Power	Secondary Sources – Egyptian Central Authority for Public Mobilization and Statistics (2014)	What is the average annual household **income** for each of the four geographical regions studied in the scope of this paper? (Cairo, Delta East, Delta West and Upper Egypt)

Appendix C

Standardized Beta Weight

King (2007) developed the LR equation for the calculation of the standardized beta weight as follows:

Standardized Beta Weight =(1/(1+EXP(-(LN(A2/(1-A2))+0.5*A3*A4))))-(1/(1+EXP(-(LN(A2/(1-A2))-0.5*A3*A4)))), where

A2 = Mean of the predicted probability of the dataset

A3 = unstandardized beta weight for a given variable

A4 = Standard deviation for a given variable

	Control	Information	Size
Mean of the predicted probability	0.406993	0.406993	0.406993
Un-standardized beta weight	-2.017	0.419	-0.203
Standard deviation	1.000291	1.000369	1.000360
Standardized Beta Weight	**-0.453**	**.101**	**-0.049**

Standardized beta equation for the group variables (Control, Information and Size):

1) Control Standardized Beta Weight: = (1/(1+EXP(-(LN(A2/(1-A2))+0.5*A3*A4))))-(1/(1+EXP(-(LN(A2/(1-A2))-0.5*A3*A4)))) = -.453

2) Information Standardized Beta Weight: =(1/(1+EXP(-(LN(A8/(1-A8))+0.5*A9*A10))))-(1/(1+EXP(-(LN(A8/(1-A8))-0.5*A9*A10)))) = .101

Size Standardized Beta Weight: =(1/(1+EXP(-(LN(A20/(1-A20))+0.5*A21*A22))))-(1/(1+EXP(-(LN(A20/(1-A20))-0.5*A21*A22)))) = -.049

25

The Importance of Training and its Impact on the Performance of Employees in Banking Sectors of Abu Dhabi, Dubai - UAE to Raise Efficiency: A Field Study on UAE banks

Burhan Mahmoud Awad Alomari*

Emirates College of Technology, ECT, Abu Dhabi, United Arab Emirates

Abstract

The study aims at measuring the impact of human resource management practices on creativity and innovation with the presence of competencies as an intermediary variable. The study highlights the importance of human resource management practices for UAE banks and explores the role of human resource management practices in enhancing the creativity and innovation of employees. To achieve this goal, six UAE banks were selected as a study area. A questionnaire was designed and distributed to a random sample of 150 respondents. The analytical descriptive method was used for analysis. Data analysis and testing were carried out using SPSS.

Some of the most important outcomes of this study are: Human resource management practices such as compensation and benefits, employment, empowerment and human resources planning have a positive impact on innovation. Compensation, benefits, employment, training and development, also have a positive effect on creativity. Human resource management practices have a positive impact on training. The study recommends that giving the UAE banks the priority of human resource management practices is of great importance in their dimensions according to the scale of human resource management practices that are interested in achieving innovation and creativity for employees within the banks. The further studies are suggested related to human resources management practices and creativity and innovation because of their impact on achieving competitive advantage.

Keywords: Human resources; Management; Employee performance; Training; Industrial; Banking sectors; Abu Dhabi; UAE

Introduction

The subject of the training of human resources and private managers and their development is important issue for any organization, especially banks, where the human element is the main engine of the resources of these organizations [1]. Especially, when we talk about the quality of the skills and abilities of knowledge that commensurate with the nature of the work of the organization in which it operates, and training with an effective impact on the profitability of the human element through the process of administrative efforts. It is necessary to maintain efficient work of the high strength to any level of manager and those who work under his/her supervision in terms of raising the level of skills and help to instill confidence in the hearts of workers and improve the quality of work [2].

Any organizations that do not pay attention to the subject of training or where there is no continuous improvement through training programs will find themselves in trouble as a result of the many changes that occur in the surrounding [3]. Every change requires the organization re-examination composition skills, knowledge and abilities of its human resources to fit with the new environmental requirements of all private commercial banks wherever the environment is altering [4].

A senior leader in commercial banks must be effective and the effectiveness can be measured by the performance of the leaders and managers. Therefore, the ability to align and motivate teams to drive business results is crucial to their success [5]. The Strategic Leaders training Program, through The Competing Values Framework, will challenge them to adopt a new way of thinking that will increase their impact as leaders and managers. For over 60 years the competing values of their framework has been used by the world and well-known commercial companies to drive innovation, create high-performance cultures, explore and expand into old and new markets, and improve

overall quality through the training programs to enhance their work and their staff [6]. This training program explores the critical components of effective management and leadership in order to learn how to make better decisions under pressure, improve a better and good leadership approach in increasingly complex and mixed environments like UAE, develop talent more effectively and lead with more creativity, energy, and intensity [7]. The idea of cultivating and leveraging individual and organizational capabilities will be emphasized throughout the best training program. Then, this would emerge with an action plan to help them advance their career and drive positive results in their organization wherever they are and in any administrative site [8].

Research Terms

1. Human Resources Management is working for organizations powers or human resources management. It specializes in attracting staff, selection, training, evaluation and rewarding employees. It also follows the leadership and culture of the organization to ensure its compliance with labor laws. If the staff is willing to conduct collective negotiations with human resources management, their role is the initial communication with the staff representatives (usually with trade unions).

***Corresponding author:** Burhan Mahmoud Awad Alomari, Emirates College of Technology, ECT, Abu Dhabi, HR Department, Millennium Tower, Sheikh Hamdan Street, P. O. Box: 41009, Abu Dhabi, United Arab Emirates
E-mail: burhan.alomari@ect.ac.ae

2.　Training: Whether the organization seeks to train its individuals, employed or enrolled in work, to increase knowledge, skills or abilities or ideas necessary for the performance of specific actions in accordance with its goals or it intends to change the behavior of workers through organizational procedure in order to increase and improve their efficiency and performance, especially management training of supreme departments in any institution.

3.　Banks: Commercial banks represent the largest section in commercial system sector in the second division in the sequence. The central bank proceeds out of control and monitor bank activities and affect their ability to create cash deposits. Commercial Bank was identified as an institution that deals in debt or credit and bank deposits called gets the debts of third parties and gives against which promises to pay on demand or after a short-term. This credit provided by the bank falls within its assets because it really represents it to others.

4.　Efficiency: The ability to achieve goals activates or does things properly.

5.　The performance: A set of activities performed by an individual, who reflects the level of efficiency in accomplishing the tasks and duties entrusted to him. Term productivity is known as a measure of the ability of enterprises to achieve the output of the input, also known as the possibility of achieving the largest possible amount of output from a given quantity of inputs.

6.　Emirates College of Technology which provide courses in teaching and training in the same field and other courses like Management, Human Resources and financial studies.

Emirates College of Technology was founded in the center of Abu Dhabi and it showed rapid growth and development in 1993 after receiving recognition from the Ministry of Education in the United Arab Emirates. It was launched to keep pace with developments in technology and business of modern life: it is the day to prove it as one of the oldest institutions that has a long proud history in the region.

In addition, the college not only provides bachelors' and diploma programs in many disciplines but it also prides itself by providing bachelor's programs in business, science and financial management, public relations and HRM (in English) as well as health information management and industrial management. The Emirates College of Technology gives a golden chance to its students to capture knowledge that will help them meet the challenges of the challenging developments in the local and international markets.

Emirates College of Technology is accredited by the Ministry of Higher Education and Scientific Research in the United Arab Emirates. It boasts a teaching crew that contains the authors from more than 16 different countries of the world and they are the people with a great deal of enormous contribution to the development of knowledge, professional service, teaching and supervision.

The college keeps the pace with the culture of the region. The lectures are held in three separate buildings and each one has a high number of students. The students can also choose shifts consistently within: weekend-days – morning and evening which helps them to adapt their programs according to the curriculum for the need of all students [9-12].

Emirates College is aware of the fact that the activities of students outside the auditorium are an essential part of the experience. They enjoy the college student community, a medley of environment, where they are configured for long-term friendships and integrated into a variety of social, cultural and sporting activities to enable them to develop their skills and the abilities to become downright professionals [13].

On the other hand, the programs offered as well as the future programs provide a good opportunity to the students who prefer to study in the country with a view to travelling abroad to get a diploma or bachelors' degree. Emirates College has enabled its graduates to complete their higher studies in bachelors that are furnished in the same colleges or in the local universities, Arab or Western, or in Canada, America and other countries with various programs [14].

With a platform for high-quality curriculum in addition to the body of distinctive teaching, infrastructure and facilities of the highest level, make room for students to have big dreams. It lets them share their unique talents, and makes them feel proud of being the part of a fertile culture [15].

There are several colleges and universities in Abu Dhabi and in the rest of the state of emirates that are all able to offer diverse academic programs and trainings. They enjoys a high reputation for efficiency and has copious administrative and academic competencies.

About Emirates Institute for Banking and Financial Studies which is specialized in the training of bank employees and other people of the UAE banking and financial study and also provides bachelors' in more than one specialties [16].

Emirates Institute, specifically for National Banking and Financial Studies, is a foundation that is fundamentally interested to train commercial bank employees. Aims to contribute to the strategic plans and furnishes economically in the UAE country through the development of human resource by increasing their performance through the technological process for the last several years. It has also participated in the teaching programs according to British and Canadian Academic systems and has such are put educational institutional experience process that is eligible to do the international teaching work and academic training [17]. It has progressed rapidly through the effective use advanced technologies and the evolution of this institution has been honorably recognized by the ministry of higher education and it has initiated three branches in the United Arab Emirates.

Emirates Institute for Banking and Financial Studies was founded in 1983 which provides educational programs, training courses, banking training services and financial solutions at a world-class level in three centers and it occupies a strategic planning system in Sharjah, and Abu Dhabi and Dubai. And as a part of commitment to resettlement initiative, Emirates Institute for Banking and Financial Studies in UAE centers supports UAE nationals by providing high-level training facilities and by encouraging job growth in the financial services and banking sector [18].

It was the integration of the Emirates Institute for Banking and Financial Studies worldwide with various institutes and leading universities of the world that are developing better programs and courses in the field of banking and financial services in UAE [19].

The Emirates Institute for Banking and Financial Studies has come forward in bringing about a major development in the career of thousands of students and professionals, who, working in the field of banking and finance, has been supported from trained academics and leading experts.

Emirates Institute for Banking and Financial Studies has seen significant growth over the past years, especially in terms of the number of students, trainees and academic training programs, websites and members of the faculty, staff, alumni and others.

Every year, the institute receives thousands of students and trainees who are interested in learning and training from across the UAE. It provides a wide range of educational opportunities in the banking and financial support through the experiences and research based programs and it dispenses the high-end facilities in the field in UAE [20].

Research problem

Through my work, both in teaching and management training in UAE, now and before, I strongly believe that the research problem stems from the weaknesses and deficiencies in the training programs followed by inadequate productivity in banking institutions in the UAE. According to the developments and technological changes and renewable rapid makes, it is imperative to render follow-up to the organizations and the preparation of training programs. It is feasible to limit the research problem by exploring the following questions:

1. What is the role of training in increasing the efficiency of staff performance?

2. What extent of benefit from training courses obtained by the staff?

3. What is the appropriate training period to take advantage of high efficiency training courses?

The research aims to identify the reality of the training process in productivity and banking sector in the United Arab Emirates - Abu Dhabi and Dubai and whether those institutions concerned with the development of human resources, especially the middle and upper class and the administration. It also aims to shed light on the following points:

1. Identify the convictions of those who are the in charge of the management of these institutions on the issue of training and how much importance they attach to it for the benefits of their staff.

2. Identify deficiencies or weaknesses in the existing training programs and their negative effects on the performance of employees, leaders and management, the makers of the administrative decisions.

3. To determine, if the management of these institutions follow-up with the environmental changes and take them into account when preparing for training programs.

The importance of the study

The importance of this research is the importance of the subject of training and human resource development through these things:

1. The growing value of this subject as a result of the need for training programs and the need to cope with the nature of the economic, environmental and technological changes demands that it should be treated in a befitting manner. Furthermore, the growth of a competitive mass marketing in this area and the developments in the surrounding environment so as to improve the performance of individuals and management calls for earnest handling.

2. Taking into account the subject of cost, the cost of training is much less than the cost of the negative performance of leaders and management and unqualified personnel in the long run.

Reliability and validity of the tool

The veracity of the material and the content of the tool for research questionnaire were ascertained after the thorough inspection by the supervisor of expert scientific research. In the second place it was presented for inspection to a group of specialists and experts in the field of scientific research.

Research hypothesis

In order to sniff out proper answers and solutions to the scientific problems that were raised in this research and to achieve the desired goals, the research seeks to test the validity of the following hypothesis:

The hypothesis

H1: A statistically significant relationship between human resources and training needs exists in banking sectors in the city of Abu Dhabi and Dubai.

H2: Secondly, a statistically significant relationship between human resources and defining the goals of training programs have existence in banking sectors in the city of Abu Dhabi and Dubai.

H3: Thirdly, there is a statistically significant relationship between human resources and the implementation of training in banking sectors in the city of Abu Dhabi and Dubai.

H4: Lastly, A statistically significant relationship is found between human resources and the evaluation and follow-up of the effectiveness of training in banking sectors in city of Abu Dhabi and Dubai

1. There is a statistical significance of the relationship between training and increase in the efficiency of staff performance.

2. There is a statistically significant relationship between the training period and efficiency.

3. There is statistically major link between training and the advancement of staff performance.

There are considerable differences between the training and development of the staff performance relationship and branches for this hypothesis is the following assumption:

The research variables

The research variables are shown in Figure 1.

Research Methodology

Research includes two aspects

1. The theoretical side: the adoption of the approach and descriptive analysis takes advantage of references, books and articles on the subject of the search.

2. The practical side: to ensure a field study of the reality of the training programs used by commercial banks to collect data. The information related to the data was collected through a questionnaire that was designed and distributed to the employees in a number of banks in the city of Abu Dhabi - United Arab Emirates.

Society and the research sample

Five commercial banks in the city of Abu Dhabi and the Emirates Institute for Banking and Financial Studies in Abu Dhabi, Sharjah and Dubai: banks and training centers are:

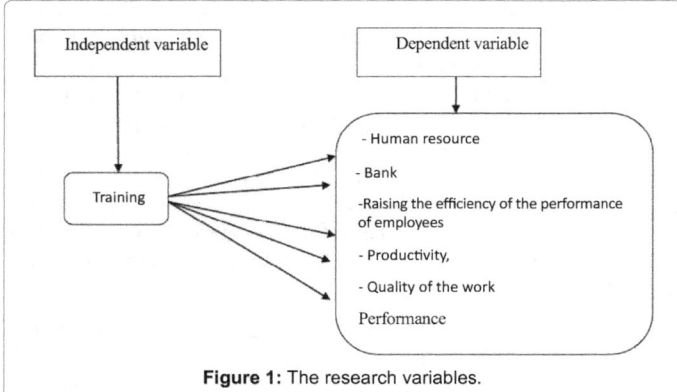

Figure 1: The research variables.

1.   (1) Union National Bank, (2) Emirates Bank, (3) Bank of Sharjah, (4) First Gulf Bank, and (5) Abu Dhabi National Bank.

2.   Emirates Institute for Banking and Financial Studies (EIBFS) and Emirate College of Technology (ECT)

Statistical analysis methods and stability of scientific research tool

The data were subjected to statistical analysis using the following methods:

Statistical and descriptive methods: (averages, standard deviation)

Statistical methods evidentiary: (Pearson correlation coefficient, test z)

The most important findings of the study revealed the following facts:

1. There is a relationship between the administrative development and all of the functional up gradation process. Transfers and operations that take place on the same administrative level between the administrative leadership, and the plans to develop for follow-up jobs in these banking institutions were selected.

2. The lack of accurate and complete information for management development plans and career development has been observed. The bank management is not getting enough information about the programs in order to help managers to let them know the importance of management development and opportunities available at management level.

3. The banks that have been subjected to the study unanimously agree that the development contributes to increase the practical and theoretical capabilities and helps acquire new job skills in the job field of the candidate. It helps them to carry out their work more efficiently.

4. Need and importance of training is not identified in a scientific way, despite the awareness of the importance of the management of the process.

5. The large number of trainees under the supervision of one coach reflects negativity on the quality of the training process.

6. Training process quality reflected positively on the quality of banking services.

7. The presence of a statistic significance of the study, effect of human resources management policies and the efficient performance of employee's were observed.

8. It was pointed out that the incentives and financial rewards in the system of the commercial banks it don't help individuals who attended the training programs. The financial incentives in previous years were much better, according to some opinions.

Data Analysis

This study aims to assess the impact of human resources in identifying training needs for bank staff, defining the goals of training programs, increasing the efficiency of the performance of the staff, the implementation of training and evaluation and follow-up the effectiveness of training in bank sectors in UAE and Abu Dhabi. Therefore, the results of the study have been presented and analyzed in this section. The study uses a descriptive analysis to describe the training needs of the responding employee, requirements and abilities through training programs. The research hypothesis were presented and tested by ANOVA and it was used to measure the differences between the sample groups, Pearson Correlation was used to explore the correlation between the study variables (dependent and independent variables), and Stepwise multiple regression was used to test the hypothesis.

Stability of the study tools

Stability tools of this study have been tested by using Cranach's alpha, in Table 1 that shows that the values are higher than 0.64 which mean that the study tool is stable. Dimension alpha's value Identifies that the training need is 0.79. It also defines that the need of training program is 0.82 that implies the implementation of training programs is 0.74 and the follow-up of training effectiveness 0.83, while the total is 0.86.

Table 1 indicates that 79.17% of the study samples were male and the remaining (20.83%) respondents were female. The study findings show that the most of the bank staff of the listed banks are from men and the reason might be to the job nature of these sectors. It also shows that 40.05% of the samples are older than 45 years, and 35.37% aged from 35- and less than 45, which gives us 24.76% between the ages of 25 – and less than 35, and 3.63% under the age of 25. The findings of this table show that the majority of the respondents lie in the third level, few of the respondents were from the second level which indicates that 39.05% of samples are holding a Bachelor degree, 30,4% of them hold a master and, 20.95% of respondents with a college diploma, and 8.57% of them hold a high school diploma , and 0.95% of them hold a PhD. So the most respondents had a bachelor degree. It means that most of the workers who work in this sector are graduates and this is a clear evidence to validate the current study.

Stability of the study tools

Table 2 shows that 61.17% of the study samples are male and the remaining (38.83%) respondents are female. These findings show that the most employees in the listed banks are men and the reason might be the job nature of the sector. It also showed that 39.05% of the sample are equal to or older than 45 years, and 32.38% aged from 35- and less than 45, 24.76% are between the ages of 25 – and less than 35, 3.81% are under the age of 25. The findings of this table reveal that the majority of

No	Dimension	Alpha's value
1	Identify training needs	0.79
2	Identify the Training programs needed	0.82
3	The implementation of training	0.74
4	The follow up of training effectiveness.	0.83
	Total	0.86

Table 1: Characteristics of the respondents.

the respondents lie in the third level, few of the respondents are from the second level and it indicates that 39.05% of samples are holders of a bachelor degree, 30,49% of them have a diploma, 20.95% of respondents are with a high school diploma, and 8.57% of them posses a master's degree, and 0.95% of them hold a PhD. So the most respondents who work in firms are graduates and this is a clear evidence for the validity of the study. This Table 2 clarifies that 52.38% of the of the respondents have an experience of 15 years or more, 19.05% of respondents have less than 5 years experience, and 17.14% have experience range from 11 to 15 years., and 11.43% of them ranging in experience between 5-10 years. The findings showed that the least respondents are from the last level. Majority of the respondents whose experience is more than 15 years, illuminate that there are 63.81% of the sample of the study is staff, 28.57% are Chiefs,5.71% are serving as Deputy Director and 1.90% of those serving as Director.

Table 3 shows that's there is a statistically noteworthy link between human resources management and training needs in banks in the city of Abu Dhabi and Dubai. As Table 3 shows that, with the exception of paragraphs 2 and 6, all paragraphs got arithmetic mean greater than 3.00 and got significant observation level less than 0.05, i.e., all those paragraphs are of statistical significance. Paragraph No. 5 came first with 4.17 arithmetic mean, which means that the greater impact of the human resources management is in the area of providing the requirements for training. Paragraph 3 which measures human resources management is to assist and identify bank training needs in the short term that came in last place among the statistically accepted paragraphs 3.65 arithmetic mean. Paragraph 2, which measures the

help of human resources management in identifying required training needs in the long run, although it got a arithmetic mean greater than 3.00 but it got an observation level greater than 0.05, i.e., it's not statistically significant. Paragraph 6, which measures human resources management, is to assist and identify individual needs which got arithmetic mean less than 3.00 and it is not statistically significance. All paragraphs unanimously got (3.51) arithmetic mean, which is greater than 3.00, and 0.00 observation levels, which is less than 0.05, i.e. Statistically significant relationship between human resources management and training needs in bank sectors in both Abu Dhabi and Dubai.

Table 4 shows there is a statistically significant relationship between human resources and defining the goals of training programs in bank sectors in the city of Abu Dhabi and Dubai. As Table 4 shows that, with the exception of paragraphs 8, all paragraphs got arithmetic average greater than 3.00 and got significant observation level less than 0.05, i.e., all those paragraphs are of statistical significance. Paragraph No. 9, which measures human resources management help in analyzing and processing goals to determine the quality of training programs came first with 3.93 arithmetic mean. Paragraph 12, which measures latest software that are suitable and appropriate in terms of the objectives that have been previously selected for training programs in Abu Dhabi and Dubai bank sectors come in the last place, among the statistically accepted paragraphs with 3.82 arithmetic average. Paragraph 8, which measure the work of the human resources management to determine the goals through training programs, although it got an arithmetic mean greater than 3.00 but it got an observation level greater than 0.05 which is not statistically significant. All paragraphs without exception got 3.74 with arithmetic mean, which is greater than 3.00, and 0.00 observation levels, which is less than 0.05. The data show a statistically significant relationship between human resources management and defining the goals of the training programs in the banking sectors in both Abu Dhabi and Dubai with a relationship between a training programs and its competence.

Table 5 shows that there is a statistically significant relationship between human resource management and the implementation of training in banking sectors in the city of Abu Dhabi and Dubai. Table 5 shows that, with the exception of paragraphs 20 and 22, all paragraphs got arithmetic mean greater than 3.00 and got significant observation level less than 0.05, i.e., all those paragraphs are of statistical significance. Paragraph No. 13 measures the work of human resource management to maintain training programs that come first with (4.03) arithmetic mean. Paragraph 19 have a written guide for the procedures on how to use the human resources management system in enhancing training programs that comes in the last place among the statistically accepted paragraphs with 3.60 arithmetic mean. Paragraph no 20 measure the difficulties in dealing with the human resources when implementing training programs in banking sectors and it got 3.00 with arithmetic mean but it's not statistically significant. Paragraph

Personal Dimension	Variable	Frequency	Percentage %
Gender	Male	56	61.17
	Female	44	38.83
	less than 25	6	4.11
	25 – less than 35	28	24.76
	35 – less than 45	36	32.38
	Equal or more than 45	43	39.05
	Secondary	25	20.95
	Diploma	33	30.48
	BS	43	39.05
	Master	10	8.57
	PhD	3	0.57
	less than 5	21	19.05
	5-10	14	11.43
	11-15	19	17.14
	More or equal 15	49	52.38
	Supervisor	4	1.90
	Chief supervisor	6	5.71
	managers and staff	30	28.75
		67	63.81

Table 2: Description of the characteristics of a study sample.

	Phrases	Arithmetic average	Standard deviation	t Value	Significance observation level
1	Human resources management help in defining that the training needs at the unit level	3.74	1.16	5.21	
2	Human resources management helps in identifying banks training needs in the long term.	3.06	1.54	0.32	
3	Human resources management helps in identifying training needs for the short term in the bank sectors.	3.65	1.09	4.90	
4	Human resources management helps in identifying training requirements according to the job description of the bank sectors.	3.97	0.74	10.75	
5	Human resources management provides training requirements for bank employees.	4.17	0.64	14.42	
6	Human resources management helps in identifying individual needs to do the required job in the bank.	2.43	1.30	-3.63	

Table 3: Arithmetic averages, standard deviation, value and significant observation level in defining training.

	Phrases	Arithmetic average	Standard deviation	t Value	Significance observation level
7	The training program is linked to the practical work in the bank	3.84	1.16	6.48	0.00
8	I reflected my participation in the training program on the practical application in the bank.	3.02	1.52	0.08	0.74
9	I developed my knowledge and career evolved in the bank as a result of the training	3.93	1.04	8.46	0.00
10	My participation in the training program helped me to improve my performance and career at the bank.	3.91	1.07	7.82	0.00
11	Increasing the size of my achievements at my work as a result of practical training programs already taken.	3.89	1.10	7.44	0.00
12	The evaluation of the training of equipment (Software) consider appropriate in terms of the objectives that have been developed and previously selected for organization training programs	3.82	1.16	6.48	0.00
Total		3.74	0.80	8.32	0.00

Table 4: Arithmetic average, standard deviation, show the value and observation level related to relationship between training, goals and performance efficiency of the bank staff.

	Phrases	Arithmetic average	Standard deviation	t Value	Significance observation level
13	Human resources management assist training programs and the innovation and the renewal and modernization in work field	4.03	1.02	9.34	0.00
14	Human resources management and itsimplementation based on identified training methods and courses leads us to the continued evaluation of the performance of the bank.Works.	3.84	1.11	6.93	0.00
15	Human resources management increase staff efficiency through training programs to became aware through training programs on some legislation and administrative laws that should be taken in the banking system.	3.65	1.18	5.16	0.00
16	Human resources management increase bank efficiency through training programs have helped us in achieving our life skills that fall within the banking work and banking systems.	3.75	1.04	6.83	0.00
17	Human resources management increase the bank productivity through the implementation of training programs helped improve our relationships and the treatment with superiors and colleagues in the bank which I work with.	3.65	1.21	4.94	0.00
18	Equipment (Hardware) used in training programs to achieve the reason of training implementation and contributed to the improvement and orientation towards the banking profession.	3.74	1.09	6.16	0.00
19	There is a written guide to use procedures on how to use the human resources management in training programs and to increase staff efficiency through training considered in the banking system.	3.60	1.22	4.51	0.00
20	There is no difficulty in dealing with the human resources management when implementing training programs to increase bank staff efficiency.	2.73	1.57	-1.64	0.00
21	Human resources management affects the staff commitment toward training programs to increase the bank productivity	3.98	1.07	8.59	0.10
22	There is no resistance from some staff to the update on the applied training programs toward Equipment (Hardware) used in training programs to achieve the reason of training implementation and contributed to the improvement and orientation in the banking profession.	2.92	1.44	-0.67	0.00
	Total	3.57	0.68	7.98	0.50

Table 5: The arithmetic average, standard deviation, the value and private observation level related to setting the goals of training programs.

no. 22, which measure the resistance from some staff to the applied training programs update, got 3.00 with arithmetic mean. However, it's not statistically significant. All paragraphs with one accord got 3.57 with arithmetic mean, which is greater than 3.00, and 0.00 observation level, and less than 0.05. It reveals that there is a statistically significant relationship between human resources and implementation of training in the banking sectors in Abu Dhabi and Dubai.

Table 6 shows that there is a statistically remarkable association between human resources and the follow up training evaluation for effectiveness of banking employees in the city of Abu Dhabi and Dubai. Table 6 also shows, with the exception of paragraphs 23, 29 and 34, that all paragraphs got arithmetic mean that is greater than 3.00 and got significant observation level less than 0.05. All of these paragraphs are of statistical significance. Paragraph no 30 shows the extent to which human resources adopt a methodology in the employment of trainees which come first with (3.98) arithmetic mean. Paragraph 27 highlights that human resources management organizes training programs to fit bank staff in the last place among the statistically accepted paragraphs with 3.59 arithmetic mean. Paragraph 23 measures the relationship between training and improving the performance of employees. One of the elements considered by human resource is continuously providing periodic reports monitoring training effectiveness. It got a 3.00 arithmetic mean which is not statistically significant On the

other hand, paragraph no 29, measures human resources adapting a competitive program for bank staff to fill posts for the future and making a competitive and effective program for staff to fill job posts with (3.00) arithmetic mean which is not statistically significant. Paragraph 34 measuresthe standard tools of monitoring staff behavior at work after implementing the training programs and it got 3.00 with arithmetic mean which is not statistically significant. All paragraphs, in complete agreement got 3.34 with arithmetic mean. It is greater than 3.00 and 0.00 observation level, which is less than 0.05, that shows that there is a statistically significant relationship between human resources and the evaluation and follows up of training efficiency in Abu Dhabi and Dubai banks.

Research result and finding

In addition to the descriptive analysis that has been applied in order to understand better characteristics of the study, some statistical tests were also used to examine and explain the relation between the independent variable (training) and dependent variables, such as Human recourses, Banks, Raising the efficiency of the performance of employees and Productivity,

Following is a review of the results:

1. There is a statistically significant relationship between training

	Phrases	Arithmetic average	Standard deviation	t Value	Significance observation level
23	The relationship between training and improving the performance of employees one of the elements consider by human resource management	1.95	1.46	-6.33	0.00
24	Standards to measure the effectiveness of training one of the concerns of human resource management	3.84		6.88	0.00
25	People working on the human resources management have different specialization to deal with training in the bank.	3.66	1.19	4.89	0.00
26	human resources personnel have a periodically training to develop abilities capabilities, and bank staff skills	3.71	1.04	6.04	0.00
27	The human resources management organized training programs to fit bank staff.	3.59	1.22	4.31	0.00
28	training courses increases job satisfaction for staff working in the bank	3.71	1.11	5.64	0.00
29	human resources management making a competitive program for bank staff to fill posts in the future	1.88	1.21	-8.08	0.00
30	human resources management follow a certain methodology in recruiting trainee to fit the bank job responsibilities	3.98	1.09	7.86	0.00
31	Equipment (Hardware) are appropriate for training organization to fit training programs needed by the bank	3.90	1.26	6.88	0.00
32	Equipment (Software) are appropriate and available in the for training organization to help you learn all what you need from your training courses.	3.90	1.26	6.32	0.00
33	Human resources management can detect the deficiency and difficulties that the bank suffers could help you to solve problems	3.88	1.06	7.29	0.00
34	Is the use of the human resource standard tools will compete to monitor working staff behavior and attitudes after implementing the training courses.	1.92	1.31	-7.25	0.00
	Total	3.34	0.55	5.20	0.00

Table 6: There is a statistically remarkable association between human resources and the follow up training evaluation for effectiveness of banking employees in the city of Abu Dhabi and Dubai.

and human resource needs in banks in Abu Dhabi and Dubai cities. The study identifies training needs at the banking sector and helps to identify the needs of training in the banks selected in the study for short term, commensurate with the job description, and provides conditions for training. However, it does not help to identify training needs of the banks in the long term, and does not help to determine individual needs.

2. There is a statistically significant relationship between training and defining the goals of training programs in the banking sector in the city Abu Dhabi and Dubai, where this system works to clarify goals through human resource and training programs, it also helps to analyze and process and goals to determine the quality of the training programs. Moreover, it helps to achieve staff training requirements, and the used of equipment (Hardware) is considered appropriate in terms of the objectives that have been developed and previously selected for bank training programs. Nonetheless, it does not work on measuring goals through training programs and human resources.

3. There is a statistically notable link between training and human resources and the implementation of training in the city of Abu Dhabi and Dubai banks. Here, it manages the implementation of training programs that are based on the ways of training which were originally identified to increase the efficiency of bank staff through necessary training programs. It increases the efficiency of the banks through training and expands the productivity. The equipment and hardware used in training programs help in the implementation of effective training. There is a written guide for the procedures used by training institution and how to use the system to practically affect the obligation of staff through training programs. However, there is a difficulty in dealing with the system while implementing the training program through human resource, and there is resistance by some of the staff members to update that training programs when applied by the human resource department.

4. There is a statistically significant relationship between training and human resources management and training evaluation and the follow up of the effectiveness of the banking sectors in the city of Abu Dhabi and Dubai. The place where the banking system provides standards for measuring the effective training to the working personnel who have different specializations, demonstrates better output. Periodical training has a vital role to develop the abilities and skills of the workers. Indispensable training programs for the organization increase job satisfaction for bank staff who learn the system to use new methodologies in the training centers like hardware, equipment and software and so on used in a way with the requirements of the training programs, and used the software to be appropriate with the requirements of the training programs through the human resource department, the system of human resource discovers there are difficulties and mistakes that the banks suffer from. But the human resource system and the training department does not provide regular or special reports that cover monitoring training effectiveness and does not work competitively to employ staff to vacant posts; the human resource system and training department do not use standard tools to continue working behavior after the implementation of training programs implemented.

5. There is a statistically significant connection between the training and human resources management productivities. If the training doesn't pay attention to the quality of service, and does not give adequate instructions to the employees, its effect is nullified. If it does not address the challenging situation created by economic problems in the country these days, it shows a lack of familiarity with the regulations and laws and its effect is reduced to the point of nothing. Furthermore, it generates the ignorance of the advantages and disadvantages of banking products, frequent inconvenience of sales representatives who try to force the customer to buy a new product in order to obtain the maximum amount of the commissions.

6. On the other hand, for self-development the bank's academy

is working to support the employees in the improvement of performance and enhancement of skills and abilities through a series of innovative and sophisticated ways.

Recommendations

1. Banks must provide personal development plans along with skills enhancement programs to double the use of time. The trainees must be exposed to learn communication skills and a chance to plentifully communicate with others. Training should impart better presentation skills, and workshops should refine professional development to enhance the intercommunication skills to support the participants to converse effectively with their managers about their career plans. They must be encouraged to take responsibility for the development of their careers in a manner that fits their individual needs. They can works on the support of experienced leaders in the development of a clear vision and an integrated hands-on in-service training. The training on project management supports the understanding of the definition and the use of project management as well as the role and responsibilities of the strategic projects scams.

2. Banks must identify the tasks and duties of each employee and it should be determined before sending any staff to the training courses which must correspond to his nature of job. This practice can help in achieving optimum results from training courses.

3. Banks in UAE must consider training conditions like training time, location, facilities and materials available and the number of trainees in each batch.

4. Banks must work in improving skills and performance through taking into account the age, sex, educational level and experience of the trainees.

5. A bank must invest in the development of the skills of its workers. There are a number of ways to train the staff, but the need for more attention by the commercial banks need to pay more attention to improve the career bring out the best performance in creative ways conforming the needs of customers or clients.

References

1. Al-Azzawi, Abbas J (2016) The Development of Human Resources Management, Concept, Strategy. Organizational Location, Oman, Dar Yazouri, Jordan.

2. Armstrong M (2006) Strategic Human Resource Management: A Guide to Action. London: Kogan Page.

3. Michael A (2006) Performance Management: Key Strategies and Practical guide lines. (3rd edn), Kogan Page.

4. Atkinson J, Feather N (1966) Theory of Achievement Motivation. New York, NY: Wiley.

5. Banjoko SA (2010) Human resources management. Lagos: Saban Publishers.

6. Egwurudi PC (2008) Job Satisfaction: Effect on job characteristics. Unpublished Mcs Dissertation University of Lagos, Nigeria.

7. Evans MG (2006) Organisational behavior: The central role of motivation. Journal of Management 12: 203.

8. Eze N (2009) Sources of Motivation among Nigerian managers. Journal of Social Psychology 125: 341-345.

9. Jibowo AA (2007) Effect of Motivators and hygiene factors on job performance among extension workers in the former.

10. Kumar K (2009) Linking the 'Big Five' Personality Domains to Organizational Citizenship Behavior.

11. Gary K (2008) Fundamentals of Human Resource Management. International Edition, Rearson.

12. Mani V (2010) Development of Employee Satisfaction index scorecard. European.

13. Miner J (2006) Organizational Behavior 4: From Theory to Practice. Armonk, NY: M.E. Sharpe.

14. Tom R, Adrian W (2008) Contemporary Human Resource Management: Text and Cases. (3rd edn), Pearson.

15. Hadjim TJ, Mohsen VA, Hashim AF (2006) Human Resource Management, Strategic, Integrated Entrance. Oman, Warraq for Publishing and Distribution, Jordan.

16. Kamdar D, Dyne LV (2007) The Joint Effects of Personality and Workplace Social Exchange Relationships in Predicting Task Performance and Citizenship Performance. Journal of Applied Psychology 92:1286-1298.

17. Torrington D, Hall L, Taylor S (2008) Fundamentals of Human Resource Management Managing People at Work. Pearson, USA.

18. Tzeng H (2002) The influence of nurses' working motivation and job satisfaction on intention to quit: an empirical investigation in Taiwan. International Journal of Nursing Studies 39: 867-878.

19. Wood S, Menezes L (1998) High commitment management in the UK: evidence from the Workplace Industrial Relations Survey and Employers' Manpower and Skills Survey. Human Relations 51: 485-515.

20. Yazdani BO, Yaghoubi NM, Giri ES (2011) Factors Affecting the Empowerment of Employees. European Journal of Social Sciences 20: 267-274.

26

Service Quality Gap Analysis: Comparative Analysis of Public and Private Sector Banks in India

Sai Akhilesh P*[1] and Vinay CV[2]

[1]*School of Management, NIT Warangal, Telangana, India*
[2]*Andhra Pradesh Productivity Council, Hyderabad, Telangana, India*

Abstract

As economic globalization intensifies competition and creates a climate of constant change, winning and keeping customers has become all the more important. Now a days banks have realized that cost of attracting a new customer is much more than retaining existing customers, so banks are more emphasizing upon customer satisfaction. These days customers demand for top quality services and products served with minimum wait time, so customers prefer techno- savvy banks as well bankers. This paper attempts to make a comparative analysis of level of customer satisfaction towards the services provided by YES Bank and UCO bank. The study has been conducted in Warangal city based on questionnaire method and a sample of each 30 customers and employees of respective banks has been selected using convenient sampling method. The servqual model analysis is conducted with its all five service dimensions and Gap analysis. This study concludes that private sector banks are more preferred by majority of the customer as they emphasize more upon relationship building with their clients and are better equipped with modern infrastructure as compared to public sector banks.

Keywords: Banks; Quality service; Customer satisfaction; The servqual model; Gap analysis

Introduction

The banking sector in India plays a significant role and it's rapidly growing from few decades. Banks will provide a variety of services ranging from opening a savings account, current account, internet banking, retail banking, financial consulting, providing loans, locker facilities, foreign money transfer etc. The banks have to satisfy the customers belonging to all different classes. A study on the comparative analysis of services of private and public sector bank and customer's satisfaction is very important. Such analysis will provide the banks with a quantitative and qualitative estimate of their services as perceived by their customers. Servqual Model is chosen in our study to assess the service quality and customer satisfaction. Servqual can be used to measure service quality in variety of service settings and can be used to compare with the competitors. This model of service quality identifies the reasons for any gaps between customer expectations and perceptions. The banks are chosen to identify the service quality gaps and customer perception and satisfaction in which Servqual model will fit to do the better gap analysis and to identify the factors for poor quality service.

Literature Review

The Servqual model was developed by a group of American authors, Parsu Parasuraman, Valarie Zeithaml and Len Berry in1988 for measuring the customer expectations of service quality in term of the five dimensions. Many of the management researchers has given their views in terms of service quality, customer service etc. The four dimensions of service quality namely, attitude, competence, tangibles and convenience are very important in the view of the customer's differentiation and also the bank managers should enhance the skills and attitudes of the employees to initiate a better customer-service culture which is revealed by the Koushiki Choudhury [1] in their research. Sandip Gosh Hasra and Srivastava [2] also suggested about the attention factor in their study that the bank should pay the attention to dimension of service quality and assurance-empathy to increase the loyalty to a company, willingness to pay, customer commitment. The public sector banks are facing the poor service quality in terms of tangibility, lack of responsiveness, empathy and on the other hand private sector banks are far better which is noted by the Sudesh [3] and also his study revealed that management of banks should pay more attention to the potential failure points and to provide better solutions to the customer problems. The Expectation and perception of service quality in old and new generation banks was observed by Joshua and Koshi [4,5] in their research study that the performance of all service quality dimensions of the new generation banks are better than old generation banks.

Servqual model

The main instrument in analyzing the service quality is "The gap model" of service or Servqual model which is developed by Parshuraman et al. [6]. This model is mainly used to determine average gap score (between customer's perceptions and expectations) for each service attribute and also to evaluate the company's service quality.

The five servqual dimensions are:

- **Tangibles**-Appearance of physical facilities, equipment, personnel, and communication materials.

- **Reliability**-Ability to perform the promised service dependably and accurately.

- **Responsiveness**-Willingness to help customers and provide prompt service.

- **Assurance**-Knowledge and courtesy of employees and their ability to convey trust and confidence.

- **Empathy**-Caring, individualized attention the firm provides its customers.

***Corresponding author:** Sai Akhilesh P, School of Management, NIT Warangal, Warangal-506004, Telangana India, E-mail: akhibt@gmail.com

The study has few of the limitations like the project is limited to 2 months only. The sample size is small and people are unlikely to provide accurate answers for the collection of data.

Methodology

The SERVQUAL model questionnaire was to evaluate the customer's service quality gap analysis and data is collected through

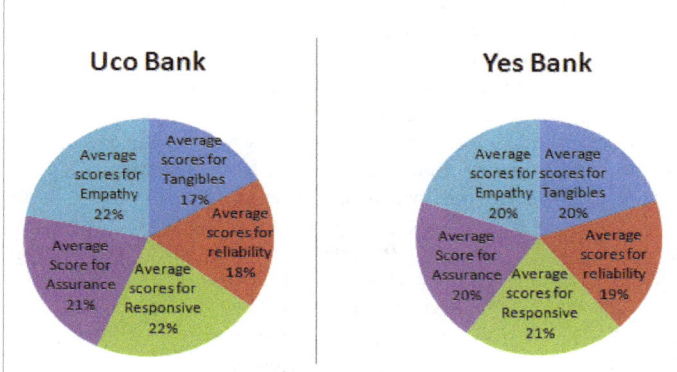

Figure 1: Service Quality differences between UCO Bank and Yes Bank.

survey in the selected Private and public sector bank in Warangal district in Andhra Pradesh. The data is collected for customers' expectations and customers' perception each consisting of 21 questions of 5 dimensions. The respondents were asked to rate their expectations and perceptions of service offered by the respective banks. A seven point Likert scale is linked to this study to evaluate the service quality. The useful survey data is also collected from the related books of marketing, magazines, catalogs, newspapers and also from the Internet.

Results and Discussions

The Table 3 represents the attributes having the highest gap scores observed from the Table 1 and the Unweighted gap score from the Table 2. There exist highest gap between customer expectations and perceptions of bank services in these attributes. This indicates the customers are not satisfied with the few of the services in these attributes. Hence it was observed that the more gaps are identified in empathy dimensions in the UCO bank. The Table 6 represents the attributes having the highest gap scores observed from the Table 4 and the Unweighted gap score from the Table 5. There exist highest gap between customer expectations and perceptions of bank services in these attributes. This indicates that the customers are not satisfied with the few of the services in these attributes. Hence it was observed that the more gaps are identified in Responsiveness dimensions in the YES bank. Figure 1 shows the Pie chart explaining

Statements	Exception	Perception	Service gap (E-P)
Tangibility	6		
Modern looking equipment	6.3	4.6	1.4
Physical Facility	6	3.6	2.7
Employees are well dressed	6.2	4.4	1.6
Materials are visually appealing		4.1	2.1
		Avg Gap score	1.95
Reliability	6.2		
Delivers service at promised time	6	4	2.2
Interest in solving problem	6	3.5	2.5
Perform service right first time	6.5	4.9	1.1
Follows the promised time	6.3	3.8	2.7
Maintain error free records		4	2.3
		Avg Gap score	2.16
Responsiveness	6.3		
Tell you about performance of service	6.9	3.9	2.4
gives prompt service	6.73	3.7	3.2
Willingness to help	6.8	4.4	2.33
Not busy to respond queires		4.2	2.6
		Avg Gap score	2.6325
Assurance	6.9		
Instills confidence	6.6	3.3	3.6
Safe transactions	6.2	4	2.6
Employees are consistently courteous	6.1	3.2	3
Employees have enough knowledge		5.2	0.9
		Avg Gap score	2.525
Empathy	6.9		
Gives individual attention	6.6	3.2	3.7
Conveinent operating hours	6.3	4.2	2.4
Gives personal attention	6.3	4.2	2.1
Best interest in heart	6.3	3.6	2.7
Understand customer's specific needs		4.1	2.2
		Avg Gap score	2.62

Analysis of Public Sector Bank- UCO Bank

Table 1: Gap Analysis Score- UCO Bank.

NO.	Dimensions	Gap scores
	Average scores for Tangibles	
1	Average scores for reliability	2
2	Average scores for Responsiveness	2.1
3	Average Score for Assurance	2.6
4	Average scores for Empathy	2.5
5	TOTAL	2.6
	Average Unweighted Score	11.8

Table 2: Average Gap Score of UCO Bank.

No.	Attributes	Dimensions	Gap scores
1	Gives individual attention	Empathy	3.7
2	Instills Confidence	Assurance	3.6
3	Gives prompt service	Responsiveness	3.2
4	Best interest in Heart	Empathy	2.7
5	Physical Facility	Tangibility	2.7

Table 3: Highest Gap Scores of UCO Bank

Statements	Expectation	Perception	Service gap(e-p)
Tangibility			
Modern looking equipment	6.4	5.1	1.3
Physical Facility	6.5	5	1.5
Employees are well dressed	6.5	4.7	1.8
Materials are visually appealing	6.4	5	1.4
		Avg Gap score	1.5
Reliability			
Delivers service at promised time	6.5	4.7	1.8
Interest in solving problem	6.3	4.9	1.4
Perform service right first time	6.3	5.3	1
Follows the promised time	6.7	5	1.7
Maintain error free records	6.6	5.2	1.4
		Avg Gap score	1.46
Responsiveness			
Tell you about performance of service	6.6	5	1.6
gives prompt service	6.9	5	1.9
Willingness to help	6.9	5.3	1.6
Not busy to respond queires	6.8	5.3	1.5
		Avg Gap score	1.65
Assurance			
Instills confidence	6.9	4.9	2
Safe transactions	6.6	4.7	1.9
Employees are consistently courteous	6.5	4.9	1.6
Employees have enough knowledge	6.1	5.5	0.6
		Avg Gap score	1.525
Empathy			
Gives individual attention	7	5.5	1.5
Convenient operating hours	6.8	5	1.8
Gives personal attention	6.3	5.2	1.1
Best interest in heart	6.5	4.7	1.8
Understand customer's specific needs	6.4	5	1.4
		Avg Gap score	1.52

Analysis of Private sector bank- YES BANK

Table 4: Gap Analysis Score-Yes Bank.

the Service Quality differences between UCO Bank and Yes Bank.

Conclusion

Banks have to understand the changing needs of customers, their aspirations and expectations to create a brand value. Banks should also have a strong customer relationship management system that would indicate the worth of the customer and be able to understand their needs while interacting with them, so as to cross sell their products. This research survey concludes the service quality gay analysis is having more gaps between customer expectation and perception of service quality in the UCO bank. The bank has to reduce this gap giving individual personal attention to understand the customer specific needs and in the YES bank more gap is identified for Responsiveness. To manage growth and continuity in business, human resources play an important role. The new generation private sector banks and foreign banks enjoy a lead in this regard when compared to PSBs and old generation private sector banks. Banks may follow a feedback system to know the customer expectations for improving the level of customer satisfaction to maximum level. Remarks on service responsiveness and empathy should be continuously obtained from customers. This will enhance their service quality to a large extent.

No.	Dimensions	Gap scores
1	Average scores for Tangibles	1.5
2	Average scores for reliability	1.4
3	Average scores for Responsiveness	1.6
4	Average Score for Assurance	1.5
5	Average scores for Empathy	1.5
	TOTAL	7.5
	Average Unweighted Score	1.5

Table 5: Average Gap Score of Yes Bank.

No.	Attributes	Dimensions	Gap scores
1	Instills confidence	Assurance	2
2	gives Service	Responsiveness	1.9
3	Safe Transactions	Responsiveness	1.9
4	Employees are well dressed	Tangibility	1.8
5	Delivers service at promised time	Reliability	1.8

Table 6: Highest Gap Scores of Yes Bank.

Acknowledgement

The author was thankful for the guidance and support from the Professors and other staff of the School of Management, NIT Warangal for providing the necessary facilities for the preparation of the paper and supporting for completion of the research article. The research article is a result of the Quarter system based Academic Curriculum Mini Projects in the NIT Warangal.

Conflict of Interest

The manuscript represents the valid work and I hereby confirm that the disclosure made above are complete and correct to the best of my information and belief. I shall not be participating in the discussion and decision making of this matter. The author certifies that they have NO Affiliations or involvement in any organization or entity with any Conflicts of interest in the subject matter or materials discussed in this manuscript.

References

1. Choudhury k (2007) Service quality dimensionality: A study of the Indian banking sector. Journal of Asia-Pacific Business 8: 21-38.

2. Chandrakala S (2009) Effective role of CRM in Banking Sector. Banking Finance.

3. Sudesh (2007) Service quality in banks-A study in Haryana and Chandigarh. NICE Journal Business 2: 55-65.

4. SERQUAL model, from http://www.scribd.com/doc/25356471/Servqual-Model

5. Al-Fazwan (2005) Assessing Service Quality in a Saudi Bank. Journal of King Saud University 18: 101-115.

6. Service quality model from http://www.slideshare.net/anujtoma/service-quality-servqual-model.

27

Management Accounting Systems in New Zealand Regional Family Businesses: Organisational Identity and Strategic Alignment

Julia Wu[1]*, Ahsan Habib[2] and Joy Kuhns[3]

[1]*Department of Accounting & Information Systems, College of Business & Law, University of Canterbury, New Zealand*
[2]*School of Accountancy, Massey University, Auckland, New Zealand*
[3]*Ara Institute, Christchurch Campus, New Zealand*

Abstract

This paper explores how and why some small and medium size family businesses can survive in an environment that is full of uncertainties. We content that family businesses have an inherent resilience, constructed through its organisational identity that may render continuous competitive advantages and enable family businesses to meet the challenges and to take the opportunities embedded in turbulent conditions. Based on thirteen interviews of family businesses' owners and managers, we found that the constitution of family business as an organisational identity denotes the strategic choices.

Keywords: Management accounting; Family business; Strategy; Interview; Organisational identity theory

Introduction

The main message of our paper is that family businesses have an inherent resilience, constructed through its organisational identity that may render continuous competitive advantages and enable family businesses to meet the challenges and to take the opportunities embedded in turbulent conditions. In turn, the ability to identify and react to those opportunities and challenges is attributable to how family businesses utilise management accounting information to assist their strategic decision making.

This study draws on the theoretical perspectives of organisational identity [1,2] and strategic management accounting [3,4] to explore the dynamics of family businesses. While these theoretical frameworks are rooted in and have usually been referred to in the context of large and highly professional firms, we believe they are even more relevant to family businesses. Collectively, the family members, non-family employees and other stakeholders constitute the organisational identity (the meaning of who they are or are not) of 'family business'. The construction of such organisational identity is an ongoing process of symbolic interactions conducted internally within the family businesses, and externally with suppliers, customers and the wider social community. The unique family component of this organisational identity may create a competitive advantage for these businesses that their non-family businesses do not have. Strategic business intelligence, i.e., strategic management accounting information, can assist family businesses to utilise their competitive advantage in surviving and succeeding in turbulent environments.

Drawing on Rubin and Rubin's [5] responsive interview model, we interviewed 13 Family business owners and managers who told stories of their businesses. Our interview participants are all from the Canterbury and Tasman regions, and are located in the central-east and north of South Island. A significant backdrop to our research is the earthquakes that have affected these regions[1]. It has been long recognised that family businesses strive for non-financial goals [6,7].

Many suggest that because of the pursuit of family-oriented objectives, it is unrealistic to assume that family businesses priorities a profit-maximising agenda [8]. Drawing on qualitative interview data, we argue that family businesses can evoke the 'family' and 'business' aspects as well as to embrace the founders/owners' entrepreneurial and leadership perspective in their organisational identity. Therefore, family businesses owners and managers can balance their vision of business performance and family values in setting their strategic goals. Our interview data reveal that although many systems were informal, these family businesses utilise management accounting information to assist in sustaining their strategic position in their competitive environment. We contend that instead of a traditionally emphasised 'planning and control' approach toward incremental growth, the fundamental strategic concern of family businesses is how to assist these firms in being flexible to react to both opportunities and challenges embedded in their external environment.

Our paper aims to utilise an alternative theoretical underpinning to discuss the dynamics of family businesses supported by insightful qualitative evidence. It is the hope that our research will contribute to the wellbeing of family businesses and be of value to practitioners who aspire to a career in a family business. We also aim to shed light on the practical value of theory. Our findings are, therefore, useful for academics, professional consultants, advisors and regulators.

The remainder of the paper proceeds as follows. Section 2 summarises the related literature on organisation identity, strategic management accounting and their relevance to family businesses. The following Section 3 explains the research design choices including the data collection and approach used in its analysis. The main findings are presented in Section 4. We conclude the paper by summarising the

---

[1]An earthquake occurred in Christchurch on 22 February 2011 at 12:51 p.m. local time and registered 6.3 on the Richter scale. The earthquake caused widespread damage across Canterbury, killing 185 people. Christchurch's central city and eastern suburbs were among the worst affected, with damage to buildings where the infrastructure had already been weakened by the magnitude 7.1 Canterbury earthquake of 4 September 2010 and its aftershocks.

*Corresponding author: Julia Wu, Department of Accounting and Information Systems, College of Business and Law, University of Canterbury, Private Bag 4800, Christchurch 8041, New Zealand, E-mail: julia.wu@canterbury.ac.nz

practical and academic implications of our findings and ideas for future research.

Literature Review and Theoretical Underpinning

Our literature review does not intend to rehash the extant literature from both a theoretical and empirical perspective to distinguish family businesses from their non-family counterparts. In recent years, family business research studies based Socioemotional Wealth theory draw scholar's attention to the behavioural aspects and strategic choices made by these firms [9]. Zellweger et al. [10] point out that SEW literature touches on an identity-based rationale of decision making, but surprisingly very little further development in the research literature links the organisational identity of family businesses with their behaviours.

Following this view, we provide a possible alternative theoretical underpinning of family business is the organisational identity. The uniqueness of family businesses that are embedded in this organisational identity fits well with the concept of competitive advantage articulated in the strategic management literature. We start our literature review with an introduction of the organisational identity theory. The discussion of the link between organisation identity and strategy is followed by a review of the key concepts of strategic management accounting that we believe have assisted family businesses to survive, revive and succeed in turbulent conditions.

Organisational identity

Organisational identity is defined as the characteristics that are "central, enduring, and distinctive" (CED) to the organization [1]. The meaning that the members' consensually construct through their interactions with each other and with people outside of the organisation. The defining characteristics of the organisation are 'central' as they are essential rather than peripheral. 'Enduring' means that an organisational identity constitutes a set of stable elements that endure over time, rather than those that are ephemeral. The defining characteristics of organisational identity are described as 'distinctive' because the identity stakes out how the organisation is both similar to, and different, from other organisations. The concept of organisational identity is well suited for our research because it offers a comprehensible theoretical foundation for the *raison d'être* of the family business in explaining the uniqueness of these entities [11]. Our paper also draws on the following two notions that are derived from organisational identity.

A family business represents a type of "hybrid-identity organisation" [1]. It is the intentional amalgamation of two organisational forms – the 'family' and the 'business'. These would normally be mutually exclusive. The hybrid-identity, therefore, denotes an inherent tension between two different sets of rules or scripts, including culture-specific social expectations for how family businesses are expected to operate [12]. This tension explains the pursuance of non-financial goals of family businesses [10]. Because of the strong 'family' traits embedded in the daily life of these organisations, Hall [13] disapproves the claim that family businesses make 'irrational' choices to priorities their family-oriented objectives. We further argue that the tension between the family-oriented component and the business-oriented component of a family business identity functions similarly in the multi-identity at an individual level. People play multiple roles in the society. Some roles are processed by the same person and may create conflicts - for instance, being a teacher as well as being an assessor of the same subject and same group of students. Different identities embedded

in different roles are organised into a salient hierarchy therefore can be enacted respectively depending on the circumstances [14,15]. The family business as an organisational identity is very capable of invoking both the family-oriented and business-oriented perspective to adapt to different circumstances.

The organisational identity theory is rooted in the individual level role-based identity theory. The organisation identity of a family business is initially seen as being extended from the individual founder (or the founder family) who creates the business [2,16,17], and this individual level identity becomes one of the essential elements that constitute the organisational identity over time [18]. In the case of small family businesses and new ventures, such identities are mostly shaped by the founder and the entrepreneur's set of values, norms and personality through their actions and communications [19].

The theoretical underpinning of our paper lies in the theory of organisational identity and concepts that are related to the constitution of organisational identity. We contend that the theory of organisational identity provides suitable explanations of the behaviours of family businesses by recognising (a) the collective and consensual perceptions of family members as well as non-family employees in how they view what their business means; and (b) the influence of the funders who usually set the tone of the family business identity. Our interview data support the view that the 'family business' *per se* gives rise to an organisational identity, which influences the strategic decision-making of the family business.

A strategic view of family businesses' organisational identity

Strategic management literature suggests that the real key to business success lies in its ability to develop a competence that is distinctive and difficult to replicate. A clear and strong organisational identity is believed to be critical for corporate success [20]. Organisational identity denotes the consensual and collective cognition and beliefs of organisational members as well as of their external stakeholders. This eventually guides their actions. Several scholars have documented the interplay between organisational identity as a relatively stable collective cognitive construct and the dynamic aspects of strategy [21-24]. However, research studies that use strategic management as an organising framework in family businesses are sparse [25].

Do family businesses possess competitive advantages? Scattered evidence and discussions have emerged. Habbershon and Williams [26] conceptualise that "familiness" is the idiosyncratic, firm-level bundle of resources and capabilities resulting from a family factor that potentially leads to the competitiveness of family firms. Kansikas et al. [27] conclude that familiness gives rise to resources that can be grouped under three dimensions: structural (network ties), relational (trust, norms, obligations, identification) and cognitive (shared vision, shared language). Webb et al. [28] suggest that entrepreneurship and leadership styles provide explanations of how family firms make decisions. Frank et al. [29] criticise that in the construction of 'familiness' there is a failure in coupling the system of 'family' as well as 'enterprise' (p: 128).

We believe the missing piece of this puzzle is the organisational identity of the family business. Marketing scholars surmise that the relevance of an appropriate organisational identity is one of the critical factors in the success of small businesses in competitive markets [30]. Zellweger, et al. [31] point out that the familiness-oriented perspective and the business-oriented perspective have constituted the meaning of being a family business into an organisational identity that is describable, as well as communicable both internally and externally. Family business owners and founders may create a "family business meta-identity" to address who they are as a family business [32] to contribute to success of the business, as well as to the well-being of the family [33]. We posit that this organisational identity *per se* is the key competitive advantage of family businesses. The central, enduring and distinctive defining characteristics are socially constructed by the families behind these organisations and their stakeholders in incorporating both family functions and business functions. Our interview data reveal that family businesses can survive and succeed in turbulent environments through the constant balancing and prioritising of both family-oriented and business-oriented objectives.

Strategic management accounting (SMA)

During the interview data collection and analyses, we found SMA to be particularly relevant for making sense of the business information utilised by our interview participants. We invited interviewees to identify all potential factors that may have shaped their business practice. A firm's business value, strategic goals and competitive environment are just some of these potential aspects. As our data collection and analyses progressed, we increasingly realise that the themes and plots embedded in the interviewee data all point to the strategic goals of these family businesses. Paradoxically, most of the family businesses that were referred to in our research were neither large nor professional. All but one interviewee implied that his firm had established a separate management accounting function. From a strategic view, how do they know their strategic positioning is correct? How do they survive in the radically-changing competitive environment?

The term 'strategic management accounting' was introduced by Simmonds [3] and is defined as 'the provision and analysis of management accounting data about a business and its competitors, for use in developing and monitoring business strategy'. The discussion of what constitutes SMA has largely drawn on Porter's [34,35] strategic management typology. Porter [34] suggests that differentiation, cost leadership and focus are the strategies that provide firms with the ability to attain a competitive advantage and outperform rivals in an industry. Firms adopt different strategies and then usually implement different tactics including management accounting practices to sustain their competitive position [35,36]. Empirical evidence on the practice of SMA has commonly been collected via interviews or case studies in large professional organisations who have a well-established management accounting function in support of formal strategic planning and control [37,38]. Mintzberg and Waters [39] suggest that senior managers typically deal with unpredictable situations so they strategize in ad-hoc, flexible, dynamic, and implicit ways. Therefore, strategic management is a continuous and emergent activity [39]. Lord [40], based her case study on a New Zealand bike manufacturer and criticised that the textbook version of SMA as a function of a firm's management accounting department was completely disconnected from actual practice. As per Lord [40], in responding to pressures caused by external factors beyond their control, firms might have already intuitively applied SMA practices without the involvement of firm's accounting department or their equivalent. We see our paper as an empirical extension of Lord [40]. Our qualitative evidence suggests that the survival, revival, and prospering of family businesses in turbulent environment are living evidence of the success of their strategies and in the utilisation of SMA techniques.

Methodology and Research Design

Constructionist responsive interviewing

The responsive interviewing technique developed by Rubin and

Rubin [5] is adopted as the model for the research design. The responsive interviewing model has its roots in interpretive constructionism [5]. In constructionism, researchers focus on meaning and power because their epistemological position dictates that meaning and power are all that one can claim to know. Constructionism research is aimed at accounting for the ways in which phenomena are socially constructed [41]. The initial interview questions are expressed in a broad way to give the interviewees the opportunity to answer from their own experience [5]. The interviewee's answers then direct the researcher as to what to pursue further. The openness revealed after the interviewees start to describe their experience, makes it possible - even natural - for the interviewer and interviewee to become conversational partners in suggesting topics, concerns, and meanings that are important to the themes under exploration. Based on this design, the interviewee is virtually taking the interviewer though his/her experience. Essential to the responsive interviewing model is that the interviewer and interviewee are in a relationship in which there is mutual influence in both directions.

In our investigation, a questionnaire of thirteen interview questions was prepared with three broad themes that are related to the context and nature of management accounting systems (MAS) in family businesses. The main interview questionnaire was prepared for interviewees who were founders and owners of family businesses. We then adapted the main interview questionnaire to suit the managers and management accountants who do not own an equity interest in the family firm, without changing the structure and subject matter. The interview questions were semi-structured, allowing a certain level of scope limitation, as well as a certain degree of openness for responses by the interviewees [42]. Conceptually, to explore the shared values or norms of the interviewees, the interviewer often asks the interviewee to describe a typical event or ordinary occurrence [5]. The interviews give the interviewees the opportunity to describe what is important to them. The data collected via these questions is contextual and demonstrates a sense-making process by interviewees in perceiving what has happened, why those events happened and the intentional factors which justify their behaviour in response to the events. The interview questionnaires can be found in the Appendix A.

Thirteen interview questions are organised into three broad sections, namely (1) the business and the family, (2) values and strategy and (2) MAS. We argue that it is important to understand the how and the why of certain MAS being utilised by family businesses in the context of their specific historical development, organisational setting and their prospects. The traces and clues of the stories revealed in the interviews show the progress of individual family businesses, their values, strategic goals, and reflect the salience of the family and the business agenda. These businesses provided rich descriptions of the how and the why in their utilisation of different types of MAS.

Recruitment of interview participants and data collection

The population of interest includes owners, managers and in-house management accounting practitioners who regard themselves as controlling, managing and/or working for a family business in New Zealand. These roles are not mutually exclusive. We started with convenience sampling. The first few participants were recruited from the existing professional networks of the researchers. Then the existing participants were invited to refer other participants from among their acquaintances and business networks. Between November 2015 and April 2016, 13 interviews were carried out. Except for interviewee 02 (who was on the executive team of a family owned and operated not-for-profit organisation), all the interviewees held an ownership interest and also participated in the decision making and operation of their family business. All data gathered in the study is strictly confidential and all the participants were assured of complete anonymity in any publication of the research results. The interviewees were numbered from 01 to 13. The basic information of the interviewees is summarised in Table 1.

Findings and Discussions

The meaning of 'family business' as an organisational identity

In the construct of the meaning of the family business as an organisational identity there is an understanding that there is a shared meaning which is shared and understood cohesively by people who are interacting with these organisations. The most directly-relevant people are the founders or founder families of these businesses. For the start-up (or first generation) family business, the vision, mission and strategy and the management of the business are firmly controlled by the founders. The founders also set the tone of the organisational culture that denotes the behaviours of other family members, employees and external stakeholders. So what does the family business mean to the founders? Interviewee 08 described their business as:

It's my little castle. Apart from my family, it's my purpose for living. For them (my family), it's like home, we've been here that long… [Interviewee 08]

Interviewee 08 was very passionate when talking about the stories of his family and his business. His account incorporated several aspects of meanings that the interviewees ascribed to their family businesses. The insights provided by the interviewees in substantiating the meaning of the business to the families and to themselves encompasses following themes:

- "Livelihood": the source of income that has supported the family financially;

- "Home": a place where family members support and/or interact each other;

- "Passion": a career of choice and something they always love to do;

- An extension of the founders/owners' personal Identity: a representation of who they are and what their whole life is about.

Several interviewees specifically identified that the business had been the 'livelihood' (Interviewee 01) and supported the family financially. It seemed to be a logical and basic expectation, but interviewee 05 suggested that she had a 'love-hate' relationship with her furniture shop. She said:

Well, the retail business has been a lifeline for everybody, because it has supported me and my children. But it has also been a real drain on the family, because we don't make enough to be able to hire staff. [Interviewee 01]

In addition to the income generated from the family businesses, Interievee 03 revealed a second theme that was shared by other four interviewees. I.e., the family business is seen as a 'home', a reference point where they interact and function as a family. Interviewee 03 suggested:

[…] it was a very good income. It would have put our family in the top five per cent of income earners in New Zealand in the early to late 1990's. Given that one of our children had developmental issues, it gave me a freedom to put a lot extra effort into my family without detracting from the input that I put into the business. […] It gave me the time to be a complete person. Not just a business man but to be a father, and to do things for my family, which have been considerable. As I said, it would not have been possible if I had been an employee or in a larger business. For me, it is incredibly important from that aspect. [Interviewee 03]

It is noteworthy that even interviewee 03 (compared with interviewee 05) was satisfied with the level of income generated by the family business. His emphasised that the flexibility and time allowed by the business was of greater importance to him in fulfilling his family duty. Interviewee 04 at the time of interview, operated a factory with his wife and two daughters. He said:

On the whole the great thing about this business, of course, has been the fact that it has involved my wife and both of our daughters. It is the business where we can as a family work together on something. This business is pretty much a split between my passion of building and running the machine, and of course the carpets are our own design. It's also been (the) provision for quite a bit of our family for a number of years. The satisfaction is of course, still being able to be involved in engineering, developing machinery that sort of thing. [Interviewee 04]

Interviewee	Industry	Gender	Year of founding	Family control/ownership	Non-family employees	External investors
01	Professional service	Male	1997	A married couple (a son involved)	Yes	Yes
02	Not-for-profit	Male	2009	A married couple (the only son involved)	Yes	No
03	Professional service	Male	1999	A married couple (the only son involved)	No	No
04	Manufacturing	Male	2003	A married couple (two daughters involved)	No	No
05	Retail	Female	1995	A mother (all three daughters involved)	No	No
06	Professional service	Female	2003	A brother and a sister	Yes	No
07	Retail	Male	1887	Six generations of the same family	Yes	No
08	Hospitality	Male	1978	A married couple (all three children involved)	Yes	No
09	Manufacturing	Male	1965	A married couple (all three children involved)	Yes	No
10	Hospitality	Female	1994	A married couple (both sons and parents involved)	Yes	No
11	Retail	Male	2004	A married couple	Yes	No
12	Manufacturing	Female	2001	A married couple and the brother of the husband	Yes	Yes
13	Manufacturing	Male	1999	A married couple	Yes	No

Table 1: Basic information of interviewees.

Interviewee 06 operated a professional services agency with her brother. She, too, shares the same emotion towards their business, and regards it as something they always wanted to do together as a family:

For us, I guess, it is the idea of being our own boss and doing it successfully. It's always been our epitome of how we want to work. For our parents… Oh! They are very emotionally invested in terms of (the fact) that we are their two children. For them seeing us working together, it is a kind of dream for them as well. [Interviewee 06]

Both interviewee 04 and interviewee 06 provided the third theme which was shared by several other interviewees. These interviewees describe the meaning of the business as their own passion and life-long career. Another example was suggested by interviewee13:

The business is owned by the family trust. The lady you met downstairs (in the showroom), she is my wife. I am the main man here. I drive it. I am now a pensioner. Theoretically I am already retired…But I enjoy it. I enjoy the purpose of it. I enjoy the challenge of it. Interviewee13

The fourth theme is that their family business represents their families and themselves, i.e., it is an extension of owners/founders families' identity.

Our findings show evidence of how the meaning of a 'family business' is constructed. The 4 themes identified by our interviewees represent the defining characteristics of a family business as perceived by our participants. We suggest that these themes should be viewed as an interdependent and combined entirety capturing the core functions of family businesses. Thus, these themes give rise to the organisational identity of 'family businesses'. According to Albert and Whetten [1] and, Whetten [43], an organisational identity is central, enduring and distinctive. The meaning of the interviewees' family businesses implies the central and essential purpose in establishing and operating these organisations. The actual family businesses involved in our research have different longevity (Table 1) and are at different stages of the organisational life cycle. Yet our participants can identity these shared meanings. The core functions of family businesses as a combined set of properties ultimately differentiate these organisations from their non-family counterparts, as an occupation, as well as being in the family per se.

The organisational identity of 'family business' as an competitive advantage

So far, we have explained how the organisational identity of 'family business' is formed by plotting our interview data along the theoretical constructs proposed by Albert and Whetten [1], and Whetten [43]. We further argue that such an organisational identity per se give rise to a competitive advantage for family businesses.

First, our interview data validates the fact that family businesses are hybrid-identity organisations [1], as the above-mentioned themes of the shared meaning underpinning the organisational identity encompass the pursuance of both financially-oriented goals and family-oriented goals. We contend that applying the entrepreneurial and leadership qualities of the founders to the individual level, Jones [19], should also be included in the mix. In additional to the conflicts embedded in the hybrid of organisational identity [10,12], the interview quotes shown earlier vividly describe how these different aspects of the family business identity are complementary to one another. Albert and Whetten [1], and Whetten [43] propose that the organisational identity functions in a similar fashion to the identity at the individual level. Following this notion, the enriched and dynamic organisational identity traits can be arranged and rearranged into salient hierarchies that allow a family business to enact different aspects of the identity in order to adapt to different circumstances. We therefore argue that the heterogeneity of family businesses reflects nothing but the different salience of the organisational identity mix. Furthermore, this hybrid-identity and the salience of it create a competitive advantage for family businesses.

Second, Zellweger, et al. [31] suggest that an organisational identity has the potential to enhance strategy if it is describable and communicable both internally and externally. Our interview data suggests that the meaning of family businesses is internally shared by managers and employees. The identity of the family business is also externally displayed to, and thus perceived by, other stakeholders.

Interviewee 07 is a fourth generation shareholder and a Director of a family owned enterprise. During the interview, he told a story of how his family business 'survived, revived and prospered again'. His family business experienced a devastating fire and also experienced the on-going challenges caused by the Canterbury earthquakes. He described the difficult time right after the fire:

So from a very early age, I saw my parents and my relations struggling. They were struggling but decided they would not walk away because the firm, as I said, was really insolvent. It had little to come and go on. There was a great deal of public sympathy and support for the firm to continue in business. They were encouraged. The board decided that (the) business should continue, and through blood, sweat and tears. I mean through blood, sweat and tears! [Interviewee 07]

He continued with a detailed description of how overseas suppliers were willing to continue shipping stock to the shop knowing the business was insolvent. Many years later, the Canterbury earthquakes damaged some of their business premises which needed to be demolished and rebuilt within a short time. Again, the family business experienced disruption. Interviewee 07 suggested that their business had to get through the most difficult time after the earthquake and was prepared for the rebuild despite the uncertainties posed by the infrastructure and the geographical and demographical changes caused by the earthquakes.

Interviewee 12 also suggested that the special bond between the family business and their employees assisted her and her husband in getting through difficult times. She said:

At some point in our lowest period some of our staff came in and worked for no pay. We (the family) worked for no pay. (Not only) managerial (staff) but also the factory staff. That's one of the unique things. [Interviewee 12]

Interviewee 02 is the only non-family member of a family owned and operated not-for-profit organisation, who participated in our interview. He clearly articulated the organisational identity in how he perceived it as non-family member. He said during the interview:

It's (the business is) their life. They spend all of their time on it. They have no other purpose other than to develop this organisation. It's totally their life. Yep… Well, I guess. The positive side of that…it means there is 100% commitment over there. It means their passion for the business rubs off on other people, so it creates a very positive attitude. At the moment, I don't think the business can exist without them because they are the… What is the word I am looking for? They are the business! I can only put it in that way. (Laugh)

[…]we have a very strong relationship. I am involved with them on a leadership team, what we call 'the core leadership team', which meets roughly once a month. We have very honest, open discussions with each other.
[Interviewee 02].

In summary, our data shed light on the theory that 'family business' as an organisational identity is a competitive advantage that has contributed to the resilience and flexibility of these business. We further contend that the strategic planning and the utilisation of MAS of family business are also related to and affected by the organisational identity.

Business strategies incorporating the identity of family business

During the interview, we invited our participants to describe their business values, competitive environment and reputation. The findings of interviewees' perception of business values are summarised in Table 2.

The interview quotes (Table 2), on the one hand, highlight that the business value articulated by these family business owners and managers is largely drawn on building the relationship with stakeholders and the reputation of the family businesses. These business values and strategy are motivated and addressed by their organisational identity, as shown in the representative quotes. On the other hand, it can be concluded that all the family businesses being referred to in our research adopted 'differentiation' and/or 'focus' strategies [35]. According to Porter [35], when firms adopt a differentiation strategy it is aimed at delivering high quality to customers; and if customers perceive this product or service as different from other products, consumers are willing to pay more. To our surprise, although all these family businesses were from different industries, all of them have described their industry as highly competitive; their businesses, and they themselves, had a very good reputation in the industry.

We also invited interviewees to comment on their midterm to long term business plans and how they would achieve them. The interview findings about business plans are summarised in Table 3.

Management accounting systems denoting the business strategies of family business

Although interviewees were from different industries, at different ages, and were motivated by different reasons, most of them would want their business to grow. We then encouraged our interviewees to identify the broad range of MAS that they had used in their operations, as much as they could. The flexibility provided by the semi-structured interview design allows interviewees to disclose what they believe is important to them and often showcases hidden facets of their organisations [44]. In analysing the interview data, it became apparent that although informal, interviewees had utilised many elements and techniques of SMA to achieve their competitive advantage and to sustain their competitive strategies. We found that it was particularly intriguing that quite a few accounts of MAS were well aligned with the interviewee's discussion of their business values – i.e., competitive strategies and advantages, although they might merely be subconsciously describing what was apparent and important to them [45-49]. To discuss and justify the following findings, the MAS identified by interviewees as being utilised in their businesses are presented alongside the competitive advantages identified by our interviewees previously (Table 4).

The commonly adopted MAS elements and techniques were:

- Performance evaluation and management (key resources, including employees);

Interviewee	Industry	Business values and strategy	Representative quote
01	Professional service	Quality of service	You are only as good as your last contract.
02 (non-family member)	Not-for-profit	Faith and ethics	[…] their faith is a significant value to them. I think 'integrity' is a big value. They like to be transparent as much as possible. And 'accountability' is a big value to them as well. So they like systems around them, which ensure accountability to their membership.
03	Professional service	Personal service and competence	A high level of personal service to our clients. Creating an employee-fulfilling environment. And opportunities for the owners to develop their strengths.
04	Manufacturing	Honesty and integrity	Honesty and integrity!
05	Retail	Quality	We have to rely on the best service and the best product.
06	Professional service	Quality of service	It is all about being able to deliver the work to the highest level and get the work out of the door for our clients who are on board[...] "Being well regarded" is what we are proud of as well. Our values are right at the heart of it.
07	Retail	Quality merchandise	It has been built on quality merchandise, supplying to the middle to upper market, mainly the middle. Our emphasis was very much the middle (market). But we are able to sell, because of our image and reputation, some very high end merchandise, too. Considered as 'expensive' in New Zealand but not on a world scale. That merchandise policy is backed up by our high level of staff knowledge, and customer service.
08	Hospitality	Personalised service and quality of service	We are very careful to make sure that people are looked after the right way. "Personalise" is the word! Satisfied customers and return costumers. The most valuable is return businesses.
09	Manufacturing	Honesty and excellence	Honesty and excellence
10	Hospitality	Community and family value	It is a community hub. I think customers like seeing us here, knowing it's us running it. We've been doing it for so long. People's children are coming back. Things change so much, but they really like coming back to the same thing, sons and grandchildren, an integral part.
11	Retail	Specialty	[…] our value is that we know what we are talking about. We are specialists. We only take on employees who know what they are talking about in **my** industry.
12	Manufacturing	Determination, innovation, and loyalty	"Determination, innovation, and loyalty"
13	Manufacturing	Honesty and Integrity	We are as straight as a die. I don't say that to just create "PR". And the golden rule is that we treat people how we want to be treated.

Table 2: Business values and strategy.

Interviewee	Short to midterm plan	Long term plan	How to achieve it
01	Selling out the current consulting business	Focusing on other businesses and initiatives	• Growing the current business by taking on a few more contracts
02	Accommodating the fast-growing membership	Transforming into a more comprehensive organisation	• Moving to new business premises; • Establishing a professional management team
03	Increasing and replacing revenue source	Being able to retire from business	• Purchasing fee-based business • Continuously training and developing skills
04	Expanding overseas	Selling out the business and working on other business initiatives	• Marketing and networking • Excellent product quality and design
05	Closing down the retailing business	Establishing and growing the new business	• Taking on more contracts
06	Doubling the turnover	Becoming "the best regarded" independent marketing agency	• Recruiting "like-minded" clients and employees • "Simplest structures and processes to get the job done to the highest level so we can strike" • "leading edge in terms of technology, processes, systems"
07	Rebuilding the business	Staying profitable and being privately owned by the family	• Incurring debts • Remaining profitable • Keeping up a good reputation
10	Handing over the business management and operations to the two sons	(not identified)	• Creating a succession plan
11	Selling out the business	Being able to retire from business	• Increasing profit
12	Expanding overseas	Creating a succession plan for existing family Directors to retire	• Growing the business overseas through influencing industrial and health and safety standards in the targeted overseas countries • Establishing a professional management mechanism
13	Doubling the turnover	Being able to retire from the business	• Purchasing and installing new production machinery • Establishing a performance-based remuneration system

Both interviewee 08 and interviewee 09 have retired from their operational positions. Interviewee 08 did not answer this question from a business operation perspective, but described some details of his will in leaving his wealth to the family. The interview of interviewee 09 was not recorded. Therefore we decided not to quote any text from the notes taken during the interview with interviewee 09.

Table 3: Business plans.

- Ongoing profitability analysis (customer level and job level) and pricing review;

- Customer relationship management;

- Competitor analysis;

- Quality management; and

- Capital investment planning

It is the underlying rationale of observing competitors, financing capital expenditure and remunerating on the desired behaviour that give rise to a seamless justification that these MAS have been utilised for their exact competitive strategies. The conventionally-emphasised planning and control driven by forecasting and budgeting techniques and cost management were not emphasised by interviewees. Instead, some interviewees explicitly precluded the idea of setting a budget, instead suggesting that cash flows were constantly monitored against spending. Interviewee 11 suggested:

We don't funnily enough have a budget. I have it set in my mind but no formal budget, except for cash flow. Cash flow, you cannot do without it. We are constantly watching cash flow.

[Interviewee 11]

The MAS identified by the interviewees as being utilised in their family business by no means represents the exemplars of 'state of the art' design and execution of MAS for strategic purposes, but instead, there was usage of some unsophisticated procedures and practices - for example, the accounts provided by interviewee 01 and interviewee 13 (Table 4). Yet, some of the MAS identified by interviewees are professional and sophisticated. For example, interviewee 12 described quite comprehensive analyses in the preparation for tendering. Interviewee 04 and interviewee 06 suggested that customised computer

systems had been acquired to provide information to assist their core operating activities. Not all interviewees provided descriptions whereby their intuitive utilisation of MAS could be identified, for instance interviewee 05 and interviewee10 (Table 4). We acknowledge their management approach could be common among small businesses, but compared to the entirety of interview findings, we do not believe their approach has a pervasive influence on our overall conclusion.

In summary, motivated by the meaning of the family businesses, owners and managers want to see their businesses growing. The constitution of family business as an identity denotes the strategic choices. The organisational identity *per se* also gives rise to a competitive advantage. Family businesses have utilised many elements and techniques of MAS and SMA to discharge their competitive advantage and to sustain their competitive strategies. It was particularly intriguing that many of the MAS were well aligned with the family businesses' competitive strategies and advantages. The MAS identified by interviewees (although many are unsophisticated procedures and practices) are purposeful and suitable for their strategies.

Concluding Remarks

This study attempts to explore the dynamics of family business based on an alternative framework – the organisation identity. We plotted our qualitative data along the theoretical construct of organisational identity and contend that the meanings perceived by family business owners, founders and managers constitute the identity of these organisations. The shared meanings of the family business as an organisational identity is central, enduring and distinctive [1]. It captures both family-oriented and business-oriented goals and blends with the founders/owners' entrepreneurial and leadership characteristics. The stable constructs of the organisational identity gives rise to the idiosyncratic competitive advantage of family businesses so that these firms are flexible and resilient.

Interviewee	Industry	Competitive advantages (Table 2)	How to achieve growth (Table 3)	MAS utilised	Representative quote
01	Professional service	Quality of service	Growing the current business by taking on a few more contracts	• Monitoring competitors • Strategic pricing	So we do look at the market. We look at what other consultancy companies are charging and we match that. There is a mechanism where the pricing of the job is variable.
02	Not-for-profit	Faith and ethics	• Moving to a new business premises; • Establishing a professional management team	• Key internal control • Customer management	Within their members in terms of giving as well. So they don't know who gives what. They don't treat people differently based on financial giving. Only the bookkeeper and I know who gives what. The Trust Board doesn't know either.
03	Professional	Personal service and competence	• Purchasing fees • Continuously training and developing skills	Customer profitability analysis	We are charging fees on a weekly basis. [...] recoveries are probably our principal financial concern. When we charge the clients, we look at the efficiency of that particular work. We take steps if we feel that we are not efficient by ways of communicating with our clients, and ways that we can improve that.
				Employee performance evaluation	Q: And… how often do you review the pricing? A: Six-monthly. They are reviewed with our reviews with employees Q: So you have six-month employee reviews. What do you discuss in those reviews? A: We discuss their remuneration. We discuss their recoveries of costs on jobs. We discuss the professional standard of their work. We discuss their career development.
04	Manufacturing	Honesty and integrity	• Marketing and networking • Excellent product quality and design	Customised job-based system with comprehensive accounting functions	[...]it is very good at tracking jobs, tracking the raw materials…It is a great system that allows you recording all the samples' information. Because for us, samples are everything. They are all over the world. (laugh) So no matter who rings us or emails us asking about the samples, we know exactly what it is. It is customised to our particular business. It has the ability to record the job in progress. And also the financial aspects, of course, taking deposits and following that right through.
05	Retail	Quality	• Hiring staff	Not identifiable	[...] it's in my head, if he says "do you have this?" I know I have this or that. It's probably a terrible way to do it.
06	Professional service	Quality of service	• Recruiting "like-minded" clients and employees	Employee performance evaluation	We are both involved in recruitment and performance reviews, which we do at least once a year, in terms of salary review and performance review, including setting goals for the next twelve months to achieve the next level of financial rewards. This is to make sure that we are getting the best out of our team.
			• "Simplest structures and processes to get the job done to the highest level so we can strike" • "Leading edge in terms of technology, processes, systems"	• Job-based system • Customer relationship management	[...]We log it with an individual job number. Whether they are for a potential new client or an existing client. They are all logged in our system. And in each job, we take timesheets against the actual hours spent, so we have a good ability to look at our real time costs, the hours spent against the actual types of work. [...]usually flag what stage our projects are at in terms of quoting. [...]Being able to look at the real time spent on jobs is vital for future quoting, and to be able to substantiate prices when being challenged in dealing bigger organisations, you know, being accountable for things.
08	Hospitality	Personalised service and quality of service	(did not identify)	• External hotel starring and rating programme • Employee performance evaluation • Reservation system • Restaurant costing system	Our other most important people are our reservationists. We have full control of it (the reservations). Those girls get paid on a percentage of how much we get each month. Behind the screen, that is all going on. We are working flat out and slot people around because we have approximately fifteen room types. That's where the money comes from.

Interviewee	Industry	Competitive advantages (Table 2)	How to achieve growth (Table 3)	MAS utilised	Representative quote
10	Hospitality	Community and family value	(Handing the business to two sons. not operation related)	• Quality management	Quality is most essential.[…]Suppliers often offer us cheaper products, not necessarily good, not our priority. We have had the same menu for many years and know the ingredients. Sometimes they stop stocking and have to look for another supplier. We do staff training - choosing good ingredients for a start. Stock is dated and rotated[…]as part of the brewery food safety plan. We fill out the temperature required every day in a little book.
11	Retail	Specialty	Increasing profit	(Some general internal control principles are identified, but no systematic approach)	Can I use the word 'haphazard'? It's when I remember to do it. There is no sort of[…] huh[…]calendar day in which I say to myself, "this is what you should do."
12	Manufacturing	Determination, innovation, and loyalty	• Growing the business overseas through influencing industrial and health and safety standards in the targeted overseas countries • Establishing a professional management mechanism	• Competitor analyses (substitute products life-cycle) • Pricing review	The product does have a long (lifespan) […] Electrical signs do need replacing every 5 years. We've just done the costing, (our product will last) over 30 years. We've just worked out how to save the country 50 million dollars by every single school in New Zealand getting rid of electrical 'exit' signs and putting our products in. So we know exactly what that saves. (We are) reviewing our pricing all the time, I'm trying to think about the latest change we have just made. […]Yes, with the latest exchange rates changes in America we could keep, we could just be earning more now, but instead of the fact that we are earning more we are giving them a reduction in price just so that we can be competitive, so we are constantly (doing this).
13	Manufacturing	Honesty and Integrity	• Purchasing and installing new production machinery	Monitoring cash flows and capital investment planning	I look at Xero (an accounting software) every month, and you can see the cash flow. Our stock doesn't vary. It varies from top to bottom by twenty grand in year. So I can see the cash surplus down the bottom. I will tell you how I do it. Our depreciation is about five or six thousand dollars a month. So I think I would spend five or six thousand dollars (a month) on new equipment (laugh)!
			• Establishing a performance based remuneration system	Profit-sharing (to be implemented)	Well, I am putting that in. Yeah. I am not sure how am I going to structure it, because I want also to have an incentive for volume as well as gross profit. I don't want them to say 'look we did fifty grand last week. And we made sixteen percent gross profit.' I would rather they say that 'we did two-hundred grand last week, and made forty percent gross profit (the targeted gross profit).'

Table 4: MAS utilised by family businesses.

Our paper also relates theory to practice. We posit that the organisational identity of family businesses also motivates and symbolises the strategic choices of these firms in distinguishing themselves through superior quality and reputation. To achieve such strategies, family businesses focus on building the relationships internally and externally with their stakeholders through the deliberate and meaningful communication of the meaning of their organisational identity. The utilisation of MAS and SMA techniques has contributed to their survival, revival and success. We believe the practical implications of this are of interest to current and future family business owners and managers, as well as business advisors who directly benefit from the wellbeing of these organisations. We also hope to contribute to the understanding of the family business by broad communities in appreciating the importance of these organisations.

We encourage researchers to continue building and testing the model of the organisational identity of family business. Future testing of this model will allow researchers to determine whether this model indeed provides a valid avenue of building knowledge of family businesses. The construct of the family business as a cohesive and stable organisational identity can be of benefit for several areas of business research in addition to strategic management and management accounting. Marketing, human resources, entrepreneurship and leadership research may also draw on the constructs of organisational identity of family businesses.

This paper suffers from the limitations commonly shared by much qualitative research, in that it is based on face-to-face interviews. As the interview data was collected from regions in New Zealand, the findings may suffer from a lacking of generalisability. The convenience and snowball sampling methods may have only recruited interviewees who are familiar with the subject matter, thus are more comfortable in reflecting on their experience. The interview responses are what are believed to be true and important from the interviewee's perspective, rather than being verifiable facts. The current research design does not include family business stakeholders other than the owners and managers. The perceptions and behavioural choices of these stakeholders, for instance employees, are of great importance to the understanding of family business identity.

Acknowledgements

We would like to thank all our interviewees for their participation in the research.

References

1. Albert S, Whetten DA (1985) Organizational identity. Research in Organizational Behavior 7: 263-295.

2. Dyer WG, Whetten DA (2006) Family Firms and Social Responsibility: Preliminary Evidence from the S&P 500. Entrepreneurship Theory and Practice 30: 785-802.

3. Simmonds K (1981) Strategic Management Accounting. Management Accounting (British) 59: 26-29.

4. Simons R (1990) The role of management control systems in creating competitive advantage: new perspectives. 15: 127-143.

5. Rubin HJ, Rubin IS (2005) Qualitative interviewing: the art of hearing data, (2nd edn.), Thousand Oaks, California: Sage Publications.

6. Chua JH, Chrisman JJ, Sharma P (1999) Defining the Family Business by Behavior. Entrepreneurship: Theory & Practice 23: 19-39.

7. Zellweger TM, Astrachan JH (2008) On the Emotional Value of Owning a Firm. Family Business Review 21: 347-363.

8. Westhead P, Cowling M (1997) Performance contrasts between family and non-family unquoted companies in the UK. International Journal of Entrepreneurial Behaviour & Research 3: 30 - 52.

9. Gomez-Mejia LR, Makri M, Kintana ML (2010) Diversification Decisions in Family-Controlled Firms. Journal of Management Studies 47: 223-252.

10. Zellweger TM, Nason RS, Nordqvist M, Brush CG (2013) Why Do Family Firms Strive for Nonfinancial Goals? An Organizational Identity Perspective. Entrepreneurship: Theory & Practice 37: 229-248.

11. Whetten DA, Foreman PO, Dyer WG (2013) Organizational identity and family business. In: Melin L, Nordqvist MM, Sharma P (eds.), The Sage handbook of family business. Sage Publications, pp. 480-497.

12. Kraatz M, Block E (2008) Organizational implications of institutional pluralism. In: Kraatz M, Oliver C, Suddaby R, Sahlin-Andersson K (eds.), Handbook of organizational institutionalism. Sage Publication, London, UK, pp: 243-275.

13. Hall A (2012) Family Business Dynamics: A Role and Identity Based Perspective. Cheltenham: Edward Elgar.

14. Stryker S (1980) Symbolic Interactions: A social Structural Version. Menlo Park, CA.

15. Stets JE, Burke PJ (2009) Identity Theory. Oxford University Press, New York.

16. Haveman HA, Khaire MV (2004) Survival beyond succession? The contingent impact of founder succession on organizational failure. Journal of Business Venturing 19: 437-463.

17. Schein EH (1983) The role of the founder in creating organizational culture. Organizational Dynamics 12: 13-28.

18. Dyer GW (1988) Culture and Continuity in Family Firms. Family Business Review 1: 37-50.

19. Jones GR (2007) Creating and managing organizational culture. In: Organizational Theory, Design and Change. Upper Saddle River, NJ: Pearson, pp: 176-196.

20. Collins JC, Porras JI (2005) Built to last: successful habits of visionary companies. London: Random House.

21. Dutton J, Dukerich J (1991) Keeping an eye on the mirror: Image and identity in organizational adaptation. Academy of Management Journal 34: 517-554.

22. Gioia DA, Thomas JB (1996) Identity, Image, and Issue Interpretation: Sensemaking during Strategic Change in Academia. Administrative Science Quarterly 41: 370-403.

23. Ravasi D, Schultz M (2006) Responding to Organizational Identity Threats: Exploring the Role of Organizational Culture. The Academy of Management Journal 49: 433-458.

24. Kjærgaard AL (2009) Organizational Identity and Strategy: An Empirical Study of Organizational Identity's Influence on the Strategy-Making Process. International Studies of Management & Organization 39: 50-69.

25. Sharma P, Chrisman JJ, Chua JH (1997) Strategic Management of the Family Business: Past Research and Future Challenges. Family Business Review 10: 1-35.

26. Habbershon TG, Williams ML (1999) A Resource-Based Framework for Assessing the Strategic Advantages of Family Firms. Family Business Review 12: 1-25.

27. Kansikas J, Laakkonen A, Sarpo V, Kontinen T (2012) Entrepreneurial leadership and familiness as resources for strategic entrepreneurship. International Journal of Entrepreneurial Behavior and Research 18: 141-158.

28. Webb JW, Ketchen DJ, Ireland RD (2010) Strategic entrepreneurship within family-controlled firms: Opportunities and challenges. Journal of Family Business Strategy 1: 67-77.

29. Frank H, Lueger M, Nosé L, Suchy D (2010) The concept of "Familiness": Literature review and systems theory-based reflections. Journal of Family Business Strategy 1: 119-130.

30. Abimbola T, Vallaster C (2007) Brand, organisational identity and reputation in SMEs: an overview. Qualitative Market Research: An International Journal 10: 341-348.

31. Zellweger TM, Eddleston KA, Kellermann FW (2010) Exploring the concept of familiness: Introducing family firm identity. Journal of Family Business Strategy 1: 54-63.

32. Shepherd D, Haynie JM (2009a) Birds of a feather don't always flock together: Identity management in entrepreneurship. Journal of Business Venturing 24: 316-337.

33. Shepherd D, Haynie JM (2009b) Family Business, Identity Conflict, and an Expedited Entrepreneurial Process: A Process of Resolving Identity Conflict. Entrepreneurship Theory and Practice 33: 1245-1264.

34. Porter ME (1980) Competitive Strategy: Techniques for Analysing Industries and Competitors. New York: The Free Press.

35. Porter ME (1985) Competitive Adtantage: Creating and Sustaining Superior Performance. The Free Press, New York.

36. Simons R (1987) Accounting control systems and business strategy: an empirical analysis. Accounting, Organizations and Society 12: 357-374.

37. Roslender R, Hart SJ (2003) In search of strategic management accounting: theoretical and field study perspectives. Management Accounting Research 14: 255-279.

38. Dixon R (1998) Accounting for strategic management: a practical application. Long Range Planning 31: 272-279.

39. Mintzberg H, Waters J (1985) Of Strategies, Deliberate and Emergent. Strategic Management Journal 6: 257-272.

40. Lord BR (1996) Strategic management accounting: the emperor's new clothes? Management Accounting Research 7: 347-366.

41. Burr V (1995) An introduction to social constructionism/Vivien Burr. Routledge, London, New York.

42. Wengraf T (2001) Qualitative Research Interviewing. Thousand Oaks, California Safe Publication.

43. Whetten DA (2006) Albert and Whetten Revisited: Strengthening the Concept of Organizational Identity. Journal of Management Inquiry 15: 219-234.

44. Qu SQ, Dumay J (2011) The qualitative research interview. Qualitative Research in Accounting and Management 8: 238-264.

45. Chrisman JJ, Chua JH, Litz RA (2004) Comparing the agency costs of

family and non-family firms: Conceptual issues and exploratory evidence. Entrepreneurship: Theory & Practice 28: 335-354.

46. Harms H (2014) Review of Family Business Definitions: Cluster Approach and Implications of Heterogeneous Application for Family Business Research. International Journal of Financial Studies 2: 280-314.

47. KarraN, Tracey P, Phillips N (2006) Altruism and agency in the family firm: exploring the role of family, kinship, and ethnicity Entrepreneurship. Theory and Practice 30: 861-877.

48. Le Breton-Miller I, Miller D, Lester RH (2011) Stewardship or Agency? A Social Embeddedness Reconciliation of Conduct and Performance in Public Family Businesses. Organisational Science 22: 704-721.

49. Senftlechner D, Hiebl MRW (2015) Management accounting and management control in family businesses: Past accomplishments and future opportunities. Journal of Accounting & Organizational Change 11: 537-606

28

The Credibility of the Somali Central Bank: Independence, Transparency, and Accountability

Husein Mohamed IRBAD*

Lincoln University College, Mogadishu Centre, Malaysia

Abstract

The very purpose of this study is to review the credibility of the Somali central bank: its independence, transparency, and accountability. The reason why, this study was conducted is that there was no previous study in its kind regarding the credibility of the central bank of Somalia by looking at its independence, transparency and accountability. The first objective of this study is to find out if central bank of Somalia is credible in terms of political, financial, and monetary policy independence. The second objective is to examine the types and degree of transparency and to settle ways to measure the transparency of the Somali central bank. The third objective is to find out if there are clear and well defined financial accountability structures in the central bank (CB) of Somalia. In this study, central bank independence (CBI), transparency, and accountability was measured to find out whether these elements can influence or possibly could have some positive effects on central bank credibility. The questionnaire used in this research is a self-administered dichotomous scale. Data was analyzed by using Statistical package for social sciences (SPSS) in descriptive statistics. The target population of this study was 32 respondents from the banking industry in Mogadishu. The result of this study became 55.78 mean averages with a Std. Dev. 5.235. The overall mean averages for a total of 30 questions became 1.859 and overall Std. Dev. 0.1745 which meant the result showed greater abnormality and data distribution positively skewed to the right. The central bank of Somalia has no independence.

Keywords: Independence; Monetary policy; Credibility; Political independence; Financial independence; Central bank; Transparency; Accountability

Introduction

In recent years, central banks have substantially changed their specific characteristics and attributes and number of countries that has developed such banks has increased. At the end of the 19th century, there were only 18 such banks that changed their operating structures, while by the beginning of the 21st century the number has increased to 173. Apparently, the first central banks were owned by the governments but fortunately some governments continuously incorporated and lastly developed functions that gave those banks the possibility made them the bank of the banks of the 20th century. These central banks have made their historic role for they were assigned changes during the 1990s as they were gradually become independent from their governments' control. Due to transformations 34 central banks adopted new statues. The structural changes of central banks happened because of two main reasons: in the first place, over the past decade 34 industrial and developing countries enacted legislations that allowed the increase of their central banks' operational independence. Also, independence in making decisions on monetary policy has been increased. This trend has been caused by three main factors: (1) the institutionalization of the European Central Bank (ECB) in 1999. (2) The stabilization programs of some emerging market countries. (3) The economic shift of former communist countries attempted to build market economies. In the second place, reforms have been made to increase transparency of monetary policy and accountabilities of central banks. As a formal principle, these reforms reflected an attempt to incorporate price stability into monetary policy. These two main reasons: enactment legislations allowing central banks' independence and reforms increasing transparency of monetary policy and accountabilities of central banks are supposed to make it easier for the public and elected representatives to monitor their central banks [1].

Over the past 20 years, separation between central bank independence and political process has been a great objective. All over the world, there are many countries that have implemented some institutional reforms which gave their CBs more independence from the political process [2,3]. Some work has been done on time inconsistency on monetary policy, together with Rogoff [4] who suggested that the theoretical rationale for these central banks reforms is under the idea that credibility of the inflation policy depends on central bank with more inflation adverse preferences. Around the world policy makers, academics and observers has reached a consensus that the goals of monetary policy should be established by the political authorities but the implementation of the monetary policy with its goals should be free from political control and interventions from politicians. The achievability of both stable prices and maximum sustainable employment depend the consistency of the economic growth rate and the expansion of its productive capacity. Achieving monetary policy working with substantial time lags requires monetary policy makers taking a longer term perspective when making their decisions-only an independent CB with a mandate to achieve the best possible economic outcomes in the longer term is best able to take such perspective. When CB policy makers are subject to short term political influence to achieve short term economic output and employment gains only favoring and helpful in political election campaigns-such political interference in monetary policy generates and leaves behind an inflationary pressure that deteriorates economy's longer term prospects [5]. The institutional device associated with lower inflation is the central bank independence;

***Corresponding author:** Irbad HM, Lincoln University College, Mogadishu Centre, Malaysia, E-mail: Cirbad10@yahoo.com

independence also brings time consistent monetary policy. Central bank transparency (CBT) is absolutely crucial for it makes central bankers accountable and more credible in the eyes of the public. Transparency brings greater advantages such as reputability and flexibility on the credibility of the central banks. Transparency also attracts the private sector to infer central bank's monetary policy decisions [6].

According to Siklos, Spinesi and Williams [7-9] the independence of the Central Bank from the government is an autonomy arrangement which is beneficial to the society but the CB cannot be completely independent from the government. Other authors such as, Gabillon and Martimort [10] Yang [11] and Mixon and Upadhyaya [12] believe that the proponents and opponents of central bank autonomy cannot agree on why such arrangement is so beneficial to society. Forder [13] Suggests convenience policy on the central bank's autonomy when some governments are convenient to the CBI policy; while Cukierman A [14] and Eijffinger and de Haan [15] view that the CBI can reduce inflation. Siklos, Bohl, and Wohar Implied the financial stability system, its measurement and its implications with a monetary policy strategy aiming low and stable inflation and to look for prospects of price level targeting must be given special focus. Croitoru [16] debates that there is a possibility for the central bank to act against the increase of effusive asset prices, since they can result severe financial crises and possibly throwing the economy into liquidity trap. So the central bank must prefer moderate and stable inflation to lower and stable inflation.

In the case of Somalia, the central bank independence (CBI) is under question – without independence there can be no transparency and accountability either. Somalia hasn't had access to international financial markets since late 1980s. Only the CB can enable Somalia to take the necessary measures to access international financial markets by settling arrears with creditors and to build track record of public financial management in the long term to warrant debt relief. CB is responsible to help Somalia by ensuring the following major tasks: (1) developing monetary and exchange rate policies and money supply regulations, (2) advising macroeconomic issues to government and to monitor economic indicators regularly, (3) to be the financial agent in the issuance of debt, (4) giving licenses to commercial banking services and other banks and to give legal protection for their operations, (5) drafting new central bank Act, (6) drafting new Commercial Banking Law, (7) setting sound payment systems. The absence of the above mentioned seven major tasks proves the functionality of the Somali central bank (SCB) is below the bottom line of the graph. Without a fully functional CB of Somalia, the Somali business context faced a huge risk and the private sector of the Somali business could not continue to generate positive multiplier effects. So there is a need to

rebuild a credible CB of Somalia under the following three directions: independence, transparency, and accountability.

Credibility is defined by Oxford Advanced Learner's Dictionary [17] as "the quality that somebody or something has that makes people believe or trust them." central bank credibility (CBC) is the legitimacy of the CB, central bank independence (CBI) supported by the public, Competence Monetary Policy, Keeping the Unemployment Rate to a Minimum Level, Promising the Expectations of the Private Sector in Price Stability, the Appreciation of the Private Sector to the Objectives of the Policy Makers, the Effectiveness of the CB itself, and Keeping the Inflation Low [18]. "The central bank is credible if people believe it will do what it says" [19]. The researcher believes (FORDER) is measuring credibility while (Blinder) is defining it.

The definition of this study was derived from Blinder [19] that defines central bank credibility (CBC) as people believe the central bank will do what it says. So the gab is the Somali Central Bank (SCB) needs credibility through independence, transparency, and accountability (Figure 1).

Generally, central bank independence must be beyond the political agenda, accountability should be upon society; transparency is to be fulfilled its task in a more efficient and complex communication mechanism [20].

Independence is the most important element because transparency, accountability, and the communication channels become crucial only after granting independence to the central banks [21]. "Independent central banks, as a result, find it easier to keep inflation under control because their societies more willingly accept the sacrifices that come along with a tight monetary policy" [22]. The first attempt to evaluate central bank independence, the index was based on two pillars: political independence and financial independence measured only in 12 industrial countries which covered nine variables: final authority, the presence of the government representative in the central bank board, the degree in which the government appoints the board members, board members' number, board members' tenure, central bank governor's tenure, financial and fiscal independence, the authority which stipulates the check and balances of the board members, and the authority which determines the profit distribution Bade and Parkin [23]. In the second attempt Grilli et al. [24] developed an evaluation of central bank independence based on two pillars: economic independence and political independence measured in 18 developed countries that covered five variables: budgetary deficit monetary financing; monetary policy instruments; governor's and board members' appointments;

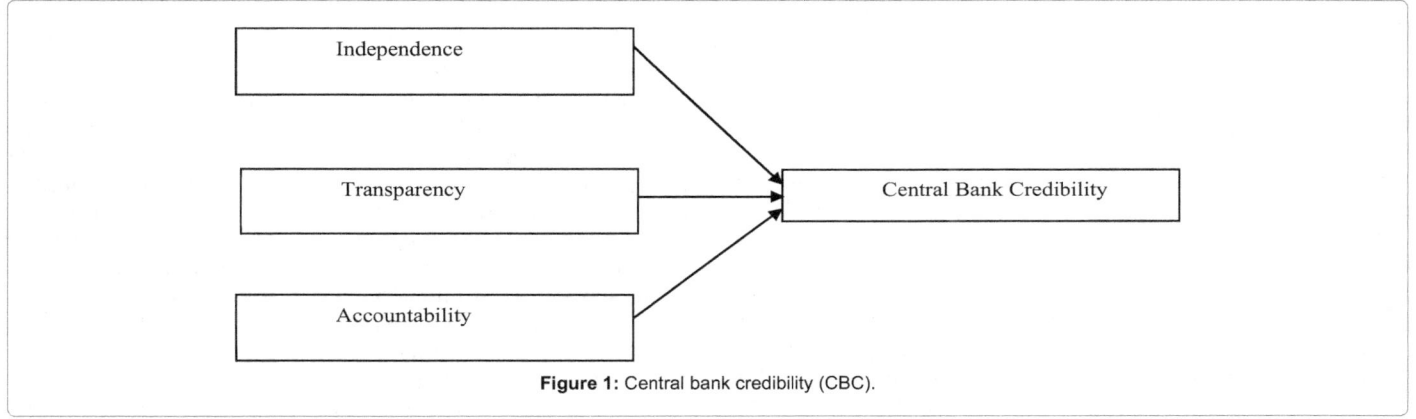

Figure 1: Central bank credibility (CBC).

the relationship between central bank and the government; and the fundamental law.

The first attempt in measuring central bank transparency an index which offered 11 variables regarding the supply of information, the understanding of the monetary policy process, procedural transparency and central bank autonomy and responsibility was established [25]. Eijffinger et al. [26] has distinguished five types of transparency: political, economic, procedural, policy and operational. Eijffinger and Geraats used a normalization technique the minimum score being 0 and the maximum score 1.

The first attempt to evaluate the degree of central bank accountability an index upon 21 developed countries which had a simple four variables was made concerning: the external monitoring of the central bank, publishing the meetings of the monetary policy council, publishing central Bank information in regular publications and the existence of an overridden mechanism in case of certain shocks [27].

When the central bank of Somalia was reopened in 2006 until the present time in 2015, its functionality is limited. The CB is operating under an old, in the mid of the 20th century decree Law N0 6 of 18 October 1968. Vision of the CB of Somalia is to: foster monetary stability, maintain the value of the Somali shilling, promote the economic growth of the republic, and contribute to the financial and economic policies. The reality is that the CB of Somalia cannot reach global financial markets because the bank has no functional regulator to attract private sector investors. The CB of Somalia lacks the following: legal and regulatory framework, strong property rights culture, enforceability of collateral contracts, and accessible credit information and sound financial structure. There are two other central banks (the CBs of Somali land and Punt land) though they are not in a position to perform key central functions of typical instruments necessary to conduct monetary policy yet they are challenge to the CB of Somalia. Because of the limited functionality of CB of Somalia, the Somali remittances companies are the main actors of the Somalia's financial sector. These remittances companies have large network of agents that give service all towns in the country.

Without a fully functional CB of Somalia, the Somali business context faced a huge risk and the private sector of the Somali business could not continue to generate positive multiplier effects. So there is a need to rebuild a credible CB of Somalia under the following three directions: independence, transparency, and accountability.

1. How Somali central bank can be credible in terms of political, financial, and monetary policy independence?

2. How can be examined the types and the degree of transparency and can be settled ways to measure the transparency of the Somali central bank?

3. Does central bank of Somalia have clear and well defined financial accountability structures?

Recently, the desirability of CBI became a popular feature in monetary making institutions like CBs to attain their objectives such as price stability. Basically CBI depends on two pillars: theoretical and empirical. Before anything else, it is better to understand the roles and primary responsibilities of CBs. Central banks have four traditional roles: conducting monetary policy; preserving financial stability; supervising and regulating banks; and safeguarding payment and settlement systems. Keeping and making sure the price stability and financial stability is the first primary responsibility a CB has to do.

The CB should have both instrument independence and full financial independence to achieve its main objectives. In order to avoid any conflicts of interest, the high ranking officials in the CB must have to stay long term in office; also they should not have other positions in government or in the private sector. Developed countries showed better proxies in actual independence relative to CB legal independence than developing countries. In developing countries, their behavioral independence showed two indices which are extremely and relatively more important: (1) actual VS legally mandated CB governors' turnover, (2) the CBs of developing countries are extremely vulnerable to a very high frequency of political change meaning there are high occurrences of political transitions within a short period of time leading to replacement of the CB governor [28]. Primarily, CBI can solve three inter-related problems: (1) CBI configures rationale balance between fiscal authority relatively to monetary authority not to satisfy the government's long-run budget constraints meaning both authorities; fiscal and monetary are separately independent. This separation of powers removes the possibility of inflation correspondence to the wishes of the monetary authority. (2) CBI protects citizens from transitional problems like tax distortions caused by bad political business. (3) CBI solves inconsistency problem of the monetary policy [29]. In developing countries, the TOR of Cukierman et al. [30] is significantly related to inflation [31]. There is a theoretical standard case for CBI intentionally keeping inflation bias because this bias is the consequence of the interactions between policy makers and rational public; this happens when the monetary policy makers is to care about both price stability and employment but their level of employment preference is higher than the natural level Kydland et al. [2] and Barro et al. [32]. According to Barro et al. [33], and Cukierman [34] the reason why this CBI inflationary bias is allowed to happen is the existence of two things: (1) tax distortions (2) employee unions, trying to keep the real wage above its market clearing level. Apparently, discrete policy makers create inflationary surprises trying to push employment above its natural level. The public understands and neutralizes any effect of inflation on employment because individuals acquainted the tricky temptations of the policy makers and correctly forecasts inflation. Undoubtedly, employment remains at its natural level but monetary policy is subject to a suboptimal inflationary bias. Then, the consequence becomes a severe dynamic inconsistency monetary policy under discretion. Rogoff [4] suggested that conservative CBs can reduce bias by delegating the conduct of the monetary policy but consequently there appeared some smaller inflationary bias could be remained. Ironically, both CBs and governments need a contract approach to design a monetary institution that mediates them. Apparently, this institution is made of a body – tri-partite officials from government, CB and the parliament. The responsibility of the monetary institution is to structure a contract (optimal contract) between both parties: the government and CB.

Walsh [35] proposed that an optimal contract can entirely eliminate bias if the CB is advised to make the correct output amount stabilization. Svensson [36] explained the optimal contract can be used as a means of inflation targeting. If a CB has long run price stability path and its aim is to make the output target equal to potential or the employment target equal to its natural level with the help of authority delegation to CB instrumental independence can bring the ideal institutional arrangement [37]. The CBI rationalization outlined above is mainly based within the context of an inflation bias because of the primary motive of monetary expansion in both developed and developing economies. In the case of the developed countries, wide capital markets allow their governments to borrow and finance deficits without raising the cost of borrowing too much. But in developing countries, during deficit periods, governments put powerful pressures to monetize on their CBs because of limited access to capital markets. This revenue motive for monetary expansion leaves behind a social inefficient bias [34].

To credibility, CBs anxiously seek to build their credibility especially during periods of disinflation thinking over the prioritization of two matters: (1) upward sensitivity, (2) inflation deviations to downward from its targets. For this, a CB needs to make sure not to miss the inflation target either from below or above. When a CB for example tries to connect some level of its credibility to a precautionary demand aiming to price stability, then the CB is waging to extremely restrictive average policies because theoretically there is a precautionary demand for expansion in one way and precautionary demand for price stability on the other way. These two policies; demand for expansion and demand for price stability easily tend to offset each other because the precautionary demand for expansion creates inflation bias while the other causes deflation bias. After the CB stabilizes inflation, the precautionary demand for expansion might remain to restart the risk of average inflation bias [38].

Economic policy and policies themselves fall into separate directions – economic policies can gain credibility from private agents to be effective but policies can become credible if they are effective. It is the responsibility of the central bank to develop a successful economic policy in which its viability and reliability depends on the perceptions of private agents. Credibility cannot be sustained unless economic growth and price stability is achieved. With the respect of new classical theory economic fundamentals, an independent CB can prove its capability to promoting development and economic growth [39].

Surprisingly, the emerging economies are increasingly developing the design and operation of monetary institutions (Central Banks and Currency Boards) involving monetary policy and exchange rates. The primary aim of these institutions is to influence the policy credibility. To gain financial credibility, political intervention by the government must be strictly prohibited otherwise the rational public would know the central bank financial policies are incredible and such political interventions may end up economically inconsistent liquidity trap [40].

Currency board is a monetary institution and its primary responsibility is the issuance of local currency which is fully backed by large stocks of a hard foreign reserve currency. The convertibility of the local currency must be upon demand and unlimited into the foreign reserve currency at a fixed exchange rate. Also there must be an inviolable strict line between the local and foreign currency reserve. As recommended by the IMF, the exchange rate must be written in the currency board's constitution [40,41], Hanke et al. [42] Assets payable in the foreign reserve currency and low risk interest earning securities are among the reserves held by the Currency Board. As the law may set, foreign reserve currency equals to 100 to 110 percent relative to the value of the local money stock [39].

According to Ghosh et al. [43], and Hanke et al. [42] historically, currency boards have successfully operated seventy countries. During 1990s, currency boards were operating in Argentina, Bulgaria, Bosnia, Cayman Islands, Estonia, Falkland Islands, Faroe Islands, Djibouti, and Gibraltar. The Estonian currency board was credited to having successfully stabilized the economy; the currency board of Argentine ended inflation and maintained stability during Mexican financial crises in 1994–1995; during Asian financial crises and from British to Chinese rule, the Hong Kong currency board settled and maintained stability. In the emerging economies, their currency boards proved highly

credible way to manage the exchange rates [44]. Empirical evidence is showing that countries with currency boards inflation is 4% lower than in countries with other types of exchange rates [43]. When the currency board is maintaining fixed exchange rates by having sufficient holdings of the foreign reserve currency, this means the board is giving confidence to investors and the public in general [45].

Finally, one must not confuse the responsibility of currency board with independent CB responsibilities. The currency board assists the operations of an independent CB in a complementary way which is proving to the public the monetary policy management would continue undisturbed by political intervention or any pressures from the government. Currency boards cure credibility deficit in countries where CB institutions are new or their performance is not good due to poor track record. The members in the currency boards are usually selected from the ranks of technocrats, economists, and bankers – they are appointed to stay long term in office to make sure the exchange rate policy is in the hands of independent authority free from strategic incentives to change direction toward improper deviations or wrong expansionary course [39].

To transparency and accountability, there are two views; one view says transparency is a precondition for accountability, and the other view says transparency is the result of the accountability process. Although these two views are related to each other, transparency represents the whole society including media and financial markets to ensure whether central bank has done its objectives through clarity, truthfulness, and efficiency while accountability represents a responsible behavior imposed by legislation to make the CB feel accountable as it is undertaking monetary policy actions because accountability is directly happening to the conduct of monetary policy [20].

Central Bank Independence

Central Bank Independence (CBI) can be defined full independence from the government in issuing paper money – the authorities of the central bank should be commission members chosen by the votes of the parliament and there should be no any kind of relationship or communication between the cabinet of the ministers and members of the central bank commission. The state must be obliged to collect money in a legitimate way such as taxes. There is no way the government should be allowed to lend money from those who are responsible for the issuance of it [46].

CBI represents the institutional capacity of the central bank which is typically an institutional mandate responsible to conduct monetary policy free from all kinds of political interferences from any sides including government, industry and other interest groups [1].

Central bank independence (CBI) can be only found when monetary policy officials are not involved in any kind of political or government influence to implement the monetary policy [46]. In a much different way (Blinder) has pointed out the inevitability and desirability of a close cooperation between the CB and the finance ministry in times of crises and he proposed three different settings: (1) at times of serious financial crises; (2) during the aftermath of financial crises, when the economy may be astounding and monetary policy may be unconventional; (3) in normal times when monetary policy is conventional, but he strictly recommends there must be inviolable, clear, and bright line on monetary policy between the CB and the finance ministry. (Blinder) sheds light CBs lack the independence of non-monetary policy activities such as bank supervision and relevance of authorities, for example; bank supervision and deposit insurance must be in the same hands. He concludes the rationality of the CB independence is to be against politicians creating too much inflation when they are facing elections because their aim is to produce incentives reducing inflation or keeping it low only in a short time horizon instead the monetary policy must be controlled by technocrats with long time horizons [47].

Some scholars argued for the success and better monetary policy, there must be a crafted cooperation between monetary and fiscal policies. There is a severe uncertainty that an independent central bank controls inflation unless some preconditions of fiscal policy are met. Central bank needs to examine any fiscal conditions that can support its independence. It may be the consideration of two separate equilibrium conditions: first, the real demand for money must be equal to the real supply of money; second, the real value of government liabilities must be equal to the real value of the consolidated government's surplus expected at present time. The government fiscal policy always ensures if the second condition is met [48].

The relationship between central bank independence and economic performance produced the idea of CBI empirical support with three main conclusions: Firstly, there is a negative relationship between central bank independence and long term-inflation. There is a low inflation rate in countries with independent central banks compared in countries with their central banks are subject to government control. Secondly, there is a negative relationship between central bank independence and GNP when the long term budget deficit is expressed as percentage. Countries with independent central banks have much lesser deficit than those countries with their central banks are under government control. Thirdly, the central bank independence is not affecting negatively to the production or employment during over the long term [1].

According to several studies with empirical results supporting central bank independence provided by Grilli et al. [21], Cukierman et al. [14], Alesina and Summers [49], all these studies reached the same conclusions showing that there is a negative relationship between central bank independence and average inflation. Consequently, the central bank independence improves the possibility of reaching low inflation goals without real economic costs. On the other hand, if policy makers employ incentives of expansionary fiscal policy giving the possibility of creating surprise inflations make the monetary policy implementing low inflation policy incredible in the eyes of the public [50]. The ability to halting inflation expectations at a level that can be suited with monetary policy objectives brings reward of credibility to CBs [51].

In general, CBI falls into two categories: independence of goals and independence of instruments. Goal independence refers how it is possible for the central bank to determine the goals of its activities without being involved by the government. When it comes to the instrumental independence, the central bank needs absolute freedom to select the instruments that can make possible for the bank to achieve its goals. Ćorić and Cvrlje believe this division was accepted by most of the authors in papers written in 1990s [51].

According to Lybek [52] to CBI is identified as formal and effective (actual) independence. The formal (statutory) is a type of CBI stipulated and guaranteed by legislation that could possibly be divided into three stages: when independence is established by international treaties like the european central bank (ECB); the practice of constitutional independence like the CB of Switzerland; and establishment of independence under national legislation acts. (Lybek) advocated the safeguarding of goal and instrument independence can only be

achieved when issues of personnel and financial autonomy of central bank are secured under the national legislation acts. The qualification requirements of the CB governor and board members; the nomination and appointment of the CB governor and board members; the term of office, and the dismissal of the CB governor can only happen by the approval of the legelative body.

According to Ćorić and Cvrlje [51] the CBI criteria is divided into four categories: Nomination and dismissal of the central bank governor and other members was the most important category. The independence of the central bank to define the goals of the monetary policy and the final authority in decision making was the second most important category. The third category searches up to what level the central bank defines price stability and its main goal. The fourth category measures the imposition of the central bank lending restrictions.

Apparently, there are distinctions between goal (political) and instrumental (economical) independence. CBI basically appropriated with instrumental independence comes in the first place while goal independence comes in the second place. The more the government implements monetary policy independently the more the chance the central bank would have oppertunities to solve the problem of time inconsistency, Debelle and Fischer [53].

According to Eijffinger and Haan [54] two more types of independence appeared: individual and financial independence. There is a positive solution by the presence of the government officials in the boards which empoly people but the implications of financial independence shows negative impact if the government tries to be involved in any kind of credit relations between the central bank and the government itself. The most important factor in the role of CBI is "time" to implement consistent monetary policy.

In the history of the European Central Bank (ECB), the experts outlined five types of independence as preconditions for optimum implementation of the monetary policy: institutional independence, legal independence, personnel independence, functional and operational independence, and lastly, organizational and financial independence [51].

Increasing Role of CBI

For many years, there was a problem of independence, how independence is to be measured and how CBI influences macro-economic variables. In 1970s and 1980s most of the developed countries experienced high and continuous inflation rates. Two authors, Barro and Gordon [32] explained the reason why? They proved that central banks set variables above their natural values which makes possible the balance of external and internal to happen and the result became high inflation rates. The public wanted to know the truth – they asked why such high inflation was happening, they needed explanations about the motives of the central banks, the subject of the price stability to economic growth and the reason why the economic objectives were became unrealistic? The answer was clear, there was an inconsistency of monetary policy and the behavior of central banks was motivated by political influence. The ruling parties have always been oriented to short term economic gains. It is a common knowledge to everyone the expansionary monetary policy is a unique solution but it always ignores the short term inflation effects. The solution of the problem seemed the CBI is to be increased.

Although the increase of CBI was a way tremendously intended to reduce inflation rate, after a time new reasons emerged. Cukierman [37] suggested the increased independence was due to by two factors:

(a) global and (b) regional. The idea of liberalization strongly advanced to all segments of economy, and especially influenced capital flow and the expansion of capital markets, and the need for stable macro-economic conditions was highly increased. Both domistic and foreign investors put their trust to a higher level of CBI with greater efforts focusing to prolonged price stability.

Regional contribution motives that increased independence were as follows: (1) after the institutions formerly designed safguarding nominal stability, like the European Monetary and the Bretton Woods systems have been brokendown, a new search for alternative institutions has emerged; (2) the highly independent German Bundesbank showed a good track record in assurance of nominal stability; (3) Maastricht treaty by EEC prerequisited central bank independence upgrading for the membership in the European Monetary Union, taking Bundesbank as an example; (4) after inflation has been successfully stabilized, policy makers commenced thinking over institutional arrangements which have the capabilities of reducing future inflations. Increasing central bank independence appeared a live natural way and could have a high possibility to achieve this objective; (5) the former socialist countries tried to create institutional frameworks in order to have better and orderly functioning market economies. The realization of industrial economies that legal independence is negatively related to inflation motivated the grant of substantial de jure independence to many central banks [37].

Measurement of CBI

To measure central bank independence, the following four categories can make a CB more independent: (a) the appointment of the central bank governor not by the prime minister or minister of finance but by the board of the central bank. This brings the central bank governor not to be subject dismissal and has to stay a long term in office. In the appointment process, these features are important preventing the governor of central bank pressures from politicians; (b) policy decisions of the CB must be made without direct involvement of the government; (c) the charter of the CB must give its first priority making price stability the primary goal of the monetary policy; and finally CB independence is in a higher position when the ability of the government to borrowing from CB is limited [55].

According to the pioneering work of Bade and Parking [23], the measurement of formal independence can be based on legal criteria of political (goal) and economic (instrument) independence. Later Cukierman, Webb, and Neyabti [34] developed a comprehensive index an LVAW of CBI. It is a measurement which gives a numerical weights to each question.

Bade and Parking [56] and Banaian, Laney, and Willet [57] started the first attempts at measuring central bank independence. BP divided central banks into four classes by using three dimensions of central bank structures: (1) final authority over monetary policy making; (2) no government officials in the boards of central banks; (3) board members independent of government appointment. Alesina [58] supported the work of BP introduced marginal coverage criterion inspecting the ability of monetary policy to resist the pressures of fiscal policy possibly monetize debt. Grilli, Masciandaro, and Tabellini [59] proposed an index of eight features equally weighted summation approaching interpretations of central bank laws and disagreements. Cukierman, Webb, and Neyapti [34] produced the most popular measurement of central bank independence. They considered 17 different legal attributes by using a variety of scales measurement like two or three point scales and as higher as seven point scales sometimes

in an unweighted average (LVAU) and weighted average (LVAW) [60].

Which one is beneficial for the society; a democratically elected government creating a socially high cost inflationary bias by trying to achieve objectives like high employment and easy financing of government expenditures or a consrvative central banker which has primary concerns about price stability than government does? The answer is clear. The only main objective of monetary policy that a CB should focus is the monetary policy on price stability. To be realized this focus of the bank effectively the bank must get sufficient backup of legal independence in the choice of monetary policy. Receiving explicit or implicit instructions from the government officials is strictly forbidden by laws of the central bank mandate. Sufficient personnel and financial indepenence is a gauge showing central bank legal independence which is giving the central bank the capability to resist political pressures and enough capacity to prepare constraints against the government's ability resorting inflationary financing [61].

According to Haan and Sturm [62] CBI measurement usually encounters disputes and problems like unexplicit laws that cannot make clear specifications about the line of duties between two authorites: the central bank authorities and political authorities under all possibilities. This always brings unclear indicators of actual independence compared to legal independence. Cukierman [14] believes industrial countries may show better proxies measurement for actual independence than developing countries. Therefore, Cukierman [30] and Cukierman et al. [34] developed central bank autonomy which was based on the central bank governor's term office instead on central bank laws. It is clear, this literature is turning the understanding to a higher turnover of central bank governors indicates a lower level of independence. Until now, a few studies have used the TOR of central bank governors as an idicator for CBI and the matter was concluded the existence of inflation performance between developing countries and the TOR of central bank governors. This literature has a drawback – the studies available until recently are all based on the data of Cukierman [30] and Cukierman et al. [34]. De jure and de facto indexes necessary to measure central bank independence are as follows: Political independence (final authority; the presence of the government representative in the central bank board; the degree in which the government appoints the board members; board members' number; board members' tenure; and central bank governor's tenure), Financial independence (financial and fiscal independence; the authority which stipulates the check and balances of the board members; and the authority which determines the profit distribution), this is the first attempt measured in 12 developed countries [23]. Economical independence (budgetary deficit monetary financing; and monetary policy instrumrnts), Political independence (governor's and board members' appointments; the relationship between central bank and government; and fundamental law), the second attempt measured in 18 developed countries [24]. LVAU and LVAW unweighted and weighted measures respectively (governor; monetary policy making process; monetary policy objectives; limits upon the unguaranteed borrowings; limits upon guaranteed borrowings; terms of lending; potential beneficiaries of the central bank borrowings; imposed limits upon the central banks borrowings; maturity of loans; restriction on interest rates; and prohibition on lending on primary market), measured in 68 developed and developing countries Cukierman et al. [34]. TOR (Turn over rate of central bank governor), measured in 19 developed and 39 developing countries [63].

The possible meaursement limits of CBI is usually outlined into four categories: personnel; policy objectives; policy instrumrents; and financial independence. In personnel independence, there must be legal procedures capable to limiting the government's role in appointment and dismissal of central bank governor. CBI is measured by looking at the primary monetary policy objectives of CBs to maintaining price stability. CBI is also measured by checking the policy instrument of the CB because, central banks achieve their monetary policy objevtive through policy instrument independence. Finally CBI is measured by the financial independence of a CB. There mustn't be interdependence between government and central bank in budgetry matters. This assures the determination of fiscal policy and budget of the central bank not allowed to be a subject to executive or legislative decisions [64].

Transparency

Central bank transparency (CBT) refers as an atmosphere which is favorable to the side of the public in terms of the accessibility, understandability, and timely basis of the information about the objectives of the monetary policy, its legality, institutionality, and policy framework, monetary policy decisions, the information related to monetary policy, the terms of central bank accountability, and the rationality of monetary policy and its data [65].

According to Geraats transparency is defined as, when, the information between monetary policy makers and other economic agents is symmetrical. Geraats is advocating that transparency is new and largely responsive to the best practices of central banking. Tranparency is one of the most important key features of monetary policy. In 1998, there was a survey of 94 central banks conducted by Fry, Julius, Mahadeva, Roger, and Sterne which became the most understandable survey on the conduct of monetary policy. The survey showed a greater consideration of transparency by 74% of the central banks marked transparency as a vital component of their monetary policy framework. Lack of transparency generates opacity, which leads to asymmetric information, then, the result becomes uncertainty. If both central bank and private sector have the same information about the structure of the economy, then, it appears that transparency prevails. However, transparency doesn't mean perfect information or full certainty.

The beginning of central bank transparency characterises in a number of intertwined mechanisms. First, transparency includes bulky means to pressuring the government to be more responsive to the public. Second, transparency is a primary key of accountability which is getting support from central bank independence. Third transparency enhances the communication between markets and policy decisions. In a transparent atmosphere investors are aware of policy action. In good transparency, there is less chance of financial distress caused by sharp movements of asset prices after policy changes happen. Fourth, transparency enhances policy credibility, policy flexibility, and credibilty of central bank's commitment [55].

The internal decision making process of the central bank depends on transparency. Central bank achieves its mandate through transparency that explains the uses of different instruments of monetary policy. Transparency needs well defined monetary policy strategy and a timely statistical data in the form of publications and forecasts on which the central bank bases its decisions. These days, there are academic comunities and political audiences who bases their arguments and ideas on the favorabilty of transparency in monetary policy. There are four categories on which an IMF code called "good practice on transparency in monetary and financial policies" is structured. Categories are as follows: (1) clarity of roles, responsibilities and objectives; (2) formulating open process and reporting policy decisions; (3) public availability of information policies; and (4) integrity of accountability and assurances. Inflation rate targeting has especial importance in

the operational transparency of central banks beause there could be a monetary policy action that could change, for example , the central bank financing rate – the prevailing of this matter necessitates the existence of time lag (which empirical research shows it could take 6 up to 8 quarters) between monetary policy action and the response of the inflation rate. This time lag changes the transparency into opacity and the public feels difficulty to monitor and evaluate how the central bank is doing its actual commitment to inflation rate targeting. A central bank always has a course of policy actions and the public has expectations of inflation. When the influence of public expectations and the credibilty of central bank and maintainance of its independence act accordingly the target becomes credible and the inflation expectations are reduced to minimum level. In terms of employment and ex-post real interest burden creates costly unsuccessful operations trying to bring down high inflation rates to lower target rates. If disinflation social costs gets higher the implementation of disinflationary policy politically becomes very difficult and central banks lose their instrument independence [1]. Eijffinger and Geraats [26] has distinguished five types of transparency: political, economical, procedural, policy and operational. Eijffinger and Geraats used a normalization technique the minimum score being 0 and the maximum score 1. At this moment the researcher likes to describe these five types of transparency one by one: (1) Political transparency indicates openness about policy objectives and institutional arrangements like central bank independence, contracts, and override mechanisms that clarify the motives of monetary policy makers; (2) Economic transparency focuses on economic data, policy models, and central bank forecasts. This economic information is used for monetary policy; (3) Procedural transparency gives details about the monetary policy strategy and policy deliberations account through minutes and voting records. This typical provision describes the way monetary policy decisions are taken; (4) Policy transparency is a form of policy inclination that embraces explanation of policy decisions and prompt announcements and indications of likely future policy actions; (5) Operational transparency supports operating instrument to control errors. It also prevents macroeconomic transmission disturbances. This whole process concerns the implementation of monetary policy actions.

Measurement of Transparency

According to Fry et al. [66] measurement of transparency covers a wide range of aspects on monetary policy frameworks ranging from institutional characteristics to policy focus and monetary analysis. (Fry) constructed indices in which he included a measure of policy explanations primarily based on (1) if central bank prepares explanations of policy decisions; (2) the publication preparations of forward-looking analysis; (3) assessment explanation and analysis (bulletins, speeches, and research papers). But, here, the researcher inclines to present other types of central bank transparency measures: Siklos [25] measured central bank transparency in 20 developed countries and European Central Bank. He constructed indices composed of the following 11 main variables: publication of minutes of central bank meetings; key assumptions in generating outlook; publication of committee voting record; regular information published about how monetary policy decisions are made and their justification; operational instrument of monetary policy; instrument independence; are monetary policy and operational objectives the same?; special recognition of the role of financial system stability; economic modeling procedures; forms of communication; and publication of a monetary policy strategy and limits of monetary policy. Eijffinger and Geraats [26] measured central bank transparency according to their five types division. Each has three variables. (1) Political transparency measure: is there a formal statement of the objectives of monetary policy with an explicit prioritization in case of multiple objectives? Is there a quantification of the primary objectives? Are there explicit institutional arrangements or contracts between the monetary authorities and the government? (2) Economical transparency measure: does the central bank disclose the formal macroeconomic models that uses for policy analysis? Are the basic economic data relevant for the conduct of monetary policy publicly available? Does the central bank regularly publish its own macroeconomic forecast? (3) Procedural transparency measure: does the central bank provide an explicit policy rule or strategy that describes its monetary policy framework? Does the central bank give a comprehensive account of policy deliberations within a reasonable amount of time? Does the central bank disclose how decisions on the level of its main operating instrument/target were reached? (4) Policy transparency measure: are decisions about adjustments to the main operating instrument or target promptly announced? Does the central bank provide an explanation when it announces policy decisions? Does the central bank disclose an explicit policy inclination after every policy meeting or an explicit indication of likely future policy actions? (5) Operational transparency measure: does the central bank evaluate to what extent its main operating targets has been achieved? Does the central bank regularly provide information on macroeconomic disturbances that affect the policy transmission process? Does the central bank regularly provide an evaluation of the policy outcome in light of its macroeconomic objectives? [67] developed an index based on three main pillars of central bank transparency measurement: (1) Objective measure which has five variables (clear objectives, clear priorities, clear definition, clear time horizon, and quantification); (2) Strategy measure that has three variables (announcement of the strategy, interest rate decision immediately announced and always explained, and inflation forecast); (3) Communication strategy measure which has six variables (parliamentary hearings, frequency of reports, meeting schedule, press conference/press releases, publication of minutes, and publication of individual votes).

Accountability

According to the definition of Demertzis et al. [68] accountability is defined in a combination of meaning and responsibility in which the targets of economic performance is under the care of policy makers who are bearing, can and would have been held the responsibility to make the indicators of economic performance closer to the target values set. Central bank transparency has two different rationales: economic benefits and democratic accountability [69].

Measurement of accountability

Fry et al. [66] reported two types of accountability measures: public accountability and accountability with respect to a specific target which have common characteristics of combining both transparency and responsibility. The central bank accountability measurement indices first constructed by BHK is based the following four variables: the central bank must be subject to external monitoring by the parliament; the minutes of meetings necessary to the decisions of monetary policy must be published; the central bank must publish an inflation or monetary policy report, in addition to standard central bank bulletins; and there must be a clause that allows the central bank to be overridden if certain shocks appear. Bini-Smaghi and Gros [70] measured accountability in 20 developed countries and ECB using the following measures: Ex ante accountability; Ex post accountability; and accountability procedures. Here, the researcher considers the measurement of accountability procedures and there are four variables: participation of government representative at meeting of the decision-making bodies as observers;

publication of summary minutes; publication of detailed minutes; publication of the votes of the members of the decision-making bodies. Ex ante accountability has five variables: clear definition of the objective of price stability; announcement of the operational target; announcement of the intermediate target; announcement of indicators for assessing monetary policy; and explanation of how monetary policy targets affect other policies and objectives. Ex post accountability has six variables: publication of data on intermediate target or explanation of possible deviation; publication of inflation forecast and deviation from inflation target; explanation of main policy measures and underlying reasons; explanation of how these measures affect other policies; regular public reports; and hearings in parliament.

Design

This study adopted a descriptive research design to achieve the study objectives. Descriptive study attempts to describe or define a subject, often by creating a profile of a group of problems, people, or events, through the collection of data and tabulation of the frequencies on research variables or their interaction [71]. This study uses quantitative approach which determines the relationship between an independent variable and dependent variables [72]. Survey is a research design that is used to present oriented methodology used to investigate population by selected samples to analyse and discover occupancy. Its main purposes to find out descriptions of some part of the population and explain as they are, as they were, or as they will be [73]. The justification of choosing the survey design is the rapid collection of data, and the suitability of the nature of this study. It also has been utilized to collecting primary data process of this study.

Sample

The sample size of this study is composed of 32 respondents from the banking industry in Somalia, especially in Mogadishu.

Instrument

The study made use of primary data. Primary data was collected using a semi-structured questionnaire which was administered to the management of the banking industry in Mogadishu. The questionnaire sought to obtain information pertaining to general information of the respondents, effect on central bank credibility: independence, transparency, and accountability.

Result

Independence

Independence has shown an abnormality of data distribution about five questions of central bank independence. The result is quite positively skewed to the right. The frequency of the lowest average mean question is below one. The second lowest average mean question, its frequency is below five. The third lowest average mean question has a level five frequency. The frequency level of question four which ranks the fourth position in high mean average is above five. The frequency level of the last question which has the highest high average mean is above (15) fifteen (Figure 2). The overall of high mean average of five questions of central bank independence questions is 9.19 and the Std. Dev. is 1.12.

Transparency

Transparency has indicated an abnormality of data distribution which is somewhat different from the abnormality of central bank independence. The central bank transparency questions were (15) fifteen in total but this graph has shown only eight histogram bars on central bank transparency, obviously some of the questions had same high mean average. But the interesting thing is that eight transparency questions are below level five frequencies. The rest seven central bank transparency questions which originally had high mean average of 1.94 and 1.91 have now got the highest frequency level which is above 12.5. The overall computation of high average mean of (15) fifteen central bank transparency questions is now 27.88 and the Std. Dev. is 2.882. Three questions of central bank transparency which originally had high average mean of 1.84 have just fallen the central tendency of the mean bell shaped line (Figure 3). Five transparency questions have gone left side of the central tendency mean line while seven questions have gone to the right side, so the result is positively skewed to the right.

Accountability

Accountability has proven an abnormality of data distribution about five questions of central bank accountability which is very similar to the data distribution of central bank independence. The result of data distribution is quite positively skewed to the right. Three central bank accountability questions have dramatically fallen to below frequency level of five while one question is below level (10) ten frequencies. The last central bank accountability question is somewhere between of the level of frequencies 15-20 (Figure 4). The overall of originally high mean average central bank accountability questions is now 9.19 and the Std. Dev. is 1.091.

Credibility

Credibility has given an abnormality of data distribution about five questions of central bank credibility which is basically similar to others but typically, it is quite different because four central bank credibility questions are far below the frequency level of five. The last credibility question is surprisingly skyrocketing to the highest frequency level of

(30) thirty which it is seen in the first time. This data distribution is positively skewed to the right side of central tendency line (Figure 5). The overall mean average equals 9.53 and its Std. Dev. is 1.164.

Credibility of Somali Central Bank

The credibility of Somali central bank has merely shown the greatest or overall abnormality of data distribution about (30) thirty questions answering whether central bank of Somalia is credible in which the first five questions have described central bank independence while the next (15) fifteen questions have described of central bank transparency and the next five questions are about central bank accountability. The last five questions are about central bank credibility. It is not surprise whether this graph has shown only nine histogram bars instead of (30) thirty. Let the researcher show you how this is happened. The highest original high mean average 1.97 has appeared only one time in credibility questions while the second highest average 1.94 has appeared four times: one in independence, two in transparency, and only one time in credibility. The third highest mean average 1.91 has shown seven times; five in transparency and two in credibility while the fourth highest mean average 1.88 has appeared in only and only one time in accountability questions. The fifth highest mean average is 1.87 and it has appeared only one time in central bank accountability questions while 1.84 which is the sixth highest mean average has shown itself four times, only one time in central bank independence questions and three times in transparency. 1.81, which is the third lowest mean average has happened five chances: four times in independence and transparency in equal chances, and only one time in credibility while second lowest mean average 1.78 has also had five chances to happen; four times in transparency and accountability questions by equal chances and only one chance in independence questions. The lowest mean average 1.75 has only had one chance to happen in central bank transparency questions. So everyone can see now that these nine histogram bars

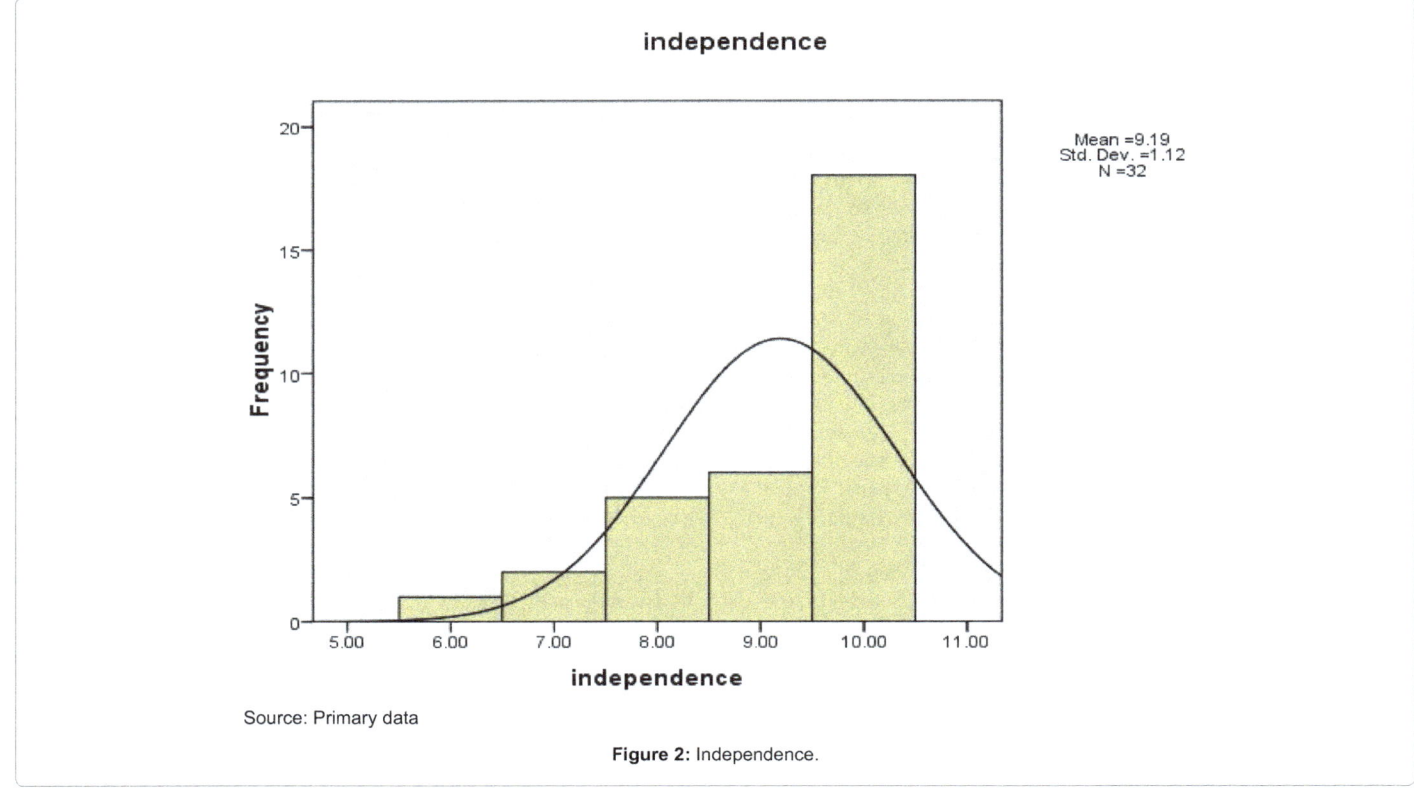

Source: Primary data

Figure 2: Independence.

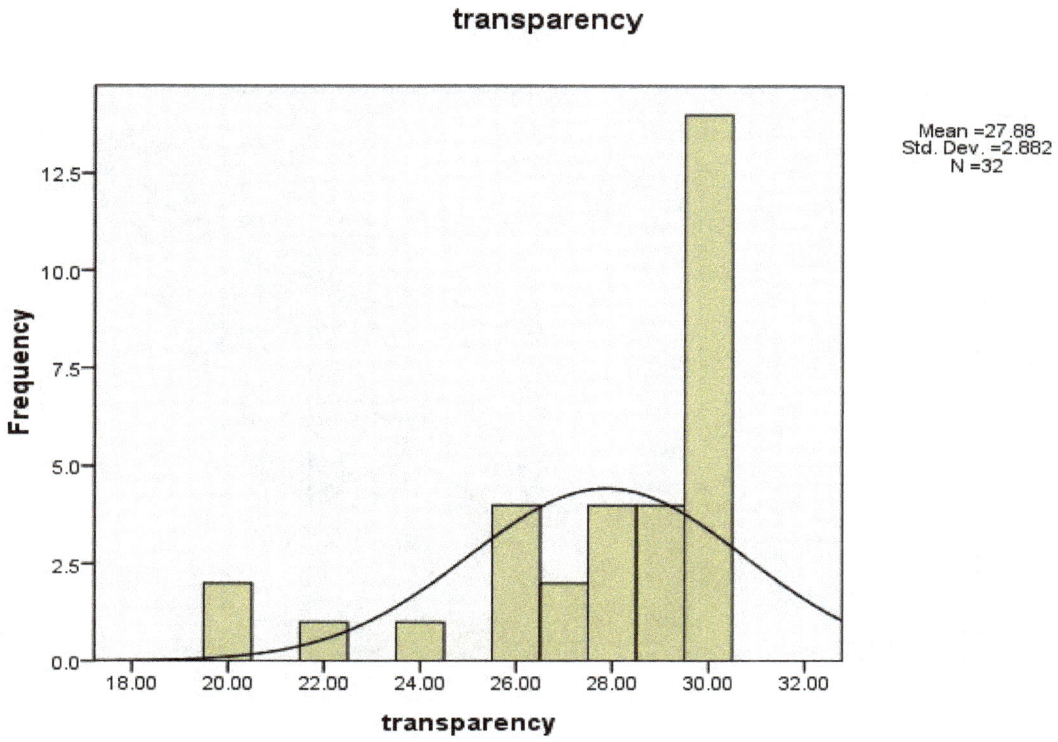

Source: Primary data

Figure 3: Transparency.

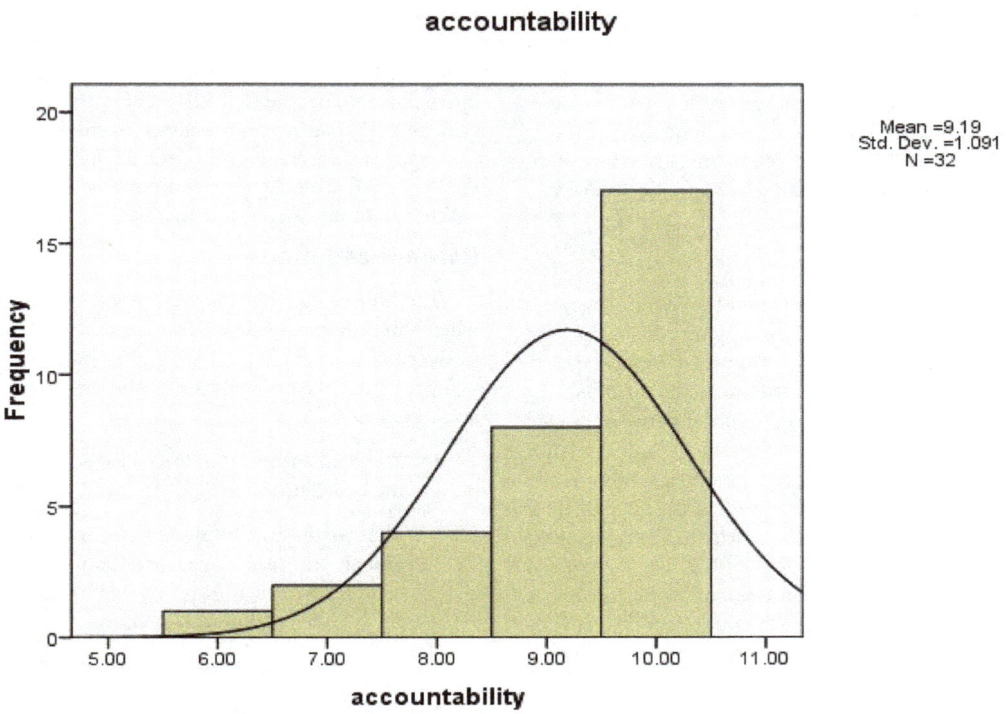

Source: Primary data

Figure 4: Accountability.

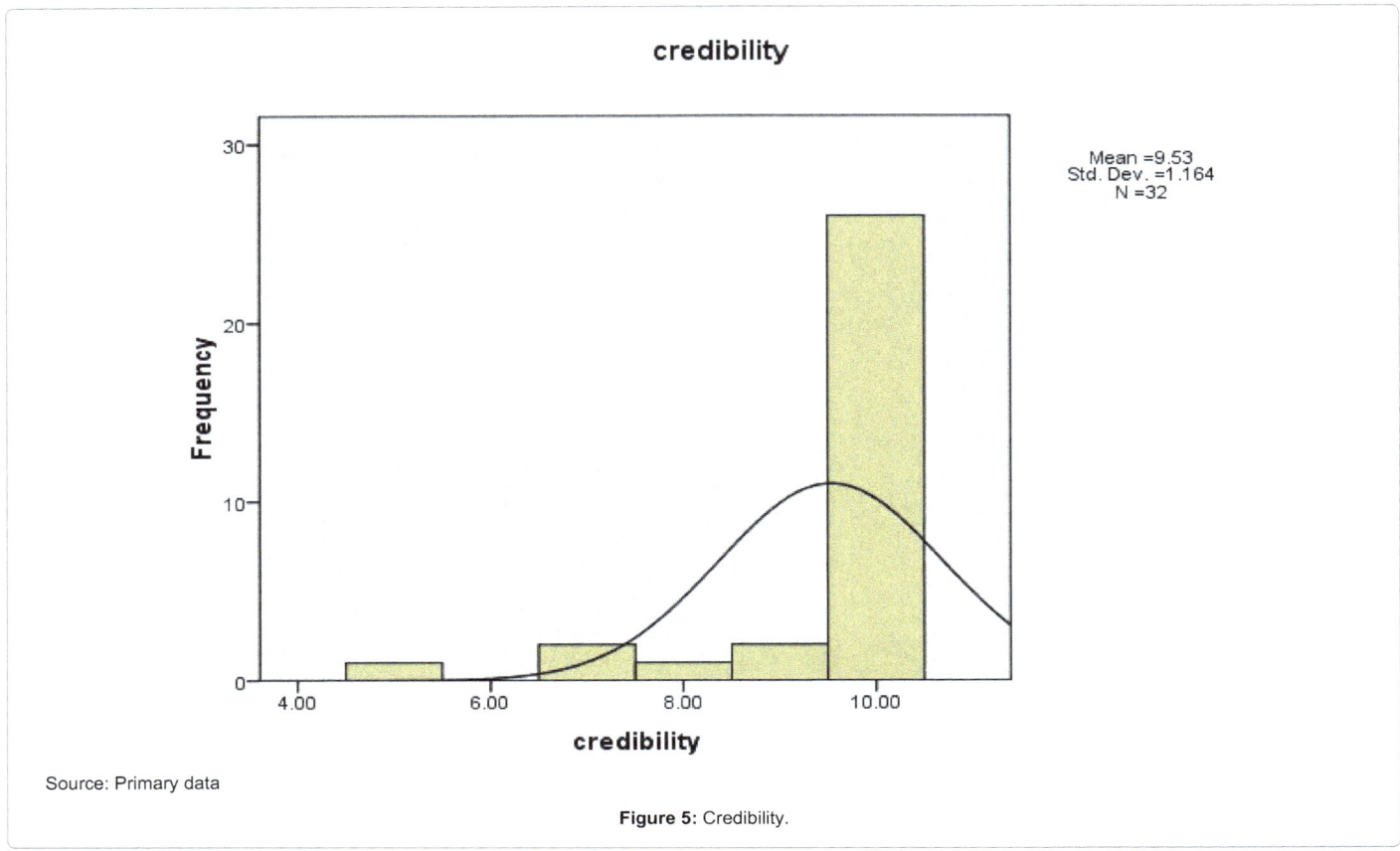

Source: Primary data

Figure 5: Credibility.

have accounted for nine mean averages: (1.97, 1.94, 1.91, 1.88, 1.87, 1.84, 1.81, 1.78 and 1.75). It appears almost (21) twenty-one questions have already gone to the right of the central tendency line in which (12) twelve of them have fallen below level twelve frequencies and nine of the twenty-one questions happened below level eight frequencies while the rest nine questions are below level five frequencies, so this abnormal data distribution is positively skewed to the right. The overall mean computation of (30) thirty questions is 55.78 and the Std. Dev. is 5.235 (Figure 6).

Discussion

The countries their central banks dominated the literature review of this research were among developed and emerging economies. The monetary policy of their central banks always supported independence, transparency and accountability and it is the independent monetary policy that necessarily established a clear tight border between central bank authority and government officials to safeguard the independence of the monetary policy because those governments themselves already implemented the CBI to represent the institutional capacity of their central banks. In Somalia, the government authority has never allowed an independent monetary policy and the idea of CBI has never been advocated in the public institutions for the interest of the public. This is the mainstream which is behind the reason why this larger discrepancy between literature review in this research and the result of the Somali central bank appeared.

Conclusion

The primary responsibility of an independent CB is to make sure and keep the price stability. To do this, the desirability of CBI became a popular feature in monetary making institutions like CBs to obtain their objectives. Only CBs that have long price stability path can make the output target equal to potential or the employment target equal to its natural level with the help of authority delegation to the instrumental independence of the CB that could bring an ideal institutional arrangement. During disinflation, CBs think over two matters in order to safeguard their credibility: upward sensitivity and inflation deviation to downward from its targets. Similarly CBI rationalization is based within the context of an inflation bias.

Recommendations

The findings of this study is indicating and suggesting the areas, where the ailing Somali central bank can look for its institutional recovery arrangements. The central bank of Somalia needs full independence which will make the bank to be transparent and accountable.

- The final authority of the CB of Somalia must be stipulated by the board members

- The board members' number, the board members' tenure, and central bank governor's tenure must be clearly stated in a central bank's statutory enacted by the parliament

- The authority of the central bank of Somalia that stipulates the check and balances of the board members must be independent

- The CB of Somalia must enjoy an economical independence which the bank determines the budgetary deficit monetary financing, monetary policy instruments, and the final authority which determines the profit distribution

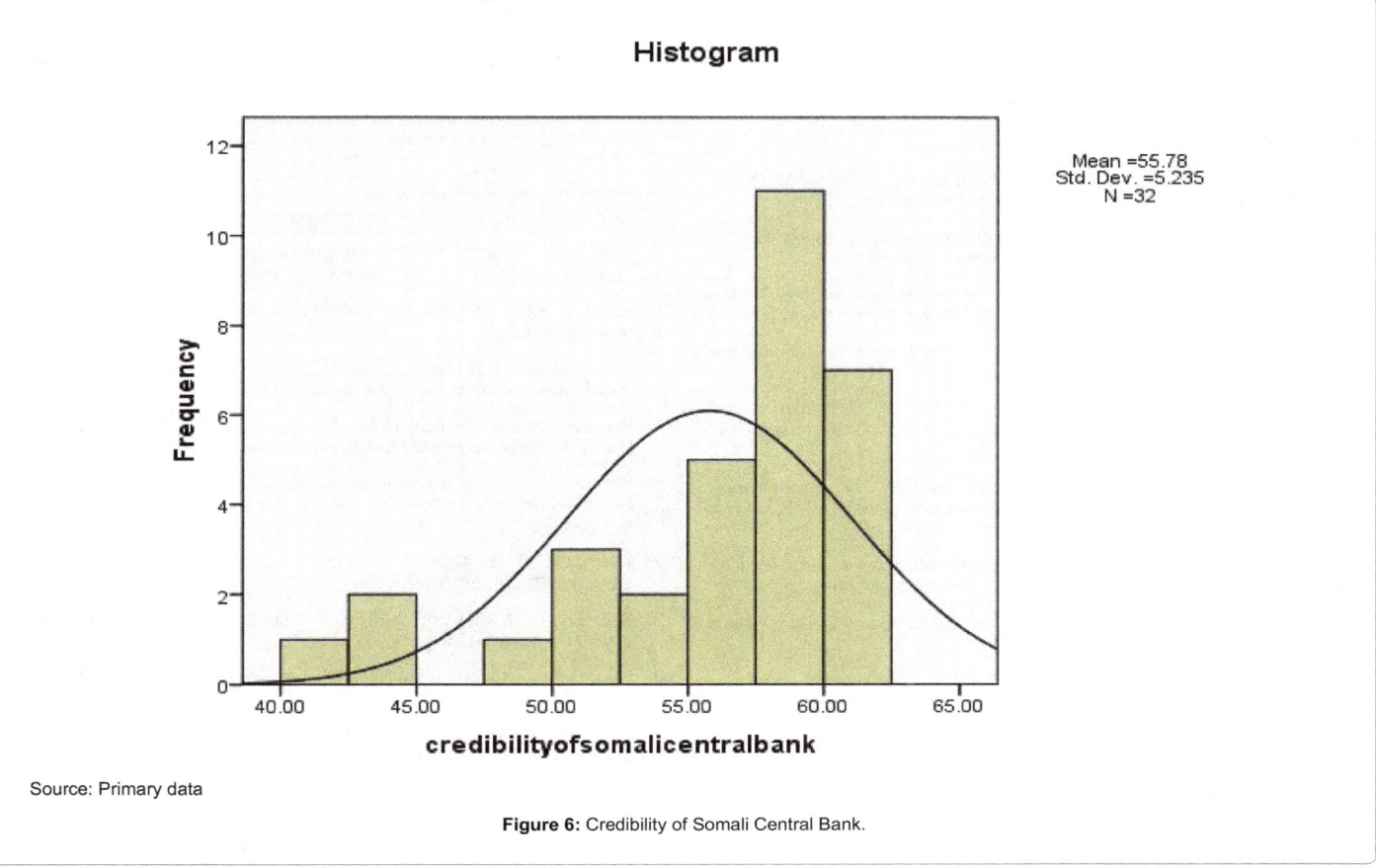

Source: Primary data

Figure 6: Credibility of Somali Central Bank.

- The governor's and board members appointments must be happened by the vote of the parliament

- As political transparency, the CB of Somalia must describe the formal objectives of the monetary policy with an explicit prioritization in case of multiple objectives. The CB of Somali has to quantify the primary objectives. the SCB must have an explicit institutional arrangements or contracts between the monetary authorities and the government

- As economical transparency, the SCB must prepare a basic economic data relevant for the conduct of monetary policy which is publicly available. The bank must use policy analyses to disclose the formal macroeconomic models. The SCB must regularly publish its own macroeconomic forecast

- As procedural transparency, the SCB must provide an explicit policy rule or strategy that describes its monetary policy framework. The bank must give a comprehensive account of policy deliberations within a reasonable amount of time. The SCB must disclose its decisions on the level of its main instrument

- As policy transparency, the central bank decisions must be about adjustment to the main operating instrument or the announcements of prompt targets. The bank must provide an explanation when it announces policy decisions. The central bank of Somalia must disclose explicit policy inclinations after every policy meeting or an explicit indication of likely future policy actions

- As operational transparency, central bank of Somalia must

evaluate how its main policy operating targets have been achieved. The bank must regularly provide information on macroeconomic disturbances that affect the policy transmission process. The SCB must regularly provide an evaluation of the policy outcome in light of its macroeconomic objectives

- The central bank of Somalia must be subject to external monitoring by the parliament

- The government should have no rights to give instructions to the central bank of Somalia

- The government should participate at meeting of the decision making bodies as observers

- The central bank of Somalia must have rights to prepare publications of the votes of the members of the decision making bodies

- The central bank of Somalia should have rights to prepare publications of statement of accountability and ultimate responsibility for monetary policy

- The central bank of Somalia should publish an inflation or monetary policy report of some kind, in addition to standard central bank bulletins/reports

- The central bank of Somalia must explain publicly to what extent it has been able to reach its objectives

- The central bank of Somalia must clearly define the objectives of price stability

- The central bank of Somalia must always and immediately announce the interest rate decisions

- The central bank of Somalia must publish the risks to the forecast and it must be better able to forecast inflation

References

1. Schwödiauer G, Komarov V, Akimova I (2006) Central Bank Independence, Accountability and Transparency: The Case of Ukraine.

2. Kydland F, Prescott E (1977) Rules Rather than Discretion: The Inconsistency of Optimal Plans. Journal of Political Economy 85: 473-492.

3. Barro RJ, Gordon D (1983) Rules, Discretion, and Reputation in a Positive Model of Monetary Policy. Journal of Monetary Economics 12: 101-121.

4. Rogoff K (1985) The Optimal Degree of Commitment to an Intermediate Monetary Target. Quarterly Journal of Economics 100: 1169-1190.

5. Bernanke BS (2010) Central Bank Independence, Transparency, and Accountability. Institute for Monetary and Economic Studies International Conference Tokyo pp: 1-16.

6. Spyromitros E, Tuysuz S (2012) Do Monetary Policy Transparency, Independence and Credibility Enhance. International Journal of Economics and Finance 4: 44-54.

7. Siklos P (2008) No Single Definition of Central Bank Independence Is Right for All Countries. European Journal of Political Economy 24: 802-816.

8. Spinesi L (2009) Rent-Seeking Bureaucracies, Inequality and Growth. Journal of Development Economics 90: 244-257.

9. Williams A (2009) On the Release of Information by Governments: Causes and Consequences. Journal of Development Economics 89: 124-138.

10. Gabillon E, Martimort D (2004) The Benefits of Central Bank's Political Independence. European Economic Review 48: 353-378.

11. Yang S (2008) Bureaucracy versus High Performance: Work Reorganization in the 1900s. The Journal of Socio-Economics 37: 1825-1845.

12. Mixon F, Upadhyaya K (2004) Examining Legislative Challenges to Central Bank Autonomy: Macroeconomic and Agency Costs Models. Journal of Economics and Business 56: 415-428.

13. Forder J (2005) Why is Central Bank Independence so Widely Approved? Journal of Economic Issues 39: 843-865.

14. Cukierman A (1992) Central Bank Strategy, Credibility and Independence. Cambridge.

15. Eijffinger SC, Haan DJ (1996) The Political Economy of Central Bank Independence. Princeton University, New Jersey.

16. Croitoru L (2012) Monetary policy : Faces unconventional , Lucian Croitoru.

17. Hornby AS (2000) Oxford Advanced Learner's Dictionary. Oxford University Press, Oxford.

18. Forder J (2004) Credibility in Context: Do Central Bankers and Economists Interpret the Term Differently? Econ Journal Watch 1: 413-426.

19. Blinder AS (1999) Central Bank Credibility: Why do we care? How do we build it? NBER Working Paper Series.

20. Dumiter FC (2014) Central Bank Independence, Transparency and Accountability Indexes: Survey. Timisoara Journal of Economics and Business 7: 35-54.

21. Oritani Y (2010) Public Governance of Central Banks: An Approach from New Institutional Economics.

22. Tognato C (2012) Central Bank Independence: Cultural Codes and Symbolic Performances. Palgrave: MacMillan.

23. Bade M, Parkin R (1988) Central Bank Laws and Monetary Policies: A Preliminary Investigation. London, Ontario, Canda.

24. Grilli V, Masciandaro D, Tabellini G (1991) Political and Monetary Institutions and Public Financial Policies in the Industrial Countries. Economic Policy: European Forum 6: 342-392.

25. Siklos P (2006) The Changing Face of Central Banking: Evolutionary Trends since World War II. Cambridge: Cambridge University Press.

26. Eijffinger SW, Geraats P (2006) How Transparent are Central Banks. European Journal of Political Economy 22: 1-21.

27. Briault CB, Haldane AG, King MA (1996) Independence and Accountability. Bank of England.

28. Cukierman A (2006) Central Bank Independence and Monetary Policymaking Institutions: Past, Present and Future. European Journal of Political Economy 24: 722-736.

29. Sousa PA (2001) Independent and Accountable Central Banks and the European Central Bank. European Integration online Papers.

30. Cukierman A (1992) Central Bank Strategy, Credibility And Independence-Theory and Evidence. Cambridge MA: MIT Press.

31. Berger H, Haan J, Eijffinger SC (2000) Central Bank Independence: an update of theory and evidence.

32. Barro RJ, Gordon R (1983) A Positive Theory of Monetary Policy in a Natural Rate Model. Journal of Political Economy 91: 589-610.

33. Barro R, Gordon R (1983) Rules, Discretion and Reputation in a Model of Monetary Policy. Journal of Monetary Economics 12: 101-121.

34. Cukierman A, Webb SB, Neyapti B (1992) Measuring the independence of central banks and its effects on policy outcomes. The World Bank Economic Review 6: 353-398.

35. Walsh CE (1995) Optimal Contracts for Central Bankers. The American Economic Review 85: 50-167.

36. Svensson LE (1997) Optimal Inflation Targets, Conservative Central Banks and Linear Inflation Contracts. American Economic Review 87: 98-114.

37. Cukierman A (2006) Central Bank Independence and Policy Results: Theory and Evidence.

38. Cukierman A, Muscatelli VA (2003) Do Central Banks have Precautionary Demands for Expansions and for Price Stability?

39. Grabel I (1999) The Political Economy of Policy Credibility: The New-classical Macroeconomics and the Remaking of Emerging Economies.

40. Schmieding H (1992) Lending Stability to Europe's Emerging Market Economie: On the importance of the EC and the ECU for East-Central Europe.

41. IMF (1996) Currency Boards Circumscribe Discretionary Monetary Policy.

42. Hanke S, Jonung L, Schuler K (1993) Russian Currency and Finance. London: Routledge.

43. Ghosh A, Gulde M, Wolf H (1998) Currency Boards: The Ultimate Fix? IMF Working Paper of the Policy Development and Review Department.

44. Caramazza F, Aziz J (1998) Flexible or flexible: Getting the Exchange Rate Right in the 1990s. IMF Economic Issues.

45. Bhattacharya R (1997) Pace, Sequencing and Credibility of Structural Reforms. World Development 25: 1045-1061.

46. Blinder AS (2012) Central Bank Independence and credibility during and after a crises.

47. Walsh CE (2011) Central Bank Independence Revisited. Economic Papers 30: 18-22.

48. Alesina A, Summers L (1993) Central Bank Independence and Macroeconomic Performance: Some Comparative Evidence. Journal of Monoey, Credit, and Banking.

49. Daunfeldt SO, Luna X (2008) Central Bank Independence and Price Stability: evidence from OECD-countries.

50. Łyziak T (2013) A note on central bank transparency and credibility in Poland.

51. Ćorić T, Cvrlje D (2009) Central bank independence:the case of croatia.

52. Lybek T (2004) Central Bank Autonomy, Accountability and Governance: Conceptual Framework.

53. Debelle G, Fischer S (1995) How Independents Should Central Banks be?.

54. Eijffinger S, Haan J (1996) The Political Economy of Central Bank Independence.

55. Dincer NN, Eichengreen B (2014) Central Bank Transparency and Independence: Updates and New Measures. International Journal of Central Banking pp: 189-253.

56. Bade R, Parkin M (1987) Central bank laws and monetary policy: A Three Decade Perspective.

57. Banaian K, Laney LO, Willett TD (1983) Central bank independence: an international comparison. Economic Review 13: 1-13.

58. Alesina A (1989) Politics and business cycles in industrial democracies. Economic Policy 8: 55-98.

59. Grilli V, Masciandaro D, Tabellini G (1991) Political and Monetary Institutions and Public financial Policies in the Industrial Countries. Economic Policy 6: 341-392.

60. Burdekin RC, Banaian K, Hallerberg M, Siklos PL (2011) Fiscal and monetary institutions and policies: onward and upward? Journal of Financial Economic Policy 3: 340-354.

61. Cukierman A (2005) Legal, Actual and Desirable Independence: A Case Study of the Bank of Israel.

62. Haan JD, Sturm JE (2001) Central bank independence and inflation in developing countries: the role of influential observations.

63. Cukierman A, Webb S (1995) Political Influence on the Central Bank: International Evidence. The World Bank Economic Review 9: 397-423.

64. Momani B, Amand SS (2014) Central Bank Independence in North Africa.

65. IMF (2000) Code of Good Practices on Transparency in Monetary and Financial Policies: Declaration of Principles.

66. Fry M, Julius D, Mahadeva L, Roger S, Sterne G (2000) Key Issues in the Choice of Monetary Policy Framework. In: Mahadeva L, Sterne G (eds). Monetary Policy Frameworks in a Global Context. London: Routledge.

67. Haan J, Amtenbrink F (2003) A Non-Transparent European Central Bank? Who is to Blame.

68. Demertzis M, Hughes HA, Viegi N (1998) Independently Blue? Accountability and Independence in the New Central Bank For Europe.

69. Blinder A, Goodhart C, Hildebrand P, Lipton, D, Wyplosz C (2001) How Do Central Banks Talk? Geneva Reports on the World Economy.

70. Bini-Smaghi L, Gros D (2000) Open Issues in European Central Banking. Basingtoke: Macmillan.

71. Cooper D, Schindler P (2000) Business Research Methods. NewYork:USA.

72. Hopkins W (2000) Quantitative Research Design. Sportscience Journal.

73. Oso YW, Onen D (2008) Guide to Research Writing proposal and Report.

29

The 21st Century Trade Union Challenges in India

Abhishek Gupta* and Neetu Gupta

Finance & Administration Department, Sardar Swaran Singh National Institute of Renewable Energy (Ministry of New & Renewable Energy, Govt. of India), Kapurthala, Punjab, India

Abstract

A trade union or labour union is an organization of workers who have banded together to achieve common goals in key areas such as wages, hours, and working conditions, forming a cartel of labour. India has the largest number of trade unions. But they have developed very slowly. In spite of the slow growth, the unions brought about some economic, political and social betterment of the workers. Economically, they have improved the lot of the workers. Politically, the unionism has produced a mighty secular anti-imperialist, anti-capitalist, equalitarian and socialistic force of national economy. Trade unionism has not influenced a variety of industries. The degree of unionisation varies widely from industry to industry. Though trade unions are of various sizes with thousands of members, yet, most of the unions are still characterized by their small size and small membership. Majority of Indian labour is illiterate, ignorant and poor. They are exploited by unscrupulous trade union leaders, which result in the following problems. In a democracy, political influence of trade unionism cannot be avoided. Through this research paper we will discuss about how in India, the historical development of trade-union movement was inseparably intermingled with political movement through liberation struggle due to the 21st Century Challenges in front of the Trade Unions.

Keywords: Organization; Common goals; Democracy; Liberation struggle; Trade unions

Introduction

India has the largest number of trade unions [1]. But they have developed very slowly. In spite of the slow growth, the unions brought about some economic, political and social betterment of the workers. Economically, they have improved the lot of the workers. Politically, the unionism has produced a mighty secular anti-imperialist, anti-capitalist, equalitarian and socialistic force of national economy. Socially they have emerged as a unique force of national integration in spite of the hindrance offered by illiteracy, rural background of the worker and their migratory character, by communalism, casteism and linguism. The chief features of the present day unionism in India are that only about 28% of the workers are unionized. The unions are getting smaller in size. Their finances are generally in bad shape. Trade union leadership faces several dilemmas. The unions often cannot make a constructive approach because of intensive inter-union rivalries and multiplicity of unions. Then, there is the heterogeneity of membership with workers from different areas, classes, castes and regions. Because of such peculiarities, it has been observed that unlike the trade unions in Sweden, Germany, the U.K., the U.S.A. Indian unions are yet weak, unstable, amorphous, fragmental and uncoordinated. The most important problems of the trade unions in India are uneven Growth: industry-wise and Area-wise, small size of unions, financial weakness, multiplicity of the unions and inter-union rivalry, leadership issue, politicaliation of the unions, democracy and leadership, management Attitude, statutory support, illiteracy and ignorance.

Uneven Growth of Unionism

Trade unionism has not influenced a variety of industries. Plantations, coals mines, food industries, textiles, printing presses, chemicals, utility services, transport and communication and commerce are the main organised industries, in which unionism has made progress [2]. The degree of unionisation varies widely from industry to industry. For example, it has been 51% in mining and 30 to 37% in transport, communication, manufacturing industries and electricity and gas, industries with a high rate of unionism are coal (61%); tobacco manufacture (75%); cotton textile (56%); iron and steel

(63%) banks (51%) insurance (33%) railways (33%) and plantation (28%). Another important feature of the unionism is that it is mainly concentrated in a few States and in bigger industrial centres. The main reason for the development of such industry-cum-centre unions has been the concentration of certain industries in particular areas. For example textile workers in Bombay, Ahmedabad, Indore, Kanpur; plantation labour in Assam, west Bengal, Tamil Nadu and Kerala; jute mill workers in Bengal, engineering workers in Calcutta, Bombay etc; workers engaged in chemical and pharmaceutical industries in Bombay and Vadodra. Trade union development in white-collar workers and in lower management cadre is even more unsatisfactory. Hardly there is any trade union activity in small scale enterprises, domestic servants and agricultural labour. Of the total labour force of about 100 lakhs, only about half of the workers are trade union members. The story of labour in the organised industry is the history of Indian labour moment. There has been no movement amongst the vast mass of labour in the primary sector and the small establishments. The lack of labour organisation in the rural sector is due to their scattered and sparse habitations, their lack in "in group" feeling, and their neglect by labour leaders. The proportion of union members to the total number of workers could be placed at about 23 per cent in sectors other than agriculture. If workers in agriculture are included, the percentage of organized labour will fall considerably.

Small Size of Unions

Though trade unions are of various sizes with thousands of members, yet, most of the unions are still characterized by their small size and small membership. The average membership per union in

---

*Corresponding author: Abhishek Gupta, Finance & Administration Department, Sardar Swaran Singh National Institute of Renewable Energy (Ministry of New & Renewable Energy, Govt. of India), Kapurthala Punjab, India
E-mail: iloveindia1909@gmail.com

India is less than 800, as compared with the U.K (17,600) the USA (9,500) [3]. The small size of the unions is due to the following factors as the fact that any seven workers may from a union under the Trade Union Act and get in registered has resulted in large number of small unions, the structure of the trade unions organisation in the country is in most cases, the factory or the unit of employment; so whenever employees in a particular factory or mine are organised, a new unions is formed. Unionisation in India started with the big employees and gradually spread to smaller employees [4]. This process is still continuing and has pulled down the average membership. Though the number of unions and union membership are increasing, average membership is declining. Rivalry among the leaders and the Central Organisations has resulted in multiplicity of unions thereby reducing the average membership. It is noteworthy that as the number of unions increases, the total membership does not increase proportionately. If rival unions could be stopped from being evolved, the average size of unions could definitely go up. Because of the small size of the unions, they suffer from lack of adequate, funds and find it difficult to engage the services of experts to aid and to advise members in time of need. Further, they cannot face the challenge of employers for long because of their weak bargaining power. Again, the small degree of unionisation further aggravates their helplessness in collective bargaining and makes them thoroughly dependent either on the political parties or on such outside personalities who happen to command political influence on the employers and the Government machinery.

Financial Weakness

Trade unions suffer from financial weakness as the average yearly income of the unions has been rather low and inadequate [5]. The average income has been low not because of the poverty of the workers but because of certain factors namely, workers are apathetic towards trade unions and do not want to contribute out of their hard earned money. The national commission on labour observed that, union organisers generally do not claim anything higher nor do the workers feel like contributing more because the services rendered by the unions do not deserve a higher fee. The members instead of making regular payment to the union make adhoc payment if a dispute arises which show a lack of commitment to the unions. Under conditions of multiplicity of unions, a union interested in increasing its membership, usually keeps their subscription rate unduly low and does not collect even that subscription regularly. To improve the financial conditions of the unions, the National Commission on Labour recommended that the minimum subscription should be raised to rupee one per month. It, however did not favour the existing arrangement of collecting one per cent or even more by way of membership fee on the ground that it would mean different amounts within each State for the same group of workers. Another method advocated is the introduction of the "Check-off system," under which an employer undertakes on the basis of a collective agreement, to deduct union dues from the worker's pay and transfer the same to the union [6]. But, this system has not found favour with certain sections. It has been alleged that if the system is adopted, the constant touch between the union and the rank-and file will be lessened. Further, no deductions can be made on this account under the payment of Wage Act. The National Commission on Labour has held "An enabling provision should be adequate. The right to demand check-off facilities should vest with the unions, and if such a demand is made by a recognised union, it should be incumbent on the management to accept". But this recommendation seems to be difficult to implement. The best solution of improving the financial; condition of the unions would be to remove trade union rivalry, by strictly adhering to the principle of "one union in one industry' [7].

Multiplicity of Trade Unions

Multiple trade unions are the biggest curse of Indian trade union movement. Existence of many unions each trying to compete with each other on membership drive and securing management support to recognise their union, not only weakens the trade union movement but also cause inter-union rivalry and disunity among the workers. The following are the major causes of multiple trade unions. Rapid industrialization has increased the pace of capital formation in India [8]. But skill formation" has not matched the capital formation. This is because we in India missed 'merchant craftsmanship" stages of capitalism and instead a predominately "agrarian labour force" was converted directly into an "industrial labour force". Accordingly, most of the trade unions were not based on "trade" specialization and instead based on generalization. Most of the trade unions were linked to the political parties. Since India have a plethora of political parties, it causes formation of number of trade unions linking with each political parties. When such political parties spilt, the trade unions also spilt. Political influence often necessitates projecting outside politicians as trade unions leaders. Since the political parties' fortune changes rapidly, the membership of unions also fluctuate. Union management relationship is a social relationship. Unfortunately, in India we the same more as a legal matter [9]. For example, as per Indian Trade Unions Act, any seven workers can form a union. Many unions are formed on this basis. Also, there is no central law which stipulates conditions for recognizing a trade union. Hence, each union is trying to 'influence management' to recognize a trade union. In order to influence them, they often take help from outside leaders and political parties and organise union as dictated by influential persons from outside. The ill-effects of multiple trade unions are also as multiplicity divide the workers on party lines instead of uniting them together which is the primary objective of trade unionism. Unscrupulous management exploits this to their advantage. Unions organized on party line are more committed to the ideology of political parties to which it is affiliated than the industrial unit and its objectives in which they work. Union's rivalries often make it difficult to settle disputes because their approach to the problem and method of settlement vary. The problem is more complicated when settlement does not suit the liking of their" political bosses" outside. Multiple trade unions also make it difficult for all of them to join together and make a single charter of demands or chalk out a common strategy of action plan. This will make their bargaining power very weak. Multiple trade unions weaken the financial status of each union. This causes severe handicap for each of them to effectively project their programmes and influence the workers.

Intra-Union Rivalry

Another vexing problem is intra-union rivalry. Trade union rivalry is acute and pervades the entire industrial scene in India. Rival unions sometimes go to the extent of even obstructing the normal conduct of trade Union activities on different pleas. A union does oppose strike by a rival on various grounds, the strike being unnecessary, uncalled for against the interests of the workers and being anti-national. Conditions are created where anti-union employer gets a chance to paint the trade union in the darkest colour and to play one against the other, causing all-round disruptions. The rivals also indulge and wild accusation which shakes worker's faith in the trade unions itself. The Standing committee of the Indian Conference, discussed the problem and recommended that, "A provision should be made in the Trade Unions Act, that when more than one per of persons claimed to be office-bearers of the same union" [10]. If the union is affiliated to any central Organisation, the latter should first try to settle the difference within its affiliates. Failing this, under the aegis of the Labour Court, an election confined to the members of the union concerned should be held." The National Commission on Labour recommended the following to reduce inter-union rivalries, i) building of internal leadership within the unions in order to eliminate party politics and outsiders; (ii) Promotion of collective bargaining through recognition of sole bargaining agents; (iii) improving the system of union recognition; (iv) encouraging union security; and (v) empowering the Labour Courts to settle inter-union disputes, if the concerned central organisation is unable to resolve these.

Leadership Issue

Another disquieting feature of the trade unions is outside leadership, i.e., leadership of trade unions by persons who are professional politicians and lawyers and have no history of physical work in the industry [11]. This is "leadership by intellectuals" rather than by workers'. It applies at the local as well as at the national level. There are several reasons for this phenomenon, namely, the rank and the file are largely illiterate; as such they cannot effectively communicate with the management; the union 's lack of formal power tends to put premium on the charmistic type of the leader, usually a politician, who can play the role of their defender of the workers against his enemies; for ensuring a measure of equation of power in collective bargaining, where the workers are generally uneducated and have a low status; for avoiding victimisation of workers office bearers of the trade unions; and at times for lack of financial resources to appoint whole time office-bearers. The National Commission on Labour gave a good deal of thought to the issue whether outside leadership should be retained. It felt that, there should be one of non-employees holding positions in the executive body of the unions as that would be a very drastic step. The commission referred to freedom of association and protection of the right to organise, and the workers' organisations to have the right to elect their representatives in full freedom.

Politicalisation

In a democracy, political influence of trade unionism cannot be avoided. However in India, the historical development of trade-union movement was inseparably intermingled with political movement through liberation struggle. In the initial stages, it helped union to record rapid growth and gain considerable influence with the government in power. In the long run, it has become a curse for undoing the very objective of trade unionism the unity among the working class. The disadvantages are dependence on outside leadership who are not committed to the organisation, exploitation of trade unions and workers' strength by political parties to meet their political objectives, multiplicity of trade unions because of the existence of multiple political parties., Any spilt in the parental political party automatically spilt the corresponding trade unionism. Examples are the spilt in communist party of India into CPI and CITU owing allegiance to CPM, inter-union and intra-union rivalry and disunity among the employees which weaken their bargaining power, exploitation of the disunity among the union by employers in their effort to play them, one against other.

Democracy and Leadership

One of the basic objectives of trade unionism is to promote industrial democracy. This objective is achieved when trade union is an organization of the workers' in practice, this rarely happens and instead less participation, openness and transparency. Decision

making is centralized Elections are often postponed and positions are filled repeatedly by nominations, rank and file are pampered with promises and seldom get near top decision-making process. Positions get worse when unions are guided by outside leader and regulated by the policies or political parties. Absence of democratic leadership reduces the effectiveness of trade unions and prevents the development of Trade Union from among the workers within the industries [12]. The disadvantages of outside leadership are obsession with political ideology or and personal interest, lack of intimate knowledge's of working conditions and workers problem, lack of stake in the survival of organisation and commitment, pre-occupation with many unions; some studies have showed that a particular political leader was president of 20 odd unions in Bombay.

Management Attitude

Management, by and large, take an unhelpful attitude. Unionism is considered by them as an anathema. Union leaders, according to managers are trouble makers. They are there to break the harmony between the management and workers. They restrict the managers; power in decision-making, question their discretion and wisdom and obstruct their "right to manage". Given this mindset, very often, they find fault with union for all difficulties faced by management; be it on low productivity, low quality, low profitability or lack of good will from customers. No doubt, some union leaders are also responsible for the negative image of their unions because of use of muscle power, money power and militant methods adopted by them which is called "irresponsible unionism". Managers also take advantage of multiple trade unions and their inter-union rivalry by playing one against another. Another area is the recognition of trade union to become a bargaining agent. Management makes use of the loopholes of the existing labour legislation in with holding or delaying the recognition. Management considers trade union a legal obligation. This does not bring faith and good will.

Statutory Support

Indian constitution considers formation of association as a fundamental right. Indian Trade Union Act allows any seven workers to join together and form a Trade union. Both give rise these file to formation of multiple trade unions which goes against the very concept of unionism-the unity workers. No central legislation now exists which makes it compulsory for management to recognize more than one unions or not to recognize anyone. This has further weakened the trade union and their bargaining power. The Indian Trade Union Act further allows 50 per cent of officer-bearers from outside the organization and 10 per cent of leadership from outside. This provision resulted politicalisation, and remote control of union activities from outside the organisations. Even the "code of discipline" only recommend recognition of trade union as a voluntary action. Recognition of trade union causes rivalry from others who are not recognized. This problem can be tackled by bringing out comprehensive central legislation covering all aspects such as Recognition, Multiplicity, Outside leadership, etc.

Illiteracy and Ignorance

Majority of Indian labour is illiterate, ignorant and poor. They are exploited by unscrupulous trade union leaders, which result in the following problems. These workers are easily brain-washed to become card holders of political parties and work for such parties at the expense of working clause interest and unity. Workers are divided on caste religion, ethnic and creed lines which goes against trade union objectives of unity and identity. Illiteracy and ignorance are also exploited by outside leaders who prevent development of leaders from within the organization. Workers are too ignorant to know their rights and often pampered with false promises by union-leaders and politicians. This is the tendency of a worker moving from one union to other with the hope that such a change will improve his economic gains. At times, they may even hold membership of more than one union.

References

1. Barber B (2003) The future of trade unions. City University Vice Chancellor's Lecture.

2. Bhopal M (2001) Malaysian Unions in Political Crisis: Assessing the Impact of the Asian Contagion. Asia Pacific Business Review 8: 73-100.

3. Cornfield D, McCammon H (2003) Labor Revitalization: Global Perspectives and New Initiatives. JAI pres, London, UK.

4. Heery E (2009) Trade Unions and Contingent Labour: Scale and Method. Cambridge Journal of Regions Economy and Society 2: 429-442.

5. Freeman RB (2005) What Do Unions Do? The 2004 M-Erane Stringtwister Edition, National Bureau Of Economic Research, Massachusetts, US.

6. Geert De Neve (2005) The Everyday Politics of Labour: Working Lives in India's Informal Economy. Social Science Press, New Delhi, India.

7. Gopal Ghosh (2005) Indian Trade Union Movement. The Peoples History Publication, US.

8. Kumar HL (2010) Law Relating to Dismissal, Discharge ard Retrenchment. Universal Law Publishing Co, Delhi, India.

9. Sabina (2008) Industrial disputes and labour laws. Alfa Publications, India.

10. PK Jalan (2004) Industrial Sector Reforms in Globalization Era. Sarup & Sons, New Delhi, India.

11. Budhwa PS, Bhatnagar J (2009) The Changing Face of People Management in India. Routledge Taylor & Francis, New York, US.

12. The challenge of employment in India: An informal economy perspective (2009) National Commission for Enterprises in the Unorganized Sector, India.

30

Price Elasticity of Electricity Demand in Iran Based on Computable General Equilibrium Model

Nosratollah Abbaszadeh[1], Ali Bahmani[2] and Mina Qavami[3]

[1]Phd of Economics, Tehran University, Iran
[2]University Teknologi, Malaysia
[3]MA of Economics, Tehran University, Iran

Abstract

Based on the CGE model and according to Social Accounting Matrix (SAM) 1380, this study simulates the impact of electricity price adjustment on demand for electricity, and the simulation results show the range of electricity elasticity of different consumers. The elasticity of Residential sector is relatively larger. However, the absolute values of the price elasticity are less than one.

Furthermore, this paper quantitatively analyses the price elasticity of different categories of users, which are classified to Resident, Agriculture, Industry and Services. The elasticity absolute value of Residents is around (1.02-0.87), that of Agriculture is around (0.013-0.015), that of Industry is around (0,013-0.032) and that of Services is around (0.02-0.031) in different scenarios.

The analytical results of this paper can provide corresponding support for the formulation of electricity pricing mechanisms for Iran.

Keywords: Electricity price; Price elasticity; CGE

Introduction

Electricity has always been regarded as one of the most essential commodities in the country, as manufacturing industries are not able to produce and households welfare would not be without it as well. In our country all forms of energy, including electricity has had a very low price over the years. Due to the low electricity prices, people did not economize in the use of electricity. Other consumer sectors such as industry used non-efficient technology due to low electricity prices compared to the prices of other factors of production and try to improve the efficiency by continuous usage of electricity power rather than other factors of production. There was no increase in electricity prices since 1384 and the prices had been remained stable in all sectors as previous year (1383) after approval of price-fixing scheme in seventh parliament and listed it in the fourth development plan. After the implementation of targeted subsidies plan from January 1389 to review the policy of subsidizing energy, Energy carriers such as electricity prices in the country rose to consumers in various sectors, especially of residential and industrial sectors and made them more sensitive to prices. This paper is an attempt to consider all economic agents behavior in a context of macroeconomic framework and assess impacts of electricity price increases in consumer demand in the various sectors and examine the use of this valuable resource that plays an important role in production process using a comprehensive model. Therefore, the aim of this paper is to examine the effects of electricity price increase on demand and estimate price elasticities using a Computable General Equilibrium Model (CGE). Since this model can balance all markets (supply and demand of goods and factors of production) and explain the relations between the sectors correctly, has more advantages than other models. Using this model, we can measure the impact of electricity price increase in different economic sectors, including residents, industry, agriculture and services accurately and estimate the price elasticity more accurately that could eventually help in the analysis and evaluation of policies and implementation of next steps in reforming the electricity price.

Questions can be posed in this context include:

- What is the price elasticity of electricity demand in different sectors?

- What is the result of comparing the price elasticity of demand in the residential, industrial and agriculture sectors?

- To answer these questions, the following two hypotheses are proposed:

- Electricity in all sectors is relatively inelastic good.

- The price elasticity of electricity demand in the residential sector is larger than the other sectors.

This paper is organized as follows: Section 2 provides an overview the literature. Section 3 deals with the methodology of the model. In this section Computable General Equilibrium Model and its database is provided. Section 4 contains the results of research, including calibration of the model and Price elasticity analysis and finally, the summery and conclusions of the study are presented.

Literature Review

General equilibrium models define a set of institutions and markets, that revenue and expenditure of each institution is equal and supply and demand in all markets is in equilibrium. It should be noted that the equations in CGE models are based on the assumption of optimizing behavior of consumers and producers in which households seek to maximize utility and producers maximize their profit. Walras equilibrium theory is the theoretical basis of these models.

The corner-stone of Walras's general equilibrium is this rule that all revenue from any activity should be equal to the amount of expenditures.

*Corresponding author:** Nosratollah Abbaszadeh, Phd of Economics, Tehran University, Iran, Email: nabbaszd@ut.ac.ir

According to this rule, all firms' products are demanded by consumers and all stock of capital and labor supplied by households is demanded by firms. Also, for a particular commodity, the firms' product must be equal to the sum of the demands of consumers and other firms. The idea of multi-sector general equilibrium model was presented in Johansen`s study in 1960 [1]. The first multi-sector practical model with endogenous prices to estimate the resource allocation was offered by him. After that, extensive studies have been done on the impact of policies such as trade liberalization, fiscal policies and other price shock policies in the form of a system of equations.

Many studies have been done in the field of electricity demand globally. The study of Huathaker [2] by using the method of least squares is one of the first studies in this field. His study suggests that the elasticity of electricity demand in the UK is low. In Atakhanova`s study [3] on the electricity market, electricity demand elasticities calculated in three residential, industrial and general in Kazakhstan. Household spending, economic restructuring, electricity prices and consumption in the previous period is considered as the most important variables in the household sector in which price elasticity of demand is very low.

Bianco [4] estimated the electricity demand function in Italy using data for the years 1970-2007. According to the results of this study, the amount of per capita income, electricity prices and the power consumption (with three lags) are involved in electricity demand function. Income elasticity is more than price elasticity and income elasticity of electricity demand is nearly 80%. Also coefficients of structural changes, energy prices and other effective variables are negative and less than one.

Heyongxiu [5] in the study on the price elasticity of electricity demand calculated the effects of price changes on consumer demand in China based on the 2007 social accounting matrix in which the value obtained for the price elasticity is less than 1 in all sectors.

Among internal studies, research carried out by Pajouyan and Mohammadi [6] can be pointed out in which electricity demand assumed as a function of the real price of electricity and substitute energy prices and GDP. The results show that the price elasticity of electricity demand is less than one and the income elasticity is greater than one.

Khiabani [7] evaluated the effects of energy price increases in Iran based on CGE model in the form of three scenarios of gasoline prices increase, all energies price increase and all energies price increase in which the prices of petrol, diesel, fuel oil and electricity prices is equivalent to world prices. The results indicate that the increase of energy prices will reduce energy overuse in the firms and households and increase inflation.

Electricity price policy on the inflation has been investigated by Eslami [8] using a computable general equilibrium model and the results show that electricity prices will increase the general level of prices and inflation and if government cash subsidies are paid from revenues resulting from the global rise in oil prices and increased foreign aid is more efficient and leads to less increase in price index.

Research Methodology

As mentioned in the previous section, the model used in this paper is Computable General Equilibrium Model (CGE). In this model, production activities, which are producing goods in the economy, their revenue earned from the sale of goods and these revenues are used to pay the factors of production and intermediate goods. Goods prices in this model are a function of the prices of factors and intermediate goods that consumer prices are quite flexible and can change in a competitive atmosphere. So suppliers and demanders in this model are price takers that equate the quantity of supply and demand in a competitive environment.

Households who are the owners of factors earn income from stock of factors (i.e. labor and capital) and spend it to buy goods, pay taxes and savings. Demand function is derived from maximizing utility given the budget constraint.

In the factor market assume the following: (1) For Labor: free mobility across activities, unemployment with fixed, activity-specific real wages and the quantity of labor supply as the market-clearing variable; and (2) For Capital: full employment but no mobility between activities and a flexible market-clearing wage for each factor-activity combination.

Government revenue is obtained from income tax, sales tax, import, and export or activity tax. This revenue is spent on government consumption expenditures or transfer payments to other domestic organs. A part of government revenue may also be transferred abroad to repay foreign debts. The remaining revenue will be saved and positive or negative savings represent the deficit or surplus in the state budget.

Other countries engage in domestic financial markets by lending funds (as loan) or invest in financial markets and receive repayment of loans, attract funds or borrow money from local government. In addition, the interaction with other countries occurs through imports and exports. The assumption of this model is that the economy is small compared with the global economy. Thus, export and import prices are set at the global level. Transfer of workers' income that employed abroad into country and vice versa shows another dimension of relation between domestic and global economy.

Mathematical statement of CGE model

The CGE model is a set of equations describing the balance between supply and demand of the economic system. In this paper, the CGE model is divided into "blocks" for prices, production and commodities, institutions, and system constraints. All endogenous variables are written in uppercase Latin letters, whereas parameters (including variables with fixed or exogenous values) have lower-case Latin or Greek letters. In the model Latin letters a and c represent activities and commodities, respectively.

Price block: This block contains six equations that determine the relation of endogenous prices and other variables.

Import price: On the import and export side, the model incorporates the "small country" assumption that world prices are exogenous.

$$PM_c = (1 + tm_c).EXR.pwm_c \qquad (1)$$

Where PM_c is the import price of commodity c in domestic currency, tm_c is the rate of import tariff of commodity c, EXR is the foreign exchange rate (domestic currency per unit of foreign currency), pwm_c is the world import price.

Export price:

$$PE_c = (1 - te_c).EXR.pwe_c \qquad (2)$$

Where PE_c is the export price of commodity c in domestic currency, te_c is the export tax rate; pwe_c is the world export price.

Absorption equation: For each commodity, absorption-total domestic spending on the commodity at domestic demander prices—is expressed as the sum of spending on domestic output and imports, including an upward adjustment for the sales tax.

$$PQ_c.QQ_c = \left[PD_c.QD_c + (PM_c.QM_c) \right](1 + tq_c) \tag{3}$$

Where PQ_c is the composite price of commodity c, QQ_c is the quantity of commodity c supplied to domestic demanders (composite supply), PD_c is the domestic price of commodity c, QD_c is the quantity of domestic output c sold domestically, QM_c is the quantity of import of commodity c, tq_c is the sales tax rate.

Domestic output value: For each commodity, domestic output value at producer prices is stated as the sum of the value of domestic output sold domestically and the export value.

$$PX_C.QX_C = PD_c.QD_c + (PE_c.QE_C) \tag{4}$$

Where PX_c is the producer price of commodity c, QX_c is the quantity of domestic output, QE_c is the quantity of export of commodity c.

Activity price:

$$PA_a = \sum_{c \in C} PX_c.\theta_{ac} \tag{5}$$

Where PA_a is the price of activity a, θ_{ac} is the yield of commodity c per unit of activity a

Value-added price:

$$PVA_a = PA_a(1 - tx_a) - \sum_{c \in C} PQ_c.ica_{ca} \tag{6}$$

Where PVA_a is the value-added price of activity a, tx_a is the tax rate for activity a, ica_{ca} is the quantity of c as intermediate input per unit of activity a.

Production and commodity block: There are ten equations in this block that describe the supply side of the model.

Activity production function: Cobb-Douglas function is used for producer technology, where QA_a is the level of activity a, ad_a is the production function efficiency parameter, QF_{fa} is the quantity demanded of factor f by activity a, α_{fa} is the value-added share for factor f in activity a.

$$QA_a = ad_a.\prod_{f \in F} QF_{fa}^{\alpha_{fa}} \tag{7}$$

Factor demand:

$$WF_f.WFDIST_{fa} = \frac{\alpha_{fa}.PVA_a.QA_a}{QF_{fa}} \tag{8}$$

Where WF_f is the average wage (rental rate) of factor f, $WFDIST_{fa}$ is the wage distortion factor for factor f in activity a.

Intermediate demand: The assumption of Leontief technology on intermediate inputs means that intermediate commodity demand (QINT) is defined as the product of the fixed (Leontief) input coefficients of demand for commodity c by activity a (ica_{ca}) multiplied by the quantity of activity output (QA).

$$QINT_{ca} = ica_{ca}.QA_a \tag{9}$$

Output function: This equation aggregates the commodity outputs by each activity.

$$QX_c = \sum_{a \in A} \theta_{ac}.QA_a \tag{10}$$

Composite supply (Armington) function: Imperfect substitutability between imports and domestic output sold domestically is captured by a CES (constant elasticity of substitution) function in which the composite commodity that is supplied domestically is produced by domestic and imported commodities Economically, this means that demander preferences over imports and domestic output are expressed as a CES function

$$QQ_c = \alpha q_c \left[\delta_c^q QM_c^{-\rho_c^q} + (1 - \delta_c^q)QD_c^{-\rho_c^q} \right]^{-1/\rho_c^q} \tag{11}$$

Where αq_c, δ_c^q and ρ_c^q are respectively the shift parameter, the share parameter and the exponent ($1\rho_c^q$) for Armington function.

Import-domestic demand ratio: This equation defines the optimal mix between imports and domestic output.

$$\frac{QM_c}{QD_c} = \left[\frac{PD_c}{PM_c} \cdot \frac{\delta_c^q}{(1 - \delta_c^q)} \right]^{1/(1+\rho_c^q)} \tag{12}$$

Composite supply for non-imported commodities:

$$QQ_c = QD_c \tag{13}$$

For commodities that are not imported, the Armington function is replaced by the above statement.

Output transformation (CET) function: Imperfect transformability between domestic output for exports and domestic sales is captured by a CET (constant elasticity of transformation) aggregation function. In economic terms, the difference between the Armington and CET functions is that the arguments in the former are inputs, those in the latter are outputs.

$$QX_c = \alpha t_c \left[\delta_c^t QE_c^{\rho_c^t} + (1 - \delta_c^t)QD_c^{\rho_c^t} \right]^{1/\rho_c^t} \tag{14}$$

Where αt_c, δ_c^t and ρ_c^t are respectively the shift parameter, the share parameter and the exponent ($1\rho_c^t$) for CET function.

Export-domestic supply ratio: This equation defines the optimal mix between exports and domestic sales as below:

$$\frac{QE_c}{QD_c} = \left[\frac{PE_c}{PD_c} \cdot \frac{1 - \delta_c^t}{\delta_c^t} \right]^{(1/\rho_c^t - 1)} \tag{15}$$

Output transformation for non-exported commodities:

$$QX_c = QD_c \tag{16}$$

For commodities that are not exported, the CET function is replaced by a statement imposing equality between domestic output sold domestically and domestic output.

Institution block: This block contains six equations that define income and expenditure of institutions of the model; households (h), government (g) and rest of world (row).

Factor income:

$$YF_{hg,f} = shry_{hg,f}(\sum_{a \in A} WF_f.WFDIST_{fa}.QF_{fa} + tr_{f,row}.EXR) \tag{17}$$

Where $YF_{hg,f}$ is the transfer of income to institution hg from factor f, $shry_{hg,f}$ is the share of the income from factor f in institution hg, $tr_{f,row}$ is the income of factor f from rest of world and hg refers to domestic institutions (households and government).

Household income:

$$YH_h = \sum_{f \in F} YF_{hf} + tr_{h,gov} + EXR\,tr_{h,row} \tag{18}$$

Where YH_h is the income to household h, YF_{hf} is the transfer of income to household h from factor f, $tr_{ii'}$ is the transfer from institution i' to institution i.

Household consumption demand:

$$QH_{ch} = \frac{\beta_{ch}(1-mps_h).(1-ty_h)YH_h}{PQ_c} \quad (19)$$

Where QH_{ch} is the quantity of consumption of commodity c by household h, β_{ch} is the share of commodity c in the consumption of household h, mps_h is the share of disposable household income to savings, ty_h is the rate of income tax.

Investment demand:

$$QINV_c = \overline{qinv_c}.IADJ \quad (20)$$

Where $QINV_c$ is the quantity of investment demand, q invbarc is the base-year investment demand; IADJ is the investment adjustment factor.

Government revenue:

$$YG = \sum_h ty_h YH_h + \sum_{c \in C} tq_c (PD_c.QD_c + (PM_c.QM_c))$$
$$+ \sum_c tm_c.EXR.pwm_c.QM_c + \sum_c te_c.EXR.pwe_c.QE_c \quad (21)$$
$$+ \sum_a tx_a.PA_a.QA_a + \sum_f YF_{g,f} + EXR.tr_{g,row}$$

Where YG is the government revenue, $YF_{g,f}$ is the transfer of income to government from factor f

Government expenditures:

$$EG = \sum_h tr_{h,g} + \sum_c PQ_c.qg_c \quad (22)$$

Where EG is the government expenditure, qg_c is the government commodity demand.

Market clearing conditions and system constraint block: This block defines the constraints that are satisfied by the economy as a whole without being considered by its individual agents. The model's micro constraints apply to individual markets.

Factor markets:

For the two factors, the closure rules are: unemployment with fixed, activity-specific real wages for labor and fixed capital use for each activity.

$$\sum_a QF_{fa} = QFS_f \quad (23)$$

Where QFS_f is supply of factor f.

Composite commodity markets:

$$QQ_c = \sum_a QINT_{ca} + \sum_h QH_{ch} + qg_c + QINV_c \quad (24)$$

Current account balance: The current-account equation imposes equality between the country's earning and spending of foreign exchange. Foreign savings (FSAV) is equal to the current-account deficit

$$\sum_c pwe_c.QE_c + \sum_{hg} tr_{hg.row} + FSAV = \sum_c pwm_c.QM_c \quad (25)$$

Savings-investment balance: This equation imposes equality between savings and investment, where the left hand side of equation refers to the total savings, the right hand refers to investment and WALRAS is a dummy variable that is zero at equilibrium.

$$\sum_{a \in A} mps_h.(1-ty_h).YH_h + (YG-EG) + EXR.FSAV = \sum_{a \in C} PQ_c.QINV_c + WALRAS \quad (26)$$

Price normalization:

$$\sum_c PQ_c.cwts_c = cpi \quad (27)$$

Where cpi is the consumer price index and cwtsc is the commodity weight in CPI.

Basic data base of CGE-SAM

Data organizing for using the CGE model is of initial important steps to build the models. The required data for these models is provided in a matrix called Social Account Matrix (SAM) in which cash flow of goods and services and also payment between sectors is reflected. SAM matrix used in this study is macro-social accounting matrix of Iran 2001 (Table 1), which is the last matrix in this field. The matrix consists of seven accounts of goods and services, activities, factors, institutions, saving-investment, taxes and rest of world. To facilitate the calculation and tracking simulation results, in this paper the matrix is aggregated regarding following characteristics.

- Account of goods and services, which includes 22 commodity groups, is aggregated to two groups of electricity and other goods that are identified by subscript c.

- Account of activities, including 21 activities, is aggregated to three activities of agriculture, industry and mining, services that are marked with subscript a.

- Account of factor in both original social accounting matrix and aggregated matrix consists of two factors, labor and capital which will be shown with subscript f.

- Account of households is introduced in two forms of rural and urban households and since the merging of enterprises and government does not create disturbance in our discussion, these two institutions have been merged. So the institutions of model are urban households, rural households, government and rest of world. This part is shown with subscript i.

Commodities		417436		397376	104733	206214				157720
Activities	1149118									
Factors		722717								1003
Households			439332		46427					15
Government			284388				37040	8965	9386	1020
S-I				51358	189639					
Income Tax				37040						
Sale Tax		8965								
Import Tax	9386									
Rest of World	124975					34783				
Total	1283479	1628125	801304	485774	349846	240997	37040	8965	9386	159762

Table 1: Macro-SAM of 2001 (unit: Billion Rials).

Sectors	5%	10%	15%	20%
Residents	-1.029	-0.958	-0.91	-0.871
Agriculture	-0.015	-0.014	-0.013	-0.013
Industry	-0.033	-0.021	-0.016	-0.013
Services	-0.031	-0.024	-0.022	-0.02

Table 2: Values of price elasticity of electricity demand.

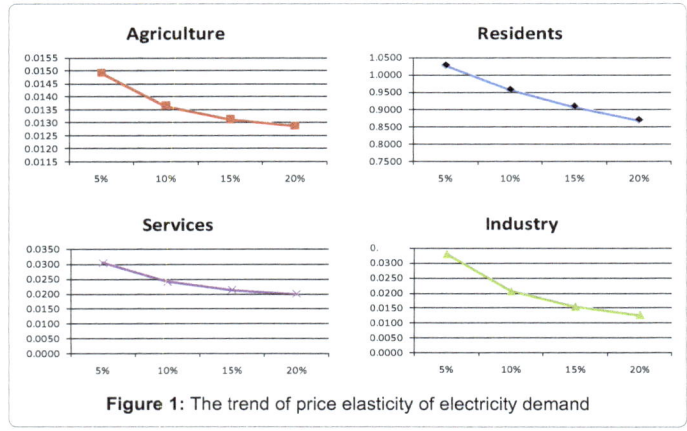

Figure 1: The trend of price elasticity of electricity demand

- Saving-Investment account represents institutions savings and on the other hand, investment demand for different goods.

- Taxes as well as production factors remained unchanged and consist of three types of taxes (income tax, sales tax, and taxes on imports).

Simulation Results

Model calibration

One of the important steps in modeling general equilibrium models is to calibrate the model. Calibration is a process of determining the parameter values so that the values of the endogenous variables for the base year to be reproduced. In fact, the aim of calibration is that general equilibrium that is presented in the form of mathematical equations should be reproduced the values of the SAM in the first run. In other words, when the general equilibrium model is solved, the same amount of social accounting matrix is obtained as the answer of the model.

CGE model has two types of parameters: the first type such as share of households and government consumption of different goods, savings rates, tax rates and etc., is called share parameters. These parameters which derived from the SAM are obtained using the GAMS software. The second type is behavioral parameters, including Armington function's elasticity and CET function's elasticity. To obtain these parameters previous studies and past research in the country or similar countries are used. In this paper import substitution elasticity (Armington function elasticity of substitution) and export elasticity of substitution (CET function elasticity of substitution) respectively 0.5 and 2 is assumed by Heyongxiu[1].

Analysis of price elasticity of electricity demand

Generally, electricity demand is in form of final demand from households and in form of intermediate demand from the firms. This section introduces the scenarios (Four Scenarios: 5%, 10%, 15% and 20% increase in electricity prices) and the effects of energy price

[1]For this purpose we use Heyongxiu [5] and Naderan and Fouladi (2006).

increases on demand based on the equation $E = \dfrac{\Delta Q/Q}{\Delta P/P}$ in all sectors is investigated.

By calibrating the model and obtained parameters and also applying above mentioned scenarios using GAMS software for the price elasticity of electricity demand the results obtained are presented in Table 2. According to this table, the price elasticity of electricity demand in all sectors is negative. It indicates the establishment of demand law for electricity. The absolute value of the elasticity in all sectors and all scenarios (except residential sector in the first scenario) is less than one and we can say electricity relatively inelastic good in all sectors. Thus, the first hypothesis of this paper is accepted. In addition, price elasticity of households demand for electricity in all scenarios is larger than the other sectors. This may be due to low price of electricity and using luxury accessories at homes that with rising prices the incentive to save and reduce the use of these materials occurs. So, the second hypothesis based on the higher price elasticity of electricity demand in the household sector relative to other sectors is accepted.

The high volatility of electricity prices results lower price elasticity in all consumption sectors. This indicates that in the early stages of rising prices greater capacity is in available for saving power consumption for people and with subsequent price increases the capacity will be decreased. This is illustrated in Figure 1.

As reference [7] Khiabani mentioned the price elasticity of electricity demand in most countries is less than one. It should be noted that the price elasticity of electricity demand in the residential sector in developed countries is usually larger, that is due to high level of welfare and use of facilities and luxury equipment. In this study the price elasticity in the residential sector is around one. From this point of view we can say that the results for the household sector are similar to studies conducted on developed countries. The results show the low electricity elasticity in other sectors in this study and similar studies as well.

Summary and Conclusions

This paper attempts to investigate the effects of electricity price increase on its demand based on the Computable General Equilibrium (CGE) model by using the 2001 social accounting matrix. Therefore, after designing the general equilibrium model and calibrating it in the GAMS software, four scenarios include 5%, 10%, 15% and 20% increase in electricity price for different consumer sectors (household, industry and mining, agriculture and services) was introduced. The results suggest that: First, the price elasticity of electricity demand in all sectors and all scenarios is negative. Second, absolute value in all sectors and all scenarios (except the residential sector in the first scenario) is less than unity that Indicates low elasticity of electricity demand. Third, elasticity in the household sector is greater than other sectors and is close to one. A comparison of these results with similar results in different countries suggests that the elasticity in the household sector in our country is very similar to developed countries. It can be due to the low price of electricity and the use of luxury equipment in this section.

Based on the above analysis it is recommended:

- As general equilibrium models provide more reliable results than other models, it is recommended that policymakers in electricity industry to increase the electricity price consider the results of this survey.

- Since more increase in electricity price leads to reduction of elasticity (compared to the past), policymakers should not expect further savings in power consumption in the second phase of targeted subsidies in comparison with first phase.

- National accounts Classification is based on the International Standard ISIC, while cost and power consumption statistical classification is based on Supplementary Regulations electricity tariffs (to separate residential, industrial, agricultural, commercial and public) that there is no connection between these two. Therefore, it is recommended that policymakers in power industry offer the electrical industry statistics in accordance with the international standards as possible.

- As this study used data from 2001 and we did not succeed to provide results in detailed breakdown of the electricity tariff, it is hoped that further research in the future provide these results producing required and up to date data.

References

1. Johansen L (1960) A Multi-sectoral Study of Economic Growth. Amsterdam, North-Holland.

2. Huathaker HS (1951) Some Calculation of Electricity Consumption in Great Britain. Journal of the Royal Statistical Society 114: 359-371.

3. Atakhanova Z, Howie P (2007) Electricity Demand in Kazakhstan. Energy Policy 35: 3729-3743

4. Bianco V, Manca O, Nardini S (2009) Electricity Consumption Forecasting in Italy Using Linear Regression Models. Energy 34: 1413-1421

5. Heyongxiu YX (2011) Electricity demand price elasticity in China based on computable general equilibrium model analysis. Energy 36: 1115-1123.

6. Pajouyan J, Mohammadi T (2000) Optimal pricing; Code for the electricity industry in Iran. Iranian Economic Journal 3: 39-117.

7. Khiabani N (2008) A Computable General Equilibrium model to assess the increase in price of energy carriers in economy. Energy Economics Studies 16: 1-34.

8. Eslami M (2010) Electricity price policy effects on inflation using a general equilibrium model. Twenty-Fifth International Conference of Power, Tehran.

Permissions

List of Contributors

Takefumi Ueno
Faculty of Management and Information Department, University of Shizuoka, Japan

Genki Sakakibara
Shizuoka Bank, Shizuoka, Japan

Sanshiro Uchino
Graduate Schools of Management and Information of Innovation, University of Shizuoka, Japan

Muhammad Hamid, Sumra Maheen, Ayesha Cheem and Rizwana Yaseen
Department of Business Administration, University of Sargodha, Pakistan

Paitoon Chetthamrongchai
Department of Marketing, Kasetsart University, Bangkok, Thailand

Lin Lin and Yu-LunHuang
Department of Banking and Finance, National Chi Nan University, Taiwan

Hsaio-Fen Hsiao
Department of Finance, MingDao University, Taiwan

Nicholas Asare, Joseph Mensah Onumah and Samuel Nana Yaw Simpson
Department of Accounting, Methodist University College, Ghana

Krisnanto U
Perbanas Institute, South Jakarta, Indonesia

Chilukuri SS
KLUBS, KL University, Guntur, Andhra Pradesh, India

Srinivas Rao K
Vivek Vardhini College of PG Studies (AN), Hyderabad, Telangana, India

Madhav VV
Department of Management, KLUBS, KL University, Guntur, Andhra Pradesh, India

Katta Ashok Kumar
Research Scholar and Assistant Professor, Saveetha University, Chennai, India

Ameni Ghenimi
Economic Sciences and Management of Tunisia, Tunisia

Khaled Oweis
Accounting Department Rafha Community College, Northem Border University, Kingdom of Saudi Arabia

Mohamed AO
Accounting Department College of Business Administration, Northem Border University, Kingdom of Saudi Arabia

Srinivasa Rao K
Assistant Professor of Commerce, Vivek Vardhini College of P.G. Studies, (Affiliated To Osmania University), Jambagh, Koti, Hyderabad-500095, India

Malyadri P
Principal, Government Degree College, Affiliated to Osmania University Patancheru, Hyderabad, Telangana State, India

Abdulazeez DA, NdibeL and Mercy AM
Federal University of Technology, Minna, Niger, Nigeria

Marta Cristina Pelucio-Grecco
PhD in Business Administration by Mackenzie Presbyterian University, Professor at Financial and Actuarial Accounting Research Institute Foundation – FIPECAFI Faculty,Brazil

Cecília Moraes Santostaso Geron
Department of Accounting, University of São Paulo, Professor at Mackenzie Presbyterian University, Rua São Bento, 545 – 5SL, São Paulo, 01011-904, Brazil

Gerson Begas Grecco
Department of Accounting, Mackenzie Presbyterian University, Rua Dr. Gabriel dos Santos, 794 – apto 111, São Paulo, 01231-010, Brazil

Katta Ashok Kumar
Business Management Department, Saveetha University, Chennai, India

Rabia Najaf
Department of Accounting and Finance, University of Lahore, Islamabad Campus, Pakistan

Khakan Najaf
Riphah International University, Islamabad, Pakistan

Timothy King
Research Officer, Accounting and Finance, Leeds University Business School, UK

Ruhua Kong
Imperial College Business School, London

Nagib Salem Mohammed Bayoud
Department of Accounting & Management, University of Tripoli, Libya

Elsayed Nasser DAA
Banking and Finance Department, Hekma School of Business, Dar Alhekma University, Jeddah, Kingdom of Saudi Arabia

Samar Rahi and Mazuri Abd Ghani
University of Sultan Zainal Abdin, Malaysia

Abdolreza Ghasempour and Mohd Atef bin MdYusof
Department of Accounting, Universiti Utara Malaysia, Sintok, Kedah, Malaysia

Sammer Mumtaz and Farheen Shafi
National College of Business Administration and Economics, DHA, Lahore, Pakistan

Fareeha Zafar
Government College University, Lahore, Pakistan

Rabia Najaf
Department of Accounting and Finance, University of Lahore, Islamabad Campus, Pakistan

Mohammad Khodaei Weleh Zagherd
Assistant Professor, University of Tehran, Iran

Mehrdad Barghi
Faculty of Management, University of Tehran, Iran

Affes H and Smii T
Department of Economics and Management Sciences, University of Sfax, Tunisia

Mostafa Bakr
Scientist and Independent Scholar

Henri Masson
Professor Emeritus, University of Antwerp, Belgium

Burhan Mahmoud Awad Alomari
Emirates College of Technology, ECT, Abu Dhabi, United Arab Emirates

Sai Akhilesh P
School of Management, NIT Warangal, Telangana, India

Vinay CV
Andhra Pradesh Productivity Council, Hyderabad, Telangana, India

Julia Wu
Department of Accounting & Information Systems, College of Business & Law, University of Canterbury, New Zealand

Ahsan Habib
School of Accountancy, Massey University, Auckland, New Zealand

Joy Kuhns
Ara Institute, Christchurch Campus, New Zealand

Husein Mohamed IRBAD
Lincoln University College, Mogadishu Centre, Malaysia

Abhishek Gupta and Neetu Gupta
Finance & Administration Department, Sardar Swaran Singh National Institute of Renewable Energy (Ministry of New & Renewable Energy, Govt. of India), Kapurthala, Punjab, India

Nosratollah Abbaszadeh
Phd of Economics, Tehran University, Iran

Ali Bahmani
University Teknologi, Malaysia

Mina Qavami
MA of Economics, Tehran University, Iran

Index